JOSEPH P. KENNEDY

A Life and Times

JOSEPH P. KENNEDY

A Life and Times

DAVID E. KOSKOFF

PRENTICE-HALL, INC.

Englewood Cliffs, New Jersey

The author is grateful for permission to quote material taken from:

The Remarkable Kennedys, by Joe McCarthy, used by permission of the author; *Halifax*, by The Earl of Birkenhead, used by his permission; Jack Newfield's *Robert Kennedy: A Memoir*, by permission of E.F. Dutton & Company, Inc.; *The Secret Diary of Harold L. Ickes*, copyright 1953 by Simon and Schuster, Inc., by permission of the publisher; Joseph F. Dinneen's *The Kennedy Family*, copyright 1959 by the author, and George F. Kennan's *Memoirs: 1925–1950*, copyright 1967 by the author, both used by permission of Atlantic-Little, Brown and Co.; the records of the Public Record Office, London, used by permission of the Controller of H.M. Stationery Office; the collection of oral history "Reminiscences" at The Oral History Collection of Columbia University, used by permission of its curators; the Jay Pierrepont Moffat Diary, by permission of Lilla Levitt and the Harvard College Library; the Diary of William Phillips, by permission of the Harvard College Library; *Front Runner, Dark Horse*, by Ralph G. Martin and Ed Plaut, copyright 1960 by its authors, used by permission of Sterling Lord Agency; and, Arthur Krock's *Memoirs: Sixty Years on the Firing Line*, copyright 1968 by Mr. Krock, used by permission of its publishers, Funk & Wagnalls Publishing Company, Inc.

Library of Congress Cataloging in Publication Data

Koskoff, David E
    Joseph P. Kennedy: A life and times.
    Bibliography: p.
    1. Kennedy, Joseph Patrick, 1888–1969. I. Title.
E748.K376K67   973.9′092′4 [B]   73-21578
ISBN 0-13-511154-4

10 9 8 7 6 5 4 3 2 1

To the memory of the late

DR. LOUIS H. NAHUM

*who guided all with whom
he came in contact into
paths of analytical thinking.*

PREFACE

An aura of the legendary surrounded Joseph P. Kennedy ever since the Irish-Catholic businessman turned his back on Al Smith and entered the circle of that Protestant aristocrat Franklin D. Roosevelt in the early 1930s. Since then a great number of myths and half-truths have revolved around him. While he made great effort to avoid the public eye after the mid-1950s, his absence from the press became conspicuous. The Presidential candidacy of John F. Kennedy in 1960 renewed interest in his father, which was only whetted by the failure of the press to follow the elder Kennedy's doings. People in "informed circles," of course, *knew* that the candidate's father was purposefully keeping in the background so that his scandalous past would not come to light, while he ordered the campaign of the mere front man, his son.

It was in this atmosphere that I first became interested in Joseph P. Kennedy in the summer of 1960, and began to delve into the sources to try to piece together the story of the career of this fascinating man. I was twenty-one at the time, a junior at Yale, and at first my "research" was on a somewhat superficial level. With the encouragement of a friendly instructor, George Langdon, I began more systematic and serious inquiry in the spring of 1961. This book has been developing and maturing in the many years since.

Over the years I have incurred substantial debt to many, perhaps most important, to my agent Oscar Collier, for enthusiasm that has lasted a decade even when my own was waning; my wife and research assistant, Charlotte; the late James M. Landis, who extended generous cooperation and encouragement beyond the call; my associate in the practice of law, Stuart M. Schimelman, who has carried more than his fair share of the burden while I prepared the final draft of the manuscript; my secretary, Carol D'Agostino, who has kept the office on an even keel during these past hectic months; Cosmo Stewart, former head of the cultural relations section at the American Department of the British Foreign Office, who suggested helpful lines of research in England and extended hospitality; and Ed Plaut, coauthor of the excellent early John Kennedy sketch in *Front Runner, Dark Horse.*

Many in the academic community have been of help to me, among them Professors James Barros of the University of Toronto; Stephen Koss of Columbia; Fred Israel of the City College of New York; Dan Anthony of the New School; D. C. Watt of the London School of Economics; Churchill's biographer Martin Gilbert; A. J. P. Taylor of the Beaverbrook Library; Lewis Kurlantzick of the University of Connecticut; and, most of all, Robin Winks at Yale. The author has been greatly influenced by the lectures of Yale's John M. Blum. Archivists imposed upon include Dr. E. Taylor Parks at the National Archives, Washington; the terrific staff at the Public Record Office in London; Elizabeth B. Drewry and her staff at the Roosevelt Library, Hyde Park, New York; Howard Gotlieb and Herman Kahn at Yale; Sylvie Turner and staff at the Kennedy Library, Waltham, Massachusetts; and the gracious people who man the manuscript collections at the Library of Congress, Harvard, Yale, Columbia, Princeton, the House of Lords, London School of Economics, Beaverbrook Library, and University Library at Cambridge, England.

Many people who figure in this story kindly gave time for interviews, including (stripped of titles) H. Meade Alcorn, Joseph Curran, Joseph F. Dinneen, James A. Farley, Joseph Kane, Emory S. Land, James M. Landis, Louis M. Lyons, Sidney A. Mitchell, Raymond O'Connell, Thomas Pappas, Ferdinand Pecora, John T. Reynolds, James Roosevelt, Walter Trohan, Ethel C. Turner, and legions more who for one reason or another preferred that their anonymity be preserved.

Various drafts of the manuscript were painfully typed by Anne Haught, Mary Ann Jenislawski, Evelyn Ullerup, Carol D'Agostino, and Joan K. Deegan.

Writing this book has been a gratifying experience in large part because of the satisfaction derived from working with these people.

DAVID E. KOSKOFF

Plainville, Connecticut

CONTENTS

Contents

JOSEPH P. KENNEDY

A Life and Times

THE STORY
OF AN IMMIGRANT

THE POTATO MEANS LIFE TO THE IRISHMAN. HIS ENEMY POTATO rot brings starvation, accompanied by utter demoralization, filth, disease, and death. An 1846 traveler in Ireland described the scourge of Erin:

> *The first appearance is a little brown spot on the leaf, which is hardly perceptible, and which gradually increases in number, and then affects the stem, assuming by degree a darker colour until it presents to you an appearance as if it had been burnt. . . . in less than a week the whole process is accomplished.*[1]

In less than a week the hopes of a nation fade.

Ireland has never been able to feed its people adequately. It exists, as one scholar points out, in a chronic state approaching famine, the particular years mentioned as famine years being those in which the symptoms become acute.[2] Consequently, every year large numbers of Irishmen must leave, and in the years of severe famine emigration reaches its peak.

Ireland has known a dozen famines, but that of 1845–1848 is the one known to Irish historians as "The Great Famine." After enduring the loss of part of its crop in 1841, 1842, and 1844,[3] in 1845 Ireland suffered the failure of almost half its potato crop.[4] In prior years crop failures had only been for one-year periods.[5] Now the failures were to be prolonged. Early in the 1846 season officials feared another lean year, but the famine that was to come was worse than anything they had imagined.

The date of the blight of the 1846 season can be pinpointed: July 12, 1846.[6] A month later a priest reported that "A blot more destructive than the simeon of the desert has passed over the land, and the hopes of the poor potato cultivators are totally blighted, and the food of a whole nation has perished." His country had become "one wide waste of putrefying vegetation."[7]

In December he wrote again:

> *Men, women, and children are gradually wasting away. They fill their stomachs with cabbage leaves, turnip tops, etc. etc., to*

1

*appease the cravings of hunger. There are at this moment more
than five-thousand half-starved, wretched beings, from the
country, begging in the streets of Cork. When utterly exhausted,
they crawl to the workhouse to die.*[8]

Mixed in with the expense accounts and general memoranda of
counsels, the fat dusty volumes of *Parliamentary Papers* contain
countless such letters. All of them describe an almost unbelievable
wretchedness.[9]

These are the times, the times of famine, when Ireland most
desperately needs to relieve her population pressure. In such periods
of trauma, the nation, like the human body, must spew out its own to
preserve itself; the famine, like the human illness, is the internal
expulsive force. For the people have no food, no work, no hopes, and
nothing to do. Nothing to do but starve. Or go.

Patrick Joseph Kennedy of County Wexford was blessed with
having been born in a corner of Ireland that was spared the worst of
the blight.[10] The house in which he lived in the village of Ballynabola
outside of New Ross still stands, a common two-room cottage of
granite stone blocks, rough inside and out. A metal roof has now
replaced the straw thatching that once covered his head. The cottage's
dirt floor and clammy stone walls make it none too inviting to
present-day Americans, but by contemporary Irish standards it was
probably comfortable.[11] From his position above the wretchedness,
Pat Kennedy could see that nineteenth-century Ireland had little to
offer. In 1848, Pat Kennedy left his home, leaving behind brothers
John and James, and sister Mary.[12]

There was probably a gathering of the clan from neighboring
districts before Pat left; historians tell us that such gatherings were
common.[13] No doubt Pat spoke on that parting day of the time in the
future when he would return to Erin. Such talk made the parting
easier, but it deceived no one. All must have known, as he walked
down the road farther and farther from his home and his loved ones,
that he was leaving forever. His destination was Boston, in the United
States.

The Irish chose to come to the United States, rather than go to
England or to a royal colony, for a number of reasons. The low fares to
England might have overcome their hatred of Britain and drawn them
to the native land, but England was already overrun with Irish
paupers. And weary of the imperial rule, Irishmen were not eager to
go to the British colonies.

The United States offered hope to the Irish. There were opportunities for work in an expanding America. It was the most menial kind of work and because it paid only a pittance, the native Americans would not do it,[14] but to the Irish the pittance represented a relatively high wage.[15] And there were already substantial numbers of Irishmen in America to welcome the newcomers to its shores. Moreover, conditions on vessels to the United States, as ghastly as they were, were still better than those on boats to Quebec and other colonies, and the trip took less time.[16] Perhaps hopes for social equality in the New World also helped bring the Irish to America.[17] Most important, though, passage to the New World was relatively cheap, as ships going to England with full cargoes frequently had to return to America with empty holds. Those not already destitute could obtain passage in the steerage by selling whatever possessions they had. In 1840 Cunard Lines set up their western terminus at East Boston, with frequent sailings from Irish ports. Though Cunard did not begin transporting immigrants until 1863, their presence drew other lines to stop at East Boston[18] and contributed to making Boston a great immigrant port. And so the Irish came to America and many of them docked at Boston.

Many died on the long voyages to America. The steerage was cramped and unsanitary, and the plagues that the Irish had fled broke out on ship.[19] Typhus, brought aboard by afflicted immigrants, was especially common. It is estimated that from 6 to 10 percent of them died during the crossing.[20] Once here, a third got off the boat utterly destitute,[21] without the two pennies needed to pay the fare from "the island," East Boston, to the city proper.[22] Perhaps that is why Pat Kennedy settled first in East Boston, close to the wharves on which he had just stepped foot. Once settled, he remained there the rest of his life. A number of factors kept the Irish in Boston: their unfitness for the pioneer life; their disillusionment with agriculture; gravitation to the Irish community in Boston; and, most of all, poverty.

While there was work for all in Boston, the choice of jobs open to Irishmen was limited. In 1850, 48 percent of the Irish in the city could be classified by occupation only as "laborers." Another 15 percent were domestic servants.[23] (The respective figures for Negroes were 20 percent and 8 percent.)[24] "None need apply but Americans" was a common phrase in Boston employment advertisements long before Pat Kennedy arrived,[25] and only very gradually did the Irish enter skilled trades. A few semiskilled trades, though, in fields crying for manpower, were open to Irishmen. Substantial numbers of the Irish worked in clothing manufacturing, in the building trades, or as smiths. Because Irishmen spent so much time in taverns, the trades associated with liquor were open to them, and many became bartenders, brewers, or barrelmakers. It was this last calling, that of cooper, that Pat Kennedy followed in the New World. As a man with a trade, Pat was better off than most of his fellow Irishmen. He married a colleen and had four children.

The Irish had no easy time in Boston. The intolerance of the Yankee community quickly demonstrated to them that the American myth was at best a half-truth. Their dismal living conditions exploded the other half.

Despite his relatively high pay, the employed laborer could not maintain a family of four, and circumstances forced the Irish to become America's first slum dwellers.[26] Whole families would sometimes live in a small, below-ground chamber, suffering from frequent flooding by water and sewage. Their low and suffocating rooms pushed the Irish out into the streets and into the taverns. There they could forget the disappointments of the New World and could remember Erin as more beautiful than it had ever been.

Filth was inescapable in the Irish neighborhoods. Sometimes 100 people shared a sink and a privy, both always in disrepair.[27] The unsanitary living conditions made the Irish community a target for every plague and illness. It was estimated that the average Irishman survived only 14 years in the New World.[28] Smallpox ravaged the Irish after 1845; they suffered cholera in 1849; tuberculosis always plagued them. Perhaps it was a plague that took the life of Pat Kennedy, who died about 14 years after his arrival, around 1862.[29]

Pushed about by circumstance all his life, Pat probably never hoped for much. But he had grounds for hope for his heirs. Pat had made it possible for his sons to be born in a land of greater opportunity than Ireland, and if there was little hope for himself, there was hope for his sons and his grandsons.

PICTURE OF
A WARD BOSS

"NOTHING IN COMMON AT ALL," EXPLAINED THE OLD-TIMER. "Fitzy and Curley were politicians—Pat Kennedy was a ward boss." He saw a fundamental difference. "Politician" was the term he applied to loudmouthed office seekers, men whom his colleague described as "all publicity and no substance." "Ward boss," on the other hand, signified the kindly father figure of the whole community, respected not only for his power but also for his wisdom and kindness. Human understanding, with the ability and willingness to help in any and all circumstances, was the forte of Pat Kennedy and a hundred like him—ward bosses up and down the East Coast. His friend and nephew Joe Kane concedes that politics helped Pat to prosper, but he quickly adds, "Pat gave away two fortunes in his day."

The old-timers differed in their opinions of the city's political leaders, and a bad word was said for most. (Of Mayor John F. Fitzgerald one man said, "I went to his funeral to make sure they buried the bastard.") But they agreed on Pat Kennedy. One man called him "the salt of the earth." Another offered, "He was a good man." A colleague corrected him. "A fine man." "A decent man," said a fourth.[1]

Pat Kennedy, son of the cooper, was born in East Boston in January, 1858,[2] and was fatherless at the age of four. His mother went to work and Pat was brought up largely by his older sisters. He was a sickly youth.[3] For a short time he attended a school run by the Sisters of Notre Dame,[4] and later he went to the Lyman School, an East Boston public school.[5] Though his education was limited, Pat read a lot, usually American history.[6]

Pat had the good fortune to grow up in a period when relations between the Yankees and Irish were relatively good. During the Civil War, the Yankees had fought slavery; the Irish had fought Britain's ally, the South; both groups had fought for the Union. An atmosphere of tolerance was created by Civil War cooperation and the longer exposure of the two groups to each other. As conditions in Ireland improved, the influx of Irish greenhorns slowed down, and this too undoubtedly helped to calm the nerves of the Yankee community. The inter-group bitterness of the 1850s and the underlying differences between the Yankees and the Irish were to some extent pushed into the back of men's minds. Temporarily forgotten, the pent-up hostility was ready to be brought to the fore again with the immigration influx of the 1880s.[7]

Pat developed into a healthy young man and went to work, perhaps as a dock hand.[8] Before long he had saved enough to buy a tavern, and became a saloonkeeper. He looked like a typical taverner. He was a stocky five feet ten inches and weighed about 185 pounds. He had a sandy complexion, dark hair, and blue eyes, and photographs of him show the luxuriously curled mustache that was the pride and joy of every gay-nineties bartender.[9]

The hard work and dismal living conditions of the Irish in the New World did not encourage temperance. Heavy enough drinkers in Ireland, the Irish in America outdid themselves. The Irishman escaped from his squalid quarters to the neighborhood tavern, the center of existence for most of the Irish immigrants.[10] Reigning over this informal community center was the saloonkeeper. When in need of help or advice, the Irishman turned to the tavernkeeper. His position as counselor and friend of all lent him power and prestige second only to the parish priest. Because of this position it is no wonder that so many saloonkeepers became ward bosses. The corner saloon and the political club were usually the same place.[11] In Boston, political powers Jerry McNamara of South Boston, Philip O'Brien of Charlestown, and James Michael Curley were all saloonkeepers at one time or another.[12] One of the most successful of these bartending ward bosses was "P.J." Kennedy, as Pat was commonly known.

When the great Irish influx of the 1880s began, Pat was already in a position to catapult himself to statewide power. When the immigrants arrived in East Boston, saloonkeeper Kennedy found them lodging and work, and gave them advice. Once they were settled, he helped solve their problems as they arose.

The newly arrived Irishman became very dependent upon the ward boss for the solution of all problems, large and small. With a little encouragement he might have been able to handle some of the simple problems himself. But to an insecure immigrant, filling out an application blank was a frightening challenge, even if he happened to be literate. Forestalling an eviction, or arranging bail, was a threat that presented awesome challenges which only friendly Pat could manage.

He saved many unemployed from starvation and straightened out all kinds of misunderstandings with the police. This kind of attention won Pat the loyalty of customers and newcomers, and brought him the substance of any ward machine: a large personal following.

This following must have developed gradually throughout the 1880s. Pat molded it into his political machine. Meanwhile, he moved up through regular channels in the party organization. By 1884 he obtained a seat on the Ward Two Democratic Committee,[13] the party's committee for the East Boston ward. Two years later, at the age of twenty-eight, he began the first of five consecutive terms in the Massachusetts House. While serving as representative, he married Mary Hickey, who sang in the church choir, and began raising a family. During Pat's third term in the legislature, in 1888, Mary gave birth to their first child, Joseph Patrick Kennedy.

That year Pat moved up to chairman of the Ward Two committee, attended the Democratic National Convention, and, according to local tradition, seconded the nomination of Grover Cleveland for President.[14] At the age of thirty he had become a power in Boston politics. When he became chairman of the Democratic committee in East Boston, his personal following took over the official party machinery in Ward Two and the party organization supplemented his personal strength.

Pat could now pick the candidates for representatives and aldermen from Ward Two. He was his own candidate for the Massachusetts Senate in '92 and '93, and was elected both times. He served the terms with neither flair nor distinction. Always a quiet man, he was never the one to spark the debate or lead the floor fight. The *Journal of the Senate* for the year 1892 shows that he made only two motions that year: he moved that the clerk supply daily newspapers for the Senate reading room, and he moved that two men be placed on the Boston Fire Department's pension rolls.[15] When one peruses the pages of the sketchy *Journal*, one finds no indication of any significant part that Pat played in the Senate.

Pat's apparently minor function in Senate activities stands in marked contrast to that of his future in-law, the colorful John F. "Honey" Fitzgerald.

Five years Pat's junior, Honey was one of the first Boston Irish to attend the famed Boston Latin School, where he became prominent in school activities. He enrolled in Harvard Medical School, but was forced to leave in his first year when his father died and he assumed obligations of support for his family. He remained fiercely family-oriented throughout his life. He became active politically, quickly rose to prominence, and joined Pat Kennedy in the State Senate in 1893. Although it was Honey's first term in the Massachusetts legislature, he took an active part in Senate debates. He was the senator who made those motions and amendments favorable to the Boston Irish, and he frequently led the Irish ranks on the Senate floor.

The voting records of the two men show that they supported the same measures. Both backed each and every bill that might have been advantageous to the Irish, the immigrant, or the laboring man. Of the 119 recorded roll calls in 1893, they differed on only four apparently insignificant votes.[16] But a difference in the scope of their interests is reflected by their committee choices. In '93 Pat served on the Committee on Street Railways and the Committee on Water Supply. These unspectacular committees were relevant to the people of the whole state. Honey served on the Committee on Election Laws and the Committee on Liquor Laws, committees whose particular relevance to Boston's Irish community is patent.[17] Pat was apparently interested in the problems of the citizens at large; Honey's interests were more narrowly confined to his constituents.

In all his affairs, Pat was always more active behind the scenes than in front of them, while the contrary is probably true of Honey. Today Pat is remembered as a quiet but solid man, while "Dr. Fitzgerald"—the name by which Honey liked to be known after Notre Dame gave him an honorary degree in 1915—is remembered as a colorful clown of dubious substance, singing "Sweet Adeline" too freely, too often. "A political Irishman of the standard type," Arthur Krock recalls him, "whose favorite topic was the anti-Irishism of the Back Bay." [18] Honey's views on foreign policy apparently never matured beyond "We are for a united Ireland and Trieste belongs to Italy." [19]

Given the great differences in the personality and temperament of Honey and Pat, it is not surprising that the two men were never close personally. Privately, Pat characterized Honey as insufferable.[20]

After the 1893 Senate term, Honey left the Senate to run for Congress, without Pat's backing, and Pat himself never again ran for elective office.[21] Pat's power depended on his ability to deliver the vote of his ward; he did not need to hold official position himself in order to exert influence. In the 20 years following his Senate career, Pat reached the apex of his political power.

While Pat served in the Massachusetts House and Senate, the

greatest political power in Boston was Patrick J. Maguire.[22] "Pea Jacket," as Maguire was known, had a political machine which was the envy of all his satellites, the lesser ward bosses. Pat was unusually close to Maguire. After the latter's death in 1896, the most powerful men in the city were Pat Kennedy; "Smiling Jim" Donovan of the South End; Joseph J. Corbett of Charlestown; Honey Fitz in the North End; and perhaps most powerful of them all, "The Mahatma," Martin Lomasney of the fabled Ward Eight.

Kennedy, Corbett, and Donovan established a working relationship and took many lesser ward bosses into their circle, which became known as the "Board of Strategy." Fitzgerald was generally excluded from the board because of his prima donna ways, and Lomasney, as a rival to the board for Maguire's power, ended up opposing it at every move, occasionally with success.

Kennedy, Corbett, and Donovan, the stalwarts of the board, headed the official Democratic organization in Boston, over which Donovan presided as chairman. The three represented the city's most potent political factor until the colorful James Michael Curley challenged and broke their power in 1913. (Curley ran that year on a reform platform.)[23] Pat was known as the "nestor of the board." A contemporary newspaper article identified him as "unquestionably one of the shrewdest men in Boston politics." He rarely made speeches, but discussed issues in a calm, constructive manner.[24] With his discreet counsel, his strong advocacy of adherence to party organization, his steady personality, and his organizational talents, Pat gave the Board of Strategy and the city's official Democratic organization the solidarity it might otherwise have lacked.

At their occasional meetings at Boston's Quincy House, the Board of Strategy chose their stooges as mayors, congressmen, and commissioners. Control of the mayor was all-important to these men, for it meant control of patronage, jobs, and contracts. Their power in their wards depended on their ability to provide favors and, most important, employment. As long as Pat had the mayor indebted to him, he could provide city jobs for his followers, and his power and connections enabled him to find work for friends in private fields as well. His house was always full of people in need of work; people who generally left satisfied. These people later repaid Pat for his kindness by voting for his choices on election day. He traded their votes to secure them, and himself, a friend in the mayor's office. And just in case all the voters did not turn out on election day, Pat used "repeaters," men who voted more than once, to insure a healthy margin in Ward Two for the candidates he favored. Joseph Kennedy remembered as a lad having heard two cronies tell Pat they had voted 128 times that day.[25] Such exaggerated civic-mindedness was not rare, and most of the bosses used "repeaters." [26]

Pat's close lieutenants were given good jobs, and he himself served in three well-paying appointive positions. In 1899 Mayor Quincy "overcame" Pat's "reluctance" (the newspapers said) and appointed him a member of the Board of Election Commissioners.[27] He held the post until 1903, though in 1902 he accepted an appointment as Wire Commissioner. Though this job probably had potential for the commissioner's personal gain, Pat was never said to have misused his office.[28] In 1905 the Wire Commissioner became a Fire Commissioner.[29]

Like his son Joe, Pat always posed as a reluctant officeholder, but these jobs, with pay that was good for the day, helped to make Pat a financial success and contributed to his prestige. They help to answer the question of what Pat got out of politics. A reporter in 1903 wrote of Pat that "Pretty much every day of his life he has witnessed something for the political betterment of Patrick J. Kennedy.[30]

Pat Kennedy was not only a longtime power in Boston politics, but also a successful businessman. Around the time of Joseph Kennedy's birth, Pat moved into a fine colonial house on Jeffries Point, the East Boston equivalent of Back Bay.[31] Perhaps as early as 1886 he had left tavernkeeping for the wholesale liquor business. When he entered the legislature that year he listed his occupation as "liquor dealer." (In subsequent years he listed his occupation as "trader.")

In any event, Pat owned two wholesale liquor houses and a coal company. In 1895 he helped to organize the Columbia Trust Company and two years later, the Sumner Savings Bank. Years later, he became president of Columbia. He accumulated a substantial estate by contemporary standards, and when he died in May, 1929, his assets were valued at $57,000.[32]

In his later years, Pat devoted his time increasingly to his business interests, and this was wise for Pat's methods of operating in politics became anachronistic long before his death. One observer commented in 1899 that Pat represented an older generation of political leader than that of the day.[33] This was true despite the fact that Pat was only five years older than Honey and two years older than the Mahatma.

There were many great changes taking place in Boston in the late nineteenth and early twentieth centuries. Newer immigrant groups were coming to the city and they were exerting an influence on Boston politics. Increased newspaper readership was opening up new avenues for office seekers, and was cutting down on the ability of the bosses to "deliver" the votes of the ward. Men with more imagination and greater understanding of the changes of the day than Pat were developing new techniques and were taking control. Honey was one of these men—he was the first Boston politician to recognize the potential of publicity. When his slogan "A Bigger, Better, Busier Boston" was posted all over the city, Honey became the first to introduce modern advertising techniques into Massachusetts politics.[34] His colorful personality and an ability to keep a staggering campaign pace gave him much of the appeal that Curley later had, and helped him to successfully oppose the Board of Strategy on more than one occasion.[35]

The early twentieth century was the time when the newer immigrant groups—Italians, Jews, Poles, and Greeks—were moving into Boston. The place of most of the Irish at the bottom of the economic ladder was taken by these people, and as the Irish moved up the ladder, many moved out of their ghettos and their former wards. Their places in society and in the slums were taken by the newer groups.

The more resourceful "pols"—Honey, Lomasney, and Curley—were able to preserve their political machines in spite of great change in the ethnic base of their wards. They were shrewd enough to utilize the newer groups for their own ends. By taking representatives of each group into their organizations, they were able to hold on to their power.[36]

A new kind of politics with new peoples, new resources, and new techniques, was replacing the quieter padrone system that "P.J." represented. By 1908, Pat was only fifty years old and would live another 21 years, but he was unable to compete in this new politics. Newspapers spoke less and less about him. Apparently control of Ward Two was never wrested from him, but he gradually, voluntarily stepped out. Because of his great personal popularity, and the almost universal respect that Pat commanded in Boston, he remained a man of some influence until his death. But after 1914, when he supported Honey in his unsuccessful bid for the Democratic party's mayoralty nomination against Curley, he apparently made no attempt to play any role in Boston politics. He represented a more purely paternalistic form of politics, and he was out of place in the loud and multi-ethnic politics of the twentieth century.

Much has been written evaluating old-time ward bosses. They traded the votes of their constituents for jobs and favors, and as brokers of interest they took commissions in one way or another. But few of the bosses milked the system.[37]

These men, for all the faults that accompanied them and their ways, fulfilled a vital social need in a day before unemployment compensation and social welfare by performing those services now handled by our welfare agencies and social workers. Because they did take care of the needs of the destitute, they retarded the implementation of social reforms that would have allowed the workingman to get help and yet preserve his dignity as a human being. But the problems of helpless people had to be met at the time, and men like Pat Kennedy saved many from desperation. It was part of the job of being a ward boss, and proponents of "good government" offered no immediate solutions to pressing problems.

Pat Kennedy was a mild-mannered man of moderate habits. He drank little—when he felt he had to take a drink for social, political, or business reasons he would drink a shot-glass of beer.[38] After his wife died in 1923,[39] he retired to Winthrop, across the harbor from East Boston, where he lived out his life with his daughter Margaret and son-in-law Charles Burke. On Sundays, Pat's fast-rising son Joe would drive out to Winthrop with his family to visit the old man.[40]

Always modest and unassuming, generous and kind, Pat was once heard to say of a politician who had double-crossed him, "He's a no-good loafer." One reporter wrote in 1937 that that was the harshest thing Pat was ever heard to say of anyone.[41] He never raised his voice in anger or used profane language.[42] The strait-laced patriarch demanded proper demeanor from his children and grandchildren. President John Kennedy later recalled that on Sunday afternoon visits to his grandfather, the old man would not even let his grandchildren wink in his presence.[43] Pat was of constant temperament[44] and liked simple foods and mild domestic cigars.[45] He could tell a good clean story.

Two days before he died, Pat's old crony Joe Corbett visited him in the hospital. He was still cheerful, with no thought that his end was near. He died peacefully, as he had lived.[46]

Joseph P. Kennedy venerated his father[47] and inherited many of his father's traits. Both were shrewd men, both had great talents for organization, both were ambitious, both had a lifelong interest in politics, both were patriarchs. But personality differences were very great. Unlike Joe, his father was always mild, quiet, a bit retiring, unassuming. He was never carried away with himself. Ethel C. Turner, who served both men as secretary at the Columbia Trust Company, remembered Joe as much more colorful and active; Pat as much more quiet and reserved.[48]

When the author asked the old-timers to compare Pat Kennedy and his famous son, only one man ventured a comment: "Joe Kennedy inherited his father's business acumen, but not his soul." [49]

THE GO-GETTER

THE YOUNG PAT KENNEDY WAS SERVING HIS THIRD TERM IN THE
Massachusetts legislature when his wife gave birth to their firstborn,
Joseph. Joe was born on September 6, 1888, in an impressive house on
Webster Street, Noodle Island's "best" street. From the start of his
life, Joe was the son of a powerful man. He was born near the top of
the Boston Irish social ladder into one of the city's "First Irish
Families." His origin must have helped him to achieve the self-con-
fidence that marked him throughout life.[1]

Joe attended a parochial school connected with the Church of the
Assumption through the seventh grade.[2] His mother had many friends
among the sisters, and his father was the most powerful man in the
community; Joe was well liked by the sisters, not only for these
reasons, but because the nuns soon discovered that the Kennedy's
charming son had an unusual aptitude for math and enjoyed figuring
out the answers to complex mathematical problems.

Joe Kennedy was equally well liked by his contemporaries. His
father's importance never prevented him from being a "regular
fellow." In an effort to live down his better home life and social status,
Joe became something of a conformist. Though he did not need
money, he sold newspapers—because the poor Irish boys who made
up the bulk of his classmates sold newspapers. Because of Pat's
position in the community, Joe was "better" than the rest of the boys,
but at the same time he was one of them. This gave him an appeal that
was heightened by athletic ability and strong personal charm. He was
able to achieve leadership of his urchin contemporaries. At the age of
eight he organized a group of boys into a military regiment to march in
a Memorial Day parade. He helped to organize a baseball team of
classmates from school. The boys called their team "the Assumptions,"
though the team had no official connection with the school. Joe was
the captain, business manager, and star, and devoted many boyhood
hours to the team and to its rivalry with "the Playfairs" and "the
Olympics." His profits as a newspaper boy went to buy him the finest
baseball equipment in East Boston. The Assumptions wore white

14

uniforms, a big English A on their breasts, and spiked shoes. With Joe as business manager, the team became a moneymaker. Baseball in those calmer days always attracted crowds, especially if the boys were in flashy uniforms. Joe rented a field for their games, and passed the hat at their first game. Afterwards they charged admission. Joe Sheehan, later one of the Kennedy's top staff members, played his first year with the Olympics; the following year Kennedy won him over to the Assumptions.

As a hobby, Joe liked to tinker with clocks. People were amazed at his ability to take parts from several broken clocks and assemble them into one running clock. Clock-making, like complex math problems, presented an inviting challenge to the bright youth. In later years, his mind was often compared to the workings of a clock.

Joe Kennedy was an industrious child. At the age of eleven he got a job as ticket-taker on the S.S. *Excelsior*, a sightseeing excursion boat. He also earned money by "spiriting away" municipal pigeons for his own flock.[3] Later, he spent his summers working as an errand boy in the Columbia Trust Company.

From the start, Joe Kennedy was interested in earning money, and his father encouraged his enterprise. Joe got satisfaction and enjoyment out of earning money, and working like the rest of the boys helped Joe to gain acceptance from his contemporaries. Being part of "the gang" always meant a lot to Joe Kennedy, and when the other boys worked he worked. He had a wholesome desire for acceptance, a desire equaled by his desire for money. He had the kind of interest in money and possessions that is often lacking in children from his financial background. Like all boys, he carted around pockets full of semi-useless objects, but his were the bulgingest pockets of all. Years later, his cousin and contemporary Joe Kane remembered that whenever he met his childhood friend on the street, Kennedy would inevitably broach the question, "How can we make some money?" [4] It is interesting that he did not turn his clock-making ability into money. Perhaps he did not do so because clock-making was an avenue closed to his playmates. Had he done so, he would have placed a second barrier between himself and his friends.

Mary Kennedy had a great respect for education and wanted her son to have the best. "Education is no burden," she would say. At the time, American Catholic doctrine on the necessity for a Catholic education had not yet rigidified; still, most Irish who thought of college at all, thought in terms of the Jesuits' Boston College, or perhaps Holy Cross. To Mary Kennedy, the best meant Harvard, and obtaining that goal would require preparation. After the seventh grade, Joe Kennedy began commuting across Boston Bay daily to pursue his studies at the famed Boston Latin School in order to prepare himself for Harvard.

Boston Latin must have presented adjustment difficulties to the Irish boy from East Boston. He was taken from an Irish neighborhood and placed in a school dominated by the Yankees, and at a time when considerable hostility existed between the two groups. But whatever difficulties Joe Kennedy had with classmates were settled long before graduation. Pat Campbell, a math teacher who later became Latin's headmaster, was impressed by the youth and took him under his wing.[5] The patronage of this popular teacher helped Joe to gain acceptance, and the importance of Pat Kennedy in Boston politics also helped. Years later, Latin baseball coach Frank Goodwin recalled this episode: Goodwin was in the habit of making snide criticisms of players who blundered, and Joe had always enjoyed Goodwin's witty barbs. But one day Goodwin's criticism fell on Joe Kennedy, and Kennedy stood up to the coach. "You have no right to make such a statement to me," the cocky lad told Goodwin. "Why not?" asked the coach. "The trouble with you, Joe, is that your father holds political office. Everybody's been toadying to you for years and you think you're better than the other boys." After discussing the incident with his father, Joe reported to Goodwin that Pat Kennedy had agreed with the coach.

While the patronage of teachers and the importance of Pat Kennedy helped Joe to gain acceptance, these factors do not account for the leadership that Joe Kennedy assumed among his classmates. That must be attributed to Joe's athletic ability and a personality that overcame the ethnic barriers that confronted him.

Joe made greater efforts to win acceptance than he should have. He neglected his studies at Boston Latin to such an extent that he had to repeat a year.[6] Despite his weak academic record, Joe's self-assurance made him popular with the faculty. Classmates remember that when the headmaster would call Joe in to reprimand him for his poor grades, the boy would turn a would-be dressing-down into a social call. There was something tremendously appealing about him.

When Joe Kennedy graduated from Boston Latin, he had compiled one of the most impressive extracurricular records in the history of the school and was clearly the outstanding personality in his class. Joe played football and basketball at Boston Latin but baseball was his forte; he captained the Boston Latin baseball team for two years. He served as colonel, the top officer of Latin's military regiment, leading it to win the Boston competition for school military units. He was also president of his class.

His senior year, Joe was awarded the John F. Fitzgerald cup—donated, of course, by Honey and awarded to the Boston high-school boy with the highest batting average at baseball. Joe had had a hit two out of every three times at bat. At the close of the school year, Honey was guest of honor at a huge party Joe Kennedy threw for his classmates at the Quincy House. So ended Kennedy's years at Boston Latin. Throughout life, Kennedy maintained affection for the school which he told Felix Frankfurter was his favorite academic institution.[7]

The following September Joe Kennedy entered Harvard. Joe had gone from an Irish community in East Boston into a Yankee community at Boston Latin, and had emerged at the top of it. Now he was to go from a Yankee community to Harvard, the Brahmin bastion. Again, Kennedy was more interested in sociability than in studies. His academic record was far from brilliant. Years later the financial wizard explained that he had been forced to switch from a major in the finance field to a music major because of his difficulties with economics. To his death, Kennedy had a great love for classical music—a love which marred his otherwise perfect philistinian façade. When SEC guests would complain about incessant symphonies, Joe would chide them with "You bastards have no love for music."

Joe's baseball ability was not unequaled at Harvard. He played first string on the freshman team, and first-string varsity in his junior year, but during his senior year a junior won Joe's position at first base.[8] Joe would not have received his letter that year, but in the last inning of the annual Harvard-Yale contest he was put in the game so that he would get the coveted felt "H." Although he struck out himself, he was the player who tagged the Yale runner out, ending the last game of his last Harvard season. The captain of the winning team had claim to the ball, but there was no love lost between Joe Kennedy and Harvard Captain Chick McLaughlin. Joe put the ball in his pocket and left the field at a run, with McLaughlin close behind.[9]

Joe did not neglect business while at Harvard. With his friend Joe Donovan, he bought a bus for $1,200 and the two set themselves up in the sightseeing business. The young men made their bus distinctive. They painted it cream and blue and neatly lettered the name

Mayflower on the side in black. Mayor Fitzgerald saw to it that Pat's boy got the prized South Station stand, though it required depriving a previous occupant. Perhaps Joe worked occasionally as barker on the bus, but he soon learned that he could do better by hiring men.[10] Their profits were great enough to permit them to buy a second bus for the following summer.

Joe also exhibited a little cockiness in the bus business, and it cost him no little money. The previous occupant of the South Station stand made so much noise that Joe finally decided to share the stand with him. Joe went to the office of Police Commissioner Stephen O'Meara and asked to see the Commissioner. O'Meara's secretary, Leo A. Rodgers, asked if he could help, but Joe would not deal with an underling: "My business is with the Commissioner." He was shown in, and displayed to O'Meara the schedules he had drawn up for himself and his competitor. O'Meara asked if the schedules were perfectly fair to both parties, and Joe assured him that they were. "In that case," O'Meara said, "you won't object to having the other bus line owner choose the alternate hours he prefers?" Joe was not in a position to object, and the other man took the better schedule. The payoff is that secretary Rodgers had been empowered to make the decision on the matter, and had been perfectly willing to let Joe choose his own hours.[11]

During the summer of 1911, between his junior and senior years at Harvard, Joe was a silent partner in the business. That summer he went to play semiprofessional ball with the Bethlehem team in the White Mountain League. He set himself up in the most expensive hotel in the area and lived well. His income as a player and his profits from the bus business were supplemented by money earned writing sports features for Boston papers.[12] Senior year Joe earned money by coaching the Harvard freshman baseball team. Early accounts of his career assert that Kennedy worked his way through Harvard; while this is untrue, it appears true that he might have done so. His profits from three summers in the bus business amounted to $5,000, a staggering amount for the early twentieth century.

Joe Kennedy took an active part in the Harvard social life. He lived in a dorm on the campus, and from his earnings he maintained himself in a style equal to that of the well-to-do Brahmins. He became a member of the Hasty Pudding Dramatic Club, the Institute of 1770, and Delta Upsilon, as well as the less prestigious St. Paul's Catholic Club and the Boston Latin Club. He served as advertising manager for an undergraduate publication. He was proud of his association with grid hero Bob Fisher and with the distinguished Professor Charles Copeland.[13] But most of his closest associates were, like himself, Boston Irish. Kennedy never gained full admittance into the mainstream of Harvard's upper-crust life, and he was never afforded entree to such exclusive Brahmin strongholds as the Fly and the Porcellian Clubs. The stodgy young Brahmins balked at accepting the cocky Irish Catholic from East Boston. Their coldness to him, their rejection of him from the "final" clubs, Harvard's most desired status symbols, stung Joe. He had always had everything he wanted, but most of all he wanted acceptance, popularity, and to be liked and desired by everyone. The Brahmins refused to accept Joe—Boston Latin's most outstanding personality—for reasons that could only have struck Joe as simple prejudice. In the final choice of "in" and "out" at Harvard, Joe Kennedy was left out.

Boston Irish resentment against "Yankees" has always been great; in Joe Kennedy, as with Honey Fitz, it was focused more narrowly upon the Brahmin aristocracy. The Brahmins rejected him from their desired company, and he, in retaliation, turned his back on them. Much of Kennedy's demeanor—his aggressiveness, his proverbial indelicacy and often vulgar diction, his scorn for aristocratic blandishments and refinements, and his frequent, almost designed manifestations of just plain bad taste—can be attributed to *his* rejection of the way of life that the Brahmins symbolized. He turned his back on their society and their ways and patterned his conduct after their opposite. He remained to his death, in taste, demeanor, and even political orientation, a rather thoroughgoing Boston Irishman. Finally, Kennedy even rejected the Brahmins' city, explaining that his principal motive for leaving Boston was aristocratic hostility to the Irish-American. Reduced to plain terms, it meant that the doors to "high society" were closed to the Kennedys.[14]

Much of Kennedy's drive and ambition must also be attributed to his desire to "show" the Boston aristocracy. He had to show them that he could go much further than the best of them, and make them regret that they, many years ago, had closed their doors to him.

Already, Joe Kennedy was seriously courting Rose Fitzgerald, the flower of Boston Irish society. Her father was by this time the equal of any political figure in the state, and Rose was his official hostess.

At the remarkable age of fifteen, Rose graduated from Dorchester High School, one of the three highest in a class of 285.[15] Honey, who looked forward to initiation into "high society," then sent her for "finishing" [16] to a Sacred Heart convent in Germany, where she studied music for a year and became "cultured" in the same way as European gentlewomen.

Rose Kennedy spent the year 1910 dreaming about and planning for her formal debut to society.[17] It was no Brahmin affair, but a Boston-Irish debut, notwithstanding which the Boston press labeled it as the social event of the season. It was an extravagant party, held in Honey's impressive mansion, the prominence and prestige of which gave Rose so much satisfaction.[18] Joe Kennedy was one of the 450 guests at the gala affair, as was Hugh Nawn, a young Harvard aviator and Joe's leading competitor for Miss Fitzgerald's attentions. Rose Fitzgerald was perhaps the prize catch among the American Irish; her suitors included not only Irish boys, but also members of the English nobility. Joe Kennedy always set out after "the best."

As little children, Joe and Rose had spent a summer at Orchard Beach together. Later, Rose would accompany her father on his political visits to Pat, and the two young people would often go to dances together, or skate together in Franklin Park. Years later, Kennedy recalled, "I was never seriously interested in anyone else." When Joe was a sophomore at Harvard, Rose returned to Boston after two years abroad. Joe went after her with the same determination that he went after money, and though Rose's courtiers included many young men with impressive lineages and impressive bank accounts, she seemed to prefer the young athlete. Handsome in the way of the Irish young, with lots of strawberry-blond hair atop six feet of lithe muscle, the dynamic Joseph Kennedy cut an attractive figure indeed.

After graduation from Harvard, Joe Kennedy worked in the counting rooms at Columbia Trust for a few months and then took a job as assistant bank examiner for the state of Massachusetts. His father's political connections got him the job despite his mediocre academic record and his poor showing in economics. The job paid $1,500, a lot of money in 1912, but Kennedy was already used to much more.

Kennedy saw that money was the foundation of power and ultimately of the social status that the Brahmins denied him. He had already set his goal at being a young millionaire,[19] and the way to make money was business. Banking, a basic factor in all business, might provide entree to any area of the financial world.[20] The job as assistant bank examiner would give him needed experience in finance, and would acquaint him with the workings of successful banking enterprises. It would also give him an opportunity to find out who the really powerful men were in Massachusetts finance. As he explained to Kane, "If you're going to get money, you have to find out where it is." Kennedy worked by "the personal equation." [21]

In the 18 months that followed, Kennedy learned the banking business and made many of the contacts to which he had looked forward. He bought an interest in the Old Colony Realty Associates, a corporation headed by his friend Henry O'Meara, and became its treasurer. He found time for two trips to Europe with bachelor friends, and he found time to court the beautiful Miss Fitzgerald. By the end of 1913 Kennedy was acquainted with the ins and outs of banking and the powerful men in it, and he was anxious to get on to bigger things than assistant bank examiner. When the opportunity presented itself he jumped.

The Columbia Trust Company was about to close its doors. Founded by Pat Kennedy and several others in 1895, Joe himself had worked there, and Pat was serving as Columbia's vice-president in 1914.[22] Stockholders of Columbia now wished to sell the neighborhood institution to First Ward National Bank, but control of Columbia stock could be picked up with some effort. The opportunity was too great for Kennedy to resist. He borrowed money from many people. Eugene Thayer, president of the Merchants National Bank, had been impressed with Kennedy and loaned him the bulk. O'Meara put up $1,200. Relatives helped out. With $45,000 of borrowed capital he bought control of Columbia's stock. The merger with the First Ward National was averted, and on January 20, 1914, Joseph P. Kennedy, age twenty-five, emerged as president of the Columbia Trust Company.

THE FIRST STEPS TO MILLIONS

Kennedy's election as president of Columbia Trust marked his start on the road to riches and the start of a career unprecedented in many ways. The press ventured that at the age of twenty-five, he was the country's youngest bank president,[23] an assertion that has been continually repeated and never challenged.

Less than ten months after assuming his new duties, Joe Kennedy wed Rose Fitzgerald. Friends of both say that Mayor Fitzgerald wanted something fancier for his prized daughter. The two men never got along well; both resented being identified as the other's in-law.[24] Kennedy's friend Edward Gallagher asserts that Kennedy was fond of

Honey "deep down," but it was only a "deep down" [25] fondness. Years later, when firmly ensconced at the top, Kennedy would treat most of the Fitzgerald clan with coldness and occasional rudeness[26]—"I can't help it that I married into an S.O.B. of a family," he told Franklin D. Roosevelt.[27]

Honey should have realized that aggressive Joe Kennedy, already a bank president, had great potential, and would someday be a man of national importance. On October 7, 1914, the couple were married by Cardinal O'Connell in the Prelate's study. "I'd always wanted to be married by a Cardinal and I was," Joe later remarked with obvious satisfaction.[28] It was a small but formal wedding. Rose's sister Agnes was the bridesmaid and Joe Donovan was best man. Following the wedding the couple took a two-week honeymoon and then settled in a $6,500 house in Brookline, a respectable "Protestant" suburb of Boston. After borrowing to get control of Columbia, Kennedy was already in debt up to his ears, but he borrowed another $2,000 for the down payment on the house. It was worth it: although the house was a comedown for Mayor Fitzgerald's daughter, to Kennedy it meant getting into the Protestant world, a fact of great significance to him.[29] The young couple immediately set out to raise a family. Exactly nine months and twenty days after their marriage, Rose Fitzgerald Kennedy gave birth to her first child. The press speculated that it would be named in honor of the Mayor.[30] The parents named it Joseph P. Kennedy, Jr. Rose thereafter settled down to her roles as mother and doyenne of young Boston-Irish "society." [31]

Joe Kennedy worked hard as president of Columbia. He had to commute daily from Brookline, well to the west of Boston, to Columbia's offices at East Boston, and then put in a long day. On the job from 8:00 A.M. to 6:00 P.M., he took no lunch break, but stayed at his desk and lunched on crackers and milk.[32]

Kennedy was popular in the immigrant East Boston in which he had grown up, and he was a popular banker. There was nothing standoffish about him. The stodginess that passes for banker's reserve was foreign to him; he worked in his shirt sleeves and mingled and joked with his poor clients. The people found him kind and helpful. Everyone received good and sympathetic treatment from Kennedy. Kennedy always understood that good personal relations were part of business success, and he slighted no one. One of Kennedy's early clients was Tom Pappas, today a prosperous, well-known Republican leader in the Boston area. Pappas remembers going to Joe Kennedy when he was sixteen. His father had just died, leaving Pappas with two small grocery stores and a number of debts. His financial problems seemed insurmountable. Kennedy made all his problems disappear. "He was wonderful to me," Pappas recalls.[33] "He made everyone's problems disappear; everyone felt that way about him," says Ethel C. Turner, Kennedy's secretary at Columbia.[34] It was a highly personal kind of business, and Kennedy was not above accepting personal favor in lieu of interest-paid-to-the-bank,[35] a matter which, by today's more refined standards, would be regarded as highly unethical.

While Kennedy maintained good personal relations with the immigrants and laborers that made up Columbia's clientele, he did not give up trying to cultivate the Boston aristocracy. He solidified his friendship with the influential people he had met as banking examiner and met new people in the Boston financial world. He also received his personal induction into politics. As a last act before leaving the mayor's office Fitzgerald appointed his son-in-law as the city's director of the Collateral Loan Company. The Collateral Loan Company was a large semipublic pawnshop established by the city to protect the poor from "loan sharks." It was perhaps the biggest pawnshop in America, and had three directors, one of whom was appointed by the mayor. After accepting the office, Kennedy spent several days going over the corporation's books and discovered sizable embezzlements. When the irregularities were exposed on December 4, 1914, he got considerable publicity throughout the state. He tried to straighten out the company's involved financial situation, but after five months of hearings, charges, and countercharges he resigned, disgusted.[36]

In 1917, all of Kennedy's efforts to cultivate the right connections finally began to pay off. Though only twenty-eight years old, he was elected a trustee of the Massachusetts Electric Company, the most powerful utility corporation in New England. Serving with Kennedy on its board of trustees were men of the stature of Charles Francis Adams. More important to Kennedy, however, was trustee Galen Stone, of the brokerage house of Hayden, Stone and Company. Later he would be very useful to Kennedy. Kennedy had been defeated for election to the board on two previous occasions, no doubt in part because of his youth. But as the company's president told him, he had been defeated in part because of hostility to Irish Catholics.[37] Kennedy had been intent on getting a seat. Why? He explained to a friend, "Do you know a better way to meet people like the Saltonstalls?"[38] He was finally named to the board on May 29, 1917, the day on which Rose

Kennedy gave birth to her second child. This one, they named for the Mayor.

Kennedy was now ready to change his occupation. On April 6, 1917, the United States had entered World War I. For one reason or another, most likely for a combination of reasons, the vigorous and athletic father of two accepted a safe berth in defense manufacturing for the duration of the war. Harvard classmates, who had rushed to enlist, resented his decision.[39]

Guy Currier, Boston attorney for Bethlehem Steel, interested Bethlehem's Charles M. Schwab in Kennedy.[40] According to Honey's biographer, the Mayor also recommended Kennedy to Schwab,[41] who finally appointed the Mayor's son-in-law assistant general manager at Bethlehem's huge Fore River Shipyards at Quincy, Massachusetts. After having played on Bethlehem's ball team six years before, Kennedy returned to their employ in a much higher capacity as second in command at Fore River with 2,200 workers under him—and at the then fabulous salary of $20,000 per year.[42] He was succeeded as president of Columbia Trust by his father.

Fore River's manager, Joseph Powell, had a first-rate assistant in young Joe Kennedy. Kennedy worked himself to ill-health on the job. Almost immediately, he noticed the lack of eating facilities for the employees, and had a big cafeteria installed where lunches were sold to the workers. It proved a moneymaker for Bethlehem.

As second man at Fore River, Kennedy came in contact with another second man also destined for fame. Assistant Secretary of the Navy Franklin D. Roosevelt and Kennedy had occasional dealings that were not too amiable. One story is told of how Roosevelt demanded that Bethlehem deliver unpaid-for ships to the Argentine government, whose credit was none too solid. Kennedy persistently refused to deliver the ships, and finally Roosevelt threatened that if Bethlehem did not deliver the ships they would be towed away by United States government vessels. They were.[43]

After the war ended, Fore River's business slowed down. When Stone offered Kennedy a job as manager of Hayden, Stone's Boston office, Kennedy jumped. He was anxious to get on to his fortune and though the job paid only $10,000 per year,[44] it had wider opportunities than a career with Bethlehem. He was already thirty, the father of three, and a long way from being a millionaire. Kennedy joined Hayden, Stone in June, 1919, a young man in a hurry to be fabulously wealthy. Besides directing Stone's office, Kennedy took a financial interest in a number of enterprises connected with the young motion picture industry. With a group of young Bostonians he bought control of a chain of 31 movie theaters in northern New England, an enterprise that the Kennedy family owned into the 1960s and may still own. Kennedy acquired the New England franchise for Universal Pictures. He dabbled in motion picture production himself on a very limited scale, and though he enjoyed it his efforts were unsuccessful.[45] He also bought heavily into Todd Shipyards, one of Fore River's competitors.[46] He was hurrying to a Todd stockholders' meeting in downtown New York when on September 16, 1920, a wagonload of bombs exploded in front of the J. P. Morgan offices. Kennedy was only a few hundred feet from the anarchist's pushcart. The explosion killed 33 and maimed more than 200; Kennedy himself was thrown to the ground by the shock.[47]

It was at Hayden, Stone, just at the start of the 1920s that Joe Kennedy learned the ins and outs of the stock market and the ways to manipulate it. In those days before market regulations, a clever operator could make a fortune in legalized swindling by trading on "inside information," or by buying and selling in such a manner as to insure profit. An operator might buy an option on an inactively traded stock, then buy and sell the stock on the open market in such a manner as to give the appearance of considerable interest in the stock. "You simply advertised the stock by trading it," Kennedy later explained.[48] When the public began buying into the company, the operator would push the price of the stock up and cash in his options. After this artificially stimulated interest died down the stock would return to its normal, lower position on the market. The operator would have made a pile, and the only losers would be the "suckers." An operator could also make a great bundle on a stock that was declining in value. One might sell large quantities of a stock on the open market—stock that the seller did not own. By so doing, the operator could further depress the value of the stock, and then buy the shares needed to deliver the stock sold at a higher price. The difference between the price at which the operator sold and the lower price at which he purchased was profit. "It's easy to make money in this market," Kennedy told a friend. "We'd better get in before they pass a law against it." [49] He followed his own advice and, with an innate sense of timing, became an accomplished master at both kinds of manipulating. By 1923 the wealthy father of five was ready to go out on his own as an independent financier, and left Hayden, Stone and Company.

Only one of Kennedy's many operations in this period has been extensively reported—an incident in which Kennedy could pose as the "good guy," and therefore spoke freely of it to journalists during the 1920s, when such doings were not so frowned upon. Walter Howey, Hearst's executive in Boston, had a large personal interest in Yellow Cab. Yellow's stock was being "bear raided"; its market value was being pushed down by manipulators from the brokerage house of Block, Maloney and Company, bringing great personal loss to Howey, Yellow's president John Hertz, and others with big stakes in Yellow Cab. In a month Block, Maloney and Company had pushed Yellow's price down from 85 to 50. At this point Howey called Joe Kennedy. The two had met in 1922 when Kennedy had solicited support for Fitzgerald's gubernatorial race from Hearst's *Boston American.* Howey went along with Fitzgerald and gave Honey considerable good publicity. Now it was Howey who needed help. He told Kennedy of Yellow's predicament and recruited him to direct a counter-manipulation on behalf of himself, Hertz, and other interested investors.

Though suffering from a bout with neuritis, Kennedy set himself up in a suite at the Waldorf-Astoria, had a ticker tape installed, and from his bedside began buying and selling Yellow's stock with brokers across the country. His goal was to offset the efforts of the opposition to drive the stock down. Kennedy stayed in the Waldorf for seven weeks, working only with his longtime personal assistant and beloved secretary Eddie Moore, for whom Edward M. "Ted" Kennedy is named. Placing orders around the country, Kennedy pushed the stock price up and down to confuse the manipulators for Block, Maloney and Company. Yellow Cab had dropped to $48.00 a share when Kennedy came in, and it was going lower and lower. He pushed it up to $62.00, then it fell to $46.00. Finally it stabilized at $50.00. Joe Kennedy's job was done. "I woke up one morning, exhausted, and I realized that I hadn't been out of that hotel room in seven weeks," he recalled years later. "My baby, Pat, had been born and was almost a month old, and I hadn't even seen her."

Kennedy had warned Hertz before he began shoring up the stock that the operation might cost Hertz and his associates $5,000,000. When he finished his job the decline in the price of Yellow Cab had been halted and the operation had cost the Hertz group relatively little. And Joe Kennedy? "Several of us emerged wealthy men," he later mused.[50]

Kennedy floated around for a couple of years doing jobs like the one for the Yellow Cab associates and manipulating for his own account. In 1924, soon after the job for Hertz, he moved his family of seven children to New York; Boston "was no place to bring up Irish children," he later told inquirers.[51] The Old Guard stubbornly refused to accept the Irish-Americans, a fact that was reinforced for Kennedy by his rejection from the Cohasset Country Club.[52] He was stung by the rejection and refused to expose his children to similar Brahmin slights. "They wouldn't have asked my daughters to join their debutante clubs," he said. "Not that our girls would have joined anyway—they never gave two cents for that society stuff. But the point is they wouldn't have been asked in Boston." [53] Though no Brahmin young man had had a more rapid rise in the city's life, Joe Kennedy felt—perhaps justifiably—slighted by Boston.

Kennedy left Boston in style. He moved his family to their new home in Riverdale, New York, in a private railway car brought to a special siding near Kennedy's home. New York had many attractions besides lack of prejudice against Irish-Americans. It was the center of the financial world, and as Kennedy was wont to say, "If you want to make money, go where the money is." [54] It had the glamor and flair that was the 1920s. It had the expensive, fashionable restaurants and nightclubs, the flashy fast living that staid Boston lacked. New York was the place to be in 1925, and Joe Kennedy would be there.

AND MILLIONS MORE

Immediately after relocating Joe Kennedy went back into business. He considered taking a plunge in Florida real estate, but when both Stone and financier Matt Brush advised against it, he abandoned the thought.[55] Instead, Kennedy went into movies. Kennedy's friend Will Hays, who had been the Republican National Chairman and Postmaster General under President Harding, was at the time president of the Motion Pictures Producers and Distributors of America.[56] Hays urged Kennedy to come into the movie business.[57] The glamor of the motion picture world appealed to Kennedy, and he had been interested in the blossoming field for some time. At Hayden, Stone, he had been agent for the financial interests that owned Robertson-Cole, an English firm that owned Film Booking Offices (FBO), an American film-producing outfit. The English organization was in difficulty due to mismanagement, and Joe Kennedy decided to buy their American affiliate.

Kennedy sold part of his interest in the Maine-New Hampshire theaters and interested several associates in the new enterprise. Currier put up $125,000, four Boston and New York bankers invested, and Mayor Fitzgerald took a small financial interest. Kennedy went to England to interest the English backers of Robertson-Cole in selling FBO. The English outfit had invested over $7,000,000 in FBO; Kennedy offered one million for it. They turned him down cold. Within a month, Lord Inverforth of Robertson-Cole arrived in Boston. "Is the deal still open?" he wanted to know. On February 8, 1926, FBO changed hands, and Joe Kennedy was in the movie business. Mayor Fitzgerald, an incorrigible publicity seeker, gave the story to the *Boston Post*, which headlined on page one:

JOHN F. FITZGERALD

IS LATEST MOVIE MAGNATE

"This is one of the biggest deals in the motion picture industry," magnate Fitzgerald told the press. He "let it be known" that the transaction was a ten million dollar deal.[58]

Kennedy represented a new type of man in the film world:[59] the Wall Streeter. Before the mid-twenties, the movies had been pretty much left to bohemians and small businessmen with an aesthetic bent. The "man on the make" who so symbolized the 1920s was noticeably absent in Hollywood. Marcus Loew, on hearing of the new owner of FBO, was skeptical: "A banker! A banker? Why I thought this business was only for furriers."[60] Kennedy himself regarded his peers—men like Loew, Louis B. Mayer, and Samuel Goldwyn—as a bunch of "pants pressers."[61]

Kennedy was a banker and, as he explained in 1928, he always approached the amusement business as a banker and a businessman.[62] He realized that the objective of any business was profits. The way to make profits was simple: he told fellow producers in a 1927 magazine article, "We must make pictures that have appeal to all."[63] Nothing can be done that appeals to all, but Joe Kennedy did the next best thing. He specialized in the mediocre that appeals to the most. With his economic approach to the industry, Kennedy was not preoccupied with "art." He and men like him contributed "commercialism" to American movies in the 1920s.

In 1926 William A. Johnson, editor of *Motion Picture World*, asserted:

> *Chances are that the captains of other industries would fail miserably if they tried to make mills and factories out of picture studios. Picture making is wholly creative, the end, without which nothing, being the capture of the public fancy. To standardize pictures is to make them dull, and so deplete the box office. . . . It is the mediocre, the economical creation that loses money.*[64]

Joe Kennedy successfully challenged this common Hollywood belief. Under his leadership, FBO stepped up its production to almost a picture a week, concentrating on westerns and melodramas—some of them composed by people of great "wasting" talent, such as young script writer Darryl F. Zanuck.[65] Kennedy ground out his trash at such a rate that FBO became a film factory, producing rather standardized economical, mediocre "creations." And they made money. While the larger producers were spending an average of $300,000 on their films, Kennedy's productions cost FBO an average of $30,000 each. Kennedy could get away with it; Johnson could not. Johnson and the vast majority of Hollywood executives thought in terms of appealing to sophisticated metropolitan audiences. Kennedy spurned competition with them and aimed to appeal to small-town viewers. They could be pleased more easily and less expensively. As Kennedy explained in 1928, when he came to Hollywood "producers were fighting to get their pictures on Broadway, New York, and State Street, Chicago. I concentrated on getting and keeping Film Booking Office's pictures on Main Street." He succeeded with films like *A Poor Girl's Romance*, *Red Hot Hoofs*, *Rose of the Tenements*, *The Dude Cowboy*, and *The Flame of the Argentine*.[66] When a journalist in 1927 flatteringly commented "You have had some good pictures this year," Kennedy was pleasantly surprised. "What were they?" he asked.[67]

As much as any other man, Joe Kennedy symbolized the alliance of Wall Street and Main Street that was the 1920s. Hays, a shrill caricature of Harding-era man, was delighted. An article in *Motion Picture World* explained that Hays had wanted Kennedy in the industry for a number of reasons, "But most of all, General Hays wanted his friend to come into the motion picture business because he regarded him as . . . a man, who, in his business ideals and concepts as in the fine character of his home life, would bring to the industry much that it has lacked in the past." [68]

Joe Kennedy turned the sick company into a profitable business. He cut costs of production to the bone. Labor costs were especially high. He explained to a journalist in 1928 that he had found that a movie accountant whose pay in any other industry would range from $5,000 to $10,000 was getting $20,000 in Hollywood. He changed that.[69]

In the summer of 1926, Kennedy allied FBO with Ideal Films Ltd. of London. The arrangement was the first genuinely reciprocal exchange of production and distribution facilities between British and American companies.[70]

Even his approach to casting showed that he had greater business sense than anyone else in Hollywood. Football hero Red Grange wanted to get into acting, and though several of the major studios had turned him down, Kennedy realized that Grange would be a box office attraction. Red's acting abilities were not in any way a relevant consideration. Kennedy asked his young sons, Joe Jr. and Jack, if they wanted to see Grange in the movies, and their enthusiastic "yes" meant a contract for Grange. Red starred in a movie about a college football hero and the film proved highly profitable. Kennedy tried to get Grange to stick to movies, but after his first film the athlete realistically appraised himself and concluded that he was a ballplayer, not an actor.[71]

Within a year, FBO was on its feet, and Joe Kennedy began looking for bigger and better things. He became the financial wizard of Hollywood. When he went there in 1926, he was scarcely a millionaire. When he left it in 1930 he was a millionaire several times over.

The *Motion Picture World* sketch of Kennedy in December, 1926, ended with, "Joseph P. Kennedy's shadow looms larger every minute." [72] By 1928 the shadow began to move. Centralization of production and distribution of films was perhaps the most important development in the movie industry in the late 1920s and the mastermind behind many of the mergers that brought centralization was Joe Kennedy.[73] In 1928, gossip-columnist Louella Parsons called him "the coming Napoleon of the movies." [74]

Late in 1927, Kennedy met David Sarnoff, strong man of Radio Corporation of America, through Boston department-store mogul Louis Kirstein,[75] and interested Sarnoff in FBO. Talkies were coming in and the major studios were contracting with RCA's competitors for sound equipment and services. RCA needed a sure outlet in Hollywood for its products, and to get it Sarnoff bought a sizable chunk of

FBO. The affiliation between FBO and RCA (and through RCA, with its affiliates, General Electric and Westinghouse) was one of the most significant associations in the industry for it formally linked film producers with sound producers, and was one of the first examples of vertical integration in Hollywood.[76]

Kennedy's longtime banking associates were not idle while Kennedy was shaping up FBO. Elisha Walker, president of Blair and Company, and the brokers from the house of Lehman Brothers, were busy buying into Pathé Pictures and Keith-Albee-Orpheum theaters. Blair and Company were the bankers for Pathé, and Lehman Brothers were the bankers for KAO. KAO itself owned controlling interest in Pathé. The Walker-Lehman associates had Kennedy appointed special advisor to Pathé in February, 1928, at the reported salary of $2,000 per week.[77] That same month, Kennedy sold a substantial interest in FBO to KAO, just one month after his sale of FBO shares to RCA.[78] The situation was shaping up for a colossal merger.

Three months later, in May, 1928, Kennedy and his associates— Walker, Lehman Brothers, and Jeremiah Milbank of the Chase National group—gained control of KAO.[79] Edward Albee, whose name symbolized vaudeville, was no great businessman and failed to see what was going on around him. He had foolishly given a large KAO stock option to his untrustworthy right-hand man, J. J. Murdock, whom Albee had placed as president of Pathé. Murdock sold the option to Kennedy, who exercised it.[80] At the same time, Kennedy approached Albee directly. He suggested that Albee sell out. Reportedly, he offered Albee $21.00 per share at a time when the stock was selling at $16.00 on the exchange. Albee declined, but changed his mind on the advice of those he thought were his friends. He sold. Three months later the stock soared to $50.00.[81]

Albee was kept on as president of KAO, and the post of Chairman of the Board was created for Kennedy. Albee announced Kennedy's association with KAO with pleasure: "Mr. Kennedy has shown in a brief but colorful career in the picture business such constructive and organization genius that we consider him a tremendous asset to our business. He is energetic, dynamic, and a straight-shooter." [82] Kennedy continued as head of FBO, and in his position with Pathé.

Though president of KAO, Albee no longer had financial control of his organization, and he failed to realize that he had sold decision-making authority with his stock. Several months later he had his awakening. One day he entered Kennedy's office to make a suggestion.

According to associates Kennedy was brief and blunt: "Didn't you know, Ed? You're washed up, you're through." Albee, at last, understood. He quit and died not long after.[83]

Before the merger of FBO, KAO, and Pathé was culminated, Kennedy went another step. Irving Rossheim, who headed Stanley movie producers, took control of First National Pictures in June of 1928, and Kennedy was appointed special advisor to First National with extensive executive authority.[84] E. B. Derr, who had worked with Kennedy at Fore River and followed him to FBO, was put in charge of management's relations with First National's stockholders.[85] Playwright Benjamin Glazer, the production advisor under Kennedy at Pathé, was made production advisor at First National as well.[86] It was widely rumored in Hollywood that with Kennedy at the helm, First National would develop "internal and operating differences," which would lead to an amalgamation of First National, Rossheim's Stanley Company, and the companies Kennedy controlled.[87] Under the terms of the contract between Kennedy and First National, announced on August 10, 1928, Kennedy was to have charge of all producing and distributing at First National for five years, at the annual salary of $150,000 per year, with an option to purchase 25 percent of First National's stock at any time during the five years.[88] Kennedy, however, was unable to bring First National into his greater scheme. He and his associates actually had control of FBO, KAO, and Pathé, but they had little power among First National stockholders. A week after the announcement of the terms of Kennedy's contract, he left First National. His friends told reporters that difficulties with stockholders on "fundamental policies of management" led to a separation by mutual consent.[89] The day the separation was announced, Kennedy and Mrs. Kennedy sailed for Europe to take a six-week vacation at the ultra-fashionable French resorts of Biarritz and Deauville.[90]

After Kennedy's return from Europe, RCA, already a chief stockholder in FBO, bought into KAO. Radio-Keith-Orpheum, RKO, emerged as a holding company in late October, 1928, controlling both FBO and KAO.[91] Kennedy resigned from FBO and KAO and held no executive position in the new RKO. He placed Hiram Brown at RKO's head, a leather magnate who knew nothing about show business but what the ticker tape told him.[92] John J. Ford, Kennedy's top executive, became RKO's general manager.[93] Before a year expired, FBO and KAO ceased to exist as separate entities, and RKO, their successor, became an RCA subsidiary. Besides his fabulous profits from FBO and

KAO stock, Kennedy was said to have received $150,000 for bringing about the merger.[94] The impression still exists in Hollywood that from the start of 1928 Kennedy was working with the (in)famous Mike Meehan as a representative of RCA.[95]

Temporarily, Pathé was left out of RKO. By this time Kennedy held the title of Chairman of the Board at Pathé, with Derr as executive vice-president.[96] Kennedy retired as active head of Pathé in May, 1930, but at Walker's request retained the title of Chairman of the Board.[97]

Derr assumed Kennedy's executive duties. It was widely rumored that Kennedy was far from done with the movie business. He and his associates were said to have had 15 million dollars still in Pathé at the time of his "retirement" and Kennedy was believed to be engineering a Pathé merger. Pathé had been comparatively idle, but just before Kennedy's resignation the studio concentrated on several big pictures and rumors of merger began to spread. Pathé stock zoomed up on the stock exchange.[98] RKO bought up considerable amounts of Pathé stock at the time. At tremendous expense to RKO, a Pathé-RKO merger was now more feasible.

In 1933, New York Congressman William I. Sirovich urged investigation of the movie industry and mergers in it. In discussing the Pathé-RKO merger, he asserted that a group was loaded down with a large block of Pathé stock then quoted at $30.00. As soon as the merger became known, this inside group pushed Pathé up to around $80.00 and sold out on the open market. RKO purchases of Pathé stock at this unwarranted level "emptied the RKO treasury." [99]

Now all that was needed to complete the formal merger of the two outfits was the mechanical approval of the stockholders. With RKO and its associates in control of both Pathé's management and Pathé stock, RKO could make formal purchase of Pathé's assets for a pittance. Pathé's assets were sold to RKO for something less than five million dollars, though the actual cost of Pathé to RKO was many times that, for it involved purchasing control of Pathé's stock at inflated prices. Those who had sold their Pathé stock to RKO did quite neatly, but those Pathé stockholders who were not in the Kennedy circle shared only in the five million dollars and felt cheated. They argued that their company was worth five times five million. Several stockholder's suits were instituted against Kennedy and other Pathé executives, charging that the Pathé officers had conspired to sell the company to RKO for an inadequate amount. But at the time stockholders' suits were extremely difficult to win, with conclusive evidence of actual fraud often needed for success. The suits fell through, and the merger was carried out.

The cost of gaining control of Pathé was equally rankling to independent stockholders in RKO. Refinancing of RKO was necessitated at least in part because of the merger. RCA's cooperation was of course necessary in the refinancing, for they controlled 22 percent of RKO's stock. A refinancing plan favorable to RCA was accepted after RKO officers made clear that the alternative was for RKO to begin bankruptcy proceedings. RCA emerged controlling 60 percent of RKO. RKO's minority stockholders, like Pathé's stockholders, felt swindled, but no complaints were heard from Kennedy, Walker, Sarnoff or Lehman Brothers. Only the little folks—the suckers—complained. They were the only ones that were hurt. It is little wonder that First National's stockholders would have none of the much acclaimed "financial wizard." Kennedy was later denounced by Wisconsin Congressman John Schafer as "the chief racketeer" in the RKO "swindle." [100]

While all of Kennedy's companies did not prosper, Kennedy unquestionably did. Under his management, Pathé's costs mushroomed far beyond its small increase in sales, and Pathé went from a profit-making company to one nearing bankruptcy. Ultimately, Kennedy managed to get his own money out of the weakened company by helping to engineer the merger with RKO.

The goal of the business executive of the 1920s was to enrich himself, not to make his company prosper. As Joe Kennedy later wrote, corporations were run for the benefit of the corporations' management, and not for the benefit of the corporate body.[101] He himself was an excellent example of the 1920s executive. Executives seemed little concerned about their duty to protect and serve the interest of the stockholders at large; such concerns were shunted aside by executives who made unfair personal use of their positions of trust. Joseph Kennedy was but a good and successful example.

Kennedy also did independent producing while in Hollywood, teaming up with Gloria Swanson. Kennedy's contact with the glamorous film star apparently started when he helped finance her film *Sadie Thompson*,[102] based on Somerset Maugham's torrid *Rain*. Thereafter they became close, both professionally and personally, and their names became linked romantically. Kennedy made no attempt to discourage such speculation. The rumors became more and more extravagant, growing over the years, including one to the effect that the glamorous film star's adopted son, "curiously" named Joseph, was not adopted at all.[103] Actually, Miss Swanson had adopted Joseph years before she had ever heard of Joseph Kennedy,[104] but the story made good telling. Hedda Hopper reported the unlikely story that Honey Fitz, himself celebrated for an alleged affair with one "Toodles," [105] had ordered his errant son-in-law out of Hollywood.[106] Kennedy thoroughly enjoyed the rumors—whether true or not, half the fun is in having it known—but Rose Kennedy was deeply hurt by the rumors, and for many years their marriage suffered.

Kennedy contracted with United Artists to produce several Swanson movies—"big" films designed for Great White Way audiences. The first was the ill-fated *Queen Kelly*, directed by the famous German director Erich von Stroheim, who was very much in vogue at the time. *Queen Kelly* was based on von Stroheim's story "The Swamp" and was set in a pre-1914 German kingdom and in German East Africa. It included some scenes involving bawdyhouses and the seduction of convent girls, which by standards of the day must have appeared rather torrid. Most of the German episode and a few scenes from the African sequence had been shot when production was halted early in 1929. The film seemed to be going nowhere, yet $750,000 had already been invested in it. Further efforts to make *Queen Kelly* manageable proved unsuccessful and brought its cost closer to a million. There was some question that the film, if completed, would get by the censors. Most important, though, "talkies" had already made *Queen Kelly* obsolete. Al Jolson had rocked the film world with his successful "talking" movie *The Jazz Singer*, and the handwriting was on the wall. "Von, the lousiest sound film will be better than the best silent film," Kennedy explained to the creative director when he had the film shelved.[107] Von Stroheim, who was later seen as Gloria Swanson's butler-husband in *Sunset Boulevard*, suffered a horrible blow to his reputation and career.

There were also colossal financial losses incidental to the scrapping of the film, and for years articles on Kennedy referred to his financial loss on the film of nearly a million dollars.[108] Even Joseph P. Kennedy, Jr., boasted to admiring friends about the shellacking his father had taken on the venture.[109]

In the late 1950s, Gloria gave a print of the film to the New York Museum of Modern Art, whose catalog noted that the film had meant "a reputed loss to Miss Swanson of $800,000." Ultimately, Gloria revealed to an interviewer that by her arrangement with Kennedy, *she* was responsible for the monies; Kennedy was repaid in full while it was she who had suffered the losses. She was tired, she explained, of subsidizing Kennedy's self-flattery.[110]

The next Kennedy-Swanson effort was more successful. *The Trespasser*, produced in 1929, was a melodrama set in Chicago's fashionable society world. In it, Miss Swanson, a stenographer, elopes with her employer, a young member of the "smart set." His parents object to his alliance with the stenographer because of her lowly origins, and an annulment is procured. After a tragic second marriage, a death, and a nervous breakdown, the couple is reunited for a happy ending. The film was widely advertised, both as "a drama of social society," and as Gloria's first "all talking and singing film." [111] It was a profitable venture, but as *Variety*'s Green and Laurie wrote, it was "not such a hit, and Gloria strolled slowly toward the studio exit." [112]

The United Artists schedule for 1930 included Gloria Swanson in *What a Widow*, a Joseph P. Kennedy production, and Kennedy's contract with United Artists called for two more Kennedy-Swanson films.[113] They were never produced. "I questioned his judgment," Gloria explained years later. "He did not like to be questioned." [114] Kennedy left the movie business; his retirement from "Gloria Productions, Inc.," and from his Pathé duties were announced at the same time.[115]

BIRTH OF THE LEGEND

The 1920s saw the coming of the talkies, the great bull market, the speakeasies and sidewalks of New York, and the rise of modern advertising and public relations techniques. The concept of "the Image," and methods for the shaping thereof, were born in the twenties. The advertising and PR men gave the period some of its wonderful hocus-pocus quality and also helped to give it its folk heroes. Sometimes, the heroes were the products of spontaneous and undirected buildups, as when the handsome Charles A. Lindbergh was transformed from the courageous aviator that he was into the superman that he was not. His PR job was done for and by an enthralled America. At other times, contrived and carefully managed public relations campaigns produced heroes, often performing miracles in the process, as when an all-around degenerate named George Herman Ruth became in the minds of Americans a symbol of American manhood and the Galahad of American women.

Joe Kennedy never became a full-fledged folk hero in the class of Lindy or The Babe, but his myth was born in much the same way as theirs. By the time he came to Washington in the early 1930s he was already a legendary figure—the product of a PR campaign that was in part spontaneous, in part contrived.

Many elements in Joe Kennedy's background, his career, and his status, made him a hero-type for the '20s that was capable of being built up. Just being a rich man made him a hero for the '20s, when wealth was equated with virtue and obtaining wealth was regarded as the noblest goal. Kennedy had been a fabulous success by what was then the most meaningful standard for success. And he had made most of his money in movies, the most glamorous enterprise in that enterprise-oriented era. Even more important was the way in which he had become a success. In the 1920s, Horatio Alger stories were supposed to provide a pattern for the young, and Joe Kennedy's fantastic rise did come surprisingly close to Alger's pattern. Though he was neither a poor boy nor an orphan, he did come from a slum neighborhood, and he was essentially a self-made man. He had been a newspaper boy; he had been beset by villains (the Brahmins); he had risen early in the morning and worked hard, shrewdly, and late; he had been alert to opportunities; a fine old man had recognized his virtues and had become his benefactor (Currier/Stone). Pluck had brought Joseph Kennedy luck. And as a result, he had obtained the golden apple of success. Pure Alger. Joe Kennedy was living proof that Dick and Newsboy could become a multimillionaire.

With this kind of background, it is little wonder that interest in Joe Kennedy was great. Newspaper articles about his companies often included colorful, half-fanciful biographical sketches of him. By 1927, feature articles on Joe Kennedy began appearing—spontaneously.

Joe Kennedy's legend was also in part contrived. It contained many details that could only have originated with Kennedy himself. The fullest of the Horatio Alger style accounts, from *American Magazine*[116] in 1928, followed interviews with Kennedy and included much erroneous information in quotations from Kennedy himself.[117] (The article's author, an unrelated John B. Kennedy, later served on Mr. Kennedy's staff.)[118] Many of the glamorous but untrue episodes are included in the columns of *New York Times* man Arthur Krock, who always had full access to Kennedy and who must have been relying on information that Kennedy gave him. Companies with which he was associated would issue professionally-written press releases chock-full of nonsense, with suggested leads like

CLIMBING THE LADDER FROM CANDY VENDOR
TO MOVIE MAGNATE[119]

Kennedy apparently did not have a full-time PR man on his payroll directing his image; stories about him are not consistent in their fabrications, and they often included items that a sensitive PR man would have kept out. But Kennedy himself, by misleading *American's* reporter, Krock, and no doubt others, took quite a hand in creating the legend of Joseph P. Kennedy.[120]

A brief composite account of the legend synthesized from the more typical pieces of the period might run something like this:

> Joseph P. Kennedy was born in 1888 in the Irish slums of Boston. At an early age he went to work peddling newspapers, and at the age of eleven he went to work on the S.S. Excelsior as ticket-taker (or candy vendor or both).

One account identifies the *Excelsior* as a vessel on the New York-Boston run, which would have meant that the tender lad was working overnight on the high seas, sharing quarters with coarse and hard seamen.

> Joe was determined to go to Harvard, and worked his way through.[121] He did so by working as a clerk in a candy store and by running a sightseeing bus business. Joe was the lecturer on the bus for three summers.[122] He became the star of the Harvard baseball team and a whiz in banking courses. Upon graduation, Joe was torn over his future.[123] Should he accept the big league baseball contract offered him?[124] Or should he take a job as assistant bank examiner, offered to him because of his outstanding performance in subjects related to banking?[125] He took the latter.

Some accounts say that Joe took the job to raise money for graduate education, but that a growing family prevented him from following through.

> It was as banking examiner that Joe really fell in love with his profession. There, he says, "I learned that the country banker serves his community as intimately as the country doctor."[126] After only 18 months as banking examiner, the Columbia Trust Company sent for him and asked him to assume its presidency.[127] At twenty-five, he became the nation's youngest bank president. Kennedy explained this success to one reporter: "How did I

become a bank president? By work, hard work. That is the only way I know." [128]

Then comes Currier, Bethlehem, and lots more hard work.

When work at Bethlehem began to slack off at the end of the war, Kennedy decided to try to sell ships to a major line. Persistent efforts to get in to see Galen Stone, president of the line, were unsuccessful, and so young Kennedy had to show ingenuity to get to the busy executive. He found out when Stone was taking a New York-Boston train ride, got on the same train, and took a seat next to Stone. He did not succeed in selling Stone the ships, but Stone was so impressed by the young stranger that he offered Joe the job of managing Stone's huge brokerage house in Boston. [129] *"He was one of the noblest figures in American business," Kennedy has said of Stone.* [130]

Finally, Kennedy went out on his own. He decided to enter the movie business, and went to England to see the backers of FBO. He had difficulty getting to see one of the bankers behind the English company. A stroke of good luck solved the problem. One afternoon Kennedy found himself in a London restaurant sitting next to the Prince of Wales, and struck up a conversation with His Highness. The next morning an unsolicited letter of introduction for Kennedy, signed by the Prince, was delivered to Kennedy's hotel. It opened all doors. [131]

As head of FBO Kennedy worked hard and made the company, and the others with which he had been associated, successful. He resolved the tangled and hostile interests in the film world. [132] *He once sold a large share in FBO to RCA's David Sarnoff in a meeting in an oyster bar. Before the first oyster was cracked, the deal had not been broached. It was completed before they left.* [133] *Kennedy is a wonderful family man with a beautiful wife and eight lovely children. He says they are his board of censors for the films he makes—"I make only clean movies."*

By the time that Joseph Kennedy assumed his duties to England, as Ambassador, he had been in the public eye much too much for such an all-good-guy account to be taken at all seriously. Some of his more questionable financial dealings had come to light, and he had shown a many-faceted personality that included some negative aspects. The legend became legends, confused and often contradictory. A 1937 *Fortune* article on Kennedy made this meaty comment on the story of the man's career:

The legends of Joe Kennedy make him at once the hero of a Frank Merriwell captain-of-the-nine adventure, a Horatio Alger success story, an E. Phillips Oppenheim tale of intrigue, and a John Dos Passos disillusioning report on the search for the big money. The truth makes him the central character of a picaresque novel of a sort not yet written.[134]

A picaresque novel, the *Encyclopaedia Britannica* informs us, involves "a real or fictitious personage who describes his experiences as a social parasite, and who satirizes the society which he has exploited." [135]

RETURN TO WALL STREET

Joe Kennedy did not avoid speculation in his days in Hollywood, but his speculative activities, like his executive services, were in movie and theater enterprises. He was always said to have been operating in an insider's pool in RKO.[136] In any event, he left Hollywood a millionaire several times over. The number five million recurs in accounts about him.[137] A 1963 *Fortune* article says that he made five million dollars in FBO and KAO stock alone.[138] His fabulous salaries of $2,000 per week from FBO, KAO, and Pathé and, briefly, $3,000 per week from First National, must have totaled considerably over a half million dollars alone in the four years. And in those pre-New Deal days most of that could be kept after taxes. One thing on which all accounts agree— Kennedy did his health no good on the job. He became a feverish smoker[139] and lost over 30 pounds in the four years.[140]

Joe Kennedy began pulling out of Hollywood as early as 1928. By 1929, his only executive duties were at Pathé and with Gloria Productions. His Pathé work was increasingly delegated to Derr, and his duties with Gloria Productions appear to have been more pleasure than business. He began to spend more time on Wall Street.

Kennedy became increasingly alarmed at the ever upward-spiraling market. A frenzied trading was making prices soar out of all relation to reality. Joe's friend Bernard Baruch publicly asserted that the market could continue upward indefinitely, but Baruch's pronouncements did not dispell his qualms. He always had an uncanny nose for trends, and he did not like what he smelled, so he followed his own admonition: "Only a fool holds out for the top dollar." [141] He pulled out. Years later he told this fanciful story:

I dropped in at a shoeshine parlor on Wall Street. The boy who shined my shoes did not know me. He wasn't fishing for information or looking for a market tip. He was the average wage earner or salaried employee playing the market like everybody

else in that day. He looked up at me as he snapped the cloth over
my shoes and told me what was going to happen to various stocks
and offerings on the market that day.
I listened as I looked down at him, and when I left the place I
thought: "When a time comes that a shoeshine boy knows as
much as I do about what is going on in the stock market, tells me
so, and is entirely correct, there is something the matter either
with me or with the market and it's time for me to get out," and I
did.[142]

Joe Kennedy was safely out of the market by the time that the world
came to an end in mid-October, 1929. Most commentators say that
Kennedy sold all his holdings before the crash,[143] but this is probably
untrue. He was already out of FBO and KAO but he was still
chairman of the board of Pathé, and no doubt kept sizable holdings in
that corporation.

When the market went down for the third time on October 29,
1929, Kennedy was sitting on top of the world. It has often been
asserted that in the crucial hours of the panic, he sold short to the tune
of 15 million dollars.[144] Kennedy students Whalen and McCarthy
doubt this and stress the near impossibility of such a feat.[145] But
Kennedy's friend Bernard "Sell-em-Ben" Smith, and Percy Rockefeller, were able to do it on the record.[146] This author doubts the story
but only because if it were true Kennedy in the 1930s would have
been worth at least 20 million dollars and estimates of his wealth at
the time rarely approached half that amount.

In the months that followed, Joe Kennedy was in the thick of some
of the most unsavory trading in the history of American business. He
unquestionably did considerable short-selling—in Paramount Pictures
stock, possibly in Anaconda Copper, and no doubt in other issues—
thus helping to aggravate and further depress the market, the
American economy, and the psychological well-being of the nation.[147]
He showed a steely disregard for the consequences of his actions to
anyone but himself; he was making money and that's what counted.
Years later he would brag about this least praiseworthy period of his
life.[148]

WINNING
WITH ROOSEVELT

BY THE END OF THE 1920s, THE FATHER OF EIGHT WAS A fabulously wealthy man, but he had worked himself too hard. He was considerably under his normal weight and he was dangerously run-down. To regain his health he had himself hospitalized. When he left the hospital it was to follow a course that he had not seriously pursued before.

Joe Kennedy had always thought about money, possessions, and great wealth, and now he had them all. But Joe Kennedy also wanted fame and power. Money was an end in itself, but it was also a means to these other ends. He wanted to be something more than simply a wealthy man; to be famous for more than just executive abilities. The way to get that fame was through politics.

Kennedy wanted fame for a number of reasons: to show the Brahmins who had snubbed him, to satisfy his own not inconsiderable vanity, and for the sake of his children. He wanted his children to respect him as a great and powerful man, not simply as a rich man. He had already seen to it that they would be well provided for; he wanted to leave them more than money. Roosevelt explained the presence in politics of the already legendary Joe Kennedy in terms of Kennedy's family,[1] and to one reporter Kennedy said as much.[2]

And so in the early 1930s the young multimillionaire was ready to get on the road to fame and power via politics.

Kennedy's previous association with politics had been extensive, though he had been out of it for several years. As a child he was always exposed to politics and its machinations in the home of his father. In 1914 he enjoyed a political job himself as a director of Collateral Loan. He took an active part in the campaigns of his father-in-law. He was a fund-raiser for Honey in Fitzgerald's campaign for Congress in 1917, and saw Honey "elected" that year only to be disqualified when election irregularities on his behalf came to light.[3] He took an active part in Fitz's campaign for governor in 1922, and though Honey was roundly defeated by Channing Cox in the Republican landslide, Joe impressed Massachusetts "pols" with his work.[4] In 1924 Catholic Al

Smith was denied the Democratic nomination for President in a convention not free from Klan influence, and many Catholics momentarily abandoned the Democratic party in retaliation. Kennedy quietly backed Robert La Follette, the Progressive party nominee. The young speculator was a generous contributor to the Progressive treasury and loaned his chauffeur-driven Rolls Royce to Burton K. Wheeler, the Progressive party's Vice-Presidential nominee, when Wheeler was campaigning in New England. In the early 1960s, Kennedy said that he had also lent his name to the Progressive's committee in Massachusetts.[5] During the '24 campaign he formed a close friendship with Wheeler, the influential Senator from Montana, that lasted until World War II.[6]

After the '24 campaign, Joe Kennedy apparently left politics. He moved from Massachusetts and became taken up with finance. Not until the early 1930s did he again become active politically. But this time he reentered on a big scale, and for the first time he would be with the winner. He sided with Franklin D. Roosevelt from the beginning.

Exactly when and how Joseph Kennedy entered the Roosevelt camp is unclear. Wheeler was early on the Roosevelt bandwagon, and his claim to have interested Kennedy in the Roosevelt candidacy[7] may have some weight. Others suggest that wealthy Catholic Frank Walker, or Henry Morgenthau, Jr., brought Kennedy into the fold.[8]

It was really an odd alliance, Roosevelt and Kennedy; Kennedy had so much more in common with Roosevelt's leading opponent, Al Smith, whom Kennedy had known slightly.[9] Both Kennedy and Smith were essentially self-made men; both were Irish-Catholics from Irish-Catholic ghettos; both were conservative Democrats. Roosevelt, on the other hand, was of well-to-do old American stock, and his political views appealed more to Midwestern agrarian radicals than to conservative Northeastern Irish. True to his heritage, from the start Honey was one of Al Smith's loudest boosters in Massachusetts.[10]

Kennedy later recalled that he had known Roosevelt during World War I, and spoke of the close friendship that had developed between the two men at the time. In pro-Roosevelt campaign literature in 1936 he said that he had realized in 1932 that the country needed "a leader who could lead" and fearful of chaos, had vowed that he would gladly give half of his fortune to preserve the other half. From his association with Roosevelt he knew that Roosevelt was that leader who would ward off the chaos that threatened his entire fortune.[11]

Actually, Kennedy had known Roosevelt only briefly during the war, and the two had had no contact throughout the 1920s. His support for Roosevelt can more convincingly be explained by his need to be on the winning team.[12] Kennedy was in a rush; he had no time to side with losers. From the start of the Presidential season Roosevelt was clearly the front-runner, and from the start Kennedy was with him. He was an important contributor to the Roosevelt campaign long before the New York governor received his party's nomination.[13]

Kennedy contributed financially and no doubt urged powerful friends to support Roosevelt, but he remained innocuous during the pre-convention period. He did no stumping for Roosevelt in Massachusetts during the primary between Smith and Roosevelt ranks, but left that to his new, unlikely, and temporary associate Jim Curley, who led the Roosevelt forces in the Bay State. Kennedy's only role was to help finance Curley's fight.[14] But Smith was something of a folk hero in the Bay State, and Honey's Smith forces easily carried.

When the Democratic nominating convention deadlocked on the third ballot Joseph Kennedy proved particularly useful to Roosevelt. On the first ballot, Roosevelt received 666 votes, well more than half, but some hundred short of the two-thirds vote needed for nomination in those days before the party's change in rules. Smith was second and Texan John Nance Garner proved a poor third. The third ballot saw the situation virtually unchanged. Roosevelt backers became convinced that Garner's support was instrumental and feared that if it did not come soon Roosevelt supporters might begin dropping away. It had happened to other first-ballot front-runners in prior years. William Randolph Hearst was backing Garner and had been responsible for bringing California into Garner's camp. His switch to Roosevelt would bring California to FDR and would start the Roosevelt bandwagon rolling again. A number of people tried unsuccessfully to get to Hearst by phone at the publisher's San Simeon mansion. He even refused to speak to James A. Farley, Roosevelt's manager. Finally Kennedy got to him. The two men had become close friends in Hollywood, and Hearst respected the younger man's judgment. Kennedy had worked on Hearst before.[15] This time he successfully played on Hearst's fears. The powerful publisher had come to be an isolationist of the first water, and Kennedy warned him that if Hearst did not support Roosevelt, dark horse Newton D. Baker, an unregenerated Wilsonian "internationalist," would likely emerge as the Democratic nominee. Arthur Krock of the *New York Times* was in Kennedy's hotel room

when the call to Hearst was put through. In 1950 he reconstructed the
conversation for Columbia University historians:

> *He said "W.R. [as Hearst's friends knew him] . . . . . . Do you*
> *want Baker?" Hearst apparently said no. He said, "If you don't*
> *want Baker, you'd better take Roosevelt, because if you don't*
> *take Roosevelt, you're going to have Baker." W.R. obviously*
> *said, "All right. Is that my choice? Could I get Ritchie?" (Bert*
> *Ritchie, Governor of Maryland.) Kennedy said, "No I don't think*
> *so. I think if Roosevelt cracks on the next ballot it'll be Baker." So*
> *Hearst apparently said, "All right, I'll turn to him."* [16]

On the fourth ballot Hearst's contact William G. McAdoo announced California's switch from Garner to Roosevelt. The convention went wild. Roosevelt went over the top, and Garner, as if by way
of consolation, received the Vice-Presidential nomination.

Many factors enter into the complex situation that is a nominating
convention, factors that make it impossible to say what might have
happened but for Hearst's switch. It seems likely that Roosevelt, well
in the lead, would ultimately have won anyway. But his supporters
might have deserted him for Smith or for one of the several dark-horse
candidates. Similarly, it is impossible to pass final judgment on the
effect that Kennedy had on Hearst. Many things, no doubt, affected
Hearst besides the urgings and argument of Joe Kennedy. Author W.
A. Swanberg makes clear in his study of *Citizen Hearst* that W.R.
"already was setting large wheels of his own in motion." [17] Other
people had spoken to Hearst on Roosevelt's behalf, and Hearst was at
the time carefully investigating the foreign policy views of FDR. It is
impossible to say that Hearst would not have swung to Roosevelt but
for Kennedy; it is likely that he would have done so anyway, though
perhaps not at that important moment. Kennedy, never one to
minimize his own role, later "admitted," "Yes, I did bring Hearst
around for Roosevelt, but you can't find any mention of it in the
history books. Hearst even sent his contribution to Roosevelt through
me." [18] While the facts do not permit Hearst's switch to be exclusively
attributed to Kennedy, it nonetheless appears that Kennedy was the
one who did finally receive Hearst's commitment for FDR.[19]

Kennedy later played a significant role in the relationship between
the President and the publisher. There is no reason to doubt that
Hearst channeled his fat contribution to the campaign treasury
through Kennedy; Kennedy was a member of the party's finance
committee that year.[20] After the election, Kennedy arranged appoint-

ments between Hearst and the President[21] and attempted to reconcile them and act as intermediary when they differed. Finally, Roosevelt and Hearst no longer had common ground, and Kennedy's function in the relationship ceased along with the Hearst-Roosevelt relationship itself. In mid-November, 1935, Roosevelt's long-time Secretary of the Interior Harold Ickes wrote in his diary:

> [T]he President also told me that Joe Kennedy had been at the White House the night before to talk about Hearst. . . . he said to Kennedy that in his opinion there was no man in the whole United States who was as vicious an influence as Hearst. Kennedy remarked that it didn't look as if there was much chance to get the two together in view of the President's opinion, and the President said that there wasn't; that he had never had very much of an opinion of Hearst.[22]

After Roosevelt secured the nomination, the candidate took a one-week vacation cruise aboard a 40-foot yawl, followed by a press boat and the yacht *Ambassadress*, holding advisors, financiers, and strategists. Joe Kennedy was honored with a berth[23] in a stateroom shared with showman Eddie Dowling. Soon Kennedy yielded his spot to his devoted secretary, Eddie Moore, who amused Dowling with his silly insistence that if everyone lived long enough, one of Kennedy's sons would be the nation's first Irish-Catholic President.[24]

Kennedy selflessly declined the honor of serving on Roosevelt's executive committee. FDR's personal secretary and the man closest to the candidate was Louis Howe. This crotchety liberal from New Bedford, Massachusetts, had taken an instinctive dislike to the conservative and wealthy Joe Kennedy.[25] Kennedy wisely realized that he and Howe could not have worked effectively together; friction between them might have proven a detriment to the Roosevelt organization, and the honor of serving on the committee was not worth this risk, so he begged off in a "self-effacing" note to the future President.[26]

He was, however, active for the candidate. Owen D. Young and Bernard Baruch were Roosevelt's most public contacts with the business community;[27] Kennedy worked more quietly in those segments of the money world that he knew best. He was credited with feats like that of immobilizing the powerful Italian-American banker, A. P. Giannini, who was under tremendous pressure to endorse incumbent Republican President Herbert Hoover for reelection, but on Kennedy's urgings refrained from doing so and instead gave silent backing to Roosevelt.[28]

Kennedy worked quietly only with regard to his work for Roosevelt within the business community. Insofar as the likely future President was concerned, his support was ostentatious.[29] He was with the candidate on his travels and was in on many strategy-making sessions. On the campaign train, he shared a cabin with brain-truster Ray Moley, and though his only title was "member of the Democratic Finance Committee," journalists wondered "Is he the Barney Baruch of the Roosevelt campaign?" Apparently his only regular function was to contact members of the finance committee in each state to solicit more funds. Besides his pre-convention contributions of unknown size, Kennedy himself gave $15,000 to the Democratic National Committee's campaign fund, "loaned" the party another $50,000, and no doubt gave still more in other unrecorded contributions.

Kennedy also gave advice in speechwriting sessions, most of which was discarded by more liberal advisors to Roosevelt. For example, Kennedy wanted Roosevelt to sidestep the question of "bimetalism." Bimetalism was the policy of making silver, as well as gold, a legal basis for United States currency. The silver-producing states were predictably eager to have bimetalism adopted, and the idea was also appealing to those who thought that bimetalism would bring some wholesome inflation to the depressed economy. The idea of bimetalism had been anathema to conservative bankers and financiers for decades. The liberals and silverites won and Roosevelt came out for bimetalism.

There were also questions of aesthetics. Kennedy, for example, wanted to write some typical New York expressions into a Topeka, Kansas, farm relief speech. Moley vetoed that one.[30]

Kennedy was not always on the minority side, though. He played a role in the drafting of Roosevelt's significant Pittsburgh address, in which Roosevelt came out for the balanced budget.[31] Although Kennedy was never a full-fledged member of Roosevelt's brain trust,[32] FDR no doubt consulted him for financial advice on numerous occasions.

In early November, just before election day, Roosevelt and Al Smith, campaigning for FDR, spoke in Boston. Kennedy arrived in Boston just before Smith's appearance; he left immediately after Roosevelt's speech.[33] Then came election day.

After devoting several months to the Roosevelt campaign, Joe Kennedy was elated at the outcome. Roosevelt's victory over the discredited Hoover had been a foregone conclusion from the start, but his smashing total was something of a surprise. Kennedy threw a huge victory party on two floors of New York's Waldorf-Astoria[34] to celebrate his arrival as a "kingmaker" in national politics. Even the Fitzgeralds took pride in that—"Everybody up there (in Boston) thinks that our Joe really was the man that made (Roosevelt) the President," his mother-in-law freely confided.[35]

The battle was over and won, and the rules of the game were clear: Joseph Kennedy was entitled to high honor. He had, wrote Moley, "Ranged himself ostentatiously on the side of Roosevelt, and after the victory thought he would be awarded with high place." [36] Kennedy sat back to await his rewards, confidently telling friends that the position would likely be Secretary of the Treasury[37]—at the time probably the most important position in the President's Cabinet. Not a bad spot for a fellow whom J. P. Morgan had seen fit to snub such a short few years before.[38] It wouldn't be long before Kennedy stepped in. And then Roosevelt made his Cabinet appointments, including William H. Woodin, an industrialist "fat cat" whose ideas on economics probably paralleled Kennedy's, for the post of Secretary of the Treasury. Perhaps some gentle efforts on Kennedy's behalf were needed. Kennedy was solicitous of the good efforts of Ray Moley, perhaps Roosevelt's most influential advisor in those early New Deal days, even offering to accumulate a "slush fund" for the brain truster.[39] It was all handled as tastefully as such a proposition can be handled and, though Moley rejected the offer, it was a "kind" gesture for Kennedy to have made. Through Frank Walker, Herbert Bayard Swope, and financier Forbes Morgan, Kennedy kept gentle pressure on Moley to find him a position in the government,[40] and though Moley knew of Kennedy's terrific work for the new President principally from what Kennedy himself told Moley that he had done,[41] Moley became the principal insider to boom Kennedy for a position. Roosevelt himself had not forgotten the Boston financier, but finding the right place for him was difficult. Howe is generally believed to have blackballed Kennedy for a meaningful position, probably with justice,[42] though Swope assured Kennedy that Howe was really "quite friendly, except he wants to keep you away from finance." [43] Howe was not the only problem. Moley, apparently with full authority from the President, tried valiantly to secure a position for Kennedy on the American delegation to an International Monetary Conference, only to be persistently told by James P. Warburg, the head of the delegation, that he did not want the delegation peopled with "hacks," and "associates for whom I would have to apologize *vis-à-vis* the Europeans." When Moley suggested that Kennedy, Baruch, and other Roosevelt obligees be put on an "Advisory Commission" to accompany the principal delegation, Warburg suggested that it be officially called "Patronesses of the Democratic Campaign." [44] At Roosevelt's nomination the State Department invited Kennedy to serve as a member of a commission to study areas of dispute between the United States and Brazil.[45] Member! Brazil!! The mere suggestion of such a thing was insulting to one who regarded himself as material for important Cabinet office, and apparently it was ignored. Scarcely better was an indirect suggestion that Kennedy head the New York office of the National Recovery Administration, and nothing even came of that.[46]

Kennedy took it all very, very badly. As early as February, 1933, Kennedy became extremely critical of the President,[47] and with the passage of time his attitude got worse. Malicious stories about the President began being credited to the transparent financier; sophisticated Washingtonians attributed Kennedy's attitude to the simple fact that he had not received his payoff.[48] According to Wheeler, Kennedy even began applying pressure for repayment of his $50,000 "loan" to the Democratic campaign[49]—a politically unthinkable thing to do. The only thing that the Kennedys "got" was the appointment of Rose's uncle as district supervisor of the Alcohol Tax Unit in Boston, and even that had required that the old man lie about his age so as to put him under the maximum age limit of 70.[50] Surely, that was not to be the payoff, was it?

In 1934, the ailing Woodin retired from his position as Secretary of the Treasury, and although Boston newspapers rumored Kennedy as the successor,[51] there was never any reason to seriously think that their hometown boy was in the running. Roosevelt named his longtime neighbor, Henry Morgenthau, Jr., to the spot. Kennedy became even more bitter. Politics and politicians, even the President, were no damn good. Especially the President!

LIQUOR BOTTLES AND LIQUOR

Kennedy returned to the business world. He encouraged a rumor that he would take over the managing of film star Greta Garbo,[52] but that never materialized. There was more money—easy money—to be made on Wall Street. Often repeated is the story of Kennedy's role in the Libby-Owens-Ford stock pool. The story of the pool is repeated here as illustrative of some of the business practices that helped make Kennedy his fortune.

A group of financiers led by Henry Mason Day of Redmond and Company and Elisha Walker, then with Kuhn, Loeb and Company, purchased 65,000 shares of stock in the Libby-Owens-Ford glass manufacturing outfit at $26.50 per share. The stock was sold to them by the Libby-Owens Securities Corporation, an outfit that specialized in the stock. L-O Securities gave the financiers options on an additional 80,000 shares at prices up to $30.30 and agreed to make no further sales of the stock for less than $35.00 during the life of the options.

The financiers set up six sham accounts at Redmond and Company, and the six accounts began buying and selling the stock to each other on the New York Stock Exchange. The impression was created that there was considerable interest in the stock. Simultaneously, false rumors were spread that Libby-Owens-Ford was going to make liquor bottles. At the time, the repeal of prohibition was just around the corner, and there was great interest in stocks associated with the liquor industry. Little by little the "suckers" bought into Libby-Owens-Ford at prices ranging up to $37.00. Indeed, business was so good that the financiers sold 20,000 shares short. They were able to cover their shorts profitably when, three days after hitting the peak at $37.00, the stock completed a drop of 16 points to $21.00.

Day testified that the "profit" to the group amounted to $395,000; Kennedy later intimated that it was much greater.[53] The participants, in order of the size of their shares, were Walker's Kuhn, Loeb and Company, 20 percent of the take; Redmond and Company, the Toledo brokerage house of Bell and Beckwith, and Kennedy, each 15 percent; Lehman Brothers, 10 percent; and 8 percent interest each for the Hyva Corporation, a Harry Sinclair front; auto man Walter P. Chrysler; and the brokerage house of Wright and Sexton. Kennedy's share, based on Day's figures, amounted to $65,805.87—a modest sum for the multimillionaire, but also not a bad take. The "profits" would have been even greater but for the generosity of the pool's floor manager, who had taken pity on a fellow insider who had misgauged the jiggling and gotten caught in a very expensive bind. The manager sold him a large block of stock at under the market price. While Kennedy's partners in the venture let their manager's "kindness" pass, Kennedy, who had never had to put up a dime, called the manager to give him a tongue-lashing for his generosity with Kennedy's profits.[54]

When the Senate Banking and Currency Committee investigated market manipulations in "Alcohol" stocks, this incident was disclosed during Day's testimony. It is a classic example of the "pool" operation, and the only documented case involving Kennedy. Day, before the Senate committee, minimized Kennedy's role in the formation and operation of the pool.

The most interesting thing about the Libby-Owens-Ford pool is when it took place—long after the stock market crash, the collapse of the Coolidge-era morality, and the advent of the Depression. It was formed at a time when federal investigators were swarming over Wall Street. Shady financial dealings in the 1920s were not practiced by everyone—many commission brokers scrupulously refrained from pools and manipulations. But those who did not temper the business-men's goal with morality were in very great numbers. Kennedy was not alone in the twenties. He was what people called "shrewd." However, by the time of the Libby-Owens-Ford jiggle in 1932, the public's toleration of and, in some circles, open admiration for amoral business activities had disappeared. As Kennedy himself later said, after the crash of the market in 1929, a "revival of the national conscience" made unthinkable business practices that had been rather common before the crash.[55] Financiers who could be appealed to on moral grounds were no longer participating in pools. That realm was left to men like Sinclair and Day, Sinclair's one-time aide, both of whom had served jail terms for briberies, and to financiers like Joseph Kennedy. He was what people began to call "ruthless."

WITH THE ELECTION OF FRANKLIN D. ROOSEVELT, THE REPEAL OF prohibition was just around the corner, and Roosevelt insiders scurried to make a buck on it.[56] Joe Kennedy was first in, and he traded on his association with the President's son James Roosevelt to grab off the best in the liquor business. Kennedy had been of help to Jimmie when the President's son had gone into the insurance business in Boston, and had delicately passed counsel to the President that a kindly interest in the health of the President's bitter antagonist, ailing Henry Ford, might have some influence in wrapping up the coveted Ford workmen's compensation policies for Jimmie.[57] These were favors that Jimmie—who could not broach such matters directly with his father—appreciated. Now Kennedy needed a favor, and Jimmie was willing to help. In September, the Kennedy entourage—Joe and Rose, their eldest son, Joe Jr., Jimmie, and his wife Betsy—sailed for England to round up Kennedy's liquor franchises.[58] They were joined on the voyage by the scintillating Kay Halle, a girlhood friend of Betsy Roosevelt, who had countless influential English connections. Miss Halle remembered the lively expedition years later.[59]

Franchises were a matter of making the right contacts, meeting the right people, and Kennedy complained bitterly to Miss Halle that she was not introducing him to "the very best people." [60] Finally, perhaps through her intervention,[61] they found themselves in the drawing rooms of the already legendary Winston Churchill. Kennedy explained his purpose.[62] The British selected their liquor distributors with very great care, and with the President's son in tow, Kennedy could be assured that he would be making precisely the right impression. James Roosevelt recalled years later that Kennedy had taken him to lunch with the head of British Distillers, no doubt to impress the Lord with his influential connections, and perhaps hoping to give the impression that the Roosevelts were "in" on the deal.[63] Nothing had to be said about the degree or kind of interest that the President's family might have in the success of Kennedy's "Somerset Importers," and the British sense of delicacy would prevent them from asking. The contacts opened up. The franchises, including the coveted Haig & Haig, flowed in.[64]

Years later another Roosevelt insider, Eddie Dowling, recalled his own scramble for a franchise:

> We knew that repeal was coming, and so all of us made a mad dash to Europe. But I'm always late for these kind of plums. I got over late. Everywhere I went Joe Kennedy had been two weeks ahead of me. So I came back without anything . . . he had it all.[65]

In 1938, a *Saturday Evening Post* article that asserted that James Roosevelt had been of help in getting Kennedy the distributorships[66] was denounced by Kennedy as "a complete and unadulterated lie." [67] "Kennedy was doing all right by himself before he ever met Jimmie Roosevelt," he was wont to say.[68] With time, the origin of Somerset gave birth to rumor that Jimmie had expected an interest in the business in exchange for his help, but that Kennedy had cut him out.[69] Both men denied it, and the two remained close throughout the Roosevelt era and beyond.[70] There were friendships lost, however, over the origin of Somerset. One Bostonian sued Kennedy for cutting him out of an alleged partnership in the distributorships.[71] More important to Kennedy, his friendship with Swope fell apart when Kennedy offered to sell Swope an interest in Somerset. Swope had expected a free ride from Kennedy, in exchange for past favors extended, only to find that Kennedy was extremely tight-fisted in allocation of "free rides." [72]

Back home, Kennedy received "medical" permits to bring in two huge shipments of Scotch prior to repeal. When prohibition was finally ended, he had this Scotch on hand and was the only man around to meet the immediate demand. Later, Joseph Hodges Choate, Jr., was commissioned by the government to investigate the issuance of liquor importing permits, and found that Somerset's permits were surprisingly large. He scaled them down, but found no evidence of any undue influence having been used in the securing of them.[73] Somerset became the importers for Dewar's Scotch, Gordon's gin, and Ron Rico rum, as well as Haig & Haig. Over the years, the company was built and managed for Kennedy by associates Ted O'Leary and Tom Delahanty, and when Kennedy sold the company in 1946, they expected a crack at the business, or a portion of the profits amassed. To their bitter disappointment, Kennedy instead sold the company to Renfield Importers for eight million dollars, pocketed the cash, and dismissed them with substantial but proportionally modest bonuses.[74]

Kennedy's real estate broker, John J. Reynolds, told the author that Kennedy never liked the liquor business.[75] He apparently regarded it as in some way morally distasteful. He himself was always known to be a sparing drinker—almost a teetotaler. When a group of friends from the Bethlehem ball team set out to get him drunk in 1911, he arranged to be served a soft drink passed off as a cocktail. Not surprisingly, Joe "drank" his colleagues under the table.

Too resilient to need a drink, too shrewd to take one, Joe Kennedy followed his father's example. He sold liquor but rarely drank it himself.

A BECKET
FOR FINANCE

FROM THE DAYS OF THE MARKET CRASH PEOPLE REALIZED THAT excessive speculation, pools and manipulations, bear raiding, and unfair use of inside information had contributed greatly to defraud thousands of individuals and to bring about the crash itself. Herbert Hoover suspected that wealthy Democrats were behind it all and had set out to embarrass his Administration. He ordered investigations that ultimately led to the grand inquest into market activities of the Senate Banking and Commerce Committee. Under the cross-examination of peppery counsel Ferdinand Pecora, the facts began to emerge. (It was Pecora who turned up the Libby-Owens-Ford jiggle.) Any doubts as to the need for securities legislation were dispelled.

The Democratic platform included a plank promising some sort of securities legislation, and it was a plank that Roosevelt intended to honor. Even Joe Kennedy had mentioned to him that some kind of regulation was needed.[1]

The first of two related acts to regulate the market was the Securities Act of 1933, designed to combat fraudulent issuance of securities. Drafted by James M. Landis and Benjamin V. Cohen, two young protégés of brain truster Felix Frankfurter, the Securities Act required corporations to file registration statements with the Federal Trade Commission before new public offerings of securities could be made by the company. More important was the Securities Exchange Act of 1934, designed to combat fraudulent trading of securities. The New Deal team of Cohen and Tom Corcoran drafted the act, which set up the Securities and Exchange Commission. Under the terms of the act, all stock exchanges and all securities traded on the exchanges had to register with the Securities and Exchange Commission. The registration forms were to be worked out by the new body and were to include all statistical information about the traded securities that was of interest to investors. The SEC was empowered to oversee trading rules and trading on the exchanges, and to nose out manipulations and other unethical market practices. It was to be composed of five members and a large staff, and was also to take over from the FTC the administration of the Securities Act of 1933.

James H. Rand, Jr., of Remington-Rand denounced the act as deliberately designed to push the nation "along the road from Democracy to Communism," a judgment in which Illinois Congressman Fred Britten heartily agreed. "The real object of the bill is to Russianize everything worthwhile," was his sophisticated comment.[2] Men of their ilk added substance to Joe Kennedy's later comment: "There has been scarcely a liberal piece of legislation during the last sixty years that has not been opposed as communistic." [3] The bill passed by a healthy majority.

The SEC was now legally in existence, but passage of the legislation was the smallest part of the mammoth task of setting up, staffing, and laying ground rules for the new independent government agency. Appointment of the members and selection of the chairman was the first task. Roosevelt asked Moley for suggestions for members, and Moley gave him a list of possibilities. Still trying to find a spot for Kennedy, Moley put his name at the top, identified with the legend "The best bet for chairman because of executive ability, knowledge of habits and customs of business to be regulated and ability to moderate different points of view on Commission." [4] Swope and Baruch kept pressure on for Kennedy.[5] Roosevelt thought it over and in mid-June, 1934, told Moley that he had virtually decided to make Kennedy chairman of the new body.[6] Then he began to waiver. Powerful Senator Duncan Fletcher, chairman of the Senate Banking and Commerce Committee, was urging Roosevelt to make Pecora chairman of the new body,[7] and Pecora publicly made known his availability for the post.[8] Friends of Landis, then serving as a member of the FTC, were waging an equally vigorous campaign on his behalf.[9] There were many objections to Kennedy. Men like Howe, who was ill and losing influence on the President, simply did not want a man with Kennedy's past in the reform Administration. More reasonable liberals feared that because of his past and his many associates on "The Street," Kennedy could not be tough enough on his old cohorts. Through Frank Walker, Roosevelt sounded out Kennedy as to his attitude on *not* being chairman, but merely serving as a member of the new commission.[10] No dice.

Moley argued Kennedy's case by impressing upon Roosevelt that it was "unwise to reject Kennedy simply because he had some professional experience in the field." [11] The experience argument was a good one, and no doubt affected Roosevelt's decision. Because of his experience as a manipulator, Kennedy knew all the tricks of the trade, and knew how to guard against them. Roosevelt, it is said, laughingly used the it-takes-a-thief-to-catch-a-thief motto in justifying the appointment. Equally important, because of Kennedy's experience he was more aware than most men were of the legitimate needs of business. A man like Pecora, less aware and less interested in the needs of business, might have administered the SEC in such a way as to seriously impede recovery from the Depression.

The experience argument, however, was not the only thing that affected Roosevelt's decision. His ultimate selection of Kennedy as chairman is reflective of both the problems that confronted Roosevelt and the way in which he worked. Reform, recovery, and relief were the problems that the government faced in the early thirties—three problems that often required conflicting remedies. Reform measures, especially needed reforms in the business world, might make it harder for businesses to prosper and to expand, and so retard recovery. Roosevelt had already seen this happen with the Securities Act of 1933, a valuable reform. The act's registration statements, prepared by FTC reformers, were long and involved. Preparation of the forms, it was ventured, would require months of arduous work gathering data and would prove too expensive for smaller outfits to issue new securities on a sound economic basis. No new stock offerings had been made in the year following the passage of the act; companies were not issuing securities for those capital investments that would stimulate the whole economy. Recovery was being retarded, and people suspected that the Securities Act and its registration statements were in some way responsible.

Kennedy believed in the need for reform in the market, but he saw recovery as the more important problem facing the government, and recovery required greater cooperation between business and the Administration than had been manifested in the FTC's registration forms. By entrusting this businessman with the administration of reform measures, and flanking him with men primarily interested in reform, Roosevelt could receive a proper consideration of both reform and recovery in the administration of the new agency. He decided on Kennedy as chairman.

Joe Kennedy wanted the job—King of "The Street"—wanted it badly, yet when Roosevelt finally made the offer, Kennedy feigned reluctance. He both insisted that he get it, and insisted that he be cajoled into accepting it. "Mr. President," he faintly protested, "I don't think you ought to do this. I think it will bring down injurious criticism." After all that had passed, Moley was not about to let Kennedy get away with that, and before Roosevelt could do the requested arm-twisting, Moley challenged Kennedy. "Joe, I know darned well you want this job. But if anything in your career in business could injure the President, this is the time to spill it." "With a burst of profanity, Kennedy," as Moley later recalled,

> defied anyone to question his devotion to the public interest or to point to a single shady act in his whole life. The President did not need to worry about that, he said. What was more, he would give his critics—and here again the profanity flowed freely—an administration of the S.E.C. that would be a credit to the country, the President, himself, and his family, clear down to the ninth child.[12]

The matter was settled: Kennedy took the job. It was understood that he would organize the SEC and then depart.

On June 28, Roosevelt stayed up late, drinking beer with Kennedy and Baruch,[13] and the next day the rumors began that Kennedy would be a member of the commission, possibly its chairman.[14] Roy Howard, of the Scripps-Howard newspaper chain, learned of the appointment and in a last-minute attempt to change the President's mind, published a front-page editorial in the *Washington Daily News* against Kennedy's appointment. Howard demanded that Farley, chief patronage-dispenser for the administration, "find something else" for Kennedy, and labeled the speculator's appointment "a slap in the face to [Roosevelt's] most loyal and effective supporters." [15] But Roosevelt had made up his mind. He rounded out the Commission with Landis, Pecora, Robert Healy, longtime chief counsel for the FTC, and George C. Mathews, who had considerable experience as the administrator of Wisconsin's progressive securities laws. Though not empowered to designate the SEC's chairman, the President saw to it that the new appointees were apprised that Kennedy was his choice.[16] When Pecora learned of the President's preference, he reacted with cold fury. There was very much more to his objection than simply having been passed over. He feared that all the efforts to reform the market would go for naught under Kennedy's administration. As investigator he had gone after Kennedy and men like him with the reformer's zeal, and he had come to regard Kennedy and his ilk contemptuously. He objected to serving under a man like Kennedy, and when he boarded the Washington train in New York on the morning of July 2, it was with the intention of fighting Kennedy's election as chairman.[17]

That sweltering afternoon the temperature rose to 93 degrees, and tempers were equally heated at the FTC building. Pecora arrived at Landis' office before 3:00 P.M. and stayed there, while Kennedy, Healy, and Mathews waited in another office four rooms down the corridor. Landis, looking very solemn, moved back and forth between the two offices. After more than an hour, Landis escorted Kennedy into the office with Pecora. Another hour passed. Then at 5:00, Kennedy, Landis, and Pecora moved into the office with Healy and Mathews. After a brief moment it was announced that a chairman, Joseph Kennedy, had been unanimously selected. A *New York Times* reporter wrote that Kennedy and Pecora appeared "as chipper as two long-lost brothers." When newsmen asked if the selection of a chairman had posed any problems, they were answered by a unanimous smile from the five commissioners.[18]

Joe Kennedy's prediction of criticism of his appointment was a sound one. Howard and Pecora were not alone; left-wing circles were aghast. The *New York Post*, in an editorial titled "The Wrong Chairman," contended that of the five commissioners Kennedy was the least fit to serve as head.[19] The *New Republic* denounced him as "that worst of all economic parasites, a Wall Street operator." [20] Its columnist John T. Flynn was incredulous: "I say it isn't true. It is impossible. It could not happen." Flynn reviewed some of the less savory aspects of Kennedy's past and concluded that Roosevelt had gone "to the bottom of the heap" to find Kennedy.[21]

Liberal insiders were equally disturbed. Roosevelt discussed the appointment of Kennedy at a Cabinet meeting on June 29, but Secretary of the Interior Harold Ickes remained dubious. "I am afraid I do not agree," he wrote in his diary,

> as to the Chairman he is going to name for the Securities Commission. He has named Joseph P. Kennedy for that place, a former stock-market plunger. The President has great confidence in him because he has made his pile, has invested all his money in Government securities, and knows all the tricks of the trade. Apparently he is going on the assumption that Kennedy would now like to make a name for himself for the sake of his family, but I have never known many of these cases to work out as expected.[22]

Corcoran told Moley "We've got four out of five anyway . . . four are for us and one is for business." [23] Jerome Frank, general counsel at the AAA, thought that merely including Kennedy on the commission was "like setting a wolf to guard a flock of sheep." [24] Time showed that the fears of men like Corcoran and Frank were unwarranted. But their fears were not placated at the time by the cheery announcement in the *Journal of Commerce* that "Brokers expressed themselves pleased . . . feeling especially that the naming of Joseph P. Kennedy is helpful to their interests." [25] No one could have guessed that Kennedy would become the Thomas à Becket of the financial world.

Outside of those men whose interest was essentially in reform, sentiment for Kennedy prevailed. Swope and Baruch approached their friend Krock and asked him to "try to give [Kennedy] a good start in his new job" [26] in Krock's influential *New York Times* column. After a searching interview with Kennedy[27] Krock's article on the new chairman must have exceeded Swope and Baruch's wildest dreams. Like Flynn, Krock gave his readers a review of Kennedy's biography, but with a somewhat different focus. He told all about how Kennedy had been "a famous ballplayer" at Harvard, and had turned down pro-ball contracts to enter business, and about the "strong admiration and friendship" that had developed between Kennedy and Roosevelt during World War I. He traced Kennedy's entire career, mentioning how Kennedy had "resolved" the tangled and hostile interests in the film business, and how he finally became "Roosevelt's campaign, business, and financial manager." [28] Kennedy was deeply grateful,[29] and thereafter a close and intimate friendship developed between Krock, perhaps the nation's most powerful journalist, and Joseph P. Kennedy.

The *Washington Post* pointed out that Kennedy's appointment would mollify business's legitimate fears that the SEC would approach its task in a hostile spirit detrimental to legitimate enterprise.[30] Syndicated columnist David Lawrence observed that the selection of Kennedy might be a bridge for cooperation between Wall Street and the government.[31] Kennedy let it be known that he had been "drafted" for the job, which made him look all the more desirable.[32]

Senator Fletcher was unconvinced. The Senate would reconvene in January, and Fletcher warned that Senate confirmation of Kennedy's appointment would depend on the record that Kennedy made before then. Kennedy, on his own part, announced that he would not ask for Senate confirmation unless he had "come through" by January.[33] The following January, without debate and inside of one minute, the Senate confirmed the appointment of Joseph P. Kennedy as chairman of the SEC.[34]

Joe Kennedy assumed his new duties on July 2, and his common-sense approach to the job immediately manifested itself. In a press conference and brief radio address on July 3, he insisted that legitimate business would not suffer from the new SEC; its goal would be to protect honest businessmen. Only the "sharpies" would be hurt. Manipulations had to cease, he insisted. He termed as "unthinkable" in the thirties, the common but unethical business practices of the twenties (in which he himself had so recently participated). He pledged a campaign against "stock market gambling," a pledge that the *Washington Post* called "unexpected in a man who has made thousands in pool operations." [35]

In his first major address, before the National Press Club on July 25, he told businessmen that they need not fear the SEC. Business would not be "harassed and annoyed and pushed around" by the SEC. Lest any of the Wall Street set feared Pecora, he assured them that "none of the members intend to push business around." He specifically commended Pecora. Recognizing that "business enterprise has been seriously wounded and needs to be nursed back to health and confidence," he asserted that the SEC would attempt to encourage legitimate operations and restore business confidence. There would be no restrictions against "proper profits," and Kennedy asserted that "There is to be no vindictiveness in [the SEC's] interpretation, no concealed punishment to those who must live under it. There are no grudges to satisfy, no venom which needs victims. The rules are simple and honest. Only those who see things crookedly will find them harsh." He appealed for the cooperation of the business community: "If we of the SEC do our job well and if we are helped by those we want to help, the New Deal in finance will be found to be a better deal for all." [36]

The speech was widely reported and widely praised as sensible and timely. The *New York Times*, which attributed the business slack to fears that the Administration would be hostile to business, called the speech reassuring.[37] The *Washington Post* commented that Kennedy's insistence that the emphasis be placed on restoring business confidence "reinforces the assertion that the commission will try to assist recovery, not to impose reforms that destroy the regulated institutions." [38] The Wall Street community was pleased by the speech.[39]

New York Stock Exchange President Richard Whitney approved Kennedy's approach, adding that "it is unnecessary to reiterate that we shall do everything to help." [40]

Kennedy demonstrated the commission's desire to cooperate with business by more than words. Exchange officials and leading business-men were called upon to join early commission conferences and were consulted on every step throughout Kennedy's administration.[41] The Wall Street community had feared the attitude of the SEC, but by the time of Kennedy's speech they had concluded that, in the words of the *Wall Street Journal*, the commission had "the apparent intention of putting knowledge ahead of action." [42] Kennedy early won acceptance of the SEC by the Wall Street community, and by so doing contributed greatly to the restoration of business confidence and to the progress of economic recovery.

More mundane problems faced the SEC in July that demanded immediate attention. The new body even lacked offices. On the morning of July 3, Kennedy and Landis met with Ickes and arranged for office space.[43] That noon the two commissioners lunched with Cohen and Corcoran; Kennedy, who had already won the approval of Landis, worked his charms on his two critics.[44]

Recruiting a large and competent staff virtually overnight posed great problems to the new commissioners. Roosevelt wanted the new body staffed strictly according to competence, and the commissioners were told to disregard the recommendations of political figures.[45] It was an "order" that brought relief to Joe Kennedy, who otherwise might have been plagued by the powerful. Farley scrupulously refrained from making "suggestions."

A part of the staff, perhaps 40 people, were brought over from the FTC and served as a nucleus around which to build. Most important of these was Baldwin Bane, general counsel of the FTC's securities division, who became executive assistant to the SEC. New men were brought in for other high-ranking positions. It is said that Kennedy's boyhood friend Joe Sheehan, a man of unquestionable abilities, was the first person appointed.[46] He became the commission's personnel director, with the extra title of "Administrative Coordinator." Cohen sought the post of general counsel to the SEC, perhaps the most important post outside that of chairman,[47] but Kennedy instead recruited his Bostonian friend John J. Burns.[48] Burns, a Harvard Law School contemporary of Landis', had already won fame as the youngest man to receive an appointment to the Massachusetts

Supreme Court. He resigned from the bench to accept the SEC position. William O. Douglas, a Yale Law School professor, began his long career of public service as director of the SEC's investigations into corporate reorganization. David Saperstein, who had served as Pecora's chief assistant during the Senate investigation, was appointed head of the SEC's trading division, in charge of nosing out pools and manipulations. James A. Fayne, a former broker and a Kennedy man, worked closely with Saperstein as a "technical advisor." [49] A concerted effort was made by the commissioners to attract able young men, accountants and attorneys, to the government service. Kennedy was always known for the unusual competence of the men under him; his underlings at the SEC attest to it. In a relatively short time the commission had recruited perhaps the ablest staff in Washington. Before Kennedy left the SEC, branch offices equally well staffed had been opened in the major financial centers: New York, Chicago, and Boston.

Of greater interest to the student are the early executive decisions of the commission. For the first three months the commission met in daylong sessions almost every day.[50] Cleavages among the commissioners were immediately clear. Kennedy's approach was at variance with the one that Pecora desired. Still eager to bare the dishonesty of the business community, Pecora insisted that corporations be required to disclose their entire financial history in registering with the SEC. This would likely expose some unethical chapter in the history of almost all American corporations, and would contribute to the further destruction of the myth of American business respectability. Psychologically, Pecora's approach would be detrimental to the resumption of business confidence, and it would adversely affect the resumption of normal business that meant recovery. His approach was calculated to further the cause of liberal reform by discrediting the commercial world and scarcely hid an aversion to big business and Wall Street finance. On specifics, his position received frequent support from Commissioner Healy.

Kennedy, on the other hand, was in no way anti-business. He argued for more limited disclosure provisions, just sufficient to inform investors. Practically, Kennedy's approach would make it easier for corporations to comply with the law and so to proceed with resumption of capital investments essential to recovery. Kennedy's position was supported by Commissioners Landis and Mathews.[51]

Pecora was given the specific task of supervising the trading division, for which he was well qualified by his experience with the investigating committee.[52] There, his zeal for exposing business dishonesty could have only a beneficial effect. But debate in the commission's executive sessions continued to be prolonged and hot. Finally the cleavage was resolved when Pecora, after six months on the SEC, accepted an appointment from Governor Herbert Lehman to the New York Supreme Court.

Ground rules for the administration of the Securities Act of 1933 were badly in need of revision, but the Securities Exchange Act of 1934 had no rules at all. It was to the administration of the latter act that the SEC first turned. On August 13, the commission issued the rules for registration of exchanges, and temporary rules for the registration of traded securities. The exchanges were required to furnish statistical data on their operations, to furnish copies of their constitutions and bylaws, and, more important, to agree to abide by the provisions of the Securities Exchange Act and to discipline or expel members that violated the act by engaging in dubious practices. Registration of traded stocks was made temporary, to give the commission more time to prepare final forms. The temporary registration forms, however, included many searching questions clearly aimed at stamping out unfair practices by insiders. Company officers and holders of more than 10 percent of a corporation's stock were required to declare the extent of their company holdings and to report any changes.[53] Under the act, short-term profits by insiders in the stock of their company reverted to the company.[54]

Kennedy pointed out that the registration statements were designed simply to insure that full information was made available to all investors. The SEC did not "guarantee" anything, and the acceptance of a registration statement was not to be interpreted as an SEC endorsement of any security. The act was designed simply to protect the investors from company insiders who might take advantage of more extensive knowledge.

The rules and forms for registrations were clearly aimed at dishonest practices, not at the ethical financier, and they were well received by the business community. The *New York Times* headlined the story of the new rules on page one with

BOARD ISSUES FIRST RULES
ON CONTROL OF EXCHANGES;
WALL ST. FEARS ALLAYED[55]

The rules and forms gave evidence that the SEC did intend, as

Kennedy asserted, to protect, not harass, honest businessmen. They had been prepared after extensive consultation with outside accountants and technical help, and after conferences with Whitney and other exchange officials. Here was evidence that the SEC intended to cooperate fully with business leaders. The Wall Streeters were equally pleased with Kennedy's announcement at the same press conference that revision of the registration forms for new issues was under-way.[56]

By January, 1935, the long-awaited revisions in the new issues forms were ready. None of the act's requirements were ignored, but the commission eliminated all requests for information not specifically required by the act and regarded as nonessential to the protection of investors. Successful efforts were made to word the questions more clearly and precisely than they had been under the old system.

In releasing the new forms, Kennedy stressed his hope that new issues would start flowing. Refunding of established corporations could be profitably done in depression times by calling in old securities and exchanging them for new ones. Corporations had been reluctant to do this because it would have entailed registering the new issues. Kennedy stressed his hope that refunding, which he regarded as the forerunner of new financing, would now begin. There was no longer any reasonable justification for hesitating on new issues. "The charge has been made that the act has been holding back the flotations," Kennedy said. "Well, this is our answer." [57]

Less than two months later, on March 7, Swift and Company led the way and registered for a large refinancing issue. Kennedy called the Swift move "a marvelous step in the right direction." The Swift's issue he loudly proclaimed as good evidence that the "capital market log-jam" was starting to break. A Swift's vice-president said that the registration had presented no real problems, and recovery salesman Joe Kennedy made sure that the press took notice. Swift's registration statement, he pointed out, was only 59 typewritten pages, as against the approximately 2,000 pages filed by Republic Steel under the old system.[58]

The Swift's issue was indeed the turning point to revival of the capital market. Days later, Pacific Gas submitted a registration statement for refinancing. Other refunding issues followed soon after, and then new financing began, as Kennedy had hoped and had predicted.

With the problems of registration statements cleared up, the SEC turned to the matter of trading rules for the several exchanges. Trading was where the most frequent abuses took place. Days after the Swift's issue, Kennedy announced that preparations were being completed for a "no quarter" campaign against stock swindlers and manipulators.[59]

Under the terms of the Securities Exchange Act of 1934, the SEC was empowered to "request" the exchanges to modify their trading rules by making those specific changes the SEC desired. If the exchanges refused, the commission was empowered to dictate the rules.[60] This principle of cooperation between the commission and the exchanges was right in line with Kennedy's own ideas as to the best way to run the SEC. The commission conferred with exchange leaders for several weeks, and then, on April 16, issued its recommendations for rules. Kennedy emphasized that the rules were experimental and would be modified if found to be unsatisfactory in any way.

The commission's 16 proposed rules, to be enforced by the exchanges, were loose ones, giving considerable leeway for interpretation. Several of them were closer to guidelines than rules, spelling out the abuses and prohibiting them in general terms. Rule 1, for example, prohibited trading by exchange members for their own accounts that was excessive in view of their resources. Rule 6 prohibited members to execute (or cause to be executed) sales in the same stock at successively higher or lower prices "for the purpose of creating or inducing a false, misleading, or artificial appearance of activity." Rule 10 prohibited specialists (members who dealt only in one or a small number of stocks) from buying or selling their specialties for accounts in which they had a direct or indirect financial interest "unless such dealings are reasonably necessary to permit such specialist to maintain a fair and orderly market." All of the flagrant and vicious abuses of the system were prohibited. The rule against bear raiding was spelled out explicitly: by rule 16 members were prohibited from executing short sales at a price lower than the previously executed regular sale.[61]

The rules, like the registration forms, were well received. A *Wall Street Journal* canvass showed a consensus among financiers for their early adoption by the exchanges. Whitney immediately announced that the suggested rules would be promptly placed before the New York Stock Exchange's governing committee.[62] They were, and they were as promptly adopted.

Joe Kennedy's job of organizing the SEC and introducing the administration of the Securities Act and the Securities Exchange Act was completed. He had also accomplished his personal goal—he had established a reputation as an able and effective public servant. He had a legacy of public service to pass on to his children. He had worked hard at the SEC, arriving early in the morning and staying late.[63] He lived alone with Eddie Moore and commuted weekly to be with his family in Palm Beach.[64] It was time for restless Joe Kennedy to move on. He was preparing to resign in the spring of 1935, but crises developed. The Supreme Court was about to review some important New Deal legislation, and Kennedy expected upsets that would adversely affect the business situation. He decided to put off his resignation until the fall. His formally submitted resignation was dated September 7, and was announced on the twelfth. On leaving the SEC, Kennedy told reporters that he had finished his last public job.[65]

Roosevelt accepted Kennedy's resignation in a letter that congratulated Kennedy for having administered the laws "so effectively as to win the confidence of the general investing public and the financial community." Newspaper comment on the work of the retiring chairman was heavy and unanimously commendatory. The *Washington Post*, in a news article, not an editorial, wrote that Kennedy was leaving the SEC,

> *acclaimed for his achievements by the professional traders of Wall Street, the bankers, the liberals, and the radicals.*
> *The opinion is widespread that Kennedy has done one of the best jobs of anyone connected with the New Deal, and has done it without bluster or publicity seeking and without leaving anyone angry with him. . . . He was able to enforce the highly-controversial 1933 securities act and the 1934 stock exchange act firmly, but without harassing or impeding legitimate, honest business operations.*[66]

More significant was the comment of John T. Flynn, the *New Republic*'s radical columnist, who performed a complete about-face,[67] and concluded "He was, I firmly believe, the most useful member of the Commission." [68]

Kennedy's contributions as chairman of the SEC were unquestionably great. He took an act that was widely regarded as unworkable, made it work, and made the moneyed interests like it. His talents organized the regulatory body and gave it machinery that has lasted with few changes right up until today. Under his administration the SEC policy was Kennedy's policy, as his successor James Landis commented.[69] It was a common-sense policy, unaffected by a doctrinaire conservative or reform bias. Kennedy always kept the goal of the legislation, abolishing unethical securities activities, in the front of his mind, but was able to implement the goal with a minimum of interference in the affairs of normal business.

He was able to sell the idea of the SEC and securities regulation to the financial community. Chester T. Lane suggested in 1951 that but for Kennedy the SEC might have been subjected to fatal attacks against it from the financial community.[70] Firm but friendly, Kennedy won acceptance for the SEC without sacrificing the principles involved, and by the time he left the Commission, Wall Street had come to appreciate what they had so violently scorned just a year before.

Kennedy's salesmanship job was even more important than the actual establishment of the body's administrative machinery, for it contributed to economic recovery from the Depression.[71] Most of his speeches were designed to restore business confidence. In them, he continually urged businessmen to take a more optimistic look at the country's financial situation, and criticized businessmen for being pessimistic. He publicly put the most favorable construction on every happening, and constantly predicted better times. Frequently he sounded like Hoover's appointees, who had proclaimed "prosperity is just around the corner" from the start of the Depression.[72] His rosy arguments were occasionally deflated by editorial writers, and he was perhaps aware that some of the reasoning in his statements was a bit specious. But Kennedy himself was sincerely optimistic; his predictions for the future differed from Hoover's mid-Depression statements in that they came at a time when the Administration was taking massive measures to bring about recovery. His speeches radiated this bright outlook and, as Kennedy was wont to say, "optimism is infectious." By helping to cheer the business community, Kennedy's many speeches could only have had a beneficial effect on recovery.

Joe Kennedy's decisions, his actions, and his words, as much as those of any other man, were responsible for restoring the capital market. This was an all-important contribution to the state of business and therefore to national recovery.[73]

NEW DEALER
JOE KENNEDY

FDR'S SECRETARY GRACE TULLY HAS WRITTEN THAT KENNEDY "certainly was never in true sympathy with the New Deal program," [1] and today the presence of conservative Joe Kennedy in the New Deal seems decidedly odd. But the New Deal program meant all things to all men—there was something in it for everyone, and much in it that Joseph Kennedy could sincerely support. In the early New Deal, the so-called first or brain-trusters New Deal of 1933–1934, Joe Kennedy could conscientiously support virtually all of the Administration's program.

Of the three New Deal goals—reform, relief, and recovery—the first New Deal was conceived mainly for recovery, and that is where Joe Kennedy would have had the emphasis. In conferences between New Deal administrators, he stressed the primary importance of recovery and showed great concern about not doing anything detrimental to recovery.[2] With American business and the economy recovered from the Depression, the need for relief would be alleviated. The New Deal's early legislative program demonstrates that such considerations were uppermost in the minds of Roosevelt's most influential advisors. The Emergency Banking Act of March 9, 1933, allowed the government to buy bank stocks. It was followed by a bill to permit the government to cut federal salaries and pensions, at a time when the business community felt that economy on the government's part would stimulate the national economic situation. The Federal Housing Administration was established to insure bank loans for housing construction, another great boon to the banker.

Business supported moderate inflation as a recovery measure, but opposed the large-scale inflation schemes put forth by Senator Huey Long, various veterans groups, the silver-state senators, and the influential radio priest Father Charles Coughlin. Kennedy too favored moderate inflation,[3] opposed the more radical proposals of the Coughlinites,[4] and had his way when the government adopted the policies he and the rest of the business community supported.

The key measure in the Administration's recovery program was the famed NRA, the National Recovery Administration, designed to harness rather than harass the cartels, and plan the national economy back to health. At the heart of the NRA were the industry codes, drafted—in theory though not in fact—by industry, labor, consumer, and government spokesmen. It represented the kind of business-government cooperation that Joe Kennedy looked forward to and attempted to institute at the SEC. Kennedy regarded national planning such as was represented by the NRA as imperative to recovery. So did the United States Chamber of Commerce, the House of Morgan, and the rest of the country. Only the discredited Herbert Hoover seemed to realize, or to be concerned with the fact that the NRA represented "fascism, pure fascism," as he put it.[5] The rest of the country was too engrossed with steps toward recovery, and put their hopes in the NRA.[6] Indeed, in his later *I'm For Roosevelt*, Kennedy called for increased governmental activity and planning, perhaps realizing that the Administration was more of an interloper in, than a planner of, the national economy.

Kennedy's attitudes about recovery pervaded every issue he touched. His approach to problems of relief is a good example. Conservatives who opposed government hiring and those who held the traditional belief that the government in hard times should economize, favored limiting federal relief efforts to the grocery dole. That was the most economical way to solve the relief problem, and those who were preoccupied with balancing the ever-expanding budget went along with Republicans, Southern Democrats, and the old-line economic thinkers in calling for a dole-oriented relief program. Roosevelt's more adventurous advisors, and especially Ickes, favored the building of huge public works, with less emphasis on the dole. Building public works would employ men on the construction projects and give work to the entrepreneurs and employees of the businesses furnishing materials. It would have considerable effect on stimulating recovery, help to alleviate the problem of relief, and cost considerably more than if the government limited relief measures to the dole.

Early in the Administration, Kennedy believed that recovery was well on its way, and spoke for the dole only.[7] But when he became convinced that recovery would be a long-term proposition, he abandoned his more short-sighted conservative friends, swung over,[8] and by 1935 was an enthusiastic supporter of the public works concept of relief.[9] Recovery of the economy was much more important to Joseph Kennedy than whether or not the budget of 1934 or 1935 was balanced. This was true of Roosevelt and the dominant wing of his advisors, as well.

Kennedy took part in many of the Administration's conferences on work relief.[10] In 1935, Congress appropriated almost five billion dollars for a public works program, and at the urgings of Secretary of the Treasury Henry Morgenthau, Roosevelt offered Kennedy the job of directing the huge expenditure. In the works program, Kennedy would have been the boss of Ickes and of Federal Relief Administrator Harry Hopkins, two rather doctrinaire liberals. Kennedy at first accepted, but then declined, explaining that he could not work satisfactorily with Ickes.[11]

Joe Kennedy was not, however, only for a New Deal for business. The New Deal was more than just a name for the program of the Roosevelt Administration; it was a national intellectual and emotional movement, a revolt against the cult of the self-made man and the drive for money and status of the 1920s. Kennedy was not oblivious to this revolt; he realized that the mores of the twenties, and the things that Joe Kennedy of the twenties had symbolized, were morally shallow. He spoke out against the corrupting business practices of the twenties—every one of which he had practiced—both at the SEC and later.[12] But he went much further. He spoke out against the values of the 1920s; against a value system that made wealth in and of itself the most respectable goal a man could set for himself. The editors of *American Magazine* would have been flabbergasted had they heard Kennedy's address to Boston Latin School students in April, 1935:

> *I am definitely convinced that the readjustments in the economic life of the nation that are going on are ordering a happier and more sensible existence for the youth of today—the greed of possession, the selfishness of personal acquisition, the vulgarity of mere wealth will not be the yardsticks by which your efforts to succeed will be measured.*[13]

Because of his affection for Boston Latin, Kennedy had sought out the brilliant and sensitive Frankfurter to "ghost" a speech for the occasion ("Will you please give me a lift? . . . I need the touch of a scholar"), yet this significant quotation does not appear in the draft that Frankfurter provided for Kennedy.[14] That, of course, does not mean that it was Kennedy's composition—he pressed Frankfurter so persistently for a draft, that one suspects that he probably requested drafts from others as well [15]—but it does mean that Kennedy selected the clause personally; understood what it meant, if he failed consciously to comprehend fully its implications; and believed, at least for the moment, in its message. Joe Kennedy—himself a creature of the 1920s—did not fear, but welcomed the new order of the 1930s. If FDR was a traitor to his class, Kennedy turned his back on his culture.

While Kennedy was primarily concerned with recovery, he supported continued reforms in the securities field. He opposed proposals to exempt from the securities laws banks that were engaged in underwriting securities, though the federal banking authorities supported the exemption.[16] He lent some qualified support to the more extreme advocates of the "death sentence" in the debate on the Public Utilities Holding Company Act of 1935, a bill which more neatly aligned liberals against conservatives than any other piece of 1935 legislation.[17] When William O. Douglas, the SEC's third chairman, attempted to bring about internal reform of the stock exchanges in 1938, Kennedy was by his side, using his influence on his many friends on Wall Street.[18]

Kennedy was unquestionably one of the more conservative men in the Roosevelt entourage—Mark Sullivan, writing in 1934, regarded him as the only one in the official family "who belongs, on the whole, on the conservative side." [19] But it was only "on the whole" that Kennedy could be pegged as a conservative; he was not a doctrinaire conservative but more simply a competent man with common sense. He was not of the ideological ilk of more typical New Dealers like Ickes or Frankfurter and his protégés—the "neo-Brandeizian" New Dealers. In that sense, his basic orientation was not that of the New Deal. But because there was nothing doctrinaire about him, Kennedy was generally able to work for the common goal in harmony with those who had different philosophical orientations. Despite considerable sub-surface friction between Kennedy and "the Left," on the surface Kennedy was able to maintain adequate relations with most of the President's more liberal advisors. He feigned an effusive affection and admiration for Frankfurter which did not fool the Justice;[20] extended hospitality to the ailing left-liberal Hopkins, who recuperated from an illness at Kennedy's Palm Beach villa;[21] contributed to election campaigns for politicians of the entire political spectrum, including that of Senator George Norris, who was not only a "left-winger," but a Republican to boot.[22]

Kennedy certainly had more than one motive for supporting so much of the New Deal program. He must have been influenced in some measure by considerations such as humanitarian concern for the poor; a conscious or subconscious desire to make amends for his own past; and even, perhaps, a desire to win the greater attentions of his chief by supporting the programs that Kennedy believed Roosevelt desired. But probably the most important reason for Kennedy's so thoroughgoing support of the New Deal was his own desire to preserve American capitalism by reforming it.

In 1933 the nation witnessed numerous food riots; 15,000 hungry and frustrated veterans swarmed over Washington; an angry mob severely beat and nearly lynched a judge who proceeded with a mortgage foreclosure. World communism was given a shot in the arm when the Soviet Union emerged as the only major world power not severely hit by depression. That year Germany, also depression-plagued, turned to Nazi dictatorship. At home, the American Communist movement mushroomed. Secret Democratic party polls showed that the Long-Coughlin quasi-fascist Union party might poll six million votes in 1936. Kennedy appreciated the threat posed by radicalism. Again and again he stressed the need to liberalize capitalism for the purpose of preserving it.[23] The removal of grievances, he explained to Reverend Joseph Thorning, was the best form of social insurance and the most effective way to prevent the emergence of totalitarianism at home.[24] Sometimes he put his thoughts rather eloquently: "A society callous to the needy is furnishing fuel for the social conflagration of tomorrow." [25] At other times he spoke crudely, as when he explained that he had become a New Deal supporter after seeing "how ugly and menacing hungry men may become." [26]

Kennedy, and American socialists and Marxists, were about the only ones in the mid-thirties who viewed the New Deal as a program to preserve capitalism. Today that is a most respectable interpretation of the New Deal. In 1936, Kennedy wrote that Roosevelt had no desire to disturb the bases of the capitalistic system, but wanted only to preserve and strengthen them.[27] That was Roosevelt's goal; it was Kennedy's goal; it was the function of the New Deal.

Kennedy's influence on Roosevelt was certainly great. Roosevelt's background and understanding of economics was at best rudimentary, and he consulted many people for advice. While Kennedy was never a full-fledged brain truster,[28] he was consulted by the President frequently on administrative matters and legislation pertaining to the national economy. According to Arthur Krock, in Roosevelt's circle, Kennedy was "unmatched for competence, imagination, and courage in the areas of fiscal and monetary economics." [29] He was a good advisor for Roosevelt because he was more flexible in his own economic thinking than most of Roosevelt's doctrinaire advisors. And he shared both Roosevelt's earnest desire to balance the budget and Roosevelt's willingness to temporarily unbalance the budget to alleviate human suffering. Roosevelt appreciated the fact that Kennedy was always a frank critic of the Administration's policies, and not a "yes man." [30] Besides advice, Roosevelt used Kennedy for all sorts of minor problems, from keeping Hearst and Coughlin sweet to studying European economic conditions.[31]

The President often toyed with the idea of making Kennedy Secretary of Commerce,[32] and on several occasions the press reported that Kennedy had been offered, or was about to be offered, the post.[33] But the job that Kennedy really wanted was Secretary of the Treasury, and on several occasions Krock boomed him for the job in his influential *New York Times* column. That post Kennedy could never have. Roosevelt told Farley, "I couldn't put Joe Kennedy in. . . . Joe would want to run the Treasury in his own way, contrary to my plans and views." [34] Kennedy and Morgenthau, once close, became less friendly; the Secretary resented both Kennedy's lobbying for his job and Krock's role in the effort to unseat him.[35]

Kennedy remained Roosevelt's top advisor on Wall Street matters until Roosevelt sent him abroad as ambassador,[36] and was responsible for the choice of Landis as his successor as SEC chairman.[37] When Landis resigned as chairman, Kennedy pushed Douglas as Landis' successor, and though Landis was urging Roosevelt to tap a different candidate for SEC chairman, the President took Kennedy's suggestion.[38] Kennedy's influence, however, was not limited to SEC problems. When Sirovich and Congressman Adolph Sabath attempted to investigate unethical deals and practices in the motion picture industry, Kennedy succeeded in having a damper put on them.[39] By further disgracing American business, Sirovich and Sabath might have retarded recovery—and in the process would have exposed mogul Joseph P. Kennedy to the bone.

Personally, relations between Joe Kennedy and the President were not as close as Kennedy would have had them. Kennedy seemed to be enamored with the charming patrician. His "personal devotion to the President is famous in Washington," wrote the *New York Times*,[40] and the correspondence files at the Roosevelt Library in Hyde Park are cluttered with letters from Kennedy asking for autographed pictures; handwritten notes—"about three lines in longhand for my children";

and similar personal souvenirs.[41] As flattered as Roosevelt may have been, he resented Kennedy's demands on his attentions, which carried to such lengths as demanding to speak to Roosevelt on the campaign trail, while the paralyzed candidate was in his bath, over "important" matters that were not important at all.[42] To other associates, Roosevelt complained that "Kennedy calls up and says he is hurt because I have not seen him." [43] "The trouble with Kennedy," he told Morgenthau, "is you always have to hold his hand." [44] To Ickes the President complained of what he called "prima donnas," and of the burden of having to "send for Joe Kennedy every few days and hold his hand." [45] It was comments such as these that led Jim Farley, writing in 1948, to conclude that Roosevelt never liked Kennedy,[46] but while Kennedy's almost childish need for manifestations of approval was tiresome, the President was able to like him in spite of his limitations, and Roosevelt enjoyed his company nonetheless.[47]

Kennedy and Roosevelt were both great haters of red tape and bureaucratic ways and inefficiencies. Though Kennedy's orientation was essentially conservative, and Roosevelt's was more-or-less liberal, both were flexible in their political views. And they were both gregarious, warm and outgoing, informal and capable of charm. They shared a very great love of life. Roosevelt was exposed only to the jolly, easygoing Joe Kennedy, not the hard and unscrupulous Joe Kennedy; he saw those aspects of the Kennedy personality that made Kennedy appealing. Roosevelt appreciated Kennedy's many favors— frequent gifts of sea foods or cases of Scotch,[48] and help in finding a suitable job for FDR's son-in-law, John Boettiger.[49] But more important, Roosevelt appreciated Kennedy's ready wit, his ability to make any gathering merry, and his stubborn refusal to be inhibited by the presence of the Chief Executive. So, when FDR insisted that Kennedy rid himself of some lady friend too much in evidence, Kennedy responded with a challenge that Roosevelt rid himself of Marguerite "Missy" LeHand, who served as much much more than just the President's secretary.[50] Journalist Joe McCarthy reports another excellent example of Kennedy's saltiness with the President: Kennedy relayed to Roosevelt and the somewhat stuffy Secretary of State Cordell Hull, a conversation he had had with Krock. Krock had expressed surprise that Alabama Senator Hugo Black had not informed Roosevelt of his brief membership in the Ku Klux Klan before Black accepted a seat on the United States Supreme Court. "Joe, when Krock said that what did you say to Krock?" asked the

President. Kennedy's reply—no doubt cleaned up for publication—was "If Marlene Dietrich asked you to make love to her, would you tell her you weren't much good at making love?" Roosevelt collapsed in laughter; Hull's jaw dropped open in amazement.[51]

Kennedy, who jealously guarded his own public dignity,[52] insisted on making inroads on the President's. Krock recalls hearing Kennedy's end of phone conversations with the President that would begin with a deferential "Mr. President" and soon lapse into a "Now-listen-to-me-boy." [53] That kind of handling of the Chief Executive, especially within earshot of the formal Krock, was proof positive of the great intimacy between Roosevelt and Kennedy. It was also a manifestation of considerable self-flattery and just a pinch of showing off for his admirer Krock.

Kennedy was an occasional visitor at the White House, stopping in the early evening or later for a beer and camaraderie with Roosevelt and his cronies.[54] He had an elevator installed at Marwood so that the crippled President could comfortably return the visits[55]—a small price to a rich and socially aspiring man for the honor of Presidential visits—and thereafter Roosevelt became an occasional caller, coming for a swim or to see a movie in Marwood's 200-seat theatre.[56] Krock, who was temporarily on strained terms with the Chief Executive, happened to be a weekend guest at Marwood on one such occasion, when the President arrived on short notice. At Kennedy's "polite suggestion" (Krock's words), the journalist exiled himself to an upstairs bedroom during the visit; Kennedy did not let on that he was "harboring the enemy"; and Krock later noted his recollections of happy carousing until well after midnight, when he fell asleep "pondering the paradoxes of the men who occupy the highest office in the land." [57] For his daily readers, though, all he revealed was that, "pursued by bores the President enjoys getting away from them and into good company" [58] with Kennedy.

Roosevelt, who enjoyed a good practical joke, used to enjoy telling this story: The President asked Kennedy to accompany him to the Shriners' Parade, climax of the Masons' annual pageantry. "I am all alone. Why don't you come join me at it?" The idea was unthinkable to any good Roman Catholic—"My God! I go to the Shriners' Parade?" Kennedy incredulously asked the President. But not to pass up a chance for the pleasure of His company, Kennedy went, taking pains, as Roosevelt put it, to keep "sliding behind the police all the time so that the photographer wouldn't get him." After the parade, he returned to the White House with the President and some high Shrine officials. At the conclusion of the evening, Kennedy accepted a ride with "one or two high-muck-a-mucks in the Shrine" and then returned to his summer home in Hyannis. A couple of weeks later, as Roosevelt told it, "I sent him a telegram. I picked any old name out of the telephone book, John Turner or something like that." The telegram read "Honorable Joseph P. Kennedy. In accordance with our delightful conversation the night of the Shriners' Parade, will it be convenient for you to go through the ceremony the first week of September? A large and distinguished gathering will be here to welcome you. Please wire as quickly as possible to Admiral Cary T. Grayson. . . . We count on your presence and the ceremonies will be made as easy for you as possible. John Turner." "I sent this off and Joe got it there and he had a fit—'My heavens, what did I say that night? I know I was perfectly sober. What could I have said?' " Then Kennedy began to suspect that the wire was a hoax, but he didn't track it down.

"About the 25th of August, I was talking to Joe on the telephone from the White House—he was still up on the Cape—and at the end of the conversation I said, 'By the way, Joe, are you going to be down here the first week in September?' Joe said, 'You blankety blank blank!' Just like that, and to the President of the United States." [59]

Richard J. Whalen, Kennedy's first biographer, reports another practical joke that goes something like this: A group of senators conspired to pass off an imposter as North Dakota's Senator Lynn J. Frazier at a senatorial stag party that Kennedy hosted at Marwood. Senator Frazier was treated like the most important guest—"It was Senator Frazier this and Senator Frazier that." A few days later, Kennedy learned that he had lavished his attentions on a nobody. Roosevelt knew how impressed Kennedy was with important personages and, in their next conversation, he gently ribbed Kennedy with a casual "Say Joe, I hear you met Senator Frazier." [60] Presidential ribbing is perhaps the only sweet ribbing, and helped to make Joseph P. Kennedy feel accepted, appreciated, liked—secure in the most "in" group in the country. It made Joe Kennedy happy.

1936

1936 WAS A BUSY YEAR FOR JOE KENNEDY. AFTER A EUROPEAN holiday he went to work as an independent management consultant. Joe Kennedy's experience and reputation as an executive, his deserved or undeserved fame for cost-cutting, his skill as a financier, and his new and national reputation for fairness, made him well qualified for such jobs. Moreover, he was an apt fellow.

Kennedy's facility for amassing fortunes is probably reflective of intelligence, and, not surprisingly, financial authorities attest to it. John Harriman, financial writer for the *Boston Globe*, has called Kennedy the second smartest man he ever knew, second only to Baruch.[1]

Kennedy's intelligence, however, is not something that one assumes because of his successes in life. It was a quality of mind that impressed most of those with whom he came in contact. Despite his mediocre academic record at Boston Latin and Harvard, Joe Kennedy had a mind that worked like clockwork. His youthful enjoyment of complex mathematical problems was an early manifestation of the mechanical way in which his mind worked. Ray O'Connell, a lawyer who worked with Kennedy on the problems of Massachusetts commerce in the mid-forties, described it this way:

If you tell Joe Kennedy a problem he'll listen quietly, and separate the wheat from the chaff while you talk. He quickly divides the problem into its components, and sees to the heart of the problem. Almost before you're finished speaking he has the answer to a problem you've struggled with for months.

O'Connell termed Kennedy's thinking process "marvelous." [2]

Apparently Joe Kennedy was born with a naturally disciplined mind—the kind generally lacking in man but found sometimes in uneducated people. It reflects a high degree of native intelligence, with which degree of education has little to do. With what Pecora called an "almost machine-like efficiency" he would cut through a maze of nonessentials straight to the crux of the matter.[3] With his unusual mental talents and his wide range of experience, it is little wonder that Cardinal Spellman called him a "genius." [4] Son-in-law Sargent Shriver referred to him as one of the most brilliant men he had ever known.[5]

This is the fellow who went to work as a management consultant in 1936. Not surprisingly, he commanded substantial fees. RCA hired him to prepare an equitable recapitalization plan on December 28, 1935. Within a month he completed the job and received a fee of $150,000 for his efforts.

RCA's financial structure had come under great criticism. It had class A preferred stockholders, class B preferred stockholders, and common stockholders. Common stock had paid no dividends in the corporation's 17-year history, and class B preferred had paid no dividends in five years. In December, RCA decided to recapitalize the company so as to bring more stockholders closer to the profits. Recapitalization almost always offended some group of stockholders, and by securing his friend Kennedy to prepare the plan, RCA's chief David Sarnoff took the onus off management's hands, and assured RCA a plan with respected, able, and authoritative sponsorship.

After a month Kennedy came up with his plan. Class A preferred stock, paying 7 percent, was to be retired and class A stockholders were to be paid $55.00 per share plus accrued dividends. Rather than pay 7 percent, RCA could take advantage of the low money market and borrow at 2.5 percent. Kennedy suggested that RCA borrow ten million dollars to pay off the class A stockholders, so that its working capital would not be drawn on too heavily. Class B stock would be replaced by a new preferred stock valued at $100.00 and paying $3.50 per year. For each B share the investor would get one and one-fifth shares of the new preferred stock, plus one share of common stock. At any time within the following five years, the new preferred could be traded for five shares of common stock. Class B stockholders would lose their unpaid accrued dividends, but would be first in line for future profits.

Kennedy regarded the plan as fair and advantageous to all classes of stockholders. RCA shareholders apparently agreed. The plan was adopted by 11,341,635 to 11,312, more than 1,000 to 1. (Such figures, while accurate, do not reveal the fact that decision-making by stockholders' proxies is almost always a Russian election.) Out of more than 300 stockholders who attended the meeting to consider the plan, only two spoke against its adoption, class B stockholders who objected to losing their accrued dividends. When shareholders asked how much Kennedy's fee would cost the company, Kennedy said, "I guess some of you will get a shock. My fee was $150,000, from which I paid $30,000 to accountants." *Time* magazine reported that "a profound silence descended." [6]

Joe Kennedy, it is said, never minded paying for competence. He always liked an able fellow that set a high price for his services.[7] He himself set the example.

The RCA plan was submitted to management on January 25, 1936. On May 2, Kennedy went to work for Paramount Pictures.

Paramount had come out of reorganization proceedings a year before that had split its stockholders into groups competing for control. Elisha Walker's Kuhn, Loeb, and Company, and Lehman Brothers owned sizable interests in Paramount, but had entered opposite camps. Kuhn, Loeb, bankers for the old management, stuck with the old crowd, while Lehman Brothers threw in with the insurgent group led by Harold Fortington. A compromise board of directors was agreed upon, but the Fortington group emerged on top. John Hertz, of Lehman Brothers, was put on the board of directors, and John Otterson, the Fortington candidate, became Paramount's president. Adolph Zukor, from the old management, was retained as chairman of the board.

The new Paramount Pictures, however, was unable to get on its feet, and the weaknesses in the old company of which the Fortington associates had complained, began to manifest themselves again. The company was losing money hand over fist. Joe Kennedy was called in by his old associates to study Paramount's setup. It turned out to be another one-month job, but Kennedy's responsibilities were much wider than those in the RCA assignment. Kennedy was to prepare a report on the whole range of Paramount's activities, making suggestions on how to revitalize the sick company. Sheehan and Fayne left the SEC to join Kennedy in his study, and his staff was expanded by Ford, and by A. B. Poole and C. J. Scollard, two of Kennedy's former Pathé colleagues.

The Paramount management got only a preliminary report from Kennedy, submitted June 10, but it was more than they had bargained for. Kennedy saw the essence of Paramount's difficulties in its management. He informed directors, "I am frank to state that it would be an inexcusable waste of money and senseless waste of our time to proceed further with the work of survey unless and until such changes are made in management as I deem an essential preliminary to any continuation of my work." [8]

He pointed at Paramount's procedures as the most ill-managed aspect of their operations. They were "incompetent, unbusinesslike, and wasteful." Kennedy saw the influence of the financier directors on studio operations as decidedly bad. "Positively and definitely good pictures" were needed, and though the executives were "quality businessmen" in their own fields, they were standing in the way of showmen who could produce such pictures. To start setting things right, Kennedy had Paramount sign up Claudette Colbert, a good thing for Paramount and an even better thing for Miss Colbert, whose agent was being blacklisted by the powerful Louis B. Mayer.[9]

Kennedy was also critical of the company's failure to make and keep sensible production schedules and its failure to plan its pictures in advance.

Kennedy urged that salaries to Paramount's executives, which he figured accounted for 19 percent of the company's expenses, be cut down. He proposed fixing their salaries at much lower levels, and the creation of a bonus plan for the top people should net earnings exceed agreed-upon totals.

Reflecting his lack of confidence in Paramount's management, he urged that the report be made public, so that stockholders would not confuse company policies with his recommendations. Management at first declined, saying that the release of the Kennedy report would be contrary to the best interest of the stockholders. Ultimately, though, the 54 page, 15,000 word report was released, perhaps because management knew it would be "leaked" anyway. Shortly thereafter changes in company management were made. Otterson left as Paramount's president; Fortington resigned his position as chairman of the executive committee. Zukor, a longtime showman, returned to active management of the company.

Kennedy had left his fee to the discretion of Paramount's board of directors. In line with his recommendation to cut executive salaries, they paid him $50,000 for the work, but a third of his pay from RCA.[10] It was worth that much and more had Kennedy's only service been to sidetrack the Sirovich-Sabath Congressional investigating committee from its planned inquiry into the shenanigans of Paramount's financier management, a service which Kennedy called to the attention of the directors.[11] No doubt the displeasure of the discredited directors from the Fortington group was partially responsible for Paramount's failure to be more generous. Thereafter, Kennedy's old friendship with Elisha Walker, principal of the "vindicated" group, would ripen to the point that Kennedy, in the '40s, thought of him as "my dearest friend," [12] while his old friend Hertz, from the "discredited" crowd, spread the story that Kennedy had double-crossed him on the Yellow-Cab jiggle assignment.[13]

The Paramount study is particularly interesting because in it Kennedy called for rejection of everything that he had helped to bring to Hollywood: Wall Street influence, excessive and unearned executive compensation, and trashy movies. The Paramount executive who bore the brunt of Kennedy's criticism was John Otterson, Paramount's president. Otterson, who knew nothing about movies, had made an excellent name for himself by running AT&T's electrical research subsidiary with battleship efficiency. His good business name, but complete lack of qualifications for motion-picture work, was reminiscent of another movie executive—leather man Hiram Brown, whom Kennedy had placed as head of RKO. Times had changed from the days when Wall Streeters could produce painfully bad pictures that were financial successes, and Paramount's management and procedures were certainly not what they should have been. But perhaps Kennedy was so very outspoken because of a subconscious and personal desire to help purge Hollywood of some of the corruptions that he had helped to bring there.

Kennedy was never one to stay in one line of work very long. An active but restless fellow, he once told Roosevelt, "I'll take any job you want me to and even work for nothing at it as long as it's interesting. I never want to be bored." [14] By mid-June he was ready to return to politics. On June 15, five days after submitting his report to Paramount, he wrote Roosevelt's secretary, "Missy" LeHand, through whom Kennedy channeled most of his correspondence to Roosevelt. He was

> *fairly free now of any business activities, and so if [Roosevelt] thinks I can be of any service to him, please let me know.*
> *I am going to take up the "bum's life" again. I am taking all the children to the Cape Wednesday of this week but shall be available if there is anything he wants me to do.*[15]

The reply, if any, to Kennedy's scarcely veiled job application is unknown, but it is clear that Kennedy did a lot of work for Roosevelt in the months that followed. That summer and fall he became one of the most hard-working boosters for the reelection of FDR.

Kennedy's work for Roosevelt's reelection had already begun before he left Paramount. By May, 1936, he had submitted a copy of the manuscript for *I'm For Roosevelt*, by Joseph P. Kennedy, largely if not entirely written by Krock,[16] to the White House for Presidential review. Roosevelt wrote Kennedy on June seventeenth, "I thought the manuscript splendid and that it will be of real service, not only from a campaign point of view but also as a distinct step in sane education of the country." [17] The book was released in August, and was a sober plea aimed at businessmen for support of the President's reelection.[18]

Most of the book was devoted to discussing recovery and to defending the increases in the national debt. It argued that the rise in the debt had been necessitated by the situation that the nation had faced in 1932. It referred to the rise as a sensible form of borrowing, and reminded people that the uses made of the money had calmed a potentially revolutionary situation. It had been a sound investment. With text and a series of statistical tables, the book compared the economic situation of the country in 1932 with that in 1936, pointing out how great recovery had been. The implication was clear: we have Roosevelt to thank for it. The increase in the national debt, which he figured amounted to no more than $120 per person, had brought about increases in the national income amounting to $190 per person. He justified the debt's increase as insurance against revolution; as money well spent for the well-being of the people; and as wholly justifiable from a business point of view because increased earnings had resulted from the borrowings.

The book credited the Roosevelt Administration with bringing about the recovery it statistically detailed.[19] It defended the Agricultural Administration Act and its crop scarcity program; devaluation of the dollar; the public works concept of relief; federal securities legislation; and Roosevelt's departures from the Democratic platform of 1932. It wholeheartedly endorsed the New Deal approach and the concept of economic planning to end depressionary cycles and periodic unemployment. It rebuked the "rugged individualists," whom it identified with the "Old Dealers," and warned that the return of such men to power would likely undo all the good of the Roosevelt years.

The book makes an effective case for the respectable thesis that Roosevelt had preserved American capitalism by taking care of the fundamental needs of the people. It was critical of rich ingrates whose fortunes had been preserved by the President's acts, and yet who rose to attack him with phrases like "regimentation."

The book presented some effective arguments and is valuable today for some sound insights into the philosophy and measures of the Roosevelt Administration. But it was designed as campaign literature and is not free from weak spots. It shied away from extended discussion of the National Recovery Act, which had already been ruled unconstitutional by the Supreme Court; the Administration's silver policy; the Social Security Act; or any other of the more controversial of the New Deal experiments.[20] It ignored the Administration's labor policies. It discussed the upturn in business and the Roosevelt measures, and drew the conclusion that the Administration's policies were responsible for the upturn. This ignored the general upturn in conditions throughout the world. It ignored the argument that recovery would have been accomplished even sooner but for the Roosevelt Administration with its parallel concern for social reforms. It gave no credit to business leaders for their part in bringing about recovery. The unbalancing of the budget it attributed to the more desirable of the New Deal expenditures—the feeding of the widows and orphans—and not to some of the more questionable Administration expenditures. And it was silent to the argument that planning and control pointed toward greater regimentation of the individual, socialism or fascism. The sober reviewer for the *Saturday Review of Literature*, former SEC official Thomas H. Gammack, asked: "Does he scoff at fears of excessive regimentation and bureaucracy because he is confident that the President can be trusted to avoid excesses or because he wants less individualism and more regulation?" [21]

Only one review picked up what today seems the most significant line in the book: "I have no political ambitions for myself or for my children." [22] The *Motion Picture Herald* pointed out that with that line Kennedy was answering an unraised question, "one suspects without consulting his subconscious." [23]

The book was generally well received.[24] Sold for a dollar, it enjoyed a wide readership. When Roosevelt finally got around to reading the published copy, he sent Kennedy a brief letter:

 Dear Joe:—
 I'M FOR KENNEDY: The book is grand.[25]

The book was only the first of Kennedy's many efforts during the campaign. The President's son Elliott Roosevelt has written that Kennedy bore the responsibility of selling Roosevelt to the business community in the 1936 campaign.[26] That was an impossible assignment. Roosevelt had gotten along fine with the financial world at the start of his term, but in 1935 the New Deal began to take a perceptible turn to the left. By 1936, the business community was almost entirely, and solidly, behind the Republican candidate. Kennedy ran "Businessmen for Roosevelt" dinners in many cities, only to find a universal coldness to his candidate among his peers. Kennedy himself wanted to drop the idea, but the President was devoted to it. Attend a dinner for Roosevelt? Some businessmen bluntly expressed their thoroughgoing hostility towards the President; others were just "busy" on the night of the dinner. Everyone had their excuses.[27] Kennedy used to boast that he was the only man with more than 12¢ in his pocket who supported Roosevelt before the 1932 convention. The assertion was plainly false, but approached truth when applied to the 1936 campaign. The dinners were unsuccessful; Roosevelt just plain could not be sold to businessmen in 1936. He had already resigned himself to getting little business support, and his campaign polemics against American Bourbons crystallized conservative business hostility toward him. In the face of this, there was little Joseph Kennedy could do.

Kennedy's personal and public advocacy of the Roosevelt candidacy was not limited to his book and his "Businessmen's Dinners." In a *New York Times Magazine* article in July, he questioned the sincerity of the businessmen who claimed to fear the government's policies. He pointed out that the big banks, all of them anti-Administration, were "loading up on government securities," belying their talk about inflation and the end of the government.[28] That same day, Kennedy urged Bostonians to support Roosevelt in a long interview by Louis Lyons published in the *Boston Globe*. He again belittled talk about runaway inflation.[29] In a *Boston Post* interview by Robert L. Norton, published in August, Kennedy spoke forcefully about the New Deal's function of preserving capitalism, and of his conviction that "planned action is imperative." [30] In September, Kennedy supported Roosevelt in articles that appeared under his name in the *New York Times Magazine* and the *Review of Reviews*, and in an interview published in the *Rostrum*.[31] He delivered a series of radio addresses on October fifth, twenty-first, and twenty-fourth.[32] His statements, no doubt "ghosted," had by this time begun to echo Roosevelt's, and he began speaking more tartly of the anti-Administration businessmen. In a brilliant speech on October twenty-first (which, Kennedy informed Roosevelt, had been partially "ghosted" by a French journalist), Kennedy warned not to let "all business get jockeyed into a position of antagonism to the rest of the nation because a few stuffed shirts have lost their silk hats. . . . We must not feel on November 4th that businessmen as a class have rebelled against the instinct of the rest of the population and have been beaten in that rebellion." He handled with great sophistication the sociological and psychological background of the hostility that the rich felt for Roosevelt. He attributed their hatred of Roosevelt (and hatred was the best word to describe it) to the fact that Roosevelt had taken the rich man, per se, off the pedestal he had occupied previously. "Before 1933," he pointed out, "the most fundamental dogma of Americanism was that to become rich was not only a worthy aim in itself, but the fulfillment of a beneficent duty toward the community." Roosevelt and his administration had done much to destroy this common belief. A reappraisal of human values had deprived the rich of their moral prestige. The faith in the rich was gone, even in the rich man himself. "All this is unconscious and all the more frightful. Being unable—and certainly unwilling—to analyze with coolness the cause of his anxiety, he seeks relief in vituperation and hatred." [33] Today the speech still gives valuable insight into the reactions of the rich man in the 1930s. Kennedy, who attributed its authorship to the Frenchman, wrote Roosevelt that he regarded the speech as "one of the greatest things in the campaign." [34]

Three days after the address, the "Progressive National Committee Supporting Franklin D. Roosevelt for President," headed by Republicans George Norris and Robert M. La Follette, Jr., sponsored Kennedy in a nationwide radio speech. It was another excellent and spirited address, in which Kennedy decried "the efforts made for low, political purposes to confuse a Christian program of social justice for a Godless program of communism." [35]

Kennedy was perhaps the only member of the Roosevelt Administration who held the universal respect of all segments of the population. While liberals saw him as the New Deal's tame capitalist,[36] businessmen regarded him as their man in the New Deal.[37] Even Father Coughlin, who denounced Roosevelt's "betrayal of America," called Kennedy the "shining star among the dim 'knights'" of the Administration.[38] Kennedy probably had little effect on the business community, but because of the esteem in which he was held, his speeches and articles must have been effective with more open-minded people. As he had predicted in the *Rostrum*, on election day Roosevelt took all but two New England states, Maine and Vermont.[39]

JOE KENNEDY ALWAYS HAD FRIENDS OF WIDELY DIFFERING POLITICAL opinions. Although his views late in life frequently threw him into camp with the far right, he remained on close personal terms with liberals like James Roosevelt and Justice Douglas.[40] The "liberal" Joe Kennedy of the 1930s was equally at ease with the men he attacked politically. His friend Hearst had fallen out with the President, and one reviewer called Kennedy's book "a savage attack on the preachings of Mr. Hearst and the Old Dealers." [41] But Kennedy remained personally friendly with Hearst and with the latter's erstwhile ally, Father Coughlin.[42] After the election, "W.R." hired Kennedy to look into the weak and tottering Hearst empire, with an eye to improving its structure and practices.

Because of the closely-held private ownership of the Hearst organization, information about Kennedy's recommendations and conclusions, and the length of his employment with Hearst, has not come to light. All that this author has found on the subject is that Kennedy's personal staff for the job was augmented by Judge Burns, and that Kennedy's own salary was a comfortable $12,500 per week.

CLEANING
THE AUGEAN STABLES

JOE KENNEDY WAS READY TO GO BACK TO WASHINGTON BY THE spring of 1937. He kept in touch with Roosevelt during '35 and '36 and made known his availability for a draft to office. A job was crying for a man with his competence, reputation for fairness, and personal popularity: chairman of the new Maritime Commission. Roosevelt had attempted to get three others to accept the job without success. His secretary, Marvin McIntyre, wanted the job, but his close ties with the shipping interests made him unacceptable.[1] On paper, Joe Kennedy was ideal for the job, and was "prevailed upon" to take it long enough to get the commission on its feet. Arthur Krock, who was in a position to know, wrote that Kennedy would probably not stay long after setting up the commission.[2] Kennedy was no doubt delighted to get back into the government, once again closely and publicly associated with the President; once again proving his talents and making headlines. The reputation of being the New Deal's trouble-shooter was a flattering one and to some extent a deserved one.

The act establishing the Maritime Commission provided that its members must have had no financial interest in the shipping industry for three years previous to appointment. This posed a problem, as Kennedy owned a sizable block of stock in Todd Shipyards. The prohibition clearly applied to him, but Congress was eager to avail the nation of Kennedy's services and passed a special resolution effectually dispensing with the prohibition in Kennedy's case.[3]

The new job proved considerably more difficult than setting up the SEC. The Maritime Commission was established by the Merchant Marine Act of 1936, and was expected to revitalize America's merchant shipping industry. Almost all of the American foreign-trade fleet was outdated and economically inefficient. The maritime labor situation was both explosive and crippling. The shipping interests, one of the most reactionary employer groups in America, were pitted against militant unions, strongly influenced by the Left, which themselves were split into bitter factions fighting for control. The shipping executives were of questionable competence.[4] American

87

shippers were unable to compete in foreign trade. The situation could not have been worse. Joe Kennedy's job was to change it all. "Such is the penalty of having once performed a miracle," wrote Krock.[5] The *New Republic*, generally unfriendly to Kennedy, conceded that his job "makes other government chiefs in Washington shudder." [6] "They tell me I've got the lousiest job in Washington," Kennedy commented. He did.

By 1936, Congress appreciated the seriousness of the state of American shipping, and responsibly regarded a stronger merchant marine as essential to American defense and commerce in times of international friction. An honest subsidy program was clearly necessary. The old system of awarding covert subsidies by way of fat "mail contracts" had led to numerous abuses and had failed to accomplish anything. New York's labor-baiting Senator-Doctor Royal S. Copeland and Congressman Schuyler Bland, of the ship-building town of Newport News, Virginia, sponsored a bill providing for open subsidies and otherwise leaving the shippers free to continue the abuses of the old system. New Deal Senator Joseph Guffey joined efforts with Senator Hugo Black, Congressman Ed Moran, and civil servant Thomas Woodward, to produce a second bill. The Guffey bill also called for unabashed subsidies to shipping, but with strong cables attached to protect the public interest and the interests of maritime labor. Their bill had the serious defect of circumscribing the actions of the subsidized shipper too closely, and it did not allow enough profit to the shipowners, operators, and builders to make shipping an attractive investment for private capital. The compromise bill that emerged from committee hearings was hardly a compromise at all; the Guffey bill prevailed on almost every point.[7]

The bill was designed, its preamble stated, "To further the development and maintenance of an adequate and well-balanced American merchant marine, to promote the commerce of the United States, to aid in the national defense, to repeal certain former legislation, and for other purposes." It created the United States Maritime Commission, abolished the mail contract subsidies, and authorized the Maritime Commission to grant new subsidies. The Maritime Commission was empowered to grant subsidies of up to one-half of shipbuilding costs for new foreign trade ships that were built in American shipyards. The subsidy was to compensate for cheaper shipbuilding costs abroad, and was designed to encourage revitalization and expansion of American shipbuilding facilities. The plans for subsidized ships were to be cleared by the Navy to insure that they were also suitable for defense purposes. The Maritime Commission also had to approve the need for the ship, its operator's reliability, and the fairness of the bid for construction. Ship operators also were eligible for subsidies of up to one-half of operating costs, again to compensate for cheaper foreign operating costs. The ships had to be used on routes deemed essential by the Maritime Commission. Subsidized vessels had to meet certain minimum labor standards set by the commission. A "recapture provision" provided for refunding to the government half of an operator's profit in excess of 10 percent of capital employed every five years. Shippers were required to maintain two separate reserve funds to provide for replacement costs, and to deposit part of their profits in each. The subsidies were to apply only on foreign-trade vessels, and companies doing both a domestic and foreign business were to keep separate books if they were to receive subsidies. In figuring costs of operation, shipbuilding industry salaries were limited to $25,000, a small amount for top executives in major outfits. Should the various subsidies fail to put an adequate American merchant marine on the waters, Title VII of the bill called for government building, operation, and ownership of merchant marine vessels.

Shipping interests were not pleased by the bill. *Marine Age*, the magazine most widely read by shipping executives, criticized the detail to which subsidized shippers were ordered, and the extent of government supervision. They warned their readers that "The Sovietizing of the American Merchant Marine is under way. The slavery of experience and ability to political dictatorship is being spread over a great industry like a wet blanket."[8] Despite the hysteria of the shipper's journal, the bill probably did circumscribe shipowners too much—there was even reference in the bill to the gold braid on uniforms—and the act was subject to criticism on a large number of particulars. Even 50 percent subsidies did not equate American costs of construction and operation with the vastly cheaper foreign costs. The five-year recapture period was unsatisfactory in a business which operated on a longer cycle. In such a risky and traditionally unprofitable business as shipping, the maximums on profits were too low to justify risking one's capital. Even without the maximums, the political vulnerability of subsidized profits would scare off many investors. Expenditure of the public money was safeguarded, but it was so hedged about as to bring no basic relief to the industry.[9]

Further, several other government agencies were left control over various aspects of the industry. In calling for amendment of the act in December, 1937, Joseph Kennedy described it as "about the worst piece of legislation that I have ever seen." [10]

This was the act that Joseph Kennedy was to administer and the situation he was to rectify. Admiral Emory S. Land, Kennedy's cohort and successor, says that Kennedy was called in "to clean the Augean Stable that was American shipping." [11] As if his task were not difficult enough, Kennedy found friction on the new commission he headed. The permanent Maritime Commission succeeded a temporary three-man board and was sworn in on April 16, 1937. Roosevelt again balanced "left-wingers" and "right-wingers." Serving with Kennedy on the commission were liberals Moran and Woodward. Because they had had a hand in the drafting of the bill, they were believed to be harsh on the industry. Title VII of the bill, allowing government ownership, operation, and construction of merchant vessels, was a Moran innovation, and he was believed to favor its implementation. Admiral Land and Admiral Henry A. Wiley rounded out the commission, and because of their military backgrounds they were regarded as conservative. The older, dignified Wiley had earned the wrath of labor by advocating company unions in the shipping industry. Admiral Land later became suspect in labor circles. Kennedy was expected to balance the commission with a heavy dose of common sense free from theoretical bias.

Wiley had served as chairman of the three-man board that had preceded the Maritime Commission, and with Kennedy assuming the chair, Wiley received a demotion that he resented.[12] The old man's disappointment, coupled with his set ways, frequently led to hot disagreements between himself and Kennedy. The commission's earliest problem was to establish a modus operandi. In the tradition of the Navy, Wiley urged that each commissioner be appointed to supervise and direct a certain branch of the commission's work. Kennedy urged that the commission consider all important matters as a body.[13] The two had many heated arguments on this and related matters, and on occasion Kennedy exploded at the Admiral with "You can't bring those God-damn quarter-deck methods into this commission." [14] At Kennedy's private urgings the commission searched for something to occupy Wiley's energies, and he was finally given the task of planning a training program for merchant seamen.[15]

Personal differences between Land and Wiley also posed problems. As a line officer, Wiley scorned staff officer Land and regarded himself as Land's better. Land and Kennedy worked closely; the two lunched together frequently, and Land served as temporary chairman during Kennedy's absences. Wiley resented Land's closeness with Kennedy.[16] There was also friction between Moran and Land.[17] Debates on most matters usually ended in three-to-two votes, with Kennedy, Land, and Woodward against Wiley and Moran. Admiral Land told the author that he suspected that Wiley sided with Moran more because of his personal feelings about Land and Kennedy than because of any sympathy for Moran's views. On labor matters the lineup was more frequently Kennedy and the Admirals against the two pro-labor civilians.[18] Kennedy generally had three votes in his pocket,[19] but debates were always hot and Kennedy soon took to skipping meetings; more often than not, Admiral Land presided at them, with Kennedy casting his vote by phone.[20]

In practice, Admiral Wiley's suggested procedure became accepted to a great extent, due to circumstances and to the different interests of the commissioners. Each commissioner did devote greater time and thought than the others to certain problems. Wiley planned his training program; Moran considered the maritime labor situation; Woodward conducted hearings on rates and regulations; Land, with Navy associates, undertook long- and short-range planning of the merchant marine and its needs and did the actual planning of ships; Kennedy supervised the business and subsidy problems of the commission.

A number of Kennedy's former associates again came with him to his new job. The post of Executive Director was created for Sheehan;[21] Woodward came to regard him as an "organizational genius." [22] Ed Moore became a dollar-a-year man at the commission, receiving his regular pay from Kennedy.[23] Judge Burns became a special advisor for the commission. Kennedy was unable, however, to persuade the shipping interests to loan him the high-priced help that he thought he needed.[24]

The most pressing problem confronting the Maritime Commission was to comply with the law by doing away with the mail contracts, settling the shippers' claims for breach of contract, and reaching new subsidy agreements, all by July 1. Because of the delay in appointing the permanent commission, the new body had only three and a half months in which to do the job. Contracts between the government and 32 outfits had to be settled, and the shipping lines put in claims totaling $165,000,000.[25]

Kennedy, Moore, and Burns set up headquarters at Marwood and set to work hammering down the claims one by one. The claims were greatly inflated. Under the Merchant Marine Act, no claims were to be honored for expected profits under the old system—the new subsidies were to take their place, and the great bulk of the damages claimed were for anticipated profits. Kennedy further hammered down the claims by using two clubs. The contracts themselves were of debatable legality, as they had been given without the competitive bidding required by law. Despite many competent legal opinions that the contracts were binding on the government, there was still some question, and the commission used the doubt effectively in bargaining with shippers. The second and heavier club was Kennedy's refusal to grant the act's new subsidies to a company until after the company had settled its old claim. This tactic was especially effective with those smaller companies that lacked financial resources.[26] In at least one case, Kennedy refused to pay one cent of the company's claim, and his decision was acquiesced to by the company, eager to receive the new bounty. Kennedy worked long hours seven days a week, and by July 1 had succeeded in dispensing with all but a few of the more complex claims from the bigger outfits.[27]

The 23 claims, totaling over $73,000,000, that Kennedy disposed of were settled for $750,000, 1 percent of the demands, plus the new subsidy agreements. Krock, *Fortune*, and most other commentators, heralded Kennedy's accomplishment of disposing of "99%" of the claims without commenting on the monetary value of the new subsidies, which accounted for most of the claims, or on the fact that most of the claims were outrageously inflated and invalid to begin with. Krock gloated over how his friend had performed another "miracle," and others were equally impressed by the many millions Kennedy had saved the country.[28] The $750,000, of course, was accompanied by the infinitely more valuable new subsidies and did not tell the whole story any more than the claimed $73,000,000 had.

It would be doing Kennedy an injustice, however, to hold the overstatements of friends against him. He had accomplished the first purpose of the law in a very short time through hard work and hardheaded business techniques. In belittling Kennedy's accomplishment, a *New Republic* commentator wrote: "What it shows is that Mr.

Kennedy caught the small, weak companies by the heels, and stuffed them through his office wringer. It also shows, however, that the big strong companies either fought him to a standstill, or else obtained about what they wanted." [29] The short time allowed the commission to settle the contracts necessitated undoubtedly rough action. The contracts had to be settled before the vessel-construction program could begin, and the dispatch with which Kennedy accomplished this must be commended in view of the seriousness of the problem.[30] Roosevelt sent Kennedy a brief note on his work: "Congratulations. It was a grand job to get those contracts out of the way on time." [31]

Another immediate problem that had to be cleared up was disposal of the dilapidated United States-owned commercial fleet. Thirty-six lines consisting of 196 government-owned vessels had been out of use for many years, and the act required the Maritime Commission to dispose of the useless ships. Most of them were of scrap value only. A few of the ships were kept by the commission; many were sold for scrap; and 33 were sold for private use.[32] By November, 1937, the commission had completed its sales program.[33]

Another problem facing the commission in 1937 was keeping clear of partisanship or entanglement in foreign wars. Kennedy himself took steps to see that the Maritime Commission remained neutral and scrupulously clear of foreign hostilities. Roosevelt and Hull wanted to aid China in resisting the aggressions of fascist Japan, and were disposed to ignore the Neutrality Act in the Far Eastern crisis. War between Japan and China had not yet been officially declared, but major battles between their armies were taking place. United States-owned vessels leased by private operators were taking war goods to China, very likely in violation of the Neutrality Act. Kennedy believed that it was important to keep clear of the crisis. In September, 1937, he conferred with Roosevelt and Hull, and finally prevailed upon Roosevelt to prohibit the transportation of war goods to the Far East on government-owned ships.[34] By Roosevelt's announcement on September 14, 1937, privately owned vessels were permitted to continue carrying such items to the belligerents, but at their own risk.[35] Kennedy's dominating effect in the decision prompted columnists Drew Pearson and Robert S. Allen to write that Kennedy, rather than Hull, was the President's chief advisor on neutrality and the protection of merchant vessels in the Far East.[36]

ANOTHER BASIC PROBLEM FACING THE COMMISSION WAS TO RECTIFY the disruptive maritime labor situation. Under the statute, the commission's only power over labor matters was to set minimum standards of wages, hours, and working conditions for maritime labor. Secretary of Labor Frances Perkins was possessive about the powers of the Department of Labor and of the National Labor Relations Board, and wanted to keep the Maritime Commission out of labor problems as much as possible.[37] But if an adequate merchant marine were to be created, the situation with regard to labor had to be calmed first. Joe Kennedy wrote the President in June, 1937, that "something must be done [about the labor situation] or else the Government is wasting money building ships." [38]

Maritime labor had had a long and colorful history. After a vigorous youth, the International Seamen's Union fell apart in the 1920s, when the union movement hit its apex. It never quite got back on its feet. The union became sedentary; its leaders corrupt. In 1934 a Norwegian ex-Wobblie, Harry Lundeberg, pulled the West Coast seamen out of the I.S.U., and out of the conservative American Federation of Labor. Lundeberg's Sailor's Union of the Pacific became an independent union. Simultaneously, left-winger Harry Bridges pulled the West Coast longshoremen out of the American Federation of Labor. Bridges' longshoremen threw in with John L. Lewis's more radical CIO. On the East Coast, militant Joe Curran led a rank-and-file revolt against the I.S.U. in 1936. His new National Maritime Union quickly outstripped the unpopular I.S.U., left the A.F. of L., and affiliated with the CIO. The I.S.U. became almost impotent. The East Coast longshoremen failed to follow the lead of their West Coast brothers, stuck with the A.F. of L. and with their head Joe Ryan. Even *Fortune* magazine regarded Ryan as a reactionary;[39] East Coast seamen from the N.M.U. had worse names for him. Dozens of splinter unions sprouted up, and factions within unions developed. By the time Joe Kennedy came to the Maritime Commission in April, 1937, the maritime unions were engaged in the bitter factional struggles that attended the rebirth of the union movement. In no other industry was the friction so great, nor was any other industry so disrupted by union factionalism. Originally cooperative, Lundeberg and Bridges, on the West Coast, broke, and friction developed between their unions. On the East Coast, A.F. of L. longshoremen and CIO seamen were maiming and killing each other in bloody waterfront battles. East and West Coast longshoremen became uncooperative with each other, and as Lundeberg's S.U.P. became more conservative, relations between the S.U.P. and the N.M.U. became strained. Curran and Lundeberg began feuding. The East Coast longshoremen remained on good terms with the I.S.U., but the old seamen's union was powerless on the East Coast. The maritime union situation was chaotic. Vessels were disturbed by "quickie" strikes over union control, and men from unfriendly unions often refused to work together. Vessels loaded by A.F. of L. longshoremen on the East Coast might not be unloaded by the CIO longshoremen on the West Coast. N.M.U. seamen might refuse to man ships loaded by Ryan's A.F. of L. longshoremen. Port hostilities left seamen disgruntled, and ship-board discipline reached new lows. In 1937, "sit-down" and "quickie" strikes in the industry were twenty times as frequent as in 1936, with fortunes in time lost.[40] Labor often disregarded its contracts because of factional disputes. With this kind of labor situation, American vessels could not be counted on to keep their schedules; vessels were apt to be tied up by quickie strikes without notice. Perishable cargoes or cargoes needed immediately could not be entrusted to American holds. Efforts to get a portion of foreign commerce for American ships and to establish an adequate and responsible American merchant marine were almost doomed to failure. Before the United States could take a meaningful part in world shipping a more peaceful situation in maritime labor was necessary. "Pro-labor" people, especially CIO partisans, wanted to let the situation run its course and stabilize itself. Reactionaries, antilabor people, and shipowners looking out for themselves wanted stern antilabor measures taken to cripple the union development and restore the placidity (and economy) of the 1920s to the maritime labor situation. Kennedy was not pro-labor, nor is there any real evidence that he had an antilabor bias. But he was for a strong American merchant marine, and he was for it as soon as possible. The growing pains of organized labor were stalling the country's maritime development. The legislation had signified the urgency of the merchant marine situation, and Kennedy was impatient to get a worthy fleet on the waters. His interest in doing his job without delay automatically and necessarily put him in opposition to the "pro-labor" people.

From the start, CIO partisans were hostile to the admirals, Wiley and Land, and were wary of Kennedy, partly because of his reputation as a wealthy conservative and partly because he owned stock in Todd.[41] In his first speech as chairman of the Maritime Commission,

Kennedy said, "There can be no excuse for costly and bitter factionalism which is harmful to everyone in the long run. No business can survive a constant threat to its services from every sort of fanciful and irresponsible cause." [42] After the repressions of the 1920s, workingmen's loyalty to the CIO and the international solidarity of the union movement were neither fanciful nor irresponsible causes to thoroughgoing labor people of the 1930s. There was bound to be trouble between Kennedy and labor.

By the fall of 1937, Kennedy was ready to take steps to end quickie strikes. He conferred with Brian McMahon, an assistant attorney general (and later a distinguished liberal Senator from Connecticut), and after the meeting wrote the President:

> [McMahon] *personally would like very much to proceed against any one guilty of refusing to obey the lawful order of the Master on the theory that that is the only way to teach those fellows a lesson.*
>
> *I am firmly convinced that such action if promptly taken would go a long way toward clearing up insubordination and generally deplorable conditions in the American merchant marine. We must all realize that the safety of the traveling public is being seriously jeopardized by the fact that discipline on many ships is practically non-existent.*
>
> *It is indeed a serious problem and I should like to have your thoughts on it at your convenience.*[43]

The same day, September 8, 1937, Kennedy wrote James Roosevelt about the labor situation, with hopes that the son would use his influence with his father to get the President to favor a stern policy. "This thing is getting terribly serious," he wrote Jimmie. "If you think it worthwhile to give it a little pressure. . . . Really though, something should be done." [44]

Roosevelt's answer, if any, is unknown, but Kennedy had the opportunity to "do something" that he had been itching for just two days later, and he was not one to pass up an opportunity. The S.S. *Algic*, a government-owned vessel leased to a private line, was hit by a seamen's strike while in the harbor at Montevideo, Uruguay. Montevideo longshoremen were on strike, and the N.M.U. seamen refused to work with the scab longshoremen that were unloading the *Algic*. In justifying their refusal to work, one *Algic* seaman explained, "They were throwing around cargo like it was hash." Others later claimed that union longshoremen had threatened violence against the American seamen if they cooperated with the scabs.[45] But sympathy for the union longshoremen was almost definitely more central to the crew's refusal to work the ship.[46] At any rate, *Algic* captain Joseph Gainard was faced with a sit-down strike. The American consul in Montevideo warned the seamen to go back to work and threatened, "if the Captain wants I will have you all put in jail." Gainard was still unable to restore discipline, but contacted Kennedy before taking up the consul's offer.[47] The chairman did not appreciate this example of the international solidarity of labor. He wired Gainard:

> *Instruct crew to proceed with your lawful orders. If they still refuse, warn crew that all still refusing to perform duty will be placed in irons and prosecuted to full extent of law on return to United States. If they still refuse, place ringleaders in irons. If other crew members still refuse duty, have them removed from ship and replace them with Americans, if available, and if not, foreign seamen. In case you experience any difficulty, request assistance local authorities.[48]*

What happened next is unclear, but 14 crewmen returned in irons and were prosecuted. Although he privately conceded that the crew's arguments might hold some water,[49] Kennedy refused to stop proceedings. With frankness he told Curran and other union leaders that he simply had to have a conviction, as an example to the seamen that such actions would not be tolerated—"otherwise, the American Merchant Marine will fold up."[50] Even Roosevelt tried to moderate Kennedy's position, only to be told that if the President's compromise proposal were to be followed, "we'll land in the shit house."[51] According to Curran, Kennedy assured him that no man would ever spend a day in jail.[52]

The case was taken from the hands of a reputedly harsh judge and was heard in Baltimore by Judge W. Calvin Chestnut, who was regarded as lenient, and a "blue-ribbon" jury of 12 businessmen. In charging the jury, Chestnut said that if they failed to bring a verdict of guilty the jury might be responsible for the lives of passengers going to sea. Upon conviction, five men were fined $50.00; nine were sentenced to two months in jail, and were released on nominal bail pending appeal. In passing sentence, Judge Chestnut said that severity in the case was not called for, as "the conduct of these men was more serious in implication than anything else." Chestnut said that those seamen who defaulted on their fines would not be sent to jail.[53] It was a victory for Kennedy, and a victory for the American merchant marine, for it ensured an end to the threat of seamen's strikes after a vessel left its home port.

Kennedy's action was approved by the *New York Times* and by most middle-of-the-road and conservative papers.[54] The *Washington Post* applauded Kennedy's action, pointing out that the men had violated their contractual agreement by striking, no matter the cause.[55] *Marine Age*, the reactionary shipper's journal, was understandably elated by what they referred to as Kennedy's "walloping throw-back to Americanism." [56] They gleefully mused over the thought that "it wouldn't take many gentle hints like that to have the CIO taking the count." [57]

Union people and labor sympathizers saw Kennedy's action only as a blow to union power, and denounced it in uncompromising terms. The *New York Post* saw it as reflective of "clear anti-labor bias," and the *Philadelphia Record* agreed.[58] Pro-labor people criticized Kennedy for having acted before investigating the merits of the walkout. A CIO pamphlet charged that Kennedy's *Algic* actions were "part of a carefully planned attack on maritime labor." [59] Vito Marcantonio, later a far-left Congressman, said "there is no question that this frame-up is part of a deep-laid scheme with the purpose of harming the N.M.U. and laying the basis for the anti-union legislation of Joseph Kennedy and the shipowners." Minnesota Congressman John T. Bernard warned, "We must link up the *Algic* case with the danger of a fascist reaction." [60] The left-wing *Nation* saw Kennedy's *Algic* stand and the legislation that followed it as, "as neat an exhibition of pre-fascist union-smashing as it has been our lot to witness." [61] Curran was widely quoted as having said he was going to get Kennedy's scalp,[62] and dozens of wires from union locals were received at the White House demanding Kennedy's removal.[63]

President Roosevelt's reaction to the whole episode is reflected by a White House office memorandum found at Hyde Park: "This office has referred all correspondence on *Algic* case to the Maritime Commission." [64]

By the time of the *Algic* episode, Kennedy had formulated his ideas on ways to permanently stabilize maritime labor. The Commission's *Economic Survey of the American Merchant Marine*, released on November 10, 1937, called for legislation to require compulsory arbitration of maritime strikes, and for laws to establish United States government training facilities for merchant seamen, another idea of long standing. Senator Copeland and others quickly complied with the commission's request for bills.[65] Kennedy backed up the requests firmly in several appearances before Congressional hearings. The *Economic Survey* suggested that the arbitration board be patterned after the Railroad Labor Board; that it have power to arbitrate all maritime labor disputes; and that long waiting periods be required before strikes or lockouts would be allowed. This would go a long way toward ending the "quickies" that were plaguing the maritime industry. The training academy, it was hoped, would turn out more competent and better disciplined seamen.[66] In his committee appearances, Kennedy stressed the chaos in the maritime industry, the frequency of union irresponsibility and instances of rudeness to passengers, and the futility of pouring money down the drain until a more reliable labor supply was established.[67]

Again, support for Kennedy's position and for the commission's recommendations came from the *New York Times*, the *Washington Post*, and other moderate journals. The bulk of editorial opinion was certainly in support of the commission's recommendations. Always thrilled over labor rebukes and possibilities of labor setbacks, *Marine Age* was once more delighted.[68]

Union spokesmen opposed the training school, suspecting that it would only be used to train scabs. Ship-school grads had always been regarded, with some justice, as "company men," and the unions did not want any more of those around. Compulsory arbitration they saw as a threat to their economic power. They had fought hard for their power and did not want it restrained. They called the compulsory arbitration bill an effectual denial of the right to strike, and though the bill was not quite that, there was some justice in their claim. With its powers to delay strikes for great lengths of time, the proposed arbitration board was in a position to deny the unions the right to call strikes on short notice, and so could make it much more difficult for seamen to strike effectively. The seamen did not have enough confidence in the beneficence of the Maritime Commission to set favorable standards of hours, wages, and working conditions to sacrifice the power they had fought so hard to achieve. They saw a tie-in between the *Algic* affair and the proposed new legislation: they suspected that the *Algic* episode was only a grandstand play to discredit maritime labor so as to create an apparent need for the legislation. Kennedy was denounced as a reactionary, a labor-baiter, and a tool of the shipowners, and Curran told N.M.U. members that the proposed laws were introduced in efforts to "hog-tie us with slave legislation." [69]

Miss Perkins testified against both proposals. She feared that the training school would infuse new men into the field, already suffering from great unemployment. She believed that the compulsory arbitration bill would further complicate the situation. She pointed out that the Railroad Labor Act had been passed after the railroad unions were stable and well organized, and so could effectively bargain with the railroads. Railroad workers had wide areas of substantial agreement with management, and the roads had experienced, reasonable personnel departments that recognized the right of collective bargaining. In contrast, maritime workers had really only been organizing since 1934; the reasonable personnel departments and the fields of substantial agreement were lacking. The stage of crystallization that the railroad industry had reached had not yet been reached in the maritime industry, and to superimpose the railroad legislation on the maritime industry would hurt the union movement and might lead to an even more disruptive labor situation. The maritime industry was not yet ripe for such legislation.[70]

The *Economic Survey* recognized the force of labor's objections. It concluded that despite some valid objections, "the Commission feels that the present situation calls for immediate affirmative action." [71] Kennedy, in his appearances before the Congressional committees, refused even to acknowledge the validity of labor's objections to the proposed laws. The unions argued that the compulsory arbitration would crush their development; Kennedy argued that the act would foster union development by serving as an impetus to solid, responsible unionization.[72] He responded emotionally to Miss Perkins' arguments:

> It is said to be *"premature"* to put into operation machinery designed to prevent strikes and lockouts in an industry which in ten months of 1937 lost approximately one million man-days of work by strikes and lockouts. . . . I submit that if the maritime industry is not *"ripe"* for conciliation and mediation of its labor disputes then it is overripe for ruin.[73]

After the hearing Kennedy told reporters "I have nothing further to say to Miss Perkins. . . . Don't you think that everything that can be said to her has been said?" Miss Perkins later attended a formal dinner at the American Embassy in London when Kennedy was Ambassador,[74] but relations between the two after that day were naturally stiff.[75]

Roosevelt refused to be drawn into the dispute, and avoided questions on Kennedy's labor policies.[76] He threw his weight on neither side.

Ultimately, greatly watered-down versions of both bills became law. A board to mediate maritime disputes was created by Congress, but their arbitration was not made compulsory and the board bore little resemblance to the one proposed. It could give little offense to labor, and its effects on the situation could only have been salutary. A training school was created, but was permitted to enroll only men with some experience in the field. Frequently the academy was enrolled to only one-fifth of its capacity.

Kennedy remained fairly aloof from the great 1930s rivalry between the A.F. of L. and the CIO. One hostile commentator wrote in August, 1937, "So far Mr. Kennedy has uttered threats against each side with great impartiality." [77] Kennedy politely but firmly rebuffed the subtle request of A.F. of L. head William Green for the public favor of the Maritime Commission,[78] and on occasion Kennedy spoke favorably of CIO leaders Lewis, with whom he always remained on good terms,[79] and Philip Murray.[80] But Kennedy's relations with the militant CIO maritime and longshoremen's unions were unquestionably poor; the docile A.F. of L. chiefs were easier for him to handle. His relations with Ryan were good,[81] and he got along well with the independent Lundeberg.[82] But Kennedy's relations with Curran and Bridges, more thoroughgoing trade unionists, were always strained. Curran recalled years later that all his life Kennedy had been used to having his own way, to giving orders and having them obeyed. When confronted with opposition he reacted like a spoiled child. And he didn't like to get backtalk from rough-and-tumble seamen. Kennedy, Curran said, was ignorant of the ways of dealing with people in a give-and-take situation.[83]

Members of the N.M.U. and West Coast longshoremen denounced Kennedy with regularity as a tool of the shipowners. And Kennedy, years later, bragged about how he had thrown a punch at Harry Bridges,[84] and had tossed Curran bodily out of his office.[85] To Curran's great friend Miss Perkins, Kennedy referred to the N.M.U. leader as a "bum." [86]

Despite the hostility that he earned in large segments of the union movement, Kennedy cannot simply be written off as unsympathetic to the seamen. He did and said a number of things on behalf of the maritime workers (as opposed to the maritime unions) and he had a sincere interest in seeing that the seamen got a fair shake from the shipowners. Besides a simple desire to see justice done, he explained to Father Thorning that "Removal of grievances is the one sure road to elimination of Communistic influence on American ships." [87] The *Economic Survey* flatly stated that the owners were "in no small measure responsible for the present unfortunate situation." Wretched conditions, unpalatable food, and excessive hours were bound to be disastrous. For 11 years owners had denied the right to organize and refused to make collective agreements. The *Survey* observed that "The shipping industry is now paying for its shortsightedness in repressing labor for so many years." [88]

Kennedy personally subscribed to this interpretation of the maritime labor situation. He thought that the primitive living quarters he found on many ships were pathetic,[89] and he told the Senate Committees on Commerce and Labor that "we found conditions on most of these ships really very bad, and justification for complaints from all the seamen." [90] He attributed the lack of discipline, at least in part, to the "deplorable conditions which justified these men to come to the point where they wanted to get something done." [91] Kennedy acknowledged the need for shipowners to "take at least one foot out of the trough." [92] Concerning American shipyards—where the labor situation was entirely different from that on the high seas—Kennedy had praise for the laborers and scorn for the management.[93]

Kennedy not only spoke for better conditions in the merchant marine, but also took steps to bring them about. Under the commission's power to set labor standards, minimum pay standards were established equal to those set by union and management negotiators on the West Coast.[94] Though the commission's announcement called the standards fair and reasonable,[95] they also stressed that the standards were minimum and were to be regarded by shippers as such.[96] The commission added an innovation new to the maritime industry: vacation pay for continuous service. Hearings were held by the commission in all the major ports, and seamen's grievances were heard. After the New York hearing, Curran said, "This is the first time the seamen have ever had a chance to say what they really think at one of these things." [97] Each subsidized vessel was subsequently visited by a committee of three, to investigate shipboard working conditions, and recommendations for changes were made in most cases. Kennedy testified that the suggestions were followed.[98] Plans for new ships were submitted to union officials, to insure that quarters were satisfactory.[99] The commission's policy was apparently to make the greatest possible improvement in conditions, in the interest of fairness and in the belief that contentment on ship leads to better discipline and greater efficiency.[100]

Despite a Christian interest in the problems of the laborer, Kennedy never manifested any meaningful sympathy for the unions, their objectives, or even the concept of organizing for bargaining purposes. As far as he was concerned, a friendly government was going to see to it that the legitimate grievances of the seamen were rectified. And that was enough for him.

Unionists, a sympathetic *Fortune* piece asserted, had good reason to rely on the unions for fair treatment. Seamen's wages and conditions had improved, degenerated, and improved, directly in proportion to union membership.[101] The seamen could be more certain of conditions by relying on their unions than by relying on a paternalistic government agency. After enduring almost inhuman conditions throughout the twenties and early thirties, seamen were now getting some measure of control over their working conditions through their unions. They were understandably opposed to anything that stood in the way of the development of the power of their unions. Kennedy could not appreciate this position. It may be significant that his sharp criticisms of management's labor policies before committee hearings were brought out through questioning from the Congressmen, and were not volunteered by the speaker, as were his scathing comments on the seamen.

In his old age, the passion of the thirties cooled in Joe Curran, though not its dedication. In a 1962 interview, he observed that Kennedy's anti-union stands were not so much the result of anti-union bias as of simple ignorance.[102] Seeing the plight of the seamen on a study tour, or reading about it, could not substitute for experiencing years of subhuman conditions. Curran believed that had Kennedy lived the seamen's life he would have more fully appreciated the desire of the seamen for strong maritime unions. *Fortune* reported that Kennedy saw the maritime labor problem in terms of the personalities involved.[103] But where maritime labor was involved, Kennedy's personal approach was out of place. The men were intent on organizing to end the age-long poverty of their craft. Kennedy could never fully appreciate why.

Moreover, the nature of the situation automatically threw Kennedy into opposition with the militant trade unionists. In union-management difficulties, the companies were more amenable to commission pressures, and while the commission formally recognized the rights of collective bargaining, its impatience was generally directed at the unions.[104] It tended to use discipline and expedition as its frame of reference for achieving stability in maritime labor relations, placing substantially less emphasis on collective bargaining.[105]

Kennedy was impressed with the urgency of getting an adequate merchant marine on the waters; genuine trade unionists were impressed with the urgency of solidifying union power with the shipowners. Kennedy and his policies stood in the way of the development of that power.

Kennedy's actions and proposals certainly were not conducive to the development of strong maritime unions. He was pro-merchant marine, and that in large part dictated his stand on labor problems. Where the interests of labor and the interests of the developing merchant marine conflicted, Kennedy's loyalty clearly lay with the latter. As a rich conservative, perhaps his value judgment in favor of the industry was a natural one. But he had been called in to develop the industry, not the unions, and kept his eye on that goal.

In 1937 and 1938, when Kennedy was head of the Maritime Commission, war clouds were rising over Europe and Asia. For strategic reasons, it was vital for the United States to stabilize its merchant marine and its maritime labor source. Kennedy's choice of emphasis must be viewed in that light.

THE MOST COMPLEX PROBLEM FACING THE MARITIME COMMISSION was planning and developing an American merchant fleet. In 1937 the American fleet numbered 3,475 vessels, over a tenth of all the vessels in the world, and nearly a fifth of the world tonnage. But that figure is deceiving. Almost all of these were coastal carriers, tugs, dredges, trawlers, oil tankers, other industry-protected ships or inland vessels on the Great Lakes and the rivers. Only 420 vessels were engaged in competition for foreign trade. With these ships, the United States ranked fourth in gross tonnage, behind Great Britain, Japan, and Germany. It ranked fifth in number of ships that could make 12 knots or better, behind Britain, Germany, Japan, and France.

More important, almost the entire American fleet was out-of-date. The life of a ship was figured at 20 years, and in 1937, 85 percent of the American fleet was over 17 years old. Of ships less than ten years old, the United States had less in tonnage than eight nations, including Italy, Norway, and Holland. As *Fortune* asserted in 1937, the United States merchant marine, "stripped of deceptive figures, turns out to be mostly a war-built fleet that is already senile and will be technically dead in four years." [106] The ships serviced 58 different routes, few of which could be termed essential to American commerce or defense.[107]

In Kennedy's first speech as head of the Maritime Commission in May, 1937, he told his listeners of America's traditional weaknesses in shipping and expressed his reasonable conclusion that

For us an adequate merchant marine has to be a new merchant marine. The question comes—what are we going to do about it? The answer is BUILD SHIPS!—the best and most modern ships—and build them RIGHT AWAY. . . . We are going to lay the keels for new fast ships. And we are going to do it NOW.

He reminded his listeners that if private enterprise did not do the job the government would. "The failure of private enterprise this time may bring about a different method of achieving this goal. If the government has to pull the whole load again, the people may want to own the tow as well as the tug." [108]

In the summer of 1937, Kennedy envisioned a first-rate foreign fleet for the American merchant marine, ultimately consisting of 300 to 350 vessels, serving perhaps a dozen vital routes.[109] His immediate goal was 95 ships, and he told a Congressional committee that he had tentative plans for 28. He contemplated a construction program over a long period. At the time, August, 1937, he did not ask for Congressional appropriations for the fleet—indeed, he asked that Congress strike out a $10,000,000 appropriation for the commission's construction program, until after a major and thoroughgoing study of the problem was made.[110]

By the fall, Kennedy had learned some of the difficulties he would encounter, and was less optimistic and enthusiastic. On September 12, he announced his personal conclusion that under the terms of the act it seemed impossible to accomplish its objectives. He indicated that construction of the 28 ships of which he had spoken might not be undertaken. The industry simply was unattractive to private capital, and Kennedy said the government did not intend to operate a fleet or to build one for others to operate. He was also critical of the shipowners, who had given him less than adequate cooperation in his efforts to develop the fleet.[111]

In November, the commission completed its overall study, the *Economic Survey of the American Merchant Marine,* and the document reiterated Kennedy's previous expression. "The conclusion seems to be inescapable that we may expect at this time no appreciable amount of new money for the subsidized lines from outside sources," the *Economic Survey* asserted.[112] When Kennedy left the Maritime Commission, contracts had been given for only one vessel,[113] and then only because Admiral Land threatened to resign unless some positive steps toward development of the fleet were taken.[114]

Kennedy's first speech at the Maritime Commission set forth a sound evaluation and a vigorous program, but Kennedy was unwilling to follow the program he had laid down. The terms of the act had specifically authorized the commission to build and/or operate vessels if private enterprise was unwilling.[115] Defense considerations made it imperative that the commission do just that. Kennedy was reluctant. He occasionally threatened the shipping interests with government ownership or operations,[116] for which the *Journal of Commerce* severely criticized him,[117] but his heart was not in his threats. He was sincerely opposed to government building or operations. He told a House committee in June, 1937,

> *We do not intend to have any government operations whatsoever. . . . As I understand this law Congress does not want to start an experiment in government ownership of shipping. Frankly, I cannot see any particular sense to government ownership. If that kind of system were intended to be developed I would not be serving you in my present position. Therefore I am trying to get a program started now that will encourage private capital to come in within the next five or twenty months. . . . I am definitely opposed to government operations.*[118]

Kennedy reiterated this position on many occasions. He did not think government operation was feasible; competent executives to run a government shipping line could not be procured on government salaries.[119] He also opposed the combination of government construction or ownership and private operation, for reasons that he never quite made clear.

Later in his term, Kennedy became very doubtful that there was any alternative to active government participation in the industry. He told a Congressional committee in January, 1938,

> Much as I oppose government ownership, nevertheless, as a practical matter to me it is inevitable, because of the impossible situation we have today. . . .
>
> I have spent hours on this thing, trying to see something out of it. And to me, there is no alternative. I see little chance of getting much new private capital into this business; I do not see what it has to offer.
>
> Therefore, I feel we are faced with government ownership within a reasonably short time. Once we begin this, I think we should go ahead with the domestic services.[120]

Yet Kennedy himself still was not for government operations. Though his conclusions left little hope for private enterprise in the field, he called for amendment of the act in the hope that private operators might be able to make a go of the business. In supporting his position, he told Congressmen:

> I think private operators might very well feel, if they were closed out today without getting what they think is a reasonable chance for a solution to their troubles, that you had done private industry a great injustice, in spite of the past record. For that reason, I say I have come to advocate giving them that chance.[121]

He proposed a number of amendments to the act, amendments that he hoped would make an entirely private fleet possible. He suggested that required down payments on ships be reduced from 25 percent of domestic cost to 25 percent of foreign cost; that construction be permitted in foreign yards where the foreign cost was less than half of domestic cost; that the salary maximum be raised or abolished; that the period for recapture of excess profits be extended from five to ten years; and that some insurance be given operators that the government would not abandon them at a later date.[122]

Kennedy stressed that even with these changes, the commission might not be able to solve the problem. "The Commission is merely indicating alterations which, in its opinion, would make the aims of the act more likely of attainment. Only experimentation can demonstrate whether or not revised legislation will enable us to achieve the objectives which the Congress had in mind." [123] He was for permitting this experimentation, though even he conceded that it would more than likely prove fruitless. He was holding out for complete private ownership and operation, when that seemed completely out of the question. "The Commission is determined to give private initiative every opportunity to succeed. . . . This is a trial and error proposition." [124] In peaceful times his approach would have been the proper one for a free enterprise society. In the winter of 1937–1938, however, times were not peaceful; major wars were threatening in both Europe and Asia. The United States did not have time for the kind of experimentation that Kennedy advocated—the kind of experimentation that even he conceded was doomed to almost certain failure. The United States needed the merchant fleet and it could not wait to give private enterprise more time to build. Only where labor was concerned did Kennedy seem to fully appreciate the urgency of the situation.

Kennedy left the Maritime Commission in the winter of 1938, and Admiral Land succeeded to the chairmanship. He immediately undertook the vigorous construction program he had been planning, building ships for government account. In his study of *The United States Maritime Commission, 1936–1940*, scholar Daniel Marx wrote "This program came just in the nick of time to provide us with a sound basis for our great wartime ship construction undertaking. It might easily have been delayed too long, as it nearly was, by any further insistence upon giving private enterprise more time to find new capital." [125]

Kennedy was called in to organize the Maritime Commission and by the end of 1937 his job was complete. Despite his lack of vision in the shipbuilding sphere, his contributions at the Maritime Commission were nonetheless significant. His ability for promotion and organization was of considerable value in breathing new life into the government's shipping agencies. The commission's predecessor, the Shipping Bureau of the Department of Commerce, had not had a private audit since 1928. Kennedy put the new Maritime Commission on a thorough businesslike basis. Admiral Land came to regard him as "an outstanding administrator, executive, and financier." [126] *The Economic Survey of the American Merchant Marine,* prepared under Kennedy's direction, provided a good basis for the commission's policy decisions for several years.[127] The *New York Times* wrote that the report was "one of the finest reports of its kind ever submitted," [128] and columnist Hugh Johnson called it a "landmark." [129]

Kennedy stayed less than a year at the Maritime Commission, but long enough to end the old subsidies, institute the new ones, direct a thorough and praiseworthy study of the merchant marine, and establish better labor conditions. He also staffed and organized a large bureaucracy. It was once more time for Joe Kennedy to move on. "This is the toughest job I ever handled in my life, without any reservations whatever," he said while at the Maritime Commission.[130] He had a still tougher job on the horizon.

A NEW DEALER
GOES TO ENGLAND

SOMETIME IN 1935, THE NEW DEAL TURNED LEFT. BASICALLY CON-
servative men like Moley and Rexford G. Tugwell were replaced in
Roosevelt's innermost circle by left-wingers of the Corcoran-Cohen
stripe. A number of factors helped to push Roosevelt farther left: the
left-wingers pulled him and the right-wingers pushed him; the temper
of Congress and of the nation was to the left; Roosevelt feared that
Huey Long was stealing too much of his thunder and too many of his
votes. Moley and others of Roosevelt's conservative advisors became
disillusioned and fell out of the picture. Kennedy, to a great extent,
also became disillusioned and privately spoke of big areas of difference
but publicly he stuck with the Administration. In 1937 he would still
describe himself as enthusiastic for the New Deal.

The tax bill of 1935 was the stroke that finally ended Roosevelt's
honeymoon with business, and it was only on tax policy that Joe
Kennedy ever publicly went to bat against the New Deal. The
Administration's fiscal policies worried him. In 1937 a serious recession
set in, which probably resulted from two related factors: (1) the
Administration balanced its budget by cutting back expenditures and
increasing taxes; (2) the increased taxes prevented industry from
making sufficient expenditures to compensate for the government's
cutback. Kennedy apparently supported Roosevelt's attempt to balance the budget,[1] but he opposed the tax policy that prevented
industry from taking up where the government left off. He probably
drew the sound conclusion that the Administration's tax policy was in
large part responsible for the recession;[2] he clearly understood the
dynamics of the national economy much better than Roosevelt
did—not a very difficult accomplishment.

Kennedy not surprisingly directed his criticism at the tax policy, and
not at the balancing of the budget. Morgenthau thought it characteristic of him to oppose any tax distasteful to business.[3] Specifically,
Kennedy's objections were directed to the capital gains tax and the
undistributed corporate income tax. Roosevelt remained dedicated to
both.

110

The now familiar capital gains tax made its first appearance long before the New Deal. By the capital gains tax profits made from the sale of investments were made taxable, though at a lower rate than income from wages. By 1937 Kennedy was calling for real modification of the capital gains tax, opposing the taxing of such income, at least at the rates used.[4] He pointed out that the tax tended to aggravate shifts in the market. It gave investors a good reason for holding on to securities—by holding on they could postpone payment of the tax. So in periods of rising stock market prices, investors would be even less apt to sell than otherwise. This would cause reduced supply of stock on the markets and therefore further increase prices and aggravate inflation. Repeal of the tax would remove the deterrent to sale of securities, and so would accelerate money; that is, it would increase the ability of investors to shift their holdings around, and so would make money for investing more readily available. These were arguments that made considerable economic sense, and still have some appeal. Kennedy should have stopped there. But he advanced other arguments that make little sense today and probably made little sense in 1937. Kennedy argued that the tax created a handicap to American investors that foreign investors did not have. The act did make it more profitable for foreigners to trade on Wall Street than Americans, but so what? Foreigners also had (and have) an advantage with the rest of the American tax scheme—any United States tax "penalizes" Americans vis-à-vis foreigners. We alone, of all nations, had such a tax, he added. But must Americans pattern their tax policies after those of other nations? He also argued that the government, as a matter of policy, should allow a man to enjoy the increment in his investments while he lived, and take its share from his heirs. The trouble with this argument is that it would be very simple for the man of capital to permanently avoid the full force of the inheritance tax, either by spending the bulk of the profits during his lifetime, or by funneling off the money into trust funds before death—as Kennedy himself did, and began doing in the 1920s. Few big investors would have ended up contributing much from their profits. To the laborer, the question seems to be, why should the fruits of a man's investments enjoy more favorable tax treatment than the fruits of his labor?

The inclusion of these somewhat specious arguments is interesting, because they would not have been advanced by a man of common sense who was also free from a theoretical or philosophical bias. To a very great extent, Kennedy of 1934–1938 was such a man—one of the few apolitical policy advisors in the Roosevelt camp. Only his arguments on the capital gains tax revealed anything other than the objectivity of the impersonal expert.[5] Kennedy remained dedicated to the idea of leaving profits from investments tax free, for either philosophical or personal reasons.

Kennedy's arguments on the undistributed corporation income tax were more satisfactory—and ultimately the tax was repealed. This was a tax on those corporate profits that were not distributed to stockholders in the form of dividends. Its proponents argued that the big corporations controlled too much of the national economy and that corporate policies of plowing profits back into the business were making the situation worse. The policy of plowing back profits also resulted in smaller dividends and, since dividends were taxed as income, the policy led to less government revenue from income taxes. Because the capital gains tax has always been smaller than the income tax, rich corporate investors have always found it advantageous to take their share of corporate profits in the form of capital gains rather than as dividends. In many cases, corporations were plowing back profits in a conscious attempt to help stockholders defeat the income tax. And in some situations, a mogul like Henry Ford of the 1920s would plow back profits into the business in an attempt to get smaller, dividend-hungry investors to sell out to himself. The tax was designed to remedy these evils. It discouraged corporations from expanding out of profits and encouraged them to distribute the profits to stockholders. It made it relatively more expedient for corporations to finance expansion out of new securities issues. The tax had, however, serious drawbacks which Kennedy outlined in his public statements. Most potent of these arguments was that the tax made it harder for the small corporation to expand, and so become a big company. Accordingly, it tended to stabilize the status quo between big and small competitors. The tax also discouraged corporations from building up a financial reserve to tide them over in unprofitable times. Corporations without such reserves would be in serious straits in case of another depression, and young corporations would be unlikely to have the needed reserves. In such cases, the tax would contribute to bringing about undesirable bankruptcies.[6]

Kennedy urged these arguments on countless occasions, both public and private. Even in his pro-Roosevelt campaign literature of 1936 he conceded that the undistributed corporate income tax was "premised upon a fallacious economic principle."[7] Such campaign-time concessions made him seem more objective about the man he was endorsing, and they set the stage for his post-election campaign against the tax. Kennedy testified before the Congressional committees and used his persuasions privately with influential Congressmen as part of an active lobby against the tax.[8] Kennedy convinced Pat Harrison, the Chairman of the Senate Finance Committee and a key man, that repeal of the tax was imperative.[9] He took the lead in organizing a series of conferences between Congressional leaders and administrative advisors on the tax burdens of corporations.[10] He argued with Roosevelt that taxes revised downward might produce more, rather than less, revenue[11] by encouraging investors to sell their holdings and by stimulating the economy in general. He must have made the point that lower taxes, especially a lower rate on undistributed profits, would leave more money available for investment, and so would stimulate recovery.

Ultimately, Congress repealed the unincorporated business tax, but maintained the capital gains tax. Had Kennedy's suggestions been followed and both taxes been repealed or substantially modified, most of the very rich would have been excused from any significant tax obligation. Corporate profits would have been poured into expansion and the rich would have taken out their share of the profits in capital gains, rather than dividends. That way they would have evaded ever paying taxes on their profits from investments—which is the only type of income that most of the very rich ever receive—so that they would never have contributed very much to the national treasury. The less rich—the salaried and working class—would have ended up paying the share of the rich. Abolition of both taxes might have helped to conquer the 1937 recession, but there were other alternatives, such as more federal spending, that would have proven equally effective.

Tax policy was the only matter on which Kennedy publicly differed with the Administration. Otherwise, he gave the New Deal considerable backing, and even supported Roosevelt's "Court-Packing" plan, the President's unsuccessful attempt to overcome an unsympathetic Supreme Court by increasing the size of the Supreme Court panel with addition of enough of his own appointees to outweigh the conservative incumbent justices. Many of Roosevelt's more finicky advisors were disturbed over use of such means to achieve the President's ends, but Kennedy attempted to round up support for the plan.[12]

At times, Kennedy even echoed the words of the anti-business New

Dealers. When Roosevelt, in the 1936 campaign, flailed economic royalists, Joe Kennedy began taking potshots at "ungrateful," "silk-hatted," "stuffed shirts." Like Roosevelt, Kennedy received much less cooperation from business in his SEC and Maritime Commission work than he had expected. When Roosevelt asserted that "most business-men can't see farther than the next dividend," Joe Kennedy could add that businessmen were "a bunch of S.O.B.'s." [13] Even when Corcoran and Company set out in late 1937 on a conscious campaign to deflate businessmen and blame them for the recession, Kennedy did not waver. Assistant Attorney General (and later Supreme Court Justice) Robert Jackson delivered a Cork-authored tirade against monopolies and monopolists that was followed by two blistering Ickes attacks on big capital. Senator Alben Barkley joined in. Business became seriously disturbed about the clear slant of these influential Roosevelt insiders. Kennedy's reaction to it all was to tell business in the person of 1,500 people at a New York Economic Club dinner to "stop bellyaching." [14] And business, in the person of the *Wall Street Journal*, took it. Their editorial the following day said " 'bellyaching' strikes us as a coarse expression when anyone tries to apply it to us . . . (but) there may be something in what he says about expending less energy in vocalizing our ventral distresses and more in exercising them away." [15] Some of Kennedy's close conservative friends, though, to whom he had spoken freely in private in critical fashion of many New Deal developments, were taken aback by the speech. Kennedy's intimate, the influential and fiercely independent columnist Frank Kent, was sharply critical of the speech, and questioned Kennedy's sincerity in his column.[16] Perhaps Kennedy had delivered the speech to curry favor with the President, whom, at that very moment, he was pressuring for still-higher honors. Kent, who was aware of an impending vacancy at the American embassy in London, and of Kennedy's great interest in the post, privately wrote Baruch "Joe wins the 1937 China Egg diamond belt prize with this one." [17]

ROBERT BINGHAM, UNITED STATES AMBASSADOR TO ENGLAND, suffered rapidly declining health through 1937, and finally returned home in the fall with his mortal illness. He did not resign, but he was hospitalized, and a successor would have to be chosen. Ambassador to the Court of St. James's was the job for Joe Kennedy. The post was the United States' most significant ambassadorial assignment from a political standpoint, and the growing possibility of war in Europe created increased popular interest and heightened importance in the post. Moreover, it was the most socially prestigious position in American government. The old American aristocracy, with its Anglophilic leanings—the aristocrats that had rejected Kennedy at Harvard —regarded the post as the nation's highest social office; its occupant was automatically placed at the very top of the nation's social ladder. And so, being appointed Ambassador to England would mean social preferment for the Kennedys and their offspring, and an opportunity to "show" the Brahmins that he could "get there" without their support. He would be their social superior. Already the lion-tamer of Wall Street, the East Boston Irishman would become the social superior of Boston's snobbiest!

Joe Kennedy wanted the post very much—to some of his friends it seemed the culmination of his ambitions[18]—and he set out to get it. He made his desires known emphatically to the President,[19] and by the summer of 1937 he was lobbying fiercely for the appointment through every available avenue. James Roosevelt spoke to the President on his behalf.[20] No doubt directly, and through Krock, he had Farley remind the President of the Party's and the President's debt to the wealthy contributor.[21] "Everybody seems to be for me but the White House," he plaintively moaned to a Virginia Senator.[22] Kent wrote Baruch, "Poor old felt-minded Joe. What a sucker he is going to look if he does not get this appointment!" [23]

It was, of course, impossible for the President to send an Irish Catholic to the Court of St. James's. But as James Roosevelt put it, "all you had to do was say something was impossible for Joe to want it." [24] Or want it all the more.

The job of Ambassador to England has always been an expensive one for the Ambassador, who is called upon to spend small fortunes for official entertainment out of his own pocket. Kennedy certainly could afford the job. He had claim to it because of past services to the President, the Party, and the Administration. He had a good reputation as a public servant. Reportedly, some New Deal insiders, jealous of Kennedy's popularity and influence, joined to sponsor him for Ambassador, to get him away from the political scene and limelight at home.[25] The argument was no doubt advanced that Kennedy was getting the Administration in hot water with labor, and that "deporting" him to England was politically expedient.[26]

Other factors, at least as important, affected Roosevelt's decision. He was suspicious of England and the English, and believed that the Irish Kennedy would not be taken in by them.[27] And the novelty of doing the impossible, of sending an Irish Catholic to the Court of St. James's, was as appealing to Roosevelt as it was to Kennedy. The President knew that with his charm and informality, Kennedy would set a healthy contrast to the striped-pants set.[28] The President decided on Kennedy and gave him his commitment. Then he began to waver. Krock reports:

> *One night I was dining alone with Kennedy at Marwood when the President's eldest son, and in that period his father's secretary, appeared. The pair retired to another room for a half hour or so, after which James Roosevelt departed and Kennedy returned to the table. It was a time when the liberals, having heard a report that the President intended to appoint Kennedy to London, were putting heavy pressure on Roosevelt. And Kennedy's report to me of his conversation with James Roosevelt implied that the President was yielding somewhat to the pressure. Kennedy was angry. "You know what Jimmy proposed? That instead of going to London, I become Secretary of Commerce! Well, I'm not going to. FDR promised me London, and I told Jimmy to tell his father that's the job, and the only one, I'll accept."* [29]

Kennedy held firm, the President with him. Roosevelt, who equaled any Boston politician in his capacity for two-facedness, made his explanations to Kennedy's detractors. Witness this remarkable conversation with Morgenthau recorded in Morgenthau's diaries:

> *The President then got started on Joe Kennedy. He said from three independent sources he had gotten the story that Floyd Odlum [a utilities representative] had offered Kennedy one million dollars to represent the utilities in Washington and that Kennedy had even gone so far as to arrange to split this million with certain parties; that he faced Kennedy with this story and that he absolutely denied it.*[30] *The President then made a startling remark that he considered Kennedy a very dangerous man and that he was going to send him to England as Ambassador with the distinct understanding that the appointment was only for six months and that furthermore by giving him this appointment any obligation that he had to Kennedy was paid for.*
> *I said, "Well, Mr. President, England is a most important post*

*and there have been so many people over there talking against
the New Deal. Don't you think you are taking considerable risks
by sending Kennedy who has talked so freely and so critically
against your administration?" The President said, "I have made
arrangements to have Joe Kennedy watched hourly and the first
time he opens his mouth and criticizes me, I will fire him." He
said two or three times, "Kennedy is too dangerous to have
around here.*[31]

Given such a start, the prospects for Kennedy's tenure as Ambassador
being successful could not have been particularly bright.

Krock broke the story of Kennedy's appointment in the *New York
Times*, to the displeasure of the President,[32] who complained that
Krock had not had the courtesy to wait until Bingham was in the grave
before announcing his successor.[33] Robert L. Norton, another of
Kennedy's journalist friends, reported in the *Boston Post* that Kennedy
was offered his choice of Secretary of Commerce or Ambassador to
England, and chose the latter largely for sentimental reasons, and for
the distinction of being the first Irish-American to represent the
United States in England.[34]

Bingham was elated with the choice of his successor,[35] and
Kennedy's appointment was well received by editorial writers. Even
the left-wing *Nation* greeted it with good-humored tolerance.[36] Editor
and diplomat Josephus Daniels wrote the President congratulating him
on the selection of Kennedy.[37] Journalists speculated on his succession
to still higher office, such as Secretary of the Treasury[38] or even the
Presidency itself.[39] In Kennedy's hometown he became the hero of the
Irish community, replacing his own boyhood idol, Mayor Pat Collins,
who had served as counselor of a legation in Britain. "Mr. Irish-American," Al Smith, publicly expressed his pleasure at Kennedy's good
fortune.[40] All the Boston newspapers featured big spreads on his
appointment, including colorful biographical sketches of interest to all
future biographers. The *Boston Post* and Hearst's *Boston American* ran
series on his career. One *Post* article, enclosed in a prominent black
border, gave a fanciful genealogy of the Kennedy clan, headlined

KENNEDY FAMILY HAS ROYAL
BLOOD ANTEDATING THE KING'S [41]

When the appointment was formally announced, Kennedy wrote
the President simply "Rose and I are deeply grateful." [42] Mrs.
Kennedy expressed her appreciation more fully:

My dear Mr. President:
I do want to thank you for the wonderful appointment you have
given to Joe. The children and I feel deeply honored, delighted
and thrilled, and we want you to know that we do appreciate the
fact that you have made possible this great rejoicing.[43]

The President responded to Rose:
To send his nomination to the Senate gave me a feeling of real
pleasure and I am glad that you both have the same feeling
about it.[44]

Joe Kennedy's appointment became known on December 9, 1937, and it was almost three months before he left for England. In the interim he had briefings at the State Department and began having discussions with Sir Ronald Lindsay, British Ambassador in Washington, over British film legislation of vital concern to American movie interests.[45]

Kennedy also worked steadily at his Maritime Commission duties right up until departure. Indeed, Father Thorning, who visited Kennedy in London in August, 1938, noted that his study was crowded with books on shipping, and that Kennedy was still devoting attention to America's maritime problems.[46]

Kennedy's successor as head of the Maritime Commission was Admiral Land. Labor opposition to Land developed before his appointment,[47] and Roosevelt gave serious consideration to appointing Lowell Mellett, a thoroughgoing New Dealer, as Kennedy's successor.[48] Kennedy pushed the Admiral across for the chairmanship.[49] Bitterly disappointed at the selection, Harold Ickes listed Kennedy in his diary as a bad influence on the President. "It was Kennedy," Ickes wrote, "who dissuaded the President from appointing Lowell Mellett as Kennedy's successor on the Maritime Commission. Kennedy was afraid that Mellett would settle the labor difficulty which he had not been able to settle, and so he persuaded the President to appoint a stooge of his own." [50] Land's primary interest was in building a fleet, and he proved to have been a sound choice when the war made heavy demands on American shipping.[51]

Kennedy sailed for England on the U.S.S. *Manhattan*, staffed by N.M.U. members, on February 23, 1938. The N.M.U. announced that it would make every effort, by good example, to change Kennedy's low opinion of American seamen during the voyage.[52] Some crew members were less than happy about serving "the enemy." A crew spokesman was quoted as having said, "Our members will give Mr. Kennedy every courtesy no matter what they think of his attempts to wreck their union." [53] Perhaps Kennedy won some of them over during the trip. He visited the crew's quarters and agreed with them that their living conditions were inadequate for human beings.[54]

AN IMMEDIATE
SUCCESS

JOSEPH KENNEDY ARRIVED IN ENGLAND ON MARCH 1, 1938, A
dark and cold day. The steady drizzle set the mood of the hour. The
small cutter that awaited him in Plymouth Harbour was buffeted by
waves higher than usual, raised up by the brisk wind.[1] The European
situation was equally dark. With Hitler menacing European peace,
England was threatened with imminent war. As he set foot on land,
Kennedy showed a nervousness[2] that was foreign to him. Kennedy had
left much of his family behind—they, together with Mr. and Mrs.
Eddie Moore, would join him shortly. He was accompanied, though,
by a young man named Harold Hinton, a journalist.

Kennedy arrived at his official residence at 4 Grosvenor Gardens,
London, and by the light of the warm fireplace the situation looked
somewhat brighter. After all, England had solid leadership and sane
direction. Cooperation among Western leaders could avert war
through negotiations with the dictatorships.

Many distinguished Americans had served as Ambassadors to the
Court of St. James's: three Adamses—John, John Quincy, and Charles
Francis—John Jay, Martin Van Buren, James Monroe, George Ban-
croft, even Benjamin Franklin. But on that first night in London,
perhaps Kennedy thought most about one of the lesser known men.

The previous life of Walter Hines Page had been but a preparation
for Page's five years as Ambassador in London. He went there in 1913
with the greatest admiration for the British, their culture, and their
political institutions; Western civilization, he believed, was based on
the Anglo-Saxon heritage. Virtually from the start of the great war,
Page saw the conflict as an unjustified assault by barbarians against
democratic ideals, civilization, and the true path of human progress.
He had no sympathy with his President's efforts to maintain neutrality,
and lost confidence in him. He sided again and again with the British
where American interests were involved, and his known sympathies
for Britain made him an ineffective spokesman for American interests.
President Woodrow Wilson lost confidence in him.

120

Page opposed all peace efforts, and was disappointed when the *Lusitania* incident failed to bring America into the war.

When America did enter the war, Wilson's war message took the same ground that Page had advocated all along. His position had been vindicated. He went to his embassy work with a new vigor and worked himself to death. He died in 1918, comforted in his knowledge that his wish to help England win the war had been fulfilled.[3]

While the war spirit was great and internationalism had its brief day, in the minds of men, Page was elevated to the highest level of visionary statesmanship. Johns Hopkins named its school of diplomacy the Walter Hines Page School of International Relations.

But when disillusionment with the war, its peace, and the part of the United States in both set in, Americans began to take another look at Walter Hines Page and his legend. Men in search of an explanation as to why America had entered the war found it in Anglophile Page. He was the guilty party, along with J. P. Morgan and a few others. He had been duped by the British propaganda; had been taken up by London society and had fallen for their story hook, line, and sinker.[4] Men reasoned that but for Page, the United States might never have entered the war. "A Walter Hines Page" came to mean an ambassador who represented the country to which he had been sent.

In March, 1938, Joseph Kennedy was facing much the same situation Page had faced 25 years before. But his background had been very different, and his reactions would be very different.

THE FIRST WEEK WAS ONE OF GETTING SETTLED, AND BECOMING familiar with the lay of the land, the employees, the buildings, the city and the powerful leaders. Kennedy viewed his new accommodations with a mixture of amusement and chagrin. He wrote James Roosevelt to tell the President that "I have a beautiful blue silk room and all I need to make it perfect is a Mother Hubbard dress and a wreath to make me Queen of the May. If a fairy didn't design this room, I never saw one in my life." He noted touches of mock austerity, as a portrait of one-time Ambassador Joseph Hodges Choate, in a red gown—". . . every time I look at him, I think I can hear him say, 'Call me a cab.' "[5] In general, Kennedy was displeased with the building and its layout.[6]

Even for an Ambassador, establishing residence in a new country is complicated by bureaucratic red tape. Mrs. Kennedy wished to bring in a French poodle and an Airedale,[7] and the Ambassador expected the usual six-month period of quarantine to be waived in view of his position.[8] The civil servants in charge, though, took the stuffy position that "the quarantine is to prevent the introduction of rabies into England and that consequently the rank of the dog's owner has nothing whatsoever to do with it. If the King himself brought in a dog it would have to spend six months in quarantine." [9]

Kennedy quickly felt put upon by the fact that every American citizen who came to England thought it his right to call and have a word with the Ambassador.[10]

In general, though, Kennedy's first week on the job was a good week, and he quickly felt at home. In no time, the English cuss word "bloody" crept into his vocabulary[11] to join his wide range of colorful American expletives. Five days after he arrived in England he took a few hours off for a round of golf and shot a hole in one, his first and a good omen.[12] Kennedy was quoted as having said, "I am much happier being the father of nine children and making a hole in one than I would be as the father of one child making a hole in nine." [13] The British press took an immediate liking to him, and the comment was widely reported. Kennedy wrote Landis, "I couldn't have done anything better to make a hit in England if I had had 25 years to discover the best answer." [14]

Three days later Kennedy created headline news again when he presented his credentials to the King wearing long trousers, instead of the more formal knee breeches.[15] Randolph Churchill reported in the *Evening Standard* that Kennedy and the less important waiters were the only civilians at the presentation in trousers.[16] Kennedy later described the ceremony as "short but a happy one that lingered long in my memory." [17]

Joe Kennedy was clearly out of the diplomatic mold. E. Wilder Spaulding writes,

> *The Londoners must have had reservations when he arrived. For he was not only the first Irish-Catholic to defile the London Embassy but he was rambunctious and ill-tempered, worse than careless with his language, vulgar in the eyes of the nicer people, anything but bashful, and filthy with American dollars. He chewed gum. He put his feet on his desk and he called the Queen "a cute trick." [18]*

He was, as Foreign Secretary Lord Halifax toasted him, "so representative of modern America," [19] and to many stuffy Britons what Halifax might have regarded as representative modern American traits were highly offensive. They noted disapprovingly, for example, the way that Kennedy rushed to be the first to dance with the Queen at a ball, preempting the position of the Dean of the Diplomatic Corps.[20] The attitude of Montagu Norman was typical of many traditionalists; according to Norman's biographer, the President of the Bank of England "disliked Kennedy as a person, partly because he was an Irish-American, a Roman Catholic, and therefore 'of bad stock,' partly because he displayed in private some of the unpleasant traits of a man permanently 'on the make.' " [21] To Lord Francis-Williams, Kennedy represented "a tycoon who seemed to me when I met him to combine all the disagreeable traits of all the very rich men I had ever met with hardly any of their virtues." [22] Stylistic differences were probably also responsible for the instinctive dislike that Sir Henry Channon had for Kennedy (". . . whose chief merit seems to be that he has nine children").[23] Sir Josiah Wedgwood, from the porcelain family and one of the most powerful liberal M.P.'s, complained to Ickes about Kennedy. The United States, Wedgwood thought, should have sent its best and had not done so. He regarded Kennedy as a rich man; unlearned in history and politics; untrained in diplomacy; and a great publicity seeker with an apparent desire to be the first Roman Catholic President.[24] William Phillips, American Ambassador to Italy, noted in his diary that when he expressed enthusiasm about Kennedy's appointment to Mrs. Shannon, wife of the British M.P., he

> *was met with a complete silence. She then described a dinner in Parliament which Kennedy attended where she had been present, and where all the M.P.'s had expressed themselves thoroughly disappointed in Kennedy; that he was not at all the type of man to represent the United States at this time. As Mrs. Shannon said, if Kennedy cannot make a good impression among M.P.'s who represent all classes and types, in what circles can he be successful?* [25]

By and large, though, Kennedy's reception with down-to-earth Britons was entirely favorable. At the Foreign Office, no doubt the first step was to check the index for older references that would give some background on the new Ambassador. A 1937 entry in the Foreign Office "minutes" introduced Kennedy as the new Chairman of the Maritime Commission, and described him as "a man of unusual ability, wealthy, businesslike, and devoted solely to the public interest, and as

head of the Security Exchange Commission he achieved a remarkable
success in circumstances of extraordinary difficulty, and there is no
man in the country better able to deal with the almost hopeless
question of American shipping." [26] After a few months at the Maritime
Commission, British negotiators reported Kennedy's "personal inclination to consult rather than conflict with legitimate British interests." [27]
This good introduction for the new Ambassador was early confirmed
by those British statesmen who had to deal with Kennedy. Oliver
Stanley, president of England's Board of Trade, quickly got into
discussions with Kennedy on films, and "gained the impression that if
Mr. Kennedy had been in London last year, the representations from
the State Department would have been of a different character—the
requests of the American film interests would not merely have been
passed on by Washington, but the State Department would have
concentrated on the points which really mattered." [28] Lord Arthur
Riverdale praised the efforts of the new and likeable American
Ambassador in letters to important American insiders,[29] and Harold
Nicolson, who later took pride in having been "the first" to warn
people against Kennedy,[30] told an American diplomat in Bucharest
how impressed he was with the new Ambassador.[31] Some of the
Foreign Office set might have held Kennedy's informality against
him,[32] but for the most part, they expected informality from an
American,[33] and enjoyed seeing it in Kennedy. Alexander Cadogan,
the highly influential Foreign Office bureaucrat, was favorably impressed.[34] Lord J. J. Astor, whose family published both the *Times*,
London's leading newspaper, and the powerful *Observer*, was "rather
taken in by 'Jo' " as he later put it.[35] His in-law, Lady Nancy Astor,
M.P. and leader of the right-leaning sociopolitical "Cliveden Set," was
disappointed that Kennedy didn't visit her country home at Cliveden
often enough.[36]

Kennedy got around a lot—"he enjoyed meeting people, especially
if they had some influence or were entertaining," said one who knew
him.[37] "He had a lot of American charm—it was charm—it may have
been slightly phony—thinking it over perhaps it was. But he always
seemed absolutely genuine. . . ." [38] The charm worked miracles, and
especially so with the British press.

British newspapers had a field day with the "Nine Child Envoy,"
and gave Kennedy's every doing significant coverage. Most British
pressmen liked Kennedy, the perfect picture of the American
go-getter as imagined abroad, and enjoyed the manifestations of his

"Americanism." [39] Kennedy took exception to an early piece about him in the popular *Daily Express* in a note to its owner, Lord Beaverbrook, which, in acknowledgment of the contemporary British disapproval of the typewriter, was handwritten.[40] A closeness thereafter developed between the two that was to last until "Beaver's" death,[41] and the *Express* more than made amends for the early offense given. At the *Daily Telegraph*, a notice was posted on the bulletin board directing that maximum coverage be given to all of Kennedy's activities.[42]

Things were going well for Kennedy. He was loudly cheered when he attended a dinner of the Canada Club on March 30.[43] His activities, his frequent speeches, even his social engagements, were widely reported.

He caused a sensation when he decided in April to end the foolish practice of presenting American debutantes to the Queen. Before he left the Maritime Commission, Kennedy was already being hounded to arrange presentations and he was irked that such demands were made on an Ambassador's time. In cooperation with Senator Henry Cabot Lodge, Kennedy arranged to break the story to the press that he would make no further presentations by publication of an exchange of Kennedy-Lodge letters in which Kennedy announced his decision.[44] The British popular press was delighted by his decision and gave it front-page coverage. Lord Beaverbrook's Hearst-like *Daily Mirror* headlined

AMBASSADOR STOPS U.S. DEBS PESTERING

The *Daily Herald* introduced the story with the lead
SOCIAL CLIMBERS TAKE TUMBLE

The *News Chronicle* proclaimed
MR. KENNEDY CUTS THE 'DEBS'; AMBASSADOR'S
BLOW TO U.S. SOCIAL CLIMBERS[45]

American newspapers circulated a poem in honor of the decision—a poem that must have had special significance for Joe Kennedy:
> *Here's to deah old London,*
> *The home of the debutante dodge—*
> *Till a Kennedy spoke to a Cabot*
> *And got a response from a Lodge.*[46]

James Roosevelt wired, "President greatly pleased . . . Congratulations! Swell job," [47] and Kent wrote the Ambassador of his delight at "that neat neat little scheme you cooked up . . . with the noble Cabot and the erudite Krock, to kick our eager, fair and panting young American debutantes in their tender, silk covered little fannies. . . . A more subtle and delightful piece of democratic demagoguery was never devised by three more cold hearted China Eggs. I salute you." [48]

Reactions to Kennedy in the United States were as good as those in England. On May 17, the *Boston Post* headlined KENNEDY TO GET HARVARD HONOR.[49] Soon after the *Boston Herald* editorialized that "this country either will select a next President of the Kennedy type or it will wish it had." A broadway play, "Leave It to Me," starring Sophie Tucker, included a good-natured joke about the size of the Kennedy family—and Kennedy's son Jack wrote his father that it got the biggest laugh.[50]

The social life was dazzling for the new Ambassador and his wife, climaxed by a weekend with the royal family at Windsor Castle in early April, 1938. Boston legend has it that as the Kennedys awaited their audience, the Ambassador commented to his wife, "It's been quite a journey from East Boston, hasn't it, Rose?" [51] The Kennedys had arrived. Shortly after the visit Cadogan found the Ambassador "very full of his Windsor week-end—lyrical about Their Majesties and the Children!" [52] In anticipation of a visit to the American Embassy by the King and Queen much later Kennedy urged the State Department to press furnishers W. J. Sloane for delivery of an Oriental rug,[53] so that he would make precisely the right impression.

The dizzying social pace had to have its effect. One diplomat of long standing in London explained to the author that "the British give every Ambassador a grand reception, and especially the American Ambassador, and the Kennedys got a particularly grand reception and fuss." [54] The word was passed to be nice, and the establishment went to work: the Kennedys were invited to house parties, dinners, golf and shooting with dukes and earls.[55] "The men usually know it's because they represent a most powerful nation, but sometimes it goes to the women's heads. Mrs. Kennedy arrived a thoroughly down-to-earth type, but after a few months, she thought she was rather grand." [56]

Kennedy, with a battery of embassy and outside ghostwriters,[57] worked hard on his first speech as Ambassador, designed for delivery before the American-oriented Pilgrims' Club, and on March 10, he submitted a draft to the State Department for clearance.[58] Hull was not pleased. Hitler's Germany had just absorbed Austria to the consternation of world leaders. Kennedy's proposed speech—including snatches like ". . . our people do not see how we could usefully participate in the adjustments of international relations . . ." and ". . . I think it is not too much to say that the great bulk of the people is not now convinced that any common interest exists between them and any other country . . ."—struck the Secretary as too isolationistic at such a time. Hull himself was then working on a statement with an "internationalist" sound to it, which conflicted with the general tenor of the Kennedy draft. At a work session, State Department staffers toned down Kennedy's draft somewhat,[59] and European Bureau chief Jay Pierrepont Moffat kept them from doing more "on the ground that an attempt to clip Kennedy's wings might well bring about a cleavage between Mr. Hull and himself far out of all proportion to small inconsistencies. . . ."[60] The revisions were wired to Kennedy. Perhaps to head off an expected complaint from Kennedy about the changes that the Department made in his speech, Hull sent the President a memorandum explaining that "almost all the best minds of those in the Department most capable of judging are unanimous in the opinion that the present draft of Kennedy's proposed speech . . . is entirely too isolationist in its every implication, or virtually so."[61] After conferring with the President, Hull wired Kennedy that he and the President still thought the speech, even as revised by the State Department, was too rigid, and suggested still further revisions. Hull made clear that his specific suggestions—"suggested for your consideration"—had been reviewed and approved by the President. He called to Kennedy's attention the thrust of the speech that he would make shortly before Kennedy's, the message of which conflicted in spirit with the Kennedy speech.[62] When the Department was done with the changes, the Kennedy speech was, as Moffat put it, "no longer the rather virile document it once was."[63]

The State Department staff was surprised at what happened next: Kennedy called to request Hull—according to Moffat, "he begged the Secretary"[64]—to postpone Hull's proposed speech, on the theory that because of Germany's absorption of Austria, Hull's statement might be distorted in England. Kennedy made no suggestion of postponing his own speech. Hull's highest ranking staff members agreed that Kennedy should be given a flat "no." "A few of them," Moffat wrote, "were quite brutal in their comment that Kennedy wanted the Secretary's speech canceled in order that his own which was more isolationist in trend would receive a better play."[65]

Both speeches went forward on schedule. On March 17 Hull

delivered his speech, the message of which was that the failure to accept international responsibilities would result, in the long run, in insecurity for the nation. Roosevelt wrote on his copy of Hull's speech "C.H.: Grand!" [66] The next day, Kennedy delivered his speech.

Kennedy's first speech as Ambassador, delivered March 18, broke diplomatic precedent: even as revised it said something. Before the Pilgrims' Club he told the English of the policy they might expect the United States to follow in the event of war.[67] He made clear that he would not be another Walter Hines Page. Asserting that the United States neither intended to attack anyone nor expected to be attacked, he insisted that the United States would act only when and if her citizens were actually threatened. Kennedy told England that she must not expect America to abandon concepts of national self-interest. He made clear to Britain's leaders that in the event of war, the efforts of English propagandists in America would not be supplemented by those of the American Ambassador, as they had been in the past. While his immediate audience was British, the speech was broadcast in its entirety to American listeners, and had been designed principally for American consumption.[68] Kennedy wrote friends at home:

> I hoped you liked my speech before the Pilgrims. I worked very hard on it, and intended it to reassure my friends and critics alike that I have not as yet been taken into the British camp. It seemed to me that it was imperative, just now, to tell our British cousins that they must not get into a mess counting on us to bail them out.[69]

While Americans took note that Kennedy had not "gone British," Britons were no less pleased by the candor of their charming new residents.

The speech was a good one and impressed world leaders. A German diplomat wrote his superiors that Kennedy was a far better speaker than his predecessor had been.[70] The history of the speech, though, was ominous in its implications for Kennedy's future relations with the Secretary of State and the President.

While Kennedy's Pilgrims' speech was designed to make clear his independence from British influence, Kennedy found himself in agreement with British leaders on most if not all of the many significant political events and situations that dominated discussion in English government circles in the spring of 1938: the *Anschluss*, Germany's absorption of the Austrian nation; England's treaty with Italy; her accord with Ireland; and the Spanish Civil War. Kennedy was quickly impressed with British Prime Minister Neville Chamberlain and his Foreign Secretary, Lord Halifax, and felt confident of his ability to work with them. "I can talk Chamberlain's language and Halifax's language," he assured Hull.[71] The ability was mutual.

Kennedy was truly impressed with Lord Halifax, his official link to the British government: he wrote friends at home that Halifax "seems to be a man of great parts—a scholar, sportsman and everything that an upper class Englishman who gives his life to public service ought to be." [72] There was obviously a great gulf in the backgrounds of the old-monied Lord and the new-monied striver, which was manifested in apparent stylistic differences. There were no doubt also deeper and more meaningful cleavages between the gentle and philosophically-religious Halifax and the less ethereal American. Nonetheless, Kennedy and Halifax shared one common characteristic that was of paramount importance in the relationship between the Ambassador and the Foreign Secretary: neither was very much interested in foreign affairs. In his sensitive biography of Lord Halifax, the Earl of Birkenhead writes that Halifax was not qualified either by knowledge or inclination for such a role as Foreign Secretary.[73] The same might have been said of Kennedy in his role as Ambassador.[74]

Presumably, Kennedy's early impression on Lord Halifax was also favorable.[75] In any event, Kennedy quickly felt at ease with the Foreign Secretary, and was soon filling Halifax's ear with such matters as his ill-regard for Ickes,[76] and his own lack of confidence in the President's domestic economic policies.[77]

ONLY DAYS AFTER KENNEDY'S ARRIVAL IN ENGLAND, EUROPE FOUND itself in the midst of a major crisis: Hitler's Germany absorbed the independent nation of Austria, a flat violation of the Versailles treaty. It was Hitler's first act of territorial aggrandizement, boldly and cleverly executed before the British and French knew what had happened. Many in Europe had expected the move, but no plans had been made for eventualities. Some, such as Kennedy, were surprised; only hours before Germany's military occupied Vienna, Kennedy wired Washington that Hitler was bluffing.[78]

British and French statesmen were in a quandary as to what to do and how to do it, giving the new American Ambassador his first glimpse of what he called "the semi-hysterical attitude which the professional diplomats here adopt whenever another foreseen step occurs." [79] Kennedy was fascinated by the developments, but saw no implications in the crisis for his own country: "The march of events in Austria made my first few days here more exciting than they might otherwise have been, but I am still unable to see that the Central European developments affect our country or my job." He did not anticipate that the West would make war over the matter and, assuming that to be the case, confidently wrote "I am sure I am right that none of these various moves has any significance for the United States, outside of general interest." [80]

Kennedy was right when he hypothesized non-action on the part of the West. Two years before, Germany had set the stage for its takeover of Austria by remilitarizing the Rhineland, Germany's border with France, in violation of the Versailles treaty. The West had let that flagrant violation of treaty commitment pass. Now, with Germany seemingly able to defend the Rhineland, there could be no easy way to intervene, and the question became whether to make war over the *Anschluss*. The stakes were high, for if the West suffered the *Anschluss* to stand, geographical barriers would make it even more difficult to halt further German aggression, in Czechoslovakia, Poland, or Southeastern Europe, where so many diplomats were anticipating further German moves.

As Kennedy predicted, the West let the matter pass without incident. It was a decision with which he himself concurred. The British were not desirous of American intervention in the crisis;[81] since it had already determined to let the matter pass, anything that the United States might do to call attention to the situation would only embarrass the Chamberlain government by highlighting its non-action. In a phone conversation with Hull on March 15, Kennedy urged the Secretary to keep America out of the Austrian affair, and to refrain from any speeches on the subject, inasmuch as nothing that the United States might do would reverse the fait accompli.[82]

With the Austrian crisis passed, Kennedy became momentarily confident that there would be peace in Europe, and he publicly prophesied on March 24 that there would be no European war in 1938.[83] Even if there were a war, he privately assured friends that he could not see that it would affect the United States very adversely.[84]

WITH GERMANY PARTIALLY APPEASED BY ITS ABSORPTION OF THE essentially German Austrian nation, England could further the cause of European appeasement by consummation of a treaty with Italy. Discussions on the treaty had been underway well before the *Anschluss*; developments in the negotiations had been in part responsible for the resignation of Anthony Eden as British Foreign Secretary, shortly before Kennedy's arrival as Ambassador. In early April, an accord was finally reached, which included Britain's recognition of Italy's conquest of Ethiopia in a war of aggression, an implicit renunciation of the principals of the League of Nations. The treaty gave England hopes of driving a wedge between Hitler and Mussolini, but with its repudiation of the League of Nation's principle of nonaggression, it was distasteful to British liberals. Halifax enlisted Kennedy's aid in "selling" the treaty to the world. The Foreign Secretary wrote Lindsay in Washington:

> *I told (Kennedy) of our progress with the Italian conversations and said that if I might speak privately to him I would like him to know how great a help it would be to us if when the result of our conversations was made public that the President could say a word in commendation of them as a contribution to peace. If, in addition, the President felt able to add something about the justification for recognizing facts in regard to Abyssinia, it would be very helpful, inasmuch as, for some reason which I had never understood, the spokesmen of the United States were generally held to be more moral than ourselves, and consequently anything falling from the President on these lines would have effect. The Ambassador said that he would willingly mention the point to the President.*[85]

Kennedy was as good as his word, urging compliance with the Foreign Secretary's request to the point of supplying Roosevelt with a draft for a suggested statement.[86] To Kennedy the Italian treaty represented, he wrote friends at home, "the high point in Mr. Chamberlain's foreign policy thus far." [87] While the President shied away from any specific endorsement of the recognition of Italy's Abyssinian conquest, he did acknowledge the Anglo-Italian Treaty as "proof of the value of peaceful negotiations." [88]

ONE OF THE FIRST MATTERS TO INTEREST THE NEW AMBASSADOR WAS the discussion then underway between Britain and negotiators for Free Ireland. Kennedy had a pretext for his involvement: before Kennedy left America for his new post, Roosevelt wrote Irish patriot

Eamon DeValera, "I have taken the course of asking my good friend, Mr. Joseph P. Kennedy, who sails today for England to take up his post as Ambassador, to convey a personal message from me to the Prime Minister, and to tell the Prime Minister how happy I should be if reconciliation could be brought about." [89] Soon after his arrival in England, Kennedy was engaged in relaying the President's polite interest; as a Boston Irishman, it was a sweet mission for him and he made the most of it. Kennedy was only in London days when the phone rang in the office of Dominions' Secretary Malcolm Macdonald, in charge of negotiations from the British side. "Hello, Malcolm? This is Joe." Macdonald was unaccustomed to having calls put through directly to him; he had not the slightest idea who was calling or how whoever it was had "gotten through," and he was disconcerted. He reacted awkwardly. "Joe Kennedy, the American Ambassador. Can I come over and see you?" Macdonald later hypothesized that Kennedy had addressed his secretary in terms like "you'd better put me through direct to him right now" with a tone that let her know that she had just better put him through.[90] In no time, Kennedy was at Macdonald's office, and began impressing upon the British Roosevelt's "keen" interest, and the important effect on American public opinion of any settlement that "Dev," the Irish leader, would acknowledge to be satisfactory.[91] The British fully appreciated this line of argument; Lindsay wrote the Foreign Office that settlement would be significant in Washington if only because

> The O's and the Macs are still numerous in Congress and throughout American political life, and politicians generally find it worthwhile to testify from time to time to their affection for Ireland and to their sympathy for Irish aspirations, even though with many it may be a somewhat academic sentiment, which may win a few votes and can hardly cost any.[92]

A key Englishman in the negotiations with Ireland told the author that Kennedy had "only marginal influence if any" upon the British position—"We already wanted and appreciated the need for a treaty"—but suggested that Kennedy might have had a role in helping to moderate the Irish position by more effectively presenting to the Irish the same arguments that the British were simultaneously making directly.[93] In the course of his involvement, Kennedy took the occasion to enlist the help of John Cudahy, U.S. Ambassador in Dublin, in attempts to secure Kennedy an honorary degree from Trinity College, Dublin, Ireland's ancient and only prestigious university.[94]

Ultimately a settlement was brought about between Great Britain and the Irish Free State. The British brought the news to Kennedy for the personal information of the President, timing their visit so that any news leakage would be too late for the evening papers. Kennedy told the emissary that he had heard the news ten days previously,[95] no doubt from the Irish side.

To Chamberlain, the accord with Ireland represented a final settlement and a triumph for appeasement: mollification through satisfaction of legitimate grievances; to DeValera, it was a mere payment on account.[96] There still remained questions burning in the Irish heart: principally, reunification of Northern Ireland and the Irish Free State under Dublin's control.[97] The treaty put the ports of southern Ireland, important to Britain's naval defense, entirely in the hands of the Irish Republic. Dour Winston Churchill asked Parliament what guarantee there was that Ireland would be cooperative over the ports in the event that Britain became involved in a war? There was no solid answer. Ultimately, when war came, Ireland remained steadfastly neutral; closed Britain's relinquished ports to the Allies; and, according to Churchill, "many a ship and many a life were soon to be lost as the result of this improvident example of appeasement." He characterized the settlement as a "lamentable and amazing episode." [98] But to most, the strategic significance of the treaty did not hit home.

Kennedy was elated at the settlement, feeling especially that it contributed significantly to British security.[99] From the Irish point of view, he thought that DeValera "seemed to me to attach too much importance to the failure to secure a solution of the partition question." [100] To the Ambassador, it represented another triumph for Chamberlain's policies,[101] and he counseled British statesmen as to how to get the greatest public-relations mileage out of the settlement in the United States.[102] Macdonald, though, was unimpressed with his advice, and graciously ignored it.[103]

In relating his efforts to Irish diplomats, Kennedy perhaps exaggerated the effect that he had had on the British position.[104] In any event, the Irish were impressed with his efforts,[105] and leading Irish-American politicians were jealous of Kennedy's claim for any credit. Jim Farley complained to Morgenthau that it had been he who had brought the Anglo-Irish situation to Roosevelt's attention, and that Kennedy had had nothing to do with the settlement.[106]

IN 1936 LEFT-WING PARTIES DEMOCRATICALLY CAPTURED CONTROL of the Spanish government. Soon after, General Francisco Franco began the long three years of bloodshed known as the Spanish Civil War. Russia and left-wingers from all over the world began sending significant aid to the legitimate "loyalist" government; Germany and Italy began assisting Franco's right-wing and Church-oriented Falange Party. In democratic nations, the stronger voice of sympathy was for the loyalists, but to Neville Chamberlain, any involvement in the Spanish War threatened to explode the whole European situation. He strove to keep Britain, and her ally France, neutral in the conflict. Joseph Kennedy was willing to assist.

Kingsley Martin writes that Kennedy was privately "horrified at any suggestion that America or Britain should help in any way the 'bunch of atheists and Communists' which he believed the Spanish government to be," [107] and left-wing circles regarded the Ambassador as decidedly pro-Franco.[108] Kennedy, though, was generally careful to phrase his position in less personal terms, perhaps, as some suspected, because he did not want to appear "too Catholic" in the event that Kennedy's own remote but hoped-for Presidential opportunities should materialize.[109] So, when the question arose of ending the American embargo on shipment of arms to Spain, where the "atheist" loyalists would have been the principal beneficiaries, Kennedy phrased his opposition carefully in wires to Hull: if the United States ended its embargo, he suggested that it would embarrass the nonintervention efforts of the Chamberlain government in England and the Daladier government in France, and then anything might happen:

> With all its faults, non-intervention [in the Spanish Civil War] has contributed towards the preservation of peace in Europe. Settlement of the Spanish problem would seem to be an essential prerequisite to any scheme for general European appeasement. The injection of any new factor into this already overcharged and delicate situation, might have far reaching consequences.[110]

In his correspondence with Roosevelt, he spoke in the same kind of terms against ending the embargo.[111] William C. Bullitt, the United States Ambassador in France, spoke along similar lines, and Roosevelt was certainly influenced by their reasoning.[112] Apparently Kennedy's only active involvement in the Spanish situation was extraofficial. The Mother Superior of the Convent of the Sacred Heart in Roehampton, England, called to his attention the plight of the sisters of her order in war-torn Barcelona, which was being bombed by Franco. Kennedy solicited the assistance of both Halifax[113] and the State Department[114] in getting the sisters evacuated. As an accommodation to the Ambassador, they were brought out on a British destroyer.[115]

Both of Kennedy's eldest sons visited Spain during the war, and came back with somewhat different impressions. John F. Kennedy, who went to Spain in the summer of 1937, developed considerable sentiment for the Loyalists: ". . . at the beginning the government was in the right morally speaking as its program was similar to the New Deal. . . . Their attitude towards the Church *was* just a reaction to the strength of the Jesuits who had become much too powerful— the affiliation between church and state being much too close." [116] Joseph P. Kennedy, Jr., who more consistently reflected his father's views, was in Spain in the summer of 1939, and found that his sympathies lay with the Franco forces.[117]

EVEN ON DOMESTIC AMERICAN POLITICS, KENNEDY FOUND HIMSELF AT one with the leaders of Britain. In the winter and spring of 1937–1938, the United States and much of the world found itself in the midst of a serious recession—"the Roosevelt depression." Kennedy was seriously concerned, both over the depression and over possible repercussions arising out of it. "A few more months of depression of values," he wrote friends at home,

> will have us and the rest of the world so deeply in the doghouse that war might seem to be an attractive out. That is the danger in world-wide depressions such as we have nowadays. Everybody gets to feeling poor and put upon at the same time. International tempers flare up. Pressure is brought to bear on those in authority to do something drastic to better the economic lot of their subjects.[118]

In the midst of this economic and emotional uncertainty, Roosevelt saw fit to deliver a class-oriented attack on the "economic royalists" at Gainesville, Georgia, calling for more economic democracy. As Kennedy saw it, the speech could only make matters worse; he exploded at Hull "Who was responsible for that Gainesville speech? Whoever [it] was ought to be horsewhipped." [119] He told the Secretary that he had just had a meeting with 18 "big bankers" (all of whom might have taken the speech as a personal attack upon themselves) and they had strongly disapproved.[120] Privately, he wrote friends, "I am distressed beyond words at conditions in the United States." [121]

KENNEDY'S PRIMARY INTEREST, EVEN AT THIS EARLY DATE, WAS NOT
so much in European relations as it was in keeping his country aloof
from them. On April 28, he wrote the isolationist Senator William
Borah:

> The more I see of things here, the more convinced I am that we
> must exert all our intelligence and effort toward keeping clear of
> any kind of involvement. As long as I hold my present job I shall
> never lose sight of this guiding principle.[122]

This interest could best be served by improving American relations
with Germany. By late spring, Kennedy had become nervous about
the European situation,[123] and if the United States had better relations
with Germany it would be less apt to enter a war against her. The
German Ambassador in London, Herbert von Dirksen, cabled Berlin
on May 31 that Kennedy on several occasions had "repeatedly turned
the conversation to the point that he would like to do his very best to
improve German-United States relations." [124] Kennedy was to leave
for a visit home shortly, but they arranged for a longer visit to take
place before he departed.

On June 14, the London *Times* reported that the previous day
Kennedy had made the round of diplomatic circles before leaving
for the United States. Among those he visited was Herbert von
Dirksen.

Kennedy's visit to von Dirksen lasted almost an hour, during the
course of which Kennedy stressed the bright side of German-American
relations, and convinced the German of his own sympathies for the
Reich.[125] He impressed von Dirksen with the fact that Roosevelt's
information on Germany was mostly unfavorable, because the President's informants were themselves ill-advised, or were afraid of the
Jews. The East Coast press, predominant in forming public opinion,
was also strongly influenced by Jews. But he, Kennedy, would
enlighten the President. Von Dirksen wrote that "although [Kennedy]
did not know Germany, he had learned from the most varied sources
that the present Government had done great things for Germany." [126]
He was interested in making a study tour of the country.[127] Kennedy
took a very dim view of conditions in the Soviet Union.

On the "Jewish question," von Dirksen reported that Kennedy
believed that

> It was not so much the fact that we wanted to get rid of the Jews
> that was harmful to us, but rather the loud clamour with which
> we accompanied this purpose. He himself understood our Jewish

policy completely; he was from Boston and there, in one golf club and in other clubs, no Jews had been admitted for the past 50 years. . . . such pronounced attitudes were quite common, but people avoided making so much outward fuss about it.[128]

In European affairs, Kennedy "repeatedly expressed his conviction that in economic matters Germany had to have a free hand in the East [Poland] as well as in the Southeast [Central Europe and the Balkans]"—one of the most basic of German demands.[129]

Kennedy's statements to von Dirksen were potentially gravely harmful. He told von Dirksen that Chamberlain was extremely anxious for a settlement with Germany.[130] If this statement was given any currency, it must have helped to confirm Germany's suspicions, and so made it more difficult for Chamberlain to drive a hard bargain with the Reich. Because of Kennedy's known closeness with Chamberlain and the confidential nature of the information, the statement (which was true) must have been noted by the German Foreign Office. Furthermore, Kennedy's expressed interest in improving German-American relations, and his statement that he thought Germany should have a free hand in the East and Southeast,[131] if given credence, might have encouraged Germany to pursue its aggressive expansionist policies.

As it was, German policy was no doubt little influenced by the series of von Dirksen dispatches. Though von Dirksen himself attached great significance to the American's statements,[132] sounder heads in *Wilhelmstrasse* suspected that Kennedy spoke loose words; that he had poor judgment;[133] and that his statements to von Dirksen, and especially his desire to visit Germany, were part of a plan to "put himself in a better position" [134] in American politics, possibly to boost himself to the Presidency.[135] Under the circumstances, Kennedy's statements may have had little or no ill effects on subsequent world affairs, but they were nonetheless ill-conceived and potentially dangerous.

Kennedy's motives for his statements to von Dirksen are of as much interest as the effect of the comments. No doubt he was sincerely interested in improving German-American relations. By June of 1938 he was pessimistic,[136] for he must have realized that a European War was imminent. He probably reached a most reasonable conclusion: that improved relations with Germany would make American entry less likely. He believed that Germany would not cease its persecution of the Jews. By suggesting to von Dirksen that it was the "loud clamor" of the persecution, rather than the persecution itself, that was so detrimental to German-American relations, he probably hoped that Germany might become more discreet. Americans would then be less aware of Germany's offenses to humanity, and so less apt to enter a war against her.

Kennedy was by no means consistent in his efforts to make people forget Germany's faults. In the pre-Munich days, both before and after his first meeting with von Dirksen, he publicly spoke out against restrictions on freedom of thought[137] and the absence of religious freedom[138] in totalitarian lands. By so doing, Kennedy helped to nullify the effects of his statements to von Dirksen, and by the same token his statements to the German helped to nullify the total effect of his public statements.

ON JUNE 15 KENNEDY SAILED FOR HOME ON THE QUEEN MARY TO attend Joe Junior's graduation from Harvard—with honors. It was an event that he did not want to miss and he wired the State Department for permission to leave his post in order to attend. He was undoubtedly aware that a Czech crisis was developing, and he had become pessimistic.[139] Arriving in New York on June 20, he paused long enough to tell newsmen he would not run for President.[140] Then it was off to Hyde Park to confer with Roosevelt.

After a long conference with his Ambassador, Roosevelt told newsmen that Kennedy had simply confirmed Roosevelt's own views of the past two years.[141] "Did he seem hopeful?" asked a reporter. Roosevelt did not answer.[142]

After the meeting Kennedy went to Boston. He dispelled current rumors that he was to receive Harvard "kudos." Good naturedly, he told reporters "But there will be one honor degree in the family. That's pretty good." [143]

Still, Kennedy must have been a little disappointed about being passed up for the Harvard "honorary." Throughout the 1930s he lobbied consistently for the recognition of university honoraries: through Baruch for an honorary from Oglethorpe College, awarded in 1937 (offered his choice of degrees, Kennedy took "Laws"); through Cudahy, for one from Trinity College, Dublin, "for the sake of my children," which was never forthcoming; through the State Depart-

ment's Breckenridge Long, via Krock, for one from Princeton
(". . . he would rather have one from Princeton than from [Oxford or
Cambridge] and would prefer one from Princeton than from Harvard . . ."), which also never materialized; and, no doubt for degrees
from other universities through other similar efforts.[144] Honorary
degrees were terrific for the ego in general, but even more important,
an honorary from a prestigious university would increase the political
stature of its recipient. An unabashed blessing. Surely, the self-made
millionaire and occupant of the nation's highest diplomatic post was
entitled to such recognition from his own alma mater. When the
rumors that Kennedy would be honored by Harvard had first begun in
mid-May, he had denied them. He would never get an honorary
degree from Harvard, he had explained, because he had refused to
sign a petition urging Harvard to honor the aged Supreme Court
Justice Louis Brandeis.[145] But this explanation, volunteered by Kennedy, was somehow unconvincing. Despite his rough-diamond demeanor, Kennedy was always thin-skinned about criticisms, personal
slights, and being passed up for anything. The papers reported that the
illness of Kennedy's second son, John, would keep Kennedy from
actually attending the graduation exercises.[146]

After a visit in Washington where he conferred with Hull,
Morgenthau, Under Secretary of State Sumner Welles, and the
President,[147] Kennedy left for England on June twenty-ninth, accompanied by his two oldest sons, Joe Junior and John Kennedy. Krock
accompanied the Kennedys on the voyage, and later recalled:

> The ship's company was gay, and there was a beautiful actress
> aboard to whom young Joe was very attentive. This annoyed the
> father, because he thought that the boy might perhaps be a little
> too impulsive and the girl be making a play for a youth of his
> prominence and wealth. Jack was also staying up late at night,
> with a girl I think his father didn't know about. So he imposed a
> curfew on the young men; they would have to be in their
> quarters in his suite by midnight or thereabouts.
>
> They made the first deadline. But the suite had a service door,
> distant from the bedrooms. So when thereafter I saw them as my
> fellow-conspirators, enjoying themselves in the ship's salons in
> the small hours of the night, I assumed they must have used this
> facility to elude the curfew.[148]

Krock makes clear, though, that Joseph Kennedy was not a disciplinar-
ian in any Calvinistic way.[149]

It was during this visit home that a strain in relations between the President and his Ambassador first came to public attention.

Kennedy's activities in London had been hailed much too much for Roosevelt, and the Chief could see that Kennedy himself was behind much of the publicity. While Harold Hinton bore the title "Private Secretary to the Ambassador," his background with the *New York Times*'s Washington bureau made him better suited for other things, and Hinton's closeness with Krock, the *Times*'s Washington bureau chief and Kennedy's biggest booster for higher office, must have made the President suspect that Hinton's functions were neither administrative nor secretarial. He knew that Moore was Kennedy's personal secretary. The British were given to understand that Hinton's function was to ghost speeches and "keep contact with the press" [150]—in short, to be Kennedy's public relations man. Roosevelt no doubt suspected as much. To the President, the very idea that his Ambassador, his agent, had a public relations man for himself on the staff, must have been offensive. There was no need for a press release at all on the decision to end court presentations, and the inference arose that Kennedy did not want his decision to go unnoticed.[151] Roosevelt's instructions to Kennedy to "please use your own judgement on release" of the story were sent two days after the American press had carried the news on page one and a day after many American papers had editorialized on it.[152] Kennedy was personally responsible for releasing the story to the press of the rescue of the Spanish nuns from Barcelona,[153] and State Department staffers noted what Moffat called his "inordinate pushing of personal publicity." [154] The Ambassador greeted any article that spoke of him in less than totally laudatory terms with fury,[155] an attitude that no doubt got back to the highest levels of the Administration.

For some reason, Kennedy was making efforts to keep his name alive, and favorably alive, back home. It all seemed to add up to something that Roosevelt did not like to see in others: Presidential ambitions. Roosevelt thought his suspicions confirmed when he learned that Kennedy had been writing frank letters to Krock[156] and other influential Americans, principally in the highest echelons of the press world, giving extensive, current, and confidential information on European developments. The letters, labeled "Private and Confidential," were in tone, content, length, and presentation, such that their recipients, important though they were in their own right, must of necessity have been flattered by such close attention from the

Ambassador. With only minor deviations, the letters were of identical text[157] and went out to a "mailing list," [158] but the recipients didn't have to know it. ("Just had another of Ambassador Kennedy's syndicated 'Private and Confidential' letters," Kent wrote fellow recipient Baruch.)[159] When Roosevelt learned of Kennedy's "correspondence," he was furious. He became convinced that Kennedy was using the Court of St. James's as a steppingstone to the Presidency. Krock, the President believed, was sparking Kennedy's Presidential boom.[160] Roosevelt was famous for souring on those who aspired to succeed him, and he was not impressed by Kennedy's transparent and Iago-like professions to James Roosevelt that "there are two things I am for—the U.S.A. and F.D.R." [161]

Kennedy probably realized that the President was "on to him"; his June twentieth disclaimer of Presidential ambitions was apparently not in response to a question, and the text of it hints at a desire to placate the President:

> I enlisted under President Roosevelt in 1932 to do whatever he wanted me to do. There are many problems at home and abroad and I happen to be busy at one abroad just now. If I had my eye on another job it would be a complete breach of faith with President Roosevelt.[162]

If Kennedy's statement was inspired by a desire to put the President at ease, his effort was unsuccessful. Roosevelt told Steve Early, his press secretary, to plant an unfavorable story about Kennedy's Presidential ambitions and activities, and Walter Trohan of the *Chicago Daily Tribune* did the job. Trohan wrote that "the chilling shadow of 1940" had fallen across the Roosevelt-Kennedy friendship. He reported the story of Kennedy's letters to Washington correspondents, and Roosevelt's resulting suspicions and displeasure, attributing his information to "unimpeachable sources." [163]

Matters like this were probably not discussed between the President and Kennedy, but relations between the two grew steadily worse in subsequent months. A couple of weeks after the Trohan story appeared, Roosevelt commented to Ickes that he did not expect Kennedy to last more than a couple of years in London, as Kennedy was the kind of man who liked to go from one job to another, dropping it just when the going became heavy.[164]

MUNICHTIME

KENNEDY WAS NO SOONER BACK IN LONDON THAN HE LEFT FOR
Ireland for a few days. The *New York Times* observed that it was a
most unusual visit, but Kennedy denied that it had any political
significance. He had come only to receive the National University's
honorary degree; it was a sentimental visit. He said that if he were
asked to make a speech at the presentation, he would likely cry in the
middle of it.[1] Kennedy was accompanied on the visit by Joe Jr., Moore,
and John B. Kennedy,[2] an unrelated journalist who had authored
laudatory pieces about the Ambassador.[3]

Kennedy diplomatically sought permission to accept the honor from
the Foreign Office. Through chargé Herschel Johnson he represented
that DeValera had suggested to Cudahy that Kennedy be given an
honorary; that Kennedy was disposed to accept, and Roosevelt had
given his blessings, but that the Ambassador wanted clearance from
Halifax. The idea of the Irish giving Kennedy a degree struck the
Foreign Office as abnormal, inasmuch as Kennedy was not accredited
to Ireland, but Sir Robert Vansittart, the high-ranking Foreign Office
civil servant, reasoned, "Even if we disliked the idea, I don't see how
we could possibly object. That being so, let us say that we shall be
very pleased if Mr. Kennedy agrees." And so they did.[4]

It was a brief but pleasant visit. Cudahy hosted a small dinner for
the Ambassador, DeValera, the Papal Nuncio, and several members of
the Irish cabinet. The following day, DeValera give Kennedy a small
luncheon, equally studded with dignitaries.[5] In his capacity as Prime
Minister, DeValera served also as Chancellor of the National University, and presented the degree, followed by a state banquet in
Kennedy's honor.[6]

Then it was back to business. Hitler's absorption of the Austrian
state proved to be the setting-of-the-stage for increased agitation for,
and ultimate accomplishment of, German territorial gains in Czechoslovakia. Austria had not appeased the hunger of the Reich.

The hybrid nation of Czechoslovakia contained substantial numbers
of culturally Germanic peoples clustered along the country's moun-

tainous border with Germany. These "Sudeten Germans," as they were known, led by Czechoslovakian Nazi Party chief Konrad Henlein, were agitating for increased local autonomy within the Czechoslovakian state throughout the late 1930s; after Britain and France "made it easy" in Austria, they dramatically stepped up their previously unrequited demands, and the Reich became increasingly boisterous about the "intolerable ill-treatment" meted out by Czechoslovakia to the Sudeten Germans, and about Germany's duty to protect the colony of Germans across the mountains in Czechoslovakia. It sounded like threat of war on the horizon. The British and French leaders were pressing Czech leaders to come to terms with Hitler, but what if an impasse resulted? Kennedy felt that the situation was not critical at the time of his return to England in July, 1938, but acknowledged that it looked touchy for the future, perhaps in the spring of 1939.[7] As history turned, the Czech crisis was then only a couple of months from the explosive stage.

Kennedy renewed his contact with von Dirksen and had another long session with the German Ambassador. He told von Dirksen that he had relayed to Roosevelt the substance of their talks in a visit with the President during Kennedy's holiday. Roosevelt, he told the German, thought "calmly and moderately" about the European situation and "would be prepared to support Germany's demands vis-à-vis England or to do anything that might lead to pacification." It seemed "obvious" to von Dirksen that Kennedy was acting on orders from the President. The United States was supporting Chamberlain's government in its efforts to secure a settlement with Germany, von Dirksen reported, and this support, he believed, would be sufficient to break Chamberlain's opposition.

Should peace efforts fail, however, and should the Czech situation explode, Kennedy warned that the United States would inevitably be drawn into the conflict on the side of England.

Kennedy expressed interest again in visiting Germany. One of his ambassadorial duties was to serve as President of the International Wheat Conference, and a Wheat Conference meeting was to be held in September in Berlin. Kennedy suggested that a visit at that time would not stimulate speculation.[8]

Von Dirksen did express some interest in Kennedy's motives for wanting to undertake the visit, but he concluded "Personally he still made a good impression on me." [9]

The picture of how diplomats deceive each other is rounded out by

Kennedy's report home on the conversation. Kennedy reported that von Dirksen had made clear that now was a good time for England to make overtures to Germany, and that von Dirksen had "implied that he hoped there was some way that we could urge the English to begin. His manner this morning was a revelation to me. He definitely gave me the impression that Hitler was decidedly in the mood to start negotiations with England." He reported von Dirksen's assertion that Germany was willing to agree on arms limitation, if England would see that her European allies were included, but that "the Germans are distrustful naturally of Russia, Czechoslovakia, and Poland." [10]

Today it is clear that Hitler never had any sincere interest in arriving at armament limitations nor was he really concerned about reaching peaceful settlements. Whether or not von Dirksen believed what he communicated to Kennedy is as open as is the answer to the converse question: Was Kennedy sincere in his expressions? The document books make clear that the German was acting on instructions.[11] In any event, von Dirksen did impress Kennedy with Hitler's willingness to negotiate, and Kennedy reported the Ambassador's statements uncritically, transmitting the enthusiasm that von Dirksen had manifested. And Kennedy, of course, had succeeded in impressing the German with his own bona fides. The two Ambassadors apparently convinced each other; neither, however, seem to have made much impression on their chiefs.

Kennedy remained at his routine work in London until August fourth, when he left to join his family at Cannes.[12] It was a good rest. He wrote to Admiral Land on August eighth, "I am vacationing at Cannes and doing little if any work. I am dictating this letter to a beautiful French girl, so if it does not make sense blame it on the French." [13] He relaxed with swimming, and yachting with the Duke of Windsor,[14] and by the twentieth of August he was back at work in London.[15]

By this time Hitler was sounding increasingly bellicose over Czechoslovakia, and with difficulties coming to a head, Kennedy had a heavy six weeks ahead of him. Kennedy's job at such times of crises was essentially reportorial, and Chamberlain kept him well informed of developments. Throughout the Czech crisis of 1938, Kennedy sent fresh dispatches frequently—sometimes every hour—and often he was at his work until three or four in the morning. On the twenty-fifth Roosevelt sent him a bit of encouragement: "I know what difficult days you are going through—and I can assure you that it is not *much* easier at this end!" [16]

On August thirtieth Kennedy first learned just how serious the Czech crisis was. He appeared surprised when Chamberlain told him that Hitler had apparently decided to invade the little nation. The Prime Minister suggested that it would be unwise for Britain to utter threats, given her unpreparedness to back them up by going to war. Kennedy agreed. Chamberlain said he doubted that the fall of Czechoslovakia would leave Hitler unstoppable. Kennedy again agreed, though he added that if that were to happen, "it will be hell."

Kennedy said that if the French went in to protect Czechoslovakia, with whom France was formally allied by treaty, and Britain went in too, the United States would follow before long. He seemed interested in helping. Did Chamberlain want Roosevelt to make a speech? He assured the Prime Minister that "he was convinced that President Roosevelt had decided to go in with Chamberlain; whatever course Chamberlain decided to adopt he would think right." [17]

Kennedy was not as pessimistic as he might have been, nor as fearful as Chamberlain was. The Prime Minister, he reported, "still is the best bet in Europe today against war, but he is a very sick looking individual. He is worried but not jittery." [18] Kennedy himself still had very great confidence in the Prime Minister's peace-making capabilities,[19] and he had come to the conclusion that Hitler's manifested belligerency was more in the nature of further bluffing than indicative that final decisions for war had been made in Berlin.[20] Even if Hitler did attack Czechoslovakia, Kennedy suspected that the Führer would try not to involve the West in any conflict.[21] He thought a momentary lessening of criticism of England in the German press was a good sign, and indicative that Germany realized that the Czech problem was being considered by Chamberlain fairly, from the German point of view.[22] Von Dirksen had made Germany's position seem something that it was not—he had made it seem slightly reasonable, which may explain why Kennedy harbored these optimistic, unrealistic beliefs.

Kennedy saw other grounds for optimism, too. He expressed the hopeful thesis that Nazism could only be imposed over a limited area; that its excessive control would bring a paralyzing economic situation if the Reich were extended over a much larger area than it already included. He conceded that this argument was not necessarily conclusive, and that much could be said on the other side,[23] but still he was hopeful.

The thought of war—or even of a crisis—over a minorities problem seemed to him to be utterly ridiculous,[24] and when his beautiful and fashionable artist-friend Ione Robinson considered returning to America because of the war threat, he assured her that nothing was going to happen.[25]

After an August thirty-first meeting with Halifax, Kennedy wired home a report.[26] Halifax was interested in possible American reactions in the event that the Czech situation did explode, and Kennedy—who had already fully discussed the matter with Chamberlain and the Foreign Secretary—asked instructions about how to answer Halifax's query.[27] After completing the wire, the Ambassador gave an exclusive telephonic interview to Hearst's *Boston Evening American*. Things weren't so discouraging as they seemed, he reported. Asked if the English public were behind the cabinet in the crisis, he answered "Yes, very strongly so." [28] Kennedy slept soundly that night.

The President and the State Department, perhaps tense from the pressure of general developments, became hot at both the request for guidance as to probable American reactions and also the exclusive interview given the Hearst press. Roosevelt sent Hull a note that Kennedy should be told that if all ambassadors were to give exclusive interviews to favored newspapers, the State Department might as well close up shop.[29] Hull began his draft of the reprimand: "For your information considerable embarrassment has been caused here by the appearance of a special telephonic interview. . . ." [30] Then he scratched it out and toned down the wire to a tactful but firm don't-do-it-again.[31] When Kennedy defended himself to the Secretary in terms of the obligation of "getting along reasonably well with the agencies," Roosevelt sent his own reprimand direct to the Ambassador.[32]

Even more alarming to the President was the inquiry with regard to possible American reactions, for it signified to the President that his Ambassador "must have been doing some talking," as he put it to Morgenthau.[33] "I know my men," he told the Secretary of the Treasury.[34]

The British and French were in a difficult position: theirs was the decision as to whether to save or abandon Czechoslovakia to the Nazis. It was a heavy burden and, understandably, they were eager to spread the responsibility. Their query as to possible American reactions was a quest for guidance that would enable them to shift at least part of the responsibility for the awesome decision to others.

Scholar Edward L. Henson, Jr., puts it this way: "The British Government had shown a distinct preference for sacrificing Czechoslovakia, and, like all those with a guilty conscience, they sought justification by securing general acceptance." [35] At the time, Moffat wrote the same thing in somewhat less charged language in his diary:

> *Few developments in the Czech crisis other than that the British seem to be maneuvering to obtain some sort of an expression of advice or opinion from us by which they could throw responsibility on us. This is an old game but Joe Kennedy seems to have fallen for it. He keeps asking on behalf of Chamberlain and Halifax what would be our reaction in every sort of contingency.* [36]

Even the man on the London streets was concerned about American attitudes and reactions, and consulted ordinary Americans living in the city as to the state of American feelings. [37] The *Yorkshire Post*, Lord Halifax's "hometown newspaper," reported that Halifax had asked Kennedy about possible American reactions, [38] and then the London *Times*'s Washington correspondent pointedly asked Hull whether discussions between Kennedy and Halifax had been a British effort to ascertain what America would do if-and-when. [39]

The President was irritated at the turn of events and especially that correct speculation had hit the press. He felt that Kennedy should "cuss out the press" for inaccurate reporting, and suspected that Kennedy himself was leaking information, perhaps in an effort to force his own hand "in his process of playing the Chamberlain game." [40] Morgenthau was completely satisfied that Kennedy "is playing with the British Foreign Office and the Prime Minister"; that he had "spilled the beans"; and, that he had brought about a situation such that "it would be very difficult for us to do anything without playing the British game. We are in the position now that anything we do now makes us a party either way, a party to their fighting or not fighting. They have us, for the moment, stymied." [41] The President himself outlined a telegram for Kennedy, [42] and Hull wired the Ambassador:

> *I feel that the recent public statements of the President and myself, which were prepared with great care, accurately reflect the attitude of this Government toward the European and world situation, and that it would not be practicable to be more specific as to our reaction in hypothetical circumstances.* [43]

He gave substantially the same response to the inquirers from the London press. [44]

Kennedy was kept thoroughly informed of developments and made extensive reports to Washington. But the English press reported his visits to the British government offices widely, headlining

VISIT FROM AMERICAN AMBASSADOR

at every opportunity. The press gave the appearance of continuous consultations between the United States and Great Britain.

The Secretary of State was perturbed about an apparent London-Paris-Washington axis that might prove embarrassing to the United States if England and France should go to war. He attributed the appearance of this axis to Kennedy, Bullitt and Ambassador Hugh Wilson in Berlin, whom he believed were representing personal as opposed to State Department policies.[45] Kennedy's advertised consultations played a big part in creating the appearance of the "alliance." They gave the public the impression that Great Britain and the United States were cooperating in a kind of understanding that did not in fact exist.[46] They created the appearance of the kind of understanding that Hull wished to avoid. Moffat noted in his diary, "Joe Kennedy's star is not shining brightly these days. He cannot move without a blare of publicity, and in tense moments like these, publicity is the thing most to be avoided."[47]

The State Department wanted to steer clear of anything approaching continuous consultations or anything that gave the appearance of them, for the same reason that it did not want to comment on possible American reactions: it did not want to share responsibility for European developments at the time of crisis. If America were too closely connected, either in fact or in the minds of the public, with the developments before the war, her position as an unconcerned neutral would be compromised, and it would be harder for her to remain aloof should war break out.[48] The State Department did not want to be involved in any way in the affair. They wanted full information on the developing situation, but did not want to be consulted. Hull wanted little or no attention drawn to the United States during the time of crisis. He did not want the United States or its representatives involved. He wanted less contact between his Ambassador and the crisis. Perhaps Kennedy did not understand this. The author has found no evidence that the State Department ever attempted to make this clear to Kennedy. Either Kennedy did not understand this, did not wish to understand it, or did not care.

After a September tenth conference between Kennedy and Halifax, the Foreign Secretary wired Lindsay that Kennedy felt it essential to take every possible step to avoid misunderstanding in Hitler's mind. The American Ambassador had wondered if it might not be possible for the Soviet government to make some move that might compel attention, such as concentrating airplanes near the frontier. On American reaction to Hitlerite aggression, Kennedy had said that American opinion was much more excited against Germany than he had ever known it—"Twenty times as excited as in 1914."

> If war should come, (Kennedy) anticipated that the immediate reaction would be a desire to keep out of it, but that, if we were drawn into it and, for example, London was bombed, he thought there would be a strong revulsion of feeling and that the history of the last war would be repeated, leading a good deal more rapidly than in the last war to American intervention.[49]

Kennedy's report of the meeting to the State Department, not surprisingly, is very different. In his wire to Hull after the meeting, he said "Halifax asked again what would be America's reaction. I said I had not the slightest idea; except that we want to keep out of war." [50]

Kennedy was misrepresenting the conversation to the State Department. Whether he fully understood the State Department's position is not clear, but his wire does make clear that he had understood the rebuke about commenting on hypothetical circumstances. Halifax's wire demonstrates that Kennedy paid that rebuke little heed.

On September 11, Kennedy suggested to Halifax that Britain might make some political use of the fact that two American destroyers were being sent to British waters.[51] Further, Halifax wrote,

> Mr. Kennedy suggested that it might be useful were he to call on the Prime Minister this evening in order to encourage German speculation regarding the fact that our two countries were apparently keeping in such close touch. I welcomed the Ambassador's suggestion.[52]

Halifax appreciated the spectacular, moral value in such visits,[53] but it was exactly the kind of attention that Hull and Roosevelt did not want drawn to American activities; the kind of "speculation" they wished to avoid.[54] Later in September Kennedy commented on his trips to the government offices to the King—"I go sometimes only to read the newspapers." The King laughed.[55] While Kennedy boasted of this "strategy" to the King, aviator Charles Lindbergh,[56] and no doubt others, he did not bother to tell Hull about it.

Theodor Kordt, chargé in Germany's London embassy, wired German Foreign Secretary Joachim von Ribbentrop on the twelfth of Kennedy's visits, and added "I learn from a reliable source, President Roosevelt has made it known through the Ambassador that Great Britain could count on the support of the United States if she should become involved in a war."[57]

Kennedy was trying to make Britain look stronger and more confident than she was, in the hope that Germany would become less belligerent in the face of a powerful enemy. His was a reasonable conclusion, and he furthered his end in a masterful conference with von Selzam, counselor of the German legation in London, on the twelfth. Kennedy told the German that after his conferences of the previous day his opinions had changed. He now was convinced that if France went to war in Czechoslovakia, Britain would too. "This time they mean business," he warned. He added that Roosevelt had assured Chamberlain of his sympathy with the Prime Minister's attitude. Kennedy stressed that he personally would try his hardest to keep America out of any war, and he made a few favorable statements about Germany. But he made clear that in the event of war, America would intervene sooner or later. "It depended on Hitler whether there was to be chaos, from which no country in the world could remain immune," wrote the German in summarizing Kennedy's beliefs.[58]

If Hitler had been troubled over the likelihood of a war, it is probable that this conversation would have had a beneficial effect on the world situation. Kennedy certainly made the possibility of war seem more threatening to Germany. Most of the statesmen of the day thought Hitler could be shaken by a display of strength. Diplomats in the German Foreign Service were impressed by such things, but the Führer had already set Germany's course.

Kennedy had only two or three hours' notice of Chamberlain's surprise visit to Hitler at Berchtesgaden, Germany, on September 14, and the French had even less.[59] The visit was hastily conceived and executed. At the intimate conference, Hitler showed his most unreasonable side to Chamberlain and presented the Briton with a still-lengthened roster of demands. After Chamberlain's return, Kennedy reported the Prime Minister's belief that Hitler would be completely ruthless in his aims and methods.[60] But what could Britain do about it? Chamberlain was satisfied that many, if not most, of the Sudeten German grievances were legitimate, and he was fearful of the consequences of resistance. Two days later, on September 19,

Kennedy expressed his own prophetic belief that "unless there is a terrific rise of public opinion all over the world, England does not propose to fight on the Czechoslovak issue." [61] Chamberlain, he reported, was in bad spirits and felt a war would mean the end of civilization—that communism or worse was likely to follow.[62]

At this point Kennedy called aviator Charles Lindbergh to London for an informed report on Germany's air strength. The two had met at Cliveden the previous May, at which time Kennedy had favorably impressed the flier. Lindbergh looked forward to seeing more of the Ambassador.[63] Later, Lindbergh had become close to Hermann Goering, the head of Hitler's air force, who had shown the American aviator much of Germany's air power,[64] making a terrific impression on Lindbergh. In September, 1938, the American was in Paris, relating his frightening views to the French with such devastating effect that, after a visit with Lindbergh, French Foreign Minister Georges Bonnet concluded that "peace had to be preserved at any price." [65] While in Paris, the American received an urgent wire from Kennedy that he come to London. He immediately responded to the Ambassador's summons.[66]

Lindbergh at once reported to Kennedy. In a long conversation with the Ambassador, he stressed the size and power of the *Luftwaffe*. He "felt certain" that Germany's air strength was greater than that of all other European countries combined, and that England and France did not have enough modern war planes for effective defense or counterattack. Kennedy asked Lindbergh to put his views in writing and on the following day Kennedy wired them to the State Department. Kennedy's wire transmitted the aviator's statement almost verbatim. His deletions are of interest though; he deleted lines like "it seems to me essential to avoid a general European war in the near future at almost any cost"; "I am convinced that it is wiser to permit Germany's eastward expansion than to throw England and France, unprepared, into war at this time." Only Lindbergh's strategic estimates and evaluations were passed on. They were grim enough, and led to the inevitable conclusion.[67]

That night Kennedy's secretary called the British Air Secretary, and advised that Lindbergh was in town and available for consultation. An appointment was quickly arranged.[68] In a later interview with Walter Winchell, Kennedy boasted that Lindbergh's information was made available to Chamberlain on Kennedy's expressed request.[69]

Lindbergh's comments reinforced the previous conclusions of

British leaders that Britain was much too unprepared to risk war;[70] they were a final factor in Chamberlain's decision to avoid war at all costs.[71] His effect on Kennedy was probably even greater. When Geoffrey Dawson, editor of the *Times,* stopped in on Kennedy on the morning of the twenty-third, he found Kennedy "very vocal and excited and full of strange oaths. He had had Lindbergh with him, (and) didn't see how we could go to war effectively." [72] Kennedy no doubt spoke in similar vein to others. An American journalist who served in London during the period told the author:

> *Kennedy kept peddling this Lindbergh story. Goering and his crowd had convinced Lindbergh they were so powerful, so he would go scare the Chamberlain people. Joe swallowed all of this and kept repeating it to Chamberlain and every other Englishman. You couldn't talk to Joe about this—he knew it all.*[73]

Lindbergh was not alone in his evaluation of the situation; others, including helicopter pioneer Igor Sikorsky, reached parallel conclusions.[74] Another celebrated early aviator, Grover Loening, wrote Kennedy that though he believed the Germans to be "bluffing like hell on the size of their air force," the *Luftwaffe* was no doubt large and effective.[75] Today, though, historians conclude that Lindbergh's evaluation was unrealistically bleak; that German aircraft production was nowhere near the volume that Lindbergh and other "knowledgeable men" posited at the time,[76] and that even what there was of the *Luftwaffe* was not well suited for an independent air offensive against Britain.[77] Scholar John E. Wood writes that

> *Hitler's* Luftwaffe *possessed neither the operational ability nor the strategic doctrine to attempt the widespread destruction of lives and industry that weighed so heavily on the minds of Britain's leaders.*[78]

According to him, the Munich conference and the resulting sacrifice of the Czech nation that followed closely on the heels of Lindbergh's visit to London "was in large part caused by dread of a form of attack that the potential enemy was not ready to undertake." [79]

At the time, the American Embassy's air experts doubted Lindbergh's evaluation. Many knowledgeable Britons were equally dubious. The brilliant but difficult anti-appeasing Vansittart and Hugh Dalton, the brilliant but difficult anti-appeasement Labour-party theoretician, agreed: "He had flown the Atlantic but what does he know about military air forces?" [80] J. L. Vachell, Britain's air attaché in Berlin, suspected that Lindbergh was unwittingly being used as a "medium for the dissemination of German propaganda," [81] and Sir John Slessor, Lindbergh's "contact" at Britain's air ministry, concluded that the American, although "absolutely honest," was "a striking example of the effect of German propaganda." [82] But Lindbergh's evaluation comported with other intelligence reaching the British and made a convenient rationale for the no-fight policy to which the Chamberlain circle had already irretrievably inclined on other than military bases. [83]

On the twenty-fourth, Kennedy called Hull on the phone and reported that Lindbergh had been called in by the British for consultations—not bothering to tell the Secretary the role that he had played in bringing Lindbergh's influence to bear—and to confirm that Hull had received the flier's report. [84] Also, he reported, there was a split in the British cabinet. Chamberlain, he said, stood for "peace at any price," but there was considerable opposition from within his own cabinet. [85] A second visit by Chamberlain to see Hitler, this time on September 22 at Godesberg, Germany, had not sufficed to clear the air; as Chamberlain had acceded to the crux of the Führer's prior demands, Hitler had cut the matter short: "I am terribly sorry, but after the events of the last few days, this plan is no longer of any use." There were then new demands, [86] and Chamberlain had returned to Britain downcast. Kennedy summarized the issue facing British leaders: "The question is peace or war." [87] On the twenty-sixth he reported that sentiment in England and in the cabinet was running against Chamberlain and the policy of appeasement. [88] No doubt largely through Kennedy's urgings, [89] the President issued a plea to world leaders to continue negotiations.

As September drew to a close, the Czechs turned a deaf ear to "final" terms and the English people prepared for war. A feeling of resignation was common; as Kennedy wrote, "If war comes they know they are going to get hell but they are now reconciled." [90] The hopes of the world for peace faded. Englishmen began digging trenches and evacuating their children from potential bombing targets. But these preparations were unnecessary; Neville Chamberlain saved the day.

Chamberlain spoke to the English people on the night of September twenty-seventh: "How horrible, fantastic, incredible that we should be digging trenches . . . here because of a quarrel in a faraway country between people of whom we know nothing. . . . If we have to fight it must be on larger issues than that. . . ." [91] The ambassadorial

circle was invited to attend a Parliament session on the afternoon of
the twenty-eighth. Chamberlain announced at the session that a
four-power conference—to be held at Munich—had been arranged.
There was still hope. Writes William L. Shirer:

> *The ancient chamber, the Mother of Parliaments, reacted with a*
> *mass hysteria without precedent in its long history. There was*
> *wild shouting and a wild throwing of order papers into the air*
> *and many were in tears and one voice was heard above the*
> *tumult which seemed to express the deep sentiments of all:*
> *"Thank God for the Prime Minister!"* [92]

Kennedy reported home "When the Prime Minister read out the
replies of Hitler and Mussolini, the cheers in the house from both sides
were terrific. Everybody feels tremendously relieved tonight." Kennedy himself hoped to get six hours' sleep that night, for the first time
in a week.[93] Roosevelt wired Chamberlain a brief message:

GOOD MAN, FRANKLIN D. ROOSEVELT [94]

Things were looking much better to Joe Kennedy, who must have
been warmed by a friendly note he himself had just received from the
President: "I want you to know that in these difficult days I am proud
of you." (Kennedy could not have known that the President had sent
precisely the same message to his Ambassadors in Paris, Berlin, and
Prague—all of the central cities of the crisis.)[95] Like almost everyone,
Kennedy too felt the sentiment his President had expressed to
Chamberlain. He told Halifax that he himself was entirely in sympathy
with and a warm admirer of everything the Prime Minister had done.[96]
Privately the thought occurred to him that the steps Chamberlain was
taking "may be the beginning of a new world policy which may mean
peace and prosperity once again." [97] With confidence and pride mixed
with braggadocio, Kennedy led Lindbergh to think that the Ambassador himself had had a large part in bringing about the Munich
conference.[98]

There was only one discordant note all day. When Kennedy left the
Parliament building after Chamberlain's exciting announcement, he
shared his cab with another diplomat. Jan Masaryk, the Czech
minister,[99] got in and they drove away. They sat quietly for awhile.
Then the Czech turned to the American. "I hope this does not mean
they are going to cut us up and sell us out." [100]

At Munich the following day the four European powers did just
that. By the terms of the "settlement," Germany was to have its

demands for the Sudetenland, the mountainous Czech border area that contained most of Czechoslovakia's German population, and most of its defenses. Czechoslovakia lost 86 percent of its chemicals; 80 percent of its cement, textiles, and lignite; 70 percent of its iron, steel, and electric power; two-thirds of its coal; and 40 percent of its timber.[101] Her entire communications system was irreparably disrupted. A prosperous and valuable ally in the fight against Hitler was left impotent to defend itself or to take any meaningful part in any war against the Reich. Germany promised to leave the rest of Czechoslovakia alone, and Britain and France made a meaningless sign of firmness to salve their own national self-concepts, by pledging to go to war for the now defenseless Czechoslovakia if Hitler broke his promise.[102] (Privately, Hitler sneered his realistic appraisal of the British and French guarantees as "worthless.")[103] Britain and France made clear to Czechoslovakia that if she wished to protest the "compromise," she would have to fight Hitler alone. Halifax's biographer writes that

> It was the dictators' hour, and although they masked with reasonable decorum both a sense of indecent triumph, and a contempt for the representatives of Western democracy, no such restraint was observed when the German leaders were alone, when Hitler derided the Prime Minister in obscene gutter language, and was said to have given a devastating imitation of his mannerisms and appearance.[104]

On his return to England, Chamberlain was acclaimed by the crowds. It was he, not the war faction, that represented the spirit of the country. By making concession after concession to Hitler's constantly increasing demands, and feigning acceptance of the unreasonable as if it were the reasonable, Chamberlain had secured for Great Britain what he called "peace with honour." The Anglican prays at evensong, "Give us peace in our time, O Lord," and Chamberlain told his countrymen, "I believe it is peace in our time." [105] The comment would come back to haunt him. Europe, though, was temporarily relieved—and Kennedy, elated. "Isn't it wonderful!" he exclaimed to Masaryk. "Now I can get to Palm Beach after all!" [106] It made little sense to Englishmen or to Joe Kennedy to go to war in 1938, as Kennedy privately put it, over a problem as insignificant as the Sudeten Germans.[107] Only Chamberlain's First Lord of the Admiralty, the war-minded Duff Cooper, resigned from the cabinet, and when Winston Churchill rose on the floor of Parliament to say "we have sustained a total, unmitigated defeat," he was hissed.[108] Kennedy thought the whole Parliament debate on the Munich Pact "singularly unimpressive." [109]

Hull congratulated his Ambassador for Kennedy's tireless efforts throughout the period (as well as several other ambassadors)[110] and Chamberlain told Kennedy that he had relied on the American for judgment and advice during the crisis more than on anyone else.[111] Kennedy felt pleased and gratified at such kind words.

Americans, by and large, were sharply critical of the Munich Pact. Churchill denounced it on a nationwide American hookup with great effect. Kennedy helped Halifax prepare a reply for the United States' radio, delivered shortly after, but the Foreign Secretary had considerably less effect on American reactions.

On a number of occasions, Kennedy defended the Munich Pact as having been a wise move for the Allies. He stressed the unpreparedness of Britain and France, which he believed had made Munich a preferable alternative to war in October, 1938.[112] Today it seems clear that war in October, 1938, was the alternative to the Munich agreement. There is also little doubt that it would have been better for the Allies had the war come then.[113]

Germany's military experts disagreed in their evaluations with their Führer, Lindbergh, and Chamberlain. They believed that a war in October, 1938, would have resulted in a quick defeat for the Reich. In 1938 Germany lacked the means to go to war effectively. Later, Field Marshal Fritz Erich von Manstein put it succinctly:

> If a war had broken out, neither our Western border nor our Polish frontier could really have been effectively defended by us, and there is no doubt whatsoever that had Czechoslovakia defended herself, we would have been held up by her fortifications, for we did not have the means to break through.[114]

"It is extremely difficult to believe," Shirer writes, "that the military chiefs in London and Paris did not know of the obvious weaknesses of the German Army and Air Force and of their inability to fight a two-front war." [115] By exaggerating the power of the enemy, Lindbergh was no doubt in part responsible for the demoralization of the British and French, and so encouraged them in their appeasement policies.

Instead of fighting a probable quick war in October, 1938, the West sacrificed one of their best allies and, with it, the key to all of central and southeast Europe.

The year that was gained, Kennedy and other appeasers later argued, gave Britain and France the time they needed to prepare for war—an argument not advanced at the time by those who sincerely thought they had made the war unnecessary. As late as December, 1950, Kennedy publicly supported this position, after scholars had already evaluated the time element more realistically. He still saw Munich as a purchase of "precious time"—"I applauded that purchase then; I would applaud it today." [116]

The year's time was to Germany's advantage, and—had Chamberlain really been thinking in such terms—the Allies should have realized that time would work against them. Because Germany was a totalitarian country, the Führer did not have to work by persuasion; the Reich was thus better able than the Allies to make use of the year. Chamberlain clearly appreciated Hitler's advantage, and there are indications that Joseph Kennedy understood it as well: Chamberlain pointed it out to him on September twenty-first; it was a central point in John Kennedy's *Why England Slept*; Joseph Kennedy almost said as much himself at the lend-lease hearings.[117] But the implications of the thought never seem to have struck home to him.

In that year of "precious time," Germany, reinforced by the riches of the Sudetenland, was able to strengthen her weaknesses. Britain and France, too, had time to build up their defenses. Between the Munich crisis and the outbreak of war a year later, Britain's armaments were greatly increased, in some areas outstripping German production. But at the same time, the Sudetenland's Skoda armaments plant, by then under German control, produced more arms than all the British armament plants combined. The gain of time, like the gain of territory and resources, was Hitler's, and he got it without losing a man.[118]

Kennedy said that the British and French needed the year to prepare, and in at least one respect he was right. They needed the year and, more important, the lessons of that year, to prepare themselves emotionally and spiritually.

Though Kennedy was all for the Munich Pact, he was never totally convinced that it meant a permanent peace and he was haunted by the thought that sooner or later war was inevitable.[119] After Chamberlain left for Munich, Kennedy told Halifax that it was legitimate to have good hopes for the Munich conference. But he recognized, Halifax wrote, "all the dangers and difficulties that still had to be surmounted." The situation, in Kennedy's view, "was one that had to be faced in a spirit of realism." [120] Nonetheless, the pact meant at least temporary peace, and when Ione Robinson asked Kennedy about the wisdom of a trip to Germany, Kennedy encouraged her to go.[121]

KENNEDY MUST HAVE BEEN EAGER TO PUBLICLY IDENTIFY HIMSELF with the spirit of appeasement. At the start of the crisis, in late August, he sought State Department permission to say at a dedication in honor of Bishop Samuel Seabury,

> *I should like to ask you all if you know of any dispute or controversy existing in the world which is worth the life of your son, or of anyone else's son? Perhaps I am not well informed of the terrifically vital forces underlying all this unrest in the world, but for the life of me I cannot see anything involved which could be remotely considered worth shedding blood for.*[122]

State Department staff members did not like the Chamberlainesque phrase,[123] largely, as Moffat put it, because "if there is one chance of avoiding war it is to make the Germans believe that other nations would take up arms against them." [124] Hull wired the Ambassador that he and the President had agreed that "under existing circumstances" it would be advisable to omit the paragraph.[125] Roosevelt was upset at Kennedy's slant, and paraphrased Kennedy's proposed text for Morgenthau as "I can't for the life of me understand why anybody would want to go to war to save the Czechs"—no doubt what Kennedy had meant[126]—and complained that "The young man needs his wrists slapped rather hard." [127]

In his first post-Munich speech, though, Kennedy succeeded in getting on record publicly in favor of the appeasement approach, and thus in identifying himself with Munich in the public eye.

At the annual Trafalgar Day dinner of Britain's Navy League, on October nineteenth, Kennedy dropped a bombshell. In the course of a rather routine speech on the need for an American Merchant Marine, he advanced what he called "a pet theory of my own." He commented briefly that "the democracies and dictators should cooperate for the common good, rather than emphasize self-apparent differences."

> *It has long been a theory of mine that it is unproductive for both the democratic and dictator countries to widen the division now existing between them by emphasizing their differences, which are now self-apparent. Instead of hammering away at what are regarded as irreconcilables, they could advantageously bend their energies toward solving their common problems by an attempt to re-establish good relations on a world basis.*

It is true that the democratic and dictator countries have important and fundamental divergencies of outlook, which in certain matters go deeper than politics. But there is simply no sense, common or otherwise, in letting these differences grow into unrelenting antagonisms. After all, we have to live together in the same world, whether we like it or not.[128]

In reporting the speech, the *New York Times* characterized it as "an excellent summary of the attitude repeatedly stated here by Prime Minister Neville Chamberlain and his cabinet colleagues."[129] It was widely at variance with Roosevelt's "Quarantine" speech of a year before, in which the President had called for the quarantining of the dictators. Diplomats the world over wondered whether the speech signaled a change in United States policy,[130] and Moffat and the Department's Adolf Berle prepared a Roosevelt radio address to undo any damage, which the President himself chose to point up considerably.[131]

Editorial reaction to Kennedy's speech was predictable. In London, the pro-Chamberlain *Times* wrote that the speech

should do much in many countries to foster the atmosphere in which the policy of the Munich declaration can work itself out towards its proper consummation . . . the final re-establishment of some better system of collective security for peace.[132]

In America, though, almost all editorial comment was opposed.[133] The *New York Herald Tribune*, commenting on British reaction, said "The British . . . take the utterances of our representatives too seriously. They are unfamiliar with the rhythm of brash public statement followed immediately by public denials."[134] The *Washington Post* observed ". . . even though inferentially, we see American diplomacy adapting itself to the Munich Agreement."[135] Both papers criticized the speech, but neither went so far as the *New York Post*:

for Mr. Kennedy to suggest that we put our stamp of approval on those policies; for him to propose that the United States make a friend of the man who boasts that he is out to destroy democracy, religion and all of the other principles which free Americans hold dear . . . that passes understanding.[136]

The problem, according to columnist Walter Lippmann, was essentially one of political ambassadors in general. As political ambassadors do not feel responsible to the State Department, they take liberties professional diplomats would not take. They forget they are agents and act as principals, to the embarrassment of their governments. Their comments, Lippmann wrote, should not be on policy matters.

> So Mrs. Kennedy should tell her husband that if the subject of their nine children and of the hole-in-one at Stoke Poges golf course is exhausted he can still talk about Alfred the Great, Shakespeare, Izaak Walton, the beauty of the English spring and the snows of yesterday.
>
> And the British, who follow this practice rigorously in their own diplomacy, will respect him all the more.[137]

Felix Frankfurter complained to Roosevelt about the speech,[138] and Colonel Frank Knox, internationally-oriented publisher of the *Chicago Daily News* spoke critically about it to Hull.[139] The Canadian Ambassador in Washington was undiplomatic enough to raise the matter with the Secretary of State, telling Hull that he was out of sympathy with "certain phrases" of the speech and "really could not understand the theory on which it was delivered." [140] Those unfriendly to Kennedy within the State Department were somewhat pleased that the speech had, in George Messersmith's words, "defeated any political ambitions which (Kennedy) may have had." [141]

From Harvard, Jack Kennedy wrote his father that the speech, "while it seemed to be unpopular with the Jews etc., was considered to be very good by everyone who wasn't bitterly anti-fascist . . . ," [142] and Kennedy himself attributed the intensity of the press attacks upon him to the influence of "internationalists," and particularly Jewish publishers and journalists.[143]

Hull was very upset over the effect of the speech. At mention of it, reported Moffat, "He loses his amiability and wishes that all ambassadors would forego all speeches." [144] Moffat himself had with apprehension passed the speech; in his diary for the day before the address, he recorded:

> Kennedy sent in a speech he is planning to make to the Navy League tomorrow night. He had spent ten days in preparing it and wanted us to vet it in one. A large part of it is an endorsement of the Chamberlain philosophy of government, but being expressly advanced as the Ambassador's personal views there was nothing to do but to pass it.[145]

Due to a press of business, Welles had approved the speech without reading it first, on the assumption that Hull would read it; Hull had approved it without thought, expecting that Welles would catch anything potentially dangerous.[146]

Moffat explained Hull's irritation in his diary: "the truth of the matter is that the Secretary dislikes calling down Kennedy and Bullitt as they have a way of appealing to the White House over his head." [147] That is undoubtedly part of what Lippmann had meant when he wrote that political ambassadors were not responsible to the State Department.[148] Because of Kennedy's access to Roosevelt, Hull apparently never gave him a thorough dressing-down; perhaps if he had done so, Kennedy might have become a more admirable diplomat.

As irritated as Hull was, Kennedy was equally irritated at the Department's reaction, and to Ambassador Phillips he "mentioned his annoyance at the Department on the occasion of his Trafalgar Day speech, which he said had been approved by the Department, yet after its delivery the press had been informed that no approval had been given." [149]

Kennedy's next speech, delivered a week later, began with the comment that "A man in public life had to be careful about what he says." He proceeded to say little at some length.[150] Where prepared speeches were concerned, it only took one incident for him to learn his lesson.

Soon afterwards, however, another incident came to light that again brought Kennedy considerable bad publicity. During the Czech crisis, a Paramount newsreel was prepared containing comments on the situation by Englishmen. It included statements by A. J. Cummings and Wickham Steed, two influential anti-appeasement journalists who denounced the foreign policy of the Chamberlain government in uncompromising terms. Out of fear that their comments might jeopardize negotiations with Germany, the British government spoke to Kennedy about having the Cummings and Steed clips removed from the film. They were removed. When the incident came to light in late November, Sir John Simon, Chamberlain's Chancellor of the Exchequer, explained to Parliament that the action had been necessary for the welfare of the nation. And it was not censorship, he said. They had simply brought the matter to Kennedy's attention, warning him of the possible repercussions the film might have at such a sensitive time. The Ambassador, said Simon, had "thought it right to communicate this warning to a member of the Hays organization . . . who in a sense of public duty and general interest decided to make certain excisions from the newsreel." The Chancellor then expressed his thanks to Kennedy. "I am glad to think that the Ambassador and ourselves were in complete accord." He was pleased that Kennedy "was good enough and thought it right to take action leading to the promotion of European peace." [151]

But the government's position, reasonable as it might have seemed, was not regarded sympathetically by England's liberal press. And American reaction was equally bad. The idea of the American Ambassador being involved in subtle forms of censorship abroad was distasteful to Americans.

Hays quickly denied that any communication had been received from his longtime friend,[152] but Kennedy made no attempt to duck the matter. He said that it was inaccurate to give the impression that he personally had taken any action that had caused the film to be changed. The government's request had simply been passed on to the Hays organization.[153] He later explained at greater length:

> *I only did what I would have done with any complaint that came to my office. . . . I referred the complaint to the Company manufacturing the product and it happened to be Paramount. I made no recommendation to Paramount to cut the scenes. I never had any conversations about it.*[154]

Kennedy was probably telling the truth. It is entirely possible that Paramount cut the film on its own accord, after receiving a complaint presented in a routine manner. It was not necessary for the Ambassador, Hays-intimate, and former Paramount consultant, to say too much. Simon's cockiness before Parliament was inappropriate; he was trying to hide behind Kennedy, who as Ambassador from a friendly nation was relatively immune from criticism in the English press. And while British editorial writers condemned the suppression of opposition opinion in outspoken terms, they treaded more lightly on Kennedy's role.[155]

American papers treated the Ambassador with somewhat less deference. Even more outspoken than the left wing[156] was the isolationist right. Said the *Chicago Daily Tribune:*

> *Our Ambassadors in London should be discouraged from playing the role of office boy of empire. Walter Hines Page got a tablet in Westminster Abbey to celebrate his success in bringing us into the war; one such tablet is enough.*[157]

It is likely that the newsreel incident brought much more bad publicity to Kennedy than was warranted under the circumstances, but it so offended Liberal and Labour party members that it irrevocably linked Kennedy with the appeasement-minded conservatives, and brought to light one of his errors as Ambassador: partisanship.

Good working relations and personal intimacy with the heads of state are excellent things for an Ambassador, whose job must be to obtain information. But diplomatic reserve also has a value—it protects the Ambassador and his country from embarrassing situations. Kennedy, capable of making himself very likeable at first meeting, was always able to establish a feeling of intimacy quickly. (Krock wrote that Kennedy uses "the personal equation.")[158] He was never known for that reserve that might be called "diplomatic." [159] Kennedy either carried intimacy too far or achieved it in a poor way for a diplomat, for with his intimacy came a personal interest in the political welfare of the Chamberlain government.

Kennedy permitted his partisanship for the Chamberlain conservatives to become widely known. Indeed, he flaunted it. To a reporter in Boston he commented that the Prime Minister's settlement of Anglo-Irish difficulties had "put Chamberlain's name at the head of British statesmen of the last three or four hundred years. . . . the man was touched with genius." [160] Churchill, Duff Cooper, Eden, and the Labourites, could not have approved of the comment.

The simple fact that the very popular American Ambassador was widely known to favor the then-present government made Chamberlain's followers more appealing to the English electorate. But besides this passive aid, Kennedy gave active aid to Chamberlain's political fortunes when he spoke in elated terms about the Prime Minister's Irish settlement. One of a variety of reasons why Kennedy had the story of the nuns' rescue from Barcelona released to the press, he later explained, was because he "wanted to depict Chamberlain and Halifax as human, good-hearted men, capable of taking an active interest in such a bona fide venture and give them credit for sending the warship after the poor women." [161] He helped Chamberlain when he endorsed the principles represented by the Prime Minister in his Trafalgar address; when he gave aid and encouragement to Chamberlain during the Munich crisis—aid that von Dirksen believed would be sufficient to break Chamberlain's opposition.[162] And the clips removed from the Paramount newsreel were bitter criticisms of the Chamberlain policies; opposition leaders suspected that they had been removed for partisan reasons.[163]

Because the Trafalgar speech was so partisan to Chamberlain, the opposition regarded it as an interference with British politics.[164] But they saw no sense in offending a powerful man and potential associate, and were naturally reluctant to attack Kennedy publicly. When the newsreel affair exploded the opposition became a little more daring. While trying to put the blame on Simon, Liberal spokesman Geoffrey Mander expressed amazement at finding "such an accommodating Ambassador." He referred to the affair as the "Kennedy incident." [165]

Kennedy had done what Lippmann had feared. He had staked his personal reputation as a prophet, and his usefulness as an Ambassador, on the destiny of one man and that man's policies.[166] (And it was, incidentally, the wrong man.) He had by his own will permanently associated himself with the ill-fated Chamberlain government and its policies. He had done what no professional diplomat would have done: he had become involved in English politics.

Kennedy compromised his position as representative of the United States by supporting Chamberlain; he did so because of a whole-hearted concurrence in the Chamberlain policies and a collection of beliefs and suppositions that he held in common with Chamberlain.

Kennedy believed that Chamberlain's action in the Irish settlement had proved to the world that Britain could be trusted in diplomatic dealings: "Now Mr. Chamberlain can go ahead with his policy of dealing with dictator nations with a reputation for fair dealing established." [167] The remark reveals a naiveté basic to Chamberlain's policy of appeasement. Kennedy apparently believed that Chamberlain had first to prove his fairness, before Germany, wronged so often by England in the past, could be expected to deal with him.

The same naiveté was exhibited again in the Trafalgar speech. Fundamental to the proposition that the democracies and dictatorships *should* work together for the common good, was the belief that they *could* work together—and Kennedy told Ione Robinson that he really believed they could.[168] Fundamental to that belief was the belief that Hitler was well within the bounds of conventional reason, and could be dealt with in approximately the same terms as any other statesman. This was the basic, fallacious, assumption of Chamberlain's policy of appeasement.

Eduard Beneš, Czech President during the Munich crisis, has described Kennedy's position as an essential entanglement in the Munich policy, an entanglement that carried with it a degree of responsibility.[169] There is much truth in Beneš' charge—Kennedy was, as Soviet Ambassador Ivan Maisky characterized him, "a trusty bulkwark of Chamberlain in all the unhappy vicissitudes of that unhappy business." [170] He consciously or unconsciously involved himself in the situation. He took it upon himself to invite Lindbergh, and to call Lindbergh's exaggerated report to the attention of the English leaders. He made suggestion after suggestion. He wanted to be associated in the decision-making, even if Hull did not want him to be. His close friendship with the members of the Chamberlain circle, his known concurrence with the views of the government in power, and his active public and private support of its policies, made it easy and perhaps not too unfair for Simon to have given some of the credit for the newsreel incident to Kennedy. Along with Simon and the other members of the Chamberlain government, Kennedy shared responsibility for the whole Munich blunder; the newsreel incident was a part of it.

Roosevelt too must share the blame for the Munich Pact. When he talked with Lindsay on September twentieth, Roosevelt spoke in an appreciative manner of Chamberlain's policy and efforts for peace. Indeed, wrote the Englishman, Roosevelt had said that he was afraid to express disapproval of Germany's actions, lest he encourage Czech resistance.[171] Later in September—largely at Kennedy's impetus[172]—he urged Hitler to hold back his armies until a conference could be arranged. He was relieved when Chamberlain brought about that conference, and after the conference was over, he sent the Prime Minister word—which he instructed Kennedy to deliver orally, rather than in writing—that "I fully share your hope and belief that there exists today the greatest opportunity in years for the establishment of a new order based on justice and on law." [173] Later, Roosevelt told Josephus Daniels that had he been in Chamberlain's shoes, he would have felt constrained to have taken the same course as Chamberlain had taken.[174]

Despite an apparent concurrence with Kennedy on the "big issue," Roosevelt was not pleased with his Ambassador's actions or the strength of Kennedy's views. After a talk with Roosevelt at the height of the crisis, Morgenthau recorded in his diary that the President had been "especially perturbed over Kennedy's apparent preference for appeasement." The President's explanation for Kennedy's attitude was inherent in the question that he posed to Morgenthau: "Who would have thought the English could take into camp a red-headed Irishman?" [175] Roosevelt regarded Chamberlain as "slippery," [176] and though he certainly did not oppose Chamberlain's policies at the time of the Munich crisis, he soon after veered to the Churchillian position.[177]

Roosevelt's interpretation of Kennedy's position, that he had been "taken into camp" by the British, was held by both liberal and isolationist commentators. Columnists Joseph Alsop and Robert Kintner, who were probably closer to Roosevelt than any other Washington newsmen and had several pipelines to inside information at the White House, reported on September nineteenth that Kennedy had become intensely Anglophilic—"Indeed, there are unfortunate signs that Kennedy is going the way of Page." They reported that he was one of the prize exhibits at Cliveden; that he was no longer popular at the White House; that he was a partisan of England and should be watched carefully.[178]

Right-wing isolationists were of the same opinion. Kennedy's more admirable statements lent currency to their suspicions that he was a propagandist for Britain. At a University of London dinner on May thirteenth Kennedy had contrasted the "spirit of tolerance and free inquiry" in the United States and Britain to the "regimented education" in dictatorship nations.[179] In the Bishop Seabury speech as finally delivered in September, he sharply condemned religious persecution.[180] Later, he publicly contrasted the American system with "Hegelian" systems,[181] and in December he referred to Hitler's latest persecution of the Jews as "the most terrible thing I have ever heard of." [182] To paranoiac isolationists like General Hugh Johnson and the editorial writers of the *Chicago Daily Tribune*, it could only have looked as if Kennedy was another Walter Hines Page preparing American public opinion for entry to war. The comments of liberal insiders Alsop and Kintner "confirmed" the suspicions of the right. To such men he must have appeared, as Hugh Johnson later charged, another British Ambassador to Washington.

In fact, Kennedy was at times too vigorous in defending Britain's interests. He criticized Morgenthau for playing "dirty ball" against the British in favor of the French,[183] and his correspondence on trade problems in 1939 occasionally hints at greater sympathy for the English position than for the American position.[184] But it is inaccurate to say that Kennedy had been "taken into camp" by the British where war and peace were concerned. Let us consider briefly the nature of the relationship between Kennedy and the leader of the English government.

Joseph Kennedy appeared very different from Neville Chamberlain. If Halifax was correct in calling Kennedy "so representative of modern America," Chamberlain was in the same sense equally representative of the English tradition. The English Prime Minister, himself the son of a British statesman, had a dignified stately air about him. Tall, lean, with graying hair, he had the look and bearing of a world leader. The restrained Englishman made quite a contrast to the gregarious self-made American businessman 20 years his junior.

The similarities of thought between the two men outweighed their more apparent differences in demeanor. Chamberlain's combination of social reform and business orthodoxy was by no means contradictory. Like Kennedy, he blended receptiveness to humanitarian appeal with a profound conservatism. The two shared a common origin and interest in commerce, and by 1938 both men had become slaves to their business mentalities. Churchill's characterization of the Prime Minister, "alert, businesslike, opinionated, and self-confident in a very high degree," [185] might have applied equally to the Ambassador.[186] Both men feared the future and especially war. They were ready to avoid war at almost any price, refusing to see (or to be concerned) that the price was Nazi domination of continental Europe, if not more.

Krock wrote that Chamberlain had early become attracted to Kennedy in an open way,[187] and one of Chamberlain's biographers wrote that Kennedy "at once enjoyed Mr. Chamberlain's confidence." [188] The affection was mutual. After hearing Chamberlain speak on the incipient Czech crisis in late March, just three weeks after his arrival in England, Kennedy wrote Baruch "I sat spell-bound in the diplomatic gallery and heard it all. It impressed me as a combination of high morals and politics such as I had never witnessed." [189] The Prime Minister struck the Ambassador as "a strong, decisive man with a realistic, practical mind, and evidently in full charge of the situation." [190] Little wonder that the two became fast friends and reliable allies. Kennedy described the relationship with characteristic color to friends: "I'm just like that with Chamberlain. Why Franklin himself isn't as confidential with me as the Prime Minister";[191] "If only they would listen to me in the White House the same way they do in Downing St." [192] Before the outbreak of war, Kennedy unsuccessfully sought the State Department's permission to sign his name to the foreword for a compilation of Chamberlain's speeches, *In Search of Peace*.[193] When Chamberlain died, Kennedy commented that he was "closer to Neville Chamberlain than I was to anybody else in England. The world will miss his sane counsel. He really gave his life that England might live." [194] Perhaps Kennedy was greatly influenced by the older man whose dignity and reserve were reminiscent of Kennedy's father, Pat. Many of the views that Kennedy reported as Chamberlain's he later expressed on his own behalf. But it was not that Kennedy had been "taken into camp." He had a great respect for Chamberlain founded on similarity of outlook, but was able to appraise the Englishman with some degree of realism. Being exposed to the views of the Prime Minister probably hastened the maturation of Kennedy's own ideas, but Chamberlain's effect was not more than that of a stimulant. Kennedy's support of Chamberlain's foreign policy was not the result of his being duped; rather, it followed naturally from their common fear of war.

Kennedy was no doubt speaking his fears when he told Chamberlain, Halifax, von Dirksen, and von Selzam that American intervention in a European war was inevitable. While he doubted that America had much stake in the war, he clearly understood that she had a stake in the peace. He knew that the desire he had expressed to Borah in April, to keep America clear of any involvement in war, was unrealistic if war were to come. But if the European situation could be quieted, no matter the price, there would be no war into which the United States might be drawn. His efforts to brighten the European picture were accordingly in the best interests, as he saw them, of the United States. He permitted himself to become entangled in the Munich policy partly because Munich was the policy of his friends Chamberlain and Halifax; partly because he enjoyed being in the thick of things and liked to be noticed there. But most important, he feared that if Chamberlain's efforts did not succeed, war would come and inevitably the United States would become an "associated power," associated in war. As he put it in December, 1938, "So long as efforts are made to keep the peace, America is naturally in a better position." [195]

Kennedy's work in support of Chamberlain's appeasement policy was consistent with his own goal: keep the United States out of war. That was his policy from the start of his career as Ambassador, and in at least one respect Kennedy's policy in 1938 was more sophisticated than the lack of policy represented at this time by Hull and Roosevelt. It was Kennedy who envisioned a positive role for the United States in keeping the peace, and who took such action as he could. Roosevelt and Hull were also interested in peace, but were reluctant to allow the United States to involve itself in efforts to insure the peace. It was

Kennedy the "isolationist" who wanted to "meddle in Europe's affairs"; Hull the "internationalist" who had a much more advanced concept of America's role in the world, wanted to sit out the crisis on the sidelines. Hull was willing, eager, at this time, to let world developments be shaped by other forces. History contains its paradoxes.

REFUGEES, TRADE, AND A HOLIDAY

KENNEDY FULFILLED HIS REPORTORIAL FUNCTION EXTREMELY well during the Munich crisis and his early ambassadorial period. His closeness with Halifax and Chamberlain had drawbacks, but gave him greater access to information on latest developments than a more restrained diplomat would have had. As a London reporter for the *New York Times* commented, Kennedy had the best contacts in the government of all the American Ambassadors since Walter Hines Page.[1] During a September twenty-sixth telephone call, Sumner Welles said to Kennedy "I can't tell you how admirably you have been keeping us informed. It couldn't be better." [2] Krock quoted an unnamed State Department official who had been in touch with all of Kennedy's reports—probably Welles—as having said that no diplomatic reports had ever been better prepared than Kennedy's, and that his wires had been invaluable in shaping American policy.[3] As we have seen, Kennedy performed his converse function, representing State Department policy, somewhat less adequately.

The job of Ambassador, though, is not all crisis work. Even during such times more routine work must be carried on. Particular demands on Kennedy's time were made by two somewhat less spectacular chores: negotiation of Hull's reciprocal trade agreement and efforts on behalf of Jewish refugees from Germany.

For Secretary of State Cordell Hull, freer trade was something of a mania, and the Trade Agreements Act of 1934 gave him the power to do something about it.[4] By the terms of the act, the Chief Executive was given power to cut tariffs at his discretion, in exchange for tariff reductions by other countries on United States products. A most-favored-nation agreement was not authorized; rather, trade agreements were to provide for favored products. If Denmark wanted the tariff on Danish cheese lowered, the President was empowered to lower tariffs on cheese, without special benefits for Danish cheese, in return for Danish reduction of tariffs on products that the United States wanted to sell abroad. By 1938, agreements had been reached with France, Brazil, Canada, Holland, and a dozen other countries. The net effect of the agreements was a general loosening of international trade and a beneficial increase in America's foreign trade, while retaining some protection for weak but potential American industries. A completed agreement with the United Kingdom, the United States' biggest customer nation, would carry the policy of the Trade Agreements Act very much further.

Kennedy's part was to participate in negotiations and help to consummate an agreement. Hull expected him to play a major role.[5] From the start it looked like an easy task to Baruch, who wrote Frank Kent that Kennedy would be "shot with luck"; the world economic situation would make consummation of the agreement relatively easy, "so you see our friend Joe will get a big medal because he is going to make another home run."[6] Kennedy himself was very optimistic that with sufficient opportunity he could hammer out a mutually acceptable agreement;[7] if he was thinking in parallel terms with Baruch, he was in for an unhappy surprise.

Protected industries in both countries were naturally not pleased with efforts to increase competition against them in their home territories. The plan had to be sold both at home and abroad. Kennedy became one of the leading salesmen in England. Soon after his arrival he addressed the annual dinner of the Association of British Chambers of Commerce. He reminded them of the benefits of freer trade and warned them of the need for economic cooperation. He urged the leading English businessmen to support a reciprocal trade treaty,[8] and he gave much the same advice to Americans. On July Fourth he addressed the American Society of London and said about international commerce, "we are finding, more and more, that nations cannot live to themselves with any more happiness or comfort than can individuals. . . . we cannot be prosperous in America if the rest of the world is suffering."[9]

As Kennedy approached the bargaining table, he sized up the situation thus:

> *Our bargaining position vis-à-vis Great Britain was an intrinsically weak one for British imports represented only about a fifth in dollar value of our exports to Great Britain. What leverage we possessed was less from the economics of the situation than from such political advantages as might accrue to the British from an Anglo-American accord.*[10]

Therefore, he privately urged on Chamberlain and other government leaders the positive political value of consummating a trade agreement; regardless of a posited minimal practical effect on trade between their countries, the psychological effect on international political developments would be great—"the more the impression could be created in Europe that the United Kingdom and the United States were getting together, the less would have to be spent on armaments,"[11] he told Chamberlain. The Prime Minister was impressed by these arguments to the point of commenting publicly in a similar vein himself.[12] Later, when negotiations with England bogged down, Kennedy tempted British leaders with a suggestion that he "anticipated that some trade agreement between America and Germany might shortly come on the tapis."[13]

An Anglo-American agreement with regard to the motion picture industry was to be an aspect of the reciprocal trade agreement, and even before he left the Maritime Commission, Kennedy had already spoken with Lindsay in Washington about this aspect of Anglo-American trade relations.[14] Because of Kennedy's intimate understanding of the problems of the movie business, Hull hoped that he would be in a good position to iron out difficult provisions of that agreement.[15] Kennedy himself handled that aspect of negotiations. At his suggestion, Arthur Houghton of the Hays office, who had accompanied Kennedy to London, remained there and was available for immediate consultation on developments,[16] and Kennedy was assisted by one of the embassy's more vigorous career men, W. W. Butterworth, who enjoyed tremendous respect in British government circles as "the live wire of the American Embassy."[17] Soon Hull determined that most other aspects of the agreement were to be worked out by British negotiators in Washington.

During Kennedy's term as Ambassador, he remained throughout a keen and persistent advocate on behalf of American movie interests, so much so as to give rise to questions as to his motives and to irritate many of those within the British Foreign Office bureaucracy.[18] In Washington, insiders like Farley and Morgenthau bantered about cutting jokes about Kennedy's preoccupation with serving Hollywood;[19] an American journalist who served in London during Kennedy's tenure told the author, "Everyone knew that Kennedy was on two missions in England: movies and liquor."[20]

Negotiations on the trade agreement went slowly, and in June the London *Times* reported that there was disappointment with the pace on both sides of the Atlantic.[21] Kennedy suspected that many of the British cabinet members were cold to the idea of the agreement in general, and in October he reported that opposition in the cabinet to the agreement was growing. Only Chamberlain was really for it, he believed.[22] And he was seriously disturbed by the department's modus operandi, and frankly put out by the failure of the State Department to keep him adequately posted, much less, to rely on himself more fully in the negotiations. As he saw it, the situation required

> *a type of trading beyond the capacity of the normal bureaucrat. It seemed that my experience in business as well as the position that I had made for myself in England fitted me particularly for the task of negotiation. I knew the men in the Cabinet who had to be prevailed upon and the influences that might be brought to bear, whereas Washington was dealing only with subordinates who were controlled by London.[23]*

On the eighteenth he wired that he had gone to negotiate but found that the English had heard the arguments with which he had been supplied by the State Department. The United States was pushing England too hard with its demands, and he was not being consulted enough:

> *Far be it for me to make any suggestions as to how those handling the trade agreement should avail themselves of the Ambassador's services, but it does seem to me that if they really want a trade agreement it might be well to have the man on the spot find out just how much further we could go without kicking the thing over.*

Wires from American negotiators had the flavor of ultimatums, and Kennedy criticized the State Department for lack of tact. He closed with "I am assuming naturally that you want to get this deal through if it is at all possible and my efforts are being directed to prevent a return ultimatum being sent back to you tomorrow."

Hull sent a cool reply the same day, and did not budge an inch on his position,[24] nor take up the Ambassador's offer of consultative services.[25] Two days later, Kennedy delivered his Trafalgar speech, after which Moffat concluded that Hull's displeasure at Kennedy was a mixture of irritations: irritation over the speech and irritation over Kennedy's participation in the trade agreement negotiations.[26]

Finally Hull decided in early November that further negotiations would be fruitless, and that he was ready to sign the draft agreement as it then stood. Kennedy called the Secretary to say that he felt certain that he, Kennedy, could extract further concessions from

Chamberlain—implicitly, that is, if the Secretary would "let him take the ball." While Hull feigned interest on the phone, he brushed off Kennedy with an "I'll let you know," and thereafter shot off a wire to the effect that he would go ahead with the deal as it then stood:[27]

> In reaching this decision, I have been influenced by your excellent telegraphic reports, particularly your comments about opposition to the agreement within the British cabinet. Your reports and assistance have been of great value and I am deeply grateful to you.[28]

"I thought I knew better," it seemed to Kennedy, "but there was nothing further that could be done." [29]

The agreement was well received on both sides of the Atlantic. The *Manchester Guardian* soberly commented:

> The Anglo-American trade agreement has been a desperately long time under negotiation. But now that it has come it is a good agreement, not so sweeping as one might have hoped, but considering the obstacles that had to be overcome from our protected interests, from the Dominions, and from depressed American industries, better than was at one time feared.[30]

In applauding the treaty on November 29, Kennedy called it "the rebirth of common sense in international economy and the first steps toward economic disarmament." [31] The following day, at Manchester, the birthplace of the free-trade concept, he waxed more eloquent. The treaty, he said, represented "one of the greatest contributions to world stability ever made." He contrasted the democratic system of trade represented by the agreement with the "regimented" trade of totalitarian countries. He hoped that the treaty would influence "other countries" to move away from the policy of economic self-sufficiency. They should follow the path of England and America:

> We know that an exchange of goods between countries, as between individuals, means better products, lower prices, and a higher standard of living. Therefore we shun the doctrine of self-sufficiency and seek to trade with other nations.

The Manchester speech was interrupted many times with shouts of "Hear, hear!" and the *Guardian* praised it and its author.[32]

Kennedy himself was one of the many who enjoyed the fruits of the reciprocal trade program; one of the first products affected (not the result of Kennedy's participation) was imported liquor, on which the American tariff was halved, thus reducing the price, but not the profit-per-bottle on Scotch sold in the United States. It was a great boon to the pocketbook of British distillers and those such as Kennedy who sold their wares in the United States.

THE PROBLEMS RELATED TO THE GERMAN REFUGEES ARE OF MORE general interest. As world sympathy for the plight of the German Jews developed, an international committee was formed, largely at Roosevelt's impetus, to consider the possibilities of evacuating Germany's Jews en masse. The committee, made up of members from Britain, the United States, and other interested nations, hoped to receive some cooperation from the German government, and planned negotiations with German officials. Kennedy served as ostensible vice-chairman of the conference that formally established the committee in July, 1938.[33] With strong financial and moral backing from the United States government, the group set up its headquarters at Evian, France, on the shores of Lake Geneva. Washington lawyer George Rublee served as the active head of the "Evian Committee," as it soon became known, and Myron C. Taylor, an executive from United States Steel, served as chairman of the American delegation to the international body. Rublee kept in close contact with the State Department, and wires between him and the State Department were frequently transmitted by the London Embassy.

The work of the Evian Committee was difficult; it required not only the cooperation of Germany, but that of prospective "recipient" nations. While Germany was reluctant to cooperate, Poland began to pressure the committee to evacuate Poland's Jews, lest Poland be "forced" to adopt anti-Semitic policies paralleling Germany's.[34] Recipient nations were either unwilling to consider the thought of being recipient nations, or were unenthusiastic, insisting that only well-financed agriculturalist Jews be sent, and no urban intellectuals or "business types." [35] Poland was unwilling to accept even Jews of Polish nationality returning from Germany.[36] When British diplomats suggested that Britain be permitted to turn over the British immigration quota into the United States to Jewish refugees from Germany, Welles explained that it would be legislatively impossible and, further, that "it would be most distasteful to Jewish leaders in America who fear any open and avowed increase of Jewish immigration because it would have the effect of increasing anti-Semitic feeling in America." [37] Kennedy was of the same mind, and explained to Halifax that the

Evian mission created "a very delicate problem" in the United States; anti-Semitic feelings might easily become activated and take shape in Ku Klux Klan-type activities.[38]

Britain's stance on the work of the Evian Committee was vital to its success, both because of Hitler's supposed concern for the British attitude and also because of Britain's influence over so many "undeveloped" colonial and protectorate territories, the logical recipients of emigrating German Jews. Only one of the possible recipient lands was Palestine, a British protectorate and the sought-after homeland of the Jews. Kennedy, in a formal way, promised Evian agents every assistance with the British.[39]

By October, 1938, Rublee was ready to make use of Kennedy's assistance and failed to get the cooperation that he had expected. He believed that it was vital for the British Empire to make a real contribution to the work of the Evian Committee; that the British Foreign Office was decidedly unsympathetic; and that the British had to be persuaded to cooperate. He complained to Welles:

> *This can only be done through Ambassador Kennedy. . . . My impression is that Ambassador Kennedy is not disposed to take a strong line. He feels that our undertaking is hopeless. He does not want to go out on it because he has other matters he considers more important.*[40]

At the time, Kennedy was in fact tied up with negotiations on the Reciprocal Trade Treaty, a matter that he perhaps thought more important or pressing,[41] and when Taylor tried to get to him about the German refugees, Kennedy repeatedly declined to see him, making rude explanations to the extent that he was "busily engaged." [42] His attitude was no doubt in part affected by his low regard for Taylor, whom he openly belittled to Halifax,[43] the influential Lord Bearsted,[44] and no doubt others.

Welles said he would try to prod the British himself, and would take the matter up with Ambassador Lindsay in Washington.[45]

The conversation between Welles and Rublee may have had some effect on Kennedy. Three days later he called Macdonald. Rumors were circulating that Britain was about to end all Jewish immigration into Palestine, and the State Department had been flooded with telegrams of protest. In his account of his conversation with the American Ambassador, Macdonald wrote that Kennedy "had been asked to bring these messages to my notice, and that he was therefore doing this informally. That was all." Macdonald assured him that the rumors were unfounded, and Kennedy said that he would try to get Americans to "hold their horses." [46]

Then in the following days Kennedy appeared to become extremely active on behalf of the refugees, making daily headlines. On October 15, and again on October 25, the papers reported that Kennedy had visited Macdonald to discuss the Palestine situation.[47] In the middle of November, after completion of the trade agreement, he apparently devoted more time to the problem and his actions paid off—at least in increased press copy. Chamberlain and Halifax had been afraid to say or do anything about the German Jews that might prompt war with Germany.[48] Any attention drawn to the Jews could only hurt the possibilities for maintaining peace. But finally Chamberlain did speak out: He said that the presence and persecution of the Jews in Germany threatened world peace, and so resettlement was advisable. The story was told on November 15 on page one of the *New York Times*, under a "Kennedy active" lead. According to the *Times*, Kennedy had been responsible for persuading Chamberlain to speak out, and had visited Chamberlain on the eleventh and had spent most of the thirteenth with Macdonald, and had been back again to see Chamberlain on the fourteenth. "It is known Mr. Kennedy talked earnestly of the need for action by Britain and all nations of the British Commonwealth," said the *Times*.[49] The State Department learned all about it when the newspaper arrived.[50]

The following day the *Times* reported that a plan for resettlement had been quickly drawn up, the result of a meeting between Chamberlain, Kennedy, Halifax, and Macdonald. The scheme, they explained, envisioned total emigration, to be executed by Britain, the United States, and other interested nations.[51] The way it was described, it seemed to be the Evian proposal. After reading the newspaper, Moffat noted in his diary, "There seems no doubt that Mr. Kennedy is negotiating on his own with the British government, but he has never so much as reported a word to the President, the Secretary, or Mr. Rublee." [52] On the seventeenth, Kennedy spent much of the morning with Macdonald discussing the plan, according to the *New York Times*.[53] That day Ambassador Lindsay called on Welles to protest, in the diplomatic way that diplomats protest, "American press reports about a plan which Ambassador Kennedy is said to be working out with England with regard to the Jews. I regretted this," Lindsay told Welles, "as it would only lead the American public to expect

more than could probably be done." Welles told the Briton openly
that Kennedy had been given no instructions with regard to his
reported activities, nor had he reported any conversations he had had
with the British on the subject.[54] That night Moffat wrote in his diary:

> *We are still in the dark as to what Kennedy is doing in London
> on refugees. Mr. Taylor is so upset that he gladly welcomed the
> President's invitation to return to London. . . . Not only have the
> papers been full of an alleged "Kennedy plan" but they have
> even gone further and announced that Mr. Kennedy would
> substitute for Mr. Myron Taylor at the meeting of the officers of
> the Intergovernmental Committee.*[55]

Roosevelt and Hull did not hesitate to tell reporters that they knew
nothing of the by then much acclaimed "Kennedy Plan"; according to
one journalist, "Hull came as near to being tart as he ever does in his
comments on Kennedy's reported activities." [56]

Roosevelt could only have believed that his Ambassador was
consciously publicity seeking, perhaps in a continued effort to further
Presidential ambitions. Kennedy's Trafalgar speech of the previous
month had brought him ill publicity and the favorable publicity on the
"Kennedy Plan" was just what the Ambassador needed to "right"
himself. FDR's suspicions were in no way allayed by *Life's* assertion
that "if his plan for settling the German Jews, already widely known as
the 'Kennedy Plan,' succeeds, it will add new luster to a reputation
which may well carry Joseph Patrick Kennedy into the White
House." [57] Kennedy was given an indirect rebuke when the Administration pointedly announced that Taylor was the government's
spokesman on the problem of Jewish refugees,[58] a matter noted by
Britain's Ambassador in Washington.[59]

All the publicity on the Kennedy Plan was not favorable. *The
Nation* blasted what they called "the Kennedy-Chamberlain Axis" in a
vindictive article in their November 26 issue. They wrote that
Chamberlain had opposed letting refugees impair the improvement in
Anglo-German relations, and that Kennedy had supported Chamber-
lain's position. Kennedy, they wrote, had consistently demonstrated
his "slightly grim determination to collaborate with the British Prime
Minister." They insisted that Kennedy had had to be sharply prodded
by the State Department before pressuring Chamberlain to help the
Jews.[60] The author has seen no documentary evidence of any such
prodding by the State Department, but the initial reactions of
Kennedy to the Evian Committee, and the initial reactions of Hull and

Roosevelt to the Kennedy Plan—lead one to suspect that *The Nation's* source was accurate. Kennedy was not interested in doing anything that might threaten the peace; indeed, another of his reasons for releasing the story of the rescue of the nuns from Barcelona was that "I wanted to emphasize that the Jews from Germany and Austria were not the only refugees in the world." [61] Further, it was only after Rublee's complaint about him to Welles that Kennedy even attempted to get into the headlines. Given an opportunity to deny the magazine's charge at a press conference, Roosevelt skirted a request for comment with a facetious remark about the existence of *The Nation.*[62]

Items like *The Nation's* led Kennedy to complain to Ione Robinson that his efforts were not getting the right sort of publicity. He told her that he was working his head off trying to help Hitler's victims, and he resented the attitude of the American press concerning his activities.[63]

Good, bad, or indifferent, the publicity had a dramatically adverse effect in the diplomatic world. Moffat, who in many ways admired Kennedy, took exception to his "inordinate pushing of personal publicity." "I doubt if he has been anything but helpful in pushing the British on the refugee matter, yet the whole tenor of the articles from London, which are apparently inspired ('planted' by or on behalf of Kennedy), gives him the entire credit of accomplishment and has infuriated the friends of George Rublee, Myron Taylor, and others, to the point where they can scarcely be civil." [64] On the other side of the Atlantic, one British diplomat who was personally close to Kennedy told the author, "I resented the publicity because it wasn't publicity for America, it was publicity for himself. Among his motives in anything he did was himself and advancement of himself." [65]

The author scanned the State Department files and the Foreign Office document books for indications as to the substance of Kennedy's position on the matter of refugees in mid-November, 1938, at the zenith of the publicity on the Kennedy Plan, and found only one relevant document, relating a Kennedy-Halifax interview of November 16. Kennedy had told Halifax that increased persecution of Jews in Germany was creating resentment in America towards Britain's appeasement policies. He agreed with Halifax as to the unfairness of such reaction. When the Foreign Secretary told him that England was then examining the possibility of finding some location where resettlement of the German Jews could be introduced (a matter which the British had been discussing for months with Rublee),

Mr. Kennedy said that the psychological effect of such a lead by

*Great Britain would be of immense value and that personally he
would like to see us going to the United States Government with
an offer of land and financial assistance and asking them to what
extent they were prepared to support the effort.*

Kennedy thought that private sources in America might well contribute 100 or 200 million dollars to support the effort.[66] Halifax reported the substance of his conversation with Kennedy to the cabinet.

Such other involvement as Kennedy might have had at the time of the proclamation of the Kennedy Plan was apparently not recorded in the documents. One high-ranking British diplomat involved in the discussions could not recall for the author that Kennedy had had any involvement in the negotiations whatsoever.[67]

Rublee, however, continued working less spectacularly. Reminiscing in 1951, Rublee said that Kennedy "did not seem very interested and never gave me any real support or assistance." [68] Kennedy was not alone, though.

*I soon found that there was not much interest in British
government circles or generally in the diplomatic corps in my
work. . . . I gathered that President Roosevelt was not seriously
interested himself. . . .[69] I felt that the lack of active support
made my chances of success very difficult. . . . I think the
Ambassador, Joseph Kennedy, thought that my mission was not
to be taken seriously because it was impossible for it to succeed.[70]*

If Kennedy did think that, his suspicions were not unwarranted. Ribbentrop was cold to the Rublee Committee, and German embassies were told that Germany had to reject on principle any collaboration with other countries on "an internal German problem." The German Foreign Minister told the British Ambassador in Berlin that cooperation with the Evian Committee was out of the question.[71] After Ambassador Wilson spoke to Baron Ernst von Weizsäcker, a high-ranking official at the German Foreign Office, about an informal visit by Rublee, Ribbentrop's reaction was that the "visit is out of the question." [72] In December, Ribbentrop explicitly instructed von Dirksen to "please maintain absolute reserve in every respect vis-à-vis the Rublee Committee." [73]

One exposed to the representatives of Ribbentrop's Foreign Office could not have been hopeful for the success of the Evian Committee; if Kennedy concluded that Rublee's goal was impossible, his conclusion was a reasonable one considering Ribbentrop's manifested attitude.

Goering, however, was much closer to Hitler than Ribbentrop, and

A late nineteenth-century photo
shows Patrick J. Kennedy,
ward boss of "Noodle Island,"
with his future in-law,
Mayor John F. "Honey Fitz"
Fitzgerald, on horseback
vacationing in North Carolina.
Privately, Pat characterized
Honey as "insufferable."

Patrick J. Kennedy

The Boston schoolboy with the
best baseball batting average
was awarded the John F.
Fitzgerald Cup, presented
(of course) by Honey. One of
the winners: Joseph P. Kennedy,
captain of the Boston Latin
baseball team, 1907.

The Harvard graduat

Good ballplayer or no, his honor, the Mayor, had expected
something better.

The nation's youngest bank president, age 25.

At work at the Columbia Trust Company.

Movie moguls: Kennedy and Jesse Lasky, 1924.

Vacationing movie-mogul and wife, en route to a European vacation, 1927.

The conservative Boston Catholic and New-Deal liberal James
M. Landis, son of Protestant missionaries, first met as members
of the SEC in 1934, and forged a lifelong friendship.

"Bad Company!" is how most of the above would have regarded
most of the above. From left: Secretary of the Treasury Henry
Morgenthau, Jr., Kennedy, Federal Relief Administrator
Harry Hopkins, Budget Director Dan Bell, Secretary of the
Interior Harold Ickes, Roosevelt's Congressional-liaison man
Charles West, brain truster Rex Tugwell, and Admiral
C. J. Peoples. The group had just conferred with Roosevelt
on the problems of the federal relief program.

Kennedy photos with FDR are relatively rare. Here they are shown with Supreme Court Justice Stanley Reed, who has just administered the oath of office to the new Ambassador to the Court of St. James's.

One Irish-American congratulates another Irish-American on his wonderful appointment. The one: Alfred E. Smith.

En route to present his credentials to the King, Kennedy is accompanied by Lt. Col. Raymond E. Lee, then military attaché; Captain Russell Willson, naval attaché; Chargé Herschel Johnson; and Sir Sidney Clive, Marshall of the Diplomatic Corps.

". . . quite a journey from East Boston."

With G. B. S.

With Joachim von Ribbentrop.

Kennedy leaves the Foreign Office after one of his many
well-publicized visits at the time of the Munich crisis.
"I go sometimes only to read the newspapers," he told the
King. The King laughed.

". . . there remained in our memory the procession of the
children of Ambassador Kennedy," Pope Paul VI recalls of
the coronation of Pius XII.

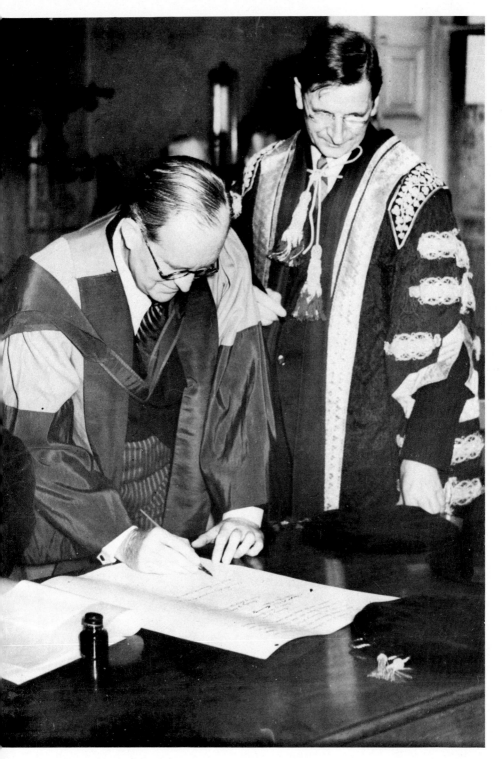

The Irish George Washington, Eamon DeValera, personally
presented Kennedy with the honorary degree of the
National University, Dublin.

Neville Chamberlain, the "umbrella man."

". . . all that stood between Hitler and the establishment of German hegemony in Europe under his dictatorship was one indomitable Englishman. . . ."

Unlikely assemblage: Governor Herbert Lehman, Lord Halifax,
Archbishop Spellman, New York political leader Newbold
Morris, Kennedy, Lady Halifax, Mrs. Lehman, Wendell
Willkie, Roosevelt confidant Frank Walker and wife,
and Kathleen Kennedy, gathered for mass at St. Patrick's
Cathedral in honor of the British peoples.

he favored cooperating with the Rublee Committee. Indeed, he demanded that Jewish emigration be promoted. Emigration, he believed, would accelerate "the Aryanization of the economy," and might stimulate Germany's export trade.[74] In January, 1939, he completed negotiations with the committee.[75] An agreement provided for the evacuation of virtually all of Germany's Jews in five years, with some money allotted to them.[76] The outbreak of the war prevented the terms of the agreement from ever being carried out; perhaps had war not come when it did, the plan might have been successful.

Years later Rublee recalled the reactions of the London diplomatic circle when they learned of his success with the Germans:

> They could hardly believe it and the attitude toward me was entirely changed. Ambassador Kennedy had returned from a winter vacation in the United States. He called me up and in an entirely new tone expressed great surprise, "How could it have happened? Why hadn't they done something like this before if they were willing to do such things?" He thought it was very extraordinary.[77]

Rublee doubted that anti-Semitism in high places cropped up as an obstacle to his work.[78] As for Kennedy himself, one high-ranking Briton who had participated in the negotiations told the author "Kennedy was not anti-Semitic." He paused and then continued, "Nor, for that matter was he pro-Semitic, except when it suited his purposes. I imagine there was a bit of the cynic in Joe." [79]

BEFORE RUBLEE'S AGREEMENT WITH GERMANY HAD BEEN REACHED, Kennedy returned home for a winter vacation. On November 29 it was announced that Kennedy had been given permission to come home for Christmas.[80] Welles told the press that the visit had no official significance,[81] and Roosevelt said it was a holiday, not a summons.[82] He declined to discuss the Paramount incident, which had just recently come to light.[83] In liberal circles, though, the rumor persisted that Kennedy was to be hauled on the carpet for his partisanship to the Chamberlain government,[84] and Farley told Morgenthau that Roosevelt was "terribly peeved with Joe. . . . I think when Joe comes back that that will probably be the beginning of the end." [85]

Kennedy was not optimistic about the European situation. Munich had not been followed by a calm, as had been hoped, but by Polish and Hungarian bites off the carcass of Czechoslovakia, an active German press campaign against Britain, intensified persecution of the German, Austrian, and Sudeten Jews, and presentation of Italian demands for French territory. Chamberlain explained the adverse turn, in part, to "the realization by Hitler that he had not had a great success at Munich, and that the gratitude of the German people for the avoidance of war had been bestowed, not on their Führer, but on the British Prime Minister." [86] Most people, though, began to suspect that the appeasers had been on the wrong track. Mahatma Gandhi, not known to be a warmonger, said "if ever there could be a justifiable war in the name of humanity, a war against Germany—to prevent the wanton persecution of a whole race—would be completely justified." Oswald Pirow, leader of South Africa's pro-Nazi "New Order party," prophesied that war would come in the spring.

Kennedy, a great one for psychological effects, publicly took issue with Pirow, but he expressed no more than doubts that European war was necessarily imminent[87]—which is hardly a cheery prophecy. In his last public statement before departing, at the Plymouth Chamber of Commerce on December 6, Kennedy acknowledged that "things are in bad shape," but he warned against the psychological effect of exaggerating the world's trouble. "We are making things worse for ourselves by adopting a defeatist attitude," he pointed out, adding that "the surest road to defeat is resignation to defeat." Perhaps Kennedy gave some courage to others when he boldly declared, "I am one of those who dares to hope we shall be able to solve the difficulties of the present." [88]

When Kennedy arrived in New York he appeared "obviously pessimistic" to reporters. He spoke frankly: "I truly think that nothing has been accomplished in the way of appeasement. But we must keep trying for peace or we shall have only two alternatives—and both are very bad: first—economic chaos, and second—war." [89] Several times he said that as a matter of strategy and policy, his country's position in the world would "be so much better if there is peace in Europe." He made his own position clear: "I am pro-peace. I pray, hope, and work for peace." Whatever were to happen, he said, the United States should steer clear of the European situation.[90] And just in case the decision of war or peace should be taken away from the United States, it should build a stronger army and navy.[91]

Kennedy's vacation-time conference in Washington with the President was probably cold. Roosevelt was not at all pleased with his

Ambassador, and Kennedy realized that much of the press criticism of him was coming from sources much too close to the President.[92] Kennedy had also noticed a tendency on the part of Roosevelt and the State Department to bypass him on certain matters, and he resented that as well.[93] He spoke to Roosevelt about these matters, but apparently neither wanted a showdown, and little came of their conversation.[94] Farley's prophecy of the beginning of the end was as yet premature. The *New York Times* report of the visit said Kennedy had told Roosevelt that he feared that the possibility of war in Europe in a few months was very great.[95]

After his Washington conferences,[96] Kennedy left for a long Palm Beach vacation with his son Jack.[97] In January he interrupted his holiday to go to Washington to speak for rearmament before a private hearing of the House and Senate Committees on Military Affairs. Press rumors as to the substance of his testimony ranged from ludicrous to fairly accurate.[98] All agreed that Kennedy and Bullitt, who testified the same day, had described the situation in gloomy terms.[99] The London *Times* correctly reported that Kennedy discussed Lindbergh's study of Germany's air power, and that he spoke about a speedup in the European armaments race.[100] The *New York Times* reported that Kennedy had predicted war in the spring,[101] and as he made like prediction privately,[102] there is no reason to doubt that he made it to the committee. He did unquestionably urge that the United States rearm, so as to be in a position to meet any eventuality.

Many had the false suspicion that the unexpected appearances of Kennedy and Bullitt before the hearing were a grandstand play by the Administration for support for a rearmament program that was really aimed at battling domestic relief problems. Both men "rushed up from Florida," the *New York Times* said, and conservative Senators who suspected that rearmament was a blind for unabashed pump-priming, pictured themselves as unimpressed by the testimony.[103] Missouri's Senator Bennett Champ Clark said he did not think anything they had said was very vital,[104] and Congressman Edward Cox of Georgia attacked their presence at the hearing.[105]

After testifying, Kennedy returned to Palm Beach. He booked passage back to his post for February 23 and hoped for a long rest. Henry Ehrlich, Washington correspondent for the *Boston Herald*, reported that Kennedy's Palm Beach home was "a virtual publicity bureau." Kennedy's house guests included influential commentators Walter Winchell and Boake Carter. Ehrlich's conclusion was that

Kennedy was considering his Presidential possibilities.[106] Ehrlich was not alone in his conclusion. The Ambassador was acting like a candidate.

Curiously, Kennedy cut short his vacation in early February, for reasons that may never become clear. Perhaps in response to increased European tensions, the British wanted their American ally on hand, and in early February, Foreign Office staff members began to stress to chargé Herschel Johnson that they wanted Kennedy back; "the Prime Minister was not urging Mr. Kennedy to do anything inconvenient—he was merely looking forward to his early return." [107] Kennedy, who hoped to prolong his visit, sent Halifax a message so cryptic that even the Foreign Office was in the dark as to its meaning: "Everything going fine on this side. Do not discuss anything over here." [108] Nonetheless, the British kept emanating the word that they wanted Kennedy back at his post, and finally Roosevelt, either in response to British requests,[109] or for reasons of his own,[110] called Kennedy in Palm Beach to urge his earlier departure.[111] When the *Queen Mary* sailed on February 9, Kennedy was on it.[112] To Breck Long it looked as if Kennedy had been "called very suddenly from his vacation in Florida and dispatched on the first boat to his post," which Long took to be some vague indication of the Roosevelt-Kennedy friction.[113] Hull had his misgivings about Kennedy's return to London, but aside from letting them be known inside the Department, he did no more than cross his fingers.[114]

The rift between Roosevelt and his Ambassador became more widely known at this time, both at home and in London. When Wisconsin Progressive Robert La Follette called for Kennedy's resignation, Carter rose to the defense. Carter was the kind of friend with whom one needs no enemies. He reported that "Roosevelt has sold out his Ambassador, lock, stock, and barrel." When Kennedy had first arrived in London, Carter wrote, he had told Chamberlain there would be no help from America if England got into war—"Thus, contrary to feeding Mr. Roosevelt's resolution to meddle in Europe, Kennedy, month after month, has bucked both the State Department and Mr. Roosevelt." Carter said that when Kennedy had come home last December, he had intended to tell Roosevelt to quit making a sucker out of him. He had not done so because friends had told Kennedy that Roosevelt would talk circles around him and charm him out of his mood, and so Kennedy had decided against a showdown. Carter was probably parroting the Ambassador when he wrote—

which, of course, does not make his statements necessarily more accurate. Though Roosevelt was much more internationally minded than his Ambassador, it was Kennedy who had been "meddling in Europe," against the wishes of the President and the State Department, and who by actions and words had encouraged British diplomats to expect American help in the event of difficulties. The valid phrase in Carter's article was that "Kennedy, month after month, has bucked both the State Department and Mr. Roosevelt." Kennedy's house guest closed his story with the assertion that Kennedy had returned to his post with a "vastly different frame of mind," and with the intention of staying at the Court of St. James's as long as possible. "He feels that he can serve America, not Mr. Roosevelt, better by sticking, than in any other job." That way, Carter explained, Kennedy would thwart the appointment of a puppet.[115]

Harry Henry, the London correspondent for the *Boston Globe* reported four days after Carter's story that the Roosevelt-Kennedy rift was well-known in informed London circles. Henry observed that the major part of United States negotiations in Europe were being conducted by Bullitt.[116] When asked to comment on the rift, Kennedy should have denied it, but instead replied "no comment to make." [117]

Why Roosevelt kept Kennedy as Ambassador is a question that will probably never be answered authoritatively. As early as November, 1938, Moffat had noted that Kennedy "must be handled with kid gloves; in fact, many people feel that he is merely looking for an opportunity to get out with a resounding attack on the administration." [118] Perhaps Roosevelt feared a showdown that would promote such an attack. Or, perhaps pure politics was uppermost in the President's mind. It is likely that Roosevelt was already thinking about a third term, and was afraid to recall his popular Ambassador for fear of pushing Kennedy and the Ambassador's fans into camp with the President's opponents. A campaign for an unprecedented third term would not be an easy one, and it would look very bad for Roosevelt if his Ambassador endorsed the Republican candidate, or if he endorsed a Democratic potential other than Roosevelt—or if the mercurial Ambassador himself ran against his chief. Ickes suspected that Roosevelt might have to turn to Kennedy for a Vice-Presidential running mate for 1940. In the event of a Garner-Farley team-up, Roosevelt might have to find a Catholic running mate to counter Farley's effect with Catholic voters, and Ambassador Kennedy seemed the likeliest choice to Ickes. Kennedy, Ickes noted, would be able to command great conservative support, and his campaign would be well financed.[119] It is possible, as Ickes suggests, that Roosevelt too thought along these lines.

It was reported that during the holiday Roosevelt had offered to make Kennedy Secretary of Commerce, but that Kennedy had turned it down.[120] Apparently there was no way to get Kennedy out of foreign affairs but to fire him. Whatever the President's motives, it must have seemed safer to Roosevelt to leave Kennedy in London than to fire him, and merely circumvent the nation's embassy at the Court of St. James's.

THE
INTERCRISIS PERIOD

KENNEDY'S THOUGHTS ON THE WORLD SITUATION RECRYS-
tallized in late 1938, and reinforced his conviction that the world had
to avoid war. While he was definitely opposed to United States entry
into any war, he could see the great likelihood of eventual United
States participation if Europe were to go to war. Even if his country
were not drawn in, any war would necessitate liquidation of British
investments in the United States, and that might have a dangerously
upsetting effect on the American economy regardless of the war's
outcome. If Britain were to lose, or the Nazis were to attain Eurasian
domination, the situation would obviously be perilous for his country.
It did not make sense to Kennedy to take these grave risks in any sort
of a crusade; if the people of Germany wanted a Nazi dictatorship, he
told Ione Robinson, the United States had no right to interfere.[1]

Kennedy saw the resolution of the dilemma in adherence to a policy
of containment and the creation of a state of coexistence. He realized
that the success of his theory required Western military preparedness
coupled with "the courageous determination of the democracies to
attend to their own knitting." [2] Otherwise, war was the only ultimate
possibility, bringing death and disaster to too many.

Back in England, Kennedy briefly became more optimistic than he
had been at home. In their first visit after Kennedy's return, Halifax
found that the Ambassador "was in good form and made even more
generous use than usual of the American vernacular to emphasize his
points." [3] To Kennedy's amazement, Rublee's mission to the Germans
had been a success, and British rearmament was underway. At first he
thought that England was looking stronger, and that Germany would
not attack.[4] On February 17, he told Hull that the chances for a
European explosion were small.[5] The following week he wired that
England regarded herself as much better prepared than she had been
at Munich and that her attitude at future round-table conferences
would be much stiffer than it had been.[6] At a meeting in March with
Bullitt and Bonnett, Kennedy did not appear pessimistic and told his

listeners that he believed Britain was fully prepared to fight.[7]
Nonetheless, Kennedy was haunted by gnawing fears that "The long
term outlook for England, whichever way you look at it, seems to me
exceedingly dark." [8]

Kennedy was kept busy in London with developments on the
Palestine situation. American Zionists were not pleased with the
rumored plans that Britain had for markedly reducing Jewish immigration into Palestine, and on February 24, Rabbi Stephen Wise and
Louis Lipsky, leading American Zionists, visited Kennedy to make
their positions known.[9] Three days later, Kennedy visited Halifax, who
briefed the Ambassador on Britain's "tentative suggestions" on
Palestine, suggestions which roughly paralleled the Zionists' fears. It
was rumored (no doubt correctly, though quickly denied) that
Kennedy told Halifax that the British plans would not be favorably
received by the American public.[10] After the conference, Kennedy
wired the State Department that he judged the British were "giving
the Arabs the better of it"; his wire shows an interest in hearing more
on the Jewish side: he had asked Dr. Wise to come by for reactions.[11]
When the Arab National League of Boston denounced Kennedy as a
"Zionist Charlie McCarthy," [12] Kennedy also conferred with Arab
spokesman Aly Maher Pasha, the Egyptian Premier,[13] and, later, with
Chaim Weizmann,[14] The Israeli George Washington.

Britain's reduction of Jewish immigration into Palestine, finally
promulgated in a White Paper issued in May, 1939, did not signify
simple unreceptivity to Jewish arguments, but rather an awareness of
competing promises that the British had made to Palestine's Arab
nationals. To the extent that it was politically influenced, it was
influenced by a desire not to push oil-rich Near Eastern Arab nations
into irrevocable alliances with Hitler. While Kennedy may have
thought that the Arabs were "getting the better of it," he found
himself very much in sympathy with the broad terms of the white
paper.[15] When it became his duty as Ambassador to present Halifax
with the mildly unfavorable reaction of the United States government,
Halifax wrote Lindsay:

> The Ambassador was concerned to point out how restrained was
> the reaction of his Government to the policy declared by His
> Majesty's Government, and expressed the view that we could
> be very well satisfied with the situation. It was very much
> more favourable in regard to this matter than he could have
> hoped.[16]

EARLY IN 1939, POPE PIUS XI DIED. KENNEDY CORRECTLY PREDICTED that his successor would be the papal Secretary of State, Cardinal Eugenio Pacelli,[17] who was ultimately chosen and took the designation Pius XII. Kennedy had met and entertained the new Pope when the Churchman had visited the United States in 1936.[18] Kennedy, first the lion-tamer of Wall Street as Chairman of the SEC and then the nation's social leader as Ambassador to the Court of St. James's, badly wanted to represent his country at the papal coronation, thus securing his status as the nation's number-one Catholic layman. Through Welles, he lobbied for the honor within the State Department,[19] and he called the President himself to request the designation.[20] Though some such as Moffat thought that the President should send a Protestant to the ceremony,[21] the President acceded to Kennedy's pleas. Excited, Rose grabbed the nearest piece of paper, a scrap of brown wrapping material, and scribbled the good news in a note to her girlhood friend Marie Greene.[22] The Kennedy family was off to Rome for the ceremonies.

The papal coronation and the new Pope made profound impact on Kennedy, who wrote Moffat:

The impression that the Coronation of the Pope and my private audience had upon me is not susceptible of description. Besides being a most saintly man, he has an extensive knowledge of world conditions. He is not pro-one country or anti-another. He is just pro-Christian. If the world hasn't gone too far to be influenced by a great and good man, this is the man.[23]

So too, the Kennedys at the coronation were long remembered in the minds of high Churchmen, including Cardinal Giovanni Battista Montini, now Pope Paul VI, who recently recalled:

It happened that the Ambassador of the United States to London, Mr. Kennedy, father of the dead President, was charged by his Government to represent the United States at the ceremony; and indeed he arrived punctually but bringing with him five children,[24] *who proceeded to occupy places that were reserved for the members of the official Missions, with the result that the arrangement of places was altered; and when there arrived the Italian Minister of Foreign Affairs, Count Ciano, the son-in-law of Mussolini, he found his seat in the Gallery of the official Missions was occupied and he began to protest, threatening to leave the Basilica and to desert the ceremony. The situation was immediately resolved; but there remained in our memory the procession of the children of Ambassador Kennedy.*[25]

When Ambassador Phillips commented to Boston's Cardinal O'Connell on the size of the Kennedy contingent, and the inconveniences necessitated by providing tickets for them all, His Eminence asked rhetorically, "Oh, will Joe ever learn!" [26]

After the ceremony, Kennedy was favored with an audience with the Pope, with whom he shared his opinions on the best way to bring about formal diplomatic recognition of the Vatican by the United States: his advice was that His Holiness had best get the American Church hierarchy in line behind recognition, lest they undercut the proposition for fear that their own power might be diminished.[27] Then the Kennedy children were ushered in, weighted down by what their proud father described as "countless packages of rosaries and holy things" for the Pontiff's blessings.[28] The Pope rose and selected as a gift for each, a rosary from a table on the side. Teddy, aged seven, told the New York *Herald-Tribune*, "He gave me the first Rosary beads from the table before he gave my sister (Patricia) any." [29] The Pope then gave Teddy his first communion, the first American child so honored. Later Rose would tell countless audiences on the hustings, "I thought that with such a start he would become a priest or maybe a Bishop, but then one night he met a beautiful blonde and that was the end of that." [30] At the time the "future bishop" told the press that he was not frightened at all. "He patted my hand and told me I was a smart little fellow." [31] Edward M. Kennedy's first press conference was a success.

The visit was not just a pleasure trip. Kennedy also spent two and a half hours with Mussolini's daughter, Countess Edda Ciano, wife of the Secretary of State. Ambassador Phillips noted the substance of the talk in his diary: Kennedy

> referred to the fact that Ambassadors these days were mere messenger boys, that the sole responsibility for world peace lay in the hands of Foreign Ministers,[32] and that here in Italy that responsibility was in the hands of a boy of thirty-five or thirty-six years of age. This was going some when he was talking to the boy's wife. However, from all appearances Edda did not seem to mind and rather enjoyed the conversation.[33]

Kennedy was unimpressed with Count Ciano, and wired Washington that Ciano had

> spent most of his time rushing girls into the corner for conversation and at the dinner he could not talk seriously for five minutes for fear that the two or three girls, who were invited in

*order to get him to come, might get out of sight. . . . I came
away with the belief that we would accomplish much more by
sending a dozen beautiful chorus girls to Rome than a flock of
diplomats and a fleet of airplanes.*[34]

His attitude was no holier-than-thou pose, explains one who worked
closely with him in London: "He was sophisticated about that; he had
a lot of girls—some in London—but those silly Italian flirta-
tions. . . ."[35] Kennedy's ultimate opinion of Ciano as the most
"pompous ass" he had ever met[36] was perhaps influenced in part by
vague rumors he had heard through the grapevine that Ciano had
reacted childishly about something—something to do with breaches of
protocol incidental to the papal coronation.[37]

Kennedy reported home that Roosevelt's influence in Italy was very
great, and that he impressed the Italians favorably:

*The President's speeches drive them absolutely crazy. My Italian
friends tell me that every time the President says anything,
nobody in the Cabinet or Government in Rome is fit to talk with
for the rest of the day.*[38]

Things looked so good and bright. Throughout the spring of 1938,
there were rumblings of difficulties within the remnant Czechoslovakian state, in which Germany was interesting itself, but these were
distant and vague. No one in the Chamberlain circle anticipated that
the world was in for another Czech crisis. London's communist *Daily
Worker* predicted in early March, 1939, that Germany would absorb
the rest of Czechoslovakia in the immediate future,[39] but "responsible" people had to agree with Neville Chamberlain, who told
Parliament on March 10 that Europe was "settling down"; Chamberlain was about to turn his attentions to disarmament. Kennedy, as we
have seen, was equally bright, and his optimism must have been
bolstered by the influence that he noted Roosevelt enjoyed in Italy.
Then it struck.[40] On March 14–15, the "nation" of Slovakia proclaimed its independence from Czechoslovakia; Czech leaders in
Berlin succumbed to Hitler's ruthless intimidation, and in the early
morning hours of March 15, signed a "treaty" placing Czechoslovakia
under German "protection." "Honoring" the "treaty," German tanks
began to roll. Hitler's orders were that they were to proceed on the
assumption that no resistance of substance was to be anticipated. By
the evening of March 15, they arrived in Prague. It was all over before
anyone knew what had happened. Kennedy rushed back to London.

Neville Chamberlain rose on the floor of Commons on March 15 to make his apologies for the Führer. He denied that aggression had been involved. Further, Slovakian independence had put an end to the state whose frontiers Britain had guaranteed at Munich; the commitments of the Munich Pact were therefore terminated. How could Britain guarantee a state which had ceased to exist? Neville Chamberlain proved Adolf Hitler right.

Joseph Kennedy was sympathetic to Britain's stance, if unsatisfied by the rationale; he explained to Halifax on his return:

> *American public opinion, like all other, was profoundly shocked, and it was very important that it should be protected, as far as might be, from jumping to entirely wrong conclusions. . . . The truth, however, as he saw it, was that nothing whatever could have prevented these recent events in Czecho-Slovakia except the decision to make war.*[41]

There was no talk of Kennedy's conviction that Britain was fully prepared to fight, nor of his policy of containment. As for the future, he had no inkling. "Where do we go from here?" he asked Chamberlain's close advisor Sir Samuel Hoare.[42] There was no answer.

In the following two days, the Briton on the street reacted angrily to his government's obvious subterfuge. Virtually all of those world leaders that had sympathized with Chamberlain at Munich learned rude lessons in mid-March, 1939. In a matter of a couple of days, his closest associates taught the Prime Minister, and when he spoke in Birmingham on March 17, his attitude was completely changed. He reproached Hitler for breach of faith and expressed his own indignation. Implicitly answering his own questions, he asked, "Is this the last attack upon a small State or is it to be followed by others? Is this, in effect, a step in the direction of an attempt to dominate the world by force?"[43]

Delivering the speech involved tremendous personal disappointment for the Prime Minister, because it meant acknowledgment that his faith in Hitler, faith that he had maintained long after Halifax and the Foreign Office had seen through the Führer,[44] had been misplaced. The fallacy of appeasement was made apparent by the subjugation of Czechoslovakia: Hitler's previous aggressiveness had not simply been an adherence to the principles of national self-determination; it had not been based on demands that should or could have been reasonably appeased. His actions, rather, had been part of a scheme that few European statesmen would consciously have furthered. Almost all of those aware of the European situation agreed that the Czechoslovakian error could not be repeated.

Only a few statesmen still thought that European peace was more important than stopping Hitler. Joseph Kennedy was one of them; he no longer toyed with concepts of "containment." Halifax reported Kennedy's reaction to Chamberlain's awakening speech of the seventeenth: "He thought the Prime Minister's speech last night was first-rate, but that to him it did definitely carry a corroboration that we should resist further German aggression." [45] Kennedy had observed, wrote Halifax, that public opinion in America was moving faster in the direction that Roosevelt was leading it—to firmness against the dictators—than he might have expected. Indeed, the Ambassador "had found American public opinion on the whole in advance of his own position." [46]

Halifax's position was "in advance" of Chamberlain's and by the twenty-fourth the Foreign Secretary's position had crystallized. Kennedy met with Halifax that afternoon and reported that the Foreign Secretary "felt that the inevitability of war sooner or later should be met right now." Kennedy's comments were apparently designed to dissuade Halifax: he had no confidence in the reliability of Britain's eastern allies:

> I told Halifax that it seemed to me that, when England and France got down to the last stages of a working agreement with Poland and possibly Rumania and Russia, in the event of acts of aggression by Hitler against them, it would become quite obvious that the assurances given might not be satisfactory to both France and England and they would find it necessary to wash their hands of the whole of Southeastern Europe. Halifax said he did not believe that was the case.[47]

Obviously, Kennedy was not eager to have firm steps taken to resist Germany's aggression, and his comments on the unreliability of all concerned may have helped convince British leaders to let the crisis pass without fighting.

Kennedy addressed the London Press Club that night and warned that there was great danger of war. He declined to elaborate, however; the situation was such that those not officially charged to speak, he said, "should keep their mouths shut." [48] Soon after, Kennedy saw U.S. Ambassador to Russia, Joseph Davies, who recorded in his diary that Kennedy was pessimistic.[49] He began to fear that Hitler had locked himself into a domestic political-economic situation that would force war on an unwilling Hitler and an unwilling world. "I'm just as convinced that [Hitler] doesn't want to fight as anybody else is," he told Hull, "but I'm not convinced as to how we can save his own situation for his own people. . . . [Hitler] has no money and he can't change all those people who are engaged in war-time activities into peace-time activities without having a terrific problem. It would be just like us if we didn't have any money to pay a deficit." [50]

Despite early hesitancies, in the months that followed, Kennedy supported the British government's moves to stiffen resistance to the dictators.

Chamberlain told Commons on March 31 that Britain would defend Poland—Hitler's posited next arena of aggression—against any attack, freely volunteering a commitment to defend the largely indefensible Poland, when he had refused to defend a highly defendable Czechoslovakia the previous September. (His resolution on that promise would shortly become clear.) After the speech, Cadogan records in his diary:

> *Halifax and I went back to F.O.–he to see Maisky (the Soviet Ambassador) and I to see Joe Kennedy. Latter very tiresome: I gave him declaration and he said it would be regarded in America as "subterfuge." I retorted rather hotly, and he promised to do his best with his beastly newsmen.* [51]

Kennedy himself reviewed those of Britain's press messages on the speech that were beamed at America,[52] and told Halifax that Roosevelt had thought the speech excellent.[53] On April 7, Mussolini's valiants "conquered" Albania. Britain prepared a guarantee of Greek independence against Italian aggression, and Kennedy advised Halifax that the declaration would be valued in the United States.[54] Chamberlain spoke in Commons on April 13, guaranteeing the independence of both Greece and Rumania, after which the *New York Times* reported that the Ambassador had congratulated Chamberlain for his assurances.[55] He told Halifax that the speech would help to dispel any belief that England put any value on Mussolini's word.[56] Kennedy himself apparently never put too much stock in the Duce's utterances. Even after his speech of the thirteenth, though, Chamberlain unfortunately still had some faith in the Italian's promises.[57] On the seventeenth Kennedy observed of the Englishman, "He has failed more in the past week than he has in the past year. He walks like an old man and yesterday talked like one." [58]

AFTER THE CRISIS, THERE WERE NO SIGNIFICANT DEVELOPMENTS until the late summer. Kennedy busied himself with negotiations on an Anglo-American barter deal, his many speaking engagements, and promoting a royal tour of the United States.

Confronted with a tense world situation in the spring of 1938, the United States began to worry about possible shortages of strategic materials. Perhaps even more central to American concerns was the fact that the United States was burdened down with a high level of surplus wheat and cotton.[59] Baruch, a nominal South Carolinian, claimed credit for the idea that if the United States could barter its surplus wheat and cotton for vital strategic resources, rubber and tin, America would obviously emerge much better off.[60] Hull let British representatives understand that he himself was not enthusiastic about the idea,[61] perhaps for theoretical reasons, but the decision was made to go forward, and on Moffat's initiative,[62] Kennedy was given the task of opening discussions.[63] Kennedy was given numerous suggestions and guidelines, but was left considerable discretion.[64]

The problem of the American wheat surplus was all well and good. Even more "strategic" to Kennedy was the problem of the American cotton surplus, in which powerful South Carolina Senator James Byrnes and his constituent Baruch, took great interest.[65] Baruch was a little sore at Kennedy over an imagined slight of the previous fall;[66] Kennedy could restore good relations with him and solidify relations with the influential Byrnes if he could "pull things off" and alleviate part of the American South's cotton surplus problem. He took a vigorous interest in the proposed barter, and began forcefully pressing the British to consider a deal.

To the British the proposal made no sense whatsoever. They had no pressing need for cotton, and none at all for wheat; could only antagonize cotton and wheat producing Commonwealth nations by importing American wheat and cotton; did not have ready supplies of either rubber or tin; did not want to undertake difficult dealings with the International Rubber Regulations Committee, that parceled out quotas for world rubber production; and did not care to spend limited foreign-exchange capital to purchase rubber or tin to barter for unwanted cotton or wheat.[67] The whole idea was distasteful to the British Treasury Department, the Board of Trade, and London's commodities markets.[68] Some sized up the barter proposal as an American "political stunt." [69] Given the British attitude, it was not an easy task for Kennedy to accomplish, and he wired the State

Department that he found little enthusiasm for the proposition anywhere.[70]

Kennedy got the British to the conference table as he had on the Reciprocal Trade Treaty, by urging peripheral political arguments: economic considerations aside, consummation of a barter at such a time would have significant effect on American opinion as to the closeness of British-American relations, which might favorably affect then-pending discussions in the American Congress on repeal or modification of the American Neutrality Act. Britain badly wanted the Neutrality Act altered in a way that might benefit Britain should war come with Germany, and Kennedy's arguments struck a responsive chord. Repeatedly, he told the British that the President took a personal interest in the success of the negotiations,[71] and that for the sake of "larger issues," the British should "clinch matters quickly on broad lines." [72] Lindsay was little impressed; he doubted that completion of the barter agreement would have any substantial effect on Congress or the Neutrality Act, and felt that "the nature of our sacrifices would never be appreciated and that the resulting gratitude would be incommensurate." [73] Both he and Halifax suspected that Kennedy "has been exerting some high pressure salesmanship." [74] At the Foreign Office, though, the only concern was the effect on Anglo-American relations of the prosecution or abandonment of an attempt to reach some kind of an agreement, the implications of which, while possibly minimal, were nonetheless clear.[75] In any event, an obstructionist attitude would certainly have some adverse repercussions,[76] if only with the friendly Ambassador Kennedy. Negotiations were opened. Many of the details of the negotiations were handled by Butterworth, but only after Kennedy dragged the British, kicking and screaming, to the conference table, proving that his intimacy with and influence upon the British heads of state had some value to his country and to his friends in South Carolina. Herbert Feis at the State Department, though not generally a fan of the Ambassador, wrote Butterworth that everyone from the President down was pleased that Kennedy had been able to get the British to at least entertain serious discussions.[77]

The British took pains from the start not to raise American hopes too high, and spoke in terms of taking perhaps 500,000 bales of cotton.[78] They were not at all interested in wheat. Kennedy expressed disappointment at the exclusion of wheat and at the limited amount of cotton, stressing the effect "on certain vital sections of the American Senate whose support he considers vital, if the isolationist campaign on the Neutrality bill is to be defeated." [79] The British, however, gently resisted what they regarded as Kennedy's "excessive pressure," and "all this extreme and seemingly unnecessary hurry." [80] Within the American Department at the Foreign Office, rumor and the degree and vigor of the Ambassador's stance gave rise to suspicions that Kennedy himself had a personal financial interest in the success of the barter.[81] They held firm to their original proposition for 500,000 bales of cotton, and by mid-June, consummation of a cotton-for-rubber agreement was about to fall into place. Kennedy acknowledged himself to be very pleased to Halifax, but kept pushing for more:

> On grounds of general policy, however, particularly connected with the Neutrality position, he urged me to do my best to get the Treasury and the Board of Trade to agree to some moderate expansion of the figures. He was, as always, very insistent, explaining all the time that he would not have tried to press for any more if it were not for the great advantage to our common cause that would certainly accrue if we were able to meet him. I asked him what exactly he wished me to suggest. . . . To this his reply was that he had originally pressed that we should take [one] million bales, but that, if we could meet him to the extent of another 150,000, in addition to the 500,000 on which we were disposed to agree, making 650,000 in all, he could represent this as a great concession and its political effect would be valuable. According to Mr. Kennedy, the United States government had made one or two concessions in the course of the negotiations which were of help to us, and he very much hoped that we could stretch our consciences and our purses so far as to meet his suggested addition.[82]

The request was brought to the British cabinet, which determined to go up to 600,000 bales of cotton. Kennedy was to be told that the upward revision "had been obtained in response to Mr. Kennedy's personal intervention." [83] Then, Kennedy began to press hard for American advantage as to terms, relative valuations of cotton and rubber, and the like,[84] all to the irritation of the British, who had never liked the idea from the start.

When the difficult negotiations were ultimately consummated,[85] many Americans, not realizing what Kennedy had been up against, were disappointed. Hull, though, graciously wired the Ambassador, "I wish to express my admiration of the skill with which you conducted this negotiation and to thank you for your great effort in the matter." [86]

⸴ Kennedy told the press that the deal represented a savings to the United States of 20 percent in the price of rubber—"a joy to us." "It hasn't been a bed of roses." [87] Privately, Kennedy realized that he had accomplished a tremendous piece of work, and that he was riding the crest of the wave. "Walt, I ought to retire now," he told Butterworth. Butterworth did not respond.[88]

THAT SPRING KENNEDY MADE SPEECHES AT VARIOUS UNIVERSITIES AND picked up honorary degrees. First, in April at the University of Edinburgh he was made an honorary Doctor of Laws. He gave the ceremony a hopeful note: "Perhaps never in history had nations been so bitter, for so long a time, without coming to open conflict." That was the most hopeful aspect of the whole situation. As war was the work of men, it was not inevitable. There was plenty of evidence to show that those on whom the final decision rested were fully aware of the consequences that would follow in the event of war, affecting the foundations of civilization itself.[89]

On May 17, he was honored at Manchester and spoke again of the need for academic freedom.[90] The following day the University of Liverpool honored him. He delivered a significant address, reflective of a rather progressive attitude about the world and its ills that was unfortunately unrealistic at the moment.

> *I dare to hope that we shall be spared the calamity of war. I find encouragement in the fact that the majority of our ills, both internal and external, spring from one cause—our failure to secure a better standard of living for the earth's people. That is a matter of economics; being a matter of economics, it is—in my opinion—capable of treatment. . . . Today we have everything that is needed to provide a decent standard of living for all. It is purely a question of exploiting the resources with which we have been endowed and assuring a just distribution of the proceeds. . . . our difficulties . . . are not the result of the penury of nature; . . . they are the result of human carelessness, human short-sightedness, human greed.[91]*

The *Times* had applauded Kennedy's Trafalgar speech the previous October, and called this the Ambassador's "latest addition to the number of his wise, humane, and sincere speeches." They wrote that

Kennedy "gives encouragement without speaking smooth things and prophesying deceits." [92] The thoughts Kennedy had expressed were good ones, but history has shown that they were out of place where Nazi aggression was concerned.

On May 26, Kennedy traveled by train to Bristol to receive an honorary from its university, accompanied by Churchill, a university officer.[93] Before the ceremony a large group of merry students kidnapped the Ambassador, and in a mock ceremony presented him with "the Degree of Fahrenheit," which a student spokesman explained represented the increased warmth between the United States and Great Britain.[94] A few days later Cambridge University conferred its prestigious Doctor of Laws on the Ambassador.

During the summer of 1939, the British royal family toured the United States. The idea of the tour was originally Kennedy's, and he was one of its most enthusiastic boosters. As early as April, 1938, Kennedy had discussed the idea of a tour of the United States with the King and Queen, and they were pleased with the proposal.[95] Roosevelt was eager to have them come, perhaps thinking, as Eleanor Roosevelt later asserted, that it would create a bond of friendship between the two countries.[96] Kennedy looked forward to working on the arrangements with the royal family, and sought State Department approval to accompany the King and Queen as personal guide and companion on the trip,[97] with the concomitant privilege of basking in the warmth of the royal couple and their spectacular publicity. He had to have expected that the State Department would politely reject his kind offer, but he did not expect that he would be completely cut out of the arrangement-making. Roosevelt himself deprived the Ambassador of that simple pleasure. Kennedy later noted:

> In August I had called on the King with a sealed letter from President Roosevelt containing an invitation to visit the United States. The King had opened the letter and read it out to me and, since the idea had originated with me and from my suggestion, I was rather annoyed at having to deliver the message without knowing its contents.[98]

In the months that followed, it was made clear to Kennedy that he was not to mix in the tour arrangements,[99] and Kennedy later complained that

> the actual details of the visit were not only arranged without reference to our Embassy but actually kept from us so that our knowledge of them, to our great embarrassment, had to be derived through the British Foreign Office.[100]

It was particularly painful for Kennedy to be unable to cope with the daily questions from the Foreign Office or the King's secretary about royal tour details. Finally Kennedy wired Hull:

> *I suppose if the President wanted me to be aware of any discussion he is having he would notify me, but if I were not advised by the Foreign Office, I would know nothing about the King's trip whatsoever. I hate to admit knowing nothing about it because that would seriously interfere, I imagine, with my prestige and contacts here.*
>
> *I suppose nothing can be done about this and that I can continue being a dummy and carry on the best I can.*[101]

In a cool reply, Hull explained that the details were being worked out in Washington simply because it was more practical to do it that way.[102] A few days later, the President wrote Kennedy:

> *I am enclosing another letter to the King. Will you be good enough to see that he gets it?*
>
> *I feel sure you will understand that the preliminary discussions about the proposed visit of their majesties next year is only in the preliminary stage and that, therefore, I am conducting it personally.*[103]

The attached letter to the King made it clear that Roosevelt was keeping a firm grip on the arrangements in Washington, which he did not let loose. Kennedy bitterly resented this bypassing of himself and his embassy. Many more such situations were to come.

While Kennedy was kept out of the arrangement-making, he remained an enthusiastic booster of the tour. On June 8, 1939, he wrote approvingly in the United States number of the London *Times* about the forthcoming royal visit to his country.[104] Soon after he described the meeting of the King and the President: "The meeting was simple and friendly, like the relations which prevail between the two people. The President held out his hand. The King grasped it. It was perhaps the most important handclasp of modern times." [105] When the royal family returned to England, Kennedy was on the greeting platform, and no one sported a bigger smile than he did.[106] The Ambassador told the American Society of London that the royal family had "made more friends for their nation than any other two people in history." [107]

The royal family did make friends for their nation. The tour unquestionably helped to strengthen Anglo-American contact and friendship, and it was resented by most of those who were more consistently concerned about keeping the United States aloof from England's expected war. Philosopher-historian Will Durant and no doubt many others viewed the royal tour as part of a campaign to prepare the United States for entry into the threatening war,[108] and whether or not it was part of some campaign, it did help to prepare the country for just that.

Kennedy's reasons for promoting a venture with such a natural effect can only be surmised. His personal affection for the King and Queen certainly played a very big part in shaping his attitude towards the royal tour. Perhaps he still thought that an apparent closeness between the United States and Britain would impress the dictators and make them less belligerent.[109] That closeness, whether "apparent" or real, would haunt Kennedy after England went to war.

Kennedy was sniped at constantly during this period by individuals and journals of all political stripes. On February 25, 1939, Germany's *Nachrichten* attacked Kennedy, Bullitt, and New York Mayor Fiorello La Guardia for "warmongering," [110] a charge later repeated in the German press.[111] To Bullitt, it was a source of mirth. He had a limited number of badge-and-sash decorations made, signifying membership in the Order of the Warmonger, and sent one by courier to his London counterpart. Kennedy, though, was extremely thin-skinned, even to criticisms from obviously controlled or irresponsible sources. Refusing to accept the decoration in the spirit in which it had been sent, Kennedy reacted irritably, and made clear to the courier that he was not at all amused.[112]

Progressive Philip La Follette attacked Kennedy with no less vehemence than the German press, but for opposite faults. There would never be peace, La Follette said, until the menace of Nazism was smashed. But the English conservatives were putting class interests ahead of national welfare by playing ball with the Nazis. Kennedy, he charged, was too friendly with these "undemocratic" elements in Great Britain.[113] He called on Roosevelt to perform a public service by immediately replacing Kennedy with "the best Benjamin Franklin he can find." [114]

A few days later Hugh Johnson took a potshot at the Ambassador before the Senate Committee on Foreign Relations: "Walter Hines Page was a British Ambassador to Washington. It would be a good idea to inquire whether we have not got another of those things at the Court of Saint Jim now. The dowagers and the duchesses—not to mention the debs—are a potent pill." [115]

In a State Department press release, Hull told the press that he thought it no serious reflection on the Ambassador to be attacked from a liberal-progressive angle one day and a reactionary on the other,[116] and the *New York Times* editorially laughed at Johnson's intimations.[117] Kennedy called Hull to thank him for his defense: "I don't enjoy doing the job where I have to have people defend me because I'd like to take a sock at this fellow (La Follette) because his conduct over here was nothing short of reprehensible." Kennedy endured Hull's playful ribbing: "You talk about the same since you changed your citizenship." [118]

Krock reported on May 4 that the coolness towards Kennedy that had existed for some time at the State Department had been replaced by the warm approval that had characterized the relationship during the early period—"his standing in the department is higher than it ever was." [119] On his own part, however, Kennedy noticed that the State Department was consulting him less and less, and he suspected and resented that he was being deliberately dealt out. Bullitt was playing a much more central role in American foreign policy, and had even begun to offer advice to the British.[120]

Kennedy's enemies in the New Deal saw to it that any and all criticisms of the Ambassador were called to Roosevelt's attention, and the President was not unaffected. *The Week*, a left-wing insider's newsletter, with a small but influential readership in both England and the United States, asked on May 17 why Roosevelt kept Kennedy as Ambassador. Its editor, Claude Cockburn, wrote:

> In his intimate conversations with the Germanophile clique which inspires The Times, Mr. Kennedy uses language which is not merely defeatist, but anti-Rooseveltian. Carried away by his pro-Franco sentiments, Mr. Kennedy . . . goes so far as to insinuate that the democratic policy of the United States is a Jewish production, but that Roosevelt will fall in 1940.[121]

The piece was reprinted in the *New York Post*,[122] many of whose readers clipped the article and sent it to Roosevelt or the State Department. Requests for official explanations were treated with light but unequivocal denials.[123] A month later, Cockburn reprinted an article by Count Carlo Sforza, a leading anti-fascist Italian, who in substance repeated Cockburn's own charges.[124] Ickes called the item to Roosevelt's attention. He recorded in his diary, "The President read this and said to me: 'It is true.' " [125] Quite possibly, Roosevelt was only telling Ickes what he knew the progressive wanted to hear. In any event, one thing is certain: Kennedy was not Roosevelt's foremost advisor on European affairs, as Krock, the Ambassador's incorrigible booster, told his readers in the *New York Times*.[126]

IN THE LATE SUMMER OF 1939, POLICY CONSIDERATIONS AGAIN became more pressing. Like Halifax, Kennedy became much less firm than he had been in April, when Britain had donned its bold front and "guaranteed" Poland against Germany and Greece against Italy, all to Kennedy's ultimate approval. But by June of 1939 the British government had weakened in resolve, and Kennedy's resolve weakened with it. Italy was making demands against France, including a demand for French territory which France could hardly entertain. Kennedy and Halifax agreed that France was being unnecessarily stiff in her relations with Italy. Halifax informed Lindsay that Kennedy had volunteered to "suggest to the President that he should from his side, and independently, counsel France to be somewhat more accommodating," [127] in her relations with the Duce.

It seemed important that France try to improve her relations with Italy, for on another front, relations between the Western allies and the Soviets, which of a sudden assumed importance, seemed to be going poorly. From the start of the Hitlerite aggression, Russia had manifested an eagerness to participate in a grand alliance against the Nazis. Their interest had been pointedly rebuffed at the time of the Munich crisis, either because the capitalist democracies did not want to soil their hands with the communists, or because they did not want any element introduced which might firm Czech resistance. Western actions and reactions at that time unquestionably influenced the Soviet attitude towards a military alliance with Britain and France. Shortly after Hitler occupied Prague, though, the West began to seek security through an alliance with the Soviets, and discussions gingerly began. Negotiations went very slowly and laboriously. Negotiators on both sides—all with justice—began to question one another's good faith. Discussions seemed to be going nowhere. Kennedy cabled Washington on June 7 that "the suspicion is beginning to dawn on the British that Russia may be taking them up a very dark road." Continued efforts to reach an agreement would be "putting coal into an engine that is not going any place." [128] With Russian cooperation looking less likely, it was necessary for the West to make every effort to placate Italy.

In late June, allied talks with Russia suffered a serious setback when *Pravda* published a bitter attack on Britain and France. Announcement of the failure of the negotiations seemed imminent, and Kennedy put the blame for the failure on Russia. "There you are!" he told English newsman George Bilainkin ("in words more colourful"). "I told you they don't want this pact. Not they." The *Pravda* attack showed that the "brink of war is a hell of a sight nearer than ever it's been." [129]

Kennedy probably convinced himself that Russian bad faith was the reason that talks were going so badly. If he had looked behind Russia's apparent attitude, however, he would have seen that there was more than one side to the story.

From the start, Kennedy had been dubious about the need or desirability of a treaty between Britain and France and Russia. In April he had explained to Davies that Russia's vested interest in fighting Hitler's eastward-creeping armies would make it vital for Stalin to fight for Poland or Rumania, with or without a pact with the West. Although he recognized the value of Russia as a military ally, there was no need for a formal treaty. Davies disagreed, and argued that Russia was eager for an agreement promising security from war. If she could not conclude a favorable agreement with England and France, she would be driven to ally herself with Germany. Kennedy saw no likelihood of this, nor did most British diplomats.[130]

Until the moment of peril (if then) Kennedy probably did not want an alliance with Russia—previously he had opposed the French pact with the Russians.[131] According to Robert Bendiner, Kennedy believed that the Nazis would continue to move east. Ultimately they would become embroiled in a war with Russia, and the two dictatorships would eliminate each other as world forces.[132] Why enter an alliance that would obligate the West to save the Communists in such a happy event? To a greater or lesser extent, Halifax and Chamberlain no doubt toyed with similar thoughts, if they never solidified a policy in that direction. After the likelihood of successful consummation of a British-Russian treaty became dim with the *Pravda* attack, Kennedy wired the State Department on July 5 that British negotiations were designed only to keep Stalin from signing up with Hitler.[133] The Russian dictator made clear in his speeches that he suspected as much. That being the attitude of Britain, Stalin had to turn elsewhere in his search for Russian security. In August, serious secret discussions began between Russia and Germany, pointing towards an alliance that might give Russia the security she sought.

It was largely the hesitations of Chamberlain and Halifax that did ultimately drive Stalin to complete an agreement with the Reich, as Davies had feared. Russian bad faith alone had not made the talks with Britain fail; rather, Britain's reluctance in the first place—a reluctance which Kennedy shared—made the Russian action inevitable.

At the end of July, Kennedy left for a vacation at Cannes.[134] Once again his vacation was interrupted by crisis. On August 21, it was publicly announced that Ribbentrop was going to Russia to visit Soviet Foreign Minister V. M. Molotov. The next day Kennedy flew back to London, arriving just in time for announcement of the consummation of Germany's speedy negotiations with the Soviets. Many of Britain's leaders attempted to appear unconcerned, but Kennedy could see that the Russian-German rapprochement meant vast economic advantage for Germany, which would enjoy access to vital Soviet commodities, affecting the Reich's war-making potential.[135]

Secure from adverse Russian action, Germany was now free to exert vicious pressure against Poland for satisfaction of its long-standing demands for Polish territory. The Poles seemed resolute, and Britain was committed to defend them. September 1 approached, the classic time for beginning war, between the gathering of the harvest and the coming of autumn rains.[136] War seemed inevitable. Kennedy wired the State Department on the twenty-third of a talk with Halifax:

> He says that England will definitely go to war if Poland starts to fight. However, I have a distinct feeling that they do not want to be more Polish than the Poles and that they are praying the Poles will find some way of adjusting their differences with the Germans at once.

(As if adjustable "differences" were really the cause of the Polish-German tension.) He quoted Halifax as saying, "My reason shows me no way out but war, but my instincts still give me hope." [137]

An hour later he wired again. He had just seen Chamberlain, who had also been on vacation. The Prime Minister's vacation had done him no good: "He looks very bad and is terribly depressed." Chamberlain had said that the specter of impending catastrophe was over him all the time; his depression transmitted itself to Kennedy:

> *He says the futility of it all is the thing that is frightful; after all they cannot save the Poles; they can merely carry on a war of revenge that will mean the destruction of the whole of Europe.*

Kennedy obviously agreed that the situation was futile.

> *I left with the feeling that the situation was dark and much worse than it was a year ago and that the only hope is for some action of the Poles in negotiating with the Germans which will make another delay possible.*

He hinted that Roosevelt might take some action that would bring about the desired "delay."

> *If the President is contemplating any action for peace it seems to me the place to work is on Beck (Polish Minister of Foreign Affairs) in Poland and to make this effective it must happen quickly. I see no other possibility.*[138]

Kennedy hoped that war might again be postponed, this time by sacrificing the Poles. Count Edward Raczyński, the Polish Ambassador, later summarized for the author: "Kennedy was generally sympathetic to Poland's plight, but Poland was of course a secondary concern to Kennedy, and to him the vista of terrific world upheaval outweighed the fate of a distant country of which he knew little. He was generally sympathetic as far as it went." [139] It didn't go very far. "Bill," he told his friend William Hillman, "I'd sell a hundred Polands down the river any day rather than risk the life of a British soldier or the loss of a British pound." [140]

Kennedy still saw the problem as a race for time—Britain needed *more* time to prepare. He was excited when commentator H. V. Kaltenborn visited him. "As I entered his private office," wrote Kaltenborn,

> *he was pacing the room in his shirtsleeves in a dramatic mood. He raised his hand and said, "You have come to me in one of the most important moments in world history! We are engaged in a fight for time! . . . Gaining time is the most important thing we can do at this point."* [141]

Kennedy was ready to sacrifice another ally for time, and he did not think Poland would bring too many hours at that. The most he expected was to "get an agreement that would last for a short time." [142] Time. He was preoccupied with it.

Kennedy apparently did not realize that the fact that "the situation was dark and much worse than a year ago" demonstrated how time could only aid Hitler. And what use would the allies make of the time anyway? Kennedy wired on the twenty-fourth: "My own belief is that the Anglo-French plans will be made when war is declared and not before. They now talk about what they might do but have not come down to making it definite. . . ." [143] That being the case, what use would England and France make of the time? Little.

It was impossible to entertain the belief anymore that Hitler was only interested in restoring Teutons to the Fatherland. After the Nazi-Soviet Pact it seemed unrealistic to think in terms of communism and nazism killing each other off. Kennedy's only argument now for avoiding war was to gain time, and we see that that argument too had flaws which were or should have been apparent to him. His real interest was not in gaining time, but rather, Kennedy's interest was in preserving peace, peace at any price.

On the twenty-fourth, Sir Horace Wilson, Chamberlain's closest advisor, visited Kennedy and urged him to get the President to put pressure on the Poles to moderate their position.[144] Kennedy told him of his previous efforts in that direction, but nonetheless relayed the substance of Wilson's position to Washington:

> Sir Horace Wilson called me this morning and told me he saw no hope for avoiding war unless the Poles were willing to negotiate with the Germans. As things stand now that is the place to apply pressure. The British are in no position to press the Poles strongly, but if anything is to be accomplished action must be taken at once, as the Prime Minister feels the blow is fairly near.[145]

Despite Kennedy's careful choice of words, the purpose of Wilson's visit was clear to Moffat: "There is no doubt that the British would like to put pressure on Poland and don't dare do so therefore they would like to get us to put such pressure and assume responsibility of a second Munich. I fear they have caught Kennedy in this net, but the fish are too wary on this side of the Atlantic." [146]

Later that same day, Kennedy decided to be more candid. He called Washington and asked openly that pressure be put on the Poles to back down. Moffat recorded in his diary that the idea had received short shrift from the President, the Secretary, and Welles on down.[147] Hull explained in his *Memoirs*, "Neither the President nor I felt any disposition to bring any pressure to bear on Poland." [148]

Nonetheless, Roosevelt may have thought that at least perfunctory efforts should be made to keep peace. Perhaps in response to

Kennedy's pleas, the President sent letters urging reasonableness to Italian King Victor Emmanuel III, Hitler, and Polish President Ignacy Mościcki. Shown a copy of the message to Victor Emmanuel, Kennedy thought it "lousy." The King counted for naught in Italy and Kennedy was annoyed that a stronger message had not been sent to the Duce.[149]

The next day Kennedy reported a conversation between Hitler and Sir Neville Henderson, the British Ambassador in Berlin. Hitler told Henderson that Great Britain should force Poland to "adjust her differences with Germany at once." His list of suggestions boiled down to one thing—Britain should abandon Poland.[150] After his conversation of the twenty-fourth Kennedy was not so bold, but he obviously still thought that everything considered, Hitler's suggestion was not a bad one: "Writing this out it looks like a ridiculous proposition to make Great Britain quit or cut away from the Poles but to hear the text [of Henderson's message] as read it seems much more reasonable." [151]

Kennedy was disturbed about the apparent desire for war that the English people were manifesting, a desire that was making it extremely difficult for Chamberlain to back down. He suggested to his friend that the Prime Minister institute war regulations then and there—"Give them a little taste of what is to come. They might not be so anxious for the Poles to refuse to negotiate and so start war." [152] But Kennedy realized that England could not back down. Not only would the abandonment of Poland break the Conservative party, but it would jeopardize the honor of Britain.[153] Even aside from such considerations, the Prime Minister was being pushed by an enraged and bellicose British public, and goaded by MPs from his own party; his hands were tied. Worse still, Kennedy strongly suspected that war was an economic necessity for Germany.[154] War seemed inevitable. At the same time, Kennedy thought that it was essential to find a way out—otherwise millions of lives would be lost and only chaos and communism would be left for the world. The way out was for the United States to lead the peace-making movement, and help Chamberlain disentangle himself from Poland. He told Chamberlain to "Get the United States now to say what it would be willing to do in the cause of international peace and prosperity." [155] But nothing came of his urgings. While Roosevelt's letters to Mościcki, Hitler, and Victor Emmanuel helped to make the dictators look bad, the President was doing nothing to make it easier for Chamberlain to drop the Poles. Kennedy liked to think that he was doing everything within his power to keep the world from a shooting war,[156] and he was displeased with his President's attitude. Years later he forgot that the English people had forced Chamberlain forward, and attributed England's entry into war to the attitude in Washington: pressure from the United States was what forced Chamberlain's hand, he told Senator Wheeler,[157] Air Secretary James V. Forrestal,[158] and no doubt others.[159]

Towards the end of August, Kennedy became briefly a little more hopeful. On the twenty-seventh he wired that Hitler was "trying through blackmail to try to squeeze the last drop of possible advantage out of Poland without war." [160] They would reach a peaceful settlement, he believed. On the twenty-ninth Hitler crystallized his terms for Henderson again. Kennedy thought that Britain's proposed answer was a little too firm.[161] But he was still hopeful. Chamberlain, he wired, "is more worried about getting the Poles to be reasonable than the Germans." In general, Chamberlain was surprisingly optimistic.[162]

Kennedy's brief optimism was a hope-against-hope. The Poles refused to be "reasonable" and on September 1, Germany invaded Poland, throwing Kennedy into a profound depression. When he called to announce the invasion, he was in such poor spirits that Roosevelt had to comfort him.[163] It was "all over" for "the party is on," he told Hull in a second telephone call that day. Asked if there was any doubt but that Britain would act, he replied, "Oh, unquestionably none." [164] Kennedy was mistaken. There then followed two days during which Chamberlain tried desperately to find another way out, until first the House of Commons[165] and then the Cabinet[166] insisted Britain's honor be preserved. There was no alternative but war.

Halifax's biographer writes that the Foreign Secretary's

> *profound belief in a future life made the disasters of this world seem by contrast transient and insubstantial. Thus armoured he could envision human afflictions with an almost unearthly calm, and face war, when it came, with complete inner tranquility, regarding the deaths of those he loved not as "utter desolation", but as softened by a sure knowledge of the immortality of their souls.*[167]

On September 3 Kennedy called Roosevelt to report that Britain was about to declare war. He read the President Chamberlain's statement with tears in his eyes. "In a state of unrelieved despair," wrote insiders Alsop and Kintner, "he foresaw dark ages, predicting that whoever won, chaos would be the war's real victor. He kept saying 'it's the end of the world, the end of everything.' " [168]

DURING
THE PHONY WAR

KENNEDY MADE NO ATTEMPT TO HIDE HIS PESSIMISM FROM THE
leaders of the Allied war effort. Count Raczyński was startled by his
gloom, and noted Kennedy's rhetorical question: "Where on earth can
the Allies fight the Germans and beat them?" [1] Kennedy was similarly
depressed when he visited King George; the King took immediate
steps to dispel his mood.[2] As the month of the war drew on, Kennedy
began to express his pessimism more frequently and more publicly,
and with less desperation in his voice. In a September 20 notation,
John Balfour, of the American desk at the Foreign Office, recorded
that "the Swiss journalist Mr. Kessler had been assured recently by
Mr. Kennedy in the presence of other journalists, that in his opinion
we should be defeated." [3] At the same time, Balfour's colleague
Berkeley Gage noted a report of a dinner at which Kennedy had
> expressed the opinion that we should be badly thrashed in the
> present war. . . . My informant [apparently Billy Hartington,[4]
> who later married Kennedy's daughter Kathleen] said that Mr.
> Kennedy appeared rather to relish expressing this opinion, which
> he attributed not to serious antagonism to us, but rather to a
> delight inherent in most Americans in seeing the lion's tail
> twisted [5] (and perhaps in twisting the lion's tail).[6]

The Ambassador's son, "Mr. Jack Kennedy, had interjected that even
if the Neutrality Act [which proscribed sale of arms to belligerents]
were repealed it would not help us much as we had not got sufficient
gold for large purchases in America." [7] With time, Kennedy's attitude
affected so many of the American Embassy staff that Lord Francis-
Williams found the atmosphere at the embassy insufferable and ceased
going there.[8]

Kennedy's communiqués to the State Department made clear that
he believed that Britain's leaders shared his pessimism. On the
eleventh, he wired that they "realize that a continuation of a war or
the maintenance of a Government on a war basis means complete
economic, financial, and social collapse and nothing will be saved after

210

the war is over." [9] On the fifteenth, he wired that Leslie Hore-Belisha, Britain's Jewish War Secretary with whom he had just lunched, was "a very blue individual," not at all optimistic. The same was true for the rest of the English government—"They have great confidence that they will stick, but I don't think they are any too optimistic about the results." [10] Toward the end of the first month, Montagu Norman had said that if the war were to proceed, "Britain as we have known her is through," [11] and in early October, Halifax had acknowledged that continuation of the war "will mean Bolshevism all over Europe." [12] When someone ventured an optimistic note—such as a comment from General Edmund Ironside that German morale was bad—Kennedy discounted it as wishful thinking.[13] Typical was his reaction to a session on September 18 with Chamberlain, in which the Prime Minister had resisted Kennedy's suggestions of the worst:

> *After listening to it all, I came away with this one impression based on my experience: when I was in the picture business whenever a new picture was being shown for the first time in the projection room a few of the topside executives would go in to look at it before it was shown to anybody on the premises and when we came out the crowd would be gathered around to see what we thought of it and in my 4 years I have never seen any executive come out that did not say the picture was "great," and in all that time I have never seen the group that waited outside for the judgement ever wrong in deciding that the tone of the executives' "great" meant that it was really lousy; so while the word was always the same the real impression was gathered very accurately. I draw a parallel from my picture experience to this conversation today. While Chamberlain did not say everything was great, he certainly did not want to give me the impression that everything was lousy, but nevertheless that is what I think it is.* [14]

He left the Prime Minister, he said, "thoroughly convinced that Chamberlain is well aware of the terrific catastrophes ahead for Great Britain." [15] After a month of a war that the British had not yet begun to fight, Kennedy summarized what he took to be the situation for the President:

> *I have yet to talk to any military or naval expert of any nationality this week who thinks that, with the present and prospective set-up of England and France on one side and Germany and Russia and their potential allies on the other, England has a Chinaman's chance. . . . I am convinced, because*

I live here, that England will go down fighting. Unfortunately, I am one who does not believe that is going to do the slightest bit of good in this case.[16]

Given Kennedy's attitude, it is little wonder that he favored getting out of the scrape as well and quickly as possible. While Britain and France did nothing whatsoever to save the Poles, Hitler's armies, aided by a Soviet grab from the East, proceeded on the speedy liquidation of Poland. Simultaneously, Hitler embarked on his "Peace Offensive," an effort to "call off the war" with Britain and France after gaining his easy acquisitions in Poland. Kennedy was not much concerned about Poland, but he was concerned about calling off the war before lives and pounds sterling, not to mention dollars, were lost,[17] and he was worried that pressure from America might steel the British against accepting a compromise. ("I was thinking to myself of the growing Jewish influence in the press and in Washington demanding continuance of the war and of the many Democrats I knew who had a tendency to believe that they could win again if the war went on but might lose if it were ended.")[18] The Ambassador embarked on his own "peace offensive." On September 11 he wired a personal plea to the President:

It seems to me that this situation may crystallize to a point where the President can be the savior of the world. The British Government as such certainly cannot accept any agreement with Hitler, but there may be a point where the President himself may work out the plans for world peace. Now this opportunity may never arise, but, as a fairly practical fellow all my life, I believe that it is entirely conceivable that the President can get himself in a spot where he can save the world and I have not thought so up to this minute. . . . I am passing this on because I think that beyond all other questions of importance in the world, this is one that the President should be thinking about to work out in his own mind what might be done at the psychological moment not to increase Hitler's prestige but possibly to bring the whole world on a peace basis.[19]

President Roosevelt himself was privately considering just such efforts,[20] but for reasons best known to himself, he resented Kennedy's interest in the same direction. Within a few hours, Hull wired the Ambassador a curt response:

The President desires me to inform you, for your strictly confidential information and so that you may be guided thereby

*without divulging this message to any one, that this Government,
so long as present European conditions continue, sees no
opportunity nor occasion for any peace move to be initiated by
the President of the United States. The people of the United
States would not support any move for peace initiated by this
Government that would consolidate or make possible a survival
of a regime of force and of aggression.*[21]

To Morgenthau, the President complained that Kennedy "has been an
appeaser and always will be an appeaser. . . . If Germany or Italy
made a good peace offer tomorrow, Joe would start working on the
King and his friend, the Queen, and from there on down to get
everybody to accept it. . . . He's just a pain in the neck to me." [22]

Whether or not their hearts were in it, the public pronouncements
of British officials made clear that they were not interested in making
peace on Hitler's terms. Perhaps word leaked to British officials in
Washington of Kennedy's interest in making peace; in any event,
three days after Kennedy's poorly received suggestion to the President, Lord Lothian, Lindsay's successor as British Ambassador in
Washington, wired Halifax, "Further evidence makes me think it very
important that the Prime Minister should take a very early opportunity to see the United States Ambassador and state emphatically to
him that H.M.G. mean to see the war through in accord with its public
declarations." [23] When Chamberlain saw Kennedy shortly after, he
interrupted the Ambassador's gloomy forebodings, flatly interjecting
that "any peace offer of the kind Germany was likely to put forward
would be immediately rejected." [24]

Though rebuffed in his efforts both at home and abroad, Kennedy
was undaunted. While the speeches of British leaders were talking
about the salvation of Poland and the demise of Nazism, Kennedy
urged Halifax not to set such impossible terms for peace, but to keep
Britain's war aims "quite general in character." Halifax summarized
the Ambassador's stance as: "To talk about the reconstitution of
Poland was, in view of the Russian action, obviously quite impossible,
and he himself was disposed to deprecate perpetual reference to the
personal elimination of Hitler." [25] It was an attitude entirely compati-
ble with the German peace offensive. At the end of the month, he
made similar argument to Sir John Simon, Chamberlain's intimate:
what, he asked Simon, were the British fighting for?

*They could not restore Poland, and even if Hitler were gotten rid
of, chaos would ensue in Germany and the country might well go*

Communist.[26] *The whole business would leave England and France mere shells. But to this Simon replied that there was no way of getting around the British public: "If they were to advocate any type of peace, they would be yelled down by their own people, who are determined to go on."* [27]

No doubt hoping to influence the President with the reasoning he had set forth to Simon, Kennedy wrote Roosevelt personally of the meeting, recounting in detail what he had told the Englishman. Just in case the President had had a change of heart, and was willing to be an agent for peace, the Ambassador suggested that

I would start thinking how you can help save face for the allies and yet at the same time be the factor in getting the position of the United States a topside one as a result of your intervention. . . . The whole problem needs a mastermind and that soon if you don't want the world's greatest calamity to fall on our friends and subsequently on us. [28]

Italy had not yet entered the war, and Kennedy urged the Italian Ambassador in London to enlist the Duce's help in finding an "honorable solution." [29] As October closed, he made what appears to be a final effort with Halifax:

He proceeded to say that, in his opinion, the consequences of indefinite continuance of the war were so serious that every effort should be made by diplomatic resources to find the way of peace. I told his Excellency that everyone would agree that peace was desirable if it could be achieved, but it was not a matter of diplomatic ingenuity. If in fact we were right, as we knew we were, in believing that the present German Government were quite untrustworthy, nothing was to be gained by deluding ourselves into supposing that any paper peace terms proposed by them could, unsupported by assurances much more solid, offer the way of peace. [30]

At the Foreign Office, Kennedy's interest was dismissed unkindly: "Mr. Kennedy is no doubt thinking of his pocket." [31]

Kennedy was certainly more pessimistic than were the members of the government, and he could only have been a depressant on their spirit, depleting their morale. In his early-September interview with the King, for example, the King attempted to dispel Kennedy's pessimistic mood, but apparently Kennedy had more effect on the King's attitude than vice versa. When Cadogan visited the King shortly after His Majesty's interview with Kennedy, Cadogan found the King "rather depressed—and a little *défaitiste*—result, I think, of a talk with Joe Kennedy." [32] Kennedy had substantially the same effect on "Chips" Channon as he had had on the King; Channon talked to himself in his diary:

> *I trust that Joe Kennedy, the jaunty American Ambassador, is wrong, for he prophesies the end of everything, and goes about saying that England is committing suicide. My reason tells me he is wrong, that everything is on our side, but my intuition warns me that he may have something.*[33]

On September 18, Kennedy asked Chamberlain "if he did not believe that the psychological trend was definitely against England at this time and that countries on the sidelines who would want to play with the victor might decide to come along with Germany?" The old and tired Prime Minister was on the verge of a war he dreaded, but managed to summon enough courage (or guile) to deny.[34] He could only have been upset and further depressed by his friend Kennedy's obvious and by then well-known attitude. On the other hand, accurate reports of Kennedy's attitude trickled back to the German Foreign Office,[35] where they could only have had a contrary effect.

Foreign Office diplomats were gravely concerned about the effect of what they early labeled as Kennedy's *"défaitiste"* talk. At the American desk of the Foreign Office, only a junior man, David Scott, had much sympathy for the American Ambassador, and even he acknowledged what he called the "disadvantages of talk of this kind." [36] To those less sympathetic, Kennedy's chatter was regarded more harshly. They could accept Kennedy holding such views himself, or reporting them to his government, but his free publication of them was intolerable. Victor Perowne of the American Desk jotted down that Kennedy

> *lays himself open to reproach when he, as the Ambassador in London of a friendly power, occupies himself in disseminating these views, and causing his family to disseminate them publicly in a way that can only give encouragement to our enemies and depress and discourage our friends.*[37]

Talking freely in such a vein to journalists or diplomats from neutral or nonbelligerent nations could only have a devastatingly adverse effect on Britain by encouraging the smaller European neutrals to "trim their sails to what they imagine to be the prevailing winds." [38] This was especially true in view of Kennedy's peculiar position:

> *The views of any United States Ambassador in London on our war chances are a matter of considerable importance and it must not be forgotten that Mr. Kennedy, rightly or wrongly, is*

regarded as having achieved a very special position here indeed and as being on terms of intimacy with the Prime Minister and other members of the Government. This belief, which is widespread, of course only enhances the importance of any views he may express and their effect.[39]

With the constancy of Kennedy's talk over time, Perowne refused to believe that it was the product of either naiveté or impersonal malaise,[40] and drew the most unkind of conclusions: Kennedy was directing a

propaganda campaign against us. The amount of indirect evidence that we have fully entitles us, I think, to regard his repeated assertions that England cannot win the war as a definite campaign. Mr. Kennedy is not the sort of man to go on talking in the sort of way that has been reported to us without an object.[41]

To Perowne and most of the Foreign Office career men, that object seemed to revolve around Kennedy's pocketbook.

An American journalist who served in London during Kennedy's tenure told the author that at the time of the Munich crisis, the British began partial mobilization, which included the "bugging" of embassy telephones, including Kennedy's. They discovered that Kennedy was making use of his "inside information" in maneuvering his own personal investments. The journalist had learned the story from Lord —— himself.[42] Lord —— demurred in response to the author's request for confirmation or denial:

I am afraid that I have no recollections of the suspicions about his personal investments when he was in this country. It may be that a number of people here felt that he was a little over-defeatist about our position in relation to the Germans and not always very understanding of our position, but more than that I am afraid I cannot say.[43]

The story, and parallel ones about Kennedy's misuse of his position for his personal financial advantage, was widely believed within London's American press community, most of whose members regarded Kennedy as ruthless, and disliked him personally on both political-policy and stylistic bases. This author tends to doubt the specific story because if it were true, everyone at the American desk would probably have been aware of the fact, and there would have been no David Scott to make occasional apologies for the Ambassador. One of Kennedy's high-ranking assistants at the time rejects such implications out-of-hand: "Kennedy was not interested in the piddling." [44] Shortly after the start of the war, though, such beliefs became common among Foreign Office staff members.

In late September, Baron Erik Palmstierna, longtime Swedish Ambassador to London, stopped in on Perowne, and casually mentioned,

> There were "funny stories" about [Kennedy] and his dealings in the city. The inference, though this was not explicitly stated, was that Mr. Kennedy's stock exchange activities, whatever they may be, are capable of being interpreted as affording evidence of anti-British proclivities on his part, as well as, of course, of a desire to make money without being too scrupulous as to the methods employed! [45]

Balfour called the story what it was, "gossip," "but gossip which very probably has more than a grain of truth in it." [46] A marginal note in a different hand adds, "Baron P. ought to know!" [47] With time, a profoundly negative regard for the Ambassador and a deeply cynical view of his motives, became, according to a then-junior man at the American desk, "an attitude well-embedded in the American department," [48] and virtually any such rumor was given currency. The Foreign Office's two top career men, Vansittart and Cadogan, rivals if not enemies, could agree, if on nothing else, on attribution of only the narrowest personal motives to the American Ambassador. [49] Even Kennedy's one friend at the Foreign Office, Scott, came to "wish that I could resist the feeling that Mr. Kennedy is thinking all the time about (1) his own financial position, (2) his political future." [50] American journalists were satisfied that Kennedy was thinking mostly about "number one": "Joe Kennedy was operating the stock market seven ways till Wednesday," one told the author. [51]

Determining the basic truth of these kinds of stories, let alone the degree of Kennedy's crisis-time speculations, will probably not be possible, at least until the private papers of stockbrokers are opened—probably never. No Kennedy material survives in the papers of Kennedy's closest friend on Wall Street, Elisha Walker. [52] The farthest that the author got in his attempt to determine the truth or falsity of the stories of Kennedy's securities dealings during his ambassadorial career, was in an interview with one very high-ranking British government official of the day. When asked whether he had heard the story related by Baron Palmstierna the diplomat replied, "A lot of people heard it—at least in the government circles." He added, cryptically, "Or perhaps even knew it." [53]

What to do about Kennedy's pessimism, and its effect on the war effort, was a subject of much discussion at the American desk. It was generally agreed that no one was going to "talk" Kennedy out of his defeatism—if events should change his mind, all well and good, but Perowne was "a little doubtful whether Mr. Kennedy is really open to conviction as his attitude seems based on some fundamental and emotional attitude of mind rather than on reason." [54] If he would only shut up about his views, that would be about as much as the Foreign Office could hope for. Serious thought was given to telling Kennedy's chargé, Herschel Johnson, informally, that rumors were circulating about Kennedy's defeatist talk, "and leave him to take the hint." [55] The suggestion was rejected as placing the chargé in an embarrassing or untenable position.[56] Another alternative was to have Lothian ask Roosevelt to tell his Ambassador to shut his mouth—a request that might be taken to be a request that the Ambassador be recalled. That course was rejected also, in part on Gage's theory that "a complaint might of course make him shut up, but in that case we shall neither know what he is thinking nor what he is telling the U.S. Government." [57] A complaint to the President would probably "confirm Mr. Kennedy's enmity without depriving him of the power to do us further harm." [58] The closest that the British ever got to determining what to do was to wire Lothian "about his indiscreet utterances in case it should later become necessary for us to ask you to drop a hint in the proper quarter." [59]

While British reactions towards Kennedy were chilling in the early days of the war, so too, Kennedy's attitude toward the British was markedly stiffening. Given his belief that the British shared his pessimism, he could only have found their refusal to give serious consideration to peace overtures as manifestation of a national death wish. And though the British insisted that they were in the war "to stay," they were not, in fact, doing very much to ready themselves for a real war. He no doubt perceived, as the celebrated British historian A. J. P. Taylor asserts, that the government was "moving into war backwards, with their eyes tightly closed." [60] The substance of Britain's articulated position, together with its actions and the "realities" of the situation, made not the slightest sense to the Ambassador, who reacted with apparent irritation. He wired Hull that there was great confusion in the British cabinet,[61] and he ridiculed the unrealistic Army staff. It seemed clear to him, notwithstanding the seeming resolution in British orations, that "they have no intention of fighting in the first place." [62] Kennedy, of course, was only critical of Britain's lack of intention to fight in view of its silly insistence that it fully intended to do just that. For his own country, Kennedy wished to ensure that the United States had no intention of fighting. He was notably upset at Americans who enlisted with the British Home Guard, out of fear that it might presage wider-scale American involvement, or, he explained to a leader of the fighting Americans, "might lead to all United States citizens being shot as *francs-tireurs* when the Germans occupied London." [63]

The day after war was declared, Brigadier Beaumont Nesbitt ran into Perowne and asked "whether I knew that Mr. Kennedy, the U.S. Ambassador, was a strong isolationist. I said I had not heard this before, I thought, and he said it had been news to him to learn it." The Brigadier had apparently heard it from Virginia Cowles, a well-known American journalist.[64] The "isolationist" diagnosis may or may not have been a bit premature, and in his discussions with British officials, Kennedy took pains not to appear such. With Americans, however, and at home, he sounded increasingly isolationistic. As early as October 2, 1939, Kennedy began warning the State Department to steer clear of the war and, particularly, to be wary of British efforts to drag America into it:

> They all contend that all they want is revision of the Neutrality Act to give them an opportunity to buy in America but I do not believe it for a minute. If Germany does not break and throw Hitler out, after the passage of the Neutrality Act they will spend every hour figuring how they can get us in.[65]

He personally warned Roosevelt against "the facility with which the Anglo-Saxon can play power politics when talking in terms of philanthropy":

> Of course the real fact is that England is fighting for her possessions and place in the sun, just as she has in the past. . . . Regardless of the God-awful behavior of the Nazis, surely the fact is that the English people are not fighting Hitler–they are fighting the German people, just as they fought them twenty-five years ago, because forty-five million Britons controlling the greatest far-flung maritime empire in the world and eighty million Germans dominating continental Europe haven't learned to live together peacefully.[66]

Clearly, Kennedy was not a partisan of the country to which he had been sent.

Kennedy was convinced that Britain had passed her peak as a world power, and that evolution on the global scale would continue in the most shrill Darwinian fashion. No matter the outcome, Britain as an Empire was done, and the United States would have to face a much different, strange world after the war.[67] It was now all-important to improve German-American relations, both, so that the United States would be less apt to be drawn into the war, and also, so that it would be easier for Kennedy's country to live in the same world as a victorious Reich. He again renewed his contact with von Dirksen.

In mid-October, the German Ambassador called on his American counterpart. Kennedy told von Dirksen that he believed that a trade agreement between their two countries was necessary, with a dollars to marks relationship more favorable to Germany. ("Kennedy added that when he developed such a line of thought regarding Germany to Hull, the Secretary of State, he found no understanding but encountered marked reserve," wrote von Dirksen.) Kennedy again brought up the subject of a trip to Germany; projecting a visit of about two weeks, "He said that he was more anxious to acquaint himself with the institutions of the new Germany than to have official conversations only." It was very important that he undertake the trip. Much could be done to improve America's relations with Germany. Kennedy told von Dirksen that the average American had more liking for the average German than for the average Englishman, and, the German Ambassador wrote:

> Today, too, as during former conversations, Kennedy mentioned that very strong anti-Semitic tendencies existed in the United States and that a large portion of the population had an understanding of the German attitude toward the Jews.

But people sympathetic to Germany were not getting access to Roosevelt, Kennedy informed von Dirksen. The German wrote that as Kennedy had the ear of the President, and approached Germany with understanding and sympathy, Kennedy believed that he could do a great deal to advance relations between the two countries. Perhaps Kennedy envisioned a role for himself as unofficial courier between the President and the Führer. Von Dirksen expressed his own hope that he might be authorized to give Kennedy the consent of the German government for the visit.[68]

Nothing ever came of these efforts. Hans Dieckhoff, Germany's Ambassador in Washington, could see little value in a visit by

Kennedy, and doubted that Kennedy could alter Roosevelt's views. He pointed out that Kennedy had wrongly summed up his own country:

> It would hardly be possible to express a more hostile and negative attitude toward Germany than is now being shown almost daily by the President and many members of the Cabinet, as well as by the entire press, radio, and film industry.

American public opinion, he advised, could not be rectified "by small palliatives," and he questioned Kennedy's motives.[69] Though Weizsäcker was agreeable to a Kennedy visit, he made clear to von Dirksen that permission from Roosevelt would have to come first.[70]

Kennedy probably hoped that Germany would make him a public invitation before consulting Washington, and that the President would find it too difficult to say "no." [71] In any event, there is no indication in the State Department files that Kennedy ever requested permission for a visit to the Reich or discussed such possibilities with the State Department. The previous May Kennedy had told the State Department that he was going to Paris for a dinner with James Mooney, a General Motors executive, and another person identified as "a personal friend of Hitler and the topside influence in the Krupps." He left-handedly sought the Department's permission to go. ("Do you see any objection to my going and have you any suggestions?")[72] At that time, Hull had told him not to go to the dinner, lest the supper receive publicity creating "erroneous impression" and "unfortunate comment." [73] That being the Department's attitude on a mere private dinner in Paris before the war started, Kennedy could certainly have forecast the Department's reaction to a formal visit to Germany by the American Ambassador in London after the outbreak of war, and it seems likely that Kennedy never bothered to inform the Department of his efforts to bring about his visit to the Reich.[74]

PROBLEMS OF REFUGEES AGAIN BECAME IMPORTANT IN THE FIRST months of the war, only now it was American refugees from Europe. Kennedy always saw things in more personal terms than Hull, and showed considerably more emotion (if not real sympathy) for London's American evacuees, than did the Secretary or the State Department staff.

On August 24, United States embassies all over Europe advised Americans to return home. Kennedy told Americans in England to return to the United States without delay, and asked that all United States nationals register at the nearest consulate.[75]

The morning that war was declared, Kennedy sent an urgent demand that American ships be diverted to England to remove American citizens. As if expecting Hull to be unreceptive, he wired: "I feel very badly for all those people who are going to wait on docks for ships to take them on trips to the West Indies and Mexico, but I am thoroughly convinced that it is much more important for the American Government to get ships here as soon as possible and get these people home." [76] Moffat regarded the wire as "very sarcastic" and did not appreciate it.[77]

Hull replied the same day that he was sending ships, but urged Kennedy to get people to safe spots in England's interior until enough vessels could be provided, and to urge shippers to use space more effectively.[78] Kennedy made a public plea asking that travelers double up, and that those with reservations share cabins with passengers lacking reservations, in the interest of getting everyone home.

To Kennedy, ships for evacuating Americans seemed unbelievably slow in arriving at United Kingdom ports;[79] to the Administration, government efforts to provide ships were only hampered by Kennedy's "wild telephonic requests and demands." [80] For such repatriation crisis as existed, Moffat knew where to lay the blame: "the panic which Kennedy complained of was due largely to his failure to get Americans out of London." [81] Breck Long, in charge of the repatriation program,[82] noted:

> [*Kennedy*] *seems to think that the only people needing repatriation are in the lobby of the American Embassy in London. . . . Kennedy has been condemning everybody and criticizing everything and has antagonized most of the people in the Administration.*[83]

When ships did arrive, Kennedy had more friction with the Department over fares for the return voyages. The liners set exorbitant prices on their cubicles, demanding fares that many of the evacuees simply did not have. The government made funds available to loan to needy Americans, but to Kennedy's great dismay, they proved "unconscionably bureaucratic" in dispensing them. When Kennedy blew off steam to the Maritime Commission's Max Truitt on the government's apparent lack of great concern and its "inefficiency" in dealing with the problem, reports of his displeasure hit the press.[84] Long noted,

*The news stories and publicity items which went out of London
with [Kennedy's] permission if not with his origination indicated
that he did not view the situation normally. Of course it is not a
normal situation, but it requires a calm head and a cooperative
brain rather than a vituperative tongue and a scattering of
energy.*[85]

The State Department sent Kennedy a stiff reprimand.[86]

Department officials observed with disapproval that many ships
were returning without a full complement of passengers[87]—which
added to their irritation over Kennedy's clamor, and perhaps led
to unkind conclusions such as Long's that "Kennedy and Bullitt
telegraphed deprecatory remarks and probably made remarks
around the Embassy that chilled public interest" in the repatriation
vessels.[88]

Kennedy showed concern for the evacuees of all nationalities that
the bureaucrats in Washington could not appreciate. He requested
that space be allowed on the ships being sent for United States citizens
for 20 injured Canadians.[89] Hull replied that this would not be possible
for a number of very sensible and valid but cold reasons, one of them
being that that would be transporting the citizens of a belligerent and
might open the ship to attack.[90] A few days later, Kennedy appealed
that a number of South Americans be allowed to occupy unused space
on American vessels, and again he received a cool reply refusing
permission.[91] Eventually, though, a number of aliens did go to the
United States on American evacuee ships,[92] and Kennedy used his
personal contacts to secure berths for the children of those influential
Britons[93] that he chose to favor.

On September 5, the British-owned *Athenia*, with 311 American
passengers on board, was torpedoed.[94] Kennedy's son, young Jack
Kennedy, was sent to the site of rescue operations to take care of
American survivors. The Ambassador requested permission soon after
to warn Americans about the dangers of sailing on the ships of
belligerents, and permission was granted.[95] When he first gave the
warning, however, he did so unjudiciously. Just before Cunard's
Aquitania sailed, a United States counsel boarded and informed the
assembled American passengers that Mr. Kennedy felt,

*It is his duty to warn American citizens taking passage on vessels
of belligerent nations that when such vessels are being convoyed,
the opposing belligerent may claim the right to sink them without
warning.*

The *New York Times* wrote that:

> The words frightened all who heard them, and fear was followed
> by a wave of indignation that culminated in the framing of a
> reply in which the passengers told Mr. Kennedy that he had
> "caused great alarm, even consternation to your fellow country-
> men aboard the Aquitania" and asking him "is it not possible for
> you to give us constructive advice in this moment of our very
> great anxiety?" [96]

The Ambassador's warning was certainly a valid one, but it was
unquestionably bad mob psychology on a group of people about to
depart on the ship of a belligerent. Why did Kennedy think it so
important to make immediate, ship-board release of his warning?
Apparently he was afraid to wait, for fear that the *Aquitania* would
suffer the fate of the *Athenia*, and that the United States might be
drawn into the conflict over a latter-day *Lusitania*. One suspects that
his interest was not only in doing "his duty to warn American
citizens," but that he was more interested in avoiding, by his
statement, the possibility of an international incident that might bring
the United States into war.[97]

By early October, the repatriation program had been essentially
completed.

WITH THE DECLARATION OF WAR, ANGLO-AMERICAN TRADE WAS
largely disrupted and Kennedy had the duty of representing American
interests. Kennedy was vigorous and aggressive in his efforts on behalf
of the American film interests; with characteristic overstatement, he
wired Hull that Britain's proposals to limit the number of dollars
Britain sent to the United States for American movies meant "the end
of the motion picture industry in the United States in its present
setup." [98] Because films were important to British morale, he believed
America could drive a hard bargain, and he fully intended to do so.[99]
Not surprisingly, Hays was very pleased with what he regarded as
Kennedy's "splendid efforts," [100] and Hull backed him up in his
approach.[101] Kennedy reported to Hull that he was being "very stiff
and hard and cold" in his film negotiations.[102] The British thought so
too; at the Foreign Office, his efforts were regarded as "extortion," and
the staff at Britain's American desk resented him for working so hard
to repatriate American movie money at a time when the British were
so very pressed for dollars badly needed for more important things.[103]

"At a time when he should have been helping to defeat Hitler," [104] one who described himself as Kennedy's friend told the author, this kind of effort was *hampering* the war against Hitler, and the British regarded it as such.[105]

Kennedy took the initiative in driving a hard bargain for the film interests, and then received Hull's concurrence in his efforts. He was somewhat more passive in his representations for other American interests. Hull seems to have had some difficulty in impressing on Kennedy the need for British cooperation with regard to America's neutral shipping. Almost immediately, Britain put heavy restrictions on the importation of American tobacco, and though Hull was rather disturbed, Kennedy made no attempt to hide his sympathy for the British position.[106] When Kennedy reported that British imports of American apples and pears would be cut Welles directed him to "make a strenuous protest," and Kennedy reported the next day that "vigorous representations" had been made.[107] Though Kennedy foresaw equally dark days for the raisin growers of America as he had seen facing the film producers, he showed little initiative on their behalf, requesting instructions as to the attitude to strike. Hull answered, "I think that your general attitude should be one of deep concern over any measure which affects trade in American products to the extent which you apprehend for raisins. . . ." [108] The document books give no hint as to what efforts Kennedy did make on behalf of the raisin growers. Perhaps history shall never know. To the British, though, Kennedy had done enough for California, the raisin state, in his representation of the movie interests; a Foreign Office minute notes that "California can't complain if we buy a few less apples or raisins!" [109]

Perhaps more serious for the United States was the disruption of the cotton-for-rubber barter deal. The cotton had been on hand in U.S. Government warehouses, and was quickly delivered, but Britain requested a prolongation of the time allotted for delivery of the rubber. Kennedy supported their position. For a man who expected the imminent collapse of the British empire, his comment that "we should not be disturbed by the prolongation of the period during which delivery of the rubber will take place," [110] does not make sense. Hull was not so agreeable.[111]

In ensuing discussions, relations between Hull and his Ambassador became tart. Viles, representative of the American rubber interests, had been in London for negotiations the previous spring, but was now unavailable. Kennedy became annoyed with the procedure of the negotiations. On November 8, he complained to Hull:

> My own belief is that Viles should be here. There is no point in trying to carry on negotiations by long distance and through third parties.
>
> While I note that you do not want the Embassy to sit in with the Committee, nevertheless, all we have been doing for the last 2 months is negotiating with them. We may not want to call this sitting in at formal meetings but the result is the same. It strikes me that Viles should get on a plane and come over here . . . he should be here until the question is settled once and for all.[112]

A reply from Hull informed Kennedy that "Viles appreciated your suggestion," and explained that the then-present situation within the Rubber Manufacturers' Association made it impossible for Viles to leave the country.[113]

By late November Hull was displeased with developments in the negotiations and wired, "It is regretted that the Department must ask you therefore to press the discussion further." A series of suggested points was included.[114]

Kennedy did not take kindly to the wire:

> I wish again to call your attention to the following situation: With all due respects to the handling of the rubber-tin situation, I believe that it is absolutely a psychological mistake to proceed the way we are proceeding.

American tactics, he believed, were a "very bad trading policy." In a visit with Macdonald the previous day, the Englishman had told Kennedy,

> That our methods were the most childish methods he had ever seen in an attempt to influence a change in Government policy and I wish to add that I think this statement is a typical British understatement. I think them worse than childish. If you want to get this thing done and done right, send Viles over here.

Kennedy expressed his belief that nothing would come of "this constant exchange of telegrams," and added once more, "I urge you to get Viles on a plane and get him over here if you ever expect to get this matter satisfactorily adjusted." [115]

Hull apparently concluded that Kennedy desired the presence of Mr. Viles. He informed Kennedy that Viles could not come because of transportation problems; because he was old and sick; and because he

was needed in the United States. His response had a decidedly chilly
tone to it:

> *Looking back over the past few years, I must say that we have*
> *the sense that our relationships with the Rubber Committee have*
> *not been badly managed. The characterization upon which you*
> *and Macdonald appear to have agreed seems to us distinctly*
> *unjustified.*[116]

In his reply, Kennedy was toned down considerably, but did not
give an inch in his earlier contentions.

> *The problem definitely is that the method of conducting these*
> *negotiations is completely wrong. You cannot fire a pea-shooter*
> *every day in the week and expect to get the results that a 16*
> *pounder will get if you fired once in a while. If the Embassy,*
> *which of course will always cooperate with American business*
> *interests and has in this case, feels definitely that the method of*
> *procedure is wrong, you either ought to take the matter out of the*
> *Embassy's hands or follow its suggestions. . . . if Viles cannot*
> *come let somebody else come.*[117]

It is likely that friction over the rubber negotiations between the
Secretary and his Ambassador would have continued, but the
following day Kennedy left for a three-month Christmas vacation in
the United States and the negotiations were completed by others.

BY THIS TIME RELATIONS BETWEEN THE PRESIDENT AND HIS
Ambassador had deteriorated still further. Roosevelt, we have seen,
was disturbed by Kennedy's views and his official conduct. He was
irritated by Kennedy's bleakness and his extreme fears for the future,
and was irked either by Kennedy's repeated efforts to call off the war
or by the tone of his urgings. Roosevelt was beginning to acquire
vision—he was moving towards a view of America's relations in the
world that was diametrically opposed to the direction in which
Kennedy's views were moving. Even if one is to discount the
President's comments to Ickes or Morgenthau, Roosevelt could not
have been satisfied as to Kennedy's loyalty. When Boake Carter wrote
that Kennedy was deliberately bucking his superior, Roosevelt could
only have been deeply disturbed, both at Kennedy's attitude and at
the vastness of Kennedy's indiscretion in boasting about it to
journalists.

On the other hand, Kennedy had grounds to believe that Roosevelt

had "sold him out lock, stock, and barrel," as he had complained to
Carter. Kennedy was aware of the fact that he was being increasingly
circumvented. Not only Bullitt was interfering with his bailiwick, but
Morgenthau was discussing matters with British officials in Washington—such as a proposal that the United States acquire the *Queen
Mary*—that must have seemed to Kennedy to be entirely outside the
Treasury's jurisdiction—and no one even saw fit to tell Kennedy about
the talks. When Kennedy learned of the *Queen Mary* discussions
through the British, he wired a curt rebuff to Morgenthau: "Let me
add that I feel that the man on the spot should certainly, in times like
this, be kept currently informed of actions in Washington vitally
affecting the country that he is stationed in and not have to learn
about such actions from the British Government." [118] He would have
been even more outraged had he known that Morgenthau had
deliberately ignored him in response to Hull's suggestion at a Cabinet
meeting that he do just that.[119] At the time of the Munich crisis,
Roosevelt had told Morgenthau that in view of Kennedy's shortcomings, "I guess my best bet is the old boy up at the British Embassy,"
Lindsay,[120] and the President also had highly confidential discussions
with Lord Murray, for Chamberlain's personal ear.[121] Soon after the
war began, the President called Winston Churchill directly by phone,
and Kennedy learned about it only when Churchill called him to send
a message back to the President. It was quite embarrassing for
Kennedy, and he resented that Roosevelt had put him in such a
position.[122] In October, 1939, the Roosevelt-Churchill correspondence
began, their letters being exchanged in sealed envelopes.[123] Kennedy
delivered them. Some of them. Increasingly, Anglo-American relations
were being directed through the British Ambassador in Washington,
rather than through the American Ambassador in London,[124] and
increasingly Kennedy had to glean more and more of his information
from return messages that the British routed through him. The British
could see what was going on, and drew the only conclusion possible:
that the President had no confidence in his Ambassador.[125] When
Kennedy complained to Roosevelt about the Administration's failure
to keep him informed, Roosevelt brushed aside the Ambassador's
grievance with pleasantries.[126]

Kennedy suspected that snipes in the press by Trohan, Alsop and
Kintner, and Kenneth Crawford, had the approval of the White House
and perhaps originated with the President himself. We know, and
Kennedy probably learned or suspected, that the President com-

plained about him to Morgenthau, Farley, Ickes, and no doubt others. The very human Kennedy reacted the way one would expect a slighted person to respond: with the petty kind of comments that Cockburn reported. On July 15, for instance, Ickes included this entry in his diary: Cudahy

> *admits that Joe Kennedy does some pretty loud and inappropriate talking about the President. He does this before English servants, who are likely to spread the news. According to John, Kennedy is vulgar and coarse and highly critical in what he says about the President. And when John cautioned him on one occasion not to talk as he was doing before the servants, Joe said that he didn't give a damn.*[127]

Later Ickes included a report on a conversation with Bullitt:

> *Recently [Bullitt] was having an interview in his office in the State Department with J. M. Patterson, publisher of the* New York Daily News, *and Doris Fleeson, Patterson's Washington correspondent, when Joe Kennedy unexpectedly came in and planted himself down. He cheerfully entered into the conversation and before long he was saying that Germany would win, that everything in France and England would go to hell, and that his one interest was in saving his money for his children. He began to criticize the President very sharply, whereupon Bill (Bullitt) took issue with him. The altercation became so violent that Patterson finally remarked that he suspected he was intruding, and he and Doris Fleeson left, but Joe continued to berate the President. Bill told him that he was disloyal and that he had no right to say what he had before Patterson and Fleeson. Joe said that he would say what he Goddamned pleased before whom he Goddamned pleased—or words to that effect. Joe's language is very lurid when it is unrestrained, as it was on this occasion. Bill told him that he was abysmally ignorant on foreign affairs and hadn't any basis for expressing any opinion. He emphasized that so long as he was a member of the Administration he ought to be loyal—or at least keep his mouth shut.*[128]

Ickes told Roosevelt on August 29 about his conversation with Cudahy and afterwards noted in his diary that "The President knows that Joe is not loyal. . . ." [129] When Morgenthau suggested, "You know, Mr. President, you can't trust Kennedy," the President responded affirmatively.[130] White House insiders Alsop and Kintner reported that Roosevelt's lingering warmth for Kennedy was chilled by reports of Kennedy's chatterings in London.[131]

Kennedy left for his vacation with an ominous word: "I am going to give the State Department information that is too confidential for cables." [132] He traveled via Lisbon, where he dined with U.S. Ambassador Herbert C. Pell, Sir Walford Selby of the British Embassy in Lisbon, and other assorted dignitaries. Selby reported home that Kennedy had expressed his opposition to American entry into the war, "in such a way as to lead me to conclude that he had little if any sympathy with the point of view of the country to which he was accredited or for the cause for which we had entered the war." Selby thereafter noted a surprisingly increased reserve in Pell's attitude towards the war situation, and suspected that the change in Pell's attitude might have been the result of "fallout" from Pell's contact with "the very 'neutral' American Ambassador in London." [133]

On his arrival in the United States, Kennedy presented a cheerful and confident facade for reporters who met him at the airport. The *Philadelphia Inquirer* reported that Kennedy was "in one of his most affable moods" when he arrived. He was the first passenger to step off the plane. Rose Kennedy broke through the lines and kissed him.[134] Kennedy told reporters that he would probably stay in London the duration of the war, but that this was his last public job.[135] On the situation in Britain, he said that London was gayer than it had been for years; he commented especially on the activity of London nightlife.[136] He assured the press that Britain did not expect the United States to fight its battles: "The British government does not have the slightest belief that the United States will get into this war . . . they understand our position perfectly." [137] Kennedy spoke like a movie executive saying "great"; apparently none of the reporters guessed that he believed the situation "lousy."

The following day Kennedy spent two hours with the President in the morning and more time with Roosevelt in the afternoon. The President told his press conference that they had discussed possible ways to expand American shipping lines by servicing routes abandoned by belligerents, and by supplying products unavailable in Europe due to disruption of transportation facilities.[138]

Kennedy was less tight-lipped. On leaving the afternoon visit, Kennedy endorsed a third term for Roosevelt. Perhaps the two discussed the Presidency during their meeting. Kennedy told reporters that the grave situation in Europe was sufficient warrant to continue Roosevelt in office. The state of affairs was such that the United States could not spare the time to break in a new man. "No matter how brilliant or earnest," no man could learn to manage national affairs in less than two years.[139] In describing the conditions that made

Roosevelt's reelection wise, Kennedy was able to voice his opinions more honestly than he had done the day before at the airport. He told reporters that if he told them what he thought about the European crisis "they would have to forego their dinners." [140] Asked how long he expected the war to last, he replied, "All I can say is that continuation of the war will be catastrophic for the political, social, and economic life of the peoples of the world." [141] American entry into the war "would mean chaos beyond anybody's dream." [142] "Nobody over there wanted war so they can't find fault with America when she insists she wants to remain neutral and stay out of the war. . . . the British were never misled as to our position." [143]

The endorsement of the third term received more comment than Kennedy's gloomy forebodings and isolationist comments on the world situation. Ickes was surprised at the endorsement;[144] even Krock was taken aback and wrote on December 12 that "Mr. Kennedy was almost the last man in the Administration from whom anti-New Dealers and New Dealers alike expected such a statement." Krock reported that those opposed to Roosevelt's reelection attributed Kennedy's endorsement to shell shock.[145]

Krock also considered the Ambassador's gloom. He quoted nameless persons as saying, "Joe is usually a bear, but this time he is a whole den." The journalist added, "Those who have talked of world conditions with the Ambassador [and Krock undoubtedly had] agree that description is perhaps an understatement. [Kennedy's view is] of the impending Dark Ages for mankind, whichever side defeats the other in the war." [146]

Krock himself expressed reservations about the third term, in which Kennedy no doubt silently concurred. His endorsement of Roosevelt was probably made in an effort to convince the President of his loyalty; Kennedy always made strenuous efforts to dispel whatever suspicions the President might have had.[147] The endorsement did not quite ring true and subsequent events made clear that Kennedy's heart was not in it.

Kennedy began to speak his views on the international scene frequently and frankly. On Decmeber 10, he attended an East Boston Church and spoke extemporaneously about keeping out of war. He included a scarcely veiled warning against British propaganda:

As you love America, don't let anything that comes out of any country in the world make you believe you can make a situation one whit better by getting into war. There is no place in this fight for us. It's going to be bad enough as it is.[148]

Afterwards in an interview with a reporter, he said:

> *After this interview is over, I hope you will leave with the
> impression that I am not too optimistic about the results if the
> United States were foolish enough to get into war. There is no
> justification, economically, socially, financially, politically, for
> the United States entering this war.*

Perhaps to make clear that his bright statements on arrival had been
insincere, Kennedy mentioned that he had done a lot of nightclubbing
in the three days since his return—"Life is dismal over there." [149]

At the Foreign Office, where Kennedy's private feelings were
well-known, press clippings of the comments were greeted mildly—"I
should not have been surprised by worse," was Cadogan's reaction.[150]
Other members of the diplomatic community, though, were aghast—
the Belgian Ambassador assured Balfour that the speech would "not
endear [Kennedy] to his European colleagues in London" [151]—and the
press reports gave the Briton on the street his first taste of Kennedy's
real stance. The unknowing felt that their friend Ambassador Kennedy
had abandoned them. *The Spectator*, an influential conservative British
weekly, called the speech "something of a shock":

> *Not, of course, that we ever expected America to come in, unless
> the situation changes catastrophically, but there would seem to
> be plenty of eminent persons in the United States to give
> isolationist advice without the Ambassador to the Court of Saint
> James's, knowing all our anxieties and all our ordeal, finding it
> necessary to join himself to the number.*[152]

The speech was another that proved embarrassing to the State
Department. Perhaps they spoke to the Ambassador about further
public statements along these lines. In any event, Kennedy remained
quiet for two months. He told newsmen, "From now on everything is
off the record. . . . There is no use in following me around any
more." [153]

Kennedy, however, spread his gloom privately. Alsop and Kintner
wrote, "To any one who comes within hailing distance, our Ambassador to England freely depicts the collapse of capitalism, the destruction of democracy and the onset of the dark ages." [154] Kennedy must
have spent much of his vacation-time impressing influential people
with the hopelessness of the situation and urging isolationism. On
December 15, he told a group of Army and Navy officers (". . . his
language being picturesque in the extreme," commented the formal

Moffat) of poor spirits among the French and British, and horrible economic conditions in both countries. Militarily, the situation was grimmer still; the Germans were building submarines faster than the British could destroy them and German air production too outran that of the British. Another year of strain could not be endured: "By the end of this year, if not before, people in England and France and all over Europe would be ready for communism." Kennedy believed the United States should reinforce itself, so as to be able to withstand the shock of European collapse. There was one hopeful note, he told the officers: "If the war should go wrong and the British Empire be defeated, Europe would be so exhausted we would have nothing to fear." [155] The remarks annoyed Colonel Knox and much of the audience.[156]

The strain of work and gloom of mood of the previous few months had adversely affected Kennedy's health. In the period since the start of the crisis he had lost 15 pounds,[157] and he needed a rest to restore himself.[158] He retired to his Palm Beach villa, and the press reported that "The Ambassador is recuperating from an illness brought on by his wartime duties in London" [159]—which was going some, inasmuch as the war had begun in London only in name. Friends were reported to have described the nature of his malaise as gastric trouble.[160] While Lothian confirmed that Kennedy was in fact not well,[161] the press reports of Kennedy's illness were greeted cynically at the Foreign Office. Perowne regarded it as a new tack in Kennedy's "*défaitiste* campaign"—"The rigours of life in London in war time are so considerable that they induce illness in certain Ambassadors, some two months after they have returned to their native lands!" [162] Balfour surmised that the gastric troubles had been "contracted no doubt at the dining tables of Mayfair," [163] a section of London celebrated for its fashionable and expensive continental restaurants. Tongue in cheek, the peppery Vansittart doubted Balfour's diagnosis: "he has always asked for special dishes—I think most of the restaurants know his foibles by now and act automatically. I wondered at one time if it was a pose but I fancy it is genuine and just the normal stomach disorder to which the successful American business men are so prone." [164]

Kennedy again emerged to public view in mid-February, with a series of newspaper interviews given at his Palm Beach home. On February 10 the *New York Journal-American* quoted him as saying:
The United States must not permit itself to be drawn into conflict, either directly or indirectly; by way of China or any

*other devious route. There is no point to our participating in the
present maelstrom in Europe.*

Kennedy apparently was not eager to have the United States loan the
Allies money either. (In correspondence and conferences with Roosevelt he had urged that it was extremely important for the United
States to keep "financially strong.") He told the *Journal-American*
reporter that the Allies had funds to carry on for an indefinite
period.[165] It went without saying that it was accordingly unnecessary
to help the Allies financially. Two days later the *Chicago Daily
Tribune* published more of the same under the headline:

"ALL HELL TO BREAK IN EUROPE"

IN 2 MONTHS, KENNEDY SAYS[166]

As Kennedy's vacation time drew to a close, speculation as to his
Presidential plans again hit the front pages. Although Kennedy's
endorsement of Roosevelt had seemingly taken Kennedy out of the
race, he made no attempt to quell fresh rumors as to his intentions. On
February 12, the *Boston Post* headlined:

KENNEDY MAY BE CANDIDATE[167]

Most high officeholders with any imagination or ambition entertain
Presidential ambitions at some time or another, if only for a brief
moment. Joseph P. Kennedy was not only ambitious and imaginative,
but also popular and self-confident. When he was first appointed
Ambassador, the world's most widely-read newspaper, the *New York
Daily News*, proclaimed him the "Crown Prince of the Roosevelt
Regime." John O'Donnell and Doris Fleeson, the *News'* Washington
correspondents, saw the appointment as indicative that Kennedy was
"F.D.R.'s personal selection as his successor to White House honors in
1940." [168] The *Boston Post, Boston American,* and *Boston Traveler*
endorsed him editorially for the Presidency early in his ambassadorial
period,[169] and papers all over the country showed remarkable interest
in a Kennedy candidacy.[170] Even if Kennedy had not previously
thought of running, the press must have put the idea in his head.
Krock, who would have known, writes that Kennedy dreamed of the
Presidency, and actively promoted his Presidential possibilities.[171] Rex
Leeper, from the Political Intelligence Department at the Foreign
Office, suspected as much, and was satisfied that "Kennedy's real
ambition is the White House, and he has a great chance of achieving
it." [172]

Never one to shun publicity, Kennedy made extra efforts to get good publicity for himself in his early ambassadorial career. His close personal contacts with reporters made this easy, and he was most solicitous of the press. Time-Life's Henry Luce, for example, could only have been favorably impressed by "a nice, a very large and very distinguished dinner party," that the Ambassador hosted for him in London, though the two were not very close at the time.[173] Kennedy was always accessible for interviews with the American press corps, varying his openness according to the strength and source of the particular reporter's references,[174] and he irritated the British by his efforts to circumvent "proper channels" in getting access for American journalists to high-ranking British officials.[175] One journalist wrote that Kennedy's Palm Beach home was a veritable publicity bureau during the winter of 1938–1939 [176] and the ring of publicity that accompanied Kennedy's every move became a constant irritant to State Department officials.[177]

Most of the "strong men" of the American press corps in London were anti-appeasers, and Kennedy's efforts to cultivate them were not notably successful. Despite Kennedy's good efforts, the American press correspondents did not frequent his embassy,[178] and the influential correspondent of one American newspaper told American newcomers not to bother with their Ambassador: "He doesn't know anything. He reads the ticker tape for the ball scores and the stock quotes and that's all he knows." [179] Leeper concluded shortly after Munich that Kennedy "has not gained the confidence of the American correspondents here and therefore has little influence with them." [180] After the start of the war, Kennedy's defeatism turned all of the American correspondents, save only William Hillman,[181] Hearst's London Bureau Chief, bitterly against him.[182] But at home, the attitude of the "men on the scene" did not filter down to the readers. The efforts of Krock and Boake Carter were supplemented by extensive and favorable coverage of Kennedy's activities in the Luce publications, and the Hearst press always gave him extravagant treatment. Hugh Johnson observed in 1938 that "somebody is doing one of the best recorded publicity jobs of pressagenting for the Honorable Joseph P. Kennedy." [183] The "somebody" seemed clear enough to New Deal insiders: in a discussion with Morgenthau, Tom Corcoran

> *got really violent in his discussion of Kennedy and Krock. He said that Krock was running a campaign to put Joe Kennedy over*

*for President; that if any prominent Catholic gets in the way he's
to be rubbed out. . . . If anybody with financial training gets in
the way, he's to be rubbed out.*[184]

Kennedy followed his press in a huge clipping collection, culling
scraps from a wide variety of papers, giving a cross-section of
American opinion. Many small-town and little-city papers were
clipped, while some of the big-city dailies were ignored. Kennedy was
sampling American opinion at large.

Kennedy could almost certainly have had the delegates from
Massachusetts in 1940,[185] and had Roosevelt stepped down, the
Ambassador would have been one of the likeliest contenders for the
Democratic nomination. There were many other possibilities—Hull,
Farley, Vice-President Garner, Senator Wheeler, Indiana Governor
Paul V. McNutt—but Kennedy had a better public image than any of
them, the result of having cultivated the press for years. He also had
better sources of campaign funds than they did. He had both
administrative and foreign policy experience, and as a conservative
associated with the New Deal, he could have appealed to both
elements in his party.[186] Of course, there were also disadvantages to
Kennedy's candidacy. Al Smith's Catholicism was incidental to his
defeat in the Presidential campaign of 1928, but in 1940 Smith's
religion was still regarded by many as having been his insuperable
impediment. All in all, Kennedy made a powerful on-paper candidate,
and friends like Grover Loening encouraged him with assurances (in
the fall of 1938) like "keep up as you are doing for another year and
you could swing the 1940 election a lot easier than you think." [187]

However appealing the idea of running for President must have
been to Kennedy, the Ambassador was not blind. He probably sensed
that Roosevelt would be a candidate again, and he saw that no contender would have much of a chance against the incumbent for the Democratic nomination. Roosevelt had a way of souring very rapidly and
very thoroughly on those who seemed interested in his job. That being
the case, Kennedy saw little sense in further threatening his position
with the Administration and the party over a hypothetical chance
at the Presidency that could not conceivably materialize in 1940.

It is likely that Kennedy put all thoughts about the Presidency out
of his mind before his return and his endorsement of Roosevelt on
December 8. But Kennedy was enjoying the speculation. Supporters in
Massachusetts were preparing to enter his name in the Common-

wealth's Presidential primary, notwithstanding his endorsement of Roosevelt. In an apparent attempt to build up suspense as to his plans, Kennedy announced on the thirteenth that he would issue a statement that evening making known his decision with regard to the Massachusetts primary.[188]

The decision was not to enter. That evening Kennedy explained that the demands for his services in London made it impossible for him to seek the Presidency: "I cannot forget that I now occupy a most important Government post, which at this particular time involves matters so precious to the American people that no private consideration should permit my energies or interests to be diverted." [189] He would not permit his name to be filed for the primary.

Mourning the loss of Kennedy's candidacy, Hearst's *Journal-American* insisted that the country needed a man *like* Kennedy for President in 1940,[190] and a Boston attorney, John F. McCarthy, Jr., who had been preparing primary papers on Kennedy's behalf, announced that he would continue to seek convention delegates pledged to the Ambassador.[191]

Political commentators were not slow to point out that Kennedy's filing in Massachusetts would have indirectly helped Roosevelt. It would have insured the loss of the Massachusetts convention delegates to Farley, the only announced candidate for the Democratic Presidential nomination. Roosevelt himself had urged Kennedy to enter the primary, arguing that it was unfair of Farley to have gone into Kennedy's home territory.[192] As early as August, 1938, the *Boston American* had asserted that a favorite-son boom for Kennedy in Massachusetts was aimed at Farley.[193] The *Boston Globe* headlined Kennedy's decision not to run with:

ENVOY'S "NO" CLEARS WAY

FOR FARLEY HERE[194]

and the Kennedy announcement was greeted with satisfaction by Farley's backers.

The advantage that accrued to Farley was of course incidental, but Kennedy did not regret this help given the Postmaster-General. The two men had never been close personally, but Farley had Kennedy's unspoken sympathies in his quest for the Presidency, as he appeared to be the strongest Democrat willing to run against Roosevelt. Farley later explained that Kennedy's sympathies for him were founded not on favor for the Postmaster-General personally, but on a philosophical opposition to the idea of any man serving three terms in the Presidency.[195] The author has found no indication that the thought of a third term was repugnant to Kennedy—who had gone along with court-packing without a whimper. It seems more likely, and quite human, that Kennedy's sympathies for Farley were based on personal considerations: on the unpleasantness that existed between Kennedy and the President. If, indeed, the Ambassador's decision rested upon higher bases, no doubt they were related to the Ambassador's differences with Roosevelt over foreign policy. But Kennedy was never excessively preoccupied with philosophical considerations; as Krock wrote, he used "the personal equation." [196]

Two days after Kennedy's announcement that he would not run, Joseph P. Kennedy, Jr., who mirrored his father's mind, announced that he would contest for a seat at the convention as a Farley delegate.[197] In response to Honey's request, Massachusetts Democratic State Chairman William Burke (who held the position until "dumped" at the insistence of Senator John Kennedy in 1956) had Joe, Jr., put on the endorsed slate as a delegate from Brookline.[198] Joe, Jr., survived a challenge to his candidacy based on the fact that he was not a registered voter in the Brookline district that he sought to represent,[199] and then, to be on the safe side, he actively campaigned for his seat at the convention in the subsequent primary, a seat that would normally have been taken for granted. He barely survived the primary.[200] Later, when the Democratic National Convention met to "draft" the "reluctant" FDR to run for an unprecedented third term, Joe, Jr., was subjected to pressures from delegation leaders, including his father's close journalist friend Clem Norton,[201] to switch from Farley to Roosevelt. Roosevelt backers put through a transatlantic call to the Ambassador, to urge him to persuade his son to "go along." The senior Kennedy turned a deaf ear.[202] Joe, Jr., turned to Krock for advice, who urged him to hold firm for Farley.[203] Finally, Joe, Jr., called the Ambassador,[204] for thoughts that, to a young man who was not a son but an alter ego, would have constituted direction from within. When the roll call was taken, it was a landslide for Roosevelt; Joseph P. Kennedy, Jr., was one of a handful to yell out "Farley!" In London, his father told Halifax that he had grave doubts that Roosevelt would win the election.[205]

OUR MOST
BOMBED AMBASSADOR

KENNEDY SAILED FOR EUROPE ON FEBRUARY 23, 1940, AFTER almost three months away from his post. His only comment on departure was, "Without question the United States should stay out of war." [1] He had grave misgivings about returning to London, and complained to diplomat Robert Murphy of "his bad health, his discontent over returning to London, his belief that everything he could do there could just as well be done by a $50-a-month clerk, that he wanted to quit but didn't see how he gracefully could before the elections." [2] In England his return was anticipated with equally grave misgivings. Kennedy's comments during his holiday had destroyed whatever lingering good will he might have enjoyed in England. He had explained to Lothian, the embassy wrote Halifax, that "he had stressed his conviction that America should stay out of the war in order that he might maintain some influence over here," [3] but at the Foreign Office no one was much impressed by the explanation. Long before Munich, Vansittart had developed a fierce dislike for anyone whom he took to be "playing Hitler's game," [4] and he was terribly worried that Kennedy would continue to press for a negotiated peace[5] and spread his gloom.

The American desk gave up on any attempt to change Kennedy's attitude. Perowne's conclusion that nothing would suffice to "alter his views except a belief that it will pay him to do or say so," was echoed by Balfour's "I don't believe we can (alter his views). He is malevolent and pigeon-livered." [6] Vansittart's opinion of the Ambassador was still harsher: "A very foul specimen of double-crosser and defeatist. He thinks of nothing but his own pocket. I hope that the war will at least see the elimination of his type." [7] The decision reached on what-to-do was to take a new stance with regard to the Ambassador; to be much less free in discussing the situation with him or with members of his staff who would have to relay any news to the Ambassador;[8] and, to spread the word that Kennedy was no longer to be "treated like an honorary member of the cabinet." [9] Cadogan sent out the decision in highly secret letters to other heads of the state.[10]

Kennedy's reception at the American Embassy was probably little better than it was at the Foreign Office. He had not become close to any of the embassy people[11] and shortly after the start of the war, Leeper wrote that, for reasons unrelated to the Ambassador's attitude, Kennedy had annoyed most of his underlings.[12] His subsequent views towards the war and his activities steeled this prior adverse disposition among significant segments of the embassy staff. Butterworth, in deepest confidence, shared his criticisms of Kennedy's vacation-time speeches with his friend, a Mr. Jebb, whose notes quickly went into the Foreign Office minute books.[13] When the Conservative journalist-politician Lord Winterton openly attacked the Ambassador at a party to the American Embassy's military attaché, General Sherman Miles, the attaché defended his chief in a fashion that "gave the impression of agreeing with Lord Winterton's opinion of Mr. Kennedy, while not wishing to appear disloyal." [14] Kennedy's Air Attaché, Colonel (later General) Raymond Lee, developed a contempt for the Ambassador that is plain from his published diary, and which, with discretion, he attempted to inculcate in other members of the American community.[15] At the time of Kennedy's return to his post, Perowne noted that the Ambassador was quite unpopular with the embassy staff and with the American press corps, to which Balfour added that he had learned that the American journalists "wax indignant at the mere mention of Kennedy's name." [16]

Even in the London press, Kennedy's reception was bad. Harold Nicolson welcomed him back in *The Spectator*:

> *He will be welcomed, as is fitting, by the large and influential Anglo-American colony in London. He will also be welcomed by the native or unhyphenated rich, who hope that he may bring with him a little raft of appeasement on which they can float for a year or so longer before they are finally submerged. He will be welcomed, of course, by the bankers and the isolationists, by the knights and the baronets. He will be welcomed by the shiver-sisters of Mayfair and by the wobble-boys of Whitehall. He will be welcomed by the Peace Pledge Union, the Christian Pacifists, the followers of Dr. Buchman, the friends of Herr von Ribbentrop, the Nürembergers, the Munichois, Lord Tavistock and the disjecta membra of former pro-Nazi organizations. A solemn gladness will even crown the brows of M. Maisky, ambassador of the U.S.S.R. Few envoys, on returning to their post, can have received a welcome of such embarrassing variety.[17]*

Kennedy's reaction to his reception was characteristic: he called a press conference. He reported to the British public on American reactions, tendering an explanation as to American isolationism. Kennedy explained that no one had yet proven to the American public that it was going to do the slightest bit of good for the United States to get into the war.

> *If isolation means a desire to keep out of war, I should say it is definitely stronger. It is not that the Americans do not want to support the Allies or that they are selfish; but there is not a single thought running through the American mind that did not run through the English mind before war was declared.*[18]

Kennedy said that the conviction in the United States that the country would enter the war was not as strong as it had formerly been. Americans, he explained, "don't understand what it is all about."[19]

Englishmen were not pleased with the Ambassador's statements. Perhaps they realized that Kennedy was speaking principally for himself. In his statements on arrival in Britain he projected as "America's" feelings his own public statements in America: "We can [not] make the situation one whit better by getting into war"; "Nobody over there wanted war so they can't find fault with America when she insists she wants to remain neutral." Britain refused to believe that he was adequately summarizing the spirit of his country.[20] A. Beverly Baxter, a journalist Member of Parliament and Churchill-intimate, attacked him in a widely circulated article in *The Sunday Graphic*:

> *When a poor demented Jewish youth killed von Rath in Paris and Hitler sent his incendiaries, robbers and murderers into the streets of Germany for revenge America knew what it was about. . . . When Germany, having reduced Czechoslovakia to helplessness, marched into Prague and ended the little republic's existence, your Nation had no difficulties in realizing what was going on.*
> *When little Dollfuss lay gasping out his life with Nazi bullets in his throat . . . When . . . When . . .*
> *Can it be true that your people did not understand?*

"My dear Ambassador," Baxter asked, "why didn't you tell them?"[21]

More than one answer could be given to Baxter's question. One Congressman answered it with the response that it was not the job of the American Ambassador to represent British interests.[22] That, however, was not the explanation that Kennedy gave to Bilainkin.

Kennedy felt at ease with Bilainkin; he knew the Englishman would respect his confidences,[23] and spoke frankly: "I have very little idea what it's really all about, and nobody else seems to have much more." [24] He had reached the conclusion that it was an imperial war—but that did not make much sense to him. Though he had early subscribed to the belief that economics was the basis of the Anglo-German friction,[25] he was unsatisfied with an economic interpretation of the war, for he told King George that he could not see that England had a valid economic interest in the disputed portions of Europe. The King was disturbed that Kennedy could not understand "the deeper motives for which Britain had entered the struggle" but could see "only that, since eastern Europe was of little use to [England] from a monetary standpoint, she might as well allow Hitler to occupy it." [26] An idealistic approach made absolutely no sense to Kennedy. To Bilainkin,

> *He defended his Boston speech of the previous Christmastime as reflecting statements no more unusual than those made in England. As he spoke, a smile revealed a tinge of bitterness. He said Britain was fighting for self-preservation, not the freedom of small nations. . . . "If I had said anything else, favoring anything else but isolation, think what our press would have said over there. They would have shouted, 'Here is another Walter Page;' 'he is a British Ambassador and not the American Ambassador any longer.' The value of what I have said to Britain, or to America, would have been vitiated. Attacks would have been wholesale. . . ." [27]*

The German press reported that Kennedy's relations with the British government had become very strained because of his comments, and although Kennedy called the German rumor "the best fairy tale I have read since Snow White," [28] he himself noted that it "soon became evident that a coolness had developed towards me in those circles, official and otherwise, whose main use for America was to embroil us in the war." [29]

Kennedy, however, did not have time to feel sorry for himself. He had just a few days' time to prepare for a visit to England by Sumner Welles. Roosevelt was unquestionably harsh on Kennedy for the Ambassador's efforts at peacemaking. Nonetheless, the President himself was attuned to just such possibilities and, early in 1940, sent Welles to visit the European belligerents to investigate—and if at all possible to encourage—prospects for a negotiated peace. Kennedy, it appears, had no direct involvement in the decision to send the Welles mission,[30] but his bleak evaluations of Britain's situation must have played some part in Roosevelt's decision to sponsor the visit, and in spirit the mission comported with everything that Kennedy had been preaching since the declaration of war and before. Though there is no reason to believe that Kennedy saw it as such, he might fairly have regarded the Welles mission as the fruit of his own efforts. While Bullitt saw Welles' trip as a blow to good order,[31] Kennedy welcomed it as an overdue step in the right direction.[32]

The British—who were unsatisfied as to the imminence of their own defeat—were not interested in a "patched up peace," [33] and suspected that the Welles mission was either the product of unsavory American partisan politics,[34] or alternately, the brainchild of their bête noire, Joseph Kennedy.[35] Vansittart urged his fellows to take firm steps to "warn President Roosevelt off any undesirable grass, before we have to receive the grass-snake, Mr. Welles," [36] but it was too hard to dissuade the President delicately, and instead the Foreign Office determined to welcome Welles while making clear to him that they were unwilling to settle for less than the humiliation of the Führer.[37] Some saw hope that the Welles visit might have a silver lining as "a useful antidote against the defeatism of people like Kennedy." [38]

Kennedy worked tirelessly on the arrangements during the short time that he preceded Welles in London, and scheduled his friend's whole visit.[39] Welles, Moffat, and entourage arrived in London on March 10, 1940. Kennedy met them at the airport, and escorted Welles to his suite at the Dorchester, where—notwithstanding a discussion as to "bugging" in which Welles commented that he assumed every hotel had its microphones, and therefore refrained from saying anything of importance in his rooms—Kennedy reported in depth to the Under Secretary.[40]

During the next two weeks, Welles visited a large number of people, usually accompanied by Kennedy and often Moffat. The latter was quite favorably impressed with Kennedy's habit of cutting short British propaganda comments with a "For Christ's sake, stop trying to make this a holy war, because no one will believe you; you're fighting for your life as an Empire, and that's good enough." [41] The Ambassador was extremely disturbed when Welles was invited to tea with the King and Queen at the Palace without him. His complaint to Welles brought a comment to a British official and an invitation for Kennedy.[42]

On the last night in London there was a stag dinner for the Welles entourage, attended by the Prime Minister, Churchill, Labour's Clement Attlee, and several other guests. Moffat noted in his diary:

Toward the end of the evening Joe Kennedy brought the talk around to actualities, and under the cloak of horseplay was able to get across many unpalatable home-truths regarding Anglo-American relations. It was superlatively done. He made it very clear that certain things, such as taking our ships into the combat area, could not be done without risking a serious flare-up. Churchill protested, but in the end agreed.[43]

Kennedy's isolationism had the value of protecting America's interests. When, at the close of the evening, Churchill commented on the toughness of the English nation, Kennedy said, "Well if you can show me one Englishman that's tougher than you are, Winston, I'll eat my hat." On this note, Moffat recorded, the party broke up.[44]

The following day Welles left. Kennedy applauded his friend's efforts in a wire to the State Department: "He did an exceptionally fine job here in getting facts from all types of people." [45] He had, however, not succeeded in eliciting much sign of willingness from the British to negotiate a peace.[46]

A visit, especially a peace mission, by an Under Secretary of State who was a close personal friend of Kennedy, was all well and good. Fact-finding missions by lesser-ranking men were a very different matter. Later, when the war in the West got really underway, Roosevelt sent a number of such missions to England. They were one way in which the President lessened his dependence on his Ambassador, but the very sending of such missions was highly offensive to Kennedy, with the inherent implication that he and his staff were incapable of providing adequate information. To others they reflected Roosevelt's lack of confidence in Kennedy.[47] In July, Knox, serving as Roosevelt's Secretary of War, decided to send Colonel William J. "Wild Bill" Donovan and journalist Edgar A. Mowrer to evaluate Britain's war situation. The White House concurred.[48] On receipt of a telegram announcing the Donovan mission,[49] Kennedy quickly wired back a spirited response:

I will render any service I can to Colonel Donovan, whom I know and like, (but) our staff, I think, is getting the information that possibly can be gathered and to send a new man in here at this time, with all due respect to Colonel Knox, is to me the height of nonsense and a definite blow to good organization.[50]

Kennedy was especially perturbed that Mowrer, a reporter with Knox's *Chicago Daily News*, was coming: "We don't need a newspaperman to make this investigation for the government and it is most embarrassing to me. I think he should be called off the complete assignment at once." [51] When Welles conveyed the Ambassador's displeasure to the President,[52] Roosevelt took it in stride—"Somebody's nose seems to be out of joint," he told Knox.[53]

With the blessings of Hull and the President, Donovan and Mowrer arrived within days thereafter, in mid-July, 1940. At the same time, Colonel Carl Spaatz led a U.S. Air Force inquiry in England. In late August missions were sent headed by General George Strong and Admiral Robert L. Ghormley. The State Department did not even notify Kennedy that Ghormley was coming; he learned of the Admiral's mission from the British, and wrote Hull, ". . . it has been a bit embarrassing to have the entire British Cabinet know that an Admiral was coming here for staff talks when nobody in the Embassy knew anything about it." [54] Later, in September, came Commander James Fife, for further inquiry. Kennedy bitterly protested the sending of these missions, to no avail, and his displeasure over them found its way into German Foreign Office files[55] and later the press.[56]

WORLD EVENTS REMAINED QUIET UNTIL APRIL, 1940, WHEN HITLER moved west for the first time, attacking Denmark and Norway. What had seemed a "phony war" to people in Britain and France revealed itself to have been a phony peace. For eight months Britain and France had taken no initiative against the Reich. Germany had taken care of Poland in short order, had enjoyed a winter to regroup, and could now turn undivided attention westward and again take the initiative. At Churchill's insistence, Britain had been preparing for a campaign in Norway, designed to cut off German access to vital ore deposits in the far north, and for the first time in the course of the war British and German forces faced each other.

Kennedy could not be optimistic. Not only the balance of tangibles seemed against England; the nation did not seem to be doing a very good job in harnessing such assets as it had. He spoke more than frankly with government leaders. John C. W. Reith of the B.B.C.

noted opinions that the Ambassador had expressed at a meeting of the two with Lord Halifax: Kennedy

> launched into a violent attack on the BBC. He continued about the service departments; about labor; about England generally. There was no doubt about it, we were thoroughly inefficient and degenerate. A meeting of US attachés had agreed that England would be beaten in the war.[57]

The day after, Kennedy reported the same sentiments to Washington:

> There is universal discontent that every branch of government service from top to bottom is being handled inefficiently. This feeling has been growing and is not only being talked about in the group that is against the government but in the group that should be for the government. . . . Everybody I meet would like to throw the Cabinet out but when you ask whom they would put in, they have not the slightest idea. . . . You know that this bearish streak of mine is not a new one. It started before Munich. Tonight a great many people here are beginning to realize that England lacks efficient leadership from top to bottom and unless there is a terrific change, and quickly, things will be as serious as one can imagine.[58]

Even Churchill did not seem so omnipotent anymore. The Norwegian campaign was going badly. The British at first routed the Germans from their positions, but failed to secure the ports, and soon found their position untenable and had to forsake the gains they had won. As First Lord of the Admiralty, Churchill took the lion's share of the blame in the largely naval campaign. Kennedy reported that "The situation in Norway, which some people are already characterizing as the second Gallipoli has caused Mister Churchill's sun to set very rapidly." [59]

While Hull asserts that he and Roosevelt did not share Kennedy's feverous gloom,[60] the President was apparently influenced by his Ambassador's reports, and when he lunched with Morgenthau on April 29, he echoed Kennedy's darkest forebodings, anticipating Britain's imminent loss—Morgenthau characterized the President's attitude as "defeatist." [61] Still, Roosevelt put on a bold front for Kennedy, and wired him on May 3, "These are bad days for all of us who remember always that when real world forces come into conflict, the final result is never as dark as we mortals guess it in very difficult days." [62] Roosevelt's comforting words fell on deaf ears. The stream of gloom, mixed with isolationist advice, continued. Soon after, Kennedy reported again on universal unrest, even in the cabinet:

Frankly the situation looks chaotic. The country is calling for more action, the opposition ministers call for taking the initiative, but outside Duff Cooper practically calling for a war with Italy, nobody has the slightest idea just how this initiative can be shown. . . . Everybody is mad and all wanting to do something and go places, but nobody has the slightest idea of what should be done.[63]

Chamberlain, Halifax, and Churchill, he reported, were all tired men, "definitely aware of just what a mess England is finding itself in."[64] His comments were largely valid, especially his conclusion that England had a Prime Minister running a war with a lack of public confidence and an angry minority party.[65.]

In fierce debate in the House of Commons on May 7 and May 8, Britain's leader of World War I, the Liberal David Lloyd George, spoke with what one observer called "a last flicker of destructive genius":[66]

He [Chamberlain] has appealed for sacrifice. The nation is prepared for every sacrifice so long as it has leadership. . . . I say solemnly that the Prime Minister should give an example of sacrifice, because there is nothing that can contribute more to victory in this war than that he should sacrifice the seals of office.

Kennedy thought that Chamberlain would weather the storm, and cabled Welles that "the real opposition is in the ranks of the Government's own supporters and it is only from them that any effective revolt can come, as the political opposition is futile and without dynamic leadership."[67] Chamberlain survived a crucial test vote, but under circumstances that made clear that his government should not continue during wartime conditions that required the support and cooperation of all elements. He summoned to himself the two logical successors: Halifax, the prestigious and longtime loyal colleague of the Prime Minister, and Churchill, his outspoken antagonist of old. Chamberlain's preference was natural and understandable, but Halifax's biographer writes that the Foreign Secretary

was acutely conscious that his great gifts were in many ways the exact opposite of those required in the fighting leader of a forlorn cause, and that he was lacking in the drive and ruthlessness which the situation demanded. He knew that Churchill was preeminent in both, and to Halifax it seemed that the whole of that turbulent life might almost have been a preparation for this moment of destiny.[68]

And so Halifax declined to take the step that would have brought him to the pinnacle of a British statesman's career, and instead yielded to the other.[69] On May 10, 1940, the reins were passed from the discredited Chamberlain to Churchill; graciously, Churchill described the fallen leader's speech as magnanimous.[70]

Taylor writes that "The Conservatives who had backed Chamberlain to the last did not forgive so easily." [71] Kennedy's reaction was typical of more than one:[72] a couple of months later, Kennedy commented to Malcolm Macdonald that the new Prime Minister was "one of the few men who has achieved his great ambition and the final mark of his success of becoming Prime Minister as a result of a great failure (the Norwegian campaign) for which he alone was responsible." [73] What seems to have struck Kennedy about the drama of succession was not the majestic self-sacrifices involved, but rather, the irony inherent in what he took to be the undeserved windfall of the successor. Though he himself had recently pointed out the need for a change in the government, once the change was made, he belittled its significance to Halifax, and no doubt to himself: "As he saw it," Halifax wrote Lothian, "the winning of the war had little to do with changes of Government, or accusations of complacency or lack of drive, it was simply a question of whether one had enough aeroplanes." [74]

The evening that Churchill took over, Kennedy called him to extend his good wishes. In a friendly telephone call, Kennedy "laughingly" (his word) reminded Churchill of Kennedy's own role in the new Prime Minister's success: through Kennedy, Roosevelt had given advance approval of Britain's mining of neutral Norwegian waters,[75] "hence Norway, hence Prime Minister." [76] Perhaps Churchill, who was acutely aware of his own share of responsibility for the Norwegian campaign, sensed that the congratulatory telephone call was really not all that friendly. In any event, relations between Kennedy and the new Prime Minister remained adequate on the surface. Below the surface, the two men never got along well.[77] The Ambassador's personal and philosophical closeness with the appeasers, his sympathies for them, his efforts on their behalf, and his continued defeatism, hampered his ability to work with the vigorous new leader. English policies had changed, and Kennedy remained as the last vestige of the old. To the President's confidant Harry Hopkins, Churchill later launched a bitter, though restrained attack on Kennedy.[78]

On his own part, Kennedy disliked Churchill, and attempted to poison the President against him with comments like Churchill "has developed into a fine two-handed drinker,"[79] or, "Churchill has in America a couple of very close friends who are definitely not on our team."[80]

Kennedy was perhaps a little jealous of Churchill's professed optimism. As the embodiment of Britain's imperial tradition, Churchill was distasteful to the Irish in Kennedy; he noted disapprovingly that Churchill referred to Cobh, in Eire, as "Queenstown," the British name for the Irish seaport.[81] He was envious of Churchill's magnificent diction, and habit of speaking even informally in cascades of oratory,[82] which stood in apparent contrast to his own limitations at turning an eloquent phrase or articulating a noble sentiment.[83] Sir Winston's approach to the war as a moral cause struck him as both self-righteous and fraudulent, and perhaps as a slap at himself.

Kennedy suspected Churchill of not being entirely frank with him; of telling him what he thought it advantageous for the American Ambassador to believe;[84] and of trying to keep him basically uninformed. He was offended that the new Prime Minister gave him not one whit the attention that he had received from Chamberlain, and he thought the explanation was personal.[85] He resented the fact that Churchill failed to note little personal things about him: Churchill would repeatedly offer Kennedy drinks, forgetting that the Ambassador was a virtual teetotaler. Churchill himself refused to be inhibited by the Ambassador's abstinence; when Kennedy pointedly commented that he had sworn off drinking and smoking for the duration of the war, Churchill responded with a "My God." "You make me feel as if I should go around in sack cloth and ashes."[86]

Kennedy strongly disapproved of the glass that was invariably seen close by the Prime Minister's side. Once when a friend asked Kennedy what kind of man Churchill was, the Ambassador replied, "Churchill is a remarkable man, or as remarkable as any man can be who's loaded with brandy by ten o'clock in the morning."[87] Kennedy predicted that when Churchill finally succeeded in bringing the United States into the war, "he'll reach for that brandy, charge his glass, lift his hand on high and say 'I have discharged my duty. Victory is ours! This is my crowning achievement. God save the King.' "[88]

Kennedy early saw deeper reasons to distrust Churchill. The Ambassador's affection for Neville Chamberlain made him wary of Churchill, who had seemed to pride himself on making life difficult for the older Prime Minister. Long before the change in government,

Kennedy thought he saw Churchill maneuvering to take power from the Ambassador's dear friend,[89] and when Churchill defended Chamberlain in the Norwegian disaster by largely taking the blame himself, Kennedy

> could not help but feel at the time that for all [Churchill's] protested loyalty to the Government, he saw in the distance the mantle being lowered on his shoulders and took pains, despite an occasional loss of temper, not to encourage too much enmity from any quarter.[90]

He was bitter that "Churchill's" loss of Norway had led to his accession, a fact that he did not tire of pointing out to people.[91] He regarded Churchill as unscrupulous,[92] ruthless and scheming, and hell-bent on dragging the United States into the war.[93] "Maybe I do him an injustice," Kennedy noted in his diary, but "he always impressed me that he was willing to blow up the American Embassy and say it was the Germans if it would get the United States in."[94] He suspected Churchill of being in touch with pro-war groups in the United States—"notably, certain strong Jewish leaders"[95]—and he was apprehensive on that account as well. He resented Churchill's freely expressed confidence that ultimately the United States would enter the war; Churchill's warnings that "after us, you will get it"; his scarcely-veiled threats about the possibility of Germany getting the British fleet.[96]

On May 13, Churchill made his maiden speech as Prime Minister, and perhaps his most famous oration:

> I have nothing to offer but blood, toil, tears and sweat. You ask, What is our policy? I will say: It is to wage war, by sea, land, and air, with all our might and with all the strength that God can give us. . . . You ask, What is our aim? I can answer in one word: Victory—victory at all costs, victory in spite of all terror; victory, however long and hard the road may be.

This, with the concomitant prospect of bankruptcy for all nations and chaos promising Bolshevism for the world, was exactly what Kennedy had feared.[97]

THE DAY THAT CHURCHILL TOOK THE REINS, GERMANY BEGAN ITS drive against the Netherlands and Belgium, the route to France that would avoid the most heavily defended portions of the "Maginot line" along France's frontier with Germany. Captain Alan Kirk, the

Embassy's Naval Attaché, saw Kennedy the day of the invasion of the Lowlands, and noted that the Ambassador was "tearing his hair." [98] It looked as if jackal Italy would soon ·join in the kill. At a late night conference on May 14, the new Prime Minister seemed to share Kennedy's pessimism. He conceded that if Italy entered the war Allied chances would be slim. Churchill said that if England fell, he would take the fleet to Canada and fight on. ("I think this is something I should follow up," Kennedy wired Hull.) The Ambassador told Hull that he had given the Prime Minister little encouragement: "I asked him what the United States could do to help that would not leave the United States holding the bag for a war in which the Allies expected to be beaten." [99] At any moment, Kennedy reported, the crack-up in France might come.[100]

Kennedy disseminated his pessimistic views over the turn of events so widely and so freely as to prompt M. Roché, from the French Embassy in London, to complain about Kennedy to the American desk at the Foreign Office, which was itself powerless to cope with the Ambassador's long-known attitude. Vansittart suggested to Balfour that in discussions with Roché, Kennedy's attitude should be dismissed in terms like "whilst we do not regard Mr. Kennedy as anti-British[101] we consider that he is undoubtedly a coward." Roché should be encouraged, though, to present his complaints instead to Ambassador Bullitt, in France, who would likely forward them to Roosevelt. With Halifax's approval, Balfour made the suggestion to Roché, making clear that Roché should keep the British role in his complaint unmentioned. Whether or not Roché followed up the suggestion we cannot know,[102] but in any event it is clear that Kennedy remained unquieted.[103]

Holland quickly fell before the Nazi *blitzkrieg,* and by May 24 the battle in Belgium was underway, not promising for the Allies, and seemed completely hopeless to Kennedy. He wired Hull:

The situation according to the people who know is very very grim. The mass of the people just never seem to realize that England can be beaten or that the worst can happen to them. . . . I do not underestimate the courage or guts of these people but from the reports brought back by American newspapermen who were with the forces in Belgium and Northern France, it is going to take more than guts to hold off the systematic air attacks of the Germans coupled with their terrific superiority in numbers.[104]

On the twenty-seventh he reported his impression that the situation could not be worse. Only a "miracle" could save the British expeditionary force in France and Belgium from being wiped out.[105] The following day Leopold, King of the Belgians, capitulated against the advice of his government, compelling the Allies to fall back to the seacoast where their position seemed impossible. Leopold was denounced by the British and French for having betrayed them;[106] Kennedy, however, respected the King for his action, and spoke up for him as "a human being, who could not stand useless sacrifice." [107]

Kennedy was right: under the circumstances it took a miracle to save the British expeditionary force from being wiped out. As the British forces fell back to the coast around Dunkirk, near the French-Belgium border, a huge fleet, largely of privately-owned small boats, many scarcely more than rowboats manned in good part by civilians, sailed from all over southeast England for the besieged port of Dunkirk, and during daylight bombings and amid the chatter of machine-gunning air-fighters, and under the cover of darkness, over a period of days ferried virtually all of the British army (and many of the French defenders) across the English Channel home to the United Kingdom. Though Churchill acknowledged that "wars are not won by evacuations," the inspirational deliverance from Dunkirk encouraged the English people to fight on under their titanic leader, who, in one of his most electric orations delivered as the last of the evacuees set foot in England, charged the nation:

> . . . *we shall not flag or fail. We shall go on to the end, we shall fight in France, we shall fight in the seas and oceans, we shall fight with growing confidence and growing strength in the air, we shall defend our island, whatever the cost may be, we shall fight on the beaches, we shall fight on the landing grounds, we shall fight in the fields and in the streets, we shall fight in the hills; we shall never surrender, and even if, which I do not for a moment believe, this island or a large part of it were subjugated and starving, then our Empire beyond the seas, armed and guarded by the British Fleet, would carry on the struggle, until, in God's good time, the New World, with all its power and might steps forth to the rescue and the liberation of the Old.*

To the British people, Churchill's deeply moving speech was a promise; to Joseph P. Kennedy, a nightmarish threat, which he fails to mention in any significant fashion in either his contemporary wires, or his discussions with British statesmen. In any event, his pessimism went unallayed. The capitulation of Belgium gave the Nazis access to the French heartland, where the French were waging battle. When Lord Camrose, owner of the *Daily Telegraph*, told Kennedy in early June that he expected the battle in France to be a long one, Kennedy responded that it was only a matter of "days before Paris is snatched!" [108] History has proven that Kennedy was again right. On June 10, with France almost prostrate, Italy abandoned her "neutrality" and attacked southeastern France. Bilainkin saw Kennedy the following day. The Ambassador appeared ill at ease and very nervous. When Bilainkin spoke about possible aid from America in the months to come, Kennedy interrupted angrily: "This is not a question of months, and you know it. It's a question of days." [109]

France, it was now clear, would fall momentarily, and Kennedy prepared as well for the imminent collapse of Britain. He was disturbed that British statesmen were making no provision for sending the nation's gold reserves and its royal family to Canada, and he took it as further evidence—for he had seen plenty of examples previously—that the British were not using foresight for possible eventualities. [110] Kennedy must have become impatient when even close friends like Beaverbrook began spouting question-begging homilies such as, "After all, if we don't think we are going to win, there is no point in going on." [111] Kennedy noted that British officials were paying him less and less attention, [112] and surmised, at least in part correctly, that this was because they couldn't take frank talk. [113]

Kennedy became preoccupied with the disposition of Britain's Navy, a fleet that might enable Hitler to cross the seas to America. As early as October, 1939, Churchill had warned him that the fleet could conceivably end up in German hands and the Prime Minister reminded him time and again of that possibility, and of the danger that such would entail for the United States. Kennedy wanted it to be made clear—and in a very sympathetic manner—why the United States could not help more than it was doing, [114] so that Britain would be less apt to feel revengeful toward the United States, and so less apt to let the fleet go to Germany. Kennedy had hoped that the Destroyer Deal, by which the United States traded Britain secondhand warships for leases on military bases in British America, would include a provision requiring Britain to send the fleet to Canada in case of surrender to Hitler, [115] and he could only have been disappointed that the idea was not taken up. He was haunted by the thought of Germany controlling Britain's fleet. On June 14, he wired Hull:

254 ⊔⊓⊔⊓⊔⊓⊔⊓⊔⊓⊔⊓⊔⊓⊔⊓ *Joseph P. Kennedy*

Now as to the British idea that they will go to Canada and continue the fight. Please remember that all decisions and speeches that are being made up to date are made in beautiful sunshining weather with the tension heavy but with very few actual casualties having been suffered by the people; to say what they are going to do when a real attack takes place would be very difficult to my ways of thinking. . . . If by any chance [Hitler] should get his hand on a substantial part of the French and British fleets and our fleet was out in Hawaii one cannot tell what he might do. It sounds ridiculous but it certainly is not a thought that can be dismissed.[116]

Later wires repeated his fears, but apparently no one in the State Department drew the conclusions from them that he wanted drawn. They too recognized the threat of Hitler but were determined to cope with him along different avenues than Kennedy envisioned.

Kennedy seemed to be the only one who was preparing for eventualities, and he could not understand why, for he believed that he was not alone in his pessimism. On June 14, the Germans took Paris. At last, many Britons began to understand what Kennedy had been talking about; he wrote Hull, "This morning for the first time many people here are realizing that they are in for a terrible time with little hope for eventual victory." [117] Days later the French and the Germans met to sign an armistice at the same spot that they had met, for the same purpose, in 1918, the vanquished now victorious. . . . Shirer writes of Hitler's great triumph:

All that stood between him and the establishment of German hegemony in Europe under his dictatorship was one indomitable Englishman, Winston Churchill, and the determined people Churchill led, who did not recognize defeat when it stared them in the face and who now stood alone, virtually unarmed, their island home besieged by the mightiest military machine the world had ever seen.[118]

Kennedy knew defeat when he saw it, and with the fall of France, he knew that he was looking at imminent British defeat. In a contemporary interview with Maisky, the Soviet Ambassador found that Kennedy

was in a state of panic. Britain was absolutely powerless before Germany, he considered. The war was hopelessly lost and the sooner she made peace with Hitler the better. He was absolutely amazed when I started to tell him that nothing was yet lost for Britain and that she had a very good chance of successfully resisting and repelling the German menace, provided of course that she stuck to her guns. As far as I had observed, the spirit of the mass of the people was unshaken. . . . there was no call to paint the picture too black. When I had done, Kennedy exclaimed: "Why you are simply an optimist. . . . I haven't heard anything like it even from the British." And small wonder. For the British Kennedy associated with were the Cliveden brand and they had no faith either in themselves or in their country's future.[119]

Churchill, like Maisky, put up a bold front, and cheerily told intimates, "We should do better without the French than with them." [120] He prepared his people to

brace ourselves to our duties, and so bear ourselves that, if the British empire and its Commonwealth last for a thousand years, men will say: "This was their finest hour."

When Hitler soon after made an offer of peace to Britain, the offer was rejected, and Churchill shortly made clear to his highest government officials that his terms for peace were still the same: unconditional surrender by Germany.

As admirable as Churchill's position may seem in hindsight, Kennedy's stance was by far the more realistic at the time. Lothian noted what he took to be a dangerous stream of defeatism developing among Americans, which he warned was "strengthening the hands of those who are now trying to withdraw supplies promised to Britain, for their own armament, on the ground that everything sent to us will be lost within a few weeks." [121] Perowne was satisfied that this was "doubtless Kennedy's influence," [122] but it was more than that: it was the result of appraisals by people better able to make an objective analysis than those immersed directly in the battle.

It was at this point that Roosevelt determined to send Colonel Donovan on his fact-finding mission to Britain. The British looked forward to Donovan's coming, as a "second crack" at influencing the evaluations of America's highest decision-makers.[123] Donovan became convinced that Britain would be able to hold off Germany, and was in other respects more optimistic than Kennedy, but the big difference between the Colonel and the Ambassador was in their attitudes as to the role the United States should play: Donovan felt the situation warranted vastly increased aid to Britain.[124] His visit had other beneficial side effects for the British: he told Kennedy that "American policy was to help in every way we can and it doesn't help these people any to keep telling them that they haven't got a chance," [125] which may have helped to quiet the Ambassador momentarily. Word got into the Foreign Office minute books that Donovan was intending to deliver very unfavorable reports about Kennedy in Washington.[126]

The fall of France left Britain alone, and the last step for Hitler's complete triumph was obvious: he must conquer Britain. In all likelihood that meant invasion of the British Isles, and Kennedy and the military community were unanimous in the correct conclusion that before Hitler attempted to cross the English Channel, he would first ready the British for panic and speedy surrender by a devastating air campaign. This would come as soon as Hitler had readied the *Luftwaffe*.[127] Kennedy began preparing himself for the anticipated air attacks, and began spending more of his time, and most of his evenings, at a 70-room country home that he rented from the American Dodge family, located some 25 miles outside of prime-target London. In an effort to discredit Kennedy's chatter, Vansittart and American-Department career men had long been whispering "coward" about Kennedy[128]—a charge that some saw as confirmed in Kennedy's frequent assertions that he would stay in London for 30 days after the bombing began, and not a moment longer.[129] Many British saw Kennedy's retreat to the country as a sign that they had had the Ambassador's number.

One high-ranking government official of the day, while insisting that he himself did not subscribe to the "cowardice" attribution, volunteered to the author an explanation as to why others did: "The government was supposed to be evacuating old people from London, but lots of them just weren't going to go; they were not going to let Hitler's bombs push them out of their city. . . . Well, you see, that kind of person is likely to expect a foreign Ambassador to stay in London, where he can get quickly to No. 10 in emergencies." [130] Another diplomat spoke in parallel terms: "Most Ambassadors stayed in London and shared it with us. It's difficult to do the job if you're not in the city, especially in wartime. But I suppose if you don't feel the cause, why die for it?" [131]

Entirely aside from considerations of self-preservation, Kennedy might fairly have thought that his position as Ambassador did not permit him to take unnecessary risks. American press correspondents in London, though, would not accept such an explanation, and were sold on Kennedy as a coward; one made an effeminate grimace while telling the author, "Kennedy didn't like the bombs." [132] Ultimately even some members of the embassy staff concluded that Kennedy "had lost his nerve." [133]

Apparently one of the few bright spots in the otherwise bleak London social season of 1940 was in directing jibes at the American Ambassador and his conduct. Even the American desk ceased to regard him as any grave peril. [134] Government insiders and those within their circles began to talk—gossip in the restrained manner of aristocratic Englishmen—about Kennedy's "fifth columning"; [135] about his associations with a former Paris model; about his "cowardice." One contemporary insider told the author:

> *I seem to remember that Kennedy greatly disliked the bombing of London and removed to a house in Sunningdale, at a safe distance outside it, and that it was a source of great pleasure and amusement when a German bomber, trying to get home quickly, jettisoned his load willy-nilly and that it happened to fall on or near Kennedy's funk-hole.* [136]

Kennedy warned Bilainkin on June 28, "They have only been skirmishing with you up to now in the air." He foresaw a real hell in the air. That too proved a valid prediction. He pointed out that there was a great lack of adequate air-raid sheltering in England, and he was of course skeptical about Britain's ability to resist attacks against the island. [137] A few days later he told Chamberlain, then serving under Churchill, that everyone in the United States thought "we shall be beaten before the end of the month." [138] By late July, Kennedy extended the term: he told neutral journalists on July 25 that Hitler would be in London by August 15. [139]

Even if England did resist the air attacks, the prospects were not hopeful. He reported on August second that the way he saw it, everything depended on the air campaign. If the Germans did well in the air, then armies and navies would not much matter, and it would all be over quickly. If the Germans did poorly in the air, "then the war will drag out with the whole world continually upset, finally resulting in the starvation of England and God knows what happening in the rest of Europe." [140] Under the circumstances, it was at best doubtful as to which alternative was preferable. Kennedy wrote that without American support "they have not got a Chinaman's chance." His wire reveals no willingness to give that support. [141]

Soon after the start of the air campaign against England in August, Kennedy advised the State Department that the time had come to begin preparing American policy "in the event" that England surrendered and Churchill fell.[142] He was unimpressed with Churchill's inspirational message to the House of Commons on August 20 ("Never in the field of human conflict was so much owed by so many to so few") and summoned neutral journalists to tell them that the Prime Minister's speech, with its references to the inevitability of increased Anglo-American cooperation and involvement, "would greatly strengthen isolationist opinion in the U.S."—news which, according to Perowne's informant, the diplomatic correspondent of the *Daily Mail*, Kennedy had "emphasized with great glee." [143] By late August, the air campaign seemed to be going badly for Britain, and Kennedy was convinced that the Germans would shortly overcome the British will. He told Bilainkin towards the end of the month that the British navy "really doesn't matter much more"; the air campaign was all that counted,[144] and that it would all be over by Christmas.[145]

On September 7, the Germans sent their first massive bombing attack on London; Kennedy shared the views of most Londoners in his one-sentence wire to Hull: "There's hell to pay here tonight." [146] The attacks were sustained, yet Britons stoutly maintained morale, and Londoners, as if as a sign of defiance to Hitler, largely refused to accede to the advice of their own government that they evacuate their aged, their women and children from the city. "The children can't go without me. I can't leave the King, and of course the King won't go," was the Queen's explanation and so she stayed, as did most. Years later, Churchill could justly take pride in his people, as he recalled from a balcony when victory came in 1945, the days when the lights had gone out, when the bombs had fallen, and no man, woman or child, had talked of abandoning the struggle.

On the eleventh, Kennedy reported home that a delayed time-bomb had exploded about 50 yards from his car in Mayfair.[147] The *New York Sun* carried a report—almost certainly fanciful—that a bomb had fallen on the grounds of Kennedy's country house bearing a disconcerting three-letter inscription on the casing: "J.P.K." [148] Whether or not it happened, the situation was not at all pleasant, and Kennedy complained to Welles that "no one in the State Department had any idea of what we were going through and seemed to care less." [149] Kennedy was probably right: Roosevelt complained to Breck Long that Kennedy, along with others, felt that since a few bombs had missed him, he was a candidate for a rest cure. The President characterized him as "a trouble-maker and as a person entirely out of hand and out of sympathy." [150] Krock, however, was more sympathetic, and portrayed, for the readers of the *New York Times*, a valiant Kennedy—"our most bombed Ambassador." [151]

After four days of the bombing of London, Kennedy reported that the war effort was very definitely being hampered; that German aircraft losses were practically nil;[152] and that high government officials expected the German invasion at any moment.[153] That day Churchill told the nation that Germany's air squadrons had nearly always been broken up, and that her losses averaged three to one in airplanes and six to one in pilots. He gave the nation the courage to fight on. Bilainkin found Kennedy unimpressed by the speech.[154] He continued to be the apostle of defeat. When the country failed to collapse immediately, he told Bilainkin on September 19, that the Germans "are not using [one-]twentieth or [one-]thirtieth of their bomber strength against Britain. [The] air war has not really begun." [155] With the wet and cold weather coming, he expected that problems of defense would become still greater, especially in London.[156]

In fact, though, the worst was already over. While Hitler's bombing raids on London continued until early winter, in mid-September the *Luftwaffe* made its last great effort. Thereafter Londoners enjoyed a marked letup. Hitler told his generals that the invasion of England was indefinitely postponed; Londoners sensed as much. In late September, Kennedy himself told Halifax that he believed the invasion was off.[157] The Ambassador relaxed enough for a light-hearted wire to the President:

> *I feel a good deal like that colored boy in the last war. You may recall that when shells began dropping around him he wailed: "Lawd, I'se in terrible trouble. You-all better send down one of your angels to help me." Whammm bang; a shell came closer and he quavered: "Things am getting worse, Lawd. I guess you-all better send down one of your saints." Then, wheee bam-bam-bammm; a flock of shells landed even closer to him and the darkey cried out: "Oh, Lawd, please hurry, and don't send your Son. You better come yourself, 'cause this is a man-size job."* [158]

There was still plenty to be pessimistic about, though: the sea campaign was going badly. Britain had again attempted to take the initiative in September, 1940, in cooperation with General Charles de Gaulle's Free French forces, in an effort to seize the important West African port of Dakar. The attempt was beaten off, Taylor writes, "with some loss and much discredit." [159] Kennedy wired that the Dakar campaign was "a bitter pill for the entire cabinet, and from my observation, for the entire country. . . ." The British propagandists, he reported,

> have concentrated all their attention on the victories in the air. They have sloughed over their losses at sea. They cannot cover up Dakar, however, and people are drawing their own conclusions.[160]

Kennedy himself drew one conclusion: the Dakar failure had been caused by exactly the same tactical blunder that had brought about the Norwegian fiasco—fleet operations too close to enemy air bases.[161] And the blame for both of them he lay at the doorstep of Winston S. Churchill.

CHURCHILL WAS NOWHERE NEAR AS PESSIMISTIC AS KENNEDY, AND tried to bolster the Ambassador's spirits. Colonel Donovan also saw the situation as far from hopeless. He reported that the large number of British airfields, and their dispersal, made it impossible for Germany to strike decisively.[162] Kennedy was quick to see the worst where it was not. (Halifax to Lothian: "He also told me that an American military observer in non-occupied France had reported an improvement of feeling between the Germans and the French. I said that this was not at all our information, which on the contrary. . . .")[163] During the first week of night bombing production was cut in half in many industries by workers going to shelters. Kennedy was convinced that the condition would be permanent, but in a week the solution of air-raid watchers was found.[164]

Perowne was concerned that the American military inquirers were exposed "to Mr. Kennedy's malign influence before being allowed to make contact with our authorities," [165] but apparently the Ambassador's influence on them was slight. Kennedy constantly tried, unsuccessfully, to persuade General Strong that the General had not seen the worst. When a large factory at Weybridge, England, was badly hit, Kennedy believed that it would have to be written off as a total loss. After speaking to the foreman, Strong concluded that in a week the factory would be producing again, and that in 25 days it would be going full-blast. Strong's prediction was off by five days.[166] When Strong returned to the United States he reported the German Air Force *had made no serious inroads on the strength of the R.A.F., that the military damage done by air bombardment had been comparatively small, and that British claims of German aircraft losses were "on the conservative side."* [167]

He was satisfied that the Germans could not beat the R.A.F. and, therefore, would not invade. Commander Fife was also much more optimistic than Kennedy,[168] as was Air Attaché Lee.[169] After his visit to England in January, 1941, Hopkins returned convinced that the British would be able to turn the tide.

Kennedy's pessimism, though, was in general warranted. He continually predicted the worst and the worst usually came. Even if the British could repulse the Germans from England's shores, there was a big difference between repulsing the Germans and defeating them. His pessimism was shared completely by Kirk, his Naval Attaché.[170] Unlike Kirk, though, Kennedy was a talkative fellow with a powerful urge to share his views, and he freely communicated them to one and all, ignoring his own admonition of December, 1938, that the "surest road to defeat is resignation to defeat." His prognostications to neutrals in the early period risked grave adverse consequences to the British; his later defeatist talk to Britons could only have helped to undermine British resistance from within. His utterances found their way into the dispatches of German officials,[171] and could only have bolstered morale in the Reich and encouraged Hitler's decision-makers. His well-known attitude made his reports to Hull and Roosevelt suspect for reliability. In August, 1939, before the beginning of the war, Ickes recorded in his diary that despite the President's own reservations about Kennedy, Roosevelt believed that Kennedy "was as good as anyone in reporting carefully what was transpiring in England and in diplomatic circles." [172] But by the fall of 1940, even that confidence was gone.

Throughout this period, Kennedy still thought about America as a possible agent for peace. He was disturbed that British statesmen were not also concerned about peace. Even Chamberlain and Halifax were opposed to any peace that would permit Hitler to save face, or leave him in power in Germany. This attitude disturbed Kennedy, and struck him as both unreasonable and gravely unrealistic.[173] He told the King, "Your Majesty is undoubtedly one of the few leaders who considers the bloodshed and sacrifices which always accompany war." [174] By and large, he complained to Welles, "there seems to be no real fire anywhere, no genius, no sense of the shambles that are to come." [175] The same could not be said of Kennedy, and he was personally keeping attuned to opportunities for peacemaking. On May 15 he warned that a collapse in France was imminent, and advised that:

> The President might start considering what he can do to save an Allied débacle. . . . any action to be effective must be conceived now. . . . My friend thinks nothing can save them from absolute defeat unless the President with some touch of genius and God's blessing can do it.[176]

After the fall of France, rumor in the press corps had it that Kennedy himself had sent an emissary ("Ben Smith, I think, was the name he mentioned"—no doubt Kennedy's pal from bear-raiding days, "Sell 'em" Ben Smith) to see Marshal Henri Pétain, leader of conquered France, and Hitler, to try to find a formula for peace.[177] As late as August, 1940, Kennedy still considered some role for the United States as peacemaker that would "save the world before it's all bashed up." [178] But he apparently never formulated any suggestions as to exactly what the United States should do, and in his dispatches he continually warned against any step that would leave the United States "holding the bag in a war in which the Allies expect to be beaten." [179]

Kennedy left no doubt in anyone's mind that he wanted the United States out of the war. After his May fourteenth meeting with Churchill, he advised the State Department: "It seems to me that if we had to fight to protect our lives we would do better fighting in our own backyard." [180] Hull and Roosevelt had also been thinking about where the fighting should take place, Hull wrote, "but we reached a different conclusion than Kennedy's. It seemed to us we should do better to keep the fighting away from our own backyard." [181]

Just in case the President and Hull envisioned an active role for America in the European war, Kennedy hoped to dissuade them by warning again and again that Britain was useless as an ally:

> . . . the preparedness for carrying on a war here is pitiful, this in spite of the fact that production and war effort are now for the first time going ahead in excellent fashion. We should know this in light of any action we in America might see fit to take. A course of action that involves us in any respect that presupposes the Allies have much to fight with except courage is, as far as England goes, I think, fallacious. The United States would have

*nothing to work with with these two countries in their present
condition. . . . The United States will have plenty to worry about
in their own country.*[182]

Shortly before the fall of France, Churchill pleaded with Roosevelt
to give the French government some indication of American support
in the hopes that the French would be inspired to fight on. Roosevelt
wrote the head of the French government, Paul Reynaud, an
inspirational message and Churchill urged Roosevelt to permit Reynaud to make the note public. Kennedy cautioned the President
against doing so—he saw "a great danger in the message as a
commitment at a later date." [183]

After the fall of France, Kennedy wired:

*Don't let anybody make any mistake; this war, from Great
Britain's point of view, is being conducted from now on with
their eyes only on one place and that is the United States. Unless
there is a miracle they realize [they] haven't got a chance in the
long run.*[184]

Later he reminded Hull, "they have not demonstrated one thing
that would justify us in assuming any kind of partnership with
them. . . ." [185]

After the bombing of England was underway he wrote:

*I was delighted to see that the President said he was not going to
enter the war, because to enter this war, imagining for a minute
that the English have anything to offer in the line of leadership
or productive capacity in industry that could be of the slightest
value to us, would be a complete misapprehension. . . . If by any
chance we should ever come to the point of getting into this war
we can make up our minds that it will be the United States
against Germany, Italy, and Japan, aided by a badly shot to
pieces country which in the last analysis can give little, if any,
assistance to cause. It breaks my heart to draw these conclusions
about a people that I sincerely hoped might be victorious but I
cannot get myself to the point where I believe they can be of any
assistance to the cause in which they are involved.*[186]

The tenor of his stance was correctly noted in the dispatches of Axis
diplomats.[187]

Kennedy even had serious reservations about helping the British
financially. After all, Britain did not have any real chance to win; aid
would be a form of encouraging what probably should not be
encouraged: continuation of a senseless struggle. And, it was vital that

the United States be kept financially strong in the event that she found herself in real trouble after the fall of Britain.

Kennedy's approach to Britain's financial problems of making war was consistently cold. He was disturbed that Britain was making her purchases in the United States with gold—an intrinsically worthless commodity. He feared that the United States might corner the gold market; other countries would then have no stake in the gold standard, and would abandon it, leaving the United States in the lurch with all the gold.[188] As he explained to Roosevelt, "it is obvious that the other countries merely regard the use of gold 'as a medium of international exchange' as meaning, sell it to the United States as quickly as you can. It is a one way street and we might as well face it." He urged Roosevelt to seek legislation to stop further gold purchases.[189]

Kennedy preferred that Britain pay for its purchases in United States dollars, which it could get by taking over American securities owned by British subjects and selling them. His approach with regard to liquidation was sound and predictably businesslike: he insisted that the Allies dispose of their securities in an orderly, gradual fashion, so as not to upset the New York Stock Exchange and threaten the American economy with depression.[190] He suggested that this could be accomplished, if necessary, by having the United States government's Reconstruction Finance Corporation loan the British money secured with the British-owned securities as collateral, the loan to be paid off by gradual liquidation of the stocks and bonds.[191] In any event, it was important that the roster of British-owned securities be kept secret, or, he argued, "you can kiss the market good-bye as far as most of these securities are concerned." [192]

Whatever Britain was to pay with, Kennedy insisted that all of her resources be completely exhausted before the United States even consider unsecured loans, something that he strongly opposed:

> *Both England and France would in my judgement be bankrupt at the end of the war. An American loan would have no chance of being repaid and would thus become a source of irritation for years to come. If as a diplomatic matter we should feel it wise to furnish financial aid to the Allies, I urged and urged strongly that we should give the money and not loan it. That was only realism, after all, and it had the virtue of making clear to the American public just exactly what we would then be doing and what it was costing us. I had no wish to pretend to the American public that we were making a loan when it was plain that bankruptcy would be the fate of the warring nations no matter who won.[193]*

Kennedy became disturbed about British pressure for unsecured credit when he knew that England's financial resources were not yet entirely expended, and wired Washington to warn against the British maneuvers.[194] After all, the United States had to think of itself.

Kennedy was concerned about his government's failure to approach the situation in this kind of businesslike fashion, and in at least two wires he used the phrase "signing a blank check" in admonishing the Administration.[195] Even the fall of France did not cause him to become sentimental where his country's material welfare was concerned. On August 2, he wired:

> *The big point I want to make, however, is that if we are contemplating doing anything besides selling to Great Britain in the ordinary course of business we should definitely have our position thoroughly understood before we go a step on the way.*

He then reiterated why the United States should have absolutely no confidence in Britain whatsoever, and without explicitly saying as much, made clear that no businessman would regard the British as a half-decent risk.[196]

On September 11, he wrote that:

> *The truth of the matter is that unless the Uited States gives them the money to continue and comes into this mess I do not believe they have a chance. And for the United States to come in and sign a blank check for all the difficulties that are faced here is a responsibility that only God could shoulder unless the American public knows what the real conditions of this battle are. I can quite appreciate their desire to help this country fight this battle but they should have a very clear notion of what the responsibility will entail for the American people to take up a struggle that looks rather hopeful on the surface but is definitely bad underneath.*[197]

Kennedy's advice on financing Britain's war effort was generally ignored in Washington, where Morgenthau—to whom Roosevelt had entrusted the task of working with the British on the problem—jealously guarded the function and resented what he took to be interference from Kennedy.[198]

KENNEDY, HOWEVER, DID NOT WANT BRITISH LEADERS TO THINK FOR A moment that he personally was not "going all out for the team." He frankly acknowledged to them that he did not want his country to enter the war under any circumstances, but otherwise from the start of the war he posed as being eager to have his country help in any other way possible. He appeared to the British to be sympathetic to repeal of the Neutrality Act,[199] in order to give Britain full access to American munitions markets, a position for which the American document books gives no verification.[200] By the time of his winter vacation of '39–'40, his view had crystallized that American and British interests were largely conflicting, yet he told Halifax that "he was anxious during his time in the United States to give any help (with Britain's financial difficulties) that might be in his power." [201] After his return he spoke in parallel terms to Montagu Norman.[202] Just before the fall of France, Churchill asked Kennedy to try to get Roosevelt to permit publication of the President's inspirational message to French Premier Reynaud. "I shall be glad to try," Kennedy responded, and at Churchill's prodding, the helpful Ambassador put through a call to the White House then-and-there. We do not know the gist of the conversation, but Kennedy's end of it was no doubt very different from the text that he wired Washington the instant that he got out of Churchill's sight, strongly urging against publication of the message.[203] He gave the appearance in London of helping to push the "Destroyer Deal," [204] as to which his real position was equivocal[205] and, on the balance, negative.[206] To the British, Kennedy made much of his position that the United States should *give* the Allies help rather than loan them help, to a greater or lesser extent disguising the uncharitable motive for his seeming charity. After a visit with the Ambassador, Scott noted Kennedy's attitude:

> *As regards the question of payment for our purchases, Mr. Kennedy's view is that America should frankly recognize that she is under an obligation to Great Britain for bearing the brunt of the war, and that this obligation should be redeemed by their giving, not lending us the money for supplies when our dollars run out.*[207]

When he finally left England, Kennedy impressed on Halifax that he was "going back determined to help you any way I can," short of a declaration of war.[208] Even after his final return to the United States, Kennedy for some reason still thought English goodwill important enough to warrant an attempt to mislead the British as to his real position. So, he got word back of "his intention to do what he can to speed up munitions to Britain." [209] As is clear from the reports already presented here, the British were unimpressed by this kind of effort.

Neither did Kennedy want the British to think for a moment that the American government was not doing everything in its power to help. If the British thought that, they might give Germany the fleet when they surrendered, both to lessen Hitler's terms against themselves and to teach the United States a lesson. Kennedy always took pains to explain why the United States was not doing more. A June, 1940, conversation with Bilainkin is no doubt typical: "They have nothing to spare in the United States of first-class material because they cannot leave the Pacific Coast unguarded." Bilainkin pressed him:

> *Kennedy's face had become more and more set, the veins showing on the neck. His answers were frank and considered. He thought for a moment and answered, "We have little to give you and it's no use pretending that we have. Take planes: we got your orders in January, and you know perfectly well that you can't begin to have mass production on a huge scale in no time. We have no army—only about 200,000 patched-up men, and that means we have no guns or tanks to spare—on a scale that would be worth while. There are only the old things."* [210]

Even the supplying of relics, like outdated American destroyers, would have to cease, he warned the British, if America entered the war; as a belligerent, the United States would not be able to spare any material aid. For that reason, he argued, England was better off with a neutral America. "If we had entered [the war] seven or eight months ago," he told Bilainkin in August, 1940, "you would by now have been lost, the slaughter of Britain would have been over." [211] Though his argument had influence on a number of British leaders,[212] Kennedy wisely doubted Halifax's candor when the Foreign Secretary parroted it back to him,[213] and Churchill warned his officials against the line of reasoning as "misleading Kennedy stuff." [214]

The gloom and keep-out warnings would undoubtedly have continued, but Kennedy returned home in October. Periodically, throughout the ambassadorial period, the press reported rumors of his resignation. In the summer of 1940 they began again. After the Democratic convention nominated Roosevelt for reelection it was widely rumored that Kennedy would be chosen the party's national chairman, to direct Roosevelt's campaign.[215] There was more than a grain of truth to the rumor, but Roosevelt himself vetoed the idea, explaining to Kennedy,

*You know how happy I would be to have you in charge, but the
general impression is that it would do the cause of England a
great deal of harm if you left there at this time. . . . I get
constant reports of how valuable you are to them over there and
that it helps the morale of the British to have you there and they
would feel that they were being let down if you were to leave.*[216]

In August the *Boston Post* called for the Ambassador's appointment as
director of the country's military preparedness operations: "Kennedy
has no place in the path of bombs and the 'blitzkrieg,' " they argued.
"He is worthy of higher honors—fuller recognition." [217] The following
month a Boake Carter column called on the President to create a
Cabinet post on National Defense for Kennedy.[218] Krock wrote in
early October, that Kennedy was

*quoted as saying he wants to return to vote, but would come
sooner if the administration displayed any interest—which it had
not yet done—in the copious notes on British rearmament
problems which he had been making for some years.*[219]

By now the circumvention of Kennedy was almost absolute.
Roosevelt was famous for bypassing his ostensibly top men, but no one
was bypassed so thoroughly, so deliberately, as was Ambassador
Kennedy. As early as April of the previous year, Harry Henry had
noted that the bulk of American diplomacy in Europe was being
carried on by Bullitt,[220] and American affairs with Great Britain were
being worked out through Lothian. Roosevelt was even requesting his
information through the British Ambassador in Washington. Kennedy
suspected that the President was doing this so that his talks with and
promises to British leaders would not appear in American records,
where they could one day be seen by a disapproving nation;[221] perhaps
his suspicions were to some extent warranted. On the other side, the
British naturally gravitated to Lothian, their own Ambassador, and
their natural bent in that direction was reinforced by their attitude
towards Lothian's American counterpart.

Kennedy did not like being circumvented,[222] and his displeasure
became known to newspaper readers.[223] He complained to Roosevelt
on August 1, "as far as I can see, I am not doing a damn thing here
that amounts to anything." [224] He was almost completely ignored in
arrangements on the Destroyer Deal and made no attempt to hide his
indignation.[225] He wired Hull: "Frankly and honestly I do not enjoy
being a dummy. I am very unhappy about the whole position and of

course there is always the alternative of resigning." [226] Roosevelt did not want that and cabled back:

> *There is no thought of embarrassing you and only a practical necessity for personal conversations makes it easier to handle details here. . . . Don't forget that you are not only a dummy but are essential to all of us both in the Government and in the Nation.* [227]

Other pats on the back came from Churchill in a wire to the President—channeled through the Ambassador—with the assertion that Kennedy "is a grand help to us and the common cause," [228] and from Hull, who wired Kennedy in September, "I want you to know the President and I appreciate the magnificent way in which you and your staff are carrying on your work and how proud we are of you and our entire personnel in London." [229] Kennedy was not fooled by this kind of attention and realized that the nice words were merely an effort to keep him sweet. After an August call from the President, he wrote Mrs. Kennedy, "I am not fooling myself and I haven't the slightest doubt that they would turn around tomorrow and throw me in the ash can. . . . I think FDR rang me up because he was afraid I would walk out and he wanted to soft-soap me." [230] His situation got worse, not better. By late September, the Roosevelt-Churchill correspondence was being transmitted exclusively via Lothian. [231]

Kennedy became almost entirely dependent on the British for his information on Anglo-American relations. He learned of Ghormley's mission through the British, and sent Washington harsh words criticizing the State Department for not keeping him informed. [232] The cable did no good. Churchill very kindly sent Kennedy carbon copies of many of his messages to Washington, and these provided most of the Ambassador's information on high-level developments in Anglo-American relations. He felt "at a loss to understand just why Churchill made a point of keeping me informed when my own government refused to do so," [233] and later bellowed at Roosevelt about the paucity of his sources of information:

> *I had to go to the British Government and say, "If you don't let me know all about this, your country is going to find me most unfriendly toward the whole situation." So I smashed my way through with no thanks to the American Government.* [234]

At that, the British were none too cooperative, and Churchill, in particular, was not showing appropriate deference. Kennedy complained to Beaverbrook on June 10 that Churchill had not seen him in three weeks, and he was quite upset about it. Beaverbrook suggested that Randolph Churchill had attempted to poison his father against Kennedy, which the Ambassador dismissed with a "To hell with him, I don't give a damn!" [235] A few days later, though, he broached the same matter with Halifax, who explained that he saw Churchill relatively little himself, ". . . that is the way Churchill works." [236] The explanation was good enough for Halifax, but not for Kennedy. Churchill was not treating Kennedy the way that one treats a powerful Ambassador, and though Kennedy realized that the Prime Minister was busy, he also knew that Reynaud was keeping Bullitt very well informed.[237] And Churchill was not the only Briton who seemed to be ignoring Kennedy. The Ambassador told Kingsley Wood, Chancellor of the Exchequer, that he was sick and disgusted that he had not been kept posted on financial matters, and he complained to Halifax that even the Foreign Minister was not keeping Kennedy adequately informed —"if it were not that I did not want to walk out under the threat of bombing, I would resign rather than put up with such nonsense." [238] The British, as well as Roosevelt, tried to keep Kennedy as little-informed as possible without generating still-increased hostility in him; when matters known to the Ambassador would mysteriously turn up in the press, suspicions would turn to Kennedy as the possible leak.[239]

Nobody seemed to be treating Kennedy like an Ambassador. He felt hopeless and frustrated in London, and there was no conceivable justification for keeping him there any longer. His stay was superfluous; the press reported that it was an open secret that he regarded his stay as superfluous. He was not being consulted on anything; his advice was not sought and when proffered was ignored; his reports were being read skeptically; he was being circumvented in every possible way. Kennedy had outlived his usefulness and wanted to come home.[240]

The President did not want him home. Twice within ten days in October, Roosevelt told the press with emphasis that Kennedy was *not* resigning.[241] Alsop and Kintner reported that Kennedy was being kept at his post because "The President regards Kennedy as likely to do less harm in London than in New York."

An emotional fellow, he has strong convictions and less than no remaining fondness for his chief. He will certainly express his opinions to every available American listener the instant he gets through the customs. He will be in a position to speak

impressively and persuasively. The President is represented as
fearing he will reduce large numbers of leaders of opinion to such
a state of hopeless blue funk that our foreign policy will be
half-immobilized by fear. In short, the President has repeatedly
urged Kennedy to remain in London in order to keep him
quiet.[242]

Krock rose to the defense, saying that implications that Kennedy was
not home because he could not be trusted to keep his mouth shut were
foolish.[243] The London *Times*'s Washington correspondent, however,
bluntly asked Hull if there was any truth to the report that Kennedy
was being discouraged from returning because of "fears and glooms."
Hull, who should have denied it in any event, replied smilingly that he
knew nothing about it.[244]

Others suspected that Roosevelt was keeping Kennedy in London
until after the election out of fear that if he came home the
Ambassador would endorse Republican nominee Wendell Willkie for
President. Kennedy's letters to Krock included "a very strong
indication that he intended to oppose the reelection of President
Roosevelt." [245] Kennedy went out of his way to promote such
speculation by talking freely in London in terms that would encourage
it. Halifax wired Lothian on October 10 that Kennedy had

told me that he had sent an article to the United States to appear
on November 1st, if by any accident he was not able to get there,
which would be of considerable importance appearing five days
before the Presidential election. When I asked him what would
be the main burden of his song, he gave me to understand that it
would be an indictment of President Roosevelt's administration
for having talked a lot and done very little.[246]

Kennedy discussed possible endorsement of Willkie with Beaverbrook,[247] and may or may not have been as open with Churchill, with
whom he at least shared his general criticisms of the President's
Administration.[248] Beaverbrook urged Kennedy to stick with Roosevelt,[249] and Churchill, by expressing an insincere hope that Kennedy
would remain as Ambassador,[250] was also obliquely telling Kennedy to
back the President. In other communications with friends at home,
Kennedy was unquestionably speaking in a similar vein.[251] According
to Randolph Churchill, Henry Luce went so far as to arrange radio
time for Kennedy's "I'm for Willkie" speech.[252]

One thing Kennedy must have known: he must have known that
Halifax, in accordance with normal diplomatic procedure, would

almost certainly wire Lothian immediately about their conversation, and that in all likelihood, Lothian would quickly have the alarming words in the President's ear. The wide degree to which Kennedy disseminated word of his displeasure makes one suspect that that was exactly what Kennedy wanted. He took special pains to see that his intentions were widely known, even inventing excuses to have suggestive messages sent to America over Hearst's International News Service wires, where he knew they would be seen at least by those in Hearst's London Bureau and probably by other handlers along the way. In an effort to protect the Ambassador against himself, Hillman declined to transmit the messages.[253] With his loyal defiance, Hillman stood in the way of the attainment of Kennedy's immediate goal: Kennedy wanted Roosevelt to get the word indirectly, and he wanted Roosevelt to get the word in time enough to do something about it. He wanted to be courted.

Finally Kennedy called Welles and said that he planned to leave England the following week; that if the State Department wanted to announce that he was being recalled for consultations it could;[254] and, Krock writes, that "he had written a full account of the facts to Edward Moore, his secretary in New York, with instructions to release the story to the press if the Ambassador were not back in New York by a certain date." [255] Kennedy had no intention of waiting for the State Department's call home. He told the press that he was going home to be with his family and, as per custom, would submit his resignation after the election.[256] Alsop and Kintner reported that London stories that Kennedy was leaving meant simply that he was refusing to stay longer.[257]

Soon after his telephone call with Welles and his public announcement, Kennedy received a wire from the State Department: he was to return home for consultations. Kennedy wired Welles:

> *Sumner, I am again indebted to you for your prompt action. I am pretty sick and sore at a lot of things but the bright spot in my whole State Department career has been your help and cooperation which I have never failed to get.*[258]

Kennedy made the diplomatic rounds and bade his final farewells— according to Lee, the Ambassador was "farewell-ing all over the place." [259] Despite Kennedy's "most complimentary" words to Lee on departure, the Air Attaché wrote his wife not to bother to look Kennedy up in Washington,[260] and regarded Kennedy's departure as an "evacuation":[261] "from a soldier's point of view, he is deserting his post at a critical time." [262] Because of its possible effect on morale, the departure of the Ambassador was decidedly bad, and Lord Reith told Lee that "if he had his way about it the British Government would not grant [Kennedy] an exit visa." [263] When Kennedy visited Reith to explain that he was leaving because "he was tired of sitting around with nothing to do," Reith thought to himself that there was plenty that Kennedy might have done: "By going about the country, visiting damaged areas, talking to people and encouraging them, Joe Kennedy might have made a position for himself such as no foreigner and few Englishmen ever had before." [264] Kennedy's reception with Labour's Hugh Dalton was probably little better. Dalton noted in his diary that Kennedy had come to say good-bye and had seemed "most effusive and complimentary." Dalton was less so: "I always regarded him as a defeatist and a crook." [265]

When Kennedy's staff left his private office on the twenty-second of October, several of those still loyal to him were in tears.[266] That night Herschel Johnson, chargé, wired Hull, "The Ambassador left London today for the United States via Lisbon and clipper service." [267]

AMBASSADOR KENNEDY

AN AMBASSADOR'S DUTIES ARE QUITE VARIED. HE IS TO MAKE
himself and his country popular in the nation to which he is assigned;
prepare frequent, accurate situation reports; represent his country and
its interests in negotiations; show a little vision in international
relations himself; and, probably most important, put over the foreign
policy of the administration that he purports to represent.

On the first of these duties, Kennedy was rather successful. He
appealed to the British with all the wiles of the Boston politician, right
down to the politician's plea for favor on the basis of regional
identification. At Bristol, England, he asserted that he could not
imagine an American coming to England without visiting Bristol—by
doing so himself he was fulfilling one of his own boyhood ambitions.[1]
Before the Society of Cymmrodorion he paid tribute to Welch
tenacity.[2] At Boston, England, he commented about the meaning of
the visit to one who was himself a "thorough Bostonian." [3] He
recounted the contributions to America of the sons of Liverpool
at—Liverpool.[4] People noted favorably the ease and willingness with
which he said "Call me 'Joe' "; he set a refreshing contrast to the
generally stuffy diplomatic circle. To England he was a breath of fresh
air. His accessibility to British as well as American newsmen, his
informality with them, his willingness to be cooperative, made the
British press well disposed to Kennedy, and they conveyed his great
personal charm to the people of Britain.

There was a chilling toward Kennedy in the British press after his
East Boston speech of December, 1939, and his relations with
government leaders grew continually more strained from the outbreak
of war until his departure. But before he left England, he had regained
his popularity with the mass of British people, who were firmly
convinced as to his sincere sympathy with them, and of his loyalty to
their cause. ("Boys," he told American journalists before leaving
London, "I'm going to say what I haven't been able to [say] for two
years. I have been saying yes when I meant no.") [5] When he left

274

Britain in October, a number of quite favorable editorials appeared. The London *Daily Herald*'s item was almost maudlin: "Forever, in deeds if not in written words, we are Allies. Largely, that is Joseph Kennedy's work. Good-by Joe! Heaven bless you! Your job is done." [6]

KENNEDY'S EARLY REPORTS TO THE STATE DEPARTMENT WERE BASED on fuller information than those of most diplomats. He was in the fullest confidence of the Chamberlain Administration, and so had complete access to their information but he did not rely exclusively on them for sources. He made some effort to consult with those not in the government circle—rebellious conservatives and other rival leaders not generally seen at ambassadorial tables.[7] He even became friendly with Labourite Ernest Bevin, for whom, despite vast differences in views as to the desirable social order, Kennedy had considerable respect.[8] The President himself acknowledged "Old Joe has the damnedest way of getting information." [9]

After his return to England in the late winter of 1940, though, the Foreign Office's policy of "closing Kennedy out" sharply curtailed Kennedy's access to information, and his own attitude restricted his circle of associations.[10] When Lee, about to take up his position at the London Embassy as Air Attaché, went to the State Department for his briefings in June of 1940, he asked Feis about whom Kennedy saw in London. The answer, more or less accurate, was "Only appeasers." [11]

Kennedy's dispatches were in the classic diplomatic tradition—gossip, accounts of conversation, scraps of unassimilated information, and opinions hastily formed and untested. He was more a reporter than an analyst.[12] He almost never included anecdotal information in them and in his prewar dispatches on the world situation he rarely elaborated on his own opinions or displayed very much of a personal bias or right-wing tinge. His occasionally critical observations of Chamberlain, his dear friend, reveal that he did not lose all objectivity, despite the fact that his own personal views were quite close to Chamberlain's. The prewar dispatches are more statistical than personal; his accounts of developments give an invaluable boost to historians trying to unravel the intricacies of the diplomacy of the period. At the height of the Munich crisis, Moffat wrote Kennedy, "Your messages have equalled the highest level of political reporting." [13]

Nonetheless, Kennedy's misleading wires to the State Department about his side of the conversations cast considerable doubts on the value of his wires to those responsible for preparing United States foreign policy. Clearly, they gave Hull no reliable information on what Kennedy himself was doing.

With the outbreak of war, Kennedy's dispatches become much less useful to the historian and more useful to the biographer. Heightening effects become noticeable for the first time; the reports become colored. More and more space and time is devoted to Kennedy's opinions, and his efforts to impress them upon the State Department. While his reports of developments give an inside story not found in the daily *New York Times*, his profound, overriding pessimism makes one suspect that the dispatches give simply *an* inside story and not *the* inside story. The State Department did not, could not, and should not have relied upon them.

Joseph Kennedy's participation in negotiations with the British left much to be desired—Messersmith characterized Kennedy's service as "vagaries" [14]—and showed that in some spheres at least, Kennedy *had* been taken in by the British. When the reciprocal trade treaty was under negotiation, he became convinced that America was pushing Britain too hard; Kennedy was ill-disposed to take the hard line the Secretary was pushing, and Hull became displeased with his Ambassador's conduct of the negotiations. When war broke out, to the serious disruption of Anglo-American trade, Kennedy made no efforts to hide his sympathy for the British on a number of points, including the British restrictions on importation of American tobacco and the inability of the British to make timely delivery of the rubber promised in the rubber-cotton trade. Kennedy argued with Hull for the British request for a prolongation of the time allotted for delivery of the rubber. He reported Malcolm Macdonald's assertion that the American methods of proceeding were childish, and added that he entirely agreed. Hull very definitely disagreed. It is hard to believe that Kennedy did not tell Macdonald of his agreement with the Englishman's assertion. The tone of the wires exchanged between the Secretary of State and the Ambassador ranges from obviously hostile to an Alphonse-Gaston politeness that if anything highlighted underlying tensions. It was only where the motion picture interests were concerned that Kennedy was truly aggressive on behalf of American commercial interests. Kennedy was eager to do well by his many good friends in that industry, and especially his close friends Walker and Hays. On other matters he was eager to do well by his many good friends in the British government; he knew and liked Board of Trade

President Oliver Stanley, but he knew neither Armstrong of the tires nor Reynolds of the cigarettes.

Kennedy was always solicitous of the good will of those with whom he came in contact. He wanted to be well liked and favorably regarded. Despite his capacity for coldness in business dealings, there was a lot of the friend-seeker in Joseph P. Kennedy. These are of course thoroughly American, human, and quite positive and worthwhile traits. But they assumed very great proportions in Kennedy and interfered with his ability to adequately represent his country or any consistent policy as Ambassador.

Mayor Fitzgerald once said that he had never met a man to whom social prestige meant less than Joe Kennedy,[15] and that was certainly the impression that Kennedy, with his rough-diamond demeanor, always tried and generally did give. ("Not that our girls would have joined anyway—they never gave two cents for that society stuff.") But that demeanor was defensive response to Brahmin slights. In fact, Kennedy desired above all to be liked and accepted by the patrician world that seemed so foreign to him. In spite of the "Call-me-Joes," Kennedy left American observers in London with the impression that he rather enjoyed hearing the full title used—"His Excellency, the United States Ambassador to the Court of St. James's," [16] and despite the ignominious termination of his service in London, in later life his inner circle encouraged all "outsiders" to pay full deference by referring to him in the third person as "the Ambassador."

Kennedy was impressed by the social aspects of the job as Ambassador and enjoyed them and especially his contacts with the royal family, and his intimacy with other "topside people." His comments on state affairs sometimes read like those of a society columnist. He noted little things such as what the Queen was wearing on his visits to the palace, and jotted down bits of social chit-chat with the royal family. Kennedy was impressed by the warmth and informality of their Majesties; he liked them and felt at ease with them. He told the Queen that she was "a cute trick" and she laughed. Kennedy early received and enjoyed the good will of the leading government officials. Chamberlain, who liked Kennedy and was naturally eager to obtain the good will of the United States, showered attention on him—much more than Roosevelt did. These people, King George, Queen Elizabeth, Chamberlain, and Halifax, were good people. They did not resent the fact that Kennedy was so thoroughly American; they appreciated it and made clear that they did. The world's very highest society was accepting Kennedy on his own terms and seemed genuinely delighted to do so. Kennedy enjoyed and was eager for their favor. The least he could do was be reasonable about rubber, especially since he was being so aggressive about movies.

"Who would have thought that the English could take into camp a red-headed Irishman?" asked Roosevelt.[17] On first thought, no one. But much in Kennedy's background and personality made it easy for the friendly English leaders to work with him; the "taking in" had much more to do with Kennedy's personal makeup than with any contrived efforts of the British. Kennedy had always been excluded from high society; it was a new and enjoyable experience for him and so he was all the more susceptible to society's blandishments. "The young man needs his wrists slapped rather hard," was the President's sound conclusion.[18] But no one in Washington ever administered the needed discipline.

The desire for acceptance and approval accounts for some of the seeming irreconcilables in Kennedy's diplomatic career, such as his encouragement of American good will tours by British leaders. The British, eager to "lock in" a powerful ally in the event of war, appreciated the propaganda effects of such visits, and were groping for gracious ways to encourage goodwill tours.[19] Kennedy was vehemently opposed to just such alliances; "goodwill" efforts of this kind could only have the effect of increasing chances for America's entry in a war that Kennedy well knew was entirely likely. Nonetheless, he personally urged American visits by British leaders. In the summer of 1938, he angled to get an official invitation for the Duke and Duchess of York to attend the World's Fair in their namesake city, New York.[20] Shortly after the Munich crisis, he urged Anthony Eden, most fashionable member, perhaps the only fashionable member, of the "Churchill" wing of the Conservative party, to accept an American invitation to address the National Association of Manufacturers.[21] Many of Eden's antagonists within the British government liked the idea, thinking that Eden's trip would hold unmixed blessings for the government crowd, by compromising Chamberlain's discreet and domesticated adversary, who would feel obliged to make apologies for the government: the trip would help the British government with American opinion, while weakening Eden at home.[22] Such a cynical explanation for Kennedy's attitude, though, does not explain why Kennedy, through Krock, saw to it that Eden met "everyone" in Washington.[23] Later, Kennedy took credit for originating the idea of the royal tour of the United States in the spring of 1939, and remained its loudest booster.[24] After the tour, he sought cooperation of the British in efforts to get the Queen to be interviewed in a widely broadcast *Herald-Tribune* radio interview.[25]

Kennedy might have rationalized this kind of effort in terms of its effect on Germany; these kinds of contacts made Britain look more dangerous to Germany, and so might conceivably have had a sobering effect on Hitler. In Dean Landis' edition of Kennedy's unpublished "Memoirs," though, there is no attempt to rationalize Kennedy's "good will" efforts on that or any other basis; the only light shed on Kennedy's reasons for urging the royal tour is in his comment to the King that "he and the Queen should visit the United States to show the American people how simple and real monarchs could be." [26] Kennedy was eager for the approval of the Britains honored by such tours, and particularly so, the royal family. He just plain liked the royal family and wanted to demonstrate his appreciation—"the mystique of the royal family got to Kennedy," one diplomat told the author.[27]

Desire for approval was no doubt in some part responsible for his "I'm for Hitler" comments to von Dirksen and other German representatives, though other reasons were probably more central to his motives.

It is perhaps not without significance that Kennedy's isolationistic comments of December, 1939, were delivered in East Boston—a community of Italian and Irish—where they could only have been precisely what the people wanted to hear. His American speeches were always very different in tone and content from his speeches in Britain. Kennedy was generally more interested in winning the favor of his audience than in convincing them to his point of view. Every audience got a slightly different shading that brought his comments closer to what they wanted to hear: he told the British one thing, the Americans another; von Dirksen one thing, Chamberlain another; the Polish Ambassador one thing, the British another; Hull one thing, Halifax another. One of Kennedy's friends attributed the content of the von Dirksen dispatches to the fact that everyone always had the feeling that Kennedy agreed with them. Why? There was always the need for current approval. There can be no other explanation for Kennedy's bizarre conduct on the matter of the publication of Roosevelt's message to Reynaud.[28]

Again, other motives were probably more central, but Kennedy's desire to cooperate, help, and be part of the goings-on, was certainly in part responsible for his ostentatious visits to the government offices at crisis times; his willingness to manufacture pro-Chamberlain publicity; his solicitousness of the Prime Minister's wishes, and ingenuity in dreaming up suggestions that might help further Chamberlain's policies; his expressed willingness to make suggestions to President Roosevelt for actions that would help Chamberlain carry out his policies. When his work proved helpful, Halifax noted that Kennedy "was gratified, I think, to feel that the efforts that he himself had made and the action itself were appreciated." [29]

Usually, Kennedy's need for approval did not conflict with his policy objectives. While Kennedy's calls on Chamberlain might have made it harder for the United States to remain aloof from the war that Kennedy feared, he could rationalize them. They did further his policy of making Britain look strong for German observers. On occasion, though, this need did result in talk that could not be reconciled with either his or Hull's policies.

Despite his forceful disclaimers later that he had never encouraged the British to expect American help or participation, Kennedy had in fact encouraged them much more than he would have had Americans know, when he assured Chamberlain privately of Roosevelt's one hundred percent support, and ventured his opinion that the United States would surely be in any war that developed.[30] Hull unquestionably did not want such comments made. They could embarrass the United States' then-foreseen nonintervention efforts, and could not be expected to have any pacifying effect on Hitler. Kennedy strongly and sincerely wanted to keep America aloof from any conflict, and yet he also wanted to encourage Chamberlain. His own policy goals as well as Hull's, required that no such assurances be spoken, yet they slipped out.

Later, Kennedy told Halifax that if Britain wanted American support in efforts to preserve Greek independence, Britain would be best off by not ignoring German efforts in Rumania.[31] This sound advice was helpful to his friend Halifax, but had the effect of encouraging the British to direct their policy with one eye on bringing the United States into the expected war, something that Kennedy privately dreaded. The behavior is strong indication that being liked may have taken precedence over the claims of policy or discretion.

KENNEDY'S POLICY GOALS CAN BE SUMMARIZED IN A WORD: PEACE. HE was, in the phrase that he lent to a Chamberlain speech, "a go-getter for peace." [32] At various times during his career Kennedy formulated different policies through which he hoped peace for the West might be preserved: maintenance of several spheres of influence allotted to the various world powers, so that each could be supreme and self-contained in his own sphere; coexistence and containment; permitting Hitler to move East, through and past Poland, so that the Nazi and Red dictatorships would remove each other from the earth in a war that would not include the West. Each of these policies might have provided a framework for Western peace, but each of them was successively proven unrealistic and was dropped by Kennedy without a qualm. Kennedy's reaction to the absorption of Bohemia and Moravia, the non-German parts of Czechoslovakia, was to try to prevent America from "jumping to the wrong conclusion"; behind his policy of coexistence and containment was not a desire to live responsibly in peace with a recognized threat, but the desire to maintain peace at any price. When the Nazi-Red pact made hopes of a non-Western German-Soviet war unlikely, Kennedy was still willing to "sell out" Poland, though his hopes for a Soviet-German war had clearly become unrealistic. He thought it necessary to dump Poland to gain time. He refused to draw a conclusion that could not be avoided: that time would not aid the Allies but could only hurt them.

Shortly after the Munich settlement, Kennedy wrote Moffat: "I have fought and battled in the cause of peace with the present Prime Minister, but, the day war is declared, I will be struggling harder for peace in America." [33] The day that war was declared, Kennedy proceeded on phase two.

KENNEDY NEVER SEEMED TO UNDERSTAND WHAT NAZISM WAS OR TO appreciate its threat. In his speeches as Ambassador, he occasionally compared Western democratic ways with totalitarian ways, always concluding that the Western systems were preferable.[34] To Claire Boothe Luce, whose influential publisher-husband Kennedy knew to be pronouncedly pro-British and anti-Nazi,[35] Kennedy said, "Remember this, we Americans can live quite comfortably in a world of English snobbery and British complacency . . . but we can't live in a world of Nazis and German brutality." [36] Later, in 1941, after suffering severe and bitter press criticism, Kennedy asserted that Nazism was "a force which seeks to destroy the rule of conscience and reason, a force which proclaims its hostility to law, to family life, even to religion itself." [37] Nonetheless, Kennedy unquestionably subscribed to much of what von Dirksen reported to be his beliefs. He believed that altogether too much emphasis was being put on the plight of the Jews—after all, they were not the only refugees in the world.[38] He resented the bellicose anti-Nazi efforts of "the Jews who dominate our press," and world Jewry in general, which threatened the peace and prosperity that he so highly valued.[39] Surely, Germany was no paradise, but from an objective point of view, was the Reich really as bad as the war faction made her out to be? Even Kennedy's Jewish friend Baruch acknowledged at the time of the *Anschluss*, "Much as I dislike saying it, the truth demands that I say that Germany is really entitled to what she is asking for," [40] and Joe Junior, in whose views the Ambassador put great stock, came back from a German tour in the fall of 1938 extremely impressed with the might and the peoples of the Reich.[41] Kennedy widely reported his young son's views,[42] and encouraged Ione Robinson to undertake her proposed trip to Germany, adding, she summarized, "that if I did go to Germany I would find that it was not such a bad place after all." [43] Kennedy did share with the Germans a gnawing, overriding fear of the left and particularly communism, and believed that the long-run threat was not Germany at all, but rather Russia.[44] When it became clear to Kennedy in the fall of 1940 that Britain's collapse was imminent, Kennedy advised Hull, Welles, and Long, that the time had come, as Long summarized it, to "take some steps to implement a realistic policy and make some approach to Germany and to Japan which would result in an economic collaboration." [45]

After his return home, Kennedy told an audience that America could not "divert the tides of the mighty revolution now sweeping Asia and Europe." [46] In a carefully worked out speech, this line cannot be written off simply as an odd choice of words to describe the Fascist phenomenon. "The mighty revolution now sweeping Asia and Europe" conjures up visions of Hitler's powerful brown-shirted army moving along, the sound of the trucks and tanks drowned out by a hundred thousand voices singing the Battle Hymn of the Republic.

Nor did Kennedy ever really understand the threat of Nazism. He never appreciated the fact that fascism glorified the making of war as an end in itself, but attributed the Reich's belligerency to economics— "They can talk to me all they want about the political aspects of everything that's happening," he told Morgenthau, "but that isn't what the trouble is." [47] When Germany's economic problems were

solved, he believed her belligerency would cease. If she controlled
Southeast Europe, either she would become economically prosperous
or collapse from overextension, and in either case the German threat
would end.[48] Kennedy was certainly sincere when he told von Dirksen
that he believed that Germany should have dominance in East and
Southeast Europe. Any other approach must have seemed a little
unreasonable as cultural and economic ties made eastern Europe part
of Germany's rightful sphere of influence; after all, he told King
George, eastern Europe was of little use to England from a monetary
standpoint.[49] Kennedy himself could see no justifiable reason for
making a war over it: "I can't make head or tail out of what this war's
all about. If you can find out why the British are standing up against
the Nazis you are a better man than I am," was his comment to
American reporters.[50]

One did not have to be an idealist to know why England was
standing up against the Nazis. Kennedy was probably right when he
said that idealism had nothing to do with Britain's entry to war. The
British public (if not all of their leaders) had become convinced that
Hitler was bent on at least European domination. Corroborating
evidence grew as Hitler's actions demonstrated the cool determination
with which he was carrying out the scheme of *Mein Kampf*. Yet
Kennedy refused to draw the requisite conclusion.

At the Lend-Lease hearings Kennedy asserted for public consumption that he believed Hitler to be bent on world domination, but
neither his dispatches nor his actions give any indication that he really
believed that. And if he had really believed it, he would have
understood what the war was all about.

When it became clear that the European war was not going to be
"called off," Kennedy became convinced that Germany would be the
victor. He repeatedly expressed his view that "words and sentiments
were no match in these days for the positive elements of strength." [51]
He projected to the war and to the relative positions of the combatants
the materialistic realism that worked so well in securities speculation,
and he could neither appreciate nor evaluate the very real effect that
bald emotion and idealism—whether deep within or merely inspired
by Churchill's perorations—had on Britain's position and thus the
overall situation. All he could see was that Britain had fewer resources
than he believed Germany to have. And that was that. He had, as
Landis told the author, "a blindness for intangibles." [52] Those who
followed the situation and Kennedy's attitude early perceived this

blindness, and noted it with varying degrees of sympathy or hostility: Balfour the day after war was declared: "I believe, however, that he wishes us well, but being himself a hustler is inclined to deprecate our less ostentatious British merits";[53] Scott, also in September, 1939: ". . . being primarily interested in the financial side of things, he cannot, poor man, see the imponderabilia which, in a war like this, will be decisive";[54] Lee, during the Battle of Britain: "Kennedy has the speculator's smartness but also his sharpshooting and facile insensitivity to the great forces which are now playing like heat lightning over the map of the world"; [55] journalist Louis Fischer after Kennedy's return home: "[Kennedy] saw the world through the bars of the dollar mark";[56] Carroll Binder, journalist and intimate of Colonel Knox, early in 1941: "[Kennedy] was a speculator and a money-maker who had no appreciation of things of the spirit";[57] the Newcastle, England, *Journal* in March, 1941: "One always felt that 'Joe' traveled widely with eyes that took in too little. . . . idealism had passed him by. . . ." [58] With the passage of time, Britons now look at Kennedy's attitude more kindly; Balfour regards Kennedy's attitude to have been "perhaps a natural outlook on the part of diplomats staying in London who looked at military facts and figures and ignored the dogged spirit of the British people." [59] Another diplomat of the day agreed: "Perhaps he was more objective than we were. . . . He said we were going to be beaten fairly freely, and we didn't believe it—we thought we were going to win. Perhaps he was more objective than we were. But you see . . ." he paused, lowered his voice, and then with quiet satisfaction added, "we did win." [60]

It must be made clear that Kennedy decidedly did not want to see a Nazi victory; indeed, he was profoundly disturbed by the British defeat that he felt certain was coming. He pointed out to the President that the British Empire,

> *through its control of the seas, had thrown a bastion about areas of the world behind which democracy had been able to survive. If Britain fell America would be left, even assuming the loyalty of the Southern Hemisphere, ringed about with totalitarian enemies. This we could hardly afford.*[61]

By 1938, Latin America was already feeling economic pressure from the Reich,[62] and Kennedy himself was aware of and warned the State Department of Nazi propaganda efforts in South America.[63]

Kennedy's concern was largely economic. He publicly acknowledged that "the economic problems of Great Britain and the United States are definitely related and interwoven," [64] and that "nations cannot live to themselves with any more happiness than individuals. . . . we cannot be prosperous in America if the rest of the world is suffering." [65] He did not relish, as he put it,

> *The prospect of our best customer beaten and finished as a Power and the attendant difficulty of arranging our place in the world with Powers who know we hate them.*[66]

In short, Kennedy understood that because of his country's innumerable economic entanglements with the British Empire, and because of the unpredictability of the Axis, a British loss would leave the United States in a much more precarious position; if nothing else, it would seriously disrupt the American economy.

A number of factors, however, led Kennedy to believe that the United States should avoid entering the war at all costs. Most obvious of these was that like almost everyone, Kennedy did not like war and did not want to have his country involved in war. War violently upset patterns of living. ("This war's raising hell with my business," he told American journalists.)[67] War's general wastefulness was repugnant to the economist in Kennedy. ("Joe thought war was irrational and debasing," says a friend. "War destroyed capital. What could be worse than that?")[68] But Kennedy's distaste for war was not based purely on economic philosophy. He himself was subjected to the fierce bombings of London in September, 1940, and he fully understood the dirtiness and the atrocities that war involved. He insisted that his country be spared what England was suffering.[69]

War also involved threat of death to one's loved ones. No one can say just how important fear for the very survival of Kennedy's nine children and especially for the lives of his two fighting-age sons may have been in shaping his reactions to the European situation. Some family friends have suggested that this was the factor that had greatest influence on Kennedy's thinking.[70] In any event, Kennedy was understandably reluctant to risk the lives and welfare of his children for a cause that he did not believe in or feel. In 1944, he would write to Beaverbrook,

> *For a fellow who didn't want this war to touch your country or mine, I have had rather a bad dose—Joe dead, Billy Hartington dead, my son Jack in the Naval Hospital. I have had brought home to me very personally what I saw for all the mothers and fathers of the world.*[71]

Most contemporary observers, though, did not attribute Kennedy's attitude to the natural apprehensions shared by the man on the street, but ascribed it to financial considerations. Financial considerations, both on a higher level and on a lower level, no doubt had great influence on Kennedy's stance.

On the higher level, Kennedy was deeply concerned about the basic economic organization of nations. He was almost terrified by the financial costs of a war which, as he saw it, would "bankrupt" all foolish enough to participate, so that regardless of what nation emerged as military victor, chaos would be the war's real victor, leading to "Bolshevism" everywhere. In a discussion with Charles Peake of the Foreign Office shortly after the outbreak of the war, Hillman explained the Ambassador's feelings in just such terms:

> *Mr. Kennedy was a professing Catholic who loathed Hitler and Hitlerism almost, though perhaps not quite, as much as he loathed Bolshevism, but he was also a self-made man who had known poverty and who did not want to know it again. Mr. Kennedy was convinced that this war unless it was soon stopped would bankrupt the British Empire and also bankrupt the United States, who would be bound to come in before it was over. Mr. Kennedy dreaded the kind of social order which he saw appearing as a result of the war. It would be Bolshevism or at least Socialism and both were dread spectres in his mind. . . . Bankruptcy and defeat, said Mr. Hillman, were obsessions now in the American Ambassador's mind and though he had tried to reason with him, he was not amenable to reason, his argument being that Hitler and the Nazis could not have lasted forever and that there was bound to be a change in regime in Germany one day if we had only let it alone.*[72]

In a last visit with Chamberlain shortly before Kennedy's final return home, the Ambassador expressed similar thoughts: "I'm still not sure of what this war will accomplish. We are supposed to be fighting for liberty and the result will be to turn the last of the democracies into socialist, communist or totalitarian states." [73] Lothian was probably close to the mark when he interpreted Kennedy's attitude as a concern for "the preservation of property, his own in particular." [74] Kennedy, however, was not alone in his view; he records that Chamberlain agreed with him,[75] as did many if not most of Britain's "privileged" class and some of the American Embassy staff. "Churchillian activists" like Lee grew weary of so many people "groaning and moaning" over probable postwar bankruptcy.[76]

There was also the matter of economics in a much more direct sense. To a reporter in 1941, Kennedy pointed out the effect that the war (and stepped-up taxes necessitated by it) had had on the wealthy Englishman: "He's been knocked entirely out of his shoes. His financial class has been obliterated." [77] He knew that if war were to come to the United States, the same would almost certainly happen to the rich American: Joseph P. Kennedy. With characteristically daring, almost designedly provocative prose, Kennedy was capable of reducing his line of argument to intensely personal terms, as in his exclamation to Bullitt that "his one interest was in saving his money for his children," [78] or in comments to American journalists like "I didn't make $9 million to see it go down the drain." [79] Talk like that convinced liberals and interventionists that Kennedy was essentially concerned with and motivated by greed. Lee noted Feis's oversimplified explanation for Kennedy's defeatism: "Because the war will lower the stock market, he said, and because Kennedy's securities are the only things he thinks about." [80]

In spite of Kennedy's loose talk encouraging that type of uncharitable conclusion, this author is convinced that Kennedy was as interested in himself as a symbol as in himself as a particular.

Kennedy could not see much likelihood of traditional America surviving a war. He had supported the policies of the New Deal, but they had led to increased collectivism in the United States, and a war would very much step up the regrettable tendency to bigger and bigger government, business, and labor units. A war effort would pragmatically force virtual nationalization of industry, capital, and labor. The war would require a long period of centralized direction at the end of which his country would be left with a staggering war debt. True, the country had recovered after World War I, but Kennedy saw a different pattern in the world of 1940. Very likely the country would embark on paths unknown, and better left untried.[81]

Kennedy had seen the effect of the war on the system of government in England with its clear warnings for America. In August, 1938, he told Father Thorning, "I find no evidence of sympathy for Marxist materialism in any sphere of public life in Great Britain." [82] But by August of 1940, after a year of intense preparation for war and a year of actual war, he was convinced that the socialists had become the dominant group in the English government.[83] The following month he reported "a definite feeling," which he himself certainly shared, that "they have not a Prime Minister but a

Generalissimo." [84] The old order was gone forever in England. It could happen in the United States. Entry into war would certainly mean the end of at least one aspect of the American way that Kennedy himself had experienced to be good: the relatively unrestrained capitalism and permissive tax structure that had permitted him and would permit others to become fabulously wealthy men would end.[85] While interventionists argued that the United States had to go to war to preserve American democracy, Kennedy concluded exactly the opposite: American democracy, and especially those aspects of American democracy that Kennedy knew and loved could be preserved only by keeping out of war.

This panoply of reasons steeled Kennedy's unreceptivity to arguments in favor of American entry, or to arguments in favor of acts that would make entry more likely, and, particularly, to talk about "saving democracy"—a consideration which he well knew had had little to do with the origins of the war or Britain's participation in it.

Basically, Kennedy was ill-disposed to crusading, feeling that if the people of Germany wanted Nazism, the West had no right to interfere.[86] More important, the American experience in World War I convinced him of the futility of crusading. The United States had been drawn into that war by British propagandists and Walter Hines Page "to make the world safe for democracy." And what happened? When the war was over, the Treaty of Versailles ignored the just claims of the Irish and other ethnic groups, and so belied much of the idealistic rationale for American participation. It was even worse than that: as Kennedy explained to Roosevelt, the treaty had forced democratic forms of government on the conquered nations and so had aligned democracy with the status quo. After the treaty, dynamic political movements necessarily had followed anti- or undemocratic courses.[87] That had been the result of crusading in 1917. In the tense moments of 1939–1941, Kennedy would have none of it. To the Queen, Kennedy explained American reactions to the European situation:

> *When they remember 1917 and how they went in to make the world safe for democracy, and look now at the crop of dictatorships, quarrels and miseries which arose from that war, they are inclined to feel, "Never Again!" And I can't say I blame them. I feel the same way myself.*[88]

"Never again" was the lesson Kennedy learned from World War I. But during the close of his ambassadorial years, Kennedy had that

I've-been-here-before feeling: history was repeating itself. Even the British propanganda was the same. "I got out the *Times*' editorial of August 5, 1914, and compared it with the one on September 4, 1939," he wrote Roosevelt, "and they are practically identical, except for the substitution of the word 'Nazi' for 'Junker.' " [89] Kennedy was seeing the 1914–1917 horror show all over again, and he had not liked it the first time.

The Irish in Eire and in America have always been extremely hostile to Britain and suspicious of British motives. In Eire, this led to strong pro-German sentiment in both world wars, which to a lesser extent was shared by those American Irish with strong ties to the "homeland." Some British diplomats thought that Kennedy's attitude was largely influenced by his Irish background.[90] The author strongly doubts this.[91] However, Kennedy did develop a suspicion of the British and their motives that was very common among the Irish of Ireland and America, as among most nationality groups that dealt with England on a colonial basis. Even before the outbreak of hostilities, this suspicion was subtly manifested in Kennedy: he told the press that the Anglo-Irish settlement had indicated that Britain could be trusted in diplomatic dealings.[92] By implication, Kennedy himself had had some doubts as to that.

After the war began, Kennedy saw many of his British associates angling to draw his country in, and his suspicions of the British— whether they were deep-down "Irish" suspicions or natural suspicions of those with competing goals—began to come to the surface and express themselves with hostility that seemed to grow with time. In 1939: "England is fighting for her possessions and place in the sun, just as she has in the past." [93] In 1940: "England never gets the impression they are licked and therefore they never can understand why they should not get the best of a trade." [94] To Claire Boothe Luce, Kennedy spoke warmly of the British, "though they snub us or sneer at us." [95] By 1941, Kennedy was embittered and had developed a vicious frame of mind [96] towards the British, exhibited in the following anecdote reported to the Foreign Office:

> *A friend of mine, Alec Tuck, was coming up from Palm Beach by aeroplane with his 14-year-old daughter. In the plane was Joe Kennedy and Franklin D. Roosevelt Junior to whom Kennedy was doing a lot of talking. In his conversation Kennedy used so many cuss words and even foul language that finally Tuck, who did not know him, turned to him and said "I wish you would*

clean up your language, sir, as my 14-year-old daughter can hear you." Kennedy turned to F.D.R. Junior and said "Who is that man?" F.D.R. Junior said "I don't know but he looks like an Englishman" (which is true). Whereupon Kennedy said, "I thought so. I hate all of those goddamned Englishmen from Churchill down." . . . Tuck told me about it himself.[97]

The idealistic approach to the war had never made much sense to Kennedy, and suspicion reinforced his conclusion: no, Britain was not fighting for the integrity of Poland nor for the dignity of the Jews. He wrote Roosevelt that she was fighting once more for her own selfish reasons—"just as she has in the past." [98] To Kennedy this was another typical European war, brought about as a result of old-world ambitions and masked in roughly the same phony ideological costume that Kennedy had seen before. Was it not the *duty* of the United States to remain aloof from this kind of petty European quarrel? Had not this country been established for something better? The United States could not permit herself to be diverted from her destiny to become instead "the tail to the kite of old world ambitions." [99]

The United States had fallen for the British line before; he did not want his country to fall for it again. "England is not fighting our battle. This is not our war," was his firm conviction.[100] American entry just did not make sense to him—"What would we get out of it?" [101]

While convinced that he had to do everything he could to keep America out of the war, Kennedy recognized that there was at least some military danger for it in a Nazi-dominated world,[102] and he could not bury his head in the sand in response to the threat. He concluded that America had to arm in case she had to fight to protect herself or her interests. It was of course necessary that America be prepared for any eventuality, and Kennedy was dissatisfied with the pace of American efforts.[103] America, he was convinced, had to prepare itself a bastion, so that when the rest of the world fell, the United States would be impregnable to the Nazis. He told himself and others that no power could successfully attack a prepared America.[104] After Britain lost, as he was convinced would happen, America could either retreat behind an impregnable military wall, or trade with a Nazi world.[105] (October, 1938: "After all, we have to live together in the same world, whether we like it or not.")

Kennedy never ceased stressing the need for preparing America. The country had to be kept powerful—financially strong as well as militarily able. Aid to Britain would help put off the inevitable collapse and so give the country more time to prepare, but it weakened America financially. For that reason it was necessary for the United States to be extremely hawkeyed about aid measures. The defeatism he injected in his wires to Hull conveyed the message that Britain could not win, from which followed the conclusion that it made little sense to waste money on her. His defeatism may have been in part calculated to discourage the giving of significant help to England.[106] He was clearly worried about excessive aid for he was convinced that "the United States will have enough troubles of its own."

Had Kennedy's suggested policies been followed, it seems likely, perhaps probable, that ultimately Germany would have defeated Britain and Russia, which the Germans foolishly invaded in the summer of 1941. Not only a repugnant ideology would have controlled Eurasia, but the United States would have been faced with a hostile world. Kennedy pretended to himself and to others that "we could go it alone," but even he was haunted by the fear of German control of the British fleet.

The soundness of isolationism as a policy for maintaining a nation's peace ultimately depends on the possibility of the particular nation being attacked, and the size of the threatened attack. If the risk is great, collective security is the wise policy. If slight, isolationism may be the wiser policy. Would the United States have been attacked? And could the United States have repulsed Hitler's armies, supplanted by the resources of the Eastern Hemisphere? Each individual's answer to those questions will turn as much on value judgments as on historical evidence.

The effect of Kennedy's suggested policies on the internal government of the United States, however, is easier to predict. Shortly after his arrival in London, Kennedy himself pointed out to Roosevelt that "America alone in a jealous and hostile world would find that the effort and cost of maintaining 'splendid isolation' would be such as to bring about the destruction of all those values which the isolation policy had been designed to preserve." [107] The United States bastioned would necessarily have been a military state, ever ready for an expected attack. The economy would have been upset, and the distribution of resources through the forces of the marketplace would have had to end in place of government allocation of labor, capital, and material resources. This situation would presumably have continued either for a long, indefinite period, or in perpetuity, and would have supplanted (not merely threatened) the American way of economic life. After a long evening's visit in November, 1940, Breckenridge Long summarized Kennedy's position in his diary: "He thinks that we will have to assume a Fascist form of government here or something similar to it if we are to survive in a world of concentrated and centralized power." [108] That was part of the price that Kennedy was prepared to pay to be free from a shooting war. Assuming that the United States was damned if it did and damned if it didn't, Kennedy thought that his country should settle for a fascistic distribution of resources, rather than waste lives and resources in a war that would only lead to chaos and probable Bolshevism. At least the profit-motive might survive, as it had in Germany.[109]

Entirely aside from questions as to the soundness of Kennedy's policies is the very fact that they were his policies, as opposed to the policies of the Department of State.

Almost from the start of Kennedy's ambassadorial career, the diplomatic records reveal that the Ambassador was inadequately reporting his activities to the State Department. Only one of Kennedy's several meetings with von Dirksen was wired to the State Department, and that wire revealed only the German's comments and omitted Kennedy's side of the conversation.[110] There is no indication in the State Department files of Kennedy's persistent efforts to bring about an official visit by himself to Germany. (Later, Kennedy told State Department officials that Hitler had twice sent him a message asking him to come to Germany for a conference—which he, "of course," had refused.)[111]

Kennedy not only failed to inform the State Department about all of his activities, the indications are strong that the Ambassador consciously misled the State Department about his activities. On August 31, 1938, for example, Kennedy and Halifax discussed what American reactions would be if Germany invaded Czechoslovakia, and Britain did not step to the defense of the Czechs. Halifax wrote Lindsay that:

> The Ambassador thought that while American opinion would be much shocked by any German aggression, it would not feel it necessary or justifiable to plunge Europe into a general war on such an issue.[112]

Kennedy's report to Hull was very different:

> I told him a great deal would depend on the attitude the President would take as to whether he thought England should

be encouraged to fight or whether he would contend that they should stay out of war until the last possible minute.[113]

This was more like the kind of reply that Hull would have wanted given, but even that was too specific for the Secretary of State. In the same wire Kennedy specifically asked for instructions as to how to handle such matters in the future. Hull replied to Kennedy's wire curtly, saying that it was not practicable to be more specific about American reactions than the President and the Secretary himself had been in their public speeches.[114]

As has been discussed in a previous chapter, Kennedy paid these instructions no heed at all,[115] and handled himself in his relations with the British in a manner totally out of step with the Secretary's wishes.

Again and again, on problems of trade or refugees, we see examples of Kennedy arguing with the State Department about their policies and attempting to reshape them. After the war began he made vigorous efforts to impress his isolationistic views on the State Department and get them accepted as official policy. His misleading reports as to his own activities and his unreliability in his representations necessitated, at the very least, circumvention of Kennedy, and more, his removal as Ambassador.

During Kennedy's early ambassadorial period, Roosevelt and Hull wanted America—and at least its ambassadors—to remain aloof from developments, while Kennedy wanted America to use its weight to preserve peace. Later, the President and Secretary became convinced of the wisdom of massive aid for the allies while Kennedy became more and more isolationistic. Positions reversed, but throughout, Kennedy pursued his own policies. Lines superfluously asking for instructions raise the suspicion that Kennedy was fully aware of what he was doing and was trying to throw Hull off the track. He was not successful; Hull suspected Kennedy of furthering personal as opposed to State Department policies.[116]

Roosevelt and Hull must share the blame for Kennedy's actions. Hull did not like disciplining Kennedy because Kennedy was a political Ambassador rather than a career diplomat and had the habit of taking matters over Hull's head directly to the President.[117] There is no indication that Roosevelt tried to keep Kennedy within "channels", that Hull ever gave Kennedy a thorough dressing-down,[118] nor even, that consistent efforts were made to guide Kennedy adequately from above.[119] Evidence of the Ambassador's failure to follow department policy is not so much derived from discrepancy between State Department orders and Kennedy actions as from Kennedy's purposefully misleading wires, which indicate that he knew that he was not following Department policies. The same, of course, is indicated by the boastful comment of the pleased Carter that "Kennedy, month after month, has bucked both the State Department and Mr. Roosevelt." [120] At the embassy it became common knowledge that Kennedy "disagrees completely with what he says are Roosevelt's policies which are leading us straight into war." [121]

After Kennedy left England, Bilainkin, who was extremely sympathetic to Kennedy, sat back and summarized "Kennedy's error in wishing to initiate policy here was that he had up against him the toughest man in the United States, Cordell Hull." [122] This was not quite accurate; Hull was very far from the toughest man in the United States, and the error in an Ambassador attempting to initiate State Department policy does not depend on the success or failure of the efforts. It is error no matter the results, and no matter the wisdom or the lack of wisdom of the Ambassador's policies. The agents of the State Department must be responsive to it if a nation is to have any kind of a consistent foreign policy. For that reason, Ambassadors must state, interpret, and advocate their government's official policy regardless of their own personal views. Bucking of the State Department should not be tolerated under any circumstances; tolerating it cannot but create an inconsistent and confused foreign policy, and so threaten a nation's welfare. The blame is not entirely Kennedy's.

FROM THE BEGINNING TO THE END OF HIS AMBASSADORIAL CAREER, the spectre of Walter Hines Page haunted Joseph Kennedy.[123] From his position as Ambassador to England, Anglophile Page had literally conspired with the British to bring America into World War I, against the wishes of President Wilson and Secretary of State Robert Lansing. To a man like Kennedy he must have seemed almost a traitor. Kennedy resented the fact that his name was always linked with Page, inviting parallels to be drawn: "Walter Hines Page got a tablet in Westminster Abbey to celebrate his success in bringing us into the war; one such tablet is enough"; "He is going the way of Page"; "He has the best contacts since Walter Hines Page"; "Walter Hines Page was a British Ambassador to Washington. It would be a good idea to inquire whether we haven't got another of those things at the Court of

St. Jim now." Even Roosevelt said, before the outbreak of war, "He's more British than Walter Hines Page." [124]

The thought of Page perhaps helped to make Kennedy even more isolationist than he would otherwise have been. In explaining his East Boston speech of December, 1939, to Bilainkin, Kennedy said, "If I had said anything else, favoring anything but isolation, think what our Press would have said over there. They would have shouted, 'Here is another Walter Page.' " [125] Kennedy was resolved that he would not be another Walter Page—he would see to it that America kept out of the war. The thought never occurred to him that refusal to follow State Department policy was the only unforgivable failure of— Walter Hines Page.

THE
GREATEST CAUSE

THE PRESIDENT "GOT THE WORD" OF KENNEDY'S INTENSE displeasure and possible endorsement of Willkie. According to Randolph Churchill, the Prime Minister had been forwarding transcripts of Kennedy's "bugged" telephone conversations to Hopkins.[1] True or not, the President did learn of Kennedy's attitude through Welles,[2] Kennedy's intimate Arthur Goldsmith,[3] possibly Lothian or others, and ultimately from the newspapers, which, on October 23, carried the rumor that Kennedy was returning to endorse Willkie.[4] Roosevelt himself credited the rumor for at least 12 days before it hit the press.[5]

Despite his earlier talkativeness, Kennedy remained tight-lipped throughout the prolonged trip home, and refused to show his hand to the group of reporters on the journey,[6] heightening suspense among the journalists and the readers of their newspapers as to his final plan. Those who knew the Ambassador best, though, were satisfied as to what his ultimate course would be: Krock never thought that Kennedy would endorse Willkie,[7] and Joseph P. Kennedy, Jr., was publicly speaking for the reelection of Roosevelt throughout the time that the Ambassador was encouraging speculation that he himself would do the contrary.[8] The Ambassador's son, ever loyal to his father, must have known something that few others—not even Roosevelt—knew. Kennedy had determined that at the end, he was not going to embarrass the President.[9]

Alsop and Kintner predicted that Kennedy would "express his opinions to every available American listener the instant he gets through customs," [10] and to guard against that, Welles urged the President to get hold of Kennedy on arrival before "any one else got at him to talk." [11] The President took steps to do just that. He had a note delivered to Kennedy when the plane landed in Lisbon, specifically requesting Kennedy to come to the White House immediately on arrival in the United States, and to make no statements to newsmen.[12] When the plane arrived in Bermuda, Kennedy received another message from the President urging Kennedy and his wife to come

296

immediately to Washington to spend the night at the White House. A third message was given Kennedy by his friend Truitt on Kennedy's arrival in New York on October 27, again from the President and again to the same effect.[13] At the American Embassy in London, Bilainkin overheard Harvey Klemmer, the Maritime Commission's agent in London, tell Kennedy on the phone, "For Heaven's sake do not say anything before you see Roosevelt at the White House, for, if you do, it will mean, politically, gravely damaging things." [14]

On arrival, Kennedy conferred with his wife and a few close friends as to what to do, but no decision was publicly announced, and the Kennedys left for Washington.[15]

Lyndon B. Johnson later claimed to have been with the President that day when Roosevelt received a telephone call from Kennedy, and Johnson recounted the President's end of the conversation to Krock: "Ah, Joe, old friend, it is so good to hear your voice. Please come to the White House tonight for a little family dinner. I'm dying to talk to you." As Johnson told Krock, Roosevelt, putting down the telephone, drew his forefinger, razor-fashion, across his throat.[16]

At dinner the same evening the Roosevelts and the Kennedys were joined by Kennedy's friends, Senator and Mrs. Byrnes. Obviously at the President's request, Byrnes began hinting about how helpful an endorsement of the President by Kennedy would be. After remaining noncommittal on the subject for quite some time, Kennedy finally blurted out his grievances. Roosevelt denied any part in the circumvention of Kennedy, heaped blame on the State Department, avowed his friendship, and otherwise charmed his Ambassador. He led Kennedy to expect further position with the Administration. Before the evening was out, Kennedy had been prevailed upon to endorse the President.[17] Perhaps, as Stewart Alsop wrote in 1960, vague hopes were held out to Kennedy that cooperation in 1940 might mean a chance for Kennedy himself to run in 1944;[18] John F. Kennedy, asked if Roosevelt had really offered his father the nod in '44, laughed it off, as if to demean it, with "I don't know—my father certainly thought he had." [19] Equally likely, Kennedy went to the meeting expecting a cajoling, receptive to the President's softening. "I can say no to that fellow on the telephone but face to face he gets me," Kennedy once said.[20] To disappointed friends, Kennedy explained that he had concluded that Willkie would get the United States into war even quicker than Roosevelt,[21] or that he had responded to his wife's pleas that abandonment of Roosevelt would stamp Kennedy an ingrate.[22]

The speech was delivered on a nationwide radio hookup on October 29, two days before the election. Kennedy personally paid the $20,786 price tag for the broadcast, rather than accept the financing of the Democratic National Committee.[23] By disassociating the speech from the National Committee, he heightened suspicions as to his message, and raised it above the usual election-time claptrap.[24]

"It is true that there have been disagreements between the President and me," Kennedy began. A half-hour later he ended with, "I urge the reelection of Franklin Roosevelt." Between the opening and closing lines of the address, Kennedy devoted himself to discussing his impressions of the world situation. His firm belief was that the "United States must and will stay out of war. . . . If we rearm fast enough we will stay out of war. It is today our guarantee of peace." Kennedy supported American neutrality and argued that "Our declaration of war would hurt England by enlarging our responsibilities here." He insisted that from his earliest days in England he had never given the English hope that the United States would enter the war, and—despite his powerful suspicions to the contrary[25]—Kennedy assured his listeners that the President had made no secret commitments to the British. Ultimately, his endorsement of the President rested on the same grounds as his previous endorsements of the third term: he stressed that the gravity of the world situation required the continuance in office of the man of experience.[26] Roosevelt wired Kennedy, "I have just listened to a great speech." [27] Even Morgenthau called Kennedy to congratulate him "on that perfectly swell speech last night." (". . . that's damn damn nice of you to bother about that. You liked it? . . .")[28]

Kennedy had done his duty for his chief. Republican Congressional leader Joseph Martin commented that Kennedy had turned out to be little more than a character reference for Roosevelt—hardly "a flaming champion of the third term candidate." [29] But the effect of the speech was great. The endorsement was restrained and comparatively free of the nonsense typical of most political speeches. Commentator Ernest K. Lindley called it the most impressive plea for Roosevelt's reelection from the conservative side.[30] *Life* later described it as probably the most effective vote-getting speech of the campaign, because—coming from Kennedy—it allayed fears that Roosevelt would involve the country in a war.[31] Those who had been exposed to Kennedy's inner thoughts, though, were not favorably impressed with his speech. Colonel Raymond Lee noted in his diary:

> *Kennedy certainly left London all primed for a vindictive and*
> *vigorous assault on Roosevelt. . . . Regardless of its effect on the*
> *campaign, it is sufficient evidence to me that Kennedy has no*
> *depth of political philosophy or political conviction whatever and*
> *is exactly the opportunist that everyone now thinks he is.*[32]

William R. Castle, one of the brains behind the keep-out-of-war America First Committee called it a "stooge" job for the President, and privately shared his suspicion that some big financial considerations must have been involved—"Everyone in Boston knows that Kennedy is money mad." [33] Even Krock found the speech "out of keeping, not only with the wholly opposite view he had been expressing privately (to me, among others), but with Kennedy's earned reputation as one of the most forthright men in public life." [34]

Immediately after Roosevelt's reelection, Kennedy submitted his resignation as Ambassador.[35] Welles begged him not to quit in a row, but Hull, eager to be rid of Kennedy, blamed men like Hopkins in Roosevelt's inner-circle for Kennedy's unhappy situation, and urged him to hold firm and quit.[36] When Kennedy visited the President, he told Roosevelt: "I think I should hand you my resignation at once. I've told you how I feel being Ambassador without anything to do. . . . to sit there doing nothing and have whatever has to be done handled through the British Embassy in Washington—I'd rather come home." The President, having gotten all he wanted out of Kennedy, was ready, as the Ambassador had predicted, to "throw him in the ash can." [37] He made no effort to dissuade Kennedy—after all that the State Department had done to the Ambassador—but requested that Kennedy's resignation not become official until Roosevelt had had time to consider a successor.[38] According to the President's appointment book, the visit lasted from 12:55 to 1:00 P.M.—a five-minute interview and the shortest length of time allotted on the President's schedule. Then, while Kennedy denied to the press that he had resigned,[39] the President left for lunch with his friend Morgenthau.[40]

Before leaving for a medical checkup in Boston, Kennedy stopped for a visit with Long at the State Department. Long noted in his diary, "I told him he ought not to talk to the press or to talk in a way that would scare the American people . . . the American people needed education in foreign affairs and that to thrust it upon them too suddenly would be disastrous. He agreed and said that he would not do that." [41] Several days later, Kennedy gave the most significant newspaper interview of his life.

Through Fitzgerald, reporter Louis Lyons of the *Boston Globe* arranged for an interview with the Ambassador at his hotel in Boston. Lyons had first interviewed Kennedy in 1936, when Kennedy was supporting Roosevelt for reelection to a second term. Kennedy was so pleased with the earlier interview that he had ordered a hundred copies of it,[42] and he remembered Lyons favorably. Kennedy was relaxed in his hotel room and spoke freely to Lyons and several others present.[43] As to some of his comments, he added, "That's off the record";[44] other portions of his discourse were by their very nature not for publication, and Kennedy no doubt assumed that no "off the record" was needed, that Lyons would use discretion to turn out a favorable piece as he had in the past. Lyons, though, left out of his article only that material that had been explicitly labeled "off the record," and presented the rest in a fashion that could only cause grave embarrassment to the Ambassador.[45]

Lyons reported that Kennedy had cut out a role as torch carrier for himself. He would lead a keep-out-of-war crusade. Kennedy would leave the East Coast shortly for California and would visit Hearst to impress the powerful publisher with his opinions.[46] He would speak to many influential people. He saw this as something of a duty: "I know more about the European situation than anybody else, and it's up to me to see that the country gets it," Kennedy had said. "I'm willing to spend all I've got to keep us out of war. . . . There's no sense in our getting in. We'd just be left holding the bag." Already, he said, "Democracy is finished in England." With labor men at the center of the government, "national socialism is coming out of it." If the United States entered the war it would experience the same thing.

Kennedy had a low impression of England's elected officials. "Now, I tell you when this thing is finally settled, and it comes to a question of saying what's left for England, it will be the Queen and not any of the politicians that will do it. She's got more brains than the Cabinet." Turning from the Queen to Eleanor Roosevelt, Kennedy volunteered "She's another wonderful woman. And marvelously helpful and full of sympathy." Nodding toward Landis, who was present during the interview, Kennedy said,

> *Jim will tell you that she bothered us more on our jobs in Washington to take care of the poor little nobodies who hadn't any influence than all the rest of the people down there together. She's always sending me a note to have some little Susie Glotz to tea at the embassy.*

Kennedy told Lyons that he supported such aid to England that would keep Britain fighting, and so give the United States time to prepare its defenses. He doubted that such aid would inevitably draw the United States into the conflict if intelligently handled. But military aid would be senseless—"What would we be fighting for?" He stressed the importance of making the most of every hour for defense works. He pointed out that the United States had not been doing that. The country, he said, had to be educated to the need for defense, and the President should be given more legislative power to mobilize for defense.[47]

The interview, and especially Kennedy's comment that democracy was finished in England, raised an international storm. Kennedy learned of the story's content before circulation of the paper, and was dubious about the wisdom of its publication. The die, however, had already been cast, and Kennedy was quoted two days later as having said, "Well, the fat's in the fire, but I guess that's where I want it." [48] After the interview became so controversial, Kennedy realized that it was not at all where he had wanted it. He asserted that all his comments had been off the record, and that the reporter had violated his confidence. After this weak disclaimer, Kennedy said that he was "going to let the whole thing drop," [49] but the press was not obliging. With his statements giving aid and encouragement to isolationists at home and Nazis abroad, the interventionist *New York Herald-Tribune* called the disclaimer unsatisfactory: Kennedy was encouraging the bad and the enemies of democracy, and discouraging the good defenders of it. His comments, they pointed out, were just what the Germans wanted to hear. Coming from the country's leading Ambassador, they contained a clear implication that the Nazis would not have to fear American intervention. He himself was contributing to the destruction of democracy by beginning with the assumption that it had already been destroyed.[50] "There is a world of difference between the realism that recognizes unpleasant facts and fights to overcome them and the emotional despair that concedes a fight before it is put to the test. . . . Despair can stab democracy in the back quite as fatally as treason." [51]

Kennedy was seriously concerned about reactions to the interview in England, and wired Beaverbrook: "The bombers may be tough in London but the ill-disposed newspapers are tougher in America. . . . Tell my friends not to pay any attention to anything they read that I say unless I sign or deliver it myself." [52] Whether due to "Beaver's" influence or to the fact that Kennedy was still (to the best of the knowledge of the British) Ambassador, the British press, for the most part, treated the interview gingerly. In the "respectable" press, Robert Waitham's restrained column in the unfriendly *News Chronicle* was about the most outspoken:

> *It would be impertinent to suggest that Ambassador Kennedy does not fully understand the implications of the word democracy or to imagine that he is less devoted to the principles of liberty than any of the rest of us. But his personal history and predilections do make it possible to wonder whether the thing he believes to be finished in England–the thing he valued and wanted to help Chamberlain preserve–is best described by the word "Democracy."* [53]

Several others took the "let's-define-our-terms" approach to "Democracy is finished in England," invariably concluding that Kennedy confused democracy with "rugged individualism," or "unrestrained capitalism," and that his understanding of the word democracy was erroneous or worse.[54] In a bitter article in the American press, Harold Laski wrote that Kennedy had discovered that British democracy was finished only when it began to reaffirm its faith.[55] Even Castle of the America First Committee privately admitted that Kennedy was "much too pessimistic and indiscreet," though he acknowledged that his committee would use Kennedy's statements for all they were worth.[56] Apparently, such reaction as there was to the *Globe* article was unanimous against Kennedy.[57] Except, that is, in Germany, where the Berlin *Boersen-Zeitung* greeted his comments favorably.[58]

Kennedy refused to deny the substantial accuracy of the statements attributed to him; indeed, to friends he marveled at Lyons' ability to report the interview with such accuracy, though Lyons had taken not a note.[59] He was not unconcerned, though, about the bad publicity. Through Judge Burns, Kennedy made efforts to get the *Globe* to print a public reprimand to its staff member,[60] or to fire Lyons.[61] The *Globe* refused. Soon after, though, Lyons left the paper to take a full-time position at Harvard, which lent fuel to Kennedy's suspicion that Frankfurter, his rival for the President's ear and an influential man at the University, had put Lyons up to doing a "hatchet-job" on him.[62] Kennedy wired Beaverbrook, "There is as much conniving on position in this country as there is in Russia." [63] While Kennedy's suspicions were probably unfounded,[64] Frankfurter took considerable delight in Kennedy's embarrassment, and sent a copy of the *Globe* clipping to

Roosevelt, just in case the President had missed it, together with a note assuring the President that Kennedy had really said much worse.[65]

Kennedy bore the *Globe* considerable ill will for having stuck by Lyons, and took Somerset's liquor advertising away from the paper. Years later he gloated about how, until he sold Somerset, the *Globe* received no advertising from Haig & Haig, Gordon's Gin, or other Somerset brands.[66]

At the Foreign Office and in informed British circles, reactions to the interview were surprisingly mild.[67] T. North Whitehead noted: "I cannot imagine how Mr. Kennedy's recent behavior should improve his political position at Washington or in the country—it rather looks as though he was thoroughly frightened when in London and has gone to pieces in consequences."[68] Perowne, unaware that Kennedy's resignation had been submitted and accepted, suspected that the comments were probably due "less to a wish to harm us than to make it impossible for him to be sent back to this unpleasantly dangerous island!"[69] Lady Astor wrote Lothian "Poor Joe Kennedy seems to have spilled the beans, but no one here is surprised as they say he talked that way to many people."[70] (The views were not surprising, wrote A. J. Cummings in the *News Chronicle*; "what is surprising is the vastness of his indiscretion.")[71] Lothian himself had already formulated a highly uncharitable view towards his American counterpart,[72] but used restraint in his public reply to the extent that he had never seen a more democratic country than wartime England. The Conservative Lothian credited the Labour Party for the fact that democracy showed no sign of weakening.[73] With the crude remarks directed at the President's wife, it is probably safe to assume that reactions in American government circles were worse.[74]

As soon as the *Globe* article was published, Kennedy left for California, to see Hearst and other influential West Coast people, and to visit his son Jack, then at the Stanford Business School. Arriving in California on November 13, he told newsmen, "The only policy I have advocated is to keep the United States out of war. . . . I will work toward that end as long as I live."[75]

In the days that followed, Kennedy visited many influential people on the West Coast, though his precise movements cannot at this point be charted. At meetings with movie moguls,[76] he gave his bleak prognostication on Britain's fate, and warned that the time had come to prepare for the future by ceasing to make pro-British and anti-Nazi films that would be offensive to the inevitable victor. He told of anti-Semitic rioting in London and warned his heavily Jewish audiences not to call attention to themselves by "warmongering," lest they be branded troublemakers, promote ill-will against American Jews, and "hurt themselves." [77] In Hollywood, rumor circulated that Kennedy had dual motives: his professed goal of keeping America out of the war and an ulterior aim—to "scare" some of the Jews and the "Jewish money" out of Hollywood, leaving a gap for his own reentry into the motion picture business.[78]

All of Kennedy's comments during this period were off the record, and so there were no extensive press accounts. Alsop and Kintner reported that Kennedy was "peddling appeasement across the country." [79] Their phrase was obviously loaded, but Kennedy took a mildly perverse pleasure in describing himself to friends as the "Number One Appeaser," [80] in view of which "peddling appeasement across the country" is probably a fair characterization of what he was doing.

Alsop and Kintner wrote that Kennedy was hard for the State Department to handle because his statements were all off the record, but they asserted that the Administration was "reported to be investigating his doings." [81] Even the London *Times,* ever friendly to Kennedy, raised its editorial eyebrow.[82]

By the end of November, Kennedy was back in Washington for another visit with Roosevelt. Kennedy was anxious to have his resignation made public. Although still unready to name Kennedy's successor, Roosevelt understandably raised no objection.[83] Kennedy made a brief statement to reporters after the meeting.

> *On November sixth I tendered the President my resignation as Ambassador. Today the President has been good enough to express his regret at my decision but he said that, not yet being prepared to appoint a successor, he wishes me to retain my designation as Ambassador until he is. But I shall not return to London in that capacity. My plan is, after a short holiday, to devote my efforts to what seems to me the greatest cause in the world today and means, if successful, the preservation of the American form of democracy: That cause is to help the President keep the United States out of the war.*[84]

Interventionist journalists heaved a sigh of relief at Kennedy's resignation, which the press celebrated with a fresh wave of attacks on him. Colonel Knox's *Chicago Daily News* discussed the resignation in an editorial headlined WELL RID OF HIM. The *New York Herald-Tribune* commented that:

> It is the simple, if perhaps unpleasant, truth that with Mr. Joseph P. Kennedy's definite disconnection from the diplomatic service a vast number of Americans, honestly concerned for their country and her freedoms, are going to breathe more easily.

Kennedy's whole diplomatic career they termed "unfortunate." [85] Alsop and Kintner reported that Kennedy's former State Department associates were "visibly relieved to be his associate no longer." [86]

Columnist Dorothy Thompson shared the barbs between Kennedy and the President. She was especially critical of Roosevelt's failure to correct Kennedy's statement that he was "helping the President":

> When the President's own Ambassador to London, Mr. Kennedy, contributes to the general defeatism, and announces that he is "helping the President," the public becomes weary, confused, and even more apathetic. There is no reprimand from Washington, and since the election, no leadership from Washington.[87]

In London, Kennedy's secretary James Seymour, solicited sympathetic treatment for his boss from leading "Press Lords," Beaverbrook, Astor, Kemsley, and Camrose,[88] and succeeded to a great extent in keeping their papers "friendly." Other journalists went to town on the former Ambassador. Janus, *The Spectator*'s columnist, reported on a touching farewell message from Kennedy:

> On the day he left England finally, a telegram addressed to the editor of [The Spectator] by name reached The Spectator office. It ran as follows: "Tried to get you unsuccessfully on telephone, cannot leave England without personally thanking you for your many kindnesses to me during my stay, and it is with real regret that I leave England—Joe Kennedy." It was a warm-hearted message. The odd thing is that the recipient, it so happened, had never had the fortune to meet Mr. Kennedy, or even so much as see him, during his stay in London.[89]

What really got under Kennedy's skin, though, was an A. J. Cummings piece designed to get under the skin, published in the *News Chronicle*:

> While he was here his suave monotonous smile, his nine over-photographed children and his hail-fellow-well-met manner concealed a hard-boiled business man's eagerness to do a profitable business deal with the dictators and deceived many decent English people.[90]

That was too much! Kennedy sent a wire addressed to Seymour at the American Embassy in London that contained an implicit threat:

> *Don't mind the attacks but resent personal observations on family in Cummings article yesterday. Even if they hated my guts I have certainly a lot of influential friends in United States who resent these attacks and what I regret exceedingly they are giving my friends in newspapers and Congress something to attack.*

Whether the wire was drafted for Seymour's eyes or those of the decision-makers in British propaganda is a matter for conjecture. Kennedy must have anticipated that the wire would be intercepted by the British government, and it was.[91]

Kennedy was not without defenders. At a time when his critics were most unrestrained, Indiana Congressman Louis Ludlow, sponsor of the most narrowly isolationistic legislation in modern American history, told his fellow congressmen, "I think I echo a sentiment that is universal this time throughout America when I say 'Thank God for Joseph P. Kennedy.' " [92] Krock, the *Boston Post*, the Hearst press, the *Kansas City Star,* the *St. Louis Post-Dispatch,* and no doubt many other journals stuck up for him.[93] In England, Kennedy was defended in Beaverbrook's Hearst-like *Express,*[94] and Bilainkin continued to have faith in his friend.[95] The *New York Daily News* and Washington *Times-Herald* decried the smear campaign against "a fine and effective Ambassador." [96] Isolationists like columnist Mark Sullivan, who expected Kennedy's information to aid their cause, began calling on Kennedy to speak publicly, and so give the nation the benefit of his judgment.[97] Senator Arthur Vandenberg, the influential Republican isolationist, agreed; Kennedy "ought to be considered one of the fundamental sources of reliable information," he argued.[98] Writing in *The Sign,* Father Thorning expressed his suspicion that the vehemence of the attack on Kennedy was part of a concerted plan,[99] and it is certainly possible that Kennedy's critics were extra-outspoken in an effort to discredit anything he might say.

Intimates of Kennedy were quoted as saying that Kennedy would launch a one-man campaign against entry soon after Christmas,[100] but for some reason this campaign never materialized.[101] Invited to head the newly formed America First Committee, Kennedy declined.[102] Instead, his public comments emphasized the need for increased defense preparations, something that most isolationists and interventionists agreed upon. "What we need in this country is less talk about going to war and more action about building up defense," he said on December 15. He reiterated this sound suggestion, mixing it with doses of isolationist advice, in a letter to Congressman Ludlow:

> As it stands today, our production for defense is nowhere near adequate for the protection of our own situation, let alone aid Britain. While our own defenses are weak, we are limited as to what we can do for Britain, even though we want to. Therefore our first obligation is to speed up defense with all our might. It would be suicidal for our country to get into war in our present state of unpreparedness.[103]

Privately, Kennedy busied himself entertaining isolationist spokesmen like Wheeler and Maryland Senator Millard E. Tydings at his Palm Beach home.[104] Krock told his readers that Kennedy was preparing a series of articles on the world situation.[105] At a Cabinet meeting in late December, Roosevelt raised the problem of domestic appeasers, specifically mentioning Kennedy.[106]

The problems that Kennedy was creating for Roosevelt were of course greater abroad than at home. Almost immediately after the *Globe* interview, Roosevelt stated publicly that the United States had to defend democracy and all it stands for. British publications were probably correct in concluding that Roosevelt was consciously answering Kennedy.[107] Soon after, Roosevelt sent Hopkins to London as his personal representative, in part to remove the distaste caused by Kennedy's reported actions.[108]

Kennedy made no public attempt to further influence public opinion until the second half of January, when he decided the time had come to "clarify" his position with a nationwide radio address. Roosevelt wanted to speak to Kennedy before the address and through Welles an appointment was arranged on short notice for the sixteenth.[109] The calm visit lasted 90 minutes. Kennedy complained about the way Roosevelt's "hatchet men" were going at him in the press but the President skirted the gravamen of the complaint with the observation that Roosevelt himself had suffered worse from the newspapers. Mostly, though, the visit was a social one,[110] and one that unquestionably had considerable effect on the Ambassador. Kennedy had had an appointment scheduled that afternoon with Wheeler, leader of the Senate's isolationist block, but attempted to avoid his old friend by simply not answering the door at his Carlton Hotel suite. Wheeler assumed the Ambassador to be asleep and prevailed upon a maid to let him into the suite, only to find the embarrassed Kennedy hiding behind the door. Kennedy explained that he had been hiding from "someone." [111]

Kennedy's speech, delivered three days later on a nationwide radio hookup, was an attempt to present a reasonable position with which no one could argue. He talked on both sides and all around the questions. The isolationist *Chicago Daily Tribune* and Hearst's *Chicago Herald American* reported it with banner headlines across the top of their front pages, and the *Chicago Daily Tribune* endorsed it editorially.[112] The London *News Chronicle* was no less pleased, observing that Kennedy had "strengthened the President's hand." [113] Its commentator, Cummings, wrote that the speech showed that Kennedy was going along with the "irresistible tide of American cooperation" with England.[114] Open to such contradictory interpretations as to win approval from both the *Chicago Daily Tribune* and the London *News Chronicle*, the speech obviously had "clarified" little.

Kennedy insisted in the speech that America should aid Great Britain even after England's financial resources were used up, so long as it comported with American self-interest. He also stressed the risk involved in any extension of aid, and he insisted that aid should not go to the point where actual military intervention became inevitable. To the amusement of those who knew better,[115] he denied having ever predicted that England's cause was lost. He regarded it as almost impossible for Germany to invade the United States, but insisted that it was equally impossible for the United States to invade Europe. He repeated his firm belief that American democracy could not withstand a long war. "We want to preserve our democracy," but "we are not going to preserve anything by getting into this war." "Why should we think getting into war would preserve our ideals, a war which would then practically leave Russia alone outside the war area, getting stronger, while the rest of the world approached exhaustion." "England is not fighting our battle. This is not our war." Kennedy closed his speech by stating that he was opposed to the proposed Lend-Lease Act.[116]

Summarizing the speech, the London *Daily Telegraph and Morning Post* ventured that it represented "general agreement with the President's policy, modified by hesitation and fears which seem out of date." [117] The London *Times* soberly commented:

> *There is disagreement on whether the speech actually clarified the discussion about giving aid to Great Britain or whether, by emphasizing the risk that the extension of further help might involve the United States in war, it increased the confusion.*[118]

Dorothy Thompson evaluated the speech in an article entitled "Mr. Kennedy vs. Mr. Kennedy." The Ambassador, she ventured, had out-Hamleted Hamlet. Instead of "To be or not to be," he had managed "to be and not to be." [119] In a battle between those for and those opposed to Roosevelt's position, Kennedy had not given effective weight to either side.

Little more light was thrown on Kennedy's position when he testified two days later before the Senate Foreign Relations Committee "against" the Administration's Lend-Lease bill. The night before his presentation he met with isolationist publishers Colonel Robert R. McCormick, and Joseph M. Patterson, and other like-minded men, and outlined a thoroughly isolationist attack on Lend-Lease that he proposed to deliver the next day.[120] After that, his five hours of testimony came as a bitter shock to Lend-Lease opponents; his equivocal comments at one point came so close to endorsement of the bill that he was roundly applauded by Administration supporters in the audience.[121] He refused to identify himself with the isolationists and said that he did not sympathize with them.[122] While he said that he opposed the Lend-Lease bill "in its present form," he said that he opposed it only because he thought the power of Congress in the field of foreign relations should be preserved. He refused to say that the bill's passage would take the United States closer to war, and he refused to say that the bill's passage was unnecessary. Indeed, he said: "It strikes me if the Congress passed this bill I shall be in favor of the bill. And as the gentleman on my left said, today there are not many powers in this bill that he feels are not already in the hands of the President." He spoke for complete aid to Great Britain short of anything that would make war inevitable. Justifiable aid to England was "entirely a question of giving us time," to prepare to defend ourselves. He refused to say what he would counsel when the United States were fully prepared. During his testimony, Kennedy continually referred back to his radio speech, as if he were on firm ground there. He acted like a shaky witness under cross-examination. At every possible chance he answered that he could venture no opinion.

Kennedy's resolution, as reflected in his *Globe* interview and in other private chats during the period, did not make a public appearance. The weak support that Kennedy gave to the Lend-Lease opponents is difficult to explain. Old-time isolationists were bitterly disappointed and never forgave Kennedy for what they took to be a "sellout." Robert F. Kennedy, a little off on his facts and interpretation, but correct in his reportage of isolationists' attitudes towards his father, later told Harry Golden, influential in the formulation of American Jewish opinion, "I think the cynics have deliberately withheld the fact that my father tipped the balance in favor of lend-lease before the Senate Foreign Relations Committee. The America Firsters thereafter called him worse names than any the liberals have ever had for him." [123]

A number of factors no doubt had influence in making Kennedy's stance so indecisive. First of these is that his resolution was never as firm as it sometimes seemed. His comments to Lyons were talk that flowed easily from the tongue of the speaker. He never expected to be quoted and so made comments that he did not care to defend publicly. "Kennedy likes to hear himself talk," Lyons told the author.

Kennedy really did fear Nazism, "a force that proclaims its hostility to law, to family life, to religion itself." He said before the Lend-Lease hearings that he believed that Hitler's goal was world domination, and so he at least acknowledged that possibility. He clearly saw that the United States had a stake in a British victory, if not a vital one. His public statement that Germany would never invade the Western Hemisphere reflected his hopes, not his firm conviction. He must have known that an invasion was altogether possible, for the United States had invaded Europe in 1918. Kennedy's firsthand experiencing of the war gave him misgivings about his own policies.

The influence of Roosevelt and the State Department over him was certainly great. The Hearst press suggested that Kennedy was left with the title of Ambassador so that the State Department could exercise some restraining influence on his public statements.[124] The value of that kind of restraint on one of Kennedy's disposition is dubious, but the President's own smile meant plenty to Joe Kennedy. Isolationist John J. O'Connor, a former Congressman, explained Kennedy's disappointing performance in just such terms: "If Roosevelt cannot win the so-called leaders over completely to his side by calling them to the White House and smiling at them, he at least does a ninety percent job on them, so that they meet themselves coming back because of the fear of offending the throne." [125]

The press criticisms of Kennedy's private talks, and especially press intimations that his position was disloyal, stung him and also helped to tone down his "for publication" comments. "I can't take criticism; I don't see how you can," he told Wheeler[126]—who could take it.

Fears of business reprisals may also have had some effect on

Kennedy. His liquor (especially Scotch whisky) business was extremely vulnerable to British reprisals. When a group of isolationists urged Kennedy to speak publicly what he was saying privately, Kennedy retorted, "Hell, if I said that I'd lose Haig & Haig!" [127] The author suspects that Kennedy gave such an explanation because he thought it would be easier for his listeners to accept than a frank admission to the extent that Kennedy had other misgivings about words he mouthed in part to please his listeners. If so, he misjudged his audience. The story spread. Many isolationists accepted Kennedy's explanation, and despised a speaker who placed personal business considerations above the national welfare.

One last factor that may have played a part in softening Kennedy's position is that put forth in Landis's edition of Kennedy's "Memoirs": "Knowing that Britain couldn't survive without the lend-lease I made no public statements against the Bill, despite my own objection to it." [128] That factor makes least sense to the author, for as Landis would have Kennedy acknowledge, the passage of Lend-Lease effectually put the United States in the war[129]—the very thing Kennedy dreaded most.

In the year between the Lend-Lease hearings and the bombing of Pearl Harbor, Kennedy largely left the public eye. He failed to join in the active campaign led by isolationists against the President's increasingly interventionist policies.[130] One of his visitors noticed that Kennedy had pushed the President's picture to an inconspicuous place in his photo gallery, placing the photographs of the Pope and the royal family in more prominent positions.[131] But Kennedy was well aware that Roosevelt could still be useful to him, and he was not burning any bridges for publication. When a columnist ventured that the Halifaxes had a sort of Rooseveltian unaffectedness, Kennedy made restitution for his jibes at Eleanor in the *Globe* interview: "Yes . . . but you and I know that no two people in the world have the charm and simplicity of the President and Mrs. Roosevelt. You can't beat them in any hemisphere." [132]

Kennedy made only two public statements between the Lend-Lease hearings and the bombing of Pearl Harbor, one on May 24 and the other a week later.

The earlier speech, addressed to the graduating class at Oglethorpe University, was perhaps the greatest speech Kennedy ever delivered, drawing on much of America's intellectual heritage for its substance. In it, Kennedy mixed concepts of the Puritan mission and of manifest destiny with quotations from Calhoun. He used contemporary "liberal" and "conservative" notions as well, to come up with an excellent "keep-out-of-war" speech, the only thoroughgoing isolationist speech he made in the period before World War II. Perhaps he felt that he had to speak his mind frankly, publicly, at least once. Wheeler called it "a very brilliant address," [133] and it was. It was a classical isolationist statement in its insistence that:

> Regardless of how this war comes out, America has a great destiny because she has youth and she has assets which nature bestowed with a generous hand. I believe that, though I believe that we shall have to fight harder and suffer more for that destiny in an Axis-dominated world. Let us not forget the American destiny; let us not be deluded by any claim that self-interest should make us guardians of the peace of the rest of the world.

Kennedy argued that America had nothing to fear from the Axis militarily:

> No country has ever been more fortunately situated for natural defense than is America. The Atlantic and Pacific Oceans constitute impregnable bastions of defense. . . . A direct attack on us would require an armada mightier than the power of man could create.

Nor did America have very much to fear economically:

> Surely, a British victory would be helpful from the viewpoint of our foreign markets. But it is nonsense to say that an Axis victory spells ruin for us. . . . From ninety to ninety-five per cent of our trade is internal. We depend less on foreign markets than any great nation. If worse came to worst, we could gear ourselves to an intelligent self-contained national economy and still enjoy a fair deal of prosperity.

Not only did the United States lack a military or economic stake in the war, Kennedy argued, but she could hope to accomplish nothing ideologically through war:

> The crusaders' argument for war is the silliest of all. I have the fullest conviction that few countries of the earth by and large want our kind of democracy. Most of them have neither the training nor the tradition for it—not even a proper understanding of it. Democracy cannot be imposed by force or otherwise. It would not last even if we were able to present them with the most up-to-date constitutional democratic system. In our very

> *attempt at this colossal crusade we would end in failure and disgrace abroad, in disillusionment and bankruptcy at home. . . .*
>
> *We cannot, my fellow Americans, divert the tides of the mighty revolution now sweeping Asia and Europe.*[134]

Clearly, "going to war will not solve anything."

War might mean disaster for America. "Most Americans say, and rightly so, war will not preserve our liberties. We may, with our eyes on the foreign scene, be insensible to the loss of our liberties right here at home." The expense of war would necessitate great changes in our way of life:

> *The modern technique of war requires such an increase in Government spending, in tax rates, in regulation and limitation of the private sphere of production, and ultimately limitations in consumption itself that a return even to our modified capitalism of today will hardly be feasible.*

And anything might happen when the war's boost to the economy ceased:

> *When the war machine has run down and the economic shock is being felt by every man, woman, and child, new and sweet-sounding slogans will fill the air. Shortcuts to utopia will be advocated on all sides.*[135]

Kennedy's speech at Notre Dame a week later must have disappointed the isolationists as much as the Oglethorpe speech had elated them. Commentary on the Oglethorpe address was unusually bitter. Claude Bowers, erstwhile United States Ambassador, wrote the President that he counted it a "fifth column" speech,[136] and the *Washington Post* used the speech as evidence that the Nazi invasion of the United States had already started.[137] Perhaps business pressures were brought to bear upon Kennedy. On May 27, 1941, the President had declared a state of national emergency, and implied increased American involvement in Britain's position. Perhaps Kennedy was impressed; in any event, he was not eager to go to bat directly against the Chief.

Kennedy's Notre Dame speech urged cooperation with the President. He called Roosevelt's proclamation of national emergency "a most historic and most solemn pronouncement," demanding "unlimited loyalty" of all Americans. "In these days of disintegrating cultures" he said, *there is much in our Western civilization that does not deserve to survive. A monopolistic capitalism, as defined by the Papal encyclicals, which freezes credit, concentrates wealth in the hands of a few, excludes labor from a share of the profits, and considers the right to property as so absolute as to be unbounded by its use, is not worth preserving. . . . An economic system which, under the cloak of organizing labor, permits subversive groups and racketeers to infiltrate into its ranks, either to serve foreign political ends or to enrich the pockets of leaders by filching from the workers their hard-earned wages, is not worth preserving. A system of education which ignores, sometimes repudiates, religion and morality is not worth preserving.*[138]

The Oglethorpe and Notre Dame speeches taken together counteract each other as guides to action. The first would impress its listeners with the soundness of the isolationist, anti-Rooseveltian position. The second speech gives support to the position of the President and the interventionists. While Kennedy's own views were closer to those reflected by the Oglethorpe address, he had once again reduced his net effect on public opinion to almost zero.

POST-MORTEM
ON A FRIENDSHIP

WHEN PEARL HARBOR was bombed, virtually all of the men who had opposed the President's policies put aside their past differences with Roosevelt and devoted their energies to the war effort. Kennedy was willing to do the same. He wired Roosevelt on December 7, 1941, "In this great crisis all Americans are with you. Name the battlefront. I'm yours to command." [1] In a volume of the President's letters edited by his son Elliott Roosevelt, it is explained that through a mixup the President never saw Kennedy's wire of December 7,[2] but Roosevelt was frequently reminded at later dates of Kennedy's availability.

Many Americans wondered why Joe Kennedy's talents were not used during the war years. So many of the men who had opposed Roosevelt's prewar policies were invited to serve. A former Liberty Leaguer, William S. Knudsen of General Motors and Republican stalwart Henry Stimson were brought into the Administration, joining Colonel Knox, who had been Alfred Landon's Vice-Presidential running mate. These men were closer in political orientation to the National Association of Manufacturers than they were to the New Deal. From the ranks of the isolationists, General Robert E. Wood and America-First head Richard Stewart served with the Armed Forces. General Creed Hammond served in an Army administrative post, and Chester Bowles headed the O.P.A. But Joe Kennedy was sidelined.

As early as January, 1941, after the *Globe* interview but before the Lend-Lease hearings, Kennedy was already looking for a door back "in," and tried a remarkable one. The British had been exploring possible American assistance in Britain's relations with steadfastly neutral Ireland; Kennedy's name, among others, had been mentioned as a possible emissary.[3] Krock, as if unaware that just such a mission had been considered, approached the British Embassy in early January with a suggestion: perhaps Kennedy could help the British in their relations with the Irish by visiting DeValera on Britain's behalf; perhaps he could prevail upon DeValera to open Ireland's ports to the

315

British.[4] Such a mission probably did not comport with Kennedy's privately held beliefs, but it would bring just the right kind of publicity needed to clear the air for Kennedy in the press, the Administration, and even the world. British officials in Washington were receptive to the idea and took it up with the State Department.[5] A few days later, when Kennedy and Roosevelt met just before the Ambassador's Lend-Lease testimony, Roosevelt mentioned to Kennedy that "he would like to have a long talk with me about the Irish situation which, according to Welles, I was the only one who could help in straightening it out."[6] The President was toying with Kennedy, tantalizing him with hopes of reentry to the inner circle in order to keep his Lend-Lease testimony innocuous. Kennedy's subsequent testimony was innocuous. Then, the talk never took place, the mission failed to materialize, and Kennedy was retired from government.

With the attack on Pearl Harbor, though, the President would need all the help he could get, and Kennedy badly wanted back in. When his offer of Pearl Harbor day was effectually ignored, he attempted to steam up interest. Five weeks after the Japanese attack, the *Boston Traveler* called for effective use to be made of his abilities.[7] Krock in the *New York Times*,[8] *Liberty* magazine,[9] and a piece in the *New York Enquirer*[10] carried similar appeals. Friends with Administration ties made direct overtures.[11] Nothing happened. After all else had failed, Kennedy wrote the President direct, this time a plea:

> I don't want to appear in the role of a man looking for a job for the sake of getting an appointment, but Joe and Jack are in the service and I feel that my experience in these critical times might be worth something in some position. I just want to say that if you want me I am yours to command at any time.[12]

Roosevelt replied on the seventh and hinted at a job in ship construction management.[13] Kennedy quickly responded.[14] He felt that the jobs of building and running the ships should be separated, and he offered advice, assistance, and possible relief.[15] Roosevelt passed the note to Admiral Land with the following notation:

> What do I do about this? My personal slant is that you should offer him a specific, definite job: a) To run a shipyard; b) to head a small hurry-up inspecting organization under Vickery to iron out kinks and speed up production in all yards doing Maritime Commission work.[16]

Land thought Kennedy would be a good man to pull the Portland, Maine, Todd shipyards out of the doldrums and told Roosevelt.[17] In phone conversations with Kennedy he also proposed to the Ambassador that Kennedy set up, administer, and manage a new shipyard; that he strengthen the management of one of the weak shipyards; or, that he head a labor board, if one should come about as in the last war.[18] But none of the proposals that were made interested Kennedy.

The rumor persisted, however, that Kennedy would return to government service. A month after Land's offer, at Roosevelt's press conference of April 14, a reporter started to ask a question: "Mr. President, speaking of newspaper stories, there is also one that Joseph Kennedy might come back to take some kind of job in connection. . . ." The President cut the reporter off: "No." "Certain papers," he started to say, but he did not finish the sentence.[19]

Two days later Kennedy visited the President. Significantly, it was for the undesirable 12:45 appointment. Too late to talk, too early to eat, it was always a 15-minute dead spot on Roosevelt's calendar. After the visit, Kennedy told reporters he had told the President that "If there is any job he thought I could do, I'd like to do it." [20] In fact, however, Kennedy was not interested in doing any job Roosevelt thought he could do. A concrete proposal for a subordinate shipbuilding position was finally made, and Roosevelt wrote Kennedy, "Land and Vickery are keen to have you do this. Will you?" [21] The job was beneath Kennedy. Kennedy was offered a job untangling railroad knots, as second man to War Transport Administrator Joseph Eastman, but he turned that down too.[22] The only jobs offered Kennedy were ones that a former head of two federal agencies, a former Ambassador, and a man with considerable regard for his own considerable abilities would not be likely to accept. Kennedy's friend Tom Woodward, still on the Maritime Commission during this period, emphatically told interviewers in 1946 that Kennedy would never have served in a subordinate position to the commission[23] he had once headed. By temperament, Kennedy was not the kind of man to make a good subordinate, and his ego would have prevented him from accepting a job as second to Land, Eastman, or anyone other than the Chief Executive himself. When James Byrnes held out to Kennedy a position in the government's relations with small business, Kennedy wrote Frank Kent, "I told him to stick it, because I feel that, in the first place, if I were of any use at all from an executive point of view, I was entitled to something I could really get my teeth into. . . ." [24] Kennedy had to have an important job, a fact that was appreciated by Roosevelt. At the President's press conference the week after his visit with Kennedy, a reporter asked Roosevelt, "Mr. President can you tell us, sir, about your conference last week with Joseph Kennedy?" Roosevelt replied: "No, I had a very pleasant talk, that was all." The reporter persisted: "Is there some thought of his being brought into the Administration?" "No, no," was the answer.[25]

Pressure from Kennedy's friends in the press and in the government for a major job for him was maintained. On April 22, the *Boston Herald* editorially supported Kennedy for a job,[26] and Krock wrote that a job was in the offing for his friend.[27] Republican Congressional leader Joe Martin, a longtime Congressman from Massachusetts, publicly urged that Kennedy be appointed "Shipping Czar," to break the shipping "bottleneck" by speeding up production. Said Martin, "An efficient, capable man of proved experience like former Ambassador Joseph P. Kennedy should be made the head of such a division and he should be given full and complete power to supervise the whole show." [28] Kennedy's Administration friends were high-pressuring for him from behind the scenes.[29]

The New York CIO became worried that the efforts of Kennedy's friends might be successful. They appealed to Roosevelt to pass up Kennedy for any key shipping position: "Kennedy's association with appeaser and pro-Nazi elements here and abroad throws grave doubt on the security of the nation's war shipping program under his management." [30] Their fears were groundless.

Under the circumstances, no important post could have been offered to Kennedy. In 1942 Roosevelt still had a large number of liberal advisors around him, men like Ickes. The liberal Hopkins had come to have perhaps the greatest influence on the President. Over ten years, antagonisms between Kennedy and these men had become too deep. They disliked Kennedy personally; they disliked what he stood for. The feelings were mutual. Kennedy could not have worked harmoniously with many of these people, and of course harmony in the Administration was most important if the goal of winning the war was to be accomplished. This was a fundamental reason why Kennedy could not have been readmitted to Roosevelt's inner coterie.

But another reason was probably more controlling. After Kennedy's diplomatic career, Roosevelt had lost confidence in Kennedy's judgment,[31] and he had plenty of personal reasons for disliking Kennedy, including memories on two continents. He had had enough of Joseph P. Kennedy. In the middle of the boom for a job for Kennedy in April, 1942, the *New York Post*, always unfriendly to Kennedy, reported that "New Dealers" were putting up a vigorous fight against an appointment for Kennedy.[32] After the publicity had died down, a sympathetic reporter, Kennedy's friend Bill Cunningham, wrote that Kennedy had been "sidelined" by "the New Deal Clique," [33] and Kennedy wrote Beaverbrook, ". . . when I saw Mr. Roosevelt, I was of the opinion that he intended to use me in the shipping situation, but the radicals and certain elements in the New Deal hollered so much that I was not even considered." [34] Neither friend nor foe seemed to realize that one of those "New Dealers" was Franklin Delano Roosevelt.

Kennedy knew it. Early in 1942, people noted that Kennedy had developed a powerful anti-Roosevelt political bias. "We have unity in that we want to win the war," he wrote Beaverbrook,

> *but unity stops there. Dissatisfaction is rife, and lack of confidence in the leaders and in Congress is definitely high and there is a great undercurrent of dissatisfaction with the appointment of so many Jews in high places in Washington. . . . if you want everyone yelling for our team, Mr. Roosevelt certainly is not attaining that end.*[35]

As soon as Roosevelt tapped Congressman Joseph Casey to run for United States Senator from Massachusetts, Kennedy went to work. A residence requirement prevented Kennedy himself from running against Casey in a primary,[36] so Kennedy sought out his cousin Joe Kane, a Boston politician of broad experience, for suggestions as to a possible horse to knock off the President's favorite. Kane came up with a lulu: John F. Fitzgerald. Honey was a human moth when it came to limelights, and though he was nearing eighty it took little effort to prevail upon him to run.[37] Kennedy wrote Beaverbrook: "I am very unhappy that I have not had a chance to do anything [in the Administration] but I've made every effort that I could [to obtain a position] and unless things get a little worse, I'm not likely to be called, so I am taking a slight interest in the politics of Massachusetts and that is giving me something to work on—at least for the time being." [38] He never did get around to telling Beaver that he was running his father-in-law against the President's handpicked choice.

At the time, Farley was directing a fight to take control of the Democratic party in New York from the New Dealers, and the two kept in close contact.[39] Kennedy used a lot of Farley's materials in

Fitz's campaign, and the candidate devoted much of his efforts to criticizing the Roosevelt Administration.[40] Hearst's *Boston American* supported him; Boston was a leading Coughlinite city and the Coughlin elements went to bat for Fitz; Honey's appeal to the Irish was infinitely greater than that of the assimilated Casey.[41] Honey looked strong.

Then Roosevelt began to show some sense. John Henry Cutler, Honey's biographer, tells it his way:

> *Two weeks before the primaries, Kane was in the Kennedy suite at the Ritz-Carlton in Boston when Congressman John W. McCormack phoned from Washington to ask Kennedy to make a speech for Casey. Kennedy refused. Twenty minutes later, according to Kane, President Roosevelt himself telephoned from Washington and made the same request. Kennedy, upset, held his hand over the mouthpiece of the phone. "What shall I say Joe?" After a quick parley, he told the President he didn't consider it proper for him to take the stump against his father-in-law.*[42]

The call, however, did wonders. A few days later Kane showed Kennedy an impressive advertising spread that he assured Kennedy would make Honey the nominee. "But can he lick Lodge?" Kennedy asked Kane. "No" was Kane's response. "And the campaign would cost between two and three hundred thousand?" Kane agreed that it would. Kennedy returned to his suite at the Ritz and was never heard from again.[43]

On primary day Casey beat Honey 108,000 to 80,000, with a third candidate polling 17,000 votes.

Kennedy's goal, however, had been accomplished. He had split the Democratic party and the bitter primary fight had insured the defeat of the President's candidate.[44] The beneficiary was the Republican incumbent, Henry Cabot Lodge. According to Krock, Kennedy substantially helped Lodge in his successful campaign against Casey.[45] A couple of months after election day, Kennedy wrote Beaver, "I was quite active in the fall campaign," [46] without elaboration.

A month after the elections, Kennedy again visited the President, for the first time in eight months.[47] Democrats had done surprisingly badly in the cities in the elections. "I did point out to him," Kennedy wrote Beaverbrook of the meeting, "that he had failed to appoint an Irish Catholic or a Catholic to an important war position since 1940.

. . . That course of action is not conducive to strengthening the Democratic Party. . . ." [48] Didn't work.

The visit raised speculation again on the possibility of a post for Kennedy. On leaving the President, Kennedy told reporters that he was still willing to serve, but doubted that there was any prospect for a job.[49] But talk began anyway.

Marquis Childs reported the following month that a job had been offered to Kennedy but that Kennedy had refused it because it was not an important enough post. Childs' interpretation of the offer was that Roosevelt was trying to bring dissident elements back into the party before the 1944 election.[50] In February, the Boston City Council petitioned Roosevelt for a high federal post for Kennedy,[51] and in April there was speculation that he would head the proposed Civilian Supply Office.[52] Later, he was suggested by Maine Senator Ralph O. Brewster as head of diplomatic matters in invaded lands.[53] Then, in 1944, it was "reliably reported" that he would enter the Cabinet as Secretary of Commerce.[54] But nothing came of it. Too many things had happened for Kennedy ever to be welcomed back into the Roosevelt fold. Kennedy was deeply hurt by his estrangement from the Chief Executive, for among its consequences, Kennedy lost his place on the great stage.[55] A society columnist noticed him at an elegant New York eatery one night in 1943, and reported that the former Ambassador was "telling all and sundry how the war should be fought." [56]

JOE KENNEDY IN
THE POSTWAR WORLD

AFTER HIS AMBASSADORIAL CAREER, JOE KENNEDY NEVER again served the nation as a major official. Early in the Truman Administration, Kennedy was seen as a likely prospect for the post of Secretary of the Navy,[1] but this never materialized, nor did anything come of speculation that he might become head of the International Bank for Reconstruction and Development.[2] In 1945 he served briefly as head of a temporary state committee to "study" (publicize a predetermined conclusion) the need for a Massachusetts Department of Commerce.[3] Later he served innocuously as a member of the First Hoover Commission to study the organization of the federal government's executive branch;[4] he took a more active role on the Second Hoover Commission;[5] he served briefly on Eisenhower's CIA Watchdog Committee.[6] But after his ambassadorial period, Kennedy was comparatively retired from public life and turned his attention again to the business world. He did so as much to keep himself occupied as for any other reason. Joseph Kennedy enjoyed making money; he did it easily. "Money making is a game with Joe Kennedy," his friend Joseph Dinneen told the author.[7] While Kennedy remained a shrewd businessman, the frantic greed and aggressiveness that had characterized his earlier business career was lacking in the businessman Kennedy of the 1940s. He was older, and was already wealthy enough. He took things easier, delegating greater responsibility to his large and competent staff in Manhattan, supervising by phone from the side of swimming pools in Hyannis Port and Palm Beach. With a fortune behind him, accumulating subsequent millions was child's play for Joseph Kennedy. "You know, I used to work hard," he told Landis in 1948. "Now I sit here by the pool and I make more money than I ever did."[8] To another friend Kennedy complained about taxes, saying that his income did not cover his living expenses. "And," he added, jabbing his finger into the other man's shoulder, "there are goddamned few people in this whole world that have a bigger income than I've got."[9]

How much money Joseph Kennedy "made" is for some reason of great interest to people. A number of factors make it impossible for

322

the Kennedy fortunes to be adequately evaluated. Much of the money, perhaps most, is and for many years has been tied up in investments that cannot be accurately appraised. How much, for example, is the Kennedy-owned Merchandise Mart worth? Is it worth the amount for which it is appraised by tax collectors? Or, is it worth 10 or 20 times the amount of annual profit it brings to the Kennedys? Is it worth the amount Kennedy paid for it? Or the amount that an eager purchaser might be willing to pay? A confusing web of mortgages makes the value of the equity even harder to evaluate. How much are 10,000 shares of a slowly traded, or even an actively traded, stock worth? One hundred shares would probably be worth approximately 100 times the last recorded price that the stock brought on the exchange. But depending on the nature and degree of the demand for the stock, 10,000 shares might be worth very much less or very much more than 10,000 times the exchange value of one share. The Kennedy fortunes are tied up in a number of such large investments, handled by a bureaucracy that dabbles in countless smaller, but equally hard to evaluate enterprises. Kennedy himself could not have made a sound evaluation of his aggregate worth without allowing a very large margin for error. The best this author can do is to repeat other people's estimates.

In tabulating the country's richest men in 1957, *Fortune* magazine listed Joe Kennedy in the $200–400 million bracket.[10] Only eight names placed in higher brackets; only 15 people were his financial equal or better. Aside from the oil magnates, Kennedy was the richest self-made man in America—not a mean accomplishment for a lad from the Irish ghetto of East Boston. By *Fortune*'s table, Kennedy was in a bracket with John D. Rockefeller, Jr., and was richer than any of the Rockefeller brothers. Subsequent to *Fortune*'s list, inflation probably increased Kennedy's worth to a greater extent than the fortunes of the other moguls, because so much of his money was in real estate, where inflation has been the steepest. Writers in the 1960s usually pegged Kennedy's worth at a cool $400 million,[11] no doubt relying on *Fortune*. The choice of the higher figure, rather than the lower $200 million, heightened the dramatic effect of the numbers, but it also took into account capital gains since 1957. Kennedy's real estate broker, John J. Reynolds, who would be in a position to know, estimated in 1960 that Kennedy had made $100 million in real estate alone.[12]

Kennedy's private statements on his worth throw little light on the subject. One journalist who published a $400 million estimate in 1960 received a call from Mr. Kennedy. Kennedy thought the article commendable, but corrected the estimate—"I'm only worth $200 million." [13] Kennedy was also capable of boasting to wealthy friends whom he expected would be impressed by such data, that he figured his net worth at something in excess of one billion dollars.

This author made no attempt to evaluate the Kennedy fortune. Without complete access to the Kennedy financial records, and adequate background in appraising, any such estimate would be presumptuous. Let it suffice to say that the Kennedys could with justice be called very wealthy people, and Joseph Kennedy properly thought of himself as such. President Kennedy's friend Paul B. "Red" Fay recalls a golf match with the Ambassador in the 1940s, when

> *we were held up on every one of the first four holes by the twosome in front of us. Mr. Kennedy was angered by the third delay, and by the fourth tie-up he was fuming. Finally, he shouted ahead, "Bill, if you want us to come through, just let us know."*
>
> *Bill nodded, indicating that he would let us know.*
>
> *"Before the depression, that guy used to be worth 35 or 40 million dollars," Joe Kennedy said. "Now he would be lucky if he could scrape together two or three millions, and he's still acting like he had it."*
>
> *"The poor fellow," I said tongue in cheek. "How does he manage?"* [14]

One last note: Joseph Kennedy himself was not worth much money at the time of his death. With inheritance taxes eating up the great bulk of large estates, Kennedy was too shrewd to die with a large personal fortune in his own name; retaining title to the funds and properties would have subjected his heirs to enormous tax claims, and Joseph Kennedy, like any wealthy man, always strove to minimize the tax bite in every way. [15] It is therefore not surprising that the inventory of his estate was not impressive in size; [16] no doubt Rose Kennedy's inventory will be equally skimpy. Kennedy must have sounded a bit defensive when he told a group of Catholic clergymen in 1947 that "Man's duty to provide for his family entitles him to make provisions for them out of his estate when he dies," [17] thus transforming tax planning into a holy act. In any event, Kennedy "made provisions" long before he died.

As early as 1926, Kennedy began funnelling off his fortune into trust funds for his children—with spendthrift clauses tied to his daughters' shares, to protect against either female squandering or hypothesized "gold-digging" husbands.[18] Much of Kennedy's real estate was purchased in the names of trusts benefiting the progeny, so that the profits would accrue directly to the heirs. The net result of this kind of tax planning was that virtually all of the Kennedy family fortune was in trusts for children, grandchildren—perhaps even for unborn great-grandchildren—long before Kennedy's demise. The oft-told story that Kennedy made each of his children millionaires early in their lives so that they could, in Kennedy's words, "Tell me where to go," is complete fabrication and traces back to the deceased. He made them millionaires in order to deny the status of "most favored heir" to the tax collector. But it would still be fair to call the Kennedy family fortunes "Joseph Kennedy's." He and his personal financial bureaucracy made it all.

If the Kennedy fortune was worth only $200 million at the time of Kennedy's death, then Joseph Kennedy clearly made the greatest part of his money in real estate. He entered the business in the 1940s.

Kennedy had dabbled a little in real estate in his pre-Columbia Trust days, but had never concentrated on it as a moneymaking venture. In 1941 he first became seriously interested in it on a large scale. In the fall of that year, Kennedy decided to sell his palatial Bronxville, New York, home. Cardinal Spellman steered Kennedy to Reynolds, one of New York's leading real estate brokers, and the agent at the time for the Archdiocese of New York. Reynolds interested Kennedy in buying real estate as a business investment. In part payment for the home, Kennedy accepted an office building in White Plains,[19] and thereafter Kennedy went into real estate big.

Always a good investment as a hedge against inflation, real estate was even more promising during the early 1940s for the man with capital. Realty prices were depressed in the early forties, but to financial observers the situation was very bright for the future.[20] Kennedy always had a nose for trends, and at the time, it was not hard to see the financial trend in real estate.

Reynolds acted as broker, purchasing agent, and chief advisor for Kennedy, and kept his eye out for good investment opportunities for his customer. Kennedy always chose business associates on whom he could rely; once the choice was made, he trusted them. Reynolds sized up opportunities, spoke to Kennedy about them, and usually made the sale, generally before Kennedy even saw his million-dollar purchases.[21]

By May of 1943, Kennedy had already built up sizable holdings in New York City.[22] That summer New York experienced what the *Herald-Tribune* called a "realty-boom," created by "wise money," and characterized by the biggest trading in big buildings since 1929. Many big financial-world names were involved; Joseph Kennedy was in on the ground floor.[23] Throughout the 1940s, Kennedy was an active real estate trader—buying low, selling high, and holding a number of the more desirable spots. Most of his investing was apparently in Manhattan, but he bought wherever there was an attractive buy. According to contemporary press reports, he acquired office buildings in São Paulo, Brazil,[24] Albany, New York,[25] Chicago, and no doubt many other cities. He was reported to have bought a sizable interest in Hialeah Race Track,[26] and was rumored in the forties to have had financial interests in other tracks. His investments in Miami-area lands, cattle, hotels, and theaters were said to total 30 million dollars in 1946,[27] and he was reported to have bought a 12-mile strip on Florida's less developed West Coast.[28] The inventory of his estate shows that at the time of his death he owned in his own name a 49.9 percent interest in 2,740 acres of undeveloped Florida lands.[29] He also invested in Texas oil lands,[30] largely because of the favored tax treatment afforded the owners of such properties, and his estate's inventory included, without valuation, "Miscellaneous equitable interests in oil and mineral property." [31]

Kennedy's most spectacular publicized purchase was his acquisition in 1945 of Chicago's Merchandise Mart, the world's largest privately owned building, second in area only to the United States Government's Pentagon.

The way in which Kennedy purchased the huge building shows a great deal about the way in which he operated his enterprises. Reynolds called the buy to his attention, and the Ambassador was immediately interested. He compared notes with other "smart money" people, such as his Bronxville associate E. Stanley Klein, who urged him to snap up the deal, and with this kind of encouragement, Kennedy sent Reynolds and John Ford to Chicago to make serious study of the building's possibilities. After reading their report, he bought the world's second largest building sight unseen.[32] He had full confidence in his advisors.

Kennedy surrounded himself with competent help, and paid them handsomely. Each one was a specialist in his field. He demanded of them the same hard work and shrewdness that he himself had displayed in his career. Once hired, Kennedy gave them considerable discretionary power, making only major policy decisions himself. In reviewing their accounts, he concerned himself with the final figure, net profit or loss. That's what counts. His good treatment of his employees accounts for the fact that most of them were with him for many years. As Reynolds puts it, he was not "chintzy" with his help.[33] His ability to select and keep thoroughly competent executives was as much at the bottom of his business success as was his own unquestionable executive ability.

Kennedy bought the Merchandise Mart for $12,500,000 from Marshall Field, its distraught owner.[34] The building had been built at a cost of $30,000,000, and Field valued it at that, but by writing it off as a tax loss, the sale of the building actually meant over 30 million dollars to him.[35] Though he certainly had the $12,500,000, Kennedy bought the building on mortgages[36] for reasons that will become clear later.

For four years, Reynolds commuted regularly to Chicago, directing alterations of the building. Air conditioning was installed at a cost of about $6,000,000. Under Marshall Field's management, much of the building had been left as loft, and this almost useless area was reconditioned for more effective use. The building was rented out for stores. Kennedy hired a public relations-press agent for the Mart. Under his ownership, it became profitable for the first time. Today its annual rents total more than the $12,500,000 for which Kennedy bought it.

While not so aggressive personally as in his youth, Kennedy by no means became "soft" in business in the forties. When New York officials began investigating rent-gouging in 1944 they found numerous complaints against Kennedy. Attorney Harry Halperin, speaking for Goodstein Brothers, clothing manufacturers, charged that soon after Kennedy bought a building at 45 West 18th Street, in 1943, his client's rent was boosted from $42,500 to $73,000 a year. The Goodsteins were presented with a five-year lease allowing the landlord, but not themselves, to cancel after two years. Kennedy's agent refused to negotiate over the terms. Not in a position to move, the Goodsteins were over a barrel and signed. Another tenant in the building, Norman Cohen, of a firm called Cohen and Goldman, complained of a rent rise from $44,000 to $81,000 per year. A third, Henry Lehrman, a manufacturer of military uniforms, complained that his rent was doubled, from $15,000 to $30,000, and that he was called upon to sign a ten-year lease. He needed time to consider whether to stay and pay or to move, and so delayed in signing. He testified that Reynolds soon told him the space had been rented to someone else. When Lehrman complained of Reynolds' failure to give him any notification, he was curtly told that none was needed. Lehrman claimed that he protested that his war contracts would be affected, to which Reynolds allegedly replied that he "didn't care about that." [37]

Soon after these colossal rent raises, Halperin complained, the city's tax assessment on the building was reduced from $1,650,000 to $1,495,000.[38] During the summer of 1944, rents in other Kennedy-owned buildings were doubled, and tenants were asked to sign long-term leases.[39]

Asked for comment about the testimony on the 18th Street building, Kennedy said that the building was held by a trust benefiting his children, and that he had "nothing to do with the building." [40] Reynolds testified several days later, and confirmed most of the unfavorable testimony of the tenants. He denied only having taken a nonchalant attitude about Lehrman's war contracts, and said that the space was still available for lease by Lehrman. He demonstrated that Kennedy's trust in him had been well placed, and loyally took the onus of rent-gouging on himself: "Why spread the name of Mr. Kennedy all over this case," Reynolds protested. "Mr. Kennedy didn't buy the property, and he never saw it. It was bought by John J. Ford of Boston, in trust for the children of Joseph P. Kennedy, and I operate it for him." [41]

Joe Kennedy no doubt appreciated Reynolds' selflessness as much as he appreciated the increased revenues from Reynolds' administration of the buildings. Reynolds, of course, found his arrangement with Kennedy rewarding. His commission on the sale of the Merchandise Mart alone totaled over a half-million dollars,[42] and over the years his commissions from Kennedy sales and purchases more than likely reached a very comfortable fortune. He apparently handled all of Kennedy's realty transactions throughout the 1940s[43] and on, until Kennedy found it financially advantageous to integrate the brokerage function into his "Joseph P. Kennedy Enterprises," thus eliminating the middleman and his commissions.

Kennedy was as shrewd as he was hard. He did virtually all his purchasing with small down payments and large mortgages.[44] With a small down payment, he could "own" the building and enjoy both the full increment in its value and the rents without putting in much of his own money. Kennedy might buy a million-dollar building, for example, putting up $100,000 of his own money and borrowing the other $900,000. Because his credit was good he could get the loans at a favorable interest rate, say 5 percent, not uncommon in those days for a man in Kennedy's position, making his interest payment $45,000 per year. The rents would bring in roughly 6 percent of the market value, or $60,000. So his annual profit would be $15,000 on a $100,000 investment, a tidy 15 percent.

Growth possibilities were even more inviting. During the inflationary period, the increments in value were many times the relatively small down payments. Kennedy, for example, purchased a building at 616 Sixth Avenue for one million dollars in 1943 or 1944, with a down payment of $200,000. He sold the building in 1946 for $1,500,000.[45] While the value of the building increased by only 50 percent, Kennedy received the full increment of $500,000 from an actual investment of only $200,000. Kennedy's profit was not 50 percent (the increase in the building's value) but 250 percent, the increase in his investment. Another building at 59th and Lexington was purchased for $1,900,000, with a down payment of $100,000. The building was later sold for $5,500,000. The profit: 3,600 percent. Other Kennedy properties have similarly increased in value, giving parallel staggering rewards. In an inflationary period, the system of buying and selling real estate with small down payments is a virtually foolproof way to make fortunes.[46] And by buying under a network of corporate names, as Kennedy did and all big investors do, the operator limits his financial risk. In case of an unexpected downturn, the operator defaults on his mortgage payments, and surrenders the building, usually losing all of his down payment. The mortgage holder is unable to receive further financial satisfaction from the building's corporate owner; the paper corporation goes bankrupt, and the operator's personal fortune is untouchable. In the 1940s, when real estate values spiraled, there were few such defaults. There was plenty of gravy in it for everyone.

The 250 percent profit on the building at 616 Sixth would have been far greater if rent control had not taken effect. In the summer of 1944 all the tenants in the building were told that on expiration of their leases their rents would double, and they were all asked to sign long-term leases. When rent control was adopted in 1945, these rent boosts were rolled back to 15 percent.[47] But for that, the building would have brought a much higher selling price than Kennedy received, and his profit would have been very much greater. *C'est la vie.*

Kennedy also made fullest use of his full-time legal staff to get the maximum legal advantages for his enterprises. He invested much of his money in fields that were favored by the tax setup, such as oil or municipal bonds.[48] While some of his business ethics may not always have been the highest, he apparently always kept within the letter of the law. His own legal staff, often second-guessed by his SEC associate, Harvard Law Dean James M. Landis, saw that he enjoyed every advantage within the letter of the law. Sometimes they would work seeming miracles, permitting Kennedy to have his cake and eat it too. In 1957, for example, his lawyers took steps to get a reduction in the tax collector's new and boosted $1,750,000 assessment of the Kennedy Building on Columbus Avenue between 62nd and 63rd Streets, New York. For years the Kennedys had protested that the appraisal was high, but when it was boosted they went to court. Under oath, the Kennedys' agent testified that the building was worth only $1,100,000. An appraiser testifying for the Kennedys asserted that their own $1,100,000 estimate was high. The tax appraisal was reduced to its previous evaluation of $1,550,000.

The following year, the land was condemned by the city for its new Lincoln Arts Center. While most of the land for the Center was acquired in blanket condemnations, a special private deal was arranged with the Kennedy family, perhaps because of their political connections. After private negotiations, Robert Moses, for the Center's Committee, agreed to pay $2,500,000 for the building. The *New York World-Telegram and Sun* blasted the deal, pointing out that the Kennedys had for years asserted that the building's true worth was $1,100,000. When the City's Board of Finance refused to go along, the matter went to court, where the lawyers for Kennedy now asserted that the higher figure was the fair one. The court apparently saw much merit in their case, and scaled down the agreed upon amount by only $97,000, to $2,403,000. In his decision, State Supreme Court Justice William C. Hecht, Jr., held that the court "cannot constitutionally deprive the owner of just compensation because the latter was greedy enough to try to pay less than its fair share of taxes." [49] The lawyers got Kennedy a low assessment for taxes; a high assessment for condemnation. Judge Hecht may have regarded the actions of the family as greedy. That's not the way that Joseph Kennedy would have regarded it. "That's business" he would say, with a shrug of the shoulders.

Besides real estate, Kennedy also dabbled in other business fields. He sold Somerset Importers in 1946, perhaps because of changes in the distribution of Scotches,[50] or because he saw the business as a possible embarrassment to his politician son. For many years a few British and Scottish families had had tight control over the distribution of Scotch, deciding who received what quantities of which brands for distribution where. Joe Kennedy could get good treatment from these people, many of whom were part of the Chamberlain coterie and could appreciate the appeasement rationale even as Kennedy applied it to America's position. But in the 1940s, Scotches came under control of the British government, and with labor in power, the rich capitalist, prewar appeaser, and wartime defeatist could not expect kid-glove handling. He sold. Reportedly, Kennedy received over $8,000,000 for Somerset.[51] In the years in which he had owned the company, he had received some profit on every bottle of Haig & Haig, Dewar's, and Gordon's Gin imported into the United States.

Kennedy also sold the old Columbia Trust Company, which the family still owned, to the Shawmut National Bank for around $500,000 in 1946.[52] But he kept his eggs in many baskets nonetheless. He was reported, for example, to have taken a financial interest in 1946 in a new sun-tanning invention, designed to give people "sun tans" without the bother of sunning themselves.[53] He publicly backed a Broadway show, Frederick Lonsdale's *Another Love Story*.[54] Though the play was *just* another love story, it was profitable. Perhaps there were other, unpublicized ventures into Broadway, and there were investments in other fields of business as well. His enterprises continued to include the Maine and New Hampshire theaters, which he had owned since the early twenties, and he added to the chain with new theater purchases.[55]

Securities transactions, unlike real estate transactions, are not generally reported in the press, and so it is not now possible to chronicle Kennedy's activities, or even to estimate the extent of his activities, in the securities markets in the 1940s and '50s. In one of his speeches, Kennedy intimated that he was speculating, but he did not specify whether or not it was in securities. He boasted to Walter Winchell that he had predicted the stock market slump that came in the summer of 1946, and that he had acted on his prediction. Winchell reported that Kennedy's acumen had enriched him with another fortune at that time. When the market hit its low, according to the columnist, Kennedy bought back in.[56]

Other areas of Kennedy's investments are probably known only to his closest business associates—men like his top executive James Fayne. He was reported in the '40s to have been investigating investment opportunities in Mexico, where his friend "Sell 'em Ben" Smith already had sizable investments,[57] and he had Landis prepare a memorandum for him on the investment picture south of the border.[58] He thought seriously about buying back into RKO.[59] He toyed with the idea of acquiring the Brooklyn Dodgers baseball team.[60] Throughout the '40s and '50s he was interested in buying into the newspaper business.[61] Through Joseph Dinneen he offered two million dollars for the *Boston Globe*.[62] Later, in 1956 he angled to purchase the failing *New York Herald-Tribune*, whose owners spurned his advances when he seemed to be driving too hard a bargain.[63]

Joe Kennedy began to live more freely in the '40s and '50s than ever before. He became a member of "café society," indulging a taste for high living that he could well afford. Scarcely a week went by in the late '40s when his name did not appear in a newspaper gossip column. He was frequently spotted by the columnists at Le Pavillon (in which he had what Whalen describes as a "not-too-silent" financial interest),[64] the Stork Club, 21, and other fashionable New York restaurants and nightspots in the company of big names from the worlds of politics and entertainment. He frequently made the rounds with designer Oleg Cassini (later dressmaker to Jacqueline Kennedy Onassis) and with singer-businessman Morton Downey. Columnists Danton Walker, Cholly Knickerbocker, Austine Cassini, Ed Sullivan, Walter Winchell, Hedda Hopper, and other society and gossip writers vied at dropping his name in their tabloid and Hearst-press columns.

Kennedy's appearances at Hialeah and Saratoga meets, usually at one of the most desirable clubhouse tables, were frequent and were noted on sports pages as well as in the gossip columns. Although strictly a two-dollar bettor, Kennedy might buy a ticket on every horse in the race, remain nonchalant through the running and calmly announce "I've got it" at the end of the race.[65]

Later, in the 1950s, Kennedy frequently appeared with young women of provocative appearance in fashionable New York nightspots. One of Kennedy's favorite restaurants was New York's stratospherically expensive La Caravelle. La Caravelle is an L-shaped restaurant, arranged so that one can sit at the end of the L and avoid being seen by the majority of patrons. Kennedy rejected these more-private tables, and always saw to it that he and his suggestive-looking young companion were seated in the center of the main part of the dining room. Joseph Kennedy was never one to scorn attention. At the same time, Kennedy remained solicitous of his public reputation as a family man. After Cardinal Spellman's blast at the Tennessee Williams-Elia Kazan film *Baby Doll* in 1957, it was banned from the Kennedy theaters. Kennedy, who had not seen the film, said: "I have been in the business forty-five years and I think this is the worst thing that has ever been done to the people and to the industry. I think it should be banned everywhere." [66]

Rose Kennedy's luncheon dates were also reported by the columnists, but there is some significance in the fact that out of literally hundreds of society and gossip columns mentioning the Kennedys reviewed by the author, only one mentions the Kennedys appearing together on a night out. There was no doubt a cooling in their relationship during the '40s and '50s, with perhaps a mellowing between them in the later '50s, when either old age or the dictates of political expediency ended the pattern that created such difficulties as existed between the lifelong couple.

Kennedy in the 1940s also emerged as a philanthropist. He had for years been a generous, quiet contributor to Catholic and mental health charities, for which he had been recognized by papal honors,[67] but in August, 1946, he made the first of a long series of spectacular contributions. One Republican pointed out that Kennedy's career as a philanthropist began at the same time as John Kennedy began his political career, when John Kennedy was running for Congress for the first time. The charity gifts always brought great publicity for John Kennedy, and for a man in Joseph Kennedy's tax bracket, they actually "cost" him but a small fraction of their value to the recipient charities. For the stature they lent to candidate John Kennedy, their cost was insignificant.

The Kennedys unquestionably made political capital of their philanthropies,[68] but other factors were probably equally responsible for Joseph Kennedy's generosity. John Kennedy's Congressional district was safely Democratic; there was no need for Kennedy to buy great publicity for political purposes in 1946. Had the publicized contributions begun just before the crucial primary in June, 1946, the cynic's thesis would have more weight. But they came in August, before the election, but after the primary. John Kennedy would have

been a "shoo-in" without the charity publicity. In the 1940s there
were many other things on Joe Kennedy's mind that impelled him to
charity.

Joseph P. Kennedy, Jr., his father's favorite, was killed on a mission
in the United States Navy in August of 1944. He had entered the
Navy's flying forces—"Wouldn't you know? *Naval aviation*, the most
dangerous thing there is!" [69] his father boasted in happier times. The
Ambassador himself addressed his son's cadet class graduation, and
perhaps from premonition broke down sobbing in the middle of his
speech.[70] Then Joe, Jr., flew off, ultimately to England, where he
completed routine maneuvers. He was ready to go on leave when the
opportunity arose for an exciting and dangerous mission. He volunteered. In *As We Remember Joe*, John F. Kennedy's book of tributes to
his older brother, John Kennedy explains that his brother knew that he
had both the experience and the guts needed for the mission, and that
he was therefore best qualified for it;[71] Krock believes that Joe, Jr.,
undertook the mission to cleanse the family of its reputation in
England for cowardice.[72] Father and son had had some differences
over the marriage of daughter-sister Kathleen to the Protestant
Marquess of Hartington and as the son prepared for his fatal flight he
asked a lady friend—or so she later told it—"If I don't come back, tell
my dad, despite our differences, that I love him very much." [73] He did
not come back. Padres came to bring the news to the family. Years
later the father wrote a journalist:

> *I've started* [As We Remember Joe] *twenty times but I still go to
> pieces every time. And this from someone who is classified by
> public reputation as being "tough". . . . Every night of my life I
> say a prayer for him. Joe is now and always will be another part
> of my life.*[74]

A month after Joe's death, the family suffered another tragedy: the
death while on maneuvers of Kathleen's recent husband, William, the
Marquess of Hartington. It was particularly difficult for the family
because it fell so close on the heels of Joe Junior's death, but more,
because of the friction that had existed within the fold over Kathleen's
marriage outside the faith. Kathleen had enjoyed many suitors,
including shipping heir Peter Grace,[75] and Winthrop Rockefeller,[76]
but had given her hand to the English nobleman, son of a leading
Protestant layman. Rose Kennedy had bitterly opposed the union,[77]
and—except for Joe, Jr.—the family was formally opposed,[78] the

adolescent Bobby rigorously so.[79] Unobtrusively, Joe Kennedy wired secret blessings to his favorite daughter: "With your faith in God you can't make a mistake. Remember you are still and always will be tops with me." [80] To Beaverbrook, he wrote: "I see now that I've lost one of my daughters to England. She was the apple of my eye and I feel the loss because I won't have her near me all the time, but I'm sure she's going to be wonderfully happy." [81] A short time after the marriage, Hartington left for the battle in France and was killed soon after. Deeply despondent, Kennedy wrote Beaver, ". . . the more I realize what a fine boy he was. His marriage to Kathleen was a real love match. Both of them braved a great deal to have one another, but I am sure that even though they only had one another for five weeks, they were extremely happy and hopeful." In the same letter:

> For a fellow who didn't want this war to touch your country or mine, I have had rather a bad dose–Joe dead, Billy Hartington dead, my son Jack in the Naval Hospital. I have had brought home to me very personally what I saw for all the mothers and fathers of the world.

He was demoralized over his own inactivity in the war: "Yet if you would ask me what I am doing to help, I would tell you nothing." [82]

Joseph Kennedy was also upset about the condition of his daughter Rosemary, and with his own handling of her unfortunate situation. Rosemary, according to most accounts, was born "slow," a slowness indicative of mental retardation that later could not be denied. As Rosemary grew to adulthood, Joseph and Rose Kennedy tried desperately to bring her along as all the others and to keep her within the family. At the right age, she was presented to the Queen, with her sister Kathleen. As she grew older, though, the accounts tell us that she became more difficult, until finally, the family reluctantly acceded to the advice of doctors that Rosemary would be happier in an appropriate institution. She was placed at St. Coletta's, a nunnery in Wisconsin whose sisters are specialists with the mentally retarded.

In those days, mental retardation was something not talked about, often taken as an ill-reflection on the parents—among the superstitious, believed to be punishment of the parent for some secret sin. "I used to think it was something to hide," Joseph Kennedy told journalist George Bookman in 1960,[83] and in the '40s and '50s the Kennedys made every effort to hide it. Contemporary accounts of the family dismissed Rosemary as the quiet one who had elected to devote her life to helping the handicapped with the sisters of St. Coletta. Not until John Kennedy's Presidential campaign in 1960—when strategy dictated frank discussion to head off ugly rumor—did the family openly acknowledge what they had tried to forget.

By 1960 the public attitude towards mental retardation had matured; even Joseph Kennedy could discuss it openly. "But then I learned," he continued to Bookman, "that almost everyone I know has a relative or good friend who has the problem of a mentally retarded child somewhere in the family. You have no idea how widespread it is. I've won more hats and neckties betting people that they have that problem somewhere among their relatives or good friends." [84] Inwardly, though, Kennedy was from that older generation that never quite felt at ease with the problem of retardation. In discussing Rosemary with the author, Landis volunteered, unasked, "Whether or not Joe thinks he's responsible for some moral fault in himself . . . I don't know." [85]

Remorse, coupled perhaps with feelings of guilt, no doubt had a great deal to do with the emergence of Joseph Kennedy, Philanthropist.[86]

In August, 1946, on the second anniversary of young Joe's death, the Kennedys presented Archbishop Richard Cushing a check for $600,000, to be used for the construction of a convalescent home for children. The check was handed over by John Kennedy (identified in the press reports as a candidate for Congress), while his parents watched. Justifiably, the gift received banner headlines on the front pages of all the Boston papers. It was the largest gift of its kind in the history of the diocese, and was the first of the Kennedys' spectacular charity contributions. The home was to be named for Joseph P. Kennedy, Jr., and was to be administered by the Franciscan Missionaries of Mary. The press reported that a Joseph P. Kennedy, Jr., Foundation would be established to make other charitable contributions.[87]

In the years that followed, the Joseph P. Kennedy, Jr., Foundation gave away many fortunes.[88] The foundation itself owns a quarter of the Merchandise Mart,[89] and its revenues from that source must be very great. As it is a charitable organization, its share of the Merchandise Mart profits are tax free. In addition, it may own part of other Kennedy buildings, and no doubt receives additional financial contributions from the Kennedys. It was the principal legatee under Joseph Kennedy's will.[90]

The great bulk of the foundation's grants for many years went to Catholic Church charities, schools, and hospitals. In 1956, the Boston diocesan newspaper, *The Pilot*, editorialized:

> No one will fail to see some significance too, in the fact that the Kennedy Foundation has consistently channelled its benefactions through the organized charities and projects of the Church. . . . When each charity, from faithful hearts, carries with it the sign and the seal of Christ's Church, who can begin to estimate its heavenly reward? [91]

Either out of gratitude, or to make sure that The Lord got *The Pilot's* message, Archbishop Cushing erected a mausoleum for the family on the grounds of a Roman Catholic child care center.[92] The Saint Coletta's order, schools and nunneries, have been one of the Kennedys' most favored charities. Mental health charities in general have been generously aided in their work, including one spectacular $12,000,000 grant made in August, 1960, for research into problems of mental retardation.[93]

The personal approach that Kennedy took in most of his activities is seen as well in the selection of his charities. There were no major contributions to general, run-of-the-mill charities like health organizations or universities. Most of the recipient charities had very special and personal appeals to Joseph Kennedy. The personal appeal to Kennedy of the Catholic and mental health charities that received most of the foundation's money is obvious.

Nowhere is the personal approach to charity more obvious than in the case of the boys expelled from West Point after a cheating scandal in 1951. The boys had been involved, most of them only by failing to inform, in helping less apt but athletic cadets to pass their exams, so as to be eligible for football. When the situation came to the attention of West Point authorities, 84 boys were expelled. Sympathy for the boys, and especially for those who had simply failed to inform, was very great across the country. Father John Cavanaugh, President of Notre Dame and Kennedy's personal friend, made a quick trip to Hyannis Port.[94] Shortly after, Father Cavanaugh made an announcement for an anonymous donor: he quoted the donor as saying: "Because I feel with millions that in the American tradition a man who makes a mistake should have a reasonable chance to rehabilitate himself I make this offer. . . . I shall pay the board, room, and tuition of the young men, Catholic or non-Catholic, among them who wish to enter the University of Notre Dame with the understanding that they meet

Notre Dame standards and academic requirements, that they need
such help, and that these young men will not participate in any form
of varsity athletics." In acknowledging the donor's offer on behalf of
the university, Cavanaugh said that "It was truly in keeping with good
Christianity and our American heritage." He estimated that the
generosity might cost the donor $250,000. The donor was quoted by
the press as having said, informally, that he was insisting on remaining
anonymous so as to avoid being branded as "a cheap publicity
seeker." [95]

There was another reason. That spring Joseph Kennedy's youngest
son, Edward M. Kennedy, had been expelled from Harvard. He had
procured a substitute to take a final exam in his name, and had been
caught. "Teddy" left school; the matter was kept quiet by university
officials; excuses were made. Joseph Kennedy could easily identify
with the parents of the West Point boys. But he could not make his
generosity public. Had the Kennedy name been used, Edward's error
would have been more likely to come to light and brought the young
man wide publicity as a cheater. At the time many suspected that Joe
Kennedy was the donor; when a gossip columnist asked Kennedy what
he knew about it he said, "They say it is a wonderful Irishman out in
St. Paul, Minnesota, Ignatius Aloysius, that is an oil man who loves
doing things on the Q.T." Thirty-one boys took advantage of his
offer.[96]

Joe Kennedy did not publicly admit to his generosity until 1960. By
that year, Edward Kennedy's transgression was too far in the past to
arouse suspicions, and in 1960 political capital could be made of the
deed. The *New York Times* told the story.[97]

Most of the aided causes were ones with a direct personal appeal to
Joseph Kennedy. It is of course easier to "feel" the desire to give
where one is most directly concerned.

Kennedy was also generous to friends, frequently in a way so as to
cause them no embarrassment. He sold some oil lands for $180,000, to
a longtime, loyal, but not wealthy friend who had to finance the
purchase. The friend told the author that he was positive that
Kennedy knew the property was worth many times the price. It was
known to be oil-bearing and turned out to be worth $5,000,000. The
friend interpreted Kennedy's business "mistake" as a conceived
attempt to inconspicuously give him a windfall.[98]

When Eddie Moore became too old to work, Kennedy kept him on
the payroll and continued to maintain him in stylish surroundings far

beyond pension standards. Soon before Moore died, close to the age of eighty, he spoke gratefully of Kennedy to Clem Norton: "Who wants a helpless old man like me around? Who but Joe Kennedy would let me end my days here in the Miami sun in the winter and Cape Cod in the summer? Why ninety-nine of one hundred men would have thrown me on the scrap heap when I got old and helpless." [99]

In 1945 Hearst-press columnist Westbrook Pegler told Kennedy about a letter he had received from a poor man in Pawtucket, Rhode Island, who had a granddaughter with a cardiac condition. Within 24 hours the granddaughter was in Lahey Clinic at Kennedy's expense.

No doubt many such stories could be collected attesting to Kennedy's generosity.[100] Like many men whose business careers were ruthless, Kennedy was capable of great generosity.

Kennedy gave for well-understood and frequently personal reasons. Examples of spur-of-the-moment or impulse generosity, as in the case of the cardiac granddaughter, are apparently rare. Kennedy generally took a businesslike approach to his charity. When he built the Joseph P. Kennedy, Jr., Hospital, it was with the understanding that the Church would keep it up. Later the Church asked him for an upkeep handout, and he firmly refused.[101] Through the Joseph P. Kennedy, Jr., Foundation, Kennedy provided for responsible administration of charity funds.

FIGHTING FOR THE
OLD ORDER

JOSEPH KENNEDY RESENTED SUGGESTIONS THAT HE BECAME more conservative with the years, and there were specific issues to which he might point to support his assertion that his political position had remained constant over time. His support for an "incentive" tax policy—the main point in his postwar domestic policy pronouncements—had been first expressed in his years as a member of Roosevelt's early, conservative New Deal and the "liberal" issues he had supported in the 1930s, continued to hold great appeal for him in the '40s and '50s. The postwar Kennedy was not a stranger to the Kennedy of the 1930s, but he became more comfortable with the Kennedy of the 1920s.

A strong strain of 1920s babbittry had lain almost (but not quite) dormant in the Joseph Kennedy of the thirties, and began to reassert itself in him. It was manifested even in Kennedy's choice of words: "This place lost its zipperoo," he said of Palm Beach.[1] Jacqueline K. Onassis chided him over his latter-day diction: "You ought to write a series of grandfather stories for children, like 'The Duck with Moxie,' and 'The Donkey Who Couldn't Fight His Way Out of a Telephone Booth.' ".[2]

Among the projects that Kennedy set out for himself in the postwar years was to see that Beaverbrook's little-known book *Success* was more widely circulated in America. The book was a series of short Alger-type biographies outlining the rise of poor boys to wealth and influence through pluck and luck—the rise of people like Joseph Kennedy and Lord Beaverbrook. Significantly, the book had first been published in 1921. Beaverbrook himself spent his formative years in Canada, and *Success* was as representative of American values of the twenties as *American Magazine* itself. Kennedy worked with *Reader's Digest* editor Paul Palmer on a preface for an American edition of the book, published by the New York house of Duell, Sloan and Pearce as *The Three Keys to Success*, by Lord Beaverbrook with an introduction by the Hon. Joseph P. Kennedy. The book apparently made no impression on the American book-buying public of 1955, and most

340

existent copies are now kept in the rare book collections of university libraries, because most of them carry the valuable presentation inscription of Joseph P. Kennedy. He was willing to underwrite the publication, he explained, because "I think (*Success*) makes a lot of sense." [3]

Kennedy of the 1930s would not have established the "Merchandisers Hall of Fame," to honor the men who had developed that art. Kennedy of the 1950s did so. Conspicuous consumption was born in the 1920s and helped to characterize it; it was the merchandiser's contribution to the era. It was the man of the '20s to whom an idea like the "Merchandisers Hall of Fame" might have appealed. Kennedy made persistent unsuccessful efforts to get people like Baruch and Illinois Governor Adlai Stevenson to participate in Merchandisers Hall of Fame functions, but they begged off,[4] and only one "big" name consented to be linked with the project: Herbert Hoover, the man of the twenties.[5]

As if making amends for a wrong of years before, Kennedy developed a closeness with former President Hoover, the man he had done so much to unseat, and came to call him and think of him as "the Chief," and developed an intimacy with him that he had never had with Roosevelt.[6] In the late '40s and early '50s, whenever Kennedy's son John made a political move, his proud father called Hoover to compare notes,[7] and when Hoover sent Kennedy a presentation photograph with a meaningless but flattering inscription, the hard-boiled financier wept.[8] The discarded President was a living remnant and reminder of those better days of long ago.

Kennedy looked back on the world of the twenties with nostalgia. It was a world with which he could identify, unlike the world of the forties and fifties. It was a simpler world, without Reds, bombs, worries about foreign affairs; a world in which a man could better himself. Kennedy looked upon it as *his* world. He became preoccupied with himself as a symbol of that world, and as an example of what it could do for others. To Dinneen, he mused about this older world he loved and lived in:

> *My world has its faults, but it brought me from the mudflats of East Boston to the Court of St. James. It brought me success and honors in business, government and the academic world—things that I never could have achieved under any of the systems of government that are offered as substitutes.*[9]

He realized that his world was either gone or going but it was his world and he was loyal to it. "I have no intention of turning my back on, and abandoning the world that I knew. It has been a good world to me and I'll fight for it." [10] And fight he would.

Just as the Kennedy of the 1930s made amends for the Kennedy of the 1920s, Kennedy of the 1940s seemed to be making amends for Kennedy of the 1930s. He must have been aware of the fact that he himself had helped to do away with the old order, simply by aiding and abetting that man Roosevelt, the executioner of the '20s ethos. So he went crusading for the old world that he had not protected before. He apparently turned down no opportunity to speak, and as a discredited former Ambassador he could not command the most desirable forums. His engagements were before such gatherings as the joint meeting of the Covington and Hot Springs, Virginia, Rotary Clubs; the second annual dinner of the Chicago Floor Covering Association; the convention of the N.B.M. (National Bedding Manufacturers); the Providence, Rhode Island, Chamber of Commerce.[11] To a man of Kennedy's pride, addressing such groups must have been a painful comedown from the New York Economic Club; one can assume that Kennedy was not making the lecture circuit for the small honorarium that after-dinner speakers receive. He was seeking a forum, any forum.

REACTION AT HOME

Kennedy's most common theme was the demise of the "profit-motive system," coupled with a call for its resurrection through reduction of taxes. Throughout the 1940s, his every speech had a direct or indirect mention of tax reform—reduction of taxes on the higher income brackets—so that the incentive of great wealth would once again motivate man and stimulate the economy. The fullest exposition of his views came in a lengthy article for the Hearst newspapers published in May, 1947.[12] It was a harsh criticism of the Truman Administration's "very sickening and discouraging political economic philosophy which has given the nation a case of first-class jitters." He called for immediate tax relief for the upper brackets so that the economy could develop as it had "prior to the confiscatory tax periods of the thirties." If the "dead hand of confiscatory taxes" were replaced by "an incentive tax policy," he predicted that business would thrive and that the nation would cease to be battered between inflation and depression. Restoration of "the virtues of thrift, incentive and enterprise" was overdue, and he pointed out that fiscal recklessness had already imposed a national debt that constituted "a bitter destiny on several entire generations of our people." Essentially he was calling for reaction. And fast!

The dreams of wealth of Henry Ford, John D. Rockefeller, and the other "captains of industry" and "robber barons" had led to activities that had made the United States great and powerful. To a large extent, the post-Depression tax policy *had* denied a man the incentive of great wealth; Kennedy insisted that by so doing, the progressive income tax had denied the nation fruits that would come from the efforts of those motivated by material desire. Henry Ford could not so easily have built his industrial empire under the new tax policy; Kennedy insisted that Ford could not have built his empire at all under the new tax policy. But more important, Kennedy argued that Ford might not have *wanted* to build his empire in the 1940s; postwar taxes were so great that his efforts could not pay off in fabulous wealth.[13] To men like Kennedy, that meant the end of the American way, and the end of great material progress for the nation.

Kennedy himself had grown rich in the heyday of the profit motive system, but he himself was hardly the ideal defender for it. He was certainly motivated by economic desires, and so was personal evidence of the effect of (for sake of shorthand, let us call it) "greed" on the individual. But the social benefits of the system could not easily be proven by using his career as an example. The greed of the captain of industry, of the inventor, the builder, the producer or manufacturer, may benefit everyone by increasing production, lowering prices, and in general stimulating the economy. Even the rich man who invests his capital in such production plays his part by enabling the production to proceed. The banker and broker play their part in that production by helping in the financing. Their efforts to benefit themselves do benefit the society at large. But virtually all of Kennedy's fortune was made in securities and real estate speculation of dubious value to society. The greed of the producer—of Joseph Kennedy, banker, shipbuilder, movie executive, business consultant—makes its contribution to American prosperity. But that work was the smallest part of the Joseph Kennedy efforts. The greed of Kennedy the lone wolf speculator, the player of trends, the man out for the really big buck and the easy buck, produced no significant benefits to society at large. He was to a large extent an "economic parasite." All too often his efforts played no part in the national machinery for production. He stood outside that machinery, making wise bets on its success or failure; making none but the most hypothetical and tenuous contribution to national production or society.

Nonetheless, the profit-motive system was "his" system, and Kennedy stood up for it as the system most suited to advancing the interests of all men. The profit-motive system was probably the most important aspect of what he regarded as the American way of life; at times he seems to have equated it with democracy itself. Thus he could deny the existence of "democracy" in a socialist-influenced England, but call the capitalistic but otherwise repugnant Boer government of South Africa "friendly to democratic principles."

The other aspects of Kennedy's policy statements of the forties—his opposition to welfare-statism and "creeping socialism"; his fear of the increased power of organized labor; his desire to keep government as "small" as possible; and his increasingly extreme isolationism—were all corollaries of his principal theme: the need to restore incentive through reduction of taxes.

The welfare-state system was the precise opposite of the profit-motive system, and even a modified welfare state required such taxes, as Kennedy saw it, as to kill incentive. He warned audiences in 1945 and 1946 that a lethargic America was being "lulled by socialism" and doing nothing "to stop the drift towards statism." [14] The signs were awesome:

> We have the spectacle at this moment, all over the country, of hundreds of thousands of jobs going unfulfilled while hundreds of thousands of men and women appeal to the state for unemployment support. The most disturbing feature of it is that so many people today are willing to ask state aid without an apology or without any realization that they may be forfeiting self-respect in doing so. . . . [15]

Already the tax burden was "sufficient to destroy all initiative." [16]

Kennedy saw organized labor as one of the most pernicious influences, and warned Colby College graduates in June, 1946, to prepare for the increased influence of it. "More and more, organized labor is going to be our influence. This means that organized labor with its conceptions of the rights of private capital will have more and more to say as to the manner in which each individual lives his life." [17] Elsewhere he pointed to the 1946 miner's strike as an example of labor irresponsibility.[18] The way to handle labor problems, he told other audiences, was to localize labor difficulties, settling them plant by plant, company by company[19]—an approach that would minimize the influence of "big labor." At every turn he urged his businessmen audiences to be active politically, to combat the trends.[20]

Kennedy had a chance to help turn the clock back as a member of the Second Hoover Commission. He had held a seat on the First Hoover Commission as one of Senator Vandenberg's appointees, but he had been the least active of the 12 members of the first commission, had attended few meetings, and had participated little in deliberations.[21] But there was an important difference between the first and second Hoover commissions: by the acts establishing the commissions, the first was to be a panel of efficiency experts, and was to keep out of policy matters; the second was invited into the world of policy. The mandate of the second commission was attractive; Kennedy became interested, and largely at the impetus of Senator Lodge,[22] he received an appointment from Republican Congressional leader Martin.

Kennedy fully took part in the work of the Second Hoover Commission. He was at most of the meetings, was frequently in Washington on commission business, and often conferred by phone with fellow commissioners. Conservative President Hoover had a large part in selecting the commission's members, and those who served on its task forces. Kennedy was much at home amongst them. The resulting policy suggestions—314 of them in all—were profoundly conservative; in effect they called for a return to the 1920s notion of limiting the function of the government to that of a policeman. Where the government offered services conceivably available from private enterprise the commission called for abolition of the government's services. Services were to be offered, the commission asserted, "only when private enterprise cannot or will not perform the function, and then only in furtherance of a justifiable government purpose." They called for sale of the TVA's steam and hydroelectric plants; for the end of TVA's chemical research; for the end of the 50-year tradition of granting power preference rights to cooperatives and municipalities.[23] They called for the end of federal aid to education, and for the end of the federal government's school lunch programs. They urged that the post office raise its rates on parcel post, and that the postal savings system be abolished. They urged that the public health service curtail its activities, and that servicemen's post exchanges be curtailed. They called for greater use by the government of private printers and shipbuilders.

Congressman Chet Holifield—the only New Deal-Fair Deal liberal on the commission—dissented from the majority reports on virtually

346 ⎍⎍⎍⎍⎍⎍⎍⎍⎍⎍⎍⎍⎍⎍ *Joseph P. Kennedy*

every significant policy question. In a *New Republic* article, he wrote: "The Commission reports fall far short of meeting the test of either thoroughness or objectivity. Frequently I was appalled by the slipshod character of the fact-finding and by the intrusion of occupational or professional self-interest." [24]

Joseph Kennedy was the commission's least frequent dissenter, entering a public dissent on only one of the commission's 314 recommendations. He fully supported the commission's effort to repeal the Roosevelt and Truman Administrations. His desire to turn back the clock was shared with Herbert Hoover and the majority of the commission.

Kennedy always spoke as a conservative at the meetings, but was more flexible and less doctrinaire than Hoover. His comments were never the kind that would provoke gut reactions from the liberal Holifield.[25] Kennedy impressed one staff member as an intelligent conservative, not a hidebound reactionary. Despite the fact that he was the commission's least frequent dissenter, he occasionally lent support to some of Holifield's positions. He saw merit, for example, in Holifield's objection that the task force on public power contained no one in sympathy with the purposes of public power—even though Kennedy himself did not sympathize with the public power advocates.[26] In the interest of obtaining an unbiased report and in the interests of fairness, he was prepared to back Holifield's unsuccessful request that the task force be expanded with the addition of liberal members.

Kennedy was especially interested in the commission's lending agencies studies, and took a hand in drafting the report on lending agencies. Curiously, his one dissent was in that report's recommendation that the Export-Import Bank be curtailed.[27] He was adamant about the report's other reactionary recommendations, though, which called for the end of the R.F.C. and of crop loans to farmers; termination of loans to veterans for farm or home improvements; tightening of loans to rural electric cooperatives; termination of loans to public housing authorities by the F.H.A.; termination of loans for local public works; and, raising interest rates on small business administration loans. In his dissent, Holifield pointed out that the commissioners did not criticize the many subsidies to big business.[28] Kennedy engaged in a heated subrosa debate with Holifield over the recommendations.[29] Holifield denounced the report as "faulty in concept and method" and supported his argument with numerous examples.[30]

SUB-CELLAR ISOLATIONISM

Joseph Kennedy's ever-present concern and most frequent speech topic, though, was that most serious threat to the profit-motive system: foreign relations. During the postwar years his views on international relations became increasingly more isolationistic and extreme. His position began to shift rightwards after the outbreak of the war in September, 1939. In his early ambassadorial period, Kennedy was capable of saying:

> *The majority of our ills, both internal and external, spring from one cause—our failure to secure a better standard of living for the earth's people. That is a matter of economics; being a matter of economics, it is—in my opinion—capable of treatment. . . . Today we have everything that is needed to provide a decent standard of living for all. It is purely a question of exploiting the resources with which we have been endowed and assuring a just distribution of the proceeds. . . . The important thing to remember is that the majority of our difficulties are man-made. They are not the result of the penury of nature; nor are they visited upon us by a vindictive fate. They are the result of human carelessness, human short-sightedness, human greed.*[31]

This attitude toward the world and its ills and to the relation between peace and prosperity, was brimming with the optimism and confidence of the progressive. In the postwar world Kennedy abandoned it. He became convinced that it was not want that caused wars but prosperity itself; that efforts "to provide a decent standard of living for all" could only end in disaster abroad and bankruptcy at home.

Kennedy himself must have recognized that his views had shifted. At the Lend-Lease hearings in 1941 he refused to identify himself with the isolationists and said that he did not sympathize with them. As late as 1944 he insisted—privately—"I am not an isolationist . . . I never have been one." [32] But by 1947 Kennedy had realized that he was in fact an isolationist. Sometime during the spring, he told Hearst-journalist Frank Conniff, "I decided to admit from now on that the term 'isolationist' described my sentiments perfectly." [33] Kennedy reached that point gradually.

During the war, Kennedy addressed 1,000 Navy inductees and pledged:

> *Our most profound minds will undertake the work of setting up
> in the post-war world a permanent system of international
> justice, so that you will not see your sons go forth to war as we
> see you go forth today.*[34]

Towards the end of the war, in an address to 800 at a National
Maritime Day dinner in Boston, he suggested giving portions of the
United States fleet to customer nations at the end of the war, as a
stimulant to America's export commerce.[35] It was, as Kennedy described it, "good business," but Krock found it necessary to defend
him and his speech against the attacks of "Nationalists," a word that
Krock defined as "1944 for 'isolationist.'"[36] A month later, Kennedy
told the American Gastroenterological Association that the United
States had to "lend a hand to pull the post-war world into some
order."[37] He and co-owner Ogden Reid offered the Whitlaw-Reid
mansion on Madison Avenue to the United Nations as a headquarters,
virtually rent free.

At the same time, Kennedy's own 1940 hesitations about "internationalism" never left him. While he was willing to entertain thoughts
of international cooperation, and even at times to sound like an
"internationalist," he himself never formulated any matured notions of
collective security; none were ever suggested that commanded his
approval; and he never manifested any willingness to sacrifice
important short-run interests for the more important long-run goal of
world peace. In 1943 he was thinking, both still and again, about
America's need to "follow the European example" and think of itself
in postwar foreign policy. To graduating students at Oglethorpe
University, he counseled by analogy:

> *We have all met at one time or another individuals who spend
> their energies on various schemes for community betterment,
> while their own house is in disrepair, their roof leaks and their
> children are without proper nourishment, discipline, or guidance.
> As a nation we must avoid this folly in the post-war era.*[38]

While he told the stomach doctors that the United States should "lend
a hand," he made clear to them that the United States shouldn't
completely open the fist:

> *But it would be stupid in our generosity to forget ourselves. Help
> the rest of the world by all means—but don't commit America to
> endless burdens. Preserve internationalism but serve America.
> Out of all this terrible turmoil some one nation should emerge
> strong enough to stand as a beacon of hope to the world.*[39]

And, the "hand" should be "lent" only on a respectable business basis. "It's all right to lend money to foreign countries," he warned the Boston Credit Men's Association in October, 1945, "but we should know what their financial position is now and what it will be later" [40]—precisely the approach that each of those Boston credit men took while dealing with their own small borrowers.

With the single exception of the loan to Finland, United States "loans" to European countries after World War I had never been repaid; Kennedy was aware of this, and hoped to guard against misleading uncollateralized loans with his admonition to Boston's credit men. At more considered moments, though, he must have realized that money would be given to Europe anyway, whether or not he was for it, and the use of the word "loan" would only make his countrymen less concerned about the size of the foreign grants. As the money would be "loaned" and not repaid, Kennedy ultimately decided that it would be best to call a gift a gift. Always suspicious of the value of foreign aid, and afraid that the government would be too generous, he hoped to keep the amount given at a minimum. Calling a never-to-be-repaid loan a gift would cost no more; rather, it would make editorial writers, the public at large, and Congressmen more aware of the size of the beneficence. The use of the word "gift" would actually help to decrease the country's foreign aid. Further, to a man who had an aversion to "entangling alliances" with foreign countries, a gift would have a psychological advantage over a loan. It would be less apt to involve the United States in other countries' affairs at a later date.

It was with this in mind that Kennedy advocated, in March, 1946, that a proposed $3,750,000,000 loan to Britain be made as an outright gift. The money should be given, he said, not because the United States "owed" the English anything, "but we have already spent about $200 billion in a war we were told would save civilization. And we had better give another four billion dollars to the same end, even though we can ill-afford to do that." But let us not deceive the American people, he said. "The truth is that financial aid to the United Kingdom, whatever name is applied to it, is and should be an outright gift." [41] The statement containing much contrary to Kennedy's prior [42] and subsequent statements, was no more than an effort to revise British aid downward,[43] and certainly must have had some affect on opinion. It was given front-page coverage in the *New York Times*,[44] received favorable play in London's *Times*,[45] and was commented upon in the *New York Herald-Tribune*,[46] among other papers.

Shortly thereafter, *Life* published the first of Kennedy's several thoroughgoing attacks on the foreign policy of the Truman Administration.[47] In *Life*, he expressed views much more attune with the dominant theme in his postwar foreign policy pronouncements. The first full exposition of his views since 1941, the article revealed a blueprint for his isolationism of the later forties and early fifties.

"Our present policy," Kennedy wrote, "involves us in world-wide minding of other people's business." It was "based on a concept that is demonstrably unworkable and perilous." It was founded on the erroneous belief that peace follows prosperity; Kennedy argued the other way, that prosperity came from peace. Accordingly, it was fruitless to invest money in foreign nations with the hope that once prosperous they would be peaceful. Kennedy suspected that the most advanced nations made the wars, and that the efforts of the United States might develop backward nations into warring nations. For all their good intentions, the high-minded optimists (the men directing State Department policies) were undermining the forces of realism (represented by men like himself) that would adequately provide for national security at all times.

Kennedy wrote that the country should wholeheartedly support the United Nations as it had been doing. However, he pointed out that the veto provisions in the U.N. Charter made it ineffective as an instrument to preserve peace through force, and he warned that the country was relying on the U.N. too much. Instead, the United States should rely on cooperation with England and the British Commonwealth.

In the United States' relations with Russia, Kennedy advocated abandonment of the then-present policy, "which seems to combine appeasement, uncertainty and double talk," in favor of "giving Russia the realism she admires." But his specific suggestions on the subject could hardly be called the substance of a "get-tough-with-Russia" policy. He suggested that the United States make clear to Russia that any actual or threatened attack on Great Britain, the west coast of Europe, the Philippines, the Western Pacific, or the Western Hemisphere would mean war. There was no suggestion, though, of American defense for the world's heartland: Central Europe, Italy, Germany, Asia, Africa. Russian imperialism in the heartland, Kennedy counseled, should be followed by immediate withdrawal of help in the reconstruction of the U.S.S.R.[48]

In this article, the elements of Kennedy's full-blown isolationism emerge, especially his hostility to the concept of foreign aid as an instrument of peace, and his willingness, later made both more explicit and more complete, to abandon most of the world to communism. Giving Stalin the policies that Kennedy advocated would have been giving the Russian dictator the "realism" he desired.

By the spring of the following year, Kennedy felt that the wisdom of his *Life* argument had been borne out. He pointed with pride to it, and characterized it as having insisted on a "tough" attitude towards Moscow that would have immediately ended the "perpetual United Nations debates." [49] It was that spring that he acknowledged to Conniff:

> I decided to admit from now on that the term "isolationist" described my sentiments perfectly. We never gave isolationism a chance. The "interventionists" had their way and look what happened. I'm proud I warned against participation in a war which could only leave the world in a worse condition than before.[50]

Given his feelings, it is little wonder that Kennedy bitterly opposed the "Truman Doctrine" of massive aid to Greece and Turkey to stave off communism,[51] and the later Marshall Plan[52] for reconstruction of Europe.

As far as Kennedy was concerned, the Western Hemisphere was an entirely different matter than the Eastern Hemisphere. His thoughts on aid for the Americas were set forth in a remarkably "radical" piece, "A Marshall Plan for the Americas," published in *Pic* magazine in October, 1948.[53] Kennedy suggested that the United States had been foolish in expending so much of its energies in the Eastern Hemisphere. Young statesmen should ask the bold question, "What price Europe?" For defense purposes, Kennedy argued, it would be wiser to concentrate on building up North and especially South America. With its rich, untapped resources, South America had necessary raw materials for defense—things worth defending.

He pointed out that relations with South America had improved "since the advent of Sumner Welles" (he would not give Roosevelt credit for anything) and counseled that the Western Hemisphere should be the core of the United States' defense efforts. Kennedy enumerated a number of specific suggestions that would contribute to making the North-South America mass more effective as a defense unit: the United States should improve transportation facilities in South America and between the two Americas; seek greater economic integration with the area by a revision of trade agreements and the encouragement of regional customs unions; begin measures to promote military integration of the area. A last and most interesting suggestion was that "We should evolve a broad program for cultural understanding between the American civilization on the one hand and the Latin-American civilization on the other, moving even beyond understanding to a basic cultural homogeneity."

Though Kennedy thought that the United States had been exerting too much effort in the Eastern Hemisphere, he did not at this time advocate forgetting about the rest of the world. He specifically disavowed advocating the breaking of ties with Europe. He simply said that the United States should make more judicious use of its funds than it had been making in the Eastern Hemisphere. Australia was worthy of United States efforts as was Africa. Though it might not be possible to hold North Africa, he pointed out that Africa's riches were in the South, where "inhabitants friendly to democratic ideals control." [54] On the other hand, Kennedy regarded China and India as "too large, too populous, too unwieldy, to be molded by us or against us." As they were of little value, "we dare not strain ourselves in their behalf."

The proud author conceded that his plan was "admittedly bold."

After this statement of October, 1948, Joseph Kennedy remained silent for over two years. In 1948 and early 1949, he saw the tide turn against him, both at home and abroad, as the domestic and international policies of the Truman Administration seemed to be "working." By the fall of 1950, though, the Truman foreign policy again appeared vulnerable.

On June 25, 1950, soldiers from North Korea crossed into the southern part of the Korean peninsula, and the Korean War began. The next day the United Nations decided to take action, and a day later, President Truman ordered American military aid for the South Koreans. His difficult decision won vigorous applause from the public and Congress. The North Koreans, with their Russian-built tanks, made good use of their surprise advantage, and pushed the South Koreans with their early United Nations reinforcements to the southeast corner of the peninsula. But by mid-September, the United

Nations was ready to take the offensive. The brilliant tactics of General Douglas MacArthur brought advance units of the United Nations to the Yalu River on November 21. Confident that mopping up operations would be quickly completed, General MacArthur told his troops that they would be home by Christmas. Then, on November 26, more than 200,000 Chinese Communist "volunteers" crossed the Yalu. The picnic was over; the battle was on. In sub-zero weather, waves of Chinese hurled back the United Nations armies. Complete disaster threatened. Americans now became less sure that Harry Truman's policies had been the correct ones. Serious doubts began to be voiced. The first voice to be heard was that of Joseph P. Kennedy.

"Where are we now?" he asked students at the University of Virginia on December 12, 1950. The brilliant and effective speech, drafted by James M. Landis,[55] contained Kennedy's answer to the question. It was the most influential speech of his entire public career. He insisted that foreign aid had accomplished nothing and that the United Nations was virtually useless. He argued that "Korea" could not be won, and he questioned whether it was even worth winning, in order "to achieve Mr. Syngman Rhee's concept of democracy." Then he advocated that Europe too was not realistically defensible. "The truth is that our only real hope is to keep Russia, if she chooses to march, on the other side of the Atlantic." [56] For the first time in a public statement he advocated United States defense only for the Western Hemisphere. In his *Life* article of 1946, he had also supported defense of the rim of Europe, the Philippines, and the Western Pacific Islands. By the time he wrote his *Pic* article in 1948 he was prepared to consider abandonment of Europe, but he still showed a live interest in Southern Africa and Australia. Now he was prepared to quit them as well. The restrained interest expressed in the Eastern Hemisphere in his statements of the 1940s may have been partially feigned in an effort to maintain "respectability." But it is also likely that the trend of world events affected him, hardening his isolationist viewpoint and making it still more extreme.

More significant than the change in degree of his opinion was the change in public reactions to his opinions. His articles for *Life*, the Hearst syndicate, and *Pic*, had provoked only minor reactions from the public.[57] Kennedy's many speeches had received inside-page coverage in local papers, but had generally been ignored by the major wire services. They received virtually no editorial comment, not even from the tabloids and the Hearst press. In the 1940s Americans remembered two major world wars. They were ready to see if international cooperation would keep their country at peace any better than isolationism had. Against this vastly dominant public attitude, Kennedy's statements were like shouting into a windstorm. No matter how professionally his statements were prepared, nor how valid aspects of the argument may have been, he was unable to have any major effect on public opinion.

In 1951, Kennedy's position was more extreme than it had ever been before. But for the first time since 1941, he was striking a responsive chord among the people. He was far out in right field, but the balls seemed to be going that way. Every major newspaper reported the speech. The *New York Times* reprinted the complete text, as did *Vital Speeches*. And *Pravda*.[58] John O'Donnell of the *New York Daily News* endorsed his position,[59] as did the *New York Daily Mirror*.[60] The *Journal-American* modestly reported that Kennedy had arrived at "the same inescapable conclusions reached by the Hearst newspapers." [61] But the far Right was not alone in its approval. Though he rejected Kennedy's argument on the whole, Walter Lippmann sympathized with much of Kennedy's approach,[62] and the *Wall Street Journal* endorsed it with qualifications. In printing long excerpts from the speech, the *Journal* wrote, "We offer Mr. Kennedy's speech as the starting point for a discussion which has been too long suppressed." [63] Six days later the *Journal* printed 17 letters to the editor, all of them supporting Kennedy's stand. The *Journal* explained that no critical letters had been received.[64]

Once more, for the first time since the Oglethorpe graduation address of May, 1941, Kennedy was denounced by his critics in excessive terms. He must have been disturbed at the tone of the critical reactions, but at the same time he must have been more than a little pleased at having provoked them. They showed that he was being taken seriously. In their widely syndicated column the Alsop brothers reminded their readers of how Kennedy had advocated "giving the world to Nazi Germany." "In the same manner in 1950," they wrote, "Kennedy has just crawled out of his richly upholstered burrow to advocate giving the world to the Soviet Union." [65] The outspokenness of their attack and those of like-minded critics was reflective of the fact that Kennedy and his position could no longer be ignored. Senator William Jenner and several other Congressmen cited it favorably.[66] Congressman John Rankin referred to Kennedy, after a reference to Herbert Hoover, as "another great American." [67] Congressman Paul W. Shafer of Michigan ventured that "His philosophy appears to agree with that of George Washington." Kennedy and the men of similar views, Shafer said, were not isolationists but "conservationists," conserving "our blood and treasure." The conservationist, he went on, "is in allegory an American eagle; watchful, sane, faithful, fierce." [68]

After the first batch of letters printed by the *Wall Street Journal*, critical letters began to be received, always outnumbered by favorable ones. One of the critical letters explained the paucity of similar letters by saying that Kennedy's suggestions were too incredible to warrant comment.[69] In 1945, they would have been, but by December of 1950, his vulnerable position was an appealing one to many of his countrymen.

The wide publicity that the speech received was an indication of the growing isolationist sentiment in America. The causes of this rebirth of the isolationist impulse among Americans are worthy of brief review, as they very likely affected Kennedy and made his own position more extreme than it had ever been before.

The "failures" of the Truman policy in the Far East were shaking to Americans. In December, 1949, Chiang Kai-shek's Chinese Nationalists fled mainland China and the Chinese Communists came to power. Americans had been unaware of the perilous situation Chiang's supporters had been in, and his failure came as a great blow to them. The fortunes that America had given Chiang to prop up his regime had been wasted. The policy of containment of communism had failed very dramatically. Korea followed six months later, and American soldiers began fighting the most unattractive kind of warfare. They fought not to defeat their enemy but only to permanently reestablish an older boundary. The losses were mounting. And for what? To preserve the southern end of a small peninsula from communism, thousands of Americans were dying of their wounds and freezing to death. And Americans were fighting virtually alone, without the aid of meaningful numbers of British, French, and other United Nations forces. What had United States giveaway programs accomplished, if the country's "allies" were to react that way? It appeared, as Kennedy charged, that they had not bought foul weather friends.[70] With the explosion in Korea, it became clear to many Americans for the first time that the United States had not "solved" anything by engaging in foreign wars. World War I had led to the Second World War, and World War II had been no more successful than its predecessor in making the Eastern Hemisphere "safe for democracy."

Partisanship also had a great influence in bringing about the turn to isolationism. President Truman's unexpected reelection victory over Thomas Dewey in 1948 brought home to Republicans that the "bipartisan" foreign policy of the 1940s had narrowed Republican alternatives and possibly cost them an election. By the winter of 1950–51, bipartisanship was virtually dead. In the sense that "partisanship" meant loyalty to the Republican party, Kennedy was obviously unaffected, but he could well be a partisan in the battle to rid his nation of Harry Truman and his crowd.

All of these factors affected Joseph Kennedy and helped to push him farther out on the limb, and the same factors account for the wide coverage and frequently favorable comments that followed his University of Virginia address.

One week later, Kennedy's friend Herbert Hoover added his voice to Kennedy's. When the former President spoke on December 20, he called for withdrawal from Korea and all of Asia, Africa, and continental Europe.[71] His position was less extreme than Kennedy's, however. He was willing to keep England, Australia, and all of the Pacific and Atlantic islands within the American defense perimeter. *Life* magazine illustrated the differences between the views of Kennedy, Hoover, and the Truman Administration with graphs that highlighted the extremism of Kennedy's view.[72]

Senator Robert Taft joined the debate, essentially in support of the Hoover thesis. Defenders of the Truman policy were not slow to appear. Two days after Kennedy's speech, Dewey spoke supporting the essence of the Truman foreign policy. John Foster Dulles, the major Republican foreign policy advisor to Secretary of State Dean Acheson, joined in defense of the Administration. Acheson was of course the most important defender. For several months, a major foreign policy address was made by a prominent speaker every few days. Attacking, defending, questioning fundamental principles of American foreign policy began that winter for the first time in 11 years.

Kennedy had said all that he had to say for the moment in his University of Virginia speech. But he followed the debate more closely than he had followed any other major development in years. The collection of clipping scrapbooks at the Joseph P. Kennedy offices is arranged chronologically, with a half-dozen extra topical volumes. One of them is labeled on the binding, "Great Debate, Major Speeches." In it are the documents of the debate itself, the addresses of Hoover, Taft, Dewey, Dulles, Acheson, Truman, Generals Dwight D. Eisenhower and Omar Bradley. Most of the clippings have been underlined in red pencil with comments written on the margins. The comments do not appear to have been written in Kennedy's hand, but their very existence indicates that Kennedy took a special interest in the exact content of each of the speeches.

Kennedy's own statements during the year 1951 were sporadic and less spectacular. When Truman fired General MacArthur for insubordination, Kennedy (like most of the isolationists) lent the General moral support in a radio appearance in April, 1951.[73] The following month a European trip led to a number of press interviews: Europeans by and large apparently thought along the same lines as the Bob Taft wing of the Republican party.[74] Towards the end of the year, he made the last major public address of his life. The "great debate" had languished by mid-1951 and Kennedy attempted to revive it in his address to the Chicago Economic Club in December, 1951. Kennedy said that the United States' foreign policy had proved "a total failure." The country's far-flung commitments had dissipated its strength and weakened its authority. He attributed much of the country's weakness to the United Nations, calling it "valueless" as an instrument of policy. He again called for a general disentanglement from the United States' far-flung commitments.[75]

Once more the *Journal-American* applauded Kennedy's "devastating analysis." [76] The *New York Daily News* discussed the speech in an editorial entitled "BULL'S-EYE BY J. P. KENNEDY." [77] The *Chicago Daily Tribune,* ever the isolationist's Bible, also approved.[78] Again, *Pravda* reported the speech at length, identifying its author as "just another imperialist." [79]

But Kennedy could not revive the great debate. People had decided that the Truman foreign policies were sound ones, and were unwilling to continue the reexamining process. The denunciations of Kennedy's position were both few and restrained.[80] The shift in public opinion had once more made Kennedy's views too incredible to warrant comment, and the great debate was over.[81]

JOSEPH KENNEDY'S ISOLATIONISM DEVELOPED SLOWLY OVER THE

period 1938 to 1950, but his matured position was classic American isolationism. The "neo-isolationism" of Taft or MacArthur was a cluster of ideas and emotions related to isolationism, but it was closer to Truman's position than it was to that of the 1940 America-Firsters. There was nothing "neo" about Joe Kennedy's isolationism; his was the most parochial approach to foreign policy—it was isolationism with a vengeance. In its spelled-out form his position showed itself to be made up of many traditional American notions, juggled and elaborated upon by Reader's Digest editor Paul Palmer, Landis, his other editorial assistants, and himself. It is fruitful to trace the development of Kennedy's position chronologically—beginning in 1620.

The Puritans either arrived with a concept of the mission of America or quickly developed one. They left Europe with a definite distaste for European mores, and wanted to help correct the sins of Europe. America could do that in one way: America's mission was simply to exist, pure and uncorrupted, as an inspiring example to Europe. If this were to be accomplished, they would have to keep themselves uncontaminated by European influences, which necessitated a healthy degree of isolation. Joseph Kennedy fervently believed this, and argued that by avoiding "never ending commitments abroad," the United States would be able to avoid the "contagious germs" of foreign communism. He cited a Westinghouse executive as authority for the assertion that already a third of the American people had "swallowed the communist line." [82] In his speeches he sometimes noted the pernicious influence that English government trends had on American government trends, a particularly alarming fact in light of the ascendency of leftish governmental philosophy in England.[83]

The Puritans believed that if they could remain uncontaminated, ultimately Europe would see the wonders of their new-world society, and the Old World would then change its ways and pattern its society after their own. Joseph Kennedy expressed the thought in its pure seventeenth-century form. It would be much wiser, he argued, to

> *permit communism to have its trial outside the Soviet Union if that should be the fate or will of certain people. In most of these countries a few years will demonstrate the inability of communism to achieve its promises, while throughout this period the disillusioned experimenters will be observing the benefits of the American way of life, and most of them will seek to emulate it. With communism once a demonstrated failure, its appeal to the unfortunate and discontented will disappear.*

The most effective way to beat communism was "merely to continue to be the land of free enterprise which our forefathers made it in order to attain a lasting prosperity inspiring to the dejected peoples of other nations." [84] That was the mission of America, and its success was within grasp.

Eighteen twenty-three was the year of the Monroe Doctrine, which soon came to mean that the United States would protect South America from the colonial powers of Europe. Ever after, those Americans who advocated limiting United States' relations with the Eastern Hemisphere have nonetheless kept a protective eye on South America. American isolationists argued that their concern for South America was based on defense considerations, though it is hard to see why Argentina is any more vital to the defense of the United States than Spain or England. In a man like Joseph Kennedy there was an emotional attachment to South America that made it "ours" and therefore, something the United States should defend.

The "Manifest Destiny" concept grew to maturity in the 1840s. Its essence was that the United States had a great destiny in the New World because of her natural resources. Its destiny would be fulfilled regardless of events in the rest of the world; it was destined by God to make the North American continent a paradise. The thought could not have been expressed more succinctly than it was by Joseph Kennedy, one hundred years later, at Oglethorpe College in 1940: "Regardless of how this war comes out, America has a great destiny because she has youth and she has assets which nature bestowed with a generous hand." [85]

In the years between 1880 and 1900, the Social Darwinists arranged the Monroe Doctrine, isolationist sentiment, and Manifest Destiny, into a vigorous program. A one-way understanding was entertained by men who thought that Europe should keep out of the Americas and that the Americas should keep out of Europe. "It takes a good deal of imagination to find reasons why the Monroe Doctrine imposes any obligation on us to assume a police power in the rest of the world," said one such, Joseph P. Kennedy, in 1947. [86]

During the same period, Manifest Destiny became a more aggressive and dynamic concept. At that time the scope of the United States' empire was first envisioned as expanded from North America to include South America as well. Unabashed American imperialists looked forward to the envelopment of South America and the emergence of a super U.S.A. They envisioned the kind of relationship between the Americas that Joseph Kennedy outlined in his *Pic* article. Because of their confidence in the supremacy of the Anglo-Saxon, they too called for "a broad program for cultural understanding between the American civilization on the one hand and the Latin-American civilization on the other, moving even beyond understanding to a basic cultural homogeneity." [87]

If this were all that there was to Joseph Kennedy's isolationism it could be written off as an unrealistic but quaint and idealistic bit of Americana. But Kennedy's isolationism was hardly pure idealism; it also had a cynical, unabashedly selfish side to it. Kennedy argued in letters to friends that America had to lose its idealistic tinge; the United States had to think first, last, and always of itself.[88] The United States had to be selfish with its resources if it was to have a responsible defense policy. While he often stressed a belief that his policy was best for humanity, he was certain that it was best for the United States from a defense standpoint. It is probable that much of his talk along mission-of-America lines was oratorical window dressing, injected by his ghost writers, and that it did not adequately reflect what was in the forefront of his mind. Primarily, Kennedy was worried about defending the United States from communism; he was concerned about defense for the United States—not for the rest of the world. The sad part is not Kennedy's cynicism but the fact that it was in defense that his policy was most vulnerable.

Many of the neo-isolationists formulated concepts of defense which began to approach the situation in the real world. Yet even where defense was concerned, Kennedy had dug in behind the mental trenches of the nineteenth century. He envisioned an American Gibraltar, surrounded by the several-thousand-mile moats of the Atlantic and Pacific oceans. If America were built into an impregnable fortress, he believed, it would not have to fear a war with communism; the United States would be home safe.

Kennedy's program completely ignored one recent invention— the aeroplane. Geologists and geographers had long appreciated the United States' economic interdependence with Eurasia, but in the 1940s the air-minded began to elaborate upon its military interdependence with the Old World. Even Lindbergh, who certainly sympathized with Kennedy's objectives, asserted in 1947 that "no earthly distance is adequate defense against the latest weapons of science." Space annihilating aircraft reduced the defense value of the geographic moat, and left America with little more natural security than the insular security of nineteenth-century England. And while airplanes could span oceans, radar could not. In order to be adequately protected against surprise attack, the United States needed to have radar stations in Europe and Asia.[89] Furthermore, in 1950 aircraft had developed only so far: the Russians could strike directly at any part of the United States across the North Pole, while the United States could not reach the truly vital areas of the U.S.S.R. except from bases outside the American hemisphere.[90] To prevent Russian aggression against the United States itself, or to meet it in case of attack, the United States had to be able to threaten Russia with devastating retaliatory action, and in 1950 crippling retaliation could only be undertaken from United States bases along the rim of the Soviet Union. With the Kremlin aggressively pursuing its expansionist policy, most Americans reached the inescapable conclusion expressed by General Eisenhower: "Any thought of retiring within our own borders will certainly lead to disaster for the U.S.A."[91] Joseph Kennedy refused to take cognizance of the world situation and the strategic factors that made Eisenhower's conclusion the only sound one. Kennedy's shortsightedness was thoroughgoing; it was almost a deliberate myopia.

SCHOLAR SELIG ADLER, WHO HAS MADE AN EXTENSIVE STUDY OF isolationism, attributes some of the isolationist's myopia to innate selfishness.[92] Another interesting theory is suggested by Arthur M. Schlesinger, Jr., who attributes the shortsightedness to "the death-wish of the capitalists."[93] Whatever its cause, there can be no doubt that the occupational disease of the professional isolationist is denial, just as that of the internationalist may be paranoia.[94]

Why a man of Kennedy's practicality continued to embrace isolationism in the face of the military and political realities of the postwar world remains an intriguing question. Undoubtedly some of the appeal of isolationism to Kennedy lay in the fact that it was the traditional American foreign policy. Even more important, however, experience "convinced" him—and throughout the 1940s seemed to continue to prove—the wisdom of isolationism. Before World War II Kennedy had feared that American entry into war would accomplish nothing; at best America could only clear the slate for a new, possibly worse and more threatening form of European imperialism. Kennedy could see that his fears had been borne out. "We put $258 billion into the last war," he told a Boston audience in 1947. "We were told it was going to wipe Fascism off the face of the earth. It probably has, but look what it left us." [95] Just as he had predicted, the war had left the world with a worse menace than before. Most Americans concluded that Stalinist Russia posed a threat to the United States, and for most the Second World War had demonstrated the obsolescence of isolationism. But Kennedy drew the same conclusion from the World War II experience that he had drawn after World War I: "Never again!" Experience continued to bear out his argument in the 1940s. Soon after the end of World War II he had warned that America should not fritter away her resources in postwar global spending; that the policy of containment of communism had to fail in enough places to make the total policy a crushingly expensive failure.[96] No one had listened. Then there was the fall of Czechoslovakia in 1948 and the fall of China in 1949, representing millions upon millions of wasted dollars. What was the sense of it all? He could easily have concluded that he had again been proven right. If America had only followed his policy—the traditional American foreign policy—it could have kept those millions for more worthwhile purposes, and avoided the meaningless war in Korea.

Perhaps there was even some of the Anglophobia of the pre-World War I Boston Irishman in Kennedy's isolationist leanings, helping to equate in his mind "isolationism" with "bailing out England." He perhaps noticed the scarcity of British troops on the Korean lines, a scarcity that could only make him again question the value of any alliance with the British.

The matter of being an Irish-American contributed to Kennedy's isolationism in another, more important way. The position of the Irish-American in Boston was a complex one that left Joseph Kennedy supersensitive about his origins. He insisted, "I was born here. My children were born here. What the hell do I have to do to be an American?" [97] A need to assert and reassert his Americanism may have helped to motivate Kennedy to take the most narrowly American approach in foreign policy. Isolationism helped to identify Kennedy with traditional America, and proclaimed that his only concern was for America. In his University of Virginia speech, Kennedy was saying in effect, "give up the rest of the world—all I care about is America." There could be no doubt as to where the loyalties of such a person lay. No other avenue could so dramatically prove that Joseph Kennedy was an American.[98]

Most important to explaining Kennedy's foreign policy views, though, was his fear for the profit-motive system, and his preoccupation with restoring the late nineteenth-century American economic system to which he attributed his own success and his country's greatness. Internationalism posed perhaps the greatest threat of all to the traditional American economic system because it was the subtlest threat. Even modified internationalism would necessarily have a staggering price tag attached to it; its cost would inevitably require still-higher taxes, giving the coup de grâce to the incentive system. If the United States would stop its wild global spending, though, and cease to shore up the rest of the world, the American tax load would be significantly lightened; the United States would then be on the road to return to the traditional domestic American scene that had prevailed long before. Reversing the trend of American foreign policy was a prerequisite to reversing the trend of American domestic tax and economic policy.

The interplay between Kennedy's domestic and foreign policy views was probably typical of most postwar isolationists. In the last days immediately before the United States entered the Second World War, one by one the liberals deserted isolationism. Even Senator Norris, the isolationist's isolationist, overcame the prejudices of a lifetime to support the President's foreign policies. Those old-time Progressives like Wheeler and Senator Gerald P. Nye who stuck with isolationism became increasingly more conservative. Adler concludes that postwar isolationism became "the seminal power of the reaction against twentieth century changes in American life." [99]

THE SENATOR FROM WISCONSIN

The relation of domestic and foreign policy issues also had less obvious connections: pink-baiting Wisconsin Senator Joseph McCarthy was concerned with domestic problems, but his appeal to isolationists was extremely great. Isolationists necessarily professed confidence in American might; to them, McCarthy explained the country's otherwise unexplainable military reverses: treason. It was a convincing explanation to evangelical conservatives like Joseph Kennedy, who saw their advice being discarded in both domestic and foreign fields, in favor of policies that could only lead to disaster. McCarthyism also provided an avenue through which such men could emphatically disassociate themselves from the "fellow travelers," who, like them, were preaching abandonment of the Eastern Hemisphere to

Stalin.[100] And at the end, McCarthy, like the isolationists, had the same goal: purging American culture and politics of the contamination of foreign ideologies.

While McCarthy and his methods were repugnant to those with much sensitivity to civil liberties, Kennedy was never much interested in civil liberties. Like McCarthy, he could well feel that crisis situations—personal or national—demand heavy-handed treatment. True, McCarthy was discrediting liberals and the Truman Administration, but Kennedy was not one to be too very disturbed about that. After all, these were the people—the liberals and the Truman "Fair Dealers"—who were leading the nation down the path destined for destruction.

Not surprisingly, Joseph Kennedy became an avid supporter and generous contributor to the Wisconsin Republican. The Senator would visit Kennedy at the Cape,[101] and in Chicago he became socially friendly with Eunice Kennedy Shriver and her husband Sarge, who managed Kennedy's Merchandise Mart.[102] Eunice and Pat Kennedy would drop in to chat with the Senator in his Washington office when they were in town,[103] and the Wisconsin Senator dated the eligible Patricia.[104] The father, completely taken up with McCarthy, helped him with influential contacts like Krock[105] and Cardinal Spellman[106] and telephoned him with endless advice, which McCarthy, out of gratitude and genuine affection, endured.[107] Finally, as an accommodation to Joseph Kennedy, McCarthy arranged his staff so as to create a position on it for Robert Kennedy,[108] which the son, notwithstanding reported second thoughts of Senator John Kennedy, eagerly accepted. Joe and Bobby proudly attended the Senator's wedding.[109]

When Gardner "Pat" Jackson, a campaign worker for John Kennedy, tried to get the senatorial hopeful to denounce McCarthy in his 1952 election campaign, Joseph Kennedy became livid. He was not opposed to McCarthy, he shouted at Jackson and the small group of campaign workers; he had contributed to McCarthy's campaign. He charged that Jackson, liberals, union people, and Jews were trying to ruin Jack's career. "I can't estimate how long he poured it out on me," Jackson later recalled. "It was just a stream of stuff—always referring to 'you and your sheeny friends.' " [110] Joseph Kennedy had a strong enough touch of right-wing paranoia to be a thoroughgoing McCarthyite.

McCarthy's excesses finally made him repugnant to virtually all, yet even in the 1960s Kennedy refused to minimize his relationship with the late Senator, nor indicate regrets over it. In a 1961 interview, his voice wavered and his eyes became clouded as he began to discuss the last bleak days of Senator Joseph McCarthy. The interviewer attributed Kennedy's reaction to his well-known loyalty to friends. [111] Another possible explanation would be loyalty to self—to Kennedy's own views. Kennedy approved of McCarthy in the early 1950s for well-understood reasons and deeply felt emotions. The shift in public opinion after that year did not affect him; he did not change his mind.

PRESIDENTIAL POLITICS
IN THE POSTWAR PERIOD

Given Kennedy's policy views, it might seem surprising that he did not lend open support to Republican Presidential candidates in the 1944, 1948, or 1952 elections. He failed to do so.

By 1944, Kennedy had become completely disenchanted with FDR. Personal reasons no doubt had most to do with the disenchantment, but there were also valid ideological disagreements between the two, over both tax and foreign policy outlooks. As the Presidential election of 1944 approached, Kennedy wrote Beaverbrook:

Short of a miracle, the New Deal is finished. . . . People are getting fed up with promises and conversation and for my part, I believe that the winning of the war is not only the movement of manpower and winning battles, but on seeing that every part of the homefront moves forward in the general scheme of things. The President says he is concerned with winning the war. He definitely is. It is just a question of what the definition of the term "winning the war" is. I feel it is much more comprehensive than battles. [112]

Rumors began to circulate that Kennedy was silently supporting Roosevelt's Republican opponent, Thomas E. Dewey. The Boston News Bureau finally published a report in the closing days of the campaign that Kennedy had purchased $25,000 worth of radio time and would use it to make a public endorsement of Dewey—"unless he changes his mind."

Roosevelt well knew how to get Kennedy to change his mind. Without losing a minute, he invited Kennedy to Washington for a visit. Surely Kennedy must have realized that the President only called for him when he wanted something, but crass as it would be, Presidential flattery was all it took to satisfy him. After the meeting Kennedy told newsmen that Roosevelt had asked him to make a study of Henry J. Kaiser's "jobs for all" program. He said that he had not discussed politics with the President; he denied that he had plans to speak for Dewey on the radio; he declined to predict the election outcome.[113]

One wonders how Kennedy reacted when FDR died on April 12, 1945. Three days later he spoke before the Guild of St. Appolonia, in Boston, and said that the new President, Harry Truman, was "a courageous man of great common sense, an American to his finger-tips." [114] The newspaper report of his speech does not indicate whether or not Kennedy mentioned Franklin Delano Roosevelt.[115] Privately, Kennedy felt great sympathy for the new President, whose task it would be to try, he wrote Beaverbrook, "to carry out the policies of a man who is dead who, even if he were alive, couldn't carry them out himself." [116]

If his initial reaction to Harry Truman was favorable, Kennedy quickly cooled toward the new President. Efforts by Kennedy's friends to get him a federal office were resisted by Truman[117] and, to make matters worse, if anything could have been worse, Truman's domestic and foreign policies were radically at variance with Kennedy's. As far as Kennedy was concerned, Truman was doing everything wrong— not just most things but everything. He threw in with the "dump-Truman" group in the Democratic party. Kennedy had a high regard for General MacArthur, and in a speech in October, 1946, he praised the General's administration of occupied Japan.[118] The following January, Danton Walker reported that Kennedy had joined Henry Luce on the MacArthur-for-President bandwagon.[119] Kennedy's friend Cholly Knickerbocker (Igor Cassini), who was in a better position to know and may have been writing with sanction from Kennedy, reported later that spring that Kennedy was "supposedly mapping a campaign to bolster [Justice William O.] Douglas as a dark horse Presidential entry." [120] Despite differences in their political outlook—certainly as great or greater than those separating Kennedy and Truman—Kennedy and Douglas were always close personally and, according to Krock, Douglas was always Kennedy's first choice for President.[121]

When Harry Truman received his party's nomination in 1948, Joe Kennedy could not have been pleased. Two factors probably prevented him from publicly coming out for Dewey, again the Republican Presidential nominee: son John Kennedy was running for reelection as a Democrat; and, Kennedy personally had little use for Dewey.[122] Kennedy said nothing throughout the election period.[123]

The election of 1948 was a confusing one. Drawing from normally Democratic voters, two third-party candidates entered the Presidential race: Strom Thurmond, on the "Dixicrat" ticket, who threatened to pull all of the South out of the Democratic column; and Henry Wallace on the "Progressive" ticket, who threatened to pull liberal Democratic votes away from Truman across the nation. With that lineup, Truman's chances looked bleak. Like prognosticators everywhere, Kennedy shared the view that with the Democrats so fragmented, any Republican would beat Truman[124]—who stunned all of the "pros" in an upset victory over Republican Dewey.

In 1952 Kennedy's first choice for President was unquestionably Taft. When Taft died in 1953, Kennedy called his death, "the greatest tragedy to befall the American people in the loss of a statesman, since the assassination of Abraham Lincoln." [125] On both domestic and foreign policy, the conservative Republican's views more closely paralleled Kennedy's than did the views of any other national political leader. (Asked "Is your father still a Democrat?" John Kennedy thought for a moment and replied, "Yes, you might call him a Taft Democrat.") [126] The views of Truman and the dominant wing of the Democratic party were repugnant to him, and John O'Donnell correctly reported that Kennedy was "privately but sincerely" against an Eisenhower candidacy.[127] After his "conservative" speech of December, 1951, the *Chicago Daily Tribune* wrote an editorial captioned HOW MR. KENNEDY CAN REALLY HELP. They publicly wondered why Kennedy expressed such views in Chicago, rather than in Massachusetts where they could do some good. They called on Kennedy to lead a Democrats-for-Taft campaign in the Bay State and New England.[128] Cholly Knickerbocker reported in February, 1952, that Kennedy would undoubtedly come out publicly for Taft.[129] It is unlikely that Cassini would have written such without Kennedy's prior knowledge. Perhaps Kennedy toyed with the idea of endorsing Taft, but he could never have done so. "Loyalty" to the Democratic party had nothing to do with it—Kennedy always kept his eye on things closer to home than party labels.[130] That election year, John Kennedy would be running for the Senate in a close race as a Democrat, and Joseph Kennedy could not embarrass him by publicly working for the selection of a Republican Presidential nominee.

Kennedy unquestionably gave quiet financial aid to Taft in Taft's pre-convention fight against Eisenhower. After the Republican "liberals" beat the Republican "conservatives," and Taft bowed to Eisenhower, Kennedy returned to the Democratic cheering squad.

Though the ideas of the Democratic Presidential nominee, Adlai Stevenson, were hardly ones with which Kennedy could sympathize, he had long been friendly with the Illinois governor; had contributed financially to his gubernatorial campaign,[131] and gave him the same indulgence that he allowed to other loyal family friends like Douglas. "I discovered Adlai Stevenson," he boasted to liberal associates.

The Ambassador went to bat for Stevenson.[132] He wrote Beaverbrook—whose Canadian newspapers might have influence on the election in border states:

> When they brought [Eisenhower] home and he took off that uniform, he was the most complete dud we have had for a candidate in my fifty years of Presidential elections. . . . Eisenhower is a complete washout himself. . . . he doesn't know enough to be President. . . .
> Now as to Stevenson, he received the only honest draft anyone has ever heard of in American politics. He is a great friend of mine and of the family. He personally did not want the job, but . . . Unquestionably he would be a great man for the United States. He and I don't see eye to eye on foreign policy, but I told him before he was a candidate that he had better run on that policy now because four years from today anybody who advocated the present policy couldn't get elected county sheriff.[133]

Kennedy seriously expected Stevenson to win the election by a healthy margin,[134] and when the party found itself in serious financial difficulty midway through the campaign, he quietly bailed it out.[135] Though sincerely disappointed at Eisenhower's handy victory over Stevenson, Kennedy made the best of it, and took the first post-election opportunity to say that Eisenhower's victory was "a clear mandate for change in foreign policy." [136]

KENNEDY WAS AT FIRST HOPEFUL THAT THE EISENHOWER ADministration would bring about a foreign policy more in line with his own views. In a newspaper interview in February, 1953, he was reported to have detected a tone of firmness in Eisenhower's foreign policy attitude, a firmness, he said, that had long been absent on top levels. He gave some advice on how things should be run:

> Other nations, since World War II, have been asking America to assume world leadership. . . . What they have really wanted,

and have been getting, is our wealth not our leadership. What I
hope we are going to give them is more of our leadership and less
of our wealth. . . . The drain on our resources is threatening our
economy. We are so dissipating the patrimony of our future
generations. . . . The money has not brought friends. . . . I
have no patience with the theory that we have to support hard
up western nations or they will surrender to communism. . . . In
the countries we surrendered to Stalin at Yalta, resistance to
bolshevism has not been killed.[137]

By the fall of 1954 it was apparent that there was no fundamental
difference between the Truman and Eisenhower approach to foreign
policy, and Kennedy had thoroughly soured on the Eisenhower
Administration. He made a last statement on foreign policy, especially
critical of Secretary of State John Foster Dulles' "globe-trotting,"
which he said was adding to the "sense of anxiety abroad." No one
listened.

One of the recommendations made by the Hoover Commission
called for the establishment of a joint Congressional committee to
quietly oversee the work of the CIA and other governmental
intelligence agencies. Fears that Congressmen would leak information
led the Eisenhower Administration to appoint a board of civilians
instead. The board, headed by Dr. James R. Killian, Jr., of MIT, was
composed of Kennedy, Admiral Richard L. Conolly, Generals James
H. Doolittle and John E. Hull, ex-Secretary of Defense, Robert A.
Lovett, and steel executives Benjamin F. Fairless and Edward L.
Ryerson.[138]

Kennedy was a brief but active member of the CIA Watchdog
Committee and fully participated in all committee activities.[139] But
because of the confidential nature of their work, no specific information has been made public on substantive matters before the board, or
on Kennedy's reactions to specific events or situations.

Joseph Kennedy served only six months on the CIA Watchdog
Committee. In 1956 John Kennedy was interested in his party's
Vice-Presidential nomination; having a father connected with the
Eisenhower Administration might create complications for him. In
the interest of his son's future, Joseph Kennedy resigned from the
committee.[140]

During the 1950s, Joseph Kennedy's public statements and activities
were increasingly curtailed in the interests of his son's ambitions. The
Kennedys decided to push their front-runner for the Presidency, and

by playing a part in public life, Joseph Kennedy could only have embarrassed his son, whose publicly espoused views were so different from his own. But for his son, Joseph Kennedy might have endorsed Robert Taft for President in 1952. For John Kennedy, he retired from the CIA Watchdog Committee. After 1956, he remained silent to the press. Kennedy even passed up attending the twenty-fifth anniversary of the SEC, in 1959; he knew that anything he said or did would remind the public of himself.[141] In the interests of the family, Joseph Kennedy made the supreme sacrifice: he retired from public life, remained quiet, and permitted himself to be eclipsed by his fast-rising son.

THE
FAMILY

THE RELATIONSHIP BETWEEN JOSEPH KENNEDY AND HIS FAMILY
was normal but exaggerated; family considerations were carried to an
unparalleled extreme in him. His feverish drive for money and status
must be attributed in great part to a desire to pave a golden way for
his children.[1] Later, when Kennedy entered the government service,
the family was still in the forefront of his mind; he explained to a
reporter shortly before beginning at the SEC that he was accepting
the job, and the loss of opportunities for additional fortunes, because
he sought a public service legacy for his family.[2] Roosevelt believed
that that was his motivation.[3] Family considerations were also said to
be behind his great interest in the ambassadorship. Kennedy told a
reporter in 1937 that he believed that "the only thing I can leave them
that will mean anything is my good name and reputation." [4]

When the time came for Jack Kennedy to move onto the national
stage, in 1956 when he sought his party's Vice-Presidential nomination, Joseph Kennedy—an incorrigible headline-hunter—made the
supreme sacrifice and stepped aside. His self-imposed exile was, as
reporter Fletcher Knebel calls it, "a rare display of self-effacement." [5]

Of course, Kennedy was not entirely selfless. There were always the
two interests working simultaneously in him—self and family—almost
merged as one. Kennedy, one old friend asserts, saw the family as an
extension of himself.[6]

One of his sons was just that—an extension of Joseph P. Kennedy.
Joseph P. Kennedy Junior was the oldest of his father's sons and the
apple of Joe Senior's eye. To a great extent he epitomized the traits,
both positive and otherwise, that became the hallmark of his three
younger brothers and perhaps of the decade that they dominated.

The dynamic youth had the same kind of record at Choate
preparatory school as his father had had at Boston Latin—he was tops
in everything that hinted at leadership potential. At Harvard, he far
excelled his father, and was one of the outstanding personalities of the
class of 1938. Though out of his element in the brilliant circle around

London Professor Harold Laski,[7] he was quick of mind and stood well in his class at Harvard, to the great satisfaction of his father. ("Besides doing a good job it means additional prestige and that all helps in the long run.") [8] His one disappointment lay in being denied, in his senior year, the Harvard "H" awarded to those football players who played in the Harvard-Yale game. Despite—perhaps because of—his father's pressures, the coach left Joseph Junior out of the game. The father took the disappointment worse than the son and reacted with cold fury.[9]

After Harvard, Kennedy persuaded his son to enter Harvard Law School as the best avenue to politics. Politics was Joe Junior's interest, and he prepared himself for it by classes in London with the celebrated Laski, immensely fashionable in intellectual circles; his sometime positions at the London and Paris embassies; his extensive travels; Harvard Law School—he even took elocution lessons. Confidently, he expressed his Presidential ambitions.[10] Joe Junior made an early political start, always echoing his father's position. When his father soured on FDR, Joe Junior, aged twenty-three, became a vociferous Farley backer; when the Ambassador's ultimate course for Roosevelt was clear, Joe Junior made several Boston-area speeches on Roosevelt's behalf, including one on the same podium as the President himself.[11] While Joe Senior urged isolationism privately, Joe Junior became active in the isolationist movement on the Harvard campus,[12] though he avoided affiliation with the important "America First Committee," perhaps, his biographer suggests, because it was headed by Robert D. Stuart, a Yale law student no older than himself.[13] He shared his father's apprehension that Jews, out of their highly personal hatred of Hitler and Nazi anti-Semitism, would bring about a situation where the whole world would go to hell.[14]

Joe Junior's initiation as a candidate, running for a seat to the Democratic National Convention of 1940, has been discussed previously. His only other bid for elective office was in his contest for presidency of the Cadet Club at naval officer's training school, a contest which, according to his biographer, he won through the clever strategy of having the other candidate's "votes" assigned to duty on the eve of balloting.[15]

In personality and character, Joseph P. Kennedy Junior was remarkably like his father, epitomizing the Senior's shrillest traits, particularly so in his drive to advertise his masculinity. From the picture painted in his biography, Hank Searls' *The Lost Prince*, it appears that Joe Junior was one of the first kids on the block to know the pleasures of the flesh, a priority and preeminence that he apparently maintained to the end. Searls dots his manuscript with strippers, showgirls, and similar types, culminating in a relationship with someone else's wife which Searls portrays as love.[16] Joe Junior was pugnacious and enjoyed brawling, which, as a Harvard student, he and athletic friends would provoke for sport in lower-class barrooms.[17] His normal sibling rivalry with his younger brother Jack, who by virtue of the age-span of the children was his only familial competitor, could fairly be described as vicious, with some of Searls' examples sounding almost sadistic.[18] As children, he punished his kid brother with beatings; [19] as late adolescents, by literally stealing Jack's "easy-mark" dates away from the tables of the Stork Club.[20] Jack, living in the shadow of his domineering brother, less aggressive and more nearly capable of sensitivity, fought back at an early age with perceptive, mock characterization of his brother as the "manly youth." [21] The manly youth savored the man's world fully; enjoyed the flashy life of nightclubs,[22] gambling in general,[23] and the race track in particular,[24] and a real man's cigar. He was temperate only in his use of alcohol which, according to Searls, he never much liked,[25] reflecting his father's general abstinence.

From his mother, Joe Junior inherited a devotion to his religious faith that was formalistically impeccable. He was a regular churchgoer [26] and climbed the stairs of Saint Peter's on his knees[27] perhaps as much for the satisfaction of accomplishment as for the satisfaction of penance. He became president of the Holy Name Society of his cadet class, and regularly roused his mates for chapel—Catholic or otherwise—with douses of cold water. (When the padre asked Joe to use more discretion, Joe pointed out that Jews too had saveable souls, and playfully chided the priest for "anti-Semitism.") [28]

The competitive spirit and willingness to take risks characteristic of all of the Kennedy children was earliest manifested in the firstborn. Edgar Mowrer, the *Chicago Daily News* journalist, recalled in his memoirs his first meeting with Joe Junior, on the ski slopes. Joe Junior was a novice at skiing, and was skiing in fast company, but repeatedly tried to step into the lead. After he crashed for the third time, the party slowed down, for fear that the Ambassador's son might do himself serious injury.[29] Joe also shared and showed the fierce family loyalty of his brothers. Even a slur in jest on the integrity of Joe's beloved grandfather, Honey Fitz, was greeted with wild reaction.[30]

Joe Junior was gregarious and quick to smile, and his tremendous doses of Irish charm made him easily likeable. Even his father's bitter foes liked him. (Felix Frankfurter: "And I also liked Joe." Interviewer: "Joe Junior?" Frankfurter: "Joe Junior. I never liked Joe Senior. Does anybody like Joe Senior? Have you ever met anybody except his family?" Interviewer: "Oh, I guess James Landis probably." Frankfurter: "Maybe Jim Landis. Sure, he was his bread and butter. Poor bread and poor butter.")[31] Able to make a conquest of the likes of Frankfurter and Laski, Joe Junior was clearly, as his father described him, "the politician of the family." "He was altogether different from Jack, more dynamic, more sociable and easy going."[32] Joe Junior idolized his father,[33] the father idolized his son. In many ways, Joe Junior seemed to be Joseph P. Kennedy, all over again.

And then came World War II, with its promises of death. At the time, the American draft system worked lottery style, without student deferments—much as was later reinstituted at the initiative of Joe Junior's favorite kid brother,[34] Senator Edward M. Kennedy. Joe Junior drew a low lottery number. Rather than await the inevitable with its uncertain assignments,[35] he enlisted in the Navy. The Ambassador's old friend Admiral Kirk arranged for a private physical,[36] so that any problems would be detected in advance. The son was accepted and went off for his war service. In training and on duty many resented a seeming arrogance in the young officer, and what was fairly or unfairly taken to be signs of privilege and favor all along the way.[37] His crew noted his insistence on his full measure of deference, never yielding his earned "aye, aye Sir."[38]

Joe's younger brother Jack also entered the Navy, and by virtue of his choice of program, quickly outranked the older brother, a matter that smarted.[39] Jack's early heroism on his "PT 109," Searls suggests, left a deep mark on the older brother, seemingly as much at having been "bested" as at the horror of his young brother's ordeal.[40] The hero status in war was as important as that football letter. Joe Junior flew off to meet death in the skies. The story of his last flight, long described as a closely guarded naval secret, was reported with substantial accuracy in the contemporary London press.[41] A battleship was named in his honor.

The father answered a letter of condolence from Roosevelt's secretary, Grace Tully:

> *Of course it has been a terrible blow to us both, particularly as he was the oldest boy and I had spent a great deal of time making what I thought were plans for his future. I have learned,*

however, that God takes quite a hand in the lives of His souls on
earth.[42]

For months after, Joe Senior spent most of each day sitting alone,
listening to recordings of symphony music.[43]

In 1957 Hearst-reporter Bob Considine asked Joseph Kennedy to
tell him about his oldest son. The father thought for a few moments
and then broke into tears. "It was a terrible thing to see," Considine
said later. "He sat there at the table weeping, unable to speak or to
control himself, for almost five minutes. It seemed to the rest of us like
an hour. Finally he pulled himself together and wiped his eyes but still
he couldn't talk. He gestured toward his wife and said, 'She can tell
you about him. I can't.' " [44]

Kennedy's other favorite, his widowed daughter Kathleen, was
taken from him only three years later in an airplane crash.[45] Kennedy
was in Europe at the time, making a widely publicized study of the
Marshall Plan. He quickly returned home. Dinneen met the plane and
tried to get Kennedy's mind off of his new tragedy. "What do you
think of the Marshall Plan now that you've looked over the ground?"
he asked. After a pause, Kennedy said, "It's no use, Joe. Nothing
means anything any more. There's nothing I can say." [46]

One who knew Kathleen characterized her as "sort of sunshine,
really," [47] and her death left her father deeply despondent. He wrote
Beaverbrook, "The sudden death of young Joe and Kathleen within a
period of three years has left a mark on me that I find very difficult to
erase. . . . What a horrible mess the world is in. I am afraid I see very
little hope on the horizon." [48]

Kennedy was always wrapped up in his family. In 1943, not a bright
year for Kennedy, a reporter asked him about his family. "It is the
finest thing in my life," Kennedy answered with quiet sincerity.[49] He
was convinced that the family was his greatest accomplishment: "The
measure of a man's success in life is not the money he's made. It's the
kind of family he has raised. In that, I've been mighty lucky," he told
reporter Harold Martin.[50] His extreme pride in his children lent
substance to Freud's observation that "If we look at the attitude of
fond parents towards their children, we cannot but perceive it as a
revival and reproduction of their own, long since abandoned narcis-
sism." [51] It is almost as if Kennedy, through his sons, had renewed his
claims for privileges and honors which he had given up himself long
ago.[52] It is said that the Kennedy family ambitions stemmed from
Kennedy's desire to "show" the Boston aristocracy, and journalist

Joe McCarthy points out that through his sons, Kennedy showed them.[53]

Being a man of wealth and influence, Kennedy was able to provide each of his children with a fascinating youth and opportunities available to few others. He appreciated that that was what wealth and influence were for. From the earliest childhood get-well greeting from "your pal, Tom"—Tom Mix—it was nice to be one of Joseph P. Kennedy's children. In school you felt a little better—and your dad a little prouder—even though you had placed poorly in a racing competition, because the *New York Times* would headline, "POINTS PROVIDED BY KENNEDY BROTHERS IN SIXTH RACE DISPLACE WILLIAMS." [54] As young adults, the opportunities for personal growth were truly valuable: while his father was Ambassador in London, Joe Junior was "employed" under Bullitt at the American Embassy in Paris, permitted to make his own schedule. He was in Czechoslovakia during the Munich crisis, and on the spot for many of the other major developments in the European situation.[55] He toured Spain as a civilian during the Spanish Civil War, being brought there on a British carrier as a favor to his father.[56] A special bus was placed at his disposal by the Spanish government.[57] The *Boston Herald* reported on February 24, 1939:

> *Yesterday Joseph P. Kennedy, Jr., visited the trenches on the Madrid front and lunched with government officers. A rich luncheon, unobtainable elsewhere in Madrid, was especially prepared by the leaders "in honor of our distinguished American guest." It consisted of omelet, red sausage, roasted mutton, cheese, fruit, wine, coffee and cognac.*[58]

State Department personnel in Spain rounded up the distinguished guest's baggage.[59]

Jack Kennedy also traveled widely in Europe, with access available to few. Even before he left the Maritime Commission, Joseph Kennedy was on the phone with the State Department's Herbert Feis, arranging appropriate letters of introduction for his younger son's European tour.[60] Everywhere Jack went, the inevitable telegram preceded him: "Will appreciate any courtesy my son Jack arriving (Belgrade) today." [61] Carmel Offie, Bullitt's closest employee and intimate, recalls Jack's visits to the Paris Embassy, "Sitting in my office and listening to telegrams being read or even reading various things which actually were none of his business but since he was who he was we didn't throw him out." [62] George Kennan, later one of President

John Kennedy's closest foreign policy advisors, took the young observer's invasion of Czechoslovakia even less nicely:

> *In those days, as the German forces advanced like encroaching waves over all the borders of Bohemia, no trains were running, no planes were flying, no frontier stations existed. Yet in the midst of this confusion we received a telegram from the embassy in London, the sense of which was that our ambassador there, Mr. Joseph Kennedy, had chosen this time to send one of his young sons (John) on a fact-finding tour around Europe, and it was up to us to find means of getting him across the border and through the German lines so that he could include in his itinerary a visit to Prague.*
>
> *We were furious. Joe Kennedy was not exactly known as a friend of the career service, and many of us, from what we had heard about him, cordially reciprocated this lack of enthusiasm. His son had no official status and was, in our eyes, obviously an upstart and an ignoramus. The idea that there was anything he could learn or report about conditions in Europe which we did not already know and had not already reported seemed (and not without reason) wholly absurd. That busy people should have their time taken up arranging his tour struck us as outrageous. With that polite but weary punctiliousness that characterizes diplomatic officials required to busy themselves with pesky compatriots who insist on visiting places where they have no business to be, I arranged to get him through the German lines, had him escorted to Prague, saw to it that he was shown what he wanted to see, expedited his departure, then, with a feeling of "that's that," washed my hands of him—as I thought.[63]*

Felix Frankfurter wrote the Ambassador that both John Adams and Charles Francis Adams had had their sons on their staffs as Ambassadors in London, and urged the father to take Joe Junior to the embassy.[64] Not to be outdone by the Adamses, before the end of his tenure, he had both Joe Junior and Jack on leaves from Harvard, serving on the embassy staff in London. Subscribers to the *Boston Globe* read of Joe Junior, installed in the room next to his father's at the embassy, a red carnation in his buttonhole.[65] Jack Kennedy, outshined by his more aggressive older brother, self-effacingly described his own position as "a glorified office boy." [66] By the fall of 1939, word got back to the Foreign Office that much of the American Embassy staff was annoyed by Kennedy's "familial" conduct of diplomacy.[67] Such reactions would have surprised and dismayed the

Ambassador, for he automatically extended to his inexperienced sons the same importance that he ascribed to himself. "You cannot imagine," he confided in a Polish diplomat, "to what extent my eldest boy is able to influence the President. I should say that the President believes him more than he does me." [68]

The opportunities were of course great while Kennedy was Ambassador. In a feature story on Kennedy's wonderful family, a *New York Times* writer commented that the children "are swamped with attentions that seem to come as much from their own charm as from their father's position." [69]

After the ambassadorial period, Kennedy was still able to provide his children with fascinating opportunities. Despite their complete lack of any journalistic experience, both Jack and Teddy worked for Hearst's International News Service, starting out as foreign correspondents, the most prized positions for which professional journalists compete. Bobby Kennedy began his brief career as a journalist representing the *Boston Post* at the United States-Japanese treaty conference; the journalist's father had the reference librarian—Landis—dig out some appropriate background reading for the *Post*'s correspondent. [70]

Kennedy also insisted that each of his children be exposed to the more mundane affairs of the world, so that they would have a feel for the existence of the common man. Each was required to work for two weeks during one of their summer vacations at the Columbia Trust Company. Bobby liked the work so much that he stayed on for two extra weeks. According to Bobby's Boswell, Jack Newfield, Bobby always had a greater feeling for the lower classes than any of his brothers.

ACCEPTANCE BY THE ARISTOCRACY WAS ALWAYS A DRIVING FACTOR IN the ambitions and conduct of Joseph Kennedy, from his earliest "what better way to meet people like the Saltonstalls." The Kennedys were the first Irish-Americans at Hyannis, and arrived in Palm Beach as soon as it became fashionable[71]—just a little behind Honey Fitz himself, who became something of a court jester in the staid Florida resort. [72] Kennedy was obviously impressed with the fact that "If Kathleen and her husband were living, I'd also be the father of the Duchess of Devonshire (first lady-in-waiting to the Queen) and the father-in-law of the head of all the Masons in the world." [73]

Kennedy raised his children for acceptance into the aristocracy. Social reasons were probably in part responsible for his choice of "American" names for his children. The daughters were sent to the Catholic finishing schools run by the Sisters of the Sacred Heart, the Catholic equivalent of the Protestant's Miss Porter's School. The Sacred Heart schools were definitely closed to all but the cream of the Catholic aristocracy: people like the Kennedys, the Raskobs, and the like. While Kennedy was Ambassador, the girls attended the convent at Roehampton, England, along with Miss Hohenzollern and Miss Bourbon. Obviously impressed, *Parents Magazine* wrote that "very little science is taught but all the household arts are" [74]—and *Parents* was not referring to dustmop technique. The convents were so inherently snobbish that even the nuns in the Sacred Heart Order were divided into castes.

John Kennedy was sent for a year to the Canterbury School, a prep school run by Catholic laymen, and Bobby was sent for a while to Portsmouth Priory, a prep school run by the clergy, but all of the boys finished at fashionable Protestant prep schools, Choate and Milton, where they could be expected to meet the sons of the Protestant aristocracy on equal terms.[75] None of the children ever went to public schools or to parish parochial schools, where they might be apt to meet the common man. When John Kennedy succeeded in having a book published at the unusual age of twenty-three, his father was understandably proud. But it was not the fact that Jack had turned out a commendable piece of scholarship or his academic bent that pleased Kennedy. He wrote his son:

> You would be surprised how a book that really makes the grade with high-class people stands you in good stead for years to come. . . . I remember that in the report you are asked to make after twenty-five years to the Committee at Harvard, one of the questions is "What books have you written?" and there is no doubt you will have done yourself a great deal of good.[76]

Kennedy's children obviously received social acceptance. In 1954 D. W. Brogan wrote that Jack was as much a "Eupatrid" as his Republican colleague Leverett Saltonstall in any real sense.[77] Massachusetts Governor Paul Dever correctly described the Kennedys as the first Irish Brahmins.[78] And in spite of their upbringing, the daughters did not degenerate into society matrons. The Kennedys are more "smart set" than old aristocracy, but they are nonetheless high, high society.

Acceptance by "high-class people" meant a great deal to Joe Kennedy. Politics was one avenue that led to that acceptance. Joe Kennedy raised his sons for political careers. He told a friendly interviewer in 1948 that he believed public service should be the career of "all children of parents who can afford it." [79] According to Kennedy, his motivation for pushing his children into public service was the public interest,[80] but there was more to it than that. Public service meant great public popularity, both a substitute for and an entree to, acceptance by the Anglo-Saxon, Protestant aristocracy, and it meant a giant's helping of limelight. Moreover, Kennedy strongly suspected that "There is no aristocracy now of finance and family; now political power is the only aristocracy." [81] In *I'm for Roosevelt*, he declared, "I have no political ambitions for myself or for my children." [82] He changed his mind.

The Kennedys had a sense of mission in politics, a mission which—at least until after John Kennedy's election as President—had no kind of an ideological goal. Joseph Kennedy gave his sons the drive necessary to put themselves into positions of political power. No one ever exhibited more drive than Jack, Bobby, or Teddy Kennedy on the campaign trail, be it for Congressman, Senator, or President. Off the trail, none of them ever showed quite the same resolution.

FAMILIES OF IMMIGRANTS ARE NOTED FOR THEIR CLOSENESS. IN America the immigrants needed a solid family base to fall back on in case a hostile world threatened to overwhelm them. But by the fourth generation, this need had disappeared, and generally the tight family unit disappeared with it. The Kennedys are unique; they not only maintained this traditional closeness but heightened it. Jacqueline Onassis says, "The day you become engaged to one of them is the day they start saying how 'fantastic' you are. And the same loyalty they show to each other they show to their in-laws. They are all so proud when one of them does well." [83]

The in-laws may or may not be assimilated by the clan. Ethel Skakel Kennedy, Bobby's widow, became as much a Kennedy as any of the blood members. She acquired their love for politics and their doggedness. In Japan, Ethel was unaccustomed to the traditional Japanese kneeling position and at a luncheon turned to the Japanese woman beside her: "Are your legs getting tired?" "No, are yours?" asked the Oriental lady. Ethel's only response was a grim "I can do it as long as you can," and she did.[84] Joseph Kennedy said that though Ethel had not been born a Kennedy, she certainly "acts like a Kennedy." [85]

Jacqueline Bouvier Kennedy Onassis was out of the Kennedy mold; her sport was not the Kennedy's touch football but fox hunting, and she never developed—or even tried to develop—the Kennedy love of competition or the family's interest in politics. Her special appreciation for and interest in the more elegant side of life, and her sometimes seeming inconsideration, make her appear what one insider calls "a latter-day Hedda Gabler." Nonetheless, the patriarch admired her stout independence of personality and interests, and Jackie developed a great warmth for her father-in-law. According to her private secretary, Jackie and the Ambassador enjoyed a camaraderie in playfully seeing who could first hit a fleeing housekeeper with their lamb-chop bones.[86] In Rita Dallas' account of the Ambassador's long final illness, *The Kennedy Case*, Jackie emerges as the book's heroine, for her truly loving interest in her father-in-law.

Jackie's relations with her mother-in-law—with whom she shares many common interests and personality traits—seem to have been remarkably poor. She reportedly regarded Rose as self-centered and selfish, and rudely mimicked her mother-in-law.[87] Jackie, though, proved herself capable of the all-important fierce family loyalty as against the outside world, and under the auspices of the Ambassador and the number-one surviving son, she was accepted into the family despite her other differences. Their love for one of their own made it impossible for them to hold her independent ways against her. "They seem proud if I read more books, and of the things I do differently. The very things you would think would alienate them brings you closer to them," she once remarked.[88]

The family seems to have received graciously Jackie's new life with the urbane, divorced, sexagenarian, multimillionaire Greek shipping magnate Aristotle Onassis, perhaps having accepted Cardinal Cushing's not-too-cryptic defense of the widow's marriage to the divorced man—"Nobody would believe me if I said what I know." [89] Even Rose was impressed with the gift-bearing Greek: "You know," she reportedly said, "Joe did so many things coast to coast, but this Onassis, he did things on a worldwide basis." [90]

Jackie's life with her new husband has been horribly complicated by her never-ending struggle to protect herself and especially her children from the clamor of the press. Years ago, as an inquiring camera girl for a Washington newspaper, she interviewed the grammar-school nieces of President-elect Eisenhower. Jackie got a big story and made page one. The mother, though, was indignant that her children's privacy had been invaded, and called the editor to protest.[91] Jackie has more than done penance.

Other in-laws have been more or less assimilated according to their own personalities. Joan Bennett Kennedy, Teddy's wife, has been fairly well assimilated. She is full of sparkle and life, yet not particularly independent—just right for clan membership. "In this family, you follow the crowd," she says, and she has.[92] On the other hand, the male in-laws have been less prone to merge themselves in the clan: Peter Lawford, Patricia Kennedy's former husband, was too much of a celebrity and personality in his own right; Sarge Shriver had much too much raw ability and personal ego; while Steve Smith, Jean's husband, fit imperfectly into the now depleted circle.

Joe Kennedy always encouraged competition among the children and against others. When they played their games they did so for blood. Among themselves, their touch football games were almost fratricidal. The girls would sob after being bested in tennis by their brothers. Jacqueline Kennedy once commented to a reporter on how she would occasionally "throw" a monopoly game to end it. "Does Jack mind?" asked the journalist. "Not if I'm on the other side," answered Jackie.

Fierce competition among themselves has always ended when the Kennedys meet the outside world. Joseph Kennedy gave them unwavering loyalty toward each other. Harold H. Martin wrote in the *Saturday Evening Post* that "When an outsider threatens to thwart the ambitions of any of them, the whole family forms a close-packed ring, horns lowered, like a herd of bison beset by wolves." [93] Their family loyalty is as fierce as their competitive spirit. Illustrating both is David Hackett's much-quoted old set of "Rules for Visiting the Kennedys."

> *Now for the football field. It's "touch," but it's murder. If you don't want to play, don't come. If you do come, play, or you'll be fed in the kitchen and no one will speak to you. Don't let the girls fool you. Even pregnant, they can make you look silly. If Harvard played touch, they'd be on the varsity. Above all, don't suggest any plays, even if you played quarterback at school. The Kennedys have the signal-calling department sewed up, and all of them have A-plus in leadership. If one of them makes a mistake, keep still. Run madly on every play and make a lot of noise. Don't appear to be having too much fun, though. They'll*

accuse you of not taking the game seriously enough. . . . Don't criticize the other team either. It's bound to be full of other Kennedys, too, and the Kennedys don't like that sort of thing. . . . To be really popular you must show raw guts. To show raw guts, fall on your face now and then. Smash into the house once in a while going after a pass. Laugh off a twisted ankle or a big hole torn in your best suit. They like this. It shows you take the game as seriously as they do. But remember. Don't be too good. Let Jack run around you now and then. He's their boy.[94]

JUST AS JOE KENNEDY WAS ALWAYS A LONER IN THE WORLD, THE Kennedys were always political loners in Massachusetts, remaining aloof from the Democratic party structure, even after John Kennedy emerged as the power within it in 1956. John Kennedy had few political friends in Massachusetts; he was not close to Congressional leader John McCormack, and he was always on bad terms with his nearer rival, Governor Foster Furcolo. The nucleus of his machine was his family. They thought and worked as a unit; one friend asserted years ago that Kennedys really only trust each other. There are few secrets between them. Once during a rare lull in family conversation, Jack turned to Jackie and asked "A penny for your thoughts?"

Whereupon Jackie smiled back at Jack and—again softly, but loud enough for everyone in the room to hear—she said, "But they're my thoughts, Jack, and they wouldn't be my thoughts any more if I told them. Now would they?"

The lull in what had been conversation became dead silence now. The Kennedys all looked at one another, amazed. Then Joe Sr. laughed suddenly and said something about liking "a girl with a mind of her own—a girl just like us."

And the others laughed too. Uproariously. A good loud Kennedy laugh.[95]

The Kennedys tend to think of their relations with the outside world as a unit. People fall into two categories: those who are for the family (good); and, those who are not for the family (bad). Someone like Landis was for the family. A friend of Joseph Kennedy's from the New Deal days and an erstwhile family employee, Landis shared with the President's counsel Theodore Sorensen the duties of family ghost-writer. Landis drafted many speeches and articles for both Joseph and John Kennedy; helped on *Profiles in Courage;* wrote most of the speeches that went to make up Robert Kennedy's book *Just Friends and Brave Enemies;*[96] and even helped put together a magazine article by Eunice Kennedy.[97] Or Benjamin A. Smith, Jack Kennedy's college roommate. Jack's loss of the Vice-Presidential nomination in 1956 moved Smith as much as it did any of the blood members of the family; while Bobby was just mad, Smith shed tears.[98] When Jack was elected President, he had Smith appointed as Massachusetts Senator to fill out his own unexpired Senate term. Teddy Kennedy confidently expected Smith to step aside for himself in 1962—"Ben's for the family," he explained.[99] Ben was and did. The shortcomings of those who pass the crucial test can be overlooked. By and large, "professional pols" and big-city bosses like Charles Buckley of the Bronx and Chicago Mayor Richard Daley were in the family corner because of their faith in the "winner mystique." Devoid of any interest in touchy policy questions, "the bosses" made more comfortable companions for Jack, Bobby, or Teddy than the liberals and reformers who conceptualized or rationalized the policies of the leftish-appearing brothers. The intellectuals were for the policies; the bosses were for the family. Though Buckley was a rogue, said Bobby, you just had to love him.[100]

Those who are not for the family as a unit are bad. An offense to one of the Kennedy's is regarded as an offense to all, and in the days when such was within their power, any offense might bring retribution to the offender. Joe Kennedy inherited his father's feud with James Michael Curley, and Jack Kennedy, in 1947, was the only Massachusetts Democrat in Congress who failed to sign a petition to the President requesting a pardon for Curley.[101] Later, John Kennedy showed extreme coolness bordering on rudeness to his father's old adversary, Eleanor Roosevelt.[102] Bobby Kennedy's heroes included Joe's friends, Lindbergh and Herbert Hoover, but excluded his father's one-time associate Franklin D. Roosevelt.[103] After publication of the unfriendly *J.F.K.: The Man and the Myth,* Bobby's Justice Department investigated its author.[104] When Harvard Law School rejected the application of Teddy Kennedy, the lad's irate father stormed up to the Harvard campus and demanded an explanation from the Harvard deans. They explained that Teddy was just too far down the list for benefits-of-the-doubt to make any difference, and demonstrated their point with charts. Joe Kennedy cut them off financially thereafter. (Jack Kennedy, however, became a member of the Harvard Board of Trustees—terrific on a candidate's résumé—and continued to make unspectacular contributions.) After the Presidential election of 1960, Joe Kennedy felt that the Catholic Church had not helped his son as it should have and vowed never to give another penny to the Church.[105]

Family loyalty came before almost anything else. Which, for example, would have been more beneficial to the President's program: the nomination of Edward McCormack as Senator from Massachusetts or that of Teddy Kennedy? Their positions and degrees of support for the President's program revolved around the Massachusetts constituency and were roughly the same. By permitting the use of means which could only offend the McCormacks to secure the nomination of his brother over the favorite nephew of House Speaker John McCormack, Kennedy risked making an enemy of the Speaker; he gave offense to "The Senate" in the eyes of many tradition-minded senators; he gave Republicans all over the country an issue to use against himself and his party. All in the interests of furthering the political fortunes of his then most undistinguished brother.

Family loyalty was extended by Joseph Kennedy and his offspring to those who by virtue of their acts deserved it. Douglas, as well to the left of center as Joseph Kennedy was to the right of center, felt a deep sense of gratitude to Joseph Kennedy for early help in Douglas's career; "I loved [Joseph Kennedy] very much like an older brother," says the Justice. Joseph Kennedy responded in kind. "You know, I must be nuts," the patriarch told the Justice, "I can't understand how the two men that I admire most in public life, my son Jack and your own self, stand for ideas that I so bitterly oppose." [106] Notwithstanding the vast differences in what the two believed to be the best course for the nation and mankind, Kennedy was always ready to do his most to boost Douglas's Presidential chances in the 1940s.[107] It was personal.

Conversely, the Kennedys expected those with whom they were close to support them politically on personal bases as a matter of loyalty, regardless of "abstract" implications. Eunice could have been speaking for the family when she said that she could not imagine how anyone could fail to support John Kennedy's 1960 Presidential bid and still think of himself "as our friend." [108] Among influential conservatives, Joseph Kennedy sought support for his son Jack, running in 1960 on the most left-wing platform either party had ever before proposed, and speaking nearly as "left" himself, on just such personal bases, to the irritation of conservative publisher William Loeb[109] and no doubt others. The situation was particularly difficult for that closest of friends, dearest of intimates, the enlightened conservative Arthur

Krock. "I wanted to see Jack Kennedy President," he confided to Charles Bartlett, "I loved him all his life, and I still do." But after what must have been a horrible struggle within the *New York Times* man, be concluded "That it would be better for the country if Nixon were elected." [110] He found himself writing critically of his dear friend's son. "Well, the final point, the break with Mr. Kennedy, Sr.," Krock continued,

> I suppose, was because I had not, as he had expressed the hope, finally "come out for Jack," as he put it. So after the election was over, on just one occasion, he communicated with me. It was the inauguration period, and he had a house here, and he telephoned me very pleasantly and we had a friendly talk. I waited for him to ask me to come to see him, as I thought he naturally might, but he never did. . . . When he had his stroke, I wrote to Rose. . . . I heard nothing more.[111]

And so ended the 30-year friendship, perhaps the most important friendship, not only outwardly, but inwardly as well, to Joseph Kennedy, that he had ever shared. To Joseph Kennedy it was a matter of loyalty; to Krock, a matter of integrity.[112]

After Teddy's victory over Eddie McCormack in the Massachusetts Senatorial primary of 1962, *New York Times* columnist James Reston asserted that the Kennedy's apply different standards to themselves than they do towards others, preaching pragmatism but practicing nepotism.[113] Despite its nasty connotations, nepotism has its positive side as a manifestation of family loyalty, albeit family loyalty fraught with potential disadvantage to the public. President Woodrow Wilson refused to permit his love for family to obscure the public interest and passed over his own brother for a local postmastership after a struggle "against affection and temptation." [114] Perhaps the claims of family loyalty are stronger in newer immigrant stock, who feel a need to "stick together" as against the world. Honey had no such Wilsonian qualms: his brother Henry Fitzgerald was his chief patronage dispenser; other brothers profited from Honey's connections with liquor licenses; Joseph Fitzgerald became known as "The Human Postage Stamp" when his brother the mayor put him on the city payroll to deliver a daily traffic report from the Warren Avenue Bridge to City Hall at the then quite generous annual salary of $1,100.[115] Jack Kennedy was more like Honey than Wilson and would not turn his back on his family. Robert Kennedy's appointment as Attorney General was a clear departure from President Kennedy's announced intention of appointing purely on the basis of qualifications, with every job going to the best man for it. The same could perhaps be said of Shriver's appointment as Peace Corps head—not withstanding Shriver's unquestionably superior intellect and polish—while Steve Smith's post at the State Department was created as pure accommodation. Where the family was concerned, Jack Kennedy took a Napoleonic approach, with ability taking the back seat.

The family's preference for itself is manifested in other ways as well. Bobby, for example, measured a man by his personal as well as his public life,[116] yet refused to apply that standard to his own family. He would spit out the word "politician" as if it were the most vicious invective he knew, and yet he never seemed to realize or care that the Kennedys themselves were none too finicky in their own election techniques.

The Kennedys, however, were not alone in their application of special standards for Kennedys. The public of the 1960s also saw them through rose-colored glasses. The following story, for example, comes from a book sympathetic to the family, Joe McCarthy's excellent *The Remarkable Kennedys:*

> Teddy and Hackett rowed ashore in a dinghy to get supplies. As Teddy was paddling past a large and luxurious yacht, where several couples were enjoying a cocktail party, a man leaning over the rail of the costly craft called to him to row a little faster. Teddy advised him to mind his own business. "Come back here, and say that again," the man yelled.
>
> "Teddy spun the dinghy around so fast I almost fell out of it," Hackett told Red Fay later. "The next thing I knew, Teddy was on the yacht and the man was being thrown overboard and all the women were screaming and running below to hide in the cabins. Their husbands were running with them, to see that they were safely tucked away, I guess. By this time I'm on the yacht with Teddy. The men start to come back up to the deck to deal with us, but it's a narrow hatchway and they have to come up through it one at a time. As each guy appears, I grab him and spin him around and throw him to Teddy, and Teddy throws him overboard. In no time, all of the men—there were about eight of them—were in the water. I never saw anything like it." [117]

In anyone other than a Kennedy, the episode would demonstrate just plain immaturity and boorishness. But the Teddy involved was Teddy Kennedy and the American public ate it up—"those Kennedys have a lot of spirit," is the conclusion to be drawn from the story.

The Kennedy appeal to the public has resembled that of movie stars rather than of political figures, and most of the movie magazines featured stories on them in the 1960s. Unlike any previous American politicians, the Kennedys took a place in the American mind comparable to that enjoyed by the royal family in Britain, with a ceaseless stream of gossip satisfying the public's desire to be "in." [118] (Is it true about Ethel and Frank Sinatra?) There was even a 50-cent picture book, published in magazine format, entitled *The Kennedys— America's Royal Family.*

STEWART ALSOP, WHITE HOUSE INSIDER IN THE CAMELOT ERA, HAS appropriately described the Kennedy family as "a remarkable closed corporation," [119] and the President and Chairman of the Board of that corporation was clearly Joseph P. Kennedy. Until his stroke in 1961, he was, writes Sorensen, the vibrant center of Kennedy family life.[120] Like his own father, Joseph Kennedy was always a patriarch, but he went much further than most patriarchs. One longtime associate described him as "a horribly dominating personality," [121] and over the family he always exercised an iron will. A family friend says that "Every single kid was raised to think, First, what shall I do about this problem? Second, what will Dad say about my solution of it?" Frank Waldrop, publisher of the *Washington Times-Herald* and one-time boss of both Kathleen Kennedy and Jacqueline Bouvier, said, "Father Joe may not speak often, but when he does, that is the word. No one in the family would think of bucking him." [122] On family matters—such as whether or not Teddy should run for the Senate—his word was clearly law.

Kennedy's fatherly efforts to guide his children went far beyond those of most parents. Some family friends suggest that the word "meddle" more accurately described his efforts than "guide." Rose Kennedy says that the father paid attention to every single thing that the children did.[123] He went so far as to pick a marriage partner for daughter Eunice—according to Landis, the father's favorite surviving daughter.[124]

From an "old" Catholic family ("We're nicer than the Kennedys," his mother says, "we've been here since the 1600s"),[125] R. Sargent Shriver attended Yale where his record even surpassed that of Joe Junior at Harvard. He was selected for Yale's most prestigious organizations, attesting to his social acceptability, but he was also chosen editor-in-chief of the *Yale Daily News*, a mark of remarkable literary talent and an aesthetic bent never shown by any of the Kennedy "undergrads." He took an active part in efforts to keep America out of World War II, and then enlisted in the Navy. Shriver is a sincere, intellectual Catholic from the liberal wing of the Church. His strong social commitment, springing from his faith, manifested itself in interfaith and integrationist activity in the 1950s—long before that kind of thing was fashionable, and long before any of Joseph Kennedy's sons showed the slightest interest at all in the black man.

Joseph Kennedy took an early interest in the smart and personable Shriver and hired him onto his staff. When daughter Eunice was working on problems of juvenile delinquency for the Department of Justice, the father sent his young and eligible employee down to Washington to help her as a brain truster. They lived happily ever after.[126] Perhaps to make clear that no one was losing any daughters, Eunice toasted her new husband at the wedding: "I searched all my life for someone like my father and Sarge came closest." [127]

Joe inspired in his children many of his own characteristics—his doggedness and singleness of purpose, his interest in public affairs, his ambitiousness and love of the limelight, and, most of all, his great competitive spirit.

Much has been written about the fierce competitive spirit of the Kennedys. Perhaps this competitive nature was natural in an Irish lad like the patriarch, who fought his way to the top and made millions in the "dog-eat-dog" world. Kennedy's children did not have to fight their way to the top of either the social or financial ladder. Yet Joseph Kennedy was able to pass on this competitive spirit, and it was of course necessary in the political world. For his sons, the goal became preeminence, rather than perfection. They took to heart their father's preaching: Come in first and never settle for second best.[128] His sons developed reputations in sailboat racing as ruthless competitors and graceless losers.[129]

As youngsters, two of the children were sent away from the table in disgrace because they had not made an all-out effort to win a sailing race that afternoon.[130] Even as adults, when his sons began to see the significance of sailing victories in its proper perspective, the patriarch firmed up the win psychology. So, when Bobby and family intimate Kenneth O'Donnell were badly beaten in a sailboat race and took it lightly, Joe was outraged at their attitude. "What kind of guys are you to think that's funny?" he demanded.[131] When asked as to the

Shrivers' future expectations during the 1960 Presidential campaign, Eunice laughed it off, explaining that they had only time to work to win. She rocked the baby in her arms to a melodious chant: "win, win, win." [132]

As a boy, Jack Kennedy named his sailboat "Victura," which he explained was Latin "meaning something about winning." [133] At Harvard, Jack's plans for a spot on the swimming team were disrupted by a high fever that sent him to the infirmary. Covertly, Jack had swimmer's gear smuggled to him in the infirmary, and between the nurse's rounds he sneaked out to the pool for a few laps. He *had* to be on the swimming team. He lost a place on the team to Richard Tregaskis (author of *Guadalcanal Diary*) and as a result of his efforts was ill for the rest of the school year.[134]

Joe rewarded his children generously with money and trips for good grades in school. James MacGregor Burns, Jack Kennedy's earliest biographer, stresses that Joe was most interested in academic success as a prelude to competition in later life.[135] This author doubts that. Sports better nurtured the competitive interest.[136] The children all devoted their efforts to athletic competition, showing virtually no interest in academic competition. Only Joe Junior was ever more than a mediocre student. One suspects that the boys were more interested in athletic than scholastic honors because their father gave them an interest in athletics, and stressed the importance of succeeding in athletics that far surpassed the interest that he instilled in them in scholastics. Though his sons were always fit enough for their ages, their father hired a private calisthenic "drill sergeant" for his sons, and boating instructors. When Jack brought home schoolmate Ralph Horton, the father held up the young guest to his sons as an example of what a good golfer should be—"he'd even stretch it a little more, I think," Horton says, "to irritate them." [137] The choice of emphasis—athletics over scholarship—is made clear in Jean Kennedy's comment that "Jack turned out to be our most intellectual member of the family because he wasn't strong enough as a kid to go in for athletics as much as Joe and the other boys." [138] A factor that must have influenced the children, as well as their father, is the fact that the school-boy athlete has hero status. The school-boy scholar does not.

The emphasis on athletics in the careers of Joe's children reflected Joe's own college-day choice of emphasis. He too strove for a reputation as an athlete and turned in only mediocre academic records. Like his sons, Kennedy was always athletic; he swam, golfed, and played tennis. In his SEC days, the father was known for the same kind of athletic proselytizing for which his sons became known.[139]

In other ways, the sons reflected their father's personal choices and habits. Kennedy and all his boys cultivated grid heroes and lived in the "jock houses" during their school years. Just as Bobby and Jack relied heavily on the "Irish Mafia," their Irish-American political strategists, Joe Senior was always surrounded by his "Murphia." [140]

But reduced Irish-Yankee tensions, assimilation of the Irish into American culture, and just plain time, watered down many of Joe Kennedy's traits. The father was sometimes known in his New Deal days as "a genial stage-Irishman"; none of his children could be described in that way. John Kennedy could come out with a profanity as easily and naturally as anyone—Sorensen punctuates his memoirs with dashes representing the President's use of obscenities—but none of Joseph Kennedy's children flavored their conversation with constant vulgarities, as their father often did. The polishing process of a hundred years in America did much to smooth the rough edges from the chips off the Joe Kennedy block.

In one sphere, Joseph Kennedy refrained from imposing himself, and that was where policy views were concerned. He scrupulously refrained from attempting to indoctrinate his children.

Joe Kennedy's postwar conservatism was not a Burkian conservatism based on any theory of gradual development; rather, it was the kind of "gut" conservatism that looked backward nostalgically. His views were based on experiences in a bygone world that his sons never knew; it was an old man's conservatism, and was not likely to have had any great effect on a youth. Joe Kennedy's children were as much products of their times and environment as Kennedy himself was of his own time and environment. His views were too far out in right field for them to have had any great effect on his children.

In one of her campaign speeches of 1960, Rose Kennedy commented that her husband's and sons' views differed because "They're of a different generation." The explanation was understated; they were of a different world. Joseph Kennedy himself understood this. In reminiscing to Dinneen in 1944 about his nineteenth-century world, the father said:

> My world may pass. It can't go on forever. The world must go forward. It can't go backward. The generation that follows me may have to stand for everything that I stood against—and I realize that includes even my own sons. I made my choice among

*the philosophies offered when I was young. Each of them will
have to make his or her own choice.*[141]

In the early 1950s, the father explained to Baruch, "Jack believes each
generation must solve its own problems in its own way." The way it
was said made Baruch think that the elder Kennedy agreed with his
son.[142]

Joseph Kennedy wanted his sons to be strong, and he appreciated
that independence was an element of that strength, including
independence in thought. He therefore encouraged his sons to expose
themselves to lines of thought competing with his own. Perhaps he
hoped that ultimately, after examining the alternatives, they would
conclude that his own beliefs were "the best," but whatever the case,
he wanted his sons to reach informed conclusions.

Kennedy wrote Justice Frankfurter in 1934 that his nineteen-year-
old son, "Joe Junior is in great shape and I'd give a good deal to hear
him discuss some of his ideas with you." [143] The great thinker took an
interest in Joe Junior that delighted the patriarch. At Frankfurter's
suggestion,[144] Kennedy sent both Joe Junior and Jack to study with
Laski in England. While sending his sons to Laski would have struck
Europeans as a most sensible thing for any man to do,[145] it must have
been difficult for a somewhat parochial Boston Irishman to knowingly
expose his sons to Laski, who was not simply a Jew, but a socialist and
atheist who made little effort to mask his hostility to the Catholic
Church. On a visit to Laski's classrooms, Frankfurter seemed to take a
paternal interest in "drilling" Kennedy's eldest son.[146]

Joseph Kennedy wanted his sons to be more than himself. Much as
he wanted them to be athletes, he also wanted them to feel
comfortable competing intellectually in the way that intellectuals do,
in that world of "bright guys," thought and letters, the world of
Frankfurter and Laski from which he, by cultural limitations, was
forever barred on any but the most superficial level. If that meant that
his sons would differ with him on policy, such consequences were of
no great matter. When Rose Kennedy started to scold her sons for
taking issue with their father on some policy matter, the patriarch cut
her short: "As long as they stick together, I can take care of
myself." [147]

Joseph P. Kennedy, Jr., died before maturing his own political
stance. Kennedy's younger sons did develop political independence
from their father, which, far from resenting, the patriarch relished,

and happily demonstrated for others. Kay Halle recalls this conversation with father and Congressman-son at a cocktail party at the Drew Pearson residence early in Jack Kennedy's Congressional career:

> Suddenly Joe said, "Kay, I wish you would tell Jack that he's going to vote the wrong way." I can't even remember what bill it was, but Joe said, "I think Jack is making a terrible mistake." And then I remember Jack turning to his father and saying, "Now, look here Dad, you have your political views and I have mine. I'm going to vote exactly the way I feel I must vote on this. I've great respect for you but when it comes to voting, I'm voting my way." Then Joe looked at me with that big Irish smile, and said, "Well, Kay, that's why I settled a million dollars on each one of them, so they could spit in my eye if they wished." [148]

By the 1960 Presidential campaign, the political differences between father and son were complete. When Joseph Kennedy boasted to intimates, "Of course Jack is saying everything I don't believe in," he seemed rather proud.[149]

THE QUEEN MOTHER OF THE KENNEDY FAMILY, MRS. JOSEPH P. KENnedy, represents pre-lib woman of the highest type, and no doubt served as her sons' model of what a woman ought to be. To the outside world she was always Mrs. Joseph P. Kennedy. As for "Rose Fitzgerald Kennedy," she told an interviewer, "They use that a lot, but Mr. Kennedy doesn't like it and I don't like it particularly." [150]

The picture of Mrs. Kennedy that emerges from her biography, Gail Cameron's *Rose*,[151] is largely confirmed by handwriting analysis of Mrs. Kennedy,[152] and shows a somewhat different person than emerges from early popular pieces about the Kennedys. Rose Kennedy has a definite concept of how she should appear to others, which she projects with only rare lapses—she is, says Truman Capote, "a public perfect person." [153] Beneath her velvet glove, though, is an iron hand rivaling that of her spouse.[154] Unlike her husband, Rose Kennedy is rigidly self-controlled and self-disciplined to the extent of inflexibility, with only infrequent emotional releases. Years of training made her a formal person, orderly, fastidious, systematic, and almost "picky." Otherwise, the adjectives so commonly applied to her husband might apply equally to her: proud, self-centered and confident; determined, assertive, and shrewd; materialistic; courageous and energetic. Rose, like her husband, has terrific executive ability, an almost calculated intuition, staggering ambition and drive, a sense of self-importance, and a strong need to be where the action is. Both could be obsessive about their goals, domineering, almost tyrannical. Both shared a deep instinct for living life fully. Both were inclined to be "loners," though Rose Kennedy has an inner self-sufficiency that her husband lacked; she enjoys and needs periods of solitude. When President William McKinley called Rose's sister Agnes the most beautiful girl he had ever seen, Mrs. Kennedy says, "I knew right then that I would have to work hard to do something about myself" [155]—exhibiting the famous Kennedy competitive spirit long before there ever was a Jack, Bobby, or Teddy. The coolness and emotional detachment characteristic of Jack or Teddy Kennedy comes from their mother, not their father.

Despite a toughness the equal of her husband's, like her husband, Rose Kennedy has a strong sentimental streak in her. She explains that she wore the same dress to the Presidential inauguration of her son that she had worn to her first presentation at the Court of St. James's because styles of 1961 had reverted to the styles of 1938, a strangely unconvincing explanation from a "clotheshorse" who was never stingy at the houses of Paris' most fashionable designers.[156]

Religion has played a large part in the life of Rose Kennedy. Jack Kennedy described her as "terribly religious," [157] and at the parish church in Hyannis, fellow regulars know her as "Pope Rose." [158] When the boys were away at prep schools, she saw to it that they had prayer books and encouraged them to use them.[159] Notes went out to remind children away from home of more obscure Catholic observances that they might otherwise miss.[160] Nurses and nannies were encouraged to drop into churches with the younger children for unscheduled prayer[161] and, according to her biographer, Rose herself will sometimes pass the time under a dryer with her rosary beads.[162] She holds the rare honor of being a Papal Countess.[163] Though neither an ascetic Catholic nor, from appearances, at all intellectual about her faith, religiosity is not simply a formal thing with Rose Kennedy. Despite the hard side to her, she is capable of restrained warmth and great consideration for others, manifested by such acts as her having taken the time to write a congratulatory note to a nephew on the very night that her son was nominated for the Presidency,[164] and her well-known generosity to her orphaned niece and nephew, Ann and Joseph Gargan, as well as others. One of her closest women companions says of Rose, "I've never heard her say an unkind word about anybody, and how many women are like that?" [165] Whether from religion or breeding, it is undoubtedly an admirable trait.

Joseph Kennedy was very much less religious than his wife,[166] and not particularly learned in his faith. In his *Memoirs*, Krock reports:

> Another time when [Cardinal Spellman] and I were both guests at Palm Beach, Joe Kennedy got a special dispensation from the prelate for the use of the living room as the locus of a Requiem Mass His Eminence would perform "for the repose of my mother's soul." I suggested to Kennedy that he also invite the Governor of Michigan, Frank Murphy, a devout Catholic, who was staying at a hotel nearby.
>
> At eight o'clock the next morning we all were present, the servants standing behind the sofa where Kennedy, Murphy, and I were sitting. The Cardinal had prepared a little altar on a taboret, putting his various religious articles upon it. As he began to intone the Requiem Mass, I followed Kennedy in the ritual until it was obvious that he was making procedural errors. So I followed Murphy, who proved letter-perfect.
>
> When the Mass ended, with Kennedy, in his emotional Irish way, overwhelmed by the memory of his mother, I said, "Look here, you're not a very proficient Catholic. You made me make several mistakes and so I turned to Murphy."
>
> In a choking voice Kennedy replied, "That character (though he used a much more pungent word) ought to have been a priest."
>
> Just as he said this the Cardinal, who had forgotten something, came back to pick it up. We froze. The Cardinal pretended not to have heard the comment of the chief mourner.[167]

Krock attributes Rose Kennedy's greater strength in the face of tragedy to the fact that she is a more literal Catholic than her husband was, and more certain of the tenets of her faith than he.[168]

The biggest thing in Rose Kennedy's life, standing alongside her religion, is her children, and she made every effort to be a good mother. When a fashionable interior decorator did her room in delicate material, she had it covered up with coarser cloth, so that the room would not be off-limits for any kind of child's play. Jack Kennedy said, "while she was always very close to us, she was, at the same time, a little removed when we were kids, and still is—which I think is the only way to survive when you have nine children." The son regarded her as "a very model mother for a big family." [169]

Rose Kennedy was always a great political asset to her sons. She is perhaps the most effective campaigner in the family. Journalists Ralph

Martin and Ed Plaut write of her role in John Kennedy's 1952 Senatorial campaign:

> *Mrs. Kennedy knew exactly what to say, what to wear, what to do, no matter what the audience. A* New York Times *reporter followed and watched and said, "Mrs. Kennedy carefully selected her accessories and tailored her remarks. Thus to a group of Italian women in the North End, she was the mother of nine children, one of whom died in the war. Perhaps a single pearl necklace over a black dress would be worn. Before a Chestnut Hill group of matrons, she might don a mink stole and a few rings and certainly a different hat."*
>
> *In the car between appearances, she would put on jewelry or strip it off to fit the occasion, appearing as the daughter of Honey Fitz to one crowd and the wife of the former Ambassador to the Court of St. James's to another crowd.*[170]

Rose did less campaigning in John Kennedy's 1960 Presidential campaign, but wowed her audiences with talk-down homey chit-chat wherever she went. Campaigning in Michigan, 17 times she told audiences, "If Jack is elected, I hope baby-sitting in the White House will be one of my duties."[171] As for the religious issue, "I don't know about it nationally or as an issue, but I think religion is wonderful for children. If your child grows up with this, he has something other people lack."[172]

The author had the pleasure of hearing Mrs. Kennedy address the convention of Franco-American War Veterans, a New England organization made up of veterans of French-Canadian descent, while Teddy was running in his first Senatorial campaign. She made it entirely clear that (1) she loves French people; (2) she loves Canadians; (3) she loves Montreal, Quebec, and Paris, and is well and favorably acquainted with much of the French countryside. She also made clear that Jack and Bobby were similarly inclined, while in Teddy's book only one group rated higher than the French or the Canadians: the French-Canadians. And then she said it all over again in French; it was halting French, apparently read phonetically, but it was French. It was a nonpolitical speech, and Rose asked for no votes, but her message could not have been lost to the Franco-American veterans.[173]

Her statements on the hustings are carefully designed to make precisely the desired impression.[174] Only once is she known to have let down her guard: while campaigning for Bobby in Indiana during the

1968 Presidential campaign, when she slashed back at charges of election-buying with an ill-advised "it's our money, and we're free to spend it any way we please." [175]

Rose Kennedy enjoys the modern upper-class life style. Like thousands of Manhattan socialites, she has become nutrient conscious, even to the extent of sometimes bringing her own lunch so that she can control her diet.[176] It is a practice both healthy and fashionable. According to Capote, "The social scene, whatever that is, does matter to her." [177] She uses the word "advantages" freely,[178] and is involved with and interested in the elegant, comfortable aspects of life. She sensibly continued to attend the high-society affairs she so enjoyed after her husband's incapacitation,[179] taking pains to maintain her public image of conventional wife and mother by keeping her private social life out of the press as much as possible.[180]

Joe and Rose Kennedy were married for over half a century. In many ways Rose Kennedy was very much like Joe's own mother, Mary Kennedy. Both women were formal, deeply religious, and devoted their lives to their families. Like his own father, Joseph Kennedy married "above his station." In many ways, Joe Kennedy was remarkably like Rose's father Honey. Perhaps the similarities between Kennedy and Fitzgerald accounted for the lifelong friction between them. They had too much in common and were competing against each other in too many ways. Both men were competent fellows and veritable dynamos when it came to energy. Both had a flair for glamor and publicity, insatiable limelight hunger, and a powerful urge to "be important." Honey's Irish charm could be equalled in his son-in-law, when Joseph Kennedy wanted to turn it on. Rose married a man much like the man who had married her mother. Perhaps she got a man more like Honey than she may have wanted. Honey was known as a philanderer.

The business of women has been much overdone in the Kennedy legend. There were always girls in the picture, but never anything serious; girls were not a serious matter, but were just another thing that a rich man had, like fancy cars and caviar. Many of those with whom the author spoke mentioned the girls, but no one dwelt on them, and their identities were not significant because the separate relationships were not significant. None of the girls would be remembered today, except insofar as they might have been celebrities in their own right. If there was ever a love of his life, it was Rose Fitzgerald.

A wife, though, cannot be expected to appreciate that. Rose's handwriting shows "daggers," taken to be a sign of deep resentment or frustration within.

The Kennedy marriage did not appear to be one of passionate love, nor, given the backgrounds and expectations of the parties, was either likely to have had such a marriage. Joseph Kennedy was a machismo American living the twentieth-century American male role as he believed a man was meant to live it. Sex was an important part of his trappings. But he expected in his wife a McKinley-era lady, to whom sex and motherhood were inseparably connected, and who, as a nicer person, did not acknowledge the baser urges. Rose Kennedy was just that. Her own libido, her handwriting indicates, was ever safely under control. From the earliest the Kennedys had separate bedrooms.[181] That was the way that the proper people lived in the Edith Wharton world that Joseph Kennedy strove to enter and for which Rose Kennedy had been groomed.

Joseph Kennedy was obviously a good father in the formal sense of providing a stable home and material comfort and benefits. In some ways he was a caricature of the good family man—he was preoccupied with the well-being of his children, and despite many prolonged absences from home, he was ever interested in their activities. A real love developed between the father and his sons.[182] "Long before [togetherness] became a slogan, I guess we had it," Kennedy told journalists in 1960.[183]

The interest of the Kennedy children in politics stems from both of their parents, but principally from their father and his penchant for "politicking." The famous Kennedy-family "dinner-table debates" were largely discussions of personalities and strategies, with little analysis or debate of substantive policy issues so that the sons grew up largely insulated from important national issues, while thoroughly immersed in the salt of government: the sport and glamor of the hustings and the smoke-filled rooms. Things such as the ramifications of the New Deal had little intellectual or emotional impact on the sons; the excitement of its election contests did. While Joseph Kennedy had pronounced opinions on most matters of national policy, he was never much interested in discussing or analyzing fine points of theory; according to Henry Luce, he was not much for heady after-dinner conversations.[184] When a child's query required careful dissection of an issue, though, he responded. Kennedy was "a very remarkable teacher," Ralph Horton recalled:

> *Any of the children could ask him questions and in the greatest*
> *detail, no matter how simple or how stupid the questions might*
> *seem, the Ambassador would go to great lengths to describe it, to*
> *explain it, to explain the strengths or weaknesses of a particular*
> *policy that he was discussing.*

A basically impatient man, answering childlike questions was not easy
or pleasant for the father; it could be done only for one's own:

> *If an outsider, such as myself, would have asked the Ambassador*
> *a question, he'd be practically ignored. . . . He would just*
> *answer it rather curtly as though he didn't want to be bothered*
> *with your questions. He was only concerned about educating his*
> *own children.*[185]

Kennedy always encouraged his sons to go on and do better. In their
mature lives he still tried to direct them, but he never chastised them
when the water was over the dam. He was always in their corner. Jack
said:

> *The great thing about dad is his optimism and his enthusiasm*
> *and how he's always for you. He might not always agree with*
> *what I do, just as I don't always agree with him, but as soon as I*
> *do anything, there's dad saying "Smartest move you ever made.*
> *. . . We really got them on the run, now."* [186]

Illustrating this perfectly was the father's reaction to John Kennedy's
speech of July, 1957, on the Algerian situation. The speech was a long
and thorough indictment of France's refusal to grant concessions to
the Algerians, and hinted at the need for Algerian independence.
Jack's speech was bitterly criticized by Dulles and Acheson. Privately,
Joe Kennedy was horrified by the speech, thinking it both unsound
policy and bad politics.[187] But when his son called and wondered
aloud whether he had made a mistake, the father hid his feelings: "You
lucky mush. You don't know it and neither does anyone else, but
within a few months everyone is going to know just how right you are
on Algeria." [188] Even when his son became President, Joseph Kennedy
was on hand as number-one morale booster after any adverse turn,
pointing out the silver lining to the darkest clouds.[189]

Unlike so many self-centered men, Kennedy was willing to share the
stage with his sons. Many egocentric fathers cannot bear to have their
sons competing with them and produce sons that are lesser men. It is
significant that neither Honey nor Curley produced sons their own

equal. Arthur Schlesinger, Jr., no fan of Kennedy Senior, writes that: *Winston Churchill and Franklin Roosevelt were incontestably greater men than Joseph P. Kennedy. Yet Randolph and Franklin Jr., both men of talent and charm, seemed to have lived lives beneath their promise and capacity, while the sons of Joseph Kennedy, endowed somewhere with a capacity for self-discipline, had risen beyond their father, and no doubt, because of him.*[190]

Kennedy permitted and encouraged his sons to expand and grow. He never felt that he had to prove that he was a bigger man than his sons; indeed, he encouraged his sons to be bigger men than himself. They were, and he was pleased. In that respect, Joseph Kennedy was generous.

Joseph Kennedy was a good father in every way and respect that was under his control. Such shortcomings as the father had as a father arose from what was not in his control: principally, himself. His attitude towards the earthier things in life clearly transmitted itself to Joe Junior, Jack, and Teddy Kennedy. He made his sons as goal-directed as himself,[191] which has both its positive side and a reverse side of insensitivity as to means. One who knew and worked closely with the father in England told the author that there was an element of "exploiting rascal" in Joseph Kennedy. "I felt that he was out for various things—America, improving British-American relations, world peace, and also Joe Kennedy, as perhaps is everyone, but Joe was perhaps more cunning than most." [192] The same self-centered approach that Joseph Kennedy took to everything transmitted itself to his sons.

The trait of arrogance was different in Joseph Kennedy than in his sons. The arrogance of Joseph P. Kennedy was no less offensive because it was sham, but sham it was. Not too far below the surface, Joseph Kennedy had a deeply humble view of himself, perhaps reflected by the unusually diminutive "I" in his handwriting, and proclaimed, no doubt without awareness, in comments like "Eddie," to his friend Edward Gallagher, "six or seven times in my life the pendulum swung my way, and for that, if it hadn't fallen favorably to me, life could be quite a bit different." [193]

Joseph Kennedy's sons could be and were more secure in their own roots, and in them arrogance was inbred. Raised from the start to have everything, they became accustomed to having everything; as adults, they fully intended to go right on having everything, a matter which they made little attempt to disguise.

And last was the matter of the example that the father provided of character and ethical standards.

FATHER
AND SONS

JACK KENNEDY WAS IN AN ODD POSITION AS "SECOND SON." FORCED to compete with his older, bigger, and stronger brother, Jack generally came off second best. He was continually outshined by Joe Junior, and not surprisingly, in the same room he seemed quiet and less outgoing than Joe.

Outside of Joe's shadow, the young John Kennedy developed into a slightly mischievous adolescent, sparky enough to sign a letter to a pal "Smuttily Yours," but at the same time wholesome enough to refrain from use of real swearwords.[1] In prep school at Choate, he traveled with the ballsy "anti" kids who called themselves the "Muckers" and whose effect on the morale of impatient school administrators prodded the headmaster to make a public tirade against Jack, LeMoyne Billings, and their crowd, as "rotten apples." [2] Nonetheless, teachers liked him[3] and the headmaster wrote the Ambassador how grateful he was for the Ambassador's generosity.[4]

Appreciating his father's goals and hungry for his approval, as a Choate senior Jack was eager to cop the yearbook's most-likely-to-succeed designation, and traded votes to achieve that objective.[5] He got the title. He was.

After Choate, Jack determined to go with his Choate friends to Princeton, where he would be free of the obvious comparisons with his more dynamic older brother, then at Harvard. A before-college summer with Laski in London was cut short by an attack of jaundice, which prevented him from beginning Princeton at the start of the school year. Princeton officials at first refused to permit him to begin after the start of school, as a matter of university policy, but intervention from his father's old associate, Herbert Bayard Swope, an influential Princeton alumnus, made for an exception.[6] A Christmastime recurrence of the jaundice forced Jack to drop out, though, and when he returned to school, it was to Harvard.

At Harvard, Jack's efforts to compete in school athletics and campus politics were uniformly unsuccessful. He demonstrated only one sign of leadership potential—when he was front man in the Winthrop House Big Apple line.[7]

Jack was not his father's favorite, which had advantages as well as disadvantages. It gave him license to be somewhat more independent in thought than his older brother. While his father and Joe, Jr., were both identified with the isolationists opposed to entry into the European war, Jack Kennedy never took a public position nor affiliated with the isolationist movement. According to Payson Wild, the Harvard Professor with whom he discussed such matters, he felt very differently about the war than the other Kennedy men.[8] Another professor who spoke with all three in 1941 concluded that young Jack had a far better historical and political mind than either his father or his brother.[9]

Jack's senior thesis at Harvard, though, "Appeasement at Munich," was a document with which his father could completely agree. From the start the father encouraged his son on the project, arranging for interviews with important British government people like Lord Lothian,[10] and knowledgeable journalists including government critics.[11]

The Ambassador's belief that he could safely expose his sons to competing viewpoints was borne out in the end product. "Appeasement at Munich" presumed that the Munich "sellout" was necessary and therefore well advised, and concentrated on the state of English defenses that had made Munich "necessary." It was a whitewash of his father's friends, the English conservative leaders, and particularly of their decision not to go to war at Munichtime.[12] Jack's older brother thought the paper "seemed to represent a lot of work but did not prove anything." [13]

At his father's suggestion, the paper was expanded into *Why England Slept*, the first of John Kennedy's two best-selling books. Arthur Krock helped to polish the draft, gave it its title (adapted from Churchill's *While England Slept*), and secured an agent for it.[14] Thinking that Henry Luce's name would bring more readers than Krock's, the Ambassador rounded up the publisher to write a foreword for the book.[15]

Again John Kennedy stressed that the government leaders were not at fault for having submitted to German demands at Munich; indeed, "If Chamberlain had fought in 1938, he would have been playing into Hitler's hands." [16] The fault lay in not having prepared for the German threat by rearming sooner. And he lay the blame for that as much at the foot of the English nation as on the doorstep of No. 10 Downing Street. Jack took the book's closing paragraphs almost verbatim from one of his father's letters.[17] Skimming it through, Lothian found the book to be "a very fair and accurate picture."[18]

Published in 1940, *Why England Slept* enjoyed excellent sales. Eighty thousand copies were sold, almost equally divided between the United States and Great Britain.[19] The author's proud father rushed off copies to Churchill and Laski. Inviting a kind word, he closed his cover-letter to Laski, "if you feel like writing (Jack) a line, I know he would be delighted to hear from you." The Ambassador must have been crushed by the Professor's candid response:

> *Dear Joe:*
> *The easy thing for me to do would be to repeat the eulogies that Krock and Harry Luce have showered on your boy's work.*
> *In fact, I choose the more difficult way of regretting deeply that you let him publish it. For while it is the book of a lad with brains, it is very immature, it has no real structure, and it dwells almost wholly on the surface of things. In a good university, half a hundred seniors do books like this as part of their normal work in their final year. But they don't publish them for the good reason that their importance lies solely in what they get out of doing them and not in what they have to say. I don't honestly think any publisher would have looked at that book of Jack's if he had not been your son, and if you had not been Ambassador. And those are not the right grounds for publication.*
> *I care a lot about your boys. I don't want them to be spoilt as rich men's sons are so easily spoilt. Thinking is a hard business, and you have to pay the price for admission to it. Do believe that these hard sayings from me represent much more real friendship than the easy price of "yes men" like Arthur Krock.*[20]

After Harvard Jack spent a brief stretch at Stanford Business School[21] and then, late in 1941, entered the Navy. Because of chronic ill-health, it took some doing, including a personal recommendation from Admiral Kirk to the medical examiners written at the father's request.[22] With the Japanese attack on Pearl Harbor, the United States was at war. Jack applied for combat duty, but did not receive it until 1943, when he pulled strings with his father's old friend, Secretary of the Navy James V. Forrestal.[23] Jack emerged from the war a hero.[24]

After the war, Jack worked briefly for Hearst's International News Service, but he had little success at journalism, and did not take it very seriously. Krock saw his fellow journalist in 1945 at the establishment of the United Nations in San Francisco, and recalled years later that Jack "was having much more of a good time as a young man, however, than he was as a young reporter. He was not terribly diligent there." [25] Jack could see that journalism was no career for him, and anyway, with Joe Junior gone, the obligation of carrying the family banner in politics fell to him. He had to pick it up.

EARLY IN 1945, JOHN KENNEDY CONFIDED IN HIS FRIEND "RED" FAY, "I can feel Pappy's eyes on the back of my neck. . . . when the war is over . . . I'll be back here with Dad trying to parlay a lost PT boat and a bad back into a political advantage. I tell you Dad is ready right now and can't understand why Johnny boy isn't 'all engines ahead full.' " [26] Dad was ready. Years later he boasted about how he "made" Jack take over—"I got Jack into politics; I was the one. I told him Joe was dead and that it was therefore his responsibility to run for Congress. He didn't want to. He felt he didn't have the ability. . . . But I told him he had to." [27]

Not surprisingly, as a Presidential candidate, John Kennedy denied that he entered politics to please a doting and domineering papa, or to carry out any kind of family plan. The father's imprudent boasts and the son's self-effacing parallel comments to Fay and others were all no doubt overstated.[28] There was much more to John Kennedy's entrance to politics than merely Papa's bald insistence.[29] But directly or indirectly, the entrance was the result of Joseph Kennedy's influence; his domination was basic, not operational, and despite whatever reluctance John Kennedy had, his decision was a natural one. "Just as I went into politics because Joe died," he explained, "if anything happened to me tomorrow, Bobby would run for my seat in the Senate. And if Bobby died, Teddy would take over for him." [30] There was no need for Joe Kennedy to give any orders. Family friend James Reed recalls an evening with the Ambassador, Honey, and Jack about the time that final decisions were made: Fitzgerald

> proposed a toast to the future President of the United States—he looked right at Jack—to which everyone joined in. It was not really said in any degree of levity or frivolity. It was a serious toast, really, that was proposed to Jack and I think everyone there thought that one day Jack would be President of the United States.

Interviewer: You don't know what Jack's reaction was to that?
Reed: Rather sober reaction to it, as I remember it.
Interviewer: Did his father comment on it?
Reed: No, there was no levity involved.[31]

Early in 1946 the young ex-serviceman was back in Massachusetts and began speaking publicly, a sure sign that his decision had been made. Often his talks sounded like pure Joseph P. Kennedy. At Lynn, Massachusetts, for example, he warned his audience to guard against the spread of "socialism," such as he had seen triumph in the English elections, and he admonished them to pit their faith in the old against the new. He called for Americans to make their government "the servant and not the master of the people," [32] an interesting contrast to the line for which he is most remembered. Soon he announced the office—it would be Congressman from the Eleventh Congressional District—a "safe" seat for whichever Democrat could win the primary. His brother Joe had talked about starting there.[33] Jack Kennedy often thought about his dead brother during the campaign. "I wish Joe was around," he would sometimes say. "Joe would have been governor." Or, "I'm just filling Joe's shoes. If he were alive, I'd never be in this." John Droney, who worked in Jack's first campaign, later recalled his own entrance into politics:

> *I went up to the Bellevue, up to Fitzy's apartment, and saw Jack talking to a lot of brass—commanders, Army officers—and I thought I'd had enough of that and started to leave. Jack followed me and we talked. I told him how I felt about politics and he said he had the same feeling, but that his brother Joe had been killed in the war, his family seemed to feel he was best fitted to carry on, and he said, "Sometimes we all have to do things we don't like to do."* [34]

At first "politicking" was difficult for Jack, especially among the hard element of "professional 'pols'" that was so foreign to him. Robert Lee, then a State Senator talked about as a possible contender for the Eleventh Congressional seat, recalls his first visit with his hypothetical competitor, when a neighbor brought Jack to his house: "Jack was very shy and almost afraid to talk. My first impression was that he was a very sick boy. After I stated I could not afford to aspire for Congress, he perked up." [35] Once into the race, Jack quickly picked up confidence and poise. Still seriously bothered by his wartime injuries and his chronic ill-health, he refused to be held back by physical limitations and campaigned to the point of collapse.[36] No one campaigned harder than Jack. And no one connived more persistently than his father. When Joseph Russo, a veteran member of the Boston City Council, threw his hat in the ring, the Kennedys recruited another man with the name Joseph Russo to run and so cut into the Councilman's vote.[37] When one candidate whose presence in the race was beneficial to the Kennedys decided to withdraw, an old friend of the Ambassador's left town at the last minute with the reluctant candidate's withdrawal papers in his pocket.[38] Joe Kane served as one of Jack's strategists and paid one candidate $7,500 to "stay in or get out," depending on how the contest shaped up.[39]

One story circulated that Joe Kennedy was bragging that with the money he was spending he could elect his chauffeur to Congress. Joe Kennedy was capable of making such a boast, and the statement might have been a valid one—at the Massachusetts State House, pundits took to wearing a $20 bill in their lapels, as "Kennedy Campaign Buttons." [40] The Kennedy money did flow freely. Streetcars frequently carried four Kennedy posters, explaining why four different people were voting for Kennedy.[41] Billboard space in the district was completely tied up by the Kennedys, and the John C. Dowd Advertising Agency, Boston's leading advertising outfit, saw to it that the space was effectively used.[42] Radio advertising also overpowered the opposition candidates. Leaflets and pamphlets by the many thousands were distributed, stressing Jack's war record more than any issues. On primary day every car for hire and cab in town were carrying voters to the poll for Kennedy.

Some rumors have it that Kennedy spent $250,000 on the campaign —a staggering amount for a Congressional campaign in the 1940s. Not surprisingly, Jack Kennedy vigorously denied this. But when Joseph Kennedy wanted something he was willing to pay the price, and if he thought that a quarter of a million dollars was needed, he would have spent as much again to be sure. "Joe Kennedy is used to paying for what he gets," Kane told the author.[43] "They spent a staggering sum in the congressional race of 1946," he said, adding immediately, "but Jack could have gone to Congress like everyone else for ten cents." [44]

Kane was probably right. From Joe Kennedy, Jack inherited many things besides money—things that would very likely have put him across with a dime in expenditures. Most important of these was his name, John Fitzgerald Kennedy. The Eleventh Congressional District included sections of Mayor Fitzgerald's "Dear Old North End" and all of Pat Kennedy's "Noodle's Island." These two men were remembered and revered in their old bailiwicks. Only four years earlier, Fitz had run for Senate and had carried the Eleventh Congressional District in the primary by a landslide.[45] Moreover, Jack was the son of Joseph P. Kennedy, who had himself become something of a folk hero to the many Irish of Boston. Kennedy. Kennedy. It was a magic name that opened doors. Jim Curley, Jack's predecessor as Congressman from the Eleventh, asked "With those two names, Kennedy and Fitzgerald, how can he lose?"

Besides the money and the name, being Joe Kennedy's son had other advantages. There were allies that his father could bring John Kennedy. Years later the father described his role: "I just called people. I got in touch with people I knew. I have a lot of contacts. I've been in politics in Massachusetts since I was ten." [46] Besides his political contacts, Joe Kennedy brought his son press allies. Hearst's *Boston American* had a reporter in Kennedy headquarters every day, but not in those of the other candidates.[47]

John Kennedy amassed 42 percent of the vote in the primary, a stunning victory in a ten-man race that included a seasoned mayor, a former secretary to the beloved James Michael Curley, and a popular Boston city councilman. James MacGregor Burns, Kennedy's first biographer, attributes the terrific victory most of all to the enthusiasm of Kennedy's aides and volunteers.[48] Perhaps. But what brought them into the Kennedy camp? As journalists Ralph Martin and Ed Plaut wrote, "Always in the hovering background was the smell of Kennedy money, even when it wasn't there; the sense of Kennedy power, even when it wasn't used; the hope of Kennedy reward, even when it wasn't promised." [49] When working for Joseph Kennedy's son, one works for a winner and becomes infected with the winner's psychology.

John Kennedy, not surprisingly, attributed his success to other factors than his familial influence and wealth. "The fact that I was the only veteran running was what did it," he later commented. John Kennedy worked very hard for the nomination, campaigning tirelessly. He probably worked longer and harder than any other candidate. His father was amazed with his energy—"I did not know he had it in him," he commented. His war record was played up big, and unquestionably made him even more appealing. But everyone who comments on the campaign mentions the huge expenditures and the glamor of the name.

After the primary, Jack Kennedy could take it easier. His election in the Democratic stronghold was assured, and all the more so after the tremendous publicity that accompanied the Kennedys' $600,000 gift to the Archdiocese. The day after the election, Swope wrote the new Congressman, "My crystal ball reveals you as the center of a fascinating dream—one that carries you far and high." [50]

JOHN KENNEDY'S VIEWS IN THE 1940s ON THE MAJOR ISSUES OF THE day may have paralleled his father's, but if so, his voting record and House speeches never showed it. By the time he got very far into the 1946 campaign, Jack Kennedy began speaking more like a New Dealer and less like his father. In his voting in Congress, John Kennedy supported the loan to Britain, about which his father was equivocal; he strongly supported the Truman program of massive aid to Greece and Turkey, which his father vehemently opposed; he firmly backed the Marshall Plan, which his father was attempting to deflate. His record on foreign policy for the period 1946 to 1949 was that of an "internationalist." He opposed the tax reform bill of 1947 on the ground that the legislation would favor the rich, at a time when his father was calling for tax reforms that would restore "the rich man's function." The father feared organized labor and its political power, and would surely have supported the Taft-Hartley bill; Congressman John Kennedy voted against it at every stage. Joe Kennedy was concerned about the fact that people accepted unemployment compensation while jobs went begging; Jack Kennedy favored a bill for improved unemployment benefits. Joe Kennedy wanted stiff immigration restrictions—in the interests of protecting labor, he said—while his son supported efforts to liberalize immigration quotas. John Kennedy took an inquisitional approach to the problem of Communists in the American labor movement, but that was about the only position he took in Congress of which his father might have approved. On most issues Jack followed a straight labor-liberal line that paralleled that of the Truman Administration for which his father had so little use.

Late in the 1940s, John Kennedy's "internationalist" foreign policy stands began to switch. By 1949 isolationism began a surge that climaxed in the great debate of 1951. The forces and developments that affected public opinion clearly affected John Kennedy as well. Though he was a Democrat, he began to speak out against the Administration's foreign policy in terms that must have thrilled his father and Republican leaders.[51] The time of his open break with the

Administration is significant—immediately after the fall of Chiang Kai-shek. On January 25, 1949, he began his attack with a brief statement on the floor of Congress:

> *Mr. Speaker, over this weekend we have learned the extent of the disaster that has befallen China and the United States. The responsibility for the failure of our foreign policy in the Far East rests squarely with the White House and the Department of State.*[52]

He criticized the policies of "the Lattimores and the Fairbanks"; their concern over the imperfections of democracy in China; their tales of corruption.[53] Soon after, he continued along the same vein in a speech which suggested that those responsible for the China loss be searched out and spotlighted. The speech was delivered, appropriately, at Salem, Massachusetts. He criticized the Yalta Pact for having "given" the Kuriles to the U.S.S.R.,[54] and included in the speech a slur against General George C. Marshall. He criticized Truman for not having treated Madame Chiang with greater deference. "What our young men had saved," he concluded, "our diplomats and our President have frittered away." [55] John Kennedy was speaking as a neo-isolationist and was sounding more like his father. When he addressed a Harvard University class in November, 1950, he echoed opinions which his father could wholeheartedly support. He asserted that he could see no reason why the United States was fighting in Korea; that he thought that sooner or later the United States would "have to get all these foreigners off our backs" in Europe; that he supported the McCarran Act and felt that not enough had been done about Communists in government; that he rather respected Joe McCarthy and thought he "knew Joe pretty well, and he may have something"; that he had no great respect for Dean Acheson or indeed almost any member of Truman's "Fair Deal" Administration; that he personally was very happy that Helen Gahagan Douglas had just been defeated by Congressman Richard Nixon.[56]

John Kennedy told Congress in his speech of January 25, 1949, that "This House must now assume the responsibility of preventing the onrushing tide of Communism from engulfing all of Asia." [57] But when a vigorous stand was taken in Asia, by Truman in Korea, Jack showed no enthusiasm. He claimed to be worried about the Administration's lack of concern over Europe. In February, 1951, Senator Walter George questioned Senator Kennedy on his opinion about his father's

University of Virginia speech. Jack tactfully disassociated himself from his father's "give up the world" position. He spoke in emphatic terms of the strategic importance of Western Europe, and the likely collapse of its defenses without more American troops. But he put somewhat more emphasis on his belief, which he shared with his father, that Europeans were not doing enough to help themselves. He was for European aid, he asserted, but his terms were such as to make it unlikely to be forthcoming.[58] In 1951 he supported massive cuts in foreign aid. He represented what Adlai Stevenson called "international cooperation by elocution." His position was remarkably like that of Senator Taft.

With his belief that those responsible should be "spotlighted"; his own predilection for exposing Communists; his contempt for "the Lattimores"; his feelings about General Marshall; his unrealistic conception of Yalta; and his family's connections with Senator McCarthy; it is little wonder that Jack Kennedy sympathized with much of the Wisconsin Senator's efforts. Faced with the likelihood of having to vote on censure of McCarthy, he prepared a legalistic position to be used if necessary: he would vote to censure, but base his vote upon the activities of McCarthy-aide Roy Cohn, and not upon any of McCarthy's own failings.[59] A serious recurrence of his back troubles hospitalized him at the time of the crucial vote, and he took the opportunity to avoid the explosive issue, and failed to go on record for or against by "pairing" with another absent Senator. His longtime friend Charles Spalding was with him the day he was to be moved from his hospital to Florida. "You know," Jack said to Spalding,

> when I get downstairs I know exactly what's going to happen. . . . Those reporters are going to lean over my stretcher. There's going to be about ninety-five faces bent over me with great concern, and every one of those guys is going to say "Now, Senator, what about McCarthy?" . . . Do you know what I'm going to do? I'm going to reach back for my back and I'm just going to yell, "OWW," and then I'm going to pull the sheet over my head and hope we can get out of there.[60]

By curious coincidence, it was during that illness that John Kennedy wrote[61] his second best-selling book, *Profiles in Courage.* Later he would drily acknowledge that he had omitted himself as the topic of a chapter in the book.[62] Arthur Krock, serving on the committee that selected the Pulitzer Prize winners, worked hard to get *Profiles* the Pulitzer award.[63]

Only during the period 1949 to 1952 did John Kennedy's expressed views show much similarity to those of his father. And even then his views were much closer to those of Taft and MacArthur than to those of Joseph Kennedy. His speeches lent support to the neo-isolationists —indeed Jack suggested Taft to the Junior Chamber of Commerce as a candidate for "Man of the Year"—but John Kennedy never said anything that would identify him with his father's nineteenth-century isolationism. During those years he was probably influenced by his father's views as much as was the rest of the disheartened nation. But his reactions during the period do not indicate parental influence so much as they indicate a reaction to the general mood of the country; he was affected by the national neurosis that almost paralyzed the country at the start of the 1950s.

John Kennedy recovered about the same time as the rest of the nation did. Sometime around 1952, he returned to his generally liberal line, and his father began to make fewer statements. When John Kennedy nominated Adlai Stevenson for President at the Democratic National Convention of 1956, he spoke in glowing terms of the "chain for freedom forged by Truman and Marshall." By the late 1950s, John Kennedy could state with complete honesty that differences with his father on foreign policy were total. The son, for example, advocated amendments to the Battle Act to permit giving foreign aid to Communist countries, an idea that could only have made his father gag. According to Arthur Schlesinger, Jr., no Senator did more to promote aid to India than Senator John Kennedy,[64] and India was one of the countries that the father felt should not be aided at all. By 1959 (when he was already a Presidential candidate himself) John Kennedy had either seen through to the inherent evils in McCarthyism or had recognized the political necessity of dissociating himself from the Wisconsin demagogue, and could openly indicate anti-McCarthy sentiments.[65]

On purely domestic issues, disagreement between father and son was less complete. Jack frequently looked to his father for advice and suggestions, and the two visited frequently over the telephone.[66] As a Senator, Jack declined to follow the Democratic party line and supported most of the recommendations of the conservative Second Hoover Commission,[67] on which his father served as the least dissenting member, while the father, like his son, was receptive to most "liberal" arguments that had genuine humanitarian appeal. The son was receptive to his father's opinions with regard to confirmation of Presidential appointees.[68] Still, differences on most domestic issues were great. The father supported the oil depletion allowance that the son worked to do away with;[69] Jack was sympathetic to public power proponents while his father consistently opposed public power; Joe disagreed with his son's stand on agriculture;[70] Jack opposed loyalty oaths for teachers whereas his father would probably have supported them. Though differences between father and son were great, Sorensen tells us that "both agreed they could disagree agreeably." "You couldn't write speeches for me," the senior Kennedy told the younger's "ghost." "You're too much of a liberal. But writing for Jack is different." [71]

While Joe's effect on his son's political views was slight, his effect on Jack's political fortunes was great. Krock says, "I think from the time he was elected to Congress, [Jack] had no thought but to go to the Senate as fast as he could." [72] The earliest chance came in 1948, when the first-term Congressman, scarcely the thirty years of age constitutionally required for Senators, sized up the chances of unseating Republican incumbent Leverett Saltonstall, and decided against.[73] The next chance would not come until 1952. Jack Kennedy began planning early, and by 1949 he was traveling throughout the state laying a groundwork of goodwill.

The Senate nomination in 1952 was easy to get; Henry Cabot Lodge, the incumbent Republican, was Jack's own college hero,[74] and widely regarded as unbeatable. "When you've beaten him, you've beaten the best," the father told the son.[75]

The same thing that made the nomination easy to get made the election a hard one to win.[76] Congressman Kennedy had a mixed and undistinguished record,[77] and where he could be pinned down on an issue, he differed little from Lodge. His secretary, Evelyn Lincoln, overheard a supposedly friendly Democratic Congressman belittle her hero's chances—"He'll never win. . . . Why, he's nothing but a playboy." [78] If the comment was true as to legislative work, nothing could have been further from the truth when it came to the athletics of the hustings. The contender went in with boundless energy and the will to win—traits for which his father was famed—and he had the Joseph Kennedy magic behind him. Both father and son were brimming with confidence. The elder wrote Beaverbrook, "You know me well enough to know that we wouldn't be in it if we weren't going to win." [79]

Joseph Kennedy seriously expected Stevenson to be elected President in 1952,[80] and Massachusetts had not gone for a Republican Presidential candidate in decades. He was not worried about having his son running on a ticket with Stevenson against Lodge backed by Eisenhower. What did bother the Kennedys, though, was the possible effect of the controversial McCarthy on the Massachusetts election. McCarthy was campaigning in sympathetic areas—states like Massachusetts—for Republican friends, and the Kennedys knew that a McCarthy endorsement for Lodge would hurt Jack badly among vast segments of normally Democratic voters, without being significantly offset the other way around. McCarthy, though, was grateful for the friendship and support of the Kennedy family, and acceded to the Ambassador's hopes that he "keep out" of Massachusetts. On the other side, the Ambassador managed to keep the McCarthy issue as quiet as possible by prevailing on Stevenson to leave McCarthy's name out of Stevenson's Massachusetts appearances.[81] Meanwhile, in a memorandum, Shriver pointed out to the Illinois Governor that Stevenson could point with pride to Jack's own record of anti-communism; and could compare it favorably with that of Eisenhower's running-mate, Richard Nixon:

> *Jack took the lead in Congress—Jack got the first successful citation for perjury of a Communist labor leader. That was _____ _____. He was the man who led the Allis Chalmers strike in Milwaukee during the War. That was the strike that retarded our destroyer program. Jack cited him for perjury when he testified before the House Education and Labor Committee, and the man was convicted. He was the first fellow like that who was convicted, Mr. Nixon to the contrary notwithstanding. This was in 1947. Nixon was on that Committee with Kennedy. Kennedy was the man on that Committee that got _____ —it was not Nixon. It set a pattern. Up here this anti-Communist business is a good thing to emphasize.*[82]

Robert Kennedy issued a lengthy study showing Lodge's record as "soft" on Communism.[83]

Again, his father's wealth and influence was of very great significance to the John Kennedy victory, though perhaps it was not determinative, as it almost definitely had been in the 1948 Congressional race.

Jack Kennedy's 70,000 vote victory over Lodge can be (and has been) attributed to many factors: three years of tireless campaigning; the Kennedy tea parties; the scores of volunteers; the fact that Lodge was off campaigning for Eisenhower much of the time; the money and skills of Joseph P. Kennedy and his staff. No doubt all of these factors played a part.

Joseph Kennedy kept in the background of the campaign, but his role cannot be minimized. He passed on all key personnel members, recruiting many of the top men himself. From his New York offices he brought down Ford, Landis, and Lynn Johnson, and he recruited other key men like journalists John Harriman, the *Globe's* financial editor, and Ralph Coughlin, whom the father remembered favorably from years before. Much of the campaign was planned well ahead of time in Kennedy's New York offices.[84] Joseph Kennedy was largely responsible for attracting many Bob Taft Republicans to the Kennedy team. At the father's request, one Taft diehard set up "independents for Kennedy." [85] Joe's old friend, Basil Brewer, publisher of the New Bedford *Standard-Times* and a Taft conservative, denounced Lodge as a "Truman socialist New Dealer," and gave Jack editorial support.[86] Jack carried New Bedford by a landslide, while the rest of the Democratic ticket fared relatively poorly there.[87] John Fox, publisher of the *Boston Post*, also endorsed Kennedy. Fox had purchased the *Post* with the specific intention of helping Lodge,[88] and he tried to persuade Wilton Vaugh, the *Post's* political commentator, to direct Lodge's publicity.[89] In the last days of the campaign, though, there was a change in signals. Robert Lee and Maurice Tobin were visiting the Ambassador, Lee later recalled, when

> a telephone call came through, and [the Ambassador] had to leave the apartment to make a visit with Mr. Fox, who was then the owner of the Boston Post. The rumors were that the Post was with Lodge. About an hour afterwards, when Mr. Kennedy returned, he stated that the Post within two days would openly endorse Congressman Kennedy for United States Senator.[90]

Shortly after he reached his decision, Fox received a $500,000 loan from Joseph Kennedy for his floundering newspaper. Fox said years later, "I think in view of the extraordinarily slim margin by which Mr. Kennedy became elected, that the *Post* elected him," [91] and Martin and Plaut assert that Kennedy would almost certainly have lost had the influential *Post* endorsed Lodge instead.[92] Fox's shabby reputation and Joseph Kennedy's known cynicism in such matters gave rise to rumor that the *Post* had printed a "$500,000 editorial," but Sorensen explains that Fox made the endorsement "in order to justify the *Post's* nominal Democratic affiliation at a time when he was endorsing Eisenhower." [93]

Wherever Kennedy money could help it was used. Under Massachusetts law, one can contribute no more than $1,000 to a candidate's committee, but nothing in the law prohibits more than one committee from working for a candidate. Jack Kennedy had five committees. Seven members of the family contributed the $1,000 maximum to each of the five committees,[94] and 35 Kennedy friends put in four or five thousand each.[95] Joe would have had no trouble channeling funds into the committees through business associates and underlings.

In his financial reports, Kennedy declared expenditures of $349,646,[96] a staggering amount. And these reports rarely tell the whole story. It was widely assumed that the Kennedys had spent several million dollars to elect Jack, though people close to the campaign management feel that four or five hundred thousand dollars would be a more accurate guess.[97] Money was spent in a drenching publicity campaign—newspapers, car placards, radio ads—nothing was spared. Each one of the 250,000 people who signed the Kennedy nominating papers, for example, received a letter of thanks. The Kennedys spent so much on advertising that "you could live the rest of your life on his billboard budget alone," one labor-politician asserted.[98] A lavish eight-page campaign tabloid proclaimed on the front page:

JOHN FULFILLS DREAM OF BROTHER JOE, WHO
MET DEATH IN SKY OVER ENGLISH CHANNEL

It was delivered to hundreds of thousands of Massachusetts families.

The organizational talents of Joseph Kennedy, Landis, and the staff from the Joseph P. Kennedy offices were priceless. Early in the campaign Joseph Kennedy forced out Campaign Manager Mark Dalton,[99] and inexperienced Bobby Kennedy assumed the title. But one campaign insider later recalled, "The father was the district boss in every way. He dominated everything, even told everyone where to sit. They are just children in that house." [100] Only on basic orientation did Jack fail to follow his father's plans: Joe urged Jack to attack Lodge from the Conservative's standpoint; others urged him to attack from the Liberal's stance. He did neither.

Joseph Kennedy, for the first time in his son's political career, was something of a mixed blessing in the Senate campaign of 1952. He had always had a reputation for being anti-Semitic, and Lodge supporters fanned suspicions by distributing copies of Ambassador von Dirksen's dispatches in predominantly Jewish wards. John Kennedy countered with cries of "smear" in his own campaign literature directed at Jewish voters. F.D.R., Jr., and John McCormack, both very popular among Jewish voters, campaigned extensively for Kennedy in Jewish sections. In spite of Kennedy's mixed record on things Israeli, and Lodge's generally more pro-Israel record, Kennedy ended up sweeping the Jewish wards.

Joe Kennedy was always disturbed by the political harm that such rumors might cause his sons, and vehemently denied any anti-Semitic feelings. He pointed to his many Jewish friends,[101] his membership in a Jewish golf club, and his support of Jewish philanthropies,[102] as evidence of his open-mindedness. But his explosion to Pat Jackson, berating Jackson "and your sheeny friends" for what he suspected was a sabotage attempt on Jack's campaign, and his frequent application of ethnic slang to Jews, indicated that Joseph Kennedy was not entirely free of one hundred years of Boston Irish anti-Semitism.[103]

With the father's effect on Jewish voters countered, he must be chalked up as a vote-getting asset. With his father's name, Jack was received by small-town businessmen with an enthusiasm no other Democrat could attain, and the Taft wing of the Republican Party was apt to be attracted by any son of Joseph Kennedy.

Without his father's financial and personal resources, would Jack Kennedy have defeated Lodge in 1952? Probably not. Even with his father's wealth and influence, the victory had been slim, too slim for comfort. With this in mind, Sorensen tells us, John Kennedy began his campaign for reelection the moment he had been elected.[104]

IN THE MEANTIME, THERE WAS THAT IMPORTANT DIVERSION, THE 1956 presidential convention, where John Kennedy got his first taste of Presidential politics as a contender for the Vice-Presidential nomination, and found that he liked the taste. First elected to the Senate in 1952, by 1953 Jack was already discussing his 1956 Vice-Presidential possibilities with his father.[105] According to the literature, the father was not enthusiastic about seeking any "second-place"—"For the Kennedys," he told Krock, "it's the [outhouse] or the castle—nothing in between." [106] In fact, however, in the early campaign season he was not averse to Jack's desire to run. Eisenhower had suffered ill-health, and Kennedy wrote Beaverbrook, "I do not see how Eisenhower can possibly accept the responsibility of being a candidate. Without him the Democrats have a good chance." His bet on the nominee: "Stevenson with possibly Jack [as] Vice-President." [107] Landis told the author that Joseph Kennedy encouraged his son to go after the nod.[108] When Eisenhower surprised Kennedy by announcing for reelection, though, a whole new light was shed on the picture. Joseph Kennedy expected "Ike" to carry the day and feared that if Jack were on the Democratic ticket the whole loss would be blamed on "the Catholic issue." [109] The father backed off,[110] and to interviewers he later dissociated himself from Jack's decision to go forward.[111]

With the start of the 1956 season, John Kennedy began his quest for the Vice-Presidential nomination. It was more out of a sense of competition than for any other reason—"That's where the action is," he told Sorensen.[112] In sizing up his chances, he concluded that he had the best chance of getting the nomination on a ticket headed by Stevenson,[113] who, as a divorced man and a thoroughgoing liberal, "needed" a more-moderate Catholic on his slate more than any of the other contenders. He began to involve himself on Stevenson's behalf; gave serious consideration to entering the New Hampshire Presidential primary as a stalking horse for Stevenson,[114] and sent Stevenson tactical advice on the Governor's leading competition, Kentucky Senator Estes Kefauver[115] and New York Governor W. Averell Harriman.[116] He began to build up his own image across the country by expanding his areas for speechmaking.[117] Sorensen set to work on the "Bailey Memorandum," a document to be issued by Connecticut's Democratic State Chairman John Bailey that would prove the value of having a Catholic on the ticket.[118] In a soft-sell way, his "availability" was made known to Stevenson. Shriver wrote the senior Kennedy that he had assured Stevenson that "you were 100% behind Jack, that you gave him and his campaign everything you had even if perchance you might disagree with the basic wisdom of a decision Jack might make." [119]

When the convention came, Stevenson got the first place, and then surprised everyone: instead of picking his own running-mate, as custom would have had it, he threw the decision to the convention itself. The story of the Kennedy drive for the majority has often been told with its historic images: Bobby, pleading for his brother before the North Dakota delegation with tears in his eyes; the Massachusetts delegate in the Stetson, carrying his "Texans for Kennedy" sign; the electric moment when Senator Lyndon B. Johnson switched the Texas votes to "the fighting sailor who wears the scars of battle," pushing Kennedy into a narrow lead; and then, the ultimate disappointment of the narrow loss to Kefauver, and the solitary flight of the first-time loser from the Convention City to seek paternal solace.

The father's role in the 1956 maneuverings was not great. He had friends at the convention—men like Steelworker's Union chief David MacDonald, who lent his support to Jack as a matter of family loyalty, and influential people from a lifetime of politics who received trans-Atlantic telephone calls from the father in France.[120] But by and large, Jack and Bobby were "on their own" at the '56 convention. Later, Joseph Kennedy second-guessed the strategy: "If I had been there I would have had a recess after the first ballot and that would have given us time to organize and win." [121] But the Kennedys came to realize that things had turned out for the best. One day in 1957 Jack Kennedy reminisced about Joe Junior to Bob Considine:

> *"If he had lived he would have gone on in politics and he would have been elected to the House and to the Senate as I was. And, like me, he would have gone for the vice-presidential nomination at the 1956 convention, but unlike me, he wouldn't have been beaten. Joe would have won the nomination."* Jack paused, smiled, and added, *"And then he and Stevenson would have been beaten by Eisenhower, and today Joe's political career would be in shambles and he would be trying to pick up the pieces."* [122]

It was a victory in disguise, but it was also an undisguised victory, because of John Kennedy's success at the convention in establishing himself for the first time as a national political figure. "You know," Charles Spalding later recalled,

> it didn't suddenly occur at this moment that now he should go for the Presidency because it had been talked about before. And Mr. (Joseph) Kennedy had had it in the back of his head. But it became perfectly obvious at this point that it was possible.[123]

"It was clear to me after the 1956 convention," writes Sorensen, "that the Presidency had become his primary goal, in politics and indeed in life." [124] Jack Kennedy nicely donned the mantle of the graceful loser and actively supported the doomed Stevenson-Kefauver ticket, while his brother Bobby accompanied the Presidential candidate's entourage on its meanderings—essentially to learn.[125]

BETWEEN ELECTIONS, THERE WAS THE SENATE, BUT THERE WAS SO little time to really get into that, what with the elections. From 1946 to 1960 (indeed, to 1963), John Kennedy was continually running for election or reelection, his eyes on the necessary strategies and the necessary positions, so that there was little self left for much else, other than the relaxation between contests necessary to keep the self together. Even a close family friend such as Justice Douglas was disappointed with the performance:

> . . . *he really had a second or third rate record as a Senator. I mean he got there, and, like getting into the House, it was interesting and challenging. And in his first years there he did, I think, very little. He was very much of a playboy. He had only occasional streaks of serious work and effort. . . . he didn't seem to be interested in much of anything.*[126]

He never emerged as a significant figure in the Senate,[127] and was apparently not much interested in doing so.[128] His closest senatorial friend became Florida Senator George Smathers,[129] who like Jack, was not terribly interested in affairs of the Senate.

Douglas saw a change in Kennedy around 1958.[130] By then the last contest was underway.

Joseph Kennedy's role in the 1960 Presidential campaign was significant but very far from the central role that he had played in his son's election to the House in '46 or the Senate in 1952.[131] In the years between, Jack Kennedy developed his own political instincts and his own circle of fresh, young advisors. The Ambassador was admitted to those strategy sessions held within the confines of his estates at Palm Beach and the Cape, but more as a matter of courtesy to himself than for the benefits of his counsel, and his advice was disregarded as often as followed. His father was one of Jack's few advisors who concurred in the candidate's decision to enter the Wisconsin primary[132]—Wisconsin, backyard of John Kennedy's leading rival, Minnesota Senator Hubert Humphrey, would be a tough state for Jack, but as his father looked at it, Wisconsin could prove to be the key to the whole game: "If we win that," he wrote Beaverbrook, "we will win the nomination and the election will be much easier." [133] But Jack did not follow his father's advice that he put off formal announcement of candidacy, or that he enter the California primary.[134] It is clear that the father had hoped his son would run on a much more conservative tack than Jack took.[135] According to Sorensen, none of the father's "crowd" played any significant strategic role.[136] In 1959, Sorensen told one journalist that the Ambassador had not affected any major decision.[137]

Not that the father didn't try. In important moments, the burden of maintaining the obligatory signs of respect was heavy; the candidate grew quick with his number-one supporter: "Well, we've heard from the Ambassador. Now let's discuss what we're going to do." [138] Sorensen summed up the father's role for Martin and Plaut in 1959: "Oh he calls me up twice a month with a pep talk. . . . I know the old man likes to go among his cronies and tell them, 'We're doing this or that. . . .' But he's on the outside." [139]

The father suspected as much, and felt hurt. He expressed his puzzlement to Plaut that "The office of the President of the United States is the greatest and most important office in the world. To get that office people have the least organization." The subject was changed. The Ambassador commented on his son's kindness and consideration—just look at the kindness and consideration Jack was showing to Plaut:

> I almost fainted when I walked over here this morning from my house and saw you sitting here with him. I said to Jack, "Who's he?" and he said, "A newspaper man doing a book about me." Now what good can you do him? I gave him a list this morning—500 people to phone, all important names. You should see the names on that list. . . . All of them more important than you. Yet he sat here the whole day talking to you and he didn't call any of them. I called him twice on the phone and he said sure he'd do it and hung right up on me and went right on talking to you. You have seen more of him in one day than I have seen in three days. I came up here because I heard that he would be here this week and I haven't seen him all summer and I haven't seen him yet. Can you explain why he did that except out of consideration. He is completely unselfish.

It was a long and fruitful interview, much of it published in Martin and Plaut's *Front Runner, Dark Horse*. At the end of the visit, as Plaut was about to drive off, the Ambassador had a last word for him: "The most important thing I said to you is that to get the greatest, the most important, office in the United States men have the worse [sic] organizations. The worse [sic] organizations are those of the men who are running for President." [140]

None of this is to say that Joseph Kennedy was not an asset in the 1960 Presidential election. Hurt feelings or no, he remained his son's number-one supporter. According to Sorensen's memoir, Joseph Kennedy's full part in the tale was "neither so large as the father sometimes liked to claim nor so small as he sometimes preferred to pretend." [141] Silently, he worked behind the scenes rounding up influential backers and delegates, with some success. He had long placed insurance contracts on his vast real estate holdings where they might do the most political good, and over the years he had contributed to countless political campaigns. He called in the obligations. Steelworkers' chief David MacDonald, for example, pledged to his friend's son in October, 1959, when the father first asked.[142] The father's close personal friendship with New York City bosses Buckley and Eugene Keough paid off for his son. Through them the father masterminded the coup of New York City's delegates. Active in northern New York, he wrapped up that state's large and influential delegation. He was responsible for taking the delegates from northern New Jersey out from under Governor Robert Meyner's control (for which Meyner held a grudge against Jack). He was useful in California.[143] His many Chicago contacts enabled him to bring Mayor Daley into the Kennedy fold—according to Krock and most conservative observers, a vital man in the ultimate Kennedy victory.[144] Only rarely did Joseph Kennedy break into print, as on a visit to Nevada's leading politicians;[145] he kept out of sight of newsmen, realizing that no good could come of drawing public attention to himself.

In the days before the convention, Joseph Kennedy set himself up in the Los Angeles villa of his old friend Marion Davies, Hearst's once-upon-a-time mistress, which became the retreat for family and family insiders during the hectic convention week. When MacDonald was favored with an invitation to the Davies mansion, his cocktail was mixed by a bartender named Frank Sinatra.[146] On the day that Joseph Kennedy's son received the nomination, Theodore White tells us, "he wanted no eye distracted from his son's moment of honor." [147] As the votes were being tallied, he was packing his bags; he left Los Angeles and flew to New York, where he viewed his son's acceptance speech on the TV set at the apartment of Henry Luce—his old friend, and the most influential "newsman" in America. It was not all self-effacement; Luce regarded Kennedy's call as a business visit—an unspoken request for favorable coverage of the crucial campaign ahead.[148] As they watched Jack's acceptance speech, Luce took exception to one of the candidates comments—"Oh well, now, don't you mind that," was the father's response.[149] When the conservative publisher ventured the

relatively innocent observation that his guest's son, if elected, would
be a "liberal" on domestic matters, the candidate's advocate was quick
to pick up the challenge: "Old Joe broke in with blazing blue eyes and
many a goddamn. He said 'Harry, you know goddamn well no son of
mine could ever be a goddamn liberal.' " [150]

Joseph Kennedy's self-effacement accomplished, it was back to Los
Angeles, where Jack Kennedy faced a vital decision: selection of a
Vice-Presidential running mate. It was the first big decision of John
Kennedy's Presidential phase, and the last big decision that he made in
which Joseph Kennedy participated.

According to Charles Spalding, the inner circle of Kennedy's
strategy-makers had been so taken up with the immediate task of
winning the nomination for Jack that they had given little serious
consideration to the choice of his Vice-Presidential running mate.
"Everything else had been thought about. But to think about the
Vice-Presidency would have been to acknowledge a kind of overcon-
fidence that everybody was fighting against." Exhausted but exhila-
rated, they were both physically and intellectually in a poor position to
make the important decision.[151] In such an unstructured situation, the
strong-willed man would prevail. Joseph Kennedy urged that they get
Lyndon Johnson to accept the Vice-Presidential nod.[152]

From a bald political standpoint, Johnson was obviously the running
mate who could do most for the ticket: South balancing North,
"maturity" balancing "youth," ostensible moderate-conservative balancing ostensible moderate-liberal, Bible-belt Protestant balancing
Irish Catholic. Johnson was not easy for Bobby to accept. The Texan
had sought the Presidential nod himself; he had taken the pre-convention campaign poorly and had opened wounds. An insider at the
highest levels of government since the 1930s, Johnson was an
important man among important men, and he didn't like "to be
pushed around by a forty-two-year-old kid." [153] He had told of how he
had arranged for Jack's seat on the Senate's Foreign Relations
Committee as a personal favor to Joseph Kennedy, relating the tale in
derisive fashion to anyone who would listen. Despite his personal
admiration for Joseph Kennedy,[154] in the heat of battle Johnson
himself had made unfavorable oblique references to Joseph Kennedy's
role in pre-World War II diplomacy,[155] while some of Johnson's
backers openly spoke of Joseph Kennedy's "pro-Hitler" beliefs.[156]
Privately, he was vicious in his comments on the front-runner: in a
pre-convention visit with journalist Peter Lisagor, Johnson called John

Kennedy a "little scrawny fellow with rickets," and as Lisagor later summarized it, "God knows what other kind of diseases." "Have you ever seen his ankles?" the Texan incredulously asked the journalist. "They're about so round," he said, as he made a small circular gesture with his fingers.[157] Tales like that got back to Bobby.[158]

Joseph Kennedy was much older than Robert Kennedy, and by his seventies, he had learned how men react in battle. He appreciated the strength that Johnson's presence on the ticket would lend to his son, and he saw that his son needed the Texan. He acknowledged that Johnson's selection would give liberals and labor a temporary shock, but insisted that Johnson "will look good a couple of weeks from now." [159] Bobby told an interviewer in 1964 that Jack decided to explore the possibilities with Johnson, "especially after talking to my father." [160] The Kennedys made the approach to the proud Texan.

According to Victor Lasky, Joseph Kennedy himself called Johnson to urge him to accept.[161] Johnson had always liked the father ("I like Old Joe Kennedy. He's all right," Johnson told Lisagor, while delineating Jack's ankles).[162] He later told Senator Henry "Scoop" Jackson, "They didn't want me. They wanted you. It was the old man who wanted me." [163] No doubt for much more substantial reasons than the father's interest, Johnson accepted.

Once the die was cast, grave doubts began to plague the sons. Schlesinger writes that when the clan gathered on the eve of the decision,

> There was an air of depression at Joe Kennedy's house. Jack and Bobby were sitting gloomily around the swimming pool when their father appeared at the doorway, resplendent in a fancy smoking jacket, and said "Don't worry Jack. In two weeks everyone will be saying that this was the smartest thing you ever did." [164]

When the tally was taken on election day, Johnson had held most of the South for Jack, apparently costing him nothing. It was the smartest thing Jack had ever done.

Joseph Kennedy's value as a campaign worker was considerable, his strategic advice in the important moment was crucial; his success in adding delegates to the Kennedy team was a valuable contribution. His financial contributions were equally significant.

Joseph Kennedy's confidence in the innate superiority of his own left no doubt in his mind as to whom the best man was—it was so obvious that he could see no legitimate reason for anyone to support anyone other than John F. Kennedy, and he viewed any other contender as little better than a spoilsport.[165] Given the obvious superiority of his son, there could be but one issue in the campaign, and as a patriotic duty, one had to confront that issue. As the contest with Republican Richard Nixon got into full swing, Joseph Kennedy wrote Beaverbrook:

> I came home to find the campaign not between a Democrat and a Republican but between a Catholic and a Protestant. . . . We can lick it now. But with the Baptist ministers working in every pulpit every Sunday, it is going to be tough.
>
> All I can say is that they have a hell of a nerve to be talking about freedom for the world when we have this kind of a condition right here in our own country. It seems to me that it is more important than ever to fight this thing with everything we have. And that is what we are going to do.[166]

Translated into concrete terms it meant, spend. As early as 1959, the patriarch made clear to campaign decision-makers that the family's full financial resources were available if needed.[167]

Lack of financial worries was a very great advantage to John Kennedy, especially in the primary contests against the hard-pressed Humphrey. Kennedy could—and did—out-advertise Humphrey, but that was not all, nor even perhaps the most important advantage that Kennedy derived from finances. Humphrey had to devote much of his time, energies, and powers of concentration to raising money, while Kennedy could devote all his time to campaigning. Kennedy never had to scrimp on anything—private planes were at his command at a moment's notice, and conveyed him everywhere. Humphrey, alighting from the train, would often end up carrying his own bags. Kennedy had the money to do things right; Humphrey did not. Kennedy could afford a telethon that was properly produced; Humphrey could not, and turned out a fiasco. Humphrey came out of the Wisconsin primary $17,000 in debt and, to make matters worse, Kennedy men Abe Ribicoff and John Bailey threatened potential Humphrey contributors with retaliation if they backed the Minnesota pharmacist.[168] Theodore White described Humphrey's position in the West Virginia primary graphically:

> I remember the final Saturday morning, shortly after it was revealed that Kennedy's TV expenditures alone across the state had mounted to $34,000. Humphrey had had but four hours' sleep that morning and was up at seven, prepared to barnstorm

north from Charleston in his bus on a rainy morning; at that point one of his assistants informed him that the TV stations that had booked him for a Sunday night half hour were threatening to cancel unless they were paid that day, cash in advance, for the time. It was one of the few times I have seen the temper of that genial man snap.

"Pay it!" snarled Humphrey. "PAY IT! I don't care how, don't come to me with that kind of story!" Then, realizing that his crestfallen aide was, like himself, destitute, Hubert pulled out his checkbook at the breakfast table and said, "All right, I'll pay for it myself," and scribbled a personal check of his own.

Mrs. Humphrey watched him do so, with dark, sad eyes, and one had the feeling that the check was money from the family grocery fund–or the money earmarked to pay for the wedding of their daughter who was to be married the week following the primary.[169]

Kennedy's television expenditures dwarfed Humphrey's entire outlay. And even the obvious expenditures did not begin to tell the story of the money spent. For years Jack Kennedy had been contributing quietly but generously to West Virginia fund-raising campaigns.[170] This gave him an "in" with West Virginia's most powerful political leaders—men like Sidney Christe, whose McDowell County gave Kennedy 84 percent of its vote on primary day.[171]

The Kennedy money was probably of greatest help in the pre-convention period, when money is harder to find than after a nomination is secured. No one will ever know how much was spent. The cost for Jack's transportation alone must have been staggering. In a single day Jack might appear in Cleveland in the morning, Washington, D.C., in the afternoon, and Cleveland again at night, an example of tremendous vigor—and of money to burn. Jack had a campaign office in almost every state, and men from his payroll were sent into other states to help out local politicians, and so make powerful friends for Jack. Kennedy headquarters reported that $700,000 was spent in pre-convention campaigning, representing, no doubt, the tip of the iceberg. Estimates ranged up to 20 times that amount.[172] The Gannett papers reported that during the pre-convention period, "Kennedy's well-oiled political machine had everything but a fund-raising section. Not one appeal ever was issued to raise primary money for Kennedy. Yet the report was that multimillionaire Joseph P. Kennedy spent $7 million on this phase of the campaign alone." [173] Money was unquestionably in great part responsible for the ease with which Jack got much of his delegate support; the financial advantage alone would have permitted almost any candidate to swamp Humphrey in West Virginia. No little thing—like a gift of extinct twelve-year-old Haig & Haig—was spared if it might help establish rapport in some important quarter.

After Jack was nominated, the Kennedy millions remained behind him, ready to meet any exigency as it arose. The father was ready, willing, and able to spend. "What's a hundred million if it will help Jack?" he asked Landis.[174] Certainly nothing approaching that figure was spent, but just knowing that one had that kind of willingness behind him would give a candidate the sense of security he needed and relieve him of some of the worries that must plague less affluent candidates. Given the closeness of the 1960 election, it seems likely that Nixon would have garnered a popular majority if not an electoral college victory but for the fact that the Kennedy machine never had to pause for financial oiling. Charges that the Kennedys "bought the election," however, are misleading. Even if fund-raising was easier for the Kennedys, there was no spectacular, obvious difference in the expenditures of the Nixon and Kennedy forces. And while money is invaluable for a successful political campaign, a Presidential candidate cannot be put across with money alone.

Another of Joseph Kennedy's very great contributions to Jack was his countless press contacts, and his good press relations. Sorensen says that it was Joseph Kennedy who gave John Kennedy his "flair for public relations."[175] On his 1940 book *Why England Slept*, Jack received help from Arthur Krock[176] and Henry Luce, two of his father's friends. Luce's son later served as Joseph Kennedy's assistant on the First Hoover Commission. Joseph Kennedy had countless other friends in the newspaper business, all of whom had known Jack "since . . . ," numbering among them such press lords as Cowles, Sulzberger, and the late Philip Graham of *Newsweek* and the *Washington Post*. Joe was a financial advisor to both Hearst and J. M. Patterson, the long-deceased publisher of the *New York News*.[177] His friends included dozens of rank-and-file reporters as well. In his career, Joseph Kennedy was ever accessible to the press, took reporters into his confidence rather freely, and used social flattery to win friends in the fourth estate. This kind of treatment won him a stable of journalists and his father's technique of winning press pals was fully appreciated and employed by Jack Kennedy.[178] It paid off, not only by resulting in the all-important favorable coverage, but in less apparent ways. During the West Virginia primary, for example, Humphrey passed out copies of his speeches well before delivery, so that the reporters would have ample time to prepare their stories. The handouts were always marked with a not-for-release-until-delivery tag, and were issued only for the convenience of the press. One faithless reporter turned them over to the Kennedy forces, so that Jack could immediately counter Humphrey's prepared statements with devastating—and apparently impromptu—comments.[179]

Luce was probably Jack's greatest asset in the press. When a high-school editor asked, "Senator Kennedy, do you have an 'in' with *Life?*" Jack had a cute response: "No, I just have a beautiful wife." [180] A more honest answer would have been "Yes." Though basically conservative and Republican, Luce had known and liked John Kennedy for as long as the Ambassador and the publisher had been close. John Kennedy first attracted national attention when *Life* did a cover story on the Kennedy-Bouvier romance before their wedding. Another *Life* cover story on John Kennedy in March, 1957, identified him as "the voice of the future in the Democratic Party." John Kennedy was "Luce's kind of guy; Luce liked him deep down," one prominent man from the Luce enterprises told George Snider, a young Yale researcher. "*Life* and *Time* probably helped him win the election more than any other publication." [181] At the inauguration, the Luces were on hand as the personal guests of Joseph P. Kennedy.

Again, as in the 1952 Senate campaign, Joseph Kennedy was used as a weapon against Jack, and unlike 1952, there was no large group around in 1960 that was apt to vote for John Kennedy *because* of his father. Republican campaign directors strictly refrained from dragging John Kennedy's father into the campaign; Nixon himself was responsible for the policy.[182] Nonetheless, stories about the Ambassador's days as Ambassador made the rounds of Jews, and Drew Pearson quoted from the Dirksen dispatches in his syndicated column.[183] But again, Jewish districts gave Kennedy an overwhelming majority of their votes, and wealthy Jewish contributors funnelled countless thousands into the Kennedy coffers.

Joseph Kennedy's business reputation could not have helped his son. He was widely regarded as being ruthless and greedy, a characterization which was apt to leave the public with a sour taste that might transfer itself to his son. Some of his dealings were particularly embarrassing because they seemed to implicate his sons. The *New*

York World-Telegram and Sun expressed suspicions of political influence in the arrival of the price for which the City of New York purchased the Kennedy Building on Columbus Avenue. For several days they played the story up big, with frequent use of the word "greed." They quoted one civil servant as saying, "I'm not authorized to talk on this property. There's a lot of pressure. You can understand why." Gene Gleason, the *Telegram*'s reporter, wrote that the whole affair was "a comedy of errors," and "Basic to the 'comedy' is the fact that officials on all sides have diligently avoided stepping on the toes of the Kennedy interests." The Republican *World-Telegram* was perhaps trying to place the family in as bad a light as possible, to discredit the Presidential aspirant through his family. It certainly had the effect of putting Senator Kennedy in an embarrassing position.[184]

Remembrances of Joseph Kennedy no doubt played at least a subconscious role in liberal reluctance to accept John Kennedy in 1960. Despite the early efforts John Kennedy made to cultivate the liberal and intellectual community, most of the intellectuals shunned him in the pre-convention period. Schlesinger was one of the few to appreciate him. In his *Thousand Days*, the Harvard professor paints a poignant picture of himself, scurrying aboard the bandwagon while casting a backward glance through tear-clouded eye at himself of years gone by. He felt lonely there as the rest of the intellectuals shied away from the remarkably cold and controlled young man he backed, and rallied instead 'round one of their own: Adlai Stevenson. Kennedy just seemed so calculating—like his father. The jibe "It's not the Pope but the Pop" was widely reported and variously attributed to Stevenson, Humphrey, or Truman.

The Kennedys were jealous of the passion of Stevenson's supporters. On the surface it may have seemed like the passion of those jumping young girls, jumping for Jack, but there was obviously a difference. There was a feeling of moral rightness—perhaps there really was a moral superiority—in the Stevenson crowd. The Kennedys were jealous and resentful as a convulsive movement[185] ran through the party towards the two-time loser. Jack Kennedy could visualize his father saying, "I told you that son-of-a-bitch has been running for President every moment since 1956." [186]

As the convention approached, Truman made a national television appearance and attempted to block Jack's nomination. He made a slip in referring to the candidate as "Joseph Kennedy," which perhaps hinted at part of his real objection.[187] The Kennedy campaigners plainly regarded the father as a political embarrassment,[188] and Jack thought it wise to deny Mrs. Roosevelt's charges that his father was making large contributions and had agents lining up delegates.[189] Jack belittled the substance of her opposition to him, and attributed it to "just a matter of prejudice; it's an argument she had with my father thirty years ago" [190]—an obviously self-serving explanation, with perhaps a grain of truth to it.

Despite their great reservations, on election day liberals had no one else to turn to but John Kennedy, and presumably few were willing to vote for Nixon out of spite.

How many people voted against John Kennedy because of his father is impossible to estimate. Being his father's son unquestionably cost him some votes, and gained him none. Joe Kennedy himself, in one of his rare interviews during the campaign, sized up his effect on his son's vote-getting abilities: "Me an issue? Let's not con ourselves. The only issue is whether a Catholic can be elected President." [191]

The election of John F. Kennedy as President in 1960 was the culmination of the life of Joseph P. Kennedy. One can easily imagine him speaking, in the early winter of 1960, "beguilingly about present and past," as Schlesinger describes it.[192] All that he had dreamed about had come to pass, and he was contented. Accounts of the transition from Eisenhower-to-Kennedy make scant reference to any significant role played by the President-elect's father. The father told journalists that he was consulted for suggested names for possible appointment to only one position—Secretary of the Treasury—and that he had had no names to suggest.[193] He apparently used his influence to secure positions only for Robert Kennedy and René Verdon, the former as Attorney General and the latter as White House chef.[194] Lisagor tells this colorful anecdote about the father and his relationship with his sons: John and Robert Kennedy

> were sitting in the Kennedy compound up in Hyannis Port discussing the need to really overhaul the State Department and the Foreign Service. Ambassador Kennedy, their father, was sitting in a corner presumably reading a newspaper or a magazine and not paying much attention, but he was, in fact, eavesdropping. He heard the two boys say that they were going to really overhaul this thing, they were going to get all this tired, dead wood out of there and going to put in some new, lively young people, fresh, with a lot of get up and go about them. He listened until his patience ran thin, and then he said, "Sons, I want to tell

you that I once went to see Franklin D. Roosevelt who made
much the same kind of talk that you're making now. He lamented
the State Department. He talked about razing the whole thing
and starting from scratch. He didn't do a damn thing about it,
and neither are you." [195]

Significantly, the Ambassador was only eavesdropping—eavesdropping was symbolic of the kinds of delights he permitted himself in the period between election day and his stroke. Otherwise, the terrific pride he took in his son and in his son's accomplishments was sufficient satisfaction for him. "There!" he said more to himself than to Spalding as the two watched the President-elect on television, "Now he's doing it. Now he's doing it. He's getting to look more and more like a President every day!" [196] That was enough for Joseph P. Kennedy.

The father did play some role in helping his son to maintain relations with the Republican party: both directly and through the intervention of Herbert Hoover, he worked on the defeated Republican candidate[197] to get the new Administration underway without John Kennedy having to fear from-the-start opposition from his defeated rival. Joseph Kennedy played a significant role in keeping communications open between the President and Luce.[198] But for the most part he minded his own business, and he was not a significant participant in the excitement of the John Kennedy years. He was only an infrequent visitor at the White House,[199] and while he and the President spoke frequently on the telephone,[200] he held himself in check—no small matter for a man who had made a pest of himself on the telephones of the mighty for half a century. Spalding says that the President used to consult with his father,

But his father used to wait for the call. And it was really
touching if you knew Mr. Kennedy, who was a terribly
aggressive individual, the way he would hold himself in check
and the way he would make his recommendations to the
President—I mean with all respect, in all remarkable, I thought, in
the restraint and in the manner in which he did it.[201]

For deeply personal reasons, he showed to President Kennedy a respect that he had never shown to President Roosevelt. In any case, he had long ceased to be evangelical about his policy views, and he was no longer interested in personal power. The successes of his sons were the most important things in his life, and he was content to bask in the light of their power. With unaccustomed sensitivity, he refused to let anything—including himself—jeopardize his relationship with his sons.

In spite of the legendary Kennedy togetherness, Dean Landis told the author that Joseph and John Kennedy were not very close.[202] Until the late 1950s, John Kennedy's nearly constant illnesses—from his back, his war injuries, his adrenalin deficiency—gave his father understandable sadness. In 1935, friends noticed that Joseph Kennedy had lost considerable weight, and believed the loss to be connected with the father's constant worries over his frail son John.[203] A decade later, he wept in Krock's office, sobbing his fears that Jack was dying.[204] A decade later, the worst was past, but still chronic ill-health got in the way—"He was good and sick," says Spalding, "and so sick that it was an irritation for both of them, for his father and for himself. It threatened to get in the way of everything they were trying to accomplish." [205] While the son appreciated his father's concern and love, he applied much the same distance to his father as he applied to a controversial issue. As the Presidential campaign got underway there was a difficult maturing of the relationship. Spalding says that the father

> worked as hard as anybody, but he had to make it obvious that he had separated himself from his son, that this wasn't a puppet. That probably was something that for somebody with his temperament was a difficult thing to do. It was something that probably Jack had to establish himself, early in the game—that as his son he was going to do it his own way. So that they did arrive at a wonderful relationship, but there must have been some rocky moments for each of them because they were both very strong. . . . As a father, if you've got a son who's out there seriously contesting for the Presidency of the United States and you say, "Why don't you wear the green tie?" he's obviously got some sort of a conflict. It just has to be established pretty soon that if he's going to be effective as a national leader he's totally on his own. And I think it's hard for a father to let go of his son, just out of habit. They had to establish that between themselves and that's always a little awkward.[206]

Once established, the relationship became one of growing admiration. After the West Virginia primary, the father sat with Spalding by the poolside: "He's so different," the father told Spalding,

> "from me. I couldn't have done what he's done." He was absolutely astounded at what his son achieved. "I don't know how he did it. I don't know how he did it; I never could've done

it." . . . Then he turned, and he said, "I'm like Bobby. That's the difference." And he said, "I don't understand that kid," pointing to the President in the pool, "I don't know how he did it." [207]

It was not easy to be the son of a man such as Joseph Kennedy, particularly when the father's considerable ego demands overcame him. The father's penchant for irresponsible chatter ("What's a hundred million dollars if it'll help Jack?") often proved embarrassing to his son. Senator George Smathers remembers that soon after Jack was elected to the Senate, the father stopped in for a chat with his son's friend:

> . . . *Some day I want to come down and talk to you about Jack's finances, because he has absolutely no understanding of it and won't stop and talk with me long enough for him to understand it, and I know that you and he have seen a good deal of each other and I would like to tell you something about it, so that you might tell him what the financial situation is and where his money comes from and things of that kind.*[208]

It was the kind of comment that a son might properly resent his father making.

While Jack was wisely attempting to minimize his father's influence and effect on his career, the father was maximizing with "I got Jack into politics. I was the one. . . ." Said Jack of his 1952 campaign, "The rest of the family was in Boston helping me, but my father stayed up at the Cape the whole time." Conceded the father to the same reporter, "I was in Boston throughout." [209] Jack was annoyed.[210]

After Drew Pearson publicized the von Dirksen dispatches during the 1960 campaign, Joseph Kennedy found it necessary to inform café society that Pearson had been pushed to the top of the "get" list that he planned to pull out after the inauguration. When his talk came to Pearson's attention, the journalist reported that as well, and for good measure repeated the volume-and-page citation for the German Ambassador's telegrams.[211]

John Kennedy could only have resented his father's talk. He found himself making occasional explanations: to Pat Jackson he confided, "My father's one motive that you can understand, Pat, is love of his family." And then he added very quietly, "Although sometimes I think it's really pride." [212] When Martin Luther King's father made an impolitic statement, John Kennedy reacted wryly, "Well, we all have our fathers, don't we?" [213]

At the same time, John Kennedy developed a tremendous respect and admiration for what his father had accomplished, and often talked to Spalding about it.[214] John Kennedy's unobtrusive but strong filial feelings blossomed after his father's debilitating stroke in November of 1961. When his father most needed the return of the encouragement, loyalty, and love that he had freely given to his son, the son repaid the debt in full.[215] Kenneth O'Donnell and David Powers report the last meeting of father and son:

> . . . the President landed on the lawn in the morning and spent the whole day with his father. Early the next day, when the helicopter was waiting to take him to Air Force One at Otis Air Base and the Ambassador was on the porch in his wheelchair to see him off, the President went to his father, put his arms around the old man's shoulders, and kissed his forehead. Then he started to walk away, turned and looked at his father for a moment, and went back and kissed him a second time, something Dave had never seen him do before. It almost seemed . . . as if the President had a feeling that he was seeing his father for the last time. When the President and Dave were seated in the helicopter, waiting for the takeoff, he looked out the window at the figure in the wheelchair on the porch and for the first time in all of the years that Dave had known John Kennedy, he saw his eyes filled with tears. The President said to Dave sadly, "He's the one who made all this possible, and look at him now." [216]

This is a book about Joseph Kennedy and, as such, attempts to highlight his role in the Kennedy family story. As such, it may obscure to some extent the very different person that John Kennedy was. The obvious stylistic gulf between the terribly successful but ever parochial Boston Irishman and his worldly son[217] was symptomatic of more meaningful differences between them: differing attitudes towards their backgrounds, themselves, and higher philosophy (if either ever dwelt upon it) were significant in the relationship between them and outcropped in legitimate differences in policy orientation. At the same time, many of the son's personal characteristics were clearly traceable to "the tree from whence," including what conservative commentators regard as the most serious flaw of John Kennedy and his Administration: impatience (if not impetuosity). One who worked closely with the father at his London Embassy told the author, "Joe Kennedy always wanted to 'buy it' or 'sell it.' There was that decisiveness in him." That decisiveness had a reverse side to it: "He couldn't see that non-action might be the proper course in a situation." [218] John Kennedy had the same blindness. While it would be stretching things to attribute the father's ambassadorial shortcomings to that fault, legitimate argument might be made to the effect that it was the principal shortcoming of the Kennedy Administration's approach to foreign relations,[219] where Kennedy haste made for gross national waste.

John Kennedy's quality of all-out effort; his will to win (first, his will to win election to the Presidency, and then his will to have the team he captained win on all fronts the war between democracy and communism);[220] his determination not to accept defeat, can all be attributable to his father.[221] The irrepressible self-confidence clearly came from the father, as did his self-centered view of almost everything. The deep sense of personal loyalty—given such importance as to take precedence over other values—came from the father.

Jack Kennedy's most obvious similarity with his father was his singleness of purpose. His strong though unsuccessful push to be on the Harvard swimming team was characteristic of his entire career; reach the goal was ever in his mind. The father's singleness of purpose in his race for money was equalled by the singleness of purpose with which the son sought political honors. Nothing would get him off that track—and least of all, issues.

On the vital issues, the issues about which people get overheated, Senator John Kennedy refused to become involved—indeed, to show any substantial commitment—and his decisions were regularly motivated by simple political expediency.[222]

Kennedy's stand on Senator McCarthy was the clearest example. In the mid-fifties, Kennedy realized that he would be forced to take a stand. It would not be an easy thing to do; his state was strongly Catholic, and for the most part Catholics had the reputation of being pro-McCarthy. On the other hand, Massachusetts had at least its share of McCarthyphobes, and Jack *was* a Democrat. Reluctantly, Jack prepared a statement; it was not a stand on McCarthyism, but it ended with a vote against McCarthy. It was a beautiful example of fence-straddling that permitted Jack to have his cake and eat it too. The final vote, the great showdown, however, was postponed and when it finally came up Jack Kennedy was in the hospital. He took the opportunity to duck the issue altogether. For months after, Kennedy refused to say how he would have voted on censure. By 1956 he was able to say, when prodded, that the Senate's action on McCarthy seemed "reasonable," and later he asserted that he would have voted for censure. But on one occasion, before he made that stand, he observed to a friend that his father was cooling on McCarthy. And if his father was cooling, then "McCarthy has nobody left." [223]

The only solid stand that Jack ever took on behalf of civil liberties was his stand against loyalty oaths for teachers—he supported the position urged vehemently by the well-organized teachers' groups.

John Kennedy's Congressional positions on civil rights can best be described as "wishy-washy," with appreciative sops thrown to the Southern delegation. Even Sorensen seems to acknowledge, "Oh yes, once when Jack was very very young, he had been cynical. . . ." [224] On the significant Civil Rights Act of 1957, he voted for the amendment requiring jury trials for accused violators of the act. [225] The amendment passed narrowly and reduced the bill's effectiveness to roughly zero. No Mississippi jury had ever convicted a white man of the murder of a black, and Mississippians were regarded as having still less regard for the black's vote than for his life.

Kennedy was not against civil rights; it was simply not one of those issues that he took very seriously. Krock well knew this:

> *I never saw a Negro on level social terms with the Kennedys in all my years of acquaintance with them. And I never heard the subject mentioned. As far as the boys were concerned,[226] there certainly was no sign of any kind of racial prejudice, but there was no concern I ever heard over the plight of the Negro to the extent of having such stress placed upon it.[227]*

The *Times* man reacted awkwardly to seeing John Kennedy blossom, of a moment, into a dedicated civil rights advocate in the '60 campaign. Knowledge of the lack of candor of his old friend's son was one of the factors that made him increasingly leery of John F. Kennedy.

On Church-State questions, John Kennedy's positions also reflected the biases of the constituencies with which he sought favor. The young Congressman from Catholic Boston had been highly receptive to hierarchical pressure, as when he declined to participate in the dedication of an interfaith chapel in response to a call from Cardinal Denis Dougherty; [228] a decade later, already running for President, he prominently abstained from the formal (but to Protestants, objectionable) gesture of publicly kissing a prelate's ring, and he took a firm stance against the not-unreasonable proposition that the United States maintain regular diplomatic relations with the Vatican. [229]

As a Congressman, he opposed federal aid to education unless the bill provided for aid to parochial schools. To the *Pilot*, Boston's archdiocesan newspaper, he represented "a White Knight." They editorialized "This gentleman of youthful appearance but extremely mature intelligence fought valiantly in the interests of large groups of citizens who are merely asking for their just share. . . ." [230] But when Kennedy began eying a national, Protestant constituency, he "came around" to the position that federal aid for parochial schools was "unconstitutional"—as the Supreme Court subsequently held it to be. But in 1960, when John Kennedy opposed aid to parochial schools, the legal argument in support of the "Catholic" position he abjured was considerably stronger than it had been a decade prior, when John Kennedy had embraced the Catholic argument. In the interim, the Supreme Court's "cooperative" decision in the *Zorach* case had offset the seemingly firmer earlier stance against Church-State cooperation that the Supreme Court had taken in its decision in the *Everson* case. And in the interim, John Kennedy had turned from a Catholic constituency to a Protestant constituency. By 1960 he had become—or appeared to have become—more Protestant than the parson.

Things were little changed after the 1960 election. In January, 1961, President John Kennedy asserted that there was no need for civil rights legislation. The seeming resolution in the cause of civil rights that he had shown in his campaign, disappeared. Blacks began sending him fountain pens—so that he might eliminate whole arenas of segregation with "a stroke of the pen," as he had so recently challenged Eisenhower to do. In early 1962, when the Civil Rights revolution began to "get out of hand," he sent the Attorney General, Robert Kennedy, on a world tour—perhaps so that no Kennedys would be personally associated with the moves that the Justice Department would have to take in support of the blacks.[231] Finally, Robert Kennedy could no longer avoid a personal involvement. When Negro student James Meredith sought to break the color bar at "Old Miss," the University of Mississippi, the federal courts backed him. Mississippi Governor Ross Barnett resisted. The Attorney General did what had to be done, necessarily incurring for the Kennedys the everlasting enmity of the narrower segments of Southern white society. The only possible compensation: wrapping up the black vote forever. James Meredith locked the Kennedys into civil rights. Thereafter they became the champions of the blacks. With the black revolution well underway, in the early summer of 1963, President

Kennedy asserted that civil rights legislation was strongly needed; for the first time since his campaign for election, he again asserted that civil rights was a "moral issue." [232] The Kennedys proceeded, through many words and some acts, to secure the devotion of the black community—for Jack, for Bobby, their heirs or assigns.

In the final analysis, John Kennedy seemed little concerned about moral issues; political issues and political opportunities seemed to shape and dominate him. He appeared to be as much a creature of the political forces working on him, and as little motivated by considerations of inner satisfaction, as any twentieth-century President.

Opportunism was his hallmark; considerations of election and reelection dictated his most significant moves. Everything was turned to his political (not policy) goals. Even his marriage to Jackie was turned into a political affair, with many political leaders and every Senator on the invitation list. Plenty of campaign aides were on hand.[233] That was the Joseph Kennedy approach: keep the goal in mind. "To hell" with the rest.

John Kennedy's tenure as President was brief and not particularly productive. The Kennedy legacy in foreign affairs, overshadowed by the Vietnam war, is not a happy one. On the domestic scene his effect was scant, and little of his influence has survived beyond the nostalgic yearnings sometimes evoked by campaign oratory. Whether or not there be merit to the common claim that "Kennedy didn't know how to deal with Congress," the legislative accomplishments of his Administration were unimpressive, largely because of his own hesitation in domestic affairs, so different from his attitude on the world stage, to assert himself. To his more liberal friends—men like Justice Douglas—he would explain his reluctance to push his legislative program in pragmatic terms: "Well, you forget—I've got to be reelected." Douglas could accept that explanation; "He was very conscious of that, quite naturally." [234] Election and reelection was always the most significant concern to John Kennedy, and he went to Dallas, to meet his death, as an early salvo in his reelection bid. He lived and died on the hustings.

In view of the dismal performance of Barry Goldwater, the 1964 Republican Presidential nominee, there can be no question that John Kennedy would have been reelected in 1964 with a strongly sympathetic Congress. One can only speculate as to what might have come in the years thereafter. Justice Douglas has no doubts: "Jack's problem in '61, '62 and '63 was to be reelected in '64. And the great

achievement would have been made after '64. . . ." [235] Perhaps. But
then there might have been other considerations . . . other elections.

The death of John Kennedy was surely the hardest blow in the life
of Joseph Kennedy. He had never worried about such things as
assassinations. "I don't worry," he had told William Manchester in the
better days,

> *I know nothing can happen to him. I tell you, something's*
> *watching out for him. I've stood by his deathbed four times.*
> *Each time I said good-by to him, and he always came back. . . .*
> *When you've been through something like that back, and the*
> *Pacific, what can hurt you? Who's going to scare you?* [236]

Manchester's *Death of a President* describes the effort, simultaneously
kind and brutal, made to keep the news of the President's death from
his father, and then the heart-rending futile attempts that he made at
the last minute to attend the funeral, and the loneliness of his plight.[237]
Perhaps he was a little comforted by the kind note that his dear friend
Beaverbrook sent to Rose: "May Joe find solace . . . in the assurance
that Bobby will repeat Jack's career." [238]

DRIVEN TO ESTABLISH HIS IDENTITY AMONG AND HIS IDENTIFICATION
with his much older brothers, Joe Junior and Jack, rather than his
contemporary sisters, and frustrated by the seeming impotence of size
and age in a fiercely competitive family, Robert Kennedy became a
moody youth, a moody young man, and a moody adult. His first 40
years were a protracted adolescence from which, this author believes,
he was beginning to emerge at the time of his death. Had he been
elected President in 1980, he might have been a profoundly decent
and philosophical President, in the rank of the greats. Such, of course,
was never in the cards, and had he become President, it would have
been premature.

Born in 1925, Robert Kennedy attended countless schools, notably
St. Paul's, a fashionable Episcopal school where compulsory Protestant
chapel services chafed the assertively Catholic boy; Portsmouth
Priory, where he considered entering the priesthood;[239] and, finally,
nonsectarian Milton Academy, from which he graduated high school.
He attended Harvard, but towards the tail end of World War II left to
join the Navy, where he served uneventfully as an enlisted man. No
doubt as a courtesy to his father, he was assigned to the carrier named

in memory of Joseph P. Kennedy, Jr. Returning to Harvard after discharge from the service, Bobby was more interested in proving himself on the football field than in the classrooms. With the help of after-hours coaching from classmate Kenny O'Donnell,[240] thereafter a member of the extended Kennedy family, Bobby made the team and succeeded in winning the coveted Harvard "H" that had eluded his two older brothers by playing in the Yale-Harvard game of his senior season. Years later he would recall that final game, and the rush—the adrenalin rush that accompanied Kennedy's rush at the opposing Yale man—as "one of the high points of my life." "Except for war," the then-Attorney General told a meeting of college coaches, "there is nothing in American life which trains a boy better for life than football." [241]

After a brief stint as foreign correspondent for the *Boston Post*, it was on to the University of Virginia Law School. There he compiled a middle-of-the-class academic record and some distinction as Chairman of the University of Virginia Law Forum, to which he drew distinguished and controversial speakers on government and politics from the wide circle of his father's friends,[242] including none other than Ambassador Joseph P. Kennedy himself. One of the speakers—not from the ranks of the elder's cronies—was Negro diplomat Ralph Bunche, the first black to address the forum, whose invitation to the segregated campus created a furor. Still on file in the Law School Library is the paper Bobby wrote at law school attacking Roosevelt's "sellout" at Yalta—a profoundly conservative view adopted from his father and echoed by his brother the Congressman.[243]

Bobby's experiences in the Navy, at Harvard, and in the world of the journalists, apparently lent him little polish or way with people, and, to his credit, no phony sophistication at all. He was puritanical in his views and courageous enough to be offensive about his puritanism. Withdrawn and self-conscious while intense and feisty, he appears an awkward young man in Paul Fay's remembrances.[244] His philosophical views—whether on politics, religion, or the cosmos—had not and would not for a long time mature beyond pugnacious defense of any and all Kennedy family biases.

After his education Robert Kennedy worked briefly for the Justice Department's internal security division, and then went to work for the Senate investigating subcommittee headed by his father's friend Senator McCarthy. Three years into his crusade, McCarthy was already the most controversial man in the United States. Krock, intimately associated with the Kennedy family at the time, remembers Bobby as passionately committed to aspects of McCarthy's cause.[245] Bobby's devotion to the cause was not enough, though, to make him suffer working with Cohn, the committee's chief counsel, and he soon left the committee. Like his father, Robert Kennedy had an instinct for command that made it gravely difficult if not impossible for him to function in a subordinate position. And, to make matters worse, Cohn was a younger man than Bobby, who equalled him in abrasiveness and excelled him in basic ability.

Bobby then went to work as executive assistant to his father on the Second Hoover Commission, where he learned to understand and share his father's admiration for the discredited Republican President. The work, though, was dull, and soon Bobby returned to the McCarthy Committee (which was never dull) as counsel to the Democratic minority, a position in which he would not have to serve as Cohn's subordinate. The days were numbered for the Wisconsin Senator when finally he took on the United States Army. As his popularity ran out, his health ran out with it. His allies deserted him. Loyalty, though, was the highest virtue in the Kennedy schema, and Robert Kennedy responded to its call: he visited the discredited Senator in his final illness, and followed him to the grave in Appleton, Wisconsin.[246] Like his father, he remained loyal to the memory. Gore Vidal, *mishpochen*[247] and bête noire of the Kennedy family, reported this meeting between Bobby and actor Paul Newman:

> *The conversation was amiable until Bobby asked Newman what he was doing next. Newman said that he hoped to narrate a documentary about the late Senator McCarthy.*
> *Bobby snapped: "You shouldn't allow your name to be associated with that." Newman said: Why not? It was just a collection of film clips; there was no invention. Besides, he didn't like McCarthy and he thought it was useful, periodically, to remind people of the methods used by that divisive figure. Bobby exploded: Newman wasn't qualified to judge. He knew nothing about McCarthy. Newman said that he had followed McCarthy's career at the time; he had also read Richard Rovere's book on the subject. "Well, Rovere didn't know anything about it either," said Bobby.*[248]

Rovere's book had been favorably reviewed by Senator John F. Kennedy.[249]

With the close of the McCarthy hearings, Bobby became chief counsel for Senator John McClellan's committee of inquiry into racketeering and corruption in the labor movement. It was here that Robert Kennedy first came to national attention in his own right, hammering away at unsavories in union leadership, in the process incurring the ill will of liberals who never quite forgot. Satisfied as to the moral rightness of exposure for exposure's sake, Bobby's soul was pure as he set out to embarrass and humiliate witnesses that he knew, knew in his heart, were deserving of punishment.[250] While the publicity was wonderful, perhaps even more important, the work was good for the soul.

Critics shared Kennedy's dislike for Teamster leaders David Beck, James R. Hoffa and their ilk, but objected to the McCarthy-like use of Congress's subpoena power for other than bona fide inquiry for bona fide legislative purposes.

It was at the McClellan hearings that Ahab and the whale, Robert Kennedy and James Hoffa, first met. The clever Hoffa refused to "take the Fifth," as lesser men had, and so refuse to testify on the grounds that his testimony might incriminate himself in wrongdoing. He proved equal to the interrogation. The "prosecutor" could be sassy? So could the witness. To Bobby it smarted. Professor Monroe H. Freedman, writing in the *Georgetown Law Review*, says, "From the day that James Hoffa told Robert Kennedy that he was nothing but a rich man's kid who never had to earn a nickel in his life, Hoffa was a marked man." [251] Bobby became obsessed with Hoffa.[252] There would be no forgetting.

The hearings provided the basis for Robert Kennedy's first book, *The Enemy Within*, a study of union corruption, written largely with the help of his investigative aide John Seigenthaler, a newspaper man whose research as a journalist had first brought to light the story of corruption in the Teamsters' Union leadership. One of the complimentary copies went off to family friend Beaverbrook. By the time Beaver got around to preparing his thoughts on the book for its author, Bobby was already Attorney General.

> *In one respect, of course, your book is most disappointing. After all your efforts, Hoffa still reigns in the Teamsters' Union.*
> *The battle against* The Enemy Within *has ended in a draw, or at best a moral victory. . . . Now that there is one Kennedy in the White House and another in the Attorney-General's office, let us hope that you may not only expose the wicked but bring them to justice as well.*[253]

Bobby fully intended to do just that, and did not need Beaverbrook to tell him. Perhaps Beaver knew as much, for he scratched it all out, and then sent a more friendly message.

While building a national reputation for himself, Robert Kennedy was intimately involved in his brother's political career. From the earliest days, Bobby was involved in Jack Kennedy's election efforts: first, in 1946, himself barely of voting age, heading an office in a poor East Cambridge ward; then, in 1952, as ostensible campaign manager of his brother's Senate drive ("When Bobby came in," one insider later recalled, "we knew it was the old man taking over");[254] and, finally, as the backbone of the Kennedy-for-President drive in 1960. Most of the less pleasant aspects of John Kennedy's '60 campaign are attributed to Bobby and it is clear that in his approach to his task, Robert Kennedy was neither seeking nor winning any popularity for himself. While probably John Kennedy's most valuable human asset, Bobby's hot head and seeming insensitivity was an off-and-on embarrassment for the candidate. Journalist Jim Bishop, later vetoed as "authorized" writer on the death of the President, reported Bobby's attitude to his readers as seeing everyone as "serfs on some big Kennedy estate." [255]

To Bobby, his brother was his brother—which fact, alone, made any act in furtherance of the end a moral act. David Halberstam, who developed great admiration for Bobby, writes:

Anyone, in those simplistic days, who opposed Jack was a bad guy likely to be roughly treated; and even friends found their sensibilities trampled on. A lifetime of intelligent and dedicated service to certain principles meant nothing to Kennedy if the person was somehow blocking, or likely to help block, Jack Kennedy's presidential ambitions.[256]

One such was Humphrey, whose major though far-from-last confrontation with the Kennedys came in the West Virginia primary in 1960. Several unconnected journalists told Snider that Bobby was responsible for a systematic, crass exploitation of the religious issue; that he induced his brother to inject it into every appearance, and planted stories about it himself.[257] It is impossible to believe that the Kennedys were unaware of a curious historical fact: Al Smith had carried the West Virginia primary in 1928 by a substantial margin over Missouri Senator James A. Reed, a Protestant.[258] West Virginians did not *need* counter-bigotry. Humphrey could not confront it. Even harder for him to confront was the attack made on Humphrey for not having served in the war, made by Kennedy backer Franklin D. Roosevelt, Jr.—on Bobby's prodding.[259] Even Bobby's admiring biographer Jack Newfield concedes that the Kennedys "fouled and savaged Hubert Humphrey in West Virginia." [260] Liberals leaning to Jack blamed Bobby (the good Jack vs. the bad Bobby); those who found Jack obnoxious found his younger brother noxious. With the West Virginia primary won, Bobby mellowed for the moment. Spalding tells us that Bobby "admired the way Humphrey struggled and knew what he was up against and perhaps knew how he would have felt had it been the other way around." [261] If he felt soft that night towards his vanquished opponent, it was not to last, and when at the Democratic convention, Humphrey threw his support to his yearning mentor, Stevenson, Bobby cornered Humphrey and vowed, "We'll get you!" [262]

Since Bobby was probably the key man in the John Kennedy election victory, it would have defied political tradition to "leave Bobby out in the cold," just as Presidential appointment of a brother to high office defied political tradition. If one of those traditions were to be defied, there could be no question as to which one it would be. The only question was where to put Bobby. The Ambassador had considered having Bobby appointed to fill Jack's unexpired Senate term,[263] but when Jack felt out his brother on the possibility, as a matter of pride Bobby was adamant against: "Never! The only way I'll go to the Senate is run for it." [264] The President considered appointing him Under Secretary of Defense behind some "Establishment" name, giving him a little experience in the Defense Department, and then after a year moving him up to Secretary of Defense,[265] the number-two position in the Kennedy Cabinet. Bobby liked the idea.[266] But it was obviously out of the question: the father pointed out that no one should be asked to serve in a Presidential appointment with the President's brother as an underling.[267] Joseph Kennedy had a suggestion: Attorney General. It was really the obvious spot, and one that had been in Kennedy minds for years. It was not all spoof when Eunice in the late '50s had laughingly looked forward to the day when "Bobby we'll make Attorney General so he can throw all the people Dad doesn't like into jail. That means we'll have to build more jails." [268] The father was enthusiastic.[269] He knew there would be charges of dynasty-building; he was prepared; indeed, as Halberstam puts it, "Nothing would have pleased him more than to have founded a dynasty." [270] Advice from all fronts was adverse[271]—even from Justice Douglas,[272] a friend but also a civil libertarian, who perhaps secretly hoped that someone more sensitive to "other sides" would be

Attorney General. Finally the Ambassador suggested that the President "try it out in the press" by floating a trial balloon. He did. "When the negative outcry was loud but not deafening he decided to heed his father's advice," says author Victor Navasky.[273] According to the father,[274] Bobby himself was very reluctant—"He fought this nomination, fought it until he drove Jack and me crazy." [275] Apparently their will was stronger than Bobby's: he took the job.

The President knew the appointment would not be well-received. When asked how he would announce it, he mused, "Well, I think I'll open the front door of the Georgetown house some morning around 2:00 A.M., look up and down the street, and, if there's no one there, I'll whisper, 'It's Bobby.' " [276] His expectations were fulfilled; reactions were almost universally adverse. The appointment was an obvious departure from the President's announced intention of appointing purely on the basis of qualifications and not of nepotism, and the *New York Times* called it so.[277] ("Nepotism, my foot!" the father exploded to Bob Considine. "Why would anybody think that Bobby needs a job?")[278] Republicans pointed to his limited legal experience and complete lack of courtroom work. Liberals, remembering his connection with the McCarthy and McClellan hearings—pointed to what they regarded as his "dis-qualifications." [279]

Bobby quickly disarmed his critics by picking as his assistant attorneys general and department chiefs one of the most able and distinguished collection of lawyers to ever serve simultaneously in the Justice Department. The reputation of the Department under Robert Kennedy has remained excellent, albeit reduced since publication of Navasky's incisive study, *Kennedy Justice*. Attorney General Robert Kennedy did not improve his reputation with liberals, though, as he fought vigorously on behalf of wiretap legislation; personally approved the obscenity prosecution of Ralph Ginsburg,[280] controversial publisher of by-today's-standards tame *Eros* magazine; turned the full force of government to settling his score with James R. Hoffa; and at least by inspiration (and according to J. Edgar Hoover, by expressed direction) set the federal government on an out-of-hand "bugging" jag that extended as far as the phones of the likes of Martin Luther King, and that lasted until Johnson's Attorney General Ramsey Clark turned the earphones off. One government associate told Gore Vidal, "It's not as if Bobby were against civil liberties. . . . it's just that he doesn't know what they are." [281]

Bobby's stop-at-nothing approach to "getting" Mafiosi and other "traditional" criminals was nowhere to be found in dealing with the problem of civil rights. He was hampered by F.B.I. intransigence; by the "gentlemen's mentality" at the highest staff level; and, most of all, by his own priorities. A social illiterate, he explained to Newfield that when he became Attorney General, "I didn't lose much sleep about Negroes, I didn't think about them much, I didn't know about all the injustice." [282] And so, he put his "activist" staff into the Criminal Division or the "Get-Hoffa Squad," and "proceduralists" into the Civil Rights Division. [283] His basic strategy with Southern governors was to win minimal compliance in order to keep peace; in organized crime, it was to exploit to the maximum every possible alternative. [284] Where civil rights was concerned, Robert Kennedy showed remarkable, uncharacteristic hesitation, almost ambivalence. Blacks became impatient and were unimpressed by his ostentatious resignation from the segregated Metropolitan Club—on the heels of the resignation of the family's Massachusetts competitor George Cabot Lodge. [285] Robert Kennedy was not unsympathetic to civil rights—Navasky, who is critical of the Department's moderation in the field, credits him as one of the more positive forces for civil rights in his brother's circle. [286] But it took years before he learned to identify the Bull Connors of America with the James Hoffas. Then Robert Kennedy would become a civil rights radical.

Robert Kennedy's role in his brother's government, of course, was both less than and very much more than, Attorney General. The day-to-day operations of the Justice Department were overseen not by Bobby but by Byron "Whizzer" White, [287] while Solicitor General Archibald Cox served as the President's chief legal advisor. [288] As department head, Robert Kennedy set the Justice Department's moral tone, but he avoided confrontation with the Department's two traditionalist bulwarks, his detective, Hoover, and his lawyer, Cox, [289] so that even in moral tone his influence was watered down. On the other front, the Attorney General was clearly his brother's chief confidant, operative lieutenant, and policeman of high-level adherence to the "party line." [290] He was the Administration's principal patronage dispenser. As overall "straw boss" of the Kennedy Administration, his intervention in the problems of departments other than Justice was intimidating. [291] The President's first order in crisis was "Get Bobby." [292] When Dominican dictator Rafael Trujillo was assassinated, President Kennedy was away in France. *Time* reported that:

> *Bobby moved into a command post on the seventh floor of the*
> *State Department to oversee the implementation of a plan for*
> *U.S. support of anti-Trujillo, anti-Communist Dominicans. He*
> *okayed a move to station U.S. Navy ships near the island in a*
> *show of force. Recalling that period, President Kennedy today*
> *acts as if it had been the most natural thing in the world for*
> *Bobby to take over. "Oh yes," he says. "That's because I was out*
> *of the country." [293]*

There was at the time a Vice-President, one Lyndon Johnson, who like Bobby, would remember.

The less one liked the Kennedys, the earlier one concluded that Robert would seek to succeed John upon completion of the President's two terms in 1968. Early in the John Kennedy Administration things seemed to be pointing in the direction of the grooming and building up of Bobby for the inevitability: Bobby's role in clearing party patronage; his increased involvement in foreign affairs; the President's acknowledgment that it was "quite likely" that he might move Bobby to a different department; the eclipse of Lyndon Johnson. Historians pointed to the role of a retiring President in the selection of his party's successor-nominee, and after the 1962 Teddy-Eddie Senate race, no one could doubt the possibility that President John Kennedy might permit family loyalty to take precedence over such competing interests, if any, as he might feel in 1968. "We all worked for Jack and we have to work for Teddy," Joseph Kennedy had told his Washington sons in 1962. The lesson lingered. "We all worked for Jack and we have to. . . ."

Realizing that the speculation was unfriendly and potentially harmful, at first Bobby would emotionally deny Presidential ambitions—"This idea is so obviously untrue that it's foolish even as rumor." [294] Then, as if to discourage the dynasty speculation, the Kennedys began to encourage talk that Bobby would seek the comparatively minor office of Governor of Massachusetts. No one could resent *that*. Friendly journalists like Stewart Alsop reported that the governorship was earmarked for Bobby.[295] Bobby himself suggested it at times.[296] By 1963, family members might acknowledge the remote possibility that maybe, some day, Bobby might make the big run, but the "maybe someday" was tacked onto the Massachusetts governorship, and was at least a term removed from the termination of the Presidency of John Kennedy. One told a *Newsweek* reporter:

Bobby will quit the Cabinet in 1964 to run Jack's campaign. Then, in 1966, he'll run for governor of Massachusetts. . . . By then, we'll have the governor's term upped from two to four years. Bob will pledge himself to serve the full four years and mean it. He'll clean up the mess in Massachusetts, run for re-election in 1970, and then be ready to run for the Presidency in 1972.[297]

Sacrifice the advantage of having the incumbent President pressuring convention delegates in 1968? Knowingly wade into the tar pit of Massachusetts corruption? Risk having to buck an incumbent Democratic President in 1972, and all the other hurdles that time might interpose? For someone born and bred in politics, and trained to shoot for the top, it didn't make much sense. The picture seemed increasingly clear: 1968 would be the year. Jack would not have to apply much pressure: courtiers would spearhead the "Draft Bobby" movement; Bobby could then "accede" to the demands of the nation, and the people would do the rest for their favorite family.

The speculation died with the President at Dallas.

Newfield tells us that "During the months following the death of his brother, Robert Kennedy almost certainly experienced the classic identity crisis most of us go through during adolescence"; suffered the survivor guilt of the Japanese *hibakusha;* "and when Robert Kennedy finally awoke from his long night of mourning, his collar a size too large, he began to will himself into an avatar of his martyred brother." [298] Many pages later, "He was, from the time he woke up from his trance of grief in 1964, a candidate for President of the United States." [299] Krock, who knew Bobby from the cradle and had watched him grow like an uncle would, seems to see it somewhat less sympathetically in his simple conclusion that Robert Kennedy claimed the Presidency "as his rightful heritage." [300] Newfield sees only love and admiration for Robert's dead brother the President (and surely no cynical angle at all) in the fact that:

In his public speeches he quoted his brother with an almost morbid obsession. He started employing his brother's characteristic gestures—one hand thrust in his suit pocket, the other jabbing the air, crooked index finger extended. He began smoking the small cigars his brother favored. He began consulting his brother's circle of intellectual advisers. He let his hair grow longer. He filled his office with memorabilia of his brother. In a cathartic five-day effort, he climbed 14,000-foot Mount Kennedy in the Canadian Yukon.[301]

William V. Shannon brushed aside his tears and saw things a little clearer when he wrote that while the climb of Mount Kennedy "held a great deal of emotional significance for him . . . his concern for the private symbolism did not inhibit him from the public exploitation of it." [302] While helicopters full of news and motion picture photographers followed Bobby's tortured climb (no less so by virtue of his being roped between the first two Americans to scale Mt. Everest), Bobby attained the summit of Mt. Kennedy, and there, to be seen in *Life* magazine, performed a macabre kitsch ceremony featuring the burial of memorabilia including three PT-109 tie clasps.[303]

Robert Kennedy's inner turmoil was perhaps greater than that of most mourners by virtue of the closeness and bonds of loyalty between himself and his brother. At the same time, he wanted full press coverage of that inner turmoil. It was neither spontaneous me nor solitudinous I. It was mileage.

Whatever one's attitude, friend and foe would agree with Newfield that "He was, from the time he woke up from his trance of grief in 1964, a candidate for President of the United States."

The situation facing Presidential candidate Robert Kennedy early in 1964 was not a pretty one: that man Johnson would occupy the office at least until 1968; in all likelihood until 1972. Any effort to unseat him prematurely would probably mean the end of the political career of anyone foolish enough to try. To remain a "viable candidate" until Johnson relinquished the office would not be easy. The only sure way was obvious: become that man's Vice-President, and so, logical successor, until such time as the way was clear. Next best alternative: seek and hold high office from some "kingmaker" state. Bobby tried the one first and then the other. There was never another word said about the governorship of Massachusetts.

In and of itself, the Vice-Presidency was not an attractive office. Shannon writes that Bobby

> recognized that [Vice-President] is inherently an empty office: "There isn't anything you can do in the Vice-Presidency . . . not one damn thing . . . that you are not told to do." It also galled him to accept second place under Lyndon Johnson, whom he personally disliked. But in the nuclear age, the importance of the second place has increased because no man who is only one heartbeat away from control of the H-bomb can be counted insignificant. Moreover, since Johnson had suffered a coronary and other illnesses, the statistical chances of succeeding to the Presidency in the next four years were better than normal. To

*become Vice-President would consolidate Kennedy's position as
the second most powerful man in the Democratic Party and the
heir apparent. To allow any other man to get that position would
complicate his struggle to succeed Johnson later.*[304]

Bobby made his availability known in every way possible—short of
actually asking Johnson for it. That would have been too difficult.

Johnson didn't want him. There were surely more reasons than one:
he wanted to "win on his own"; like John Kennedy, he did not want
anyone in his inner circle with a big national following of his own; and,
most of all, the vast and long-standing reservoir of ill will between
himself and "the little snot" that was more of Bobby's making than his
own. From the time of the President's assassination, Bobby and the
Kennedys had done nothing to improve relations with the man that
now held the power. Almost immediately after Johnson's ascension,
"Bobby for Veep" boomlets began, apparently inspired by Paul
Corbin, a "Kennedy-family man" at the Democratic National Committee,[305] which Johnson could only have taken as a hostile act aimed
at depriving himself of the Presidential nominee's right to select his
own running mate. The Kennedys pointedly declined to participate in
his Administration's official functions—even those planned in honor of
John F. Kennedy—which pundits attributed to (and Johnson no doubt
took to be) an unwillingness on the part of the Kennedy family to lend
an aura of legitimacy to John Kennedy's successor. Much of the
ungenerous private talk about Johnson so common in the extended
Kennedy family, and apparently encouraged by Bobby, got back to
the new President. "All that boy has done since I became President,"
Johnson told a friend, "is snipe at me." [306] He wouldn't have
Bobby—certainly not unless he really needed him. And with Goldwater as his probable opponent, Johnson didn't need Bobby.

Even before Johnson summoned Bobby in July, 1964, to tell him
that he had found it "inadvisable" to have Bobby on his slate, Bobby's
name had been mentioned as a possible candidate for Senator from
New York. Bobby had denied any interest.[307] With Johnson's intentions clear, there was a change in plans. New York Democrats did not
seem to have anyone that looked particularly strong—unless it were
New York City's "Reform"-group oriented Mayor Robert Wagner—
and party bosses were eager for a Kennedy, both as a foil to Wagner
and to win. The "reformers" were aghast at the suggestion of
Bobby-for-Senator and struggled covertly and unsuccessfully to find a
candidate of their own. Stevenson, spiritual leader of the city's reform

movement, was said to be livid.[308] In an editorial captioned "But Does New York need him?" the *New York Times* asked why it was New York's burden "to rescue him from non-office." [309]

The Senate held little interest for Bobby,[310] but his name had to be kept politically alive indefinitely, and in any future Presidential convention, the New York delegation would be crucial to whatever outcome. The decision was to go forward. Promptly, Bobby resigned his spot on the Massachusetts delegation to the Democratic National Convention.

Robert Kennedy's 1964 Senate campaign against the respected but unspectacular incumbent, liberal Republican Kenneth Keating, was poorly organized for a Kennedy campaign, and intellectually uninspired. Liberals and reformers—including the Senior Arthur Schlesinger—largely deserted the Democratic nominee in favor of Keating. While both camps employed questionable tactics the director of the bipartisan Fair Campaign Practices Committee zeroed in his criticisms on the unfairness of the anti-Keating literature.[311]

Bobby's principal issue was Kennedyism. Stephen Hess calls the campaign a typical gathering of the Kennedy clan. Rose went back and forth between New York rallies for Bob and Massachusetts rallies for Ted, delivering substantially the same speech. It went something like this:

> *The Presidential days were cut short. Jack's enthusiasm, liveliness, ability, and faith are no longer with us. But he had bequeathed to us a wonderful legacy of purpose and of courage. Now we have [Bob/Ted] to whom he entrusted his most ardent thoughts and ideals for which he worked so hard.*[312]

She spent her fiftieth wedding anniversary in New York delivering parallel addresses.[313] Joseph Kennedy would have wanted it that way.

As much as possible Bobby affected his brother's ways and appearance.[314] Like his brother, he cluttered the texts of his speeches with the sayings of the great, and especially those of his departed brother, but, as Hess puts it, "the quotation marks stuck out awkwardly, like face cards shuffled into a deck of pedestrian thoughts." [315] To counter the carpetbag issue, Bobby and the press made a sentimental visit to his boyhood home in Bronxville, accompanied by his young nephew John-John, aged three, who was supporting his uncle's candidacy.[316]

Given the overwhelming majority of registered Democrats in New York and Goldwater's predictable debacle, Bobby attempted as much as possible to stick with the national ticket. Running as "third man" on a Johnson-Humphrey-Kennedy slate, inferentially he stressed party regularity to the majority Democrats. The wisdom of his decision was borne out when the votes were counted: Johnson's New York plurality dwarfed his own narrow margin. But the *New York Times* was mistaken when it wrote that he had been swept in on Johnson's coattails.[317] To a greater extent, he had been borne to victory on his brother's shroud.

Bored with the Senate[318] and its institutions, Senator Robert Kennedy refused to be intimidated by its unspoken rules. His brother Ted had conquered reluctant "Club" members by his silence, waiting well over a year before speaking on the floor. Senators liked that; "shows he knows his place." Unlike Ted, Robert Kennedy never distinguished himself as a "working" Senator, and his seeming eagerness to be on and out of his "Senate-phase" chafed the traditionalists who controlled the inner workings of the august body. Three weeks in office, he made his first speech.

Even during his brother's Administration, Robert Kennedy was becoming less conservative in his own policy orientation.[319] In his Senate campaign, such content as his speeches had showed a more prominent liberal slant. As Senator, he surrounded himself with left-oriented staff and appeared increasingly liberal—sometimes imaginatively so—and towards the premature end of his career, occasionally radical. His change was no doubt a mixture of conviction and expediency. Right-oriented support for Bobby was out of the question and Lyndon Johnson stood firmly astride the broad middle of the American political spectrum. There was nowhere for Bobby to move but left.[320] The years 1964–1968 showed Bobby in a flurry of activity; the emerging image of an overextended, inwardly-troubled liberal was good or bad depending on one's slant and biases. Whatever else his Senate career was, it was also a continual sparring for advantage with a host of political rivals and potential political rivals: Wagner, Wagner's successor John Lindsay, fellow New York Senator Jacob Javits, New York Governor Nelson Rockefeller, and, mostly, Lyndon B. Johnson.

Robert Kennedy's Senate office was perhaps the most active one in Washington, and unquestionably so on the political front. Despite his involvement, he threw no effective weight in the selection of candidates or the campaigns for New York City mayor in 1965 or New York governor in 1966; on the overview, his forays into New York City

Damon Runyon and Walter Winchell.

Through the years, Joseph Kennedy had fallings-out with
a great number of once intimate friends. Two of those with
whom he remained close to the end were Arthur Houghton, a
friend from movie days, and Father John J. Cavanaugh,
President of Notre Dame, shown in a 1955 shipboard photo.

"The Holy Father did me the great honor, which I think rarely, if ever, has been accorded anyone, by having his picture taken with me. I am sure that this means he approves of the life you and I lead," Kennedy wrote Beaverbrook.

"I can't help it that I married into an S.O.B. of a family,"
Kennedy told Roosevelt. Here he is shown with the
chief S.O.B. on Honey's seventy-seventh birthday.

Greeting at the airport, 196

At an embassy party, Fourth of July, 1939.

Joe, Jr., and Jack, 1938.

The sailor is Bobby, 1946.

Kennedy points out the highlights of the New Yo[rk] skyline to Teddy, 1957.

Kennedy's favorite daughter, Kathleen, served with the Red
Cross in England during the war. Her death in an airplane crash
in 1948 threw her father into a profound depression.

1953 was a year of weddings . . .

Jackie

Eunice

The baseball fan at the stadium, in better days and worse.

Bobby's Joe III and Kathleen, greeting Grandpa at the airport, 1960.

Playing peekaboo with Teddy's Kara, early 1960s.

The President-elect and father, 1960.

Seated behind the Ambassador is niece Ann Gargan, Ethel Kennedy at the steering wheel, miscellaneous grandchildren, 1961.

A man of many faces . . .

1961

1941

57

1950

and state Democratic party infighting were neither notably successful nor particularly significant. None of the Kennedys ever took much sustained interest in their party as an institution—either in cleaning it up or in building it up—and Bobby was no exception. His support for Brooklyn power-broker and Wagner-foe Stanley Steingut in the latter's 1965 quest for speakership of the New York State Assembly, in preference to what the Kennedy literature portrays to have been a more routine hack, could not qualify as any "reformist" crusade. Robert Kennedy was never part of the New York "Reform" movement except insofar as he might incorporate it into the R.F.K. movement through stratagem like his sponsorship of the Sam Silverman campaign for New York City surrogate in 1966. In truth, he was more interested in national politics.

Long before 1968 prospects seemed within the realm of possibility, Robert Kennedy was staffed and organized like a Presidential candidate; in 1967 Shannon compared Kennedy's Washington office to "a campaign headquarters along about the third week in October." [321] The *New York Times* reported in 1966 that the Robert Kennedy office generated "the largest quantity of continuous handouts that flow from any official quarter in Washington," [322] and his "major" addresses were given all of the advance publicity of a championship boxing match. The Kennedys have always used foreign "study tours" (speaking trips) as a source for publicity, and Robert's well-touted travels abroad were reported in the at-home press more thoroughly than speaking swings on the domestic trail would have been. At home campaigning in the 1966 off-election for hopefuls across the nation, Bobby was preceded by advance men to emphasize his role and popularity, sometimes to the embarrassment of his "beneficiaries." [323]

According to the literature, Edward Kennedy came to regard 1968 as "Bobby's year." It seemed so unlikely a year for Bobby, that as late as the autumn of 1966, he let his availability be known as a possible 1968 Vice-Presidential running mate for Johnson,[324] notwithstanding the continued off-again-on-again feud between himself and the Texan. Two factors impelled him to make 1968 his year: Vietnam and Eugene McCarthy.

According to Bobby's confidants, William vanden Heuvel and Milton Gwirtzman, Robert Kennedy had had his secret doubts about American Vietnam policy even during his brother's Administration.[325] Given Bobby's tendency to think of people as "goodies" or "baddies," it would not be surprising had he classified South Vietnamese dictator

Ngo Dinh Diem as the "baddie" that he was. If he did so, however, he imposed on himself the same blind public adherence to Administration line that he imposed on others. As his brother the President escalated the war from hundreds to thousands, Bobby himself became known in Washington as "Mr. Counterinsurgency" for his compulsive interest in counter-guerilla military tactics.[326] He developed a deep respect and considerable admiration for "hawkish" General Maxwell Taylor,[327] as much as any man the architect of the Kennedy-Johnson Vietnam policy, and he became an enthusiastic partner in his brother's Vietnam policy.[328] His jingoist talk like "the solution [to the Vietnam problem] lies in our winning it. This is what the President intends to do," [329] would not be noted today were it not for the subsequent change in his position.

In February, 1965, the United States was forced to make a major decision in its Vietnam policy. The collapse of the South Vietnamese government, Communist victory, and total defeat for the American cause were imminent. The United States would either have to go in heavier, much much heavier, or call it a day and a defeat. Johnson turned to his advisors—the same men to whom John Kennedy had turned. If the President thought of Robert Kennedy at all, his thoughts would have encouraged him to take the "courageous" route. We have every reason to believe that John Kennedy would have made the same decision that Johnson made: to go in still deeper.[330] From then on, there seemed no stop to the escalation, as "powerful men with powerful vanities were sucked deeper into avoidable mistakes." [331]

Robert Kennedy was not an early man in the peace movement. Many senators preceded him: first Gruening and Morse, then Fulbright, Aiken, Mansfield; George McGovern, perhaps the Senator that Robert Kennedy most respected.[332] No doubt Bobby's feelings towards Johnson affected his attitude towards what he might rationalize to be "Johnson's war." [333] Finally Robert Kennedy joined in—probably the first Senator with a sizable national following to side with the "peaceniks." [334] His matured position developed gradually: his first "dovish" speech in 1966 calling for a coalition government in South Vietnam[335] was an advance towards the pro-peace position; followed by a retreat back towards the Johnsonian direction; followed by an advance . . . a retreat . . . ultimately placing Robert Kennedy by the end of 1967 close to the forefront of the anti-war position.

Largely because of Robert Kennedy's willingness to be associated with it, "dovishness" became increasingly respectable in the year

1967. According to most of the literature, it was Allard K. Lowenstein, gadfly of the New York left, who first sought to mobilize the nation's increasing dovishness behind some yet-to-be determined "peace candidate." With all of his idealist's naiveté, Lowenstein foolishly believed that if a dove candidate did well against Johnson in the Democratic primaries, Lyndon Johnson, the President of the United States, would withdraw rather than risk ultimate defeat. He approached Bobby and urged him to make the run. Kennedy knew Lowenstein well and favorably, but the amateur's suggestion could not seriously be entertained: the odds against defeating an incumbent President in his own party were astronomical; Bobby's chances for '72 would be wasted on a hopeless cause; his political career would be ruined, like that of some Harold Stassen. That was not the kind of battle that Kennedys choose to make. Lowenstein went to others, and others, and finally to Minnesota Senator Eugene McCarthy. McCarthy demurred: it was a good idea, but the candidate ought to be Bobby.[336] Bobby's position clear, McCarthy took the challenge.

Unwilling to risk his career on a hopeless run for himself, little wonder that Bobby should have been unwilling to risk it by endorsement of another, and especially Eugene McCarthy. Cool, arrogant in a more restrained manner than Robert Kennedy, McCarthy had high-hatted the Kennedys, all of the Kennedys, ever since they had had contact and in every way possible: personally, intellectually—McCarthy even posed as a more ethereal Catholic.[337] McCarthy's personality was the antithesis of Bobby's. McCarthy had little real interest in power—he represented the platonic truth that only the grubby were interested in power. Bobby was interested in power. Intensity—even in his own staff—bothered McCarthy, as if offending some concept of balance. Bobby was intense. McCarthy's early campaign reflected the differences between them: it was strikingly low-key, poorly organized, horribly small-time, and seemingly uninspired, largely because McCarthy strove to keep it unemotional.[338] Bobby was emotional. Bobby recalled McCarthy at the 1960 Presidential convention. A key man in the "Stop Kennedy" crowd, McCarthy had arrived as a Johnson supporter, and then swung to Stevenson—anyone but Kennedy. His speech nominating Stevenson for Jack's office had been the electric moment of the whole convention. The galleries had gone wild—wild for Adlai. A Kennedy doesn't forget that kind of thing.

It would have been less than human for Bobby not to have hoped for the failure of a man such as McCarthy in a battle that he himself had viewed as unwinnable. As if consciously trying to sabotage McCarthy, he advised McCarthy not to enter the Massachusetts primary, where a private Kennedy poll showed McCarthy's popularity to exceed even Bobby's own, and instead to enter the New Hampshire primary, where another Kennedy poll showed impending disaster for McCarthy.[339] When an inquirer asked, "Senator Kennedy would you support President Johnson if he is the nominee?" Bobby had a ready answer: "That's easy, but don't ask me whether I would support McCarthy." [340] Soon after McCarthy's campaign in the New Hampshire primary got underway, the press reported that despite Bobby's agreement with McCarthy on foreign policy, he was supporting Johnson.[341]

Right away McCarthy's campaign in New Hampshire seemed to be catching hold—in spite of McCarthy's reserve. An ill-timed step-up in the war had its effect on wavering voters (and certainly on Robert Kennedy), rebounding to McCarthy's advantage. No one expected McCarthy to out-poll the President in "hawkish" New Hampshire, but he started to look surprisingly popular there. Perhaps the President *could* be unseated. As Bobby watched the army of McCarthy volunteers marching on New Hampshire he saw something very disturbing: it was *his* army—the young, the idealistic, the ones that his brother had inspired, and to whom he himself had preached courage and morality on the college campuses—deserting him and enlisting with his new rival Eugene McCarthy, rival for the political block that he had been courting, and rival for the hearts of the young. Leadership of Bobby's natural constituency was passing to Eugene McCarthy— perhaps forever. Ten days before the New Hampshire primary Lowenstein called Bobby on the telephone: "We're going to do it! We're going to do it! It's the beginning of the end for Johnson." [342] There was an awkward coolness on the other end of the phone. To Bobby it was a taunt.

He began having second thoughts. His "older" advisors, Sorensen, Pierre Salinger, and the crowd from the John Kennedy Administration, counseled restraint. Wait. '72. Teddy counseled wait. "I don't give a damn about '72. I care about Vietnam," [343] Bobby is said to have countered with emotion; marginally true, and more nearly rationalization for the complex forces working within him. The younger men in his own office urged him to "go."

When the New Hampshire votes were tallied, McCarthy had scored a remarkable triumph (albeit not a victory; Johnson received most of the delegates). He had run close to Johnson among the Democrats, and counting cross-over Republican votes, had out-polled the President of the United States. Newfield tells us that "in his own mind" (Newfield's phrase) Bobby had decided to enter the Presidential contest a week before the New Hampshire primary, and had tried unsuccessfully to get word to McCarthy through his brother Ted that Bobby would "probably" (again, Newfield's word) enter subsequent primaries.[344] The die was no doubt hardening prior to the tally in New Hampshire; it might still have been remelted. On the heels of McCarthy's stunning showing, Robert Kennedy announced, as Krock puts it, "that he would contest the nomination from the 'moral' vantage point that Eugene McCarthy had fought for and won alone." [345] To the McCarthy forces, "It was like a jackal coming to feast on the carcass after someone else had made the kill." [346] Later Bobby would acknowledge to friends that had McGovern been the candidate, rather than McCarthy, he would never have entered the race.[347]

It was an exciting thing, the last campaign of Robert Kennedy. Slow to get organized, the very disorganization of it made it even more exciting and glamorous than the well-ordered effort of John Kennedy in 1960. Also, there were ideas in it—really for the first time in any Kennedy family campaign. By 1968 the poor had been discovered, and the young had discovered themselves, while the big-city bosses were retreating, their power chipped away by a hundred forces. Previously moving left, Robert Kennedy became the spokesman for all the dispossessed—for a variety of reasons in which conviction, emotion, and lack of practical alternatives were handmaidens. Newfield tells us that the idea that Bobby could be a "voice for all the voiceless" came to Robert Kennedy only in that last campaign,[348] as he sought to forge a coalition of blacks, poor whites, youth, and intellectuals—the goal-coalition of the 1930s leftist.[349] Bobby became emotionally involved in his message. Fortunately, there was no worry about money.[350] It was a radical-chic "pipe dream." Colorful New York Reform Democrat Jerome Kretchmer recalls it:

> *Gary, Indiana. That was what a campaign should be like. We'd start every morning with these huge breakfasts in the dining room of this hotel in downtown Gary. They were supposed to be strategy sessions, right, but we just had everybody in, people off the streets. Shit, we were feeding the poor and the hungry. Whoever left last would just sign the tab and that would be it. There was no limit . . . fleets of rent-a-cars. . . . Money, shit I*

remember days when I'd be walking around with $30,000 cash in my pocket. Wonderful! And those steelworkers, I really dug them I remember the time when I drove out to meet Bobby at the airport. . . .[351]

Some of that aura came to an end when Lyndon Johnson fulfilled Lowenstein's incredible prophecy and announced that he would not stand for reelection. Soon after, the Paris Peace Talks began. Much of the fire went out of Robert Kennedy's campaign. Newfield acknowledges that with Johnson's withdrawal, Kennedy "lost his cause and he lost his enemy. For the rest of the campaign he seemed lost and drifting without direction." [352] As much as possible he attempted to pick up portions of Johnson's constituency from a "reconciliation" meeting with Johnson in early April and some obvious plays for the "hack" element momentarily liberated by the Johnson withdrawal.[353] His campaigns in Indiana and Nebraska turned "right" in response to the supposed biases of their electorates.[354]

Lurking in the background was the President's stand-in, Vice-President Hubert Humphrey, slow to announce, but Bobby's first task was to get McCarthy out of the race.[355] They locked horns in four states: Kennedy took Indiana and Nebraska; lost to McCarthy in Oregon; and then won the California primary by a clear enough margin so that McCarthy, whether he knew it or not, had been permanently knocked out of the Presidential race. With uncharacteristic diction, Bobby vowed, "I'm going to chase Hubert Humphrey's ass all over America. I'm going to chase his ass into every precinct. Wherever he goes, I'm going to go." [356] It was not to be.

Soon after, Edward Kennedy, Rose Kennedy, and Joseph P. Kennedy appeared on the television, to thank the nation for its kind expressions of sympathy on the death of Robert Kennedy. As Rose and Teddy made their statements, the patriarch was visibly moved.[357] In a widely circulated Associated Press photo of the three,[358] the father appeared very old, very lean, and very frail, a relic from the Valley of the Kings.

Much is said of the growth of Robert Kennedy. Newfield, architect of the growth-of-Bobby legend, tells us that experience stretched him and tragedy transformed him.[359] There was definitely change—growth—even if Newfield's text does not bear out the emotion and extreme of his conclusion. Bobby of the fifties was decidedly narrow and unmistakably ill-liberal. After the death of his brother he began to appreciate a more expansive world. His preoccupation with "the cult of youth," while perhaps a misplaced value,[360] was appealing to those intellectuals to whom "the love generation" struck a responsive chord. He followed the cultural heroes of the young;[361] cultivated men like grape-workers' organizer Cesar Chavez; began to read Camus;[362] even exposed himself to people like Newfield. In Newfield's memoir, Robert Kennedy sometimes seems, or seems to be thinking of himself as, the American Che. It was an improvement—a growth—from the days when he might praise war and football for their man-building effects.

Newfield says that even as a Presidential candidate, there was something vaguely adolescent about Robert Kennedy.[363] By 1968 he had reached his sophomore year.

There were many things that Bobby did not outgrow. Newfield acknowledges that "His deep, moralistic rage against evil did not change; it merely discovered new outlets." [364] He grew from being able to equate evil-and-Hoffa to being able to equate evil-and-the-slumlord, but he did not outgrow the obsessive attitude. There was always the Jesuitical streak in him—early Jesuitical (bad) and later Jesuitical (good), or vice versa depending upon the reader's bias, but in any event, Jesuitical: strong, committed, and self-satisfied about the ideals. The touch of cynicism in Joseph, John, or Edward Kennedy was totally absent in Robert Kennedy, not because of any peculiar purity in his modus operandi (which it lacked) but because of Bobby's unshakable faith in the moral rightness of his changing goals: getting Hoffa, electing Jack, getting Lyndon, electing self. He never manifested any sign that he had developed those reservations about one's own self, motives, and goals, that prevent a man from abusing such power as he might have, and he never acknowledged the applicability to himself of the traffic control signals on the ways-means thoroughfare. He never developed an awareness of the possibility of "evil" (here meaning no more than the absence of genuine fairness) in himself or his acts.[365] He was only beginning to be able to think in terms of concepts, and he moved throughout life from crisis to crisis, without developing a matured value system. He never lost his focus on self or familial aggrandizement, a fact implicitly acknowledged in Newfield's concession that Kennedy "did not fight the barons when to fight would conflict with his own self-interest." [366] He remained to the end image and opportunity oriented and eager for the political kill.

JOSEPH KENNEDY SAID THAT HIS SON BOBBY RESEMBLED HIM "MUCH more" than any of his other children,[367] and he was clearly right. In many ways the personalities of the two were remarkably similar. Both were high-strung and hyperactive; direct and outspoken; highly temperamental and sometimes tempestuous. Three of Joseph Kennedy's friends commented on the less pleasant aspects of the father's personality. Eddie Gallagher: "he was quick, explosive-tempered, though under control, abrupt. . . ." [368] Arthur Krock: "[Joseph Kennedy] of course is a very imperious man, and it must be difficult for him at times to smile and be friendly when he is under strain. . . ." [369] Bernard Baruch: ". . . while Joe's courage and independence were widely admired, the bluntness with which he often expressed his views could be abrasive and startling. . . . Joe never suffered fools gladly, nor was he particularly tolerant of those who disagreed with him." [370] The same type of comment might fairly have been made of Robert Kennedy.

Neither Joseph nor Robert were very considerate. Neither man was very articulate and neither was a good speechmaker. Prior to Robert's metamorphosis, their political orientations were remarkably similar; John Kennedy described his younger brother's politics as "essentially conservative, but not on a matter like the minimum wage" [371]—very much like Joseph Kennedy.[372] Again until his rebirth, Bobby, like his father, was not very profound. John Kennedy said that he almost never saw his father read a serious book;[373] until his emergence, few saw Bobby read at all. Neither ever developed much of an appetite for serious analysis of policy issues.

Even the descriptions of the two men in their offices are strikingly similar. The 1962 description of the Attorney General at work—tie pulled down, shirt-sleeves rolled up, hair tousled, feet on his desk—sounds like a replay of the 1934 descriptions of the Chairman of the SEC. The Attorney General, like the SEC Chairman, took no lunch hour, but would eat a snack at his desk.[374] Neither man could be a decent subordinate; both had to be in the command position. Joseph Kennedy told journalists, "Jack used to persuade people to do what he wanted. Bobby orders them to do it." [375] So did Joseph Kennedy. Both were famed for their own doggedness, and both demanded the same intensity of effort and decisiveness of their underlings as they demanded of themselves. They demanded performance. An image-shaping *Life* story on Bobby carried the legend, "Hard-headed,

Hard-driving," [376] exactly the way in which his father had been described so often in his New Deal days.

The tendency of both towards militant views [377] was pointed up in the father's famous comment, "He's a great kid. He hates the same way I do." [378] It was a colorful figure of speech, typical of the hyperbole in which Joseph Kennedy so often spoke. It was also true. The father later explained the comment: "Bobby is soft—soft on people. All I ever meant to convey is that he has the capacity to be emotionally involved, to feel things deeply, as compared with Jack and that amazing detachment of his." [379] Both Joseph and Robert Kennedy could be soft on people in the sense of being reachable by sentimental appeal (though neither was particularly sensitive), and no one can doubt that both had a capacity to become emotionally involved, to feel things deeply. Neither ever had the detachment characteristic of John Kennedy.

In both of them, the shrillest personality traits were most obvious where the family was concerned. In both of them, the family was the highest consideration. It is impossible to believe that when Senator Robert Kennedy launched his devastating tirade against bumbling Los Angeles Mayor Samuel W. Yorty at Senate committee hearings, he was not relishing it all the more from his remembrances of 1960: when the Democratic mayor had crossed party lines to endorse John Kennedy's Republican opponent, Richard Nixon. The vindictive streak in both Joseph and Robert Kennedy became particularly pronounced when called to the fore by an offense against the family. As his wife Ethel said, he "never forgets." [380]

Bobby's most obvious and constant characteristic was also characteristic of his father: singleness of purpose. To the grave, Robert Kennedy was continually being described as "ruthless" by critics of the left, right, and center of the political spectrum, and with such regularity that in sympathetic surroundings he took to mock-characterization of himself and his supposed ruthlessness. Joseph Kennedy made light of the charge: "As a person who has had the term applied to him for fifty years, I know a little about it. Anybody who is controversial is considered ruthless. If he takes a stand against something, then he's called ruthless. It's ridiculous. Any man of action is always called ruthless." [381] That was genuine advocacy. What the word really means is unwillingness to let anything stand in the way of one's goals, and that certainly described both Robert Kennedy and his father. Shannon, who avoids the word, gets at the same thing when he points to "a certain natural savagery" in Robert Kennedy, "inherited from his father." [382]

This will to win, and concomitant disregard of means, while present in John and Edward Kennedy, is most pointed in Robert and Joseph P. Kennedy. "Bobby Kennedy has to be first all the time," said John Kennedy's official White House greeter, Dave Powers.[383] Bobby seemed to regard losing as positively immoral, and his insistence on winning carried him to childish lengths. Take, for example, the friendly touch football games that he loved so much. Fletcher Knebel wrote in a favorable 1963 *Look* piece:

> *Some friends even accuse him of tampering with the rules of the game to suit the team he happens to lead. If it's a slow, big team, he prefers rules that permit passing from behind the line of scrimmage only. If his team is fast and light, he argues for a pass-anywhere rule.*[384]

After a touch game with Bobby a different journalist wrote in 1962, "Every time I went for a pass he gave me elbows, knees, the works. When our team got within one touchdown of his team, by God, he picked up the ball and said the game was over." [385] His attitude on the football field was not much different at the time of his death. Newfield reports a 1968 scrimmage:

> *After a while I joined the game on Kennedy's team, with the score tied one touchdown apiece. But soon Richard Harwood, an ex-Marine and as good an athlete as he was a reporter, beat Kennedy by two steps in the end zone, and was waiting for the ball to sail into his arms. Kennedy, then, in one of those ugly, but human lapses that remained within his nature, leaped at Harwood, jamming his palm into his face in a deliberate foul. But the much bigger Harwood still managed to make a circus catch for the winning touchdown. He then turned on Kennedy and told him, "You're a dirty player, and a lousy one, too." [386]*

The significance attached to "winning" becomes more alarming when manifested off the football field. Bobby was perhaps even more goal directed than his father. He had what Yale Law critic Alexander Bickel called "tunnel vision," seeing only ends and unconcerned about means.[387] While Bickel saw his way to backing Bobby for President in 1968, insofar as the "tunnel vision" was concerned, it was the same Robert Kennedy.

While countless examples of ends-over-means situations might be cited, the author feels that Robert Kennedy's use of the "religious issue" in the 1960 Presidential election is a particularly good example, because one can easily imagine the rage with which Bobby would have reacted had a Catholic Humphrey or a Catholic Nixon used it against a Protestant Kennedy. Richard Nixon felt that the issue was over-played by the Kennedys and used unfairly against him,[388] to insure a walloping Catholic and Jewish vote and get Protestants to lean over backwards. His impression is supported by Clinton Green, an Indiana Democratic party wheel horse. Green was confronted with a touchy religious issue in his own state, and went to greet Robert Kennedy at an Indiana airport to implore him not to raise the religious issue in his state. Bobby ignored his request. Says Green, "I realized that the Kennedy people had come to a conclusion, and were taking a calculated risk. They were going to talk about religion. They were the ones who brought up the religious issue and kept it alive. It wasn't the Republicans." [389] Even *Commonweal*, the liberal Catholic publication, took exception to Jack's replays of his confrontation with the Protestant ministers—in predominantly Catholic cities.[390] Robert Kennedy saw it as a means to an end, and that was the end of the matter. His father would surely have approved: "Let's not con ourselves," he commented. "The only issue is whether a Catholic can be elected President."

At the same time there were naturally great differences between Joseph and Robert Kennedy. For the most part, the differences were functions of the "Puritanism" so often pointed out in Robert Kennedy, and so totally foreign to his father. The father had a prominent streak of ostentation, but Bobby never developed the love (shared by his parents) for "the finer things." As Spalding puts it, Robert Kennedy "wore his riches well." "He wasn't interested in the trappings of wealth. He was interested in being able to hire a plane that would take him from Madison to Eau Claire in the middle of the night, but he wasn't interested at all in any of the irritating aspects of his wealth." [391] Spalding describes his trips with Bobby to New York's world-renowned gourmet restaurant, Le Pavillon, presided over by the demure maître, Henri Soulé:

> We'd go up there, and Mr. Soulé would come out and explain all the number of things he had under glass, and somebody'd say, "Well, do you have green beans?" So sure he had green beans. And "Do you have cold chicken?" . . . it was always amusing to go in there and have that kind of a dinner and always finish it off—instead of having, you know, some grape that had been

*treated for ten years by Mr. Soulé, Bobby would end up having
vanilla ice cream and chocolate sauce. And he always asked the
fellow for that. . . . "Do you, by any chance, have any vanilla
ice cream and chocolate sauce?" "Oh, yes, yes, we have that."* [392]

Despite the absurd intimations of the right as to improprieties with
starlets,[393] Bobby never manifested any playboyish tendencies.

A man with many faces, Joseph Kennedy had within him the man
described by C. L. Sulzberger in 1939: a backslapper, a good cusser,
and a thoroughly good fellow.[394] Bobby, though, was not at ease in a
social situation; he never developed "charm" [395] and despite the
forced demeanor demanded of office-seekers, he remained basically
shy. While both men tended to see people and issues as black and
white, the father was somewhat more tolerant of people's shortcomings, and more generous in his appraisals of them. Lasky reports an
incident in which Bobby attacked a man as "a drunken New York
fag." [396] Joseph Kennedy was tolerant of homosexuals, was friendly
with more than one, and would never have framed an argument on
such bases.

Articles on Robert Kennedy always described him as a man of
unquestionable integrity, a word rarely used to describe his father. In
many ways the son was like a character from some Cromwellian
revolution, reminiscent of Robespierre the Incorruptible; his father,
more typical of other events, and of very different people.

TEDDY KENNEDY, BORN IN 1932, WAS THE YOUNGEST AND MOST
pampered of the children of Joseph P. Kennedy. He attended Milton
Academy and, with intensive tutoring,[397] graduated to follow his
brothers to Harvard. Suspended from Harvard for his cheating
episode, he enlisted for a four-year hitch in the United States Army.
Wild as the father must have been over the cheating incident, he was
even angrier at Teddy's impetuous enlistment, contracted in the midst
of the Korean conflict. According to Ted's most recent biographer,
Burton Hersh, Joseph Kennedy had had enough of heroes, and got on
the phone to get the enlistment cut back, and to insure that his
youngest son's wartime service would be fulfilled on the European
front.[398] After his tour of duty, Teddy returned to Harvard where, it
appears from his biographies, he majored in the football field, and
minored in the pursuit of the opposite sex.[399] His mediocre undergrad-

uate academic record precluded Harvard Law School, and the father vetoed Ted's second choice, Stanford Law. Joseph Kennedy decreed that Teddy stay on the East Coast,[400] so Teddy followed brother Bobby to the University of Virginia Law School.

At law school, Ted Kennedy distinguished himself by outrunning the local constabulary in a hair-raising chase,[401] and for his prize-winning moot court argument. Otherwise, his law school record was middling. While still at University of Virginia, in 1958, he married Joan Bennett. Cardinal Spellman personally requested the honor of presiding at the wedding. As the bride and groom knelt before him, each was wired for sound movies.[402] That same year Teddy served as ostensible campaign manager in John Kennedy's Senate reelection bid.

From the time of his law school graduation in 1959 until November, 1960, Teddy's principal occupation was working for the election of John F. Kennedy as President. He was assigned a batch of western states where his services were notable for energy but not particularly effective. Nixon carried eight of them. From all appearances, they had been hopeless states to begin with.

Even before the 1960 Presidential election, Joseph P. Kennedy was looking a long way ahead. Were John F. Kennedy to become President, his seat as Senator from Massachusetts would become vacant. One family friend told journalists, "Old Joe considers that Senate seat the family's," [403] and while the Ambassador did not quite know which, if either, of his sons might want it, he did know that he wanted the family to be in a position to name the successor. The Governor of Massachusetts would name an interim Senator to serve until the 1962 elections, and whoever was blessed with the interim nod would be a strong contender for 1962. At the same time as Jack was running for President, a new Massachusetts governor would be elected. The Democratic candidate, Joseph Ward, found his campaign floundering for want of funds, and made the pilgrimage to the Joseph P. Kennedy offices in Manhattan. According to Ward, the Ambassador was blunt and to the point:

> *I'm not interested in you. I'm not interested in who's governor of Massachusetts. I'm not interested in anyone except my son Jack. I want him to be President of the United States and I'm interested in my son Bobby. I want him to be the next United States Senator from Massachusetts. Will you appoint him?*

When Ward named his own preference and stood by it, the patriarch saw no purpose in prolonging the meeting: "The Ambassador placed his fingertips on the table, stood up to his full six-one and said, "This conference is at an end.' " [404]

Ward went home empty-handed, and lost his gubernatorial bid while John F. Kennedy swept Massachusetts. One of the first problems confronting the President-elect was the matter of how to handle the touchy matter of the selection of his successor as Massachusetts Senator:[405] he could resign his seat before the inauguration of the new Massachusetts governor, placing the decision as to his Senate successor in the hands of his bitter longtime rival, Democrat Foster Furcolo; or, he could wait to resign until after the newly elected Governor, Republican John A. Volpe, took office. As big a problem was who the President should suggest. The House Speaker was putting on a push to get the interim appointment for his nephew, Massachusetts Attorney General Edward McCormack,[406] giving "Eddie" the upper hand when it came time to run in 1962. The Speaker had close ties with Joseph P. Kennedy,[407] as he had had with Honey Fitz before, but, whatever the Kennedy plans, they did not include Edward McCormack. Bobby didn't want the seat; Teddy was only twenty-eight, constitutionally disqualified from the Senate until his thirtieth birthday in 1962, when the interim appointment would expire. Ultimately the President made his decision and laid it on the line to Furcolo:[408] the President's choice, Ben Smith—the Ben Smith who had shed the tears when Jack Kennedy had been edged for his party's Vice-Presidential nomination in 1956. Furcolo was entering involuntary political retirement and seemingly had nothing to gain from cooperation, but for reasons that will probably never become clear, he put aside a decade of ill-will towards the Kennedys. Ben Smith became Senator Smith. Briefly.

Joseph P. and Edward M. Kennedy immediately began working quietly on the youth's 1962 Senate campaign.[409] Joseph Kennedy had made clear long before that he sought public service careers for his sons, and as Henry Luce put it, "Joe Kennedy was not in favor of any of his sons starting at the bottom." [410] Teddy began appearing all over Massachusetts; and building up his candidate's résumé with "study tours" abroad. The trips, Hersh writes,

> *Besides reportedly disrupting a Caribbean consulate or two as the result of this energetic young man's interest in specialized night life, furnished Kennedy with a kind of huge privately branded area of expertise on the hook he subsequently dispensed in steaks*

and chops to his thousands of Massachusetts audiences in the
pre-campaign year dawning. . . . He marketed the vast contribu-
tions of the Catholic missions in Latin America to the Holy
Name groups, pushed Israel's example to Latin America to the
B'nai B'rith bagel-and-lox Sunday brunches, extolled Latin
America the untapped market to Chambers of Commerce.[411]

Thousands of potential delegates to the 1962 Massachusetts Democratic Convention—most of whom had never so much as seen Edward
M. Kennedy—received Christmas cards from the President's brother
in 1961.[412] No doubt about it, Teddy was running. His ostensible
"employer," District Attorney Garrett Byrne, in whose office Teddy
held a desk, later told an interviewer,

> *I was hearing too much of it, so I called Ted in. He was sitting*
> *just where you are, and I called up the father and I said, "Look I*
> *have Ted here with me now. Let's settle this once and for all. Just*
> *what have you and Jack decided, if Jack gets into it at all—I*
> *don't know, but knowing that this is a close-knit family. . . .*
> *Now what is he running for?" And [the Ambassador] said, "Look,*
> *get this straight, will you? He's running for the United States*
> *Senate. Now put him on the phone." So Ted got on, and I think*
> *Mr. Kennedy must have done most of the conversation, and*
> *when he hung up, I said, "Now you know what you're running*
> *for."*

"I always knew what I was running for, Gary," was the hopeful's
response. "You were the one who wondered what I was running for,
not me." [413] When journalists asked the father what problems Teddy
might have in the Senate campaign, Joseph Kennedy put his fingertips
together and answered a cool "None." [414]

Realizing the political sensitivity of Teddy's candidacy, the Washington Kennedys spread the word through friendly reporters that they
had been reluctant. Dozens of publications reported the patriarch's
order: "You boys have what you want now, and everyone else helped
you work to get it. Now it's Ted's turn. Whatever he wants, I'm going
to see he gets it." [415] Inside journalists like Stewart Alsop reported that
Jack and Bobby had finally been "won over" when pollsters convinced
them that only Teddy could keep Jack's Senate seat out of the hands
of those Republicans.[416] It was unbelievable nonsense, for surely
everyone realized that the "Teddy Issue" would cost many more
Senate votes than Teddy might lend. Evelyn Lincoln confirms that
there was not a grain of truth to it.[417] The President's attitude,

according to James Reed, "was that Teddy had a perfect right to run for the Senate if he had the desire and if he had the ability and the inclination. He did have all of those attributes, and he had certainly the desire." [418] The President read the riot act to those of his White House staff that took poorly to the idea of the Teddy candidacy,[419] and used his good office in attempts to squash or temper the *Boston Globe*'s election-time revelation of Teddy's cheating.[420]

Right on schedule, Smith declined to run in 1962, and Teddy's competition came from Attorney General McCormack. Though also from a political family, McCormack was not simply capitalizing on a family name. After graduating first in his class at Boston University Law School, McCormack became a successful attorney. He gave up his lucrative practice to run for a seat on the Boston City Council, and in 1958 was elected the State's Attorney General. Reelected in 1960 by more than 400,000 votes, he became the Massachusetts party's top vote-getter. McCormack had, as he claimed, a record and a commendable one. Overtures to him of better things to come if he would only yield were to no avail;[421] he refused to step aside in order to further the interests of "the family." He resented that Teddy, so patently unqualified, should even presume to run, and his resentment was heightened by a gnawing suspicion that an unfair and insensitive electorate might prefer a pretty name and a pretty face to a man with a record of both personal accomplishment and public service.

Joseph Kennedy suffered his crippling stroke before the nominating convention, but by 1962 his spirit had already been passed on to his sons; his presence was unnecessary. The convention was a pushover. Fifteen Massachusetts postmasterships were vacant and each had plenty of applicants. Teddy did not have to promise anything; it was clear that none of them would go to McCormack supporters.[422] Where a tough line was necessary, Ted could be as blunt as his father, as he warned hardened "pols," "Remember: win or lose, I'm handling the patronage in Massachusetts," [423] or, vote for me and "do yourself a favor." [424] For most, that kind of talk wasn't necessary; a friendly "Jack was asking about you" [425] was enough in and of itself. The vague possibilities of reward or punishment were always present, just because the candidate was a Kennedy. One delegate told journalists, "Teddy's been an Assistant District Attorney for a year or so. He's completely unqualified and inexperienced. He's an arrogant member of an arrogant family." Smilingly, he added, "And I'm going to be with him." [426] Teddy carried the convention by a two-to-one margin.

In the historic "Teddy-Eddie" primary campaign that followed, Teddy and his aides unquestionably worked hard. He was able to take over much of the Jack Kennedy machine intact and effectively used it. His campaign was as hard fought as any and he displayed the energy and will to win that has marked all the Kennedy political endeavors. He worked hard to prove that he, Teddy, could do it too. He too could win elective office.[427] He had to prove it to himself, his brothers, his father, and the intellectuals who ranged, with but two prominent exceptions, unanimously against him.[428]

The primary quickly became vicious. McCormack picked up Teddy's unnecessary and foolish claim that he had voted in every election since he had come of age as an opportunity to reveal an embarrassing truth: that Teddy had bothered to vote in only two prior elections and one primary [429]—all contests in which his brother had been involved. It seemed to prove that Teddy's only interest in politics was personal—something with which a rich man's son might occupy his time—and it silently reinforced the lingering aura of dishonesty brought about by the recent revelation of the old cheating episode. Sorensen, Robert Kennedy, and even the President briefed and grilled Teddy so that he became thoroughly conversant with state and national problems,[430] but in his face-to-face confrontations with McCormack, the Massachusetts Attorney General went for the jugular in his slashing attacks on his opponent's qualifications.

The Kennedys, ever sensitive to charges of election-buying, were careful not to be too ostentatious in their spending. But the financial advantage played its part. Where Teddy had private, many-line switchboards, Eddie was limited to single telephones.[431] McCormack could not afford sleek, professional films like "Ted Kennedy in Italy." [432] Nor could he afford the brass bands and sound trucks that followed Teddy everywhere. When it was over, a Kennedy staffer acknowledged to Professor Murray Levin, "I have had different percentages quoted. But let us say that Mr. McCormack spent in the vicinity of $200,000. And it would not be unfair to say we outspent him six or seven to one." [433]

Teddy did work hard, but *Time* was mistaken when it asserted that "Teddy won because he staged a campaign unmatched and unmatchable in its energy, enterprise and sheer intensity of purpose." [434] As McCormack charged, just plain Edward Moore would not even have bothered to step forth. He would not have had the huge, receptive crowds everywhere he went, made up of people eager to see a fabulous Kennedy and share in the glories of the beautiful people. Teddy did not disappoint them: "So Big Bobby said to Little Bobby . . . and Ethel said . . . this reminds me of something that happened to the President . . ." etc., etc.[435] At Jewish functions, Teddy would rise when the speaker called on the President of the Brotherhood. "Oh," he would say. "I thought he was saying 'brother of the President.' " [436] It was always good for a laugh. Occasionally, Teddy would even treat his audiences to a song—"Sweet Adeline," a song ever associated in the minds of Bostonians with Honey Fitzgerald.[437]

People were grateful to a Crown Prince who let them into his storybook life, and who stooped to ask a very simple, very little favor. A thirty-year-old Edward Moore, with Teddy's "qualifications," would have been laughed at.

Teddy swept the primary and easily defeated Republican George Lodge in the general election. Lodge had much more in common with McCormack than he had with Kennedy. Another "family man," Lodge was a former Assistant Secretary of Labor, a lecturer at the Harvard Business School, and had over a decade of public service behind him. But in a state where an unknowledgeable nobody was thrice elected State Treasurer because he was named John F. Kennedy, a genuine relative was a shoo-in. After it was all over, wrote *Time*:

> Edward Moore Kennedy smiled at the TV newsmen who brandished microphones in his face. Had he yet talked over his triumph with his brother, the President of the U.S.? No, but he hoped to shortly. Had he talked to his other brother, the U.S. Attorney General? No, but he hoped to shortly. Had he talked to his father, Joseph P. Kennedy? Replied Teddy, with the quiet pride of a son who knows he has pleased a demanding parent: "Yes, I talked to him. He was extremely excited." [438]

"You can imagine how the outcome pleased Dad," Ted wrote Beaverbrook. "He stayed up the latest election night to make sure that the final victory was assured. Although he was always the one who believed the strongest that it was never in doubt." [439]

From beginning to end, the reaction of intellectuals, editors, and columnists was almost entirely opposed to Teddy. Doris Fleeson pointed out in November, 1961, that the Teddy candidacy "has had the rather odd effect of turning the old talk about the dynastic potential of the Kennedys from jest into earnest conversation." [440] "The only thing that can stop them," quipped pundit Alexander

Bickel, "is a war with Canada. And I guess it would be worth it." [441]
Archibald MacLeish, Samuel Eliot Morison, and Mark DeWolfe Howe
joined to label the Teddy candidacy "preposterous." [442] After the
primary, the *New York Times* called Teddy's victory "demeaning to
the dignity of the Senate and the democratic process." [443] Teddy's
victories over McCormack and Lodge—both clearly better qualified—
seemed, and were, just plain unfair. More significant, they were
disillusioning to some, because they seemed to mean that the voters
really did not give a jot about qualifications, records, or positions.
Disheartened, intellectuals took their disgust at the people out on
Teddy. Briton D. W. Brogan wrote in *Punch* that "a great many
people who admire the President thought this was a great deal too
much of a good thing." [444]

The Kennedys were amazed at the bitterness of the tirades; after all,
one of the Kennedy sisters explained disarmingly, "Teddy had to do
something." [445]

Elected amidst controversy that made him a national issue, Teddy
entered the Senate, at the age of thirty, with a President and an
Attorney General ahead of him. It meant a long, long time before
anything opened up ahead. According to Hersh, Teddy projected a
Senate career for himself in terms of "decades";[446] decades or not, he
must have hoped for one that would last at least until the end of the
two terms of President Robert F. Kennedy in 1976. That was a long,
long 14 years. Beaverbrook wrote him, "You have made such a
brilliant beginning that you must walk warily, so that the upward
swing may continue through the years, until you reach the summit." [447] Translated, it meant keep out of the limelight—which was
also the patriarch's advice to his youngest son.[448] Teddy publicity
would only tend to obscure, perhaps embarrass, the brothers ahead,
and would irritate the powerful Southern senators whose influence, if
favorable influence could be cajoled, might make the Senate endur-
able or even enjoyable for Teddy. No one could order Eastland,
McClellan, or Russell to "like Teddy"; he would have to win their
favor on his own, and he well knew that his familial connections and
the way in which he had entered the Senate did not help at all.

Senator Edward M. Kennedy set to work lying low; a tough job for a
Kennedy. He became a textbook model of the freshman Senator:
modest, attentive, and most important (and most difficult) deferential
to his elders and especially to powerful Mississippi Senator James
Eastland.[449] He accepted the worst Senate assignments—and worked

at them. He scrupulously avoided publicity and issues that would attract the national spotlight; waited an almost unprecedented 17 months before making his first speech on the Senate floor. Senators began to comment on a warmth, thoughtfulness, and consideration in Teddy that no one had ever before noticed in any Kennedy. Even Senate President Lyndon Johnson—a Senate man's Senate man, who had plenty of personal reasons to dislike Teddy—developed a fondness for the youngest Kennedy that lingered until Johnson's death. Gradually, wrote *Newsweek,* "the door to the Senate 'Club' inched open." [450]

Teddy's Senate career has been marred by his personal tragedies. First his brother John Kennedy was assassinated in 1963; the following year Teddy himself suffered a crippling back injury in an airplane crash that nearly cost his life. When he returned to the Senate after his recuperation, he was joined by his brother Robert Kennedy, Senator from New York. Teddy proceeded on his quiet course; Senator Robert Kennedy's disposition and his timetable made him take a more aggressive tack. While Teddy strove to maintain his role as a "Massachusetts" Senator, Robert Kennedy immediately took on the cast of a "National" Senator.

Teddy's policy positions emerged as might have been predicted: he backed the liberal policies of Presidents John Kennedy and Lyndon Johnson, producing a voting record parallel to those of most Northeastern Democratic senators. He was influential on immigration reform and in the battle to abolish the poll tax; later, on draft reform. His most memorable Senate battle, though, was personal: his fight to secure a federal judgeship for family retainer Francis X. Morrissey.

While his qualifications were spotty, Morrissey was not that much worse than so many others that John Kennedy named to the judiciary at the behest of powerful Southern senators. Nonetheless, John Kennedy backed off from naming Morrissey to a vacant federal judgeship in Boston, perhaps fearing that the charge of "cronyism" would be added to that of "nepotism." It was difficult for the President, Nicholas Katzenbach later told Victor Navasky, "because the father did not impose himself on them and this was one of the few minor things which would have made a great difference to him." [451] Instead, John Kennedy left the seat vacant—perhaps at some later time. . . . After Johnson's inauguration, Edward M. Kennedy rushed in where his brothers had feared to tread. The new President acceded to the suggestion of the Democratic Senator from Massachusetts, and brought Morrissey's name forward for appointment. Immediately, Judge Charles Wyzanski, one of the nation's most respected jurists and dean of the New England Federal Judiciary, took umbrage at the suggestion, and publicly denounced the appointment of a man whose only qualification was service to the Kennedy family.[452] Teddy fought hard and long for his friend and for his father. "It's the only thing my father ever asked of me," he later told journalists.[453] After Morrissey's disastrous appearance at the Senate's confirmation hearings, and subsequent revelation of inaccuracies in his testimony before the Senate committee that placed his veracity in question, opposition to his confirmation mounted.[454] Only when defeat seemed a near certainty did Senator Edward M. Kennedy withdraw the nomination, in an emotional and moving speech drafted by "ghost" Milton Gwirtzman.[455]

Nineteen sixty-eight was Bobby's year, Teddy later said. He was not enthusiastic about Bobby's ultimate decision to run, and according to Hersh tried to get Bobby to sound just a little more moderate on the hustings.[456] Then Bobby too was assassinated. His death transformed what still remained an uphill fight into what would have been a "sure thing," and the Bobby legend was born. When the 1968 convention assembled—Bobby's convention—the "Draft Teddy" movement was inevitable. *New York Times* man William Honan attributes its birth to that ubiquitous peacenik Lowenstein,[457] but whoever the founder, it became a groundswell-from-above when power-brokers like Mayor Daley, Ohio's Mike DiSalle, and Californian Jesse Unruh joined in. Steve Smith, David Hackett, and other Kennedy agents hurried to the Chicago convention to size up the possibilities. Senator Eugene McCarthy, Bobby's primary rival, offered to step aside for Teddy— "While I'm doing this for Teddy, I could never have done it for Bobby," [458] he told Smith.

It seems likely that with Bobby assassinated, Teddy could have obtained the Democratic nomination in 1968 much easier than Bobby might have had he lived, but ultimately Teddy backed off and refused to encourage the draft movement. At that point the draft movement fell apart, and the convention swung behind steady Hubert Humphrey. Teddy's most-quoted explanation for letting the moment pass: the enigmatic "This was Bobby's year." [459] He rationalized the decision more fully to Hersh: "On the other side was the complete loss of spirit in terms of willingness to run, I just didn't have the stomach for that, I didn't feel I was personally equipped for the race, I thought it was much too great a burden to place on my family at that time. People would be considering the candidacy for entirely the wrong reasons. . . ." [460] Perhaps Teddy himself never fully understood the reasons. In any event, according to *An American Melodrama: The Presidential Campaign of 1968*, "Kennedy did not turn down the Presidency. He took a rain check on it." [461]

Seemingly, Teddy Kennedy was affected relatively little by the assassination of John Kennedy and remained "conventional" while Robert Kennedy was undergoing his metamorphosis. Shortly after the death of Robert Kennedy, though, there were definite signs of change in him. On the positive side, with the death of his brother and the incapacitation of his father, Teddy succeeded to the head of the family. He began to spend long hours as substitute father to the huge brood left behind by his brother Robert, and as helpmate to Robert's widow.[462] He began to spend more time with his helpless father.[463] And he seemed interested in solidifying his position among his peers in the Senate.

After the 1968 elections, Edward Kennedy sought the post of Assistant Senate Majority Leader—"whip." It was an unglamorous "work" position, and surely no power base from which to build a Presidential campaign. If anything, it was a hindrance to Presidential ambitions. But it signified receipt of the respect of the United States Senate—earned respect.[464] Incumbent "whip" Russell Long had lost that respect of his colleagues; Southern oligarchs declined to protect him. A combination of disapproval of Long; sympathy for the tragedy-prone Kennedy; deference to the Democrats' likely 1972 Presidential nominee; and genuine respect for Edward Kennedy brought him election to the whip's office over Long in January of 1969.

At the same time, the death of Robert Kennedy had its negative effect on Edward M. Kennedy. As if the passing of Bobby and his father's incapacitation removed his superego, Teddy started to come apart at the seams in 1969. His inclination towards wild driving became more pronounced. He began to drink seriously and heavily— the only one of the sons of the disapproving Joseph Kennedy to show any weakness in that respect. Stories began to circulate of his rollicking until early hours with Green Berets in bars,[465] or lurching down the narrow aisle of an Arctic airplane, slurring a chant of "Ess-ki-mo-o-o-o power!!" [466] The gossip that has always revolved around Kennedy sex lives became dizzying.[467] And then in the summer of 1969 came the Chappaquiddick incident. A group of "Kennedy men" and "Kennedy girls" for an overnight on lonely Chappaquiddick Island; Teddy left to drive Mary Jo back to Edgartown; there was an inadvertent wrong turn; the car careened over the bridge; Mary Jo was lost. No one could believe an innocent explanation, and particularly dour Judge James M. Boyle.[468] It defied belief. A high-powered coterie of advisors from three-brothers-worth of Kennedys hurried to Cape Cod to try to unravel the mess and salvage a political career. Out of it came Edward Kennedy's appeal, a "Checkers speech" drafted largely by Sorensen that put a bad taste into the pens of virtually every opinion-maker in America.[469]

Evidence of the end of the Presidential possibilities of Edward M. Kennedy became more convincing when Senate Democrats again dumped their incumbent whip in January of 1971. The handwriting was on the wall well before. In the midst of the Chappaquiddick scandal, *Newsweek*'s Kenneth Crawford reported that Teddy's Senate colleagues were somewhat disappointed in him as a tactician and strategist; Chappaquiddick had ended his usefulness even as a symbol.[470] He became less effective personally as a Senator. Senators ceased to court him. Meanwhile, West Virginia Senator Robert Byrd—an old foe of the Kennedy family ever since he had led the stop-Kennedy forces in the West Virginia primary of 1960 [471]—was ingratiating himself with his fellow senators much as Teddy had. As Long's personal life had left him vulnerable, so did Kennedy's. Senate Majority Leader Mike Mansfield tacitly approved votes against Teddy, much as Georgia Senator Richard Russell had "cleared the way" for the dumping of Long in 1969. When the Democratic Senators caucused in January, 1971, they chose Robert Byrd as their "whip." Longtime Kennedy loyalists in the Senate declined to say how they had marked their secret ballots.[472] America's Kennedy phase seemed ended.

Three years later, Teddy's Presidential prospects are again live. When liberal George McGovern wrapped up the 1972 Democratic convention the Kennedys proved their party loyalty by lending Shriver to what already appeared to be a hopeless race. McGovern-Shriver carried only one state: Massachusetts, the significance of which was lost to no one. Dr. Gallup's post-election poll showed one Democrat that might have won: Edward M. Kennedy.[473]

Out of the 1972 wreckage of the Democratic party, Teddy Kennedy has emerged as the nation's most important Democrat. "Watergate backlash" would seem to have hurt any candidate lacking simon-pure reputation, yet Dr. Gallup's post-Watergate polls show little change in

Teddy's popularity [474] and, as of this writing, he must still be rated the party's leading prospect for 1976.[475] He laid low after Chappaquiddick; now memories are fading; his Chappaquiddick transgression, like his transgressions of the past, can be attributed to a "different" Edward M. Kennedy than stands before you today. He is back on the national hustings, even making appearances in the Deep South. His liberal line occasionally takes on a conservative streak, as when he backed President Nixon's illibertarian Crime Control Bill, but his speeches are not often ideological in tone. More, they stress what Honan calls "the Heritage theme." [476] Reminiscent of John Kennedy's private words of long ago, "Just as I went into politics . . . ," Teddy tells his audiences, ". . . Like my brothers before me, I pick up a fallen standard. . . ." [477]

Curiously, the configuration of Edward Kennedy's signature seems to say that he takes much more pride in the last name than in the first. At least at this stage in life, his abilities are less impressive than those of John F. Kennedy, and Teddy clearly appreciates as much. While he has become more articulate with time, he remains a poor reader and writer.[478] Like his father, he is much more dependent on his "ghosts" than was John or even Robert Kennedy; to the embarrassment of his staff, they were called upon even to write Teddy's eulogy to Robert Kennedy, without guidance from their boss as to what should be said.[479] Perhaps subconsciously following his brother Jack, when Teddy had his own serious back injury in 1964, he attempted to turn out something literary,[480] but while Jack produced *Profiles in Courage*, Teddy's route was to solicit entries for *The Fruitful Bough*, a book of tributes that he edited in honor of his father. While many portions of the book have been quoted, Teddy's own short contribution—about his father's tenderness—has yet to come to light. Honan says that Ted lacks the piercing intellect of John Kennedy;[481] he does not seem to equal even the plodding intellect of Bobby or the cunning intellect of his father. His intellectual and cultural proclivities are the most limited in the entire family,[482] and he lacks the spontaneity, creativity, and self-confidence of the others. As Honan puts it, though, he does have a talent for dramatization and leadership that may more than compensate for his less-agile mind.[483]

Teddy clearly has much more surface warmth and charm than either of his brothers; he has, his father said, "the affability of an Irish cop," [484] and John Kennedy encouraged Massachusetts politicians to "keep in close touch with Teddy. . . . He's the politician of the family, and he's going places." [485] *Newsweek* describes Ted as reminiscent of

Honey Fitz, "Given to trilling snatches of Irish ballads and thumping chums in the shoulder with heavy-fisted geniality." [486] He is obviously much more crony-dependent than were his more self-sufficient older brothers, with a definite Brendan Behan side to him.[487] At the same time, Teddy is capable of an almost unbelievable self-detachment and control of his own emotions. His self-control on the occasion of the assassination of President John Kennedy was offensive to his household help;[488] when Bobby was stricken and lay dying in Los Angeles, Honan tells us that Teddy was able to begin making funeral arrangements and to go with an aide to select a coffin.[489] And on the very day that his own son, Teddy, Jr., age twelve, underwent amputation of his leg in his fight against cancer, Teddy was able to muster the composure to appear in the role of substitute father at the wedding of Bobby's daughter Kathleen.

Edward Kennedy's personal shortcomings no doubt turn in part on his status in the family: his mother told nurse Rita Dallas that "Teddy was our surprise baby, and he's brought more joy into our lives than we ever thought possible." [490] As the youngest, he received less rigorous discipline, more tenderness and indulgence.[491] While Jack and Bobby were making careers of their own, the younger Edward Kennedy was with his father more. As he grew, he developed a powerful resemblance in personality and appearance to his dead brother Joe Junior, his father's first favorite, which further endeared him to Joseph Kennedy.[492] Unlike the early years of his older brothers, his youth was filled with the pranks of a rich man's son.[493] He developed a nose for "easy ways." While capable of the same all-out effort of all the Kennedy men, he seems to have less basic drive than any of the others, and to be less accomplishment-oriented. He failed to do for Robert Kennedy in 1968 what Robert Kennedy had done for John Kennedy in 1960. In many ways he seems the casualty of a large family; as if the strain had run out.

According to Joseph Kennedy's nurse, in his final years Teddy's approach brought the greatest excitement to his father, who seemed to live for the visits from his last-surviving son. He was told of the Chappaquiddick incident in guarded outline.[494] As Teddy's explanation was televised from the living room below him, the father was shielded from it. When the broadcast was completed, Ted, as if unaware, went upstairs to his father's bedroom and assured him, "Dad, I've done the best I can. I'm sorry." [495] Thereafter, Joseph P. Kennedy's health failed rapidly. He died during the course of the long-lingering scandal and investigation.

EPILOGUE

THE DEATH OF JOSEPH P. KENNEDY WAS LONG, DRAINING AND demoralizing, as his life had been long, vibrant, intense. The downward turn came in 1961 with a stroke which, together with relapses and heart attacks, left him almost completely incapacitated, usually helpless, throughout his final eight years.[1] The press covered the final days intensely, depriving him of the dignity of last peaceful moments, and turning his passing—despite the efforts of his family to protect him and themselves—into the garish affair that his life had been. In a sense, the story of the death of Joseph P. Kennedy is a recapitulation of the Kennedy phenomena in America.

The last days were opened with the inappropriate remarks of Cardinal Richard Cushing, who took it upon himself at a gymnasium dedication in Taunton, Massachusetts, to tell the people assembled, and thus the press, and thus the world, that Kennedy was "very close to death. I had a call from the family this morning, and it seems that the good Lord is about to take him in the foreseeable future." [2] The Boston papers gave the news banner front-page headlines,[3] and for the following week, the Kennedy compound at Hyannis, Massachusetts, was surrounded by reporters awaiting whatever fact or gossip would sell papers; it was a scene reminiscent of the crowds of press and laymen who had waited outside those same gates in November, 1960, for tidbits of nothing.

Rose Fitzgerald Kennedy, the patriarch's wife of over half a century, cancelled a planned appearance to help boost sales of "John F. Kennedy 'Flame of Hope' Candles" to aid the retarded, in order to be near her husband in his final moments. Once again the press carried photographs of Rose walking the windy, deserted beach, as they had each time that she had confronted tragedy in the past.[4]

The family gathered from all over the globe. Notwithstanding stylistic differences as broad as the ocean between Jacqueline Kennedy Onassis, the President's widow, and Joseph Kennedy, her father-in-law, Mrs. Onassis had been very close to the Ambassador.[5] He had always respected her for her spunk and wit in challenging him,

478

and they seemed to share genuine affection. Rumor had always had it that the Ambassador had saved her marriage with John Kennedy when it had floundered in the 1950s. Now the press featured glamorous photos of "Jackie" embarking and disembarking from airplanes with "John-John" and Caroline, the President's children, en route to join the family in the death watch.[6] From the earliest page-one headline, "Jacqueline Joins Family Death Vigil," [7] the press watched her intensely, carefully noting and reporting her dress throughout,[8] as at a New Frontier cocktail party.

Ultimately they were all assembled: Rose; Jackie; Eunice Kennedy Shriver, the Ambassador's surviving favorite; Jean Kennedy Smith, least known of the clan; Patricia Kennedy Lawford, divorced from her famous actor-husband; Ethel Skakel Kennedy, widow of the Attorney General; and, the new head of the family, the youngest and sole-surviving son, Senator Edward M. Kennedy. As the death watch continued, prognoses volunteered or extracted from collateral kin were rushed into the latest editions of the Boston papers and onto the wire-service teletypes.[9]

Finally it was reported that the Ambassador had died peacefully on Tuesday, November 18, 1969, at 11:05 A.M.[10] Plans for the funeral were reported in detail: it was to be a white-vestment mass, Cardinal Cushing would officiate, and Senator Edward M. Kennedy would read a tribute to his father that had been written by his deceased brother, Senator Robert F. Kennedy, and he would praise his selfless cousin Ann Gargan for her eight years of companionship with the Ambassador.[11]

The funeral was a private one, held at the Hyannis Catholic Church, and limited to family and a small number of invited friends. There was Arthur Houghton, a Kennedy intimate from his movie days; Joe Timilty, the last of Boston's Honey Fitz-styled "pols," who had guided Joseph P. Kennedy, Jr., through the 1940 Democratic National Convention; Francis X. Morrissey, small-time Boston lawyer who had been a Kennedy retainer since before anybody could remember when; Father John J. Cavanaugh, President of Notre Dame, the only college significantly aided by the Ambassador's beneficence; LeMoyne Billings, schoolboy chum of the Assassinated President; Carroll Rosenbloom, Baltimore millionaire and sportsman. The guests reflected every period and aspect of the Ambassador's widely varied career, except for his career as Ambassador.

At the widow's request, it was a white-vestment mass, emphasizing resurrection and joy after death, as opposed to the mourning emphasized by the customary black-vestment mass.[12] Cardinal Cushing, Kennedy's ancient crony, who had shared countless enjoyable hours with the Ambassador discussing politics of Church as well as politics of State, officiated, assisted by Rose's nephew, Father Joseph Fitzgerald. The Cardinal began: "Brethren: we have become a spectacle to the whole world, to angels as well as men," the message of which must have gratified the assembled members of Kennedyhood. He delivered a eulogy, a long and boring eulogy, not reflective of the intimate personal relationship that he had himself enjoyed with the deceased. As he spoke, perhaps a mind or two wandered back to that cold wintry day nine years before, when His Eminence had opened the Camelot era with his invocation, his long and boring invocation, at the inauguration of President John F. Kennedy.[13]

Morton Downey, the millionaire singer and the Ambassador's dear friend from Roosevelt days, sang the traditional Communion song. Downey's eyes watered as the President's fatherless son "John-John," age eight, haltingly recited the Twenty-third Psalm. Acolytes and pallbearers were drawn from the ranks of the Ambassador's countless grandchildren, 18 of whom had a direct role in the funeral. At the last, the patriarch was surrounded and attended by his "own flesh and blood," for which he had lived. Edward M. Kennedy, "Teddy," his voice shaking with emotion, read the assembled an essay on his father that had been written by his brother Robert Kennedy for *The Fruitful Bough*, a collection of in-memorium tributes to the late Ambassador that had been assembled by the Massachusetts Senator four years before his father's death,[14] and a poem about the Ambassador written at that time by his now-widowed spouse. He publicly thanked his cousin, the selfless Ann Gargan, who had served eight years as the Ambassador's constant companion through the tragedies that the Ambassador had endured in the '60s. Then it was over, and there was the long ride through the driving rain to the Holyhood Cemetery in Brookline, Massachusetts, not far from the first homestead that Joseph and Rose Kennedy had established in 1914.[15] At that time it had been a Protestant neighborhood—a source of no little satisfaction to the young Joseph Kennedy on the move up.[16]

Then came the largely feelingless tributes to the man of ". . . a long and distinguished record . . ."[17] led by President Richard M. Nixon and other world leaders as diverse as Ireland's political and spiritual leader Eamon DeValera, New York City Mayor John Lindsay, and each and every Massachusetts politician with either standing or pretensions of standing.[18] A widely published tribute by Merriman Smith, dean of the White House press corps, told how he had known Kennedy as "a man who long before it was chic, had battled quietly and effectively against anti-Semitism," [19] thus calling to the attention of his readers, no doubt innocently, the Ambassador's general reputation as an anti-Semite. Most major American newspapers editorialized on his passing, for the most part with assemblages of words that sounded as if they had been written by assigned staff writers merely because a famous man had died. A few were maudlin, a few wildly praiseworthy. The conservative *Chicago Daily Tribune*'s editorial told *Tribune* readers of Kennedy's support for Red-baiting Wisconsin Senator Joseph McCarthy,[20] a matter of which only the *Tribune*'s editorial writers still approved. *Newsweek* covered the death in a vicious obituary,[21] which the new head of the family publicly criticized,[22] reminding people of the fierce feud between Robert Kennedy and Kennedy-historian William Manchester.

Kennedy's most important days had been spent in England, where he had earned the title of which he and his family were so very proud: "Mr. Ambassador." [23] English intellectuals had never forgiven him for his conduct at his post and after, during what conservative British editor Iain Macleod once called "our finest hour and his meanest." [24] The English press was particularly restrained in its coverage of the death of Joseph Kennedy. In its issue immediately following Kennedy's death, London's influential weekly *Observer* featured an article headlined "Death of a Very Special Man," a sensitive piece about the passing of a long-distance runner, a solitary ascetic, who had had little formal education. In a small box, the *Observer* noted the death of America's wartime Ambassador to Great Britain, the father of a President.[25]

APPENDIX

NOTES

THE STORY
OF AN IMMIGRANT

1. *Parliamentary Papers*, 1847, XI, 4.

2. Oscar Handlin, *Boston's Immigrants*, rev. ed. (Cambridge, Mass.: Belknap Press, 1959), p. 43. Handlin cites George O'Brien, *Economic History of Ireland in the Eighteenth Century* (Dublin, 1918), p. 102.

3. William Forbes Adams, *Ireland and Irish Emigration to the New World* (New Haven, Conn.: Yale University Press, 1932), p. 217.

4. Marcus Lee Hansen, *The Atlantic Migration* (Cambridge, Mass.: Harvard University Press, 1940), p. 242.

5. *Ibid.*, p. 244.

6. *Ibid.*, p. 245.

7. *Parliamentary Papers*, 1847, XI, 4.

8. *Ibid.*, IX, 403.

9. See, for example, 1847, X, 15, 85, 180.

10. Tim Pat Coogan, "Sure and It's County Kennedy Now," *New York Times Magazine*, June 23, 1963, p. 7.

11. Joseph Roddy, "Irish Origins of a President," *Look*, March 14, 1961, p. 20. James MacGregor Burns, *John Kennedy: A Political Profile* (New York: Harcourt, Brace & Company, 1959), p. 5, lists the family home simply as New Ross.

12. Coogan, *New York Times Magazine*, p. 32. Coogan is the first writer to give the date of Pat's departure, and he does not state his source.

13. Marcus Lee Hansen, *The Immigrant in American History* (Cambridge, Mass.: Harvard University Press, 1940), p. 31.

14. *Ibid.*, p. 108.

15. Adams, *Ireland and Irish Emigration*, p. 340.

16. *Ibid.*, p. 230.

17. Arnold Schrier makes more of this than do previous writers. See his *Ireland and the American Emigration, 1840–1900* (Minneapolis: University of Minnesota Press, 1958), p. 30.

18. Handlin, *Boston's Immigrants*, pp. 48, 100.

19. Hansen, *The Atlantic Migration*, pp. 255–56.

20. *Ibid.*, p. 256, and Adams, *Ireland and Irish Emigration*, pp. 236–37.

21. Adams, *Ireland and Irish Emigration*, p. 219.

22. Burns gives the fare in *John Kennedy*, p. 5.

23. Handlin, *Boston's Immigrants*, pp. 57, 250–51.

24. Figures derived from Handlin's table in *ibid.*, pp. 250–51.

25. *Ibid.*, p. 62.

26. Adams, *Ireland and Irish Emigration*, p. 360.

27. Handlin, *Boston's Immigrants*, p. 111.

28. *Ibid.*, p. 115, cites Norman J. Ware, *Industrial Worker, 1840–1860* (Boston: 1924), p. 14.

29. Coogan, *New York Times Magazine*, p. 32, attributes the death to cholera.

PICTURE OF
A WARD BOSS

1. For years a group of old-time Boston "pols" would gather every afternoon at the Waldorf Cafeteria on Beacon Street, Boston, now demolished. The author spent two afternoons with them, April 5 and 6, 1962.

2. Pat Kennedy gave the date variously as January 14, 1858, or January 8, 1858, but the January 8 date was the one he used later in life. See the tables at the end of the *Journals of the House* of the Commonwealth of Massachusetts.

3. Interview with Pat's nephew and close political and personal friend, Joseph Kane, April 5, 1962.

4. James MacGregor Burns, *John Kennedy: A Political Profile* (New York: Harcourt, Brace & Company, 1959), p. 8. Burns does not indicate his source. Contemporary accounts of Pat Kennedy do not mention the parochial school.

5. *Boston Globe*, November 19, 1899.

6. Burns, *John Kennedy*, p. 9.

7. See Oscar Handlin, *Boston's Immigrants*, rev. ed. (Cambridge, Mass.: Belknap Press, 1959), pp. 207–229.

8. Joseph F. Dinneen writes that Pat worked first as a longshoreman. *The Kennedy Family* (Boston: Little, Brown and Company, 1959), p. 4. Kane says this is not so, and this author has not seen any references to longshoreman's work in any other source.

9. Michael E. Hennessy, *Boston Sunday Globe*, December 12, 1937, editorial section, p. 12.

10. William Forbes Adams, *Ireland and Irish Emigration to the New World* (New Haven, Conn.: Yale University Press, 1932), p. 343.

11. *Ibid.*

12. James Michael Curley, *I'd Do It Again* (Englewood Cliffs, N.J.: Prentice-Hall, Inc., 1957), p. 27.

13. Brief biography of Pat in C. D. Gillespie, *Noodle Island*, the souvenir edition of the *Argus-Advocate* (East Boston), 1897, p. 51.

14. *Ibid.* I find no substantiation elsewhere.

15. *Journal of the Senate* of the Commonwealth of Massachusetts for the year 1892, pp. 10, 90. The names of the men were Scott and Adamson—apparently neither of Irish extraction.

16. See the *Journal of the Senate* for 1893, pp. 683, 908, and 949 for the four matters on which they voted differently. Two of them are motions to postpone, one is a motion to reconsider, and one a motion to amend.

17. Pat also served on the Committee on the State House; Honey also served on the Committee on Engrossed Bills. The assignments are in the *Journal of the Senate*, 1893, p. 24 ff.

18. Arthur Krock, *Memoirs: Sixty Years on the Firing Line* (New York: Funk & Wagnalls, 1968), p. 351.

19. Joseph Casey, recorded interview by William McHugh, February 27, 1967, typescript at John F. Kennedy Library, Oral History Program.

20. Dinneen, *The Kennedy Family*, p. 8.

21. A 1908 clipping mentioned Pat as a candidate for Street Commissioner, but this author has been unable to confirm whether or not the candidacy actually materialized and assumes not.

22. Curley, *I'd Do It Again*, p. 27. See also Leslie G. Ainley, *Boston Mahatma* (Boston: Bruce Humphries, Inc., 1949), p. 76.

23. Joseph F. Dinneen, *The Purple Shamrock* (New York: W. W. Norton and Company, Inc., 1949), pp. 94–105.

24. Obituary, *Boston Herald*, May 19, 1929, p. 27.

25. Joe McCarthy, "Jack Kennedy: Heir to Power," *Look*, October 27, 1959, p. 91.

26. But see Ainley, *Boston Mahatma*, p. 58.

27. *Boston Herald*, December 22, 1899, p. 12, and *Boston Daily Globe* (morning edition), same day, p. 1.

28. Dinneen, *The Kennedy Family*, p. 4.

29. See the *Boston Daily Globe* (evening edition), February 16, 1905, p. 1.

30. Unidentified newspaper clipping dated May 10, 1903, in the archives of the *Boston Globe*.

31. Dinneen, *The Kennedy Family*, p. 4.

32. Probate records at the Suffolk County Probate Court list personal property valued at $50,874.05, and real property worth $5,950.00. Pat made a few small bequests and divided the remainder of his estate in the following manner: one-half to his already fabulously wealthy son, and one-quarter each to his two daughters, Mrs. Charles Burke (Margaret L. Kennedy) and Mrs. Charles Connelly (Loretta Kennedy).

33. Clipping dated November 19, 1899, in the archives of the *Boston Globe*.

34. Dinneen, *The Purple Shamrock*, p. 94.

35. Curley perfected many of Fitzgerald's ways, and as much as any man helped to bring Boston politics to a more advanced stage of social development. He created a city-wide machine of his own that would overwhelm the single-ward bosses.

36. Lomasney, for example, controlled three seats in the legislature, and filled them with one Irish, one Italian, and a Jew. One Greek businessman who was close to Fitzgerald asserted to the author that Honey had "a genuine interest in the new races." Interview with Thomas Pappas, Boston, April 5, 1962.

37. Lomasney died with a small estate. Honey was better off, but was famed in his day as a stock speculator. Even James Michael Curley was never personally associated with graft, and died with a small estate.

38. Kane interview.

39. Obituary, *Boston Transcript*, May 21, 1923.

40. Burns, *John Kennedy*, p. 23.

41. Hennessy, *Boston Sunday Globe*, December 12, 1937, editorial section, p. 12.

42. Dinneen, *The Kennedy Family*, p. 6.

43. Burns, *John Kennedy*, p. 23.

44. Unidentified newspaper clipping dated May 10, 1903, in the archives of the *Boston Globe*.

45. Hennessy, *Boston Sunday Globe*, December 12, 1937, editorial section, p. 12.

46. *Ibid.*

47. James A. Fayne, recorded interview by Raymond Henle, August 8, 1968, Hoover Institute Oral History Program, p. 1, typescript available at John F. Kennedy Library.

48. Interview with Ethel Turner, Boston, April 5, 1962.

49. See note 1, *supra*.

THE GO-GETTER

1. Most of the material on Kennedy's early life must be attributed to either of two newspaper series on him published at the time of his appointment as ambassador: Max Grossman in the *Boston Sunday Post* of December 12, 19, and 26, 1937, and the *Boston Sunday Advertiser* and *Boston American* of December 12 through December 19, 1937, inclusive; see also a somewhat fanciful account, John B. Kennedy's "Joe Kennedy Has Never Liked Any Job He's Tackled" in *American Magazine*, May, 1928. These sources are amplified by interviews by Richard J. Whalen noted in his *The Founding Father* (New York: The New American Library of World Literature, Inc., 1964). Unless otherwise noted, the material in this section is based on the *Post* or *American-Advertiser* series.

2. Years later, Kennedy "anonymously" paid to have the school's plumbing replaced. Whalen, *Founding Father*, p. 382, cites interview with Henry J. O'Meara.

3. Whalen, *Founding Father*, p. 21, recites a colorful anecdote related to him by a Katherine Sullivan.

4. Interview with Joseph Kane, Boston, April 5, 1962. Even as a fabulously wealthy man more than half a century later, Kennedy remained ever attune to the casual chance for making a dollar. His longtime friend Edward M. Gallagher recalls when he and Kennedy were preparing for a round of golf with a soft-drink executive (presumably Coca-Cola's James A. Farley). Kennedy cautioned Gallagher to be on good behavior—"Let's see what he has on his mind. We might get a franchise out of this." Gallagher, recorded interview by Ed Martin, January 8, 1965, p. 23, typescript at John F. Kennedy Library, Oral History Program.

5. Joseph F. Dinneen writes that "Campbell probably did more to shape Kennedy's career than any other person, and until Campbell died, Kennedy consulted him often. Away from the city, he was likely to call him long distance to discuss complex financial problems and factors involving stock market operations. Whenever he returned to Boston he never failed to visit him." *The Kennedy Family* (Boston: Little, Brown and Company, 1959), pp. 9–10.

6. Interview with Max Levine, Boston Latin's semi-official alumni secretary, Boston, February 28, 1962.

7. Kennedy to Frankfurter, March 23, 1935, MS. in Frankfurter Papers, Box 135, Library of Congress Manuscript Division, Washington, D.C.

8. *Harvard Class Book*, 1912, p. 149, and *Secretary's First Report*, Harvard College Class of 1912, pp. 71–72.

9. This account based on the *Boston American*, December 13, 1937, p. 5. Whalen, citing anonymous interviews, asserts that McLaughlin had Kennedy put in the game in response to political pressures brought to bear upon him, which threatened to deprive the captain of a Boston theatre license he was seeking. Whalen, *Founding Father*, pp. 4, 27. McLaughlin himself denied the whole incident when it was first reported in the press. *Boston Sunday Advertiser*, December 19, 1937, p. 20.

10. Early accounts of the Kennedy career always assert that Joe was the barker, though Grossman asserts to the contrary. *Boston Sunday Post*, December 26, 1937.

11. Grossman, *Boston Sunday Post*, December 19, 1937.

12. Whalen, citing an interview with Henry J. O'Meara, asserts that the articles were written for Kennedy gratis, by a fellow who enjoyed writing, while Kennedy pocketed the money. *Founding Father*, pp. 28–29.

13. See Joe McCarthy, *The Remarkable Kennedys* (New York: Popular Library, paperback ed., 1960), p. 27, and James MacGregor Burns, *John Kennedy: A Political Profile* (New York: Harcourt, Brace & Co., 1959), pp. 14–15.

14. Arthur Krock, *Memoirs: Sixty Years on the Firing Line* (New York: Funk & Wagnalls, 1968), p. 339.

15. Gail Cameron, *Rose* (London: Michael Joseph, 1972), p. 43. In the years since her sons came to prominence, Rose Kennedy has calculatingly donned a public facade with "dumb-woman" elements in it—essentially as a protection against too-searching questions. See page 396. Actually, she is quite bright.

16. *Ibid.*, p. 53.

17. *Ibid.*, p. 57.

18. *Ibid.*, pp. 40, 41.

19. It is often asserted that Kennedy's goal was to be a millionaire by the time he reached thirty-five. See, for example, *Brooklyn Eagle*, December 12, 1939.

20. "I saw, even in my limited dealings, that sooner or later the source of business was traced to the banks," he told John B. Kennedy. *American Magazine*, May, 1928, p. 146.

21. So wrote his longtime friend Arthur Krock, *New York Times*, December 13, 1938, p. 24.

22. *Boston Herald*, January 21, 1914.

23. Unidentified newspaper clipping dated November 3, 1916, at the *Boston Globe* archives.

24. Interview with Joseph F. Dinneen, Needham, Mass., July 29, 1961.

25. Gallagher oral history typescript, p. 8. According to Gallagher, there was a closeness between Honey and Joe, notwithstanding the rumors to the contrary. Honey, he felt, was less fond of Kennedy than vice versa.

26. See, for example, Cameron, *Rose*, pp. 24, 96.

27. Morgenthau Diary MS., entry of July 1, 1935, Vol. 8, p. 2, at Roosevelt Library, Hyde Park, N.Y.

28. Robert Palyfair, *Boston Globe* (evening edition), April 28, 1944, p. 5.

29. Cameron, *Rose*, p. 71. According to Cameron, Kennedy was more intent upon breaking into Protestant society than was Rose, who had "made [her] peace with it and could confidently go her own way." *Ibid.*, pp. 71, 59.

30. Unidentified clipping dated July 26, 1915, in the archives of the *Boston Herald*.

31. Cameron, *Rose*, pp. 58, 61.

32. Unidentified clipping dated November 3, 1916, in the *Boston Globe* archives. His father-in-law was also said to have lunched on crackers and milk while mayor. Perhaps both did. Or perhaps neither.

33. Interview with Thomas Pappas, Boston, April, 1962.

34. Interview with Miss Ethel C. Turner, Boston, April 5, 1962.

35. Whalen cites Henry J. O'Meara for an anecdote in which Kennedy accepted use of a car for himself in lieu of interest, only to have the auto repossessed out from under him by a prior creditor. *Founding Father*, p. 43.

36. *Boston American*, December 15, 1937, p. 8.

37. McCarthy, *The Remarkable Kennedys*, p. 27.

38. Richard Whalen, "Joseph P. Kennedy: A Portrait of the Founder," *Fortune Magazine*, January, 1963, p. 113, quotes Kennedy's longtime employee James Fayne.

39. Classmate Ralph Lowell, quoted in *Boston Sunday Advertiser*, January 12, 1964.

40. McCarthy, *The Remarkable Kennedys*, p. 28.

41. John Henry Cutler, *"Honey Fitz": Three Steps to the White House* (Indianapolis, Ind.: Bobbs-Merrill Company, 1962), p. 212.

42. Whalen, *Fortune*, January, 1963, p. 114.

43. McCarthy, *The Remarkable Kennedys*, p. 35.

44. Whalen, *Fortune*, January, 1963, p. 114.

45. Dinneen says that Kennedy was one of the backers of "The Miracle Man," one of the earliest and most successful shoestring productions. *The Kennedy Family*, p. 33. This author tends to doubt it; "The Miracle Man" was a significant American movie, and had Kennedy been associated with it, he would have mentioned it in many of his interviews.

46. Whalen cites an anonymous interview for assertion that Kennedy managed a "pool" in Todd's stock. *Founding Father*, p. 65.

47. Unidentified newspaper clipping dated September 18, 1920, in the archives of the *Boston Herald*.

48. McCarthy, *The Remarkable Kennedys*, p. 36.

49. Whalen, *Founding Father*, p. 66, cites interview with Oscar Haussermann.

50. See John B. Kennedy, *American Magazine*, May, 1928, p. 148, and Whalen, *Fortune*, January, 1963, p. 115.

51. McCarthy, *The Remarkable Kennedys*, p. 19.

52. Whalen, *Fortune*, January, 1963, p. 115.

53. McCarthy, *The Remarkable Kennedys*, p. 42.

54. Dinneen, *The Kennedy Family*, p. 18; Cutler, *"Honey Fitz"*, p. 248.

55. Grossman, *Boston Post*, December 26, 1937.

56. The motion picture industry, threatened with censorship in 36 states, preferred self-censorship and hired Hays to be top censor for the industry. Columbia's Professor William E. Leuchtenburg writes: "All the Hays office succeeded in doing in the 1920's was to add hypocrisy to sex by insisting on false moralizations and the 'moral' ending." *The Perils of Prosperity, 1914–1932* (Chicago: University of Chicago Press, 1958), p. 169.

57. Merritt Crawford, *Motion Picture World*, December 11, 1926.

58. Cutler, *"Honey Fitz,"* pp. 245–46.

59. *Motion Picture World*, December 11, 1926, p. 396.

60. The earliest source that this writer found for this oft-quoted line is *Photoplay*, September, 1927, reprinted in the *Boston Sunday Globe*, September 18, 1927, p. 1 of the news feature section.

61. Cameron, *Rose*, p. 106.

62. *Boston Globe*, October 25, 1928.

63. Quoted in *The Memoirs of Will H. Hays* (Garden City, N.Y.: Doubleday & Company, Inc., 1955), p. 396.

64. *Annals of the American Academy*, September, 1926, p. 96.

65. Mel Gussow, *Don't Say Yes Until I Finish Talking: A Biography of Darryl F. Zanuck* (Garden City, N.Y.: Doubleday & Company, Inc., 1971), p. 29.

66. See the *Film Year Book, 1927* (New York: The Film Daily, n.d.), pp. 391–92, for list of FBO films.

67. Joseph Patrick Kennedy, ed., *The Story of the Films* (Chicago: A. W. Shaw Co., 1927), pp. 16–17.

68. Crawford, *Motion Picture World*, December 11, 1926, p. 396.

69. Kennedy, *American Magazine*, May 1928, p. 148.

70. *Motion Picture World*, December 11, 1926, p. 396. See also Dinneen, *The Kennedy Family*, p. 34.

71. Red Grange, *The Red Grange Story*, as told to Ira Morton (New York: G. P. Putnam's Sons, 1953), p. 127.

72. *Motion Picture World*, December 11, 1926, p. 396.

73. In 1930, the *Annals* reviewed the pros and cons of mergers, but concluded that "recent mergers [of which Kennedy's were the most prominent] in the motion picture industry were not made for the purpose of lessening waste in production or diminishing the costs of production. Further, it is not apparent that the costs to the public are to be lessened." *Annals of the American Academy*, January, 1930, p. 92. In short: Kennedy's mergers were of no societal benefit.

74. Louella Parsons, *New York Journal*, October 25, 1928.

75. Eugene Lyons, *David Sarnoff* (New York: Harper & Row, 1966) p. 143.

76. *Literary Digest*, November 3, 1928, p. 12.

77. *New York Times*, May 8, 1930, p. 33.

78. *New York Times*, February 27, 1928, p. 17.

79. *Film Daily*, May 17, 1928; *New York Times*, May 17, 1928.

80. Abel Green and Joe Laurie, Jr., *Show Biz* (New York: Henry Holt and Company, Inc., 1951), p. 92. Green and Laurie say Kennedy bought the option from Murdock as a representative of RCA.

81. Douglas Gilbert, *American Vaudeville* (New York: McGraw-Hill Book Company, Inc., 1940) p. 394.

82. *New York Times*, May 17, 1928, p. 23.

83. Gilbert, *American Vaudeville*, p. 394. Albee himself was generally regarded as an unscrupulous fellow.

84. *New York Times*, June 13, 1928, p. 39.

85. *Film Daily*, August 12, 1928.

86. *Boston Post*, August 19, 1928.

87. *Ibid.* See also *New York Times*, August 11, 1928, p. 13.

88. *Film Daily*, August 12, 1928.

89. *Boston Post*, August 19, 1928.

90. *Ibid.*

91. Editorial comment on the emergence of RKO is synthesized in *Literary Digest*, November 3, 1928, p. 12.

92. Or so writes Joe Laurie, Jr., in *Vaudeville* (New York: Henry Holt and Company, 1953), p. 482.

93. *New York Times*, January 15, 1929.

94. *Boston Globe*, December 11, 1937. For a corporate executive to receive a private fee for merging his company with another would surely bring stockholders' suits today.

95. See Green and Laurie, *Show Biz*, pp. 92, 247.

96. *Motion Picture Almanac*, 1930, p. 187.

97. Newspaper article by Mayme Ober Peck dated May 19, 1930, in the archives of the *Boston Globe*.

98. *Ibid.*

99. See *Congressional Record*, May 12, 1933, XXXCVII, 3350–51. Sirovich literally spoke of widows and orphans, looted by swindlers, and called on Congress to "drive the looters from their executive offices," to show "all future financial manipulators that the Government of the United States will not tolerate financial racketeers, masquerading as honest men." *Ibid.*, p. 3353. Kennedy used his influence with Roosevelt to put the damper on Sirovich's inquiries. Hays, *Memoirs*, p. 460.

100. *Congressional Record*, January 18, 1940, XXCVI, 494.

101. See Kennedy's article, "Big Business, What Now?" *Saturday Evening Post*, January 16, 1937, p. 11.

102. Richard M. Hudson and Raymond Lee, *Gloria Swanson* (South Brunswick, N.J.: A. S. Barnes and Company, 1970), p. 13.

103. Whalen, for example, asserts that Gloria named Joseph after Kennedy, citing an anonymous interview. *Founding Father*, p. 94. Though Whalen interviewed Miss Swanson, he shied away from seeking confirmation. According to Kennedyphobe Victor Lasky, Miss Swanson later unsuccessfully sought financial help from Joseph Kennedy, on behalf of her son Joseph, and when the John Kennedy Presidential campaign got underway, Joseph Kennedy sent an emissary to Miss Swanson, to warn her to "keep her mouth shut." Lasky, who is fairly good on footnoting, does not cite any source at all for these most dubious assertions. Victor Lasky, *Robert F. Kennedy: The Myth and the Man* (New York: Trident Press, 1968), p. 39.

104. Hudson and Lee, *Gloria Swanson*, p. 13; Lester David, *Ted Kennedy* (New York: Grosset & Dunlap, 1971), p. 237. A 1948 photograph of Joseph Swanson bears no resemblance whatsoever to Joseph Kennedy. Photo in *Newsweek*, March 15, 1948, p. 44.

105. Cutler, *"Honey Fitz"*, pp. 215–16; Cameron, *Rose*, pp. 72–73.

106. Hedda Hopper, *From Under My Hat* (Garden City, N.Y.: Doubleday & Company, Inc., 1952), p. 168.

107. Peter Noble, *Hollywood Scapegoat* (London: The Fortune Press, 1950), p. 79. For another account of *Queen Kelly*, also sympathetic to von Stroheim, see Thomas Quinn Curtiss, *von Stroheim* (New York: Farrar, Straus & Giroux, 1971), pp. 242ff.

108. See, for example, "Mr. Kennedy, the Chairman," *Fortune*, September, 1937, p. 142.

109. Hank Searls, *The Lost Prince* (New York: The New American Library, Inc., 1969), p. 265.

110. Whalen, *Founding Father*, p. 95.

111. Publicity materials on *The Trespasser* are available at the Library of Congress's motion picture collection. A copy of the film is available at the New York Museum of Modern Art.

112. Green and Laurie, *Show Biz*, p. 268.

113. *Film Daily*, May 8, 1930.

114. Whalen, *Founding Father*, p. 96, cites interview with Miss Swanson.

115. *New York Times*, May 8, 1930, p. 33. According to Whalen, control of Pathé was wrested from Kennedy by Stuart Webb, a disgruntled business associate. Whalen, *Founding Father*, pp. 109–110 cites interview with Webb. True or not, Kennedy had

gotten all he wanted—the quick, easy dollar—and was ready to move on.

116. *American Magazine* was itself a caricature of the 1920s, and pushed the values of the shallow decade. It frequently published glamorous biographical sketches of those 1920s demigods—the successful businessmen.

117. John B. Kennedy, "Joe Kennedy Has Never Liked Any Job He's Tackled," *American Magazine*, May, 1928, pp. 32ff.

118. This writer saw John B. Kennedy identified as a Kennedy staffer in society clippings from the 1940s.

119. Suggested lead for an FBO press release dated September 29, 1928.

120. Cf. Theodore C. Sorensen, *Kennedy* (New York: Harper & Row, 1965), p. 32.

121. S. J. Woolf, *New York Times*, August 12, 1934, pp. 1, 3; *New York Times*, July 3, 1934, p. 9; FBO release of September 29, 1928.

122. Kennedy, *American Magazine*, May, 1928, p. 145.

123. *Fortune*, September, 1937, p. 138.

124. *New York Times*, June 30, 1934, p. 20; Krock, *New York Times*, July 4, 1934, p. 14; S. J. Woolf, *New York Times*, August 12, 1934, pp. 1, 3.

125. *New York Times*, July 3, 1934, p. 9.

126. Kennedy, *American Magazine*, May, 1928, p. 146.

127. *Ibid.*

128. Unidentified clipping dated November 3, 1916, apparently not from a Greater Boston paper.

129. *Fortune*, September, 1937, p. 140; Krock, *New York Times*, July 4, 1934, p. 14. Joseph F. Dinneen told the author that he had heard the story from Kennedy himself and had confirmed it with Stone. Interview.

130. Kennedy, *American Magazine*, May, 1928, p. 147.

131. Max Grossman, *Boston Post*, December 26, 1937. Whalen, citing Henry J. O'Meara as his source, credits a slightly different version of the tale. *Founding Father*, p. 71. Kennedy himself, though, would say with a smile in his later years that he did not recall the incident. McCarthy, *The Remarkable Kennedys*, p. 38.

132. Krock, *New York Times*, July 4, 1934, p. 14.

133. Kennedy, *American Magazine*, May, 1928, p. 149.

134. *Fortune*, September, 1937, p. 138. This lengthy and on the whole very favorable article was long the leading source on Kennedy. Unsigned, it was written by Robert Cantwell, who literally slaved over it day and night. When it appeared, Kennedy was unsatisfied. Louis Kronenberger, *No Whippings, No Gold Watches* (Boston: Little, Brown and Company, 1970), p. 67.

135. *Encyclopaedia Britannica*, 13th edition, XXI, 576.

136. *Time*, April 20, 1936; *North American Review*, December, 1938, p. 271; Congressman Sirovich in the *Congressional Record*, May 12, 1933, XXXCVII, 3351.

137. *Fortune*, September, 1937, p. 142; *Current Biography*, 1940, p. 451; and others.

138. Whalen, *Fortune*, January, 1963, p. 116.

139. Henry F. Pringle, "Handy Man," *Colliers*, April 8, 1939, pp. 11, 66.

140. *Current Biography*, 1940, p. 451; McCarthy, *The Remarkable Kennedys*, p. 41.

141. Whalen, *Founding Father*, p. 104, cites interview with Oscar Haussermann.

494 ⎣⎤⎣⎤⎣⎤⎣⎤⎣⎤⎣⎤⎣⎤⎣⎤ *Joseph P. Kennedy*

142. Dinneen, *The Kennedy Family*, pp. 34–35.
143. *Ibid.*
144. Eleanor Harris "The Senator Is in a Hurry," *McCalls*, August 1957, p. 119. See also Ralph G. Martin and Ed Plaut, *Front Runner, Dark Horse* (Garden City, New York: Doubleday & Company, Inc., 1960), p. 117.
145. Whalen, *Fortune*, January, 1963, p. 117; McCarthy, *The Remarkable Kennedys*, p. 46.
146. Frank L. Kluckhohn, *America: Listen!* (Derby, Conn.: Monarch Books, 1961) p. 31.
147. The author spoke to a gentleman from the brokerage house through which Kennedy short-sold large blocks of Paramount stock. For Anaconda, Whalen, *Founding Father*, p. 109, cites interview with Burton K. Wheeler.
148. Interviews April 5, 1962, and September 20, 1973.

WINNING
WITH ROOSEVELT

1. *The Secret Diary of Harold L. Ickes*, Vol. I: *The First Thousand Days, 1933–1936* (New York: Simon & Schuster, 1953), p. 173.
2. John Griffin, *Boston Sunday Post*, July 1, 1934.
3. John Henry Cutler, *"Honey Fitz"*: *Three Steps to the White House* (Indianapolis: Bobbs-Merrill Company, Inc., 1962) pp. 218, 229.
4. Charles McGlue, longtime Jim Curley cohort, managed Curley's campaign for mayor that year, and says that he worked closely with Kennedy. McGlue recalled Kennedy as having managed Honey's gubernatorial bid. Interview, Boston, April, 1962. For scanty published references to Kennedy's role in the campaign, see Cutler, *"Honey Fitz"*, p. 237; Joe McCarthy, *The Remarkable Kennedys* (New York: Popular Libary, paperback ed., 1960), p. 37.
5. Scanty and repetitious sources on Joseph Kennedy in the 1924 Presidential campaign are a *Boston Globe* interview by Louis Lyons, November 10, 1940; a Wheeler speech on March 24, 1937, in *Congressional Record* XXCI, 2675; Wheeler's *Yankee From the West* (Garden City, N.Y.: Doubleday & Company, 1962), pp. 252–53; William H. A. Carr, *J.F.K.*, (New York: Lancer Books, Inc., paperback ed., 1962), pp. 21–22. A 1960 statement about having lent the Kennedy name to the Progressives' official committee is in a *New York Post* interview-article, January 11, 1961, p. 37.
6. They split at that time because Wheeler and the isolationists were displeased about Kennedy's failure to effectively support their position. Wheeler later suspected that Kennedy was trying to sabotage him in 1924. R. J. Whalen, *Fortune*, January, 1963, p. 115. This is unlikely. Kennedy had a powerful motive for helping the Progressives: his disgust over "bigotry" in his own party. See page 425 *infra*. Wheeler himself has indicated that that was the reason why Kennedy gave his support. *New York Post*, January 11, 1961, p. 37.
7. Wheeler speech in *Congressional Record*, XXCI, 2675.
8. James A. Farley suggested Walker to the author. Interview, New York, March 3, 1962. Whalen says Morgenthau, citing anonymous interview, *The Founding Father* (New York: The New American Library of World Literature, Inc., 1964), p. 113.
9. Joseph P. Kennedy interview with Ed Plaut, October 29, 1959.
10. See *New York Times*, February 26, 1932, p. 18, and June 20, 1932, and Cutler, *"Honey Fitz"*, pp. 264–70.

11. See Joseph P. Kennedy, *I'm for Roosevelt* (New York: Reynal & Hitchcock, 1936), p. 3, and *New York Times*, August 12, 1934, VI, p. 3.

12. Wheeler explains Kennedy's support for Roosevelt in terms of Kennedy's antipathy for John J. Raskob, Smith's leading backer. *Yankee from the West*, p. 297. To the same effect is Booth Mooney, *Roosevelt and Rayburn* (Philadelphia: J. B. Lippincott, 1971), p. 28. This author finds it unlikely.

13. Farley interview. Farley points out that Kennedy had made heavy financial commitments to Roosevelt prior to Smith's formal reentry, which to some extent locked Kennedy in.

14. Unidentified newspaper clipping dated November 3, 1931, in the archives of the *Boston Herald.*

15. *New York Times*, May 9, 1932, p. 8.

16. "The Reminiscences of Arthur Krock," pp. 7–8, typescript in The Oral History Collection of Columbia University. Baker's biographer ascribes significance to the often-told story. C. H. Cramer, *Newton D. Baker* (Cleveland: World Publishing Company, 1961), pp. 253–54.

17. W. A. Swanberg, *Citizen Hearst* (New York: Charles Scribner's Sons, 1961), p. 437.

18. Ralph G. Martin and Ed Plaut, *Front Runner, Dark Horse* (Garden City, N.Y.: Doubleday & Company, Inc., 1960), p. 117.

19. Other sources on Kennedy's role in the pre-convention and convention periods and on Kennedy's role in bringing Hearst around, are Edward J. Flynn, *You're the Boss* (New York: The Viking Press, 1947), p. 84; James A. Farley, *Behind the Ballots* (New York: Harcourt, Brace & Co., 1938), pp. 31, 72; James A. Farley, *Jim Farley's Story* (New York: McGraw-Hill Book Company, Inc., 1948), p. 24; James Michael Curley, *I'd Do It Again* (Englewood Cliffs, N.J.: Prentice-Hall, Inc., 1957), p. 236.

20. James L. Wright, *Boston Globe*, September 25, 1932.

21. Roosevelt to Hearst, October 3, 1934, *FDR, His Personal Letters, 1928–1945*, ed. E. Roosevelt (New York: Duell, Sloan and Pearce, 1950), I, 424.

22. *The Secret Diary of Harold L. Ickes*, entry of November 15, 1935, I, 472.

23. *F.D.R., His Personal Letters, 1928–1945*, I, 288.

24. Or so Dowling related it to an Oral History interviewer. "The Reminiscences of Eddie Dowling" (1963), p. 312, typescript in The Oral History Collection of Columbia University. Assuming that Moore said it, history proved him only half-right; Moore's idea of an "Irish-Catholic President" was something like Joe Kennedy or Al Smith. There was nothing particularly Irish or particularly Catholic about John F. Kennedy. Moore apparently accompanied Kennedy, and thus the Roosevelt entourage, throughout the campaign, and made a favorable impression on the campaign hierarchy. Ray Moley noted that Moore's "infinite capacity to make friends made up for much of Kennedy's shortcomings in that respect." Moley, *The First New Deal* (New York: Harcourt, Brace & World, Inc., 1966), p. 380.

25. Lela Stiles, *The Man Behind Roosevelt* (Cleveland: The World Publishing Company, 1954), pp. 148–49, for a good anecdote on the first Kennedy-Howe meeting.

26. *F.D.R., His Personal Letters, 1928–1945*, I, 294.

27. Ray V. Peel and Thomas C. Donnelly, *The 1932 Campaign* (New York: Farrar & Rinehart, Inc., 1935), p. 149.

28. Marquis James and Bessie Rowland James, *Biography of a Bank: The Story of Bank of America* (New York: Harper & Brothers, 1954), pp. 359–61.

29. Moley, *The First New Deal*, p. 381.

30. James L. Wright, *Boston Sunday Globe*, September 25, 1932, editorial section, p. 3, is the most extensive reference to Kennedy's function in the campaign that the author has come across.

31. Interview with James Roosevelt, Washington, March 20, 1962.

32. Samuel I. Rosenman, *Working with Roosevelt* (New York: Harper & Brothers, 1952), p. 88.

33. Unidentified press clipping dated November 3, 1932, in the *Boston Herald* archives. This is no doubt an example of what Moley meant when he wrote that Kennedy "ranged himself ostentatiously on the side of Roosevelt." *The First New Deal*, p. 381. The value to Roosevelt of having Kennedy in Boston during his appearance was precisely zero. To Kennedy, though, it had value: he was being seen, both by Roosevelt, who could observe his fervor and loyalty, and by Boston's "pols" and financiers, who could take note of the immense power and influence of that fellow who had formerly been known as Honey Fitz's son-in-law.

34. Cutler, *"Honey Fitz,"*, p. 266.

35. Dowling oral history typescript, p. 445. Whalen uses a more colorful version of the anecdote, also based on Dowling, but channeled through a Drew Pearson column. *Founding Father*, p. 129, cites Pearson column in *Washington Post*, October 1, 1960.

36. Moley, *The First New Deal*, p. 381.

37. Whalen, *Founding Father*, p. 128, cites anonymous interview.

38. *Ibid.*, p. 103, cites interview with Henry J. O'Meara.

39. Moley, *The First New Deal*, pp. 381–82.

40. E. J. Kahn, Jr., *The World of Swope* (New York: Simon & Schuster, 1965), p. 378.

41. *Ibid.*, p. 380.

42. Oldest source for the assertion seems to be *The New Dealers*, by An Unofficial Observer (New York: Simon & Schuster, 1934), p. 355. Krock gives the story credence in *New York Times*, July 4, 1934, p. 14. It has continually been repeated ever since.

43. Kahn, *World of Swope*, pp. 378–79, cites letter, Swope to Kennedy, March 30, 1933.

44. "The Reminiscences of James P. Warburg," pp. 344, 348, 407, 410, 675–76, 684, typescript in The Oral History Collection of Columbia University.

45. Roosevelt to Acting Secretary of State William Phillips, July 31, 1933, and Phillips to Kennedy, August 5, 1933, MSS. at National Archives, Washington, in State Department file 711.3212/51.

46. Krock, *New York Times*, March 10, 1957, p. 22.

47. Moley, *The First New Deal*, p. 381.

48. Warburg oral history typescript, pp. 405, 407.

49. Whalen, *Founding Father*, p. 131, cites interview with Wheeler.

50. The cantankerous old man was fired when his deceit came to light, over Kennedy's seemingly vigorous protest to Morgenthau, made in the presence of Honey's intimate, Congressman John McCormack, and his understanding acquiescence in private. Henry Morgenthau Diary MS. at Roosevelt Library, Hyde Park, N.Y., VII, 105A—118 and VIII, 2. McCormack, incidentally, also made a moving plea for the old man while Honey's son-in-law was within hearing distance, only to pass the word later that he didn't care about the fate of Honey's brother. *Ibid.*

51. Unidentified clipping in the archives of the *Boston Herald* dated July 18, 1933.

52. *Boston Sunday Advertiser*, June 5, 1932, p. 5. Asked to comment, Kennedy said, "I'd rather yet [sic] it go. . . . I can't say a thing. The situation won't let me. I'm sorry."

53. McCarthy, *The Remarkable Kennedys*, p. 36.

54. *Hearings before Senate Committee on Banking and Currency on Senate Resolution 84 and Senate Resolutions 56 and 97, Part 14, "Alcohol Pools,"* pp. 6218–6246. The story about the manager from Whalen, *Founding Father*, p. 135, who cites an anonymous interview.

55. *Washington Post*, July 4, 1934, p. 1; *Wall Street Journal*, July 4, 1934, p. 8.

56. Despite rumors to the contrary, the closest Kennedy seems to have gotten to bootlegging was in his role as liquor purveyor to Prohibition-era reunions of his Harvard class—"he arranged with his agents to have the stuff sent in right on the beach at Plymouth. It came ashore the way the Pilgrims did," his classmate, Massachusetts Supreme Court Justice Raymond S. Wilkins told Whalen. *Founding Father*, p. 58, citing interview.

57. Dowling oral history typescript, pp. 249–255.

58. A society notice of the departure is in the *Boston Globe*, September 26, 1933.

59. Kay Halle, recorded interview by William T. McHugh, February 7, 1967, p. 3, typescript at John F. Kennedy Library, Oral History Program.

60. William V. Shannon, *The Heir Apparent* (New York: The Macmillan Company, 1967), p. 61. Shannon seems to interpret the comment as an example of social striving; this author sees a business angle in it.

61. Though years later, Miss Halle did not recall the visit to Winston Churchill at all. Interview, Washington, September 21, 1973.

62. Randolph Churchill interview with C. L. Sulzberger, noted in Sulzberger's diary entry of January 15, 1960, in his *Last of the Giants* (New York: The Macmillan Company, 1970), p. 629.

63. Interview with James Roosevelt, Washington, March 20, 1962.

64. "Don't drink Scotch, drink bourbon," Harry Truman would later say. "Every time you do [drink Scotch] you put money in Joe Kennedy's pocket."

65. Dowling, oral history typescript, pp. 490–91.

66. Alva Johnson, "Jimmy's Got It," *Saturday Evening Post*, July 2, 1938, p. 60.

67. *Chicago News*, June 29, 1938.

68. McCarthy, *The Remarkable Kennedys*, p. 47.

69. See, for example, Frank L. Kluckhohn, *America: Listen!* (Derby, Conn.: Monarch Books, Inc., 1961), p. 31.

70. James Roosevelt interview.

71. *Boston Transcript*, November 14, 1934.

72. Kahn, *The World of Swope* (New York: Simon & Schuster, 1965), p. 380.

73. *Saturday Evening Post*, July 2, 1938, p. 60.

74. Whalen, *Founding Father*, pp. 380–81, cites anonymous interviews.

75. Interview with John J. Reynolds, New York, May 28, 1962.

A BECKET
FOR FINANCE

1. Arthur Krock, *New York Times*, July 4, 1934, p. 14.

2. Arthur M. Schlesinger, Jr., *The Coming of the New Deal* (Boston: Houghton Mifflin Company, 1959), pp. 457, 463. Even Mayor Fitzgerald expressed serious reservations. See the *New York Times* of March 2, 1934, p. 37.

3. *New York Times*, October 25, 1936, p. 33.

4. Raymond Moley, *After Seven Years* (New York: Harper & Brothers, 1939), p. 286.

5. E. J. Kahn, Jr., *The World of Swope* (New York: Simon & Schuster, 1965), p. 379.

6. Moley, *After Seven Years*, p. 286-87.

7. *New York Post*, July 2, 1934, p. 19; Moley, *After Seven Years*, p. 287.

8. *New York Times*, June 29, 1934, p. 2.

9. Moley, *After Seven Years*, p. 287.

10. "The Reminiscences of Eddie Dowling" (1963), p. 366, typescript in The Oral History Collection of Columbia University. Whalen, relying on Dowling as channeled through a press interview, tells it somewhat differently. Richard J. Whalen, *The Founding Father* (New York: The New American Library of World Literature, Inc., 1964), p. 139, cites *Boston Advertiser*, January 19, 1964.

11. Moley, *After Seven Years*, p. 288.

12. *Ibid.* For Kennedy's attitude on the disclosure of the skeletons in one's closet, see pages 74-75 *infra*.

13. Presidential Press Conference 134, June 29, 1934, typescript at Roosevelt Library, Hyde Park, N.Y., Press Conferences, III, 436.

14. *New York Times*, June 29, 1934, p. 2; June 30, 1934, p. 20.

15. *Washington Daily News*, June 30, 1934, p. 1.

16. *Washington Post*, July 3, 1934, p. 1; *New York Post*, July 2, 1934, p. 19.

17. *New York Post*, July 2, 1934, p. 19. According to Moley, Landis also balked originally at the thought of Kennedy as chairman. Moley, *After Seven Years*, p. 289.

18. Paragraph paraphrased from the *New York Times*, July 3, 1934, p. 1. See also the *Washington Post*, July 3, 1934, p. 1.

19. *New York Post*, July 5, 1934.

20. *New Republic*, July 11, 1934, p. 221.

21. Flynn, *New Republic*, July 18, 1934, pp. 264-65.

22. *The Secret Diary of Harold L. Ickes*, Vol. I, *The First Thousand Days: 1933-1936* (New York: Simon & Schuster, 1953), p. 173.

23. Moley, *After Seven Years*, p. 289.

24. Matthew Josephson, *Infidel in the Temple: A Memoir of the Nineteen-Thirties* (New York: Alfred A. Knopf, 1967), p. 307.

25. *Journal of Commerce*, July 3, 1934, p. 2.

26. Arthur Krock, recorded interview by Charles Bartlett, May 10, 1964, p. 1, typescript at John F. Kennedy Library, Oral History Program.

27. Arthur Krock, *Memoirs: Sixty Years on the Firing Line* (New York: Funk & Wagnalls, 1968), p. 331.

28. Krock, *New York Times*, July 4, 1934, p. 14. Krock himself was probably not

responsible for these half-truths. A U.P. release of the previous day included some of them, as well as a yarn about how Joe's schooling funds were insufficient, which required him to work his way through Harvard. Krock probably relied on this, on previous fanciful articles on Kennedy, on movie company press releases in the *New York Times* files, and no doubt on his conversation with Kennedy.

29. Krock, *Memoirs*, p. 331.

30. *Washington Post*, July 2, 1934, p. 8.

31. *New York Sun*, July 5, 1934, p. 21.

32. *Boston Sunday Post*, July 1, 1934, and other contemporary newspapers.

33. Both in *Washington Post*, July 4, 1934, p. 1.

34. *New York Times*, January 17, 1935.

35. *Washington Post*, July 4, 1934, p. 1; *Wall Street Journal*, July 4, 1934, p. 8.

36. *New York Times*, July 26, 1934, p. 13.

37. *New York Times*, July 27, 1934, p. 16.

38. *Washington Post*, July 27, 1934, p. 8.

39. *Wall Street Journal*, July 26, 1934, p. 6.

40. *New York Times*, July 27, 1934, p. 23. Kennedy received less by way of cooperation from exchange officials than he had hoped for. Whitney, in particular, proved uncooperative. See Joseph Alsop and Robert Kintner, "Battle of the Market Place," *Saturday Evening Post*, June 11, 1938, p. 76.

41. *New York Times*, July 27, 1934, p. 23; August 9, 1934, p. 27; January 14, 1935, p. 24; June 13, 1935, p. 37.

42. *Wall Street Journal*, July 26, 1934, p. 6.

43. *Washington Post*, July 3, 1934, p. 1.

44. Asserted in *Fortune*, September, 1937.

45. Interview with Ferdinand Pecora, New York, March 13, 1962.

46. *New York Times*, May 7, 1936, p. 33.

47. "The Reminiscences of James M. Landis" (1964), p. 261, typescript in The Oral History Collection of Columbia University. According to Landis, Kennedy and Cohen later developed mutual admiration.

48. "The Reminiscences of Chester T. Lane" (1951), p. 308, typescript in The Oral History Collection of Columbia University.

49. As it ended up, Fayne worked more closely with Kennedy, and drafted many of the chairman's speeches during the period. The two were 40-year friends. Fayne too figured in some of the testimony on market manipulations before the Pecora investigations. Pearson and Allen, *New York Daily Mirror*, April 26, 1935.

50. Pecora interview.

51. *New York Herald-Tribune*, November 22, 1934, p. 27; *New York Times*, November 22, 1934, p. 31; Pearson and Allen, *Washington Herald*, November 26, 1934; Mallon, *Washington Star*, December 8, 1934, p. 2; Pearson and Allen, *New York Daily Mirror*, April 26, 1935.

52. *New York Times*, July 26, 1934, p. 23.

53. *New York Times*, August 14, 1934, p. 1.

54. Securities Exchange Act of 1934, Title I, Section 16(b).

55. *New York Times*, August 14, 1934, p. 1.

56. *Ibid.*

57. *New York Times*, January 14, 1935, p. 1.

58. *New York Times*, March 8, 1935, p. 1.

59. *New York Times*, March 25, 1935, p. 25.

60. Securities Exchange Act of 1934, Title I, Section 19(b).

61. *New York Times*, April 17, 1935, pp. 1, 35. The rules proved to be the least effective aspect of Kennedy's work. For an excellent critique, see Fred Rodell, "Douglas Over the Stock Exchange," *Fortune*, February, 1938, pp. 64, 116, 119.

62. *Wall Street Journal*, April 17, 1935, p. 1.

63. *New York Times*, January 20, 1935, IV, 7.

64. *Ibid.*

65. *New York Times*, September 21, 1935, p. 1.

66. *Washington Post*, September 21, 1935, p. 2. See also editorial, p. 6.

67. As the fascinating Mr. Flynn ultimately did in his entire political orientation, moving from radical left to radical right over a period of years.

68. *New Republic*, October 9, 1935, p. 244.

69. *Washington Post*, September 24, 1935, p. 1.

70. Lane oral history typescript pp. 282–83.

71. For similar comments on Kennedy's accomplishments at the SEC, see William O. Douglas, *Democracy and Finance*, ed. James Allen (New Haven, Conn.: Yale University Press, 1940), vii–viii, and Fred Rodell, *Fortune*, February, 1938, p. 116.

72. Kennedy's many speeches are reported and indexed in the *New York Times*. The most significant of them was his speech before the American Arbitration Association of March 19, 1935, reported the following day in the *New York Times*, p. 1, and reprinted the following year in the *Congressional Record*, XXC, 3979 ff. Comments on the speeches were generally favorable. Some critical comments are in the *Journal of Commerce*, November 17, 1934, and March 20, 1935, p. 4; *New York Herald-Tribune*, March 21, 1935, p. 16; *Daily Investment News*, March 21, 1935.

73. The author has seen only two criticisms of Kennedy's administration. Denis W. Brogan, in *The Era of Franklin D. Roosevelt* (New Haven, Conn.: Yale University Press, 1951), p. 259, writes that Kennedy "proved too amiable to carry through the necessary reforms." In *The American Stakes* (New York: Carrick & Evans, Inc., 1940), John Chamberlain calls the SEC "innocuous" under Kennedy, p. 115. The second SEC chairman, James Landis, and the third chairman, William O. Douglas, disagree with Brogan and Chamberlain.

It is true that much was left to be done by later chairmen, including internal reform of the exchanges and more adequate supervision of trading. But Kennedy did as much as could be done at the time. In 1934, selling the idea of exchange regulation was more important than carrying through needed reforms like those that were left for the Douglas administration. Had he stayed at the SEC, Kennedy might have proven "too amiable" to effectuate those reforms, but other things had to come first, and by the time the stage had been set for the more far-reaching reforms, Kennedy had departed.

NEW DEALER
JOE KENNEDY

1. Grace Tully, *FDR, My Boss* (New York: Charles Scribner's Sons, 1949), p. 157. In his *Memoirs*, Herbert Hoover groups the members of the Roosevelt Administration in three categories: New Dealers, old-line Democrats, and *really* old-line Democrats. He puts Kennedy in the third group. *Memoirs of Herbert Hoover*, Vol. III: *The Great Depression, 1929–1941* (New York: The Macmillan Company, 1952), p. 352.

2. The Hamlin Diaries, MS. at Library of Congress Manuscript Division, Washington, D.C., diary entry of September 25, 1934, XXV, 123.

3. He supported the government's policy in *I'm for Roosevelt*, and no doubt at the time, too.

4. Charles W. B. Hurd, "Insuring an 'Even Break' for Investors," *New York Times Magazine*, May 26, 1935, VII, 5.

5. The economic organization of Mussolini's Italy was strikingly parallel to the type of economic organization envisioned in the National Recovery Act. And, the NRA became a creature of big business before its brief career was ended by the Supreme Court. Big business, through the NRA codes, shaped national planning to its own ends. Clarence Darrow saw the NRA as partially responsible for the greater concentration of wealth that he observed in the mid-thirties, and feared that the country was headed for a society where every man was either a slave or a master.

6. The NRA proved to be a dismal failure as far as recovery went. Later studies indicated that it retarded rather than stimulated recovery; paradoxically, its good effects were in the field of reform. The same can be said of the entire New Deal period. Some historians, including John Morton Blum, assert that this was in the long run best for the country. Blum fears that recovery instead of reform would have led to a native American fascism, ruled by a strong and small upper-middle class.

7. *The Secret Diary of Harold L. Ickes*, Vol. I: *The First Thousand Days, 1933–1936* (New York: Simon & Schuster, 1953), entry of October 11, 1934, I, 203.

8. *Ickes Diary*, entry of October 20, 1934, I, 206.

9. John M. Blum, *From the Morgenthau Diary*, Vol. I: *Years of Crisis, 1928–1938* (Boston: Houghton Mifflin Company, 1959), p. 241.

10. *Ickes Diary*, I, 203, 206, 351; *New York Times*, April 26, 1935, p. 1; April 28, 1935, IV, 3; May 2, 1935, p. 8; May 26, 1935, VII, 5.

11. Blum, *Morgenthau Diary*, I, pp. 241, 242.

12. See, for example, Kennedy's article "Big Business, What Now?" *Saturday Evening Post*, January 16, 1937, pp. 10 ff.

13. *Boston Globe* (evening edition), April 23, 1935, p. 14.

14. Correspondence between Kennedy and Frankfurter dated March and April, 1935, together with draft of the speech is at Library of Congress Manuscript Division, in Felix Frankfurter Box 135, folder "Federal Securities Bill, Correspondence, 1934–1936." Request in letter of March 23, 1935.

15. Evelyn Lincoln on John Kennedy's speech-writing procedure: "He would ask several people to prepare some remarks for a specific occasion, then he would draw ideas from all their proposals. Yet his speechwriters were rarely aware that he had asked others to prepare material on the same subject." *My Twelve Years With John F. Kennedy* (New York: David McKay Company, Inc., 1965), p. 6.

16. *Washington Post*, July 3, 1935, p. 3.

17. The version of the bill that Kennedy publicly supported was tailored to delight the most rabid trustbuster. His support was rather qualified, and rested more on disapproval of the alternative than on support for the extreme position. The alternative, he felt, would place too much responsibility on the SEC. He was really not pleased with either version of the bill. See the *New York Times*, July 10, 1935, pp. 7, 20; July 12, 1935, pp. 6, 18; July 16, 1935, p. 25. The bill that passed was quickly held to be unconstitutional by the Supreme Court.

18. Alsop and Kintner, "Battle of the Market Place," *Saturday Evening Post*,

June 25, 1938, pp. 10 ff. Alsop and Kintner evaluate Kennedy's assistance as being less than useful. According to them, Kennedy's constant references to the political situation made Wall Streeters suspicious of his motives. See pp. 78–80.

19. *Washington Sunday Star*, November 11, 1934.

20. See, for example, fawning letter, Kennedy to Frankfurter, November 23, 1934, MS. Frankfurter Papers, Box 135.

21. Searle F. Charles, *Minister of Relief: Harry Hopkins and the Depression* (Syracuse, N.Y.: Syracuse University Press, 1963), p. 214.

22. Alfred Lief, *Democracy's Norris* (New York: Stackpole Sons, 1939), p. 489.

23. See, for example, Kennedy in the *Harvard College Class of 1912, 25th Anniversary Report*, 1937, p. 401.

24. Reverend Joseph F. Thorning, *Builders of the Social Order*, (Ozone Park, N.Y.: Catholic Literary Guild, 1941), p. 74.

25. Kennedy's speech keynoting the Greater Boston Community Fund Drive, *Boston Herald*, January 25, 1938, p. 1.

26. *Boston Sunday Post*, August 16, 1936, p. 14.

27. Kennedy, "Why I'm for Roosevelt," *The Review of Reviews*, September, 1936, p. 25.

28. Samuel I. Rosenman, *Working with Roosevelt* (New York: Harper & Brothers, 1952), p. 88.

29. Arthur Krock, *Memoirs: Sixty Years on the Firing Line* (New York: Funk & Wagnalls, 1968), p. 167.

30. *New York Times*, September 21, 1935, p. 1; and, Krock, *New York Times*, April 28, 1935, IV, p. 3. There is no way to ascertain whether or not Eleanor really told Kennedy "I want you to go right on telling Franklin exactly what you think." Pearson and Allen, *Washington Times-Herald*, September 18, 1937.

31. For Hearst, see *Ickes Diary*, I, 472; *F.D.R., His Personal Letters, 1928–1945*, ed. Elliott Roosevelt (New York: Duell Sloan and Pearce, 1950), p. 424. For Father Coughlin, see *Ickes Diary*, I, 472; Arthur M. Schlesinger, Jr., *The Politics of Upheaval* (Boston: Houghton Mifflin, 1960), pp. 24, 341; Presidential Press Conference 237, typescript at Roosevelt Library, Hyde Park, N.Y., Press Conferences VI, 150–51. After completing work at the SEC, Kennedy undertook a study trip for Roosevelt to look into recovery in Europe. See *New York Times*, October 12, 1935, p. 15, November 1, 1935, p. 33, November 15, 1935, p. 18.

32. *Jim Farley's Story* (New York: McGraw-Hill Book Company, Inc., 1948), p. 126.

33. The author has seen perhaps a dozen different newspaper items, widely separated in time, to this effect.

34. *Jim Farley's Story*, p. 115.

35. Blum, *Morgenthau Diary*, I, 318–19; Gay Talese, *The Kingdom and the Power* (New York: The World Publishing Company, 1969), p. 188.

36. Alsop and Kintner, *Saturday Evening Post*, June 25, 1938, p. 11; see also Adolf A. Berle, *Navigating the Rapids, 1918–1971*, ed. Beatrice Bishop Berle and Travis Beal Jacobs (New York: Harcourt Brace Jovanovich, Inc., 1973), pp. 141–42, 143.

37. *Washington Post*, September 24, 1935, p. 2.

38. Alsop and Kintner, *Saturday Evening Post*, June 25, 1938, p. 10; also, "The S.E.C.," an excellent history of the body in *Fortune*, June, 1940, p. 124.

39. *The Memoirs of Will H. Hays* (Garden City, N.Y.: Doubleday & Company, Inc., 1955), p. 460; see page 492, note 99, *supra*.

40. *New York Times*, August 16, 1935, p. 23.

41. This phrase is a note that the author made in his notebook while researching at Hyde Park. The author jotted down only two of the cites: Kennedy to "Missy" LeHand, January 28, 1937, in President's Personal File 207; and, a series of letters to Miss LeHand with regard to a photograph of the President and King of England in President's Personal File 207, October, 1939. Kennedy wanted the autographs of both men on the photograph. Years later, Rose Kennedy went to pains to have a photograph of John Kennedy and Soviet Premier Nikita Khrushchev autographed by both men, and incurred the President's familiar censure for approaching the Soviet leader through other than official channels. Gail Cameron, *Rose* (London: Michael Joseph, 1972), p. 165. Joseph Kennedy always took pride in the artifacts that he had of the prominent people he knew, and of other tangible evidences reflecting his own prominence. His friend Eddie Gallagher recalls how pleased Kennedy was when the principal officer of General Motors personally directed that Joe Kennedy get the third Cadillac produced following the end of the government's wartime restrictions on manufacture of private automobiles. Edward M. Gallagher, recorded interview by Ed Martin, January 8, 1965, p. 4, typescript at John F. Kennedy Library, Oral History Program. In 1955 he wrote his friend Beaverbrook of "the great honor" that the Pope had done him "by having his picture taken with me." Kennedy told Beaverbrook that it was an honor that the Pope rarely, if ever, accorded anyone. Kennedy to Beaverbrook, June 24, 1955, MS. at Beaverbrook Library, London.

42. "The Reminiscences of Eddie Dowling" (1963), p. 320, typescript in The Oral History Collection of Columbia University, reports an incident during the 1932 campaign in Minneapolis, Minnesota.

43. Arthur M. Schlesinger, Jr., *The Coming of the New Deal* (Boston: Houghton Mifflin Company, 1959), p. 542.

44. Blum, *Morgenthau Diary*, I, 241.

45. *Ickes Diary*, entry of October 9, 1936, I, 692.

46. *Jim Farley's Story*, p. 198.

47. The author asked James Roosevelt to comment on Farley's assertion. The President's son said that Roosevelt *had* liked Kennedy; that Roosevelt realized Kennedy's defects and limitations, but could like Kennedy in spite of them. He mentioned that Roosevelt visited Kennedy at Marwood on occasion. When the author suggested that these visits might have been part of "the holding of the hand," Roosevelt said "No, there was more to it than just that." Roosevelt suggested that the author speak to James Landis about Kennedy's relations with the President, pointing out that as Landis was a friend of both Kennedy and the neo-Brandeizian New Dealers, he would be in a good position to comment. Landis confirmed Roosevelt's comments. Interviews with James Roosevelt on March 20, 1962 and James M. Landis on March 3, 1962.

48. The correspondence files at Hyde Park include several thank-yous from "Missy" LeHand to Kennedy, acknowledging the gifts.

49. Pearson and Allen, *Boston Herald*, September 18, 1937. Boettiger and Kennedy remained close long after the Roosevelt-Kennedy relations grew cold. In January, 1939, after a visit with Boettiger, Harold Laski wrote Roosevelt "you must teach him that the American Ambassador at St. James is not a simple American in love with the New Deal." Laski to Roosevelt, January 15, 1939, in President's Personal File 3014, MS. at Roosevelt Library, Hyde Park, N.Y.

50. Earliest source for this anecdote seems to be *Newsweek*'s Joseph Kennedy

obituary, December 1, 1969, pp. 28–30. Later writings repeated it. Cameron, *Rose*, p. 95. The *Newsweek* account did not hint at its source, and the author's somewhat persistent efforts to pry the source out of *Newsweek* were to no avail. The author suspects that the anecdote traces back to Elliott Roosevelt, who for years had been bandying about exactly that type of tale. Curiously, Elliott Roosevelt includes parallel material in his recent *An Untold Story: The Roosevelts of Hyde Park* (New York: G. P. Putnam's Sons, 1973), p. 298; it seems most unlikely that he took it from *Newsweek*. It is entirely possible that Kennedy himself made up the repartee out of whole cloth (or nearly whole cloth) and related it to those that he thought might be impressed, by way of twofold boast: boast as to his sex life and boast as to his intimacy with the President.

51. Joe McCarthy, *The Remarkable Kennedys* (New York: Popular Library, paperback ed. 1960), pp. 53–54. Kennedy's favorite expression was represented to this author to be "Go shit in your hat!" It seems unlikely that such a man would use the phrase "making love" in an all-male gathering; he would more likely use some short colloquialism.

52. In later life, the family and associates encouraged people to refer to Kennedy in the third person as "the Ambassador." Mary Barelli Gallagher, *My Life With Jacqueline Kennedy*, ed. Frances Spatz Leighton (New York: David McKay Company, Inc., 1969), p. 106; Victor Lasky, *Robert F. Kennedy: The Myth and The Man* (New York: Trident Press, 1968), p. 364. After receiving a friendly razzing at a Harvard reunion in '37, Kennedy declined to attend reunions thereafter. Whalen, p. 197, cites interviews with classmates Ralph Lowell and Raymond Wilkins.

53. Arthur Krock, recorded interview by Charles Bartlett, May 10, 1964, p. 2, typescript at John F. Kennedy Library, Oral History Program. In his *Memoirs*, Krock says "I rose to leave, but Kennedy signaled me to remain." Page 332. Kennedy wanted Krock to witness his handling of the President.

54. Presidential Press Conference 134, typescript at Roosevelt Library, Hyde Park, N.Y. Press Conferences, III, 436.

55. Gallagher oral history typescript, pp. 13, 20.

56. Interviews with James Landis and James Roosevelt; Pearson and Allen, September 18, 1937, *Boston Herald*.

57. Krock, *Memoirs*, p. 171.

58. Krock, *New York Times*, December 12, 1937, IV, 3. See also Krock, *New York Times*, April 28, 1935, IV, 3; Charles W. B. Hurd, *New York Times Magazine*, May 26, 1935, pp. 5, 20; and, *New York Times*, September 21, 1935, p. 1.

59. Presidential Press Conference 246, typescript at Roosevelt Library, Hyde Park, N.Y. Press Conferences, VI, 251–53.

60. Richard J. Whalen, *The Founding Father* (New York: The New American Library of World Literature, Inc., 1964) p. 157, cites anonymous interview, probably either Burt Wheeler or "Senator Frazier."

1936

1. Andrew Tully, *Washington Daily News*, April 8, 1960.

2. Interview with Raymond O'Connell, Boston, April 5, 1962.

3. Interview with Ferdinand Pecora, New York, March 13, 1962.

4. John Henry Cutler, *"Honey Fitz": Three Steps to the White House*, (Indianapolis: Bobbs-Merrill Company, Inc., 1962), pp. 178–79.

5. Quoted in Ralph G. Martin and Ed Plaut, *Front Runner, Dark Horse* (Garden City, N.Y.: Doubleday & Company, Inc., 1960), p. 123.

6. Section on the RCA recapitalization is based on *Time*, February 10, 1936, p. 64, and April 20, 1936; also, *New York Times*, December 28, 1935, p. 21; January 25, 1936, p. 21; February 1, 1936, p. 19; and, April 8, 1936, p. 35.

7. Interview with John J. Reynolds, New York, on May 28, 1962.

8. *New York Times*, May 7, 1936, p. 33, and July 15, 1936, p. 27.

9. Bosley Crowther, *Hollywood Rajah: The Life and Times of Louis B. Mayer* (New York: Henry Holt and Company, 1960), p. 227.

10. Material on the Paramount reorganization is based on SEC Report on Reorganization Committees, Part I, pp. 6–64; *Time*, July 27, 1936, p. 51; and *New York Times*, May 2, 1936, p. 23; May 4, 1936, p. 33; June 13, 1936, p. 25; June 16, 1936, p. 39; July 3, 1936, p. 25; July 15, 1936, p. 27; and July 17, 1936, p. 23.

11. Richard J. Whalen, *The Founding Father* (New York: The New American Library of World Literature, Inc., 1964), p. 18, citing Paramount summary.

12. Kennedy to Lord Beaverbrook, MS. at the Beaverbrook Library, London.

13. Whalen, *Founding Father*, p. 68, cites anonymous interview.

14. Joseph F. Dinneen, *The Kennedy Family* (Boston: Little, Brown and Company, 1959), p. 69.

15. Kennedy to LeHand, June 15, 1936, MS. at Roosevelt Library, Hyde Park, N.Y. in President's Personal File 207.

16. In his *Memoirs: Sixty Years on the Firing Line* (New York: Funk & Wagnalls, 1968), Krock says "I helped him in an editorial capacity with the production of his book *I'm for Roosevelt*." Page 332. In his oral history interview for the Kennedy Library, though, Krock mentions in passing that Joseph Kennedy had "signed his name at least, to a book in the campaign of 1936, *I'm for Roosevelt*." Typescript, p. 2. Perhaps Fayne, who did considerable ghosting for Kennedy at the SEC, also had a hand in it. Landis, who ghosted many speeches for Joseph, John, and Robert Kennedy, told the author that he had had no hand in the book. See also W. E. Mullins column in the *Boston Herald*, December 14, 1950.

17. Published in *F.D.R., His Personal Letters, 1928–1945*, ed. Elliott Roosevelt (New York: Duell, Sloan and Pearce, 1950), I, 595.

18. Published by Reynal & Hitchcock, New York, 1936.

19. The recession of 1937 showed that genuine recovery had not yet been effectuated.

20. See reviews in *The Nation*, September 12, 1936, p. 314, and the *Saturday Review of Literature*, September 5, 1936, p. 12.

21. *Saturday Review of Literature*, September 5, 1936, p. 12.

22. *I'm For Roosevelt*, p. 3.

23. *Motion Picture Herald*, August 29, 1936.

24. Reviewed in the *New York Herald-Tribune*, September 6, 1936, p. 13; favorably reviewed in *Christian Century*, October 14, 1936, p. 1361, *The Nation*, September 12, 1936, p. 314, and the *Review of Reviews*, September, 1936, p. 13; unfavorably reviewed from a left-wing slant in the *New Republic*, September 23, 1936, p. 189; mixed review from a conservative slant in *Saturday Review of Literature*, September 5, 1936. Perhaps the best study is in *New York Times*, August 23, 1936, III, 1. See also *Review of Reviews*, October, 1936, for "I'm for Landon," a reply by Arthur Ballantine, Herbert Hoover's Under Secretary of the Treasury.

25. Roosevelt to Kennedy, October 10, 1936, MS. at Roosevelt Library, Hyde Park, N.Y., in President's Personal File 207.

26. *F.D.R., His Personal Letters, 1928–1945*, I, 547.

27. Arthur Krock discussed Kennedy's experiences in *New York Times*, December 17, 1936, p. 26.

28. *New York Times*, July 26, 1936, III, 1.

29. *Boston Globe*, July 26, 1936.

30. *Boston Post*, August 16, 1936, p. 14.

31. *New York Times Magazine*, September 6, 1936, pp. 1–2; *Review of Reviews*, September, 1936; *Rostrum*, September, 1936.

32. *New York Times*, October 6, 1936, p. 13.

33. *New York Times*, October 22, 1936, p. 13.

34. Kennedy to Roosevelt, October 24, 1936, MS. at Roosevelt Library, Hyde Park, N.Y., in President's Personal File 207.

35. *New York Times*, October 25, 1936, p. 33.

36. Alsop and Kintner, "Battle of the Market Place," *Saturday Evening Post*, June 25, 1938, p. 10.

37. Mark Sullivan, *Washington Sunday Star*, November 11, 1934.

38. Quoted in a Norton article in the *Boston Post*, August 16, 1936, p. 14.

39. *Rostrum*, September, 1936.

40. Page 385 *infra*.

41. *Saturday Review of Literature*, September 5, 1936, p. 12.

42. Charles J. Tull, *Father Coughlin and the New Deal* (Syracuse, N.Y.: Syracuse University Press, 1965), p. 156.

CLEANING
THE AUGEAN STABLES

1. *Time*, March 22, 1937, pp. 63–64.

2. Arthur Krock, *New York Times*, March 10, 1937, p. 22.

3. See *New York Times* of March 23, 24, 25, 26, and 30, 1937.

4. After a meeting with a group of shippers, Kennedy, with characteristic color, carped to Judge Burns "there wasn't a guy in that room who could write a check for a million dollars." Richard J. Whalen, *The Founding Father* (New York: The New American Library of World Literature, Inc., 1964), p. 191 cites interview with Francis Currie, Burns' law partner.

5. Krock, *New York Times*, March 10, 1937, p. 22.

6. *New Republic*, August 11, 1937, p. 7.

7. Comments on the Legislative history of the act based on *Fortune*, September, 1937, pp. 74 ff.

8. *Marine Age*, July, 1936, p. 18. (*Marine Age* frequently referred to the nation's capital as "Washscow.")

9. For an excellent criticism of the act, see the comments of the Maritime Association of the Port of New York, in *Marine Age*, October, 1937, p. 16.

10. *Hearings before the House Committee on the Merchant Marine and Fisheries on H.R. 8532*, December 2, 1937, p. 33.

11. Interview with Admiral Land, Washington, March 21, 1962.

12. *Ibid.* Also, Woodward, recorded interview by C. Guthrie and A. Ross, June 7, 1946, typescript at National Archives, Washington, D.C., Maritime Commission Historian's Collection, Research File 105.

13. Frederick C. Lane, *Ships for Victory* (Baltimore: Johns Hopkins Press, 1951), pp. 14–15.

14. Woodward interview.

15. *Ibid.*

16. Land interview; Woodward interview.

17. Land interview.

18. Land interview.

19. Emory S. Land, *Winning The War With Ships* (New York: Robert M. McBride Co., Inc., 1958), p. 7.

20. Land interview and Land, *Winning The War With Ships*, p. 6.

21. Land, *Winning The War With Ships*, pp. 16–17.

22. Woodward interview.

23. *FDR, His Personal Letters, 1928–1945*, ed. Elliott Roosevelt (New York: Duell, Sloan and Pearce, 1950), I, 490.

24. *Cleveland Plain Dealer*, September 27, 1937.

25. *Fortune*, September, 1937, p. 144.

26. Daniel Marx, Jr., "The United States Maritime Commission, 1936–1940" (Doctoral thesis, University of California at Berkeley, 1946), pp. 119–126, for discussion of mail contract settlements.

27. One of the claims, Admiral Land told the author, was not settled until 1953.

28. Krock, *New York Times*, July 1, 1937, p. 26.

29. *New Republic*, August 11, 1937, pp. 7–8. For a conservative criticism of Kennedy's mail-contracts work see *Journal of Commerce*, February 19, 1938, p. 2.

30. Marx, "The United States Maritime Commission," p. 125.

31. Roosevelt to Kennedy, July 10, 1937, MS. at Roosevelt Library, Hyde Park, N.Y., in FDR Office File 1705, Box 1 (1935–1937), 1937 folder.

32. Marx, "The United States Maritime Commission," p. 267.

33. There were some unpleasant consequences from the liquidation of the government's fleet. Some of the ships were sold to a scrutable Occidental in Shanghai who misrepresented the purpose to which they would be put. Shanghai was at the time at the center of the Chinese-Japanese hostilities, and the broker immediately resold the vessels to Japan, where they were scrapped and used in making arms to further Japan's war of aggression in the Orient. No doubt other vessels found their way, through devious routes, to the hands of aggressor nations. The fleet was disposed of with a little too much haste. Kennedy to Representative J. Parnell Thomas, November 24, 1937, MS. at Roosevelt Library, Hyde Park, N.Y., in FDR Official File 1705, Mis. and Memorandum; and, Kennedy to McIntyre, November 24, 1937, MS. at Roosevelt Library, Hyde Park, N.Y., in FDR Official File 1705.

34. Pearson and Allen *New York Daily Mirror*, September 26, 1937; also, *The Memoirs of Cordell Hull* (New York: The Macmillan Company, 1948), I, 557–58.

35. Hull, *Memoirs*, I, 558.

36. Pearson and Allen, *New York Daily Mirror*, September 18, 1937.

37. Memorandum from Miss Perkins to Roosevelt, March 10, 1937, MS. at Roosevelt Library, Hyde Park, N.Y., in President's Official File 1705, Box 1 (1935–1937), 1937 folder.

38. Kennedy to Roosevelt, June 19, 1937, MS. at Roosevelt Library, Hyde Park, N.Y. in President's Official File 1705, Box 1 (1935–1937), 1937 folder.

39. *Fortune*, September, 1937, p. 123.

40. Joseph P. Goldberg, *The Maritime Story: A Study in Labor-Management Relations* (Cambridge, Mass.: Harvard University Press, 1958), p. 164.

41. *New York Times*, July 22, 1937, p. 9; *Fortune*, September, 1937, p. 137.

42. Speech of May 22, 1937, before Propeller Club, reprinted in *Vital Speeches*, June 15, 1937, pp. 532, 534.

43. Kennedy to FDR, September 8, 1937, MS. at Roosevelt Library, Hyde Park, N.Y., in President's Official File 1705, Box 1 (1935–1937), 1937 folder.

44. Kennedy to James Roosevelt, September 8, 1937, MS. at Roosevelt Library, Hyde Park, New York.

45. Pamphlet, "The Story of the *Algic* Case" (New York. *Algic* Defense Committee, 1937, or January 1938).

46. The official organ of the N.M.U. proudly published a thank-you from the secretary of the Uruguayan longshoremen which attributed the success of their strike to "the great cooperation" and "splendid support" of the *Algic* crew. *N.M.U. Pilot*, October 8, 1937, p. 3. See also the *N.M.U. Pilot* of October 29, 1937, p. 1.

47. Joseph A. Gainard, *Yankee Skipper* (New York: Frederick A. Stokes Company, 1940), pp. 89–90.

48. *Marine Age*, September, 1937, p. 18.

49. Interview with Joseph Curran, New York City, April 10, 1962.

50. *N.M.U. Pilot*, December 17, 1937, p. 1. Also, "The Story of the *Algic* Case," p. 13, and Curran interview.

51. Arthur Krock, who was listening at Kennedy's end, reports that Kennedy had said "we'll land in the ——— ———," and hints that the missing words refer to an "ignoble but functional edifice to which Kennedy was wont to refer." *Memoirs: Sixty Years on the Firing Line* (New York: Funk & Wagnalls, 1968), pp. 332–33. The author carelessly sought permission of Krock's publisher to quote *Krock* as having quoted Kennedy as having said "we'll land in the shit house," only to be told by the gentleman at the other end of the telephone that *"Mr. Krock does not say shit house."* Kennedy, however, was wont . . . , and the publisher acknowledged that the author's guess as to the missing words was no doubt correct.

52. Curran interview.

53. *N.M.U. Pilot*, December 17, 1937, p. 1; December 27, 1937, p. 1; "The Story of the *Algic* Case," pp. 13–14.

54. *New York Times*, October 30, 1937, p. 18.

55. *Washington Post*, September 12, 1937, III, 8.

56. *Marine Age*, September, 1937, p. 18.

57. *Marine Age*, October, 1937, p. 18

58. *New York Post*, October 21, 1937, p. 18; *Philadelphia Record*, October 6, 1937.

59. Pamphlet, "The Maritime Commission vs. the Seamen" (Washington: C.I.O. Maritime Committee, 1939), p. 9.

60. Both quotations from *N.M.U. Pilot*, January 7, 1938, p. 1.

61. "Kennedy vs. the C.I.O.," *The Nation*, February 26, 1938, p. 234.

62. *New York Times*, October 26, 1937, p. 15. Denied by Curran, *New York Times*, November 2, 1937, p. 15.

63. The wires are at Roosevelt Library, Hyde Park, N.Y., in President's Official File 1705—Miscellaneous.

64. Memorandum dated October 27, 1937, at Roosevelt Library, Hyde Park, N.Y., in President's Official File 1705—Miscellaneous.

65. An earlier bill, introduced by Senator Guffey and Congressman Bland, calling

for compulsory arbitration died when Kennedy opposed it on the grounds that it was premature.

66. U.S. Maritime Commission, *Economic Survey of the American Merchant Marine* (Washington, D.C.: Government Printing Office, November, 1937), pp. 48–51.

67. Kennedy discussed labor at several Congressional Committee hearings: *Senate Committee on Commerce and the Committee on Education and Labor, Hearings on Sen. 3078*, December 8, 1937, pp. 24–36; *Hearings on Sen. 3078*, February 16, 1938, p. 1; *Hearings on Sen. 3078*, January 16, 1938, p. 776. Also, *House Committee on the Merchant Marine and Fisheries, Hearings on H.R. 8532*, December 2 and 3, 1937, pp. 14–31.

68. A large number of editorial reactions are collected in *Hearings before the Senate Committee on Commerce and the Committee on Education and Labor on Sen. 3078* (1938), pp. 1021–1062. They were introduced by Senator Copeland and were no doubt edited to favor his own antilabor position.

69. *N.M.U. Pilot*, January 22, 1938, p. 24.

70. *Senate Committee on Commerce and the Committee on Education and Labor on Sen. 3078*, February 4, 1938, pp. 964–985.

71. *Economic Survey*, pp. 48–49.

72. *Hearings on Sen. 3078*, December 8, 1937, p. 26.

73. *Hearings on Sen. 3078*, February 16, 1938, p. 1172.

74. *New York Times*, July 17, 1938, XII, 3.

75. *Current Biography*, 1940, asserts that Kennedy's opinions on Miss Perkins grew less and less printable. See also *Time*, February 28, 1938, p. 18.

76. See the following Presidential Press Conferences: 414, December 7, 1937, 10, 398; 158, February 18, 1938, 11, 174; 453, April 22, 1938, 11, 464, all at Roosevelt Library, Hyde Park, N.Y.

77. *New Republic*, August 11, 1937, p. 9.

78. Exchange of letters is in *Press Releases of The United States Maritime Commission*, PR 102, August 25, 1937; *Marine Age*, October, 1937, p. 30.

79. Interview with UAW official, Milford, Conn., 1962.

80. Interview with Kennedy by Morris DeHaven Tracy in *Boston Traveler*, January 24, 1938, p. 3.

81. Curran interview.

82. *Senate Hearings*, January 16, 1938, p. 778.

83. Curran interview.

84. Joe McCarthy, *The Remarkable Kennedys* (New York: Popular Library, paperback ed., 1960), p. 12.

85. Bill Cunningham, *Boston Herald*, August 16, 1942, p. 26. Cunningham was one of a handful of newsmen to whom Kennedy spoke openly after his interview with Louis Lyons of November, 1940, possibly because Cunningham's reports were always sympathetic and favorable to Kennedy. Labor leaders to whom the author spoke laughed at the claim.

86. *Ibid.*

87. Joseph F. Thorning, *Builders of the Social Order* (Ozone Park, N.Y.: Catholic Literary Guild, 1941), p. 74.

88. *Economic Survey*, pp. 46–47.

89. Thorning, *Builders of the Social Order*, p. 74.

90. *Senate Hearings*, December 8, 1937, p. 35.

91. *House Hearings*, December 2 and 3, 1937, p. 31.

92. *Senate Hearings,* December 8, 1937, p. 36.

93. *Senate Hearings,* February 16, 1938, p. 1169.

94. Goldberg, *The Maritime Story,* p. 195.

95. Pamphlet, "The Maritime Commission vs. the Seamen" (Washington: CIO Maritime Commission, 1939), p. 6.

96. Goldberg, *The Maritime Story,* p. 195.

97. Quoted in *Fortune,* September, 1937, p. 127.

98. *Senate Hearings,* December 8, 1937, p. 35.

99. *Ibid.*

100. Marx, "The United States Maritime Commission," p. 383.

101. *Fortune,* September, 1937, p. 126.

102. Curran interview.

103. *Fortune,* September, 1937, p. 138.

104. Goldberg, *The Maritime Story,* p. 182.

105. Paraphrased from Goldberg, *ibid.,* p. 194.

106. Statistics from *Fortune,* September, 1937, pp. 61, 163–64.

107. *Ibid.,* p. 164.

108. Speech before the Propeller Club, May 22, 1937, in *Vital Speeches,* June 15, 1937, pp. 532–35.

109. *Hearings before the Subcommittee of the Committee on Appropriations, House of Representatives, 75th Congress, 1st Session, on the 3rd Deficiency Appropriations Bill, for 1937, June 15, 1937,* pp. 223, 244.

110. *New York Times,* August 17, 1937, p. 8.

111. *New York Times,* September 13, 1937, p. 1.

112. *Economic Survey,* p. 36.

113. United States Maritime Commission, report to Congress, 1938, p. 1.

114. Land, *Winning the War with Ships,* p. 8.

115. Title VII of the act.

116. See, for example, *New York Times,* June 20, 1937, VII, 3 ff.

117. "Mr. Kennedy's Record," *Journal of Commerce,* February 19, 1938, p. 2.

118. *Hearings on the 3rd Deficiency Bill,* June 15, 1937, pp. 244–45.

119. Henry Ehrlich, *Boston Herald,* October 3, 1937.

120. *Hearings before Senate Committee on Commerce and the Committee on Education and Labor, on Sen. 3078,* January 26, 1938, p. 760.

121. *Hearings before House Committee on the Merchant Marine and Fisheries, on H.R. 8532,* December 2, 1937, p. 28.

122. *Hearings on Sen. 5078,* December 8, 1937, pp. 16–19; *Hearings on Sen. 3078,* February 16, 1938, pp. 1163–4.

123. *Hearings on Sen. 3078,* December 8, 1937, pp. 14, 30.

124. *Hearings on Sen. 3078,* December 8, 1937, p. 30.

125. Marx, "The United States Maritime Commission," p. 93.

126. Land, *Winning the War with Ships,* p. 6.

127. Marx, "The United States Maritime Commission," p. 69.

128. *New York Times,* January 8, 1938, p. 3.

129. *Newsweek,* November 22, 1937, p. 40. But see the unfavorable review of it by the pro-labor New York Maritime Council in the *Pilot,* November 19, 1937, p. 5.

130. *Time,* November 22, 1937, p. 20.

A NEW DEALER
GOES TO ENGLAND

1. *New York Times,* October 16, 1937, p. 1.

2. See Kennedy's comment in a speech of March, 1938, about his "bearishness" on the American economy in the *New York Times,* March 25, 1938, p. 1; also, the *Cleveland Plain Dealer,* September 27, 1937.

3. John M. Blum, *From the Morgenthau Diary,* Vol. I: *Years of Crisis: 1928–1938* (Boston: Houghton Mifflin Company, 1959), p. 441.

4. According to the *New York Times,* Kennedy was not calling for complete abolishment of the tax, but only substantial reduction of it. *New York Times,* October 16, 1937, p. 1.

5. Kennedy's objections to the capital gains tax are outlined in his article "Big Business, What Now?" *Saturday Evening Post,* January 16, 1937, p. 80. Baruch wrote Kennedy his congratulations on the piece. Baruch to Kennedy, January 16, 1937, MS. in Baruch Papers, Princeton University Library, Princeton, N.J., Vol. 40.

6. *Ibid.* See also Joseph P. Kennedy, *I'm for Roosevelt* (New York: Reynal & Hitchcock, 1936), pp. 75–76; *New York Times,* October 16, 1937, p. 1; and, speech by Representative Treadway on April 13, 1937, *Congressional Record,* XXCI, pp. 3415–16.

7. *I'm for Roosevelt,* p. 76, and *New York Times Magazine,* September 6, 1936, p. 2.

8. Blum, *Morgenthau Diary,* I, 441.

9. *Ibid.*

10. *New York Times,* November 25, 1937, p. 26.

11. Presidential Press Conference 407, October 29, 1937, typescript at Roosevelt Library, Hyde Park, N.Y., Press Conferences, X, 304.

12. Telegram from Kennedy to Bernard Baruch, March 4, 1937, MS. in Baruch Papers, Princeton University Library, Vol. 40, solicits Baruch's support for the plan. Copy of same, dated March 3, is at Roosevelt Library, Hyde Park, N.Y., in President's Personal File 207.

13. Or so it was said at the time of President John Kennedy's crisis with "Big Steel." The author has not discovered a contemporary citation, but the comment is not out of character.

14. *New York Times,* December 8, 1937, pp. 1, 22.

15. *Wall Street Journal,* December 9, 1937, p. 4. See also the *Wall Street Journal,* December 15, 1937, p. 4; a letter to the editor from LeGrand B. Cannon in the *New York Times,* December 19, 1937, IV, 9; and, Walter Lippmann, *New York Herald-Tribune,* December 9, 1937.

16. Kent, *Baltimore Sun,* December 8, 1937; *Wall Street Journal,* December 9, 1937, p. 4. After publication of the column, Kennedy was in touch with Kent, who wrote Baruch: "Joe Kennedy sent me Herbert's [presumably a reference to Swope] letter to read. It is amazing. He did tell him his speech was a 'courageous utterance,' and that the business men needed to be told exactly what he had told them. I am shocked at this exhibition of duplicity.

"When I see you remind me to tell you who called me up from Washington yesterday to congratulate me on the Kennedy story. You will be surprised. More duplicity. What a world! Is there such a thing as a degree for Doctor of the Double

Cross? If so, I have a couple of candidates." Kent to Baruch, December 17, 1937, MS. in Baruch Papers, Princeton University Library, Vol. 40.

17. Kent to Baruch, December 8, 1937, MS. in Baruch Papers, Vol. 40.

18. Interview with James Roosevelt, Washington, March 20, 1962.

19. Arthur Krock, recorded interview by Charles Bartlett, May 10, 1964, p. 3, typescript at John F. Kennedy Library, Oral History Program.

20. Morris DeHaven Tracy's report of a Kennedy interview in the *Boston Traveler*, January 24, 1938, p. 1.

21. Clipping of a Robert L. Norton article dated January 25, 1938, in the *Boston Herald* archives.

22. Kent to Baruch, June 14, 1937, MS. in Baruch Papers, Vol. 40.

23. *Ibid.*

24. James Roosevelt interview.

25. P.A.S. release, published December 24, 1937, in the Dearborn, Mich., *Weekly Independent*, the Langhorne, Penn., *Advance*, and other small papers.

26. *New York Post*, December 15, 1937. See also Heywood Broun's column in the *New York World-Telegram and Sun*, April 13, 1938.

27. Or so James Farley told the author. Interview, New York, March 3, 1962. Roosevelt, knowing with whom he spoke, could well have said as much to the Irish-American Farley.

28. James Roosevelt interview.

29. Arthur Krock, *Memoirs: Sixty Years on the Firing Line* (New York: Funk & Wagnalls, 1968), p. 333. In a December 16, 1937 letter to Baruch, Krock wrote that Kennedy was under very heavy pressure not to take the post, "but I am sure he will." MS. in Baruch Papers, Princeton University Library, Vol. 40.

30. This author seriously doubts that there was any substance to the rumor, and suspects that Roosevelt related it to Morgenthau knowing that it was just the kind of thing that Morgenthau liked to hear about his self-styled rival for head of the Treasury.

31. Morgenthau's diary entry of December 8, 1937, MS. at Roosevelt Library, Hyde Park, N.Y., in Morgenthau Vol. 101, p. 69. It worked: Morgenthau's own conclusion was, "I certainly will be glad to have him out of Washington and I take it that is the way the President feels." *Ibid.*

32. *F.D.R.: His Personal Letters, 1928–1945*, ed. Elliott Roosevelt (New York: Duell, Sloan and Pearce, 1950), II, 743.

33. Gay Talese, *The Kingdom and the Power* (New York: The World Publishing Company, 1969), pp. 188–89. For Krock's rejoinder, see his *Memoirs*, p. 333. According to Talese, Krock was settling an old score with Bingham, who had made somebody else editor of a Louisville, Kentucky, newspaper upon acquiring its ownership. Talese, p. 188. It seems more likely that Krock was merely printing a scoop before someone else did. Robert L. Norton, writing in the *Boston Post*, reported that Krock had had the appointment in the *Times* even before Secretary of State Cordell Hull knew of it. *Boston Post*, January 25, 1938. That is most unlikely: the appointment would have had to have been cleared with the British, through the State Department, before being firmed up.

34. Robert L. Norton, *Boston Post*, December 9, 1937. Also, *Boston Globe*, December 9, 1937; and, *U.S. News* (Washington), December 10, 1937.

35. Barry Bingham to Roosevelt, December 11, 1937, MS. at Roosevelt Library, Hyde Park, N.Y., in President's Personal File 716. Also, *New York Times*, December 21, 1937.

36. *The Nation*, December 14, 1940, p. 593. The far right, however, suspected that Roosevelt was exiling the only good man in Washington, during a recession, as some part of a maniacal plot. Krock, *New York Times*, December 12, 1937, IV, 3; and, R. deRoussy de Sales, "Joe Kennedy," *L'Europe Nouvelle*, June 25, 1938, p. 677.

37. *Roosevelt and Daniels*, ed. Carroll Kilpatrick (Chapel Hill: University of North Carolina Press, 1952), p. 172.

38. *U.S. News* (Washington), December 13, 1937; and, James T. Williams, Jr., *Chicago Daily News*, December 18, 1937.

39. John O'Donnell and Doris Fleeson, *New York Daily News*, December 10, 1937; *The Times* (London), December 10, 1937, p. 16; Max R. Grossman, *Boston Post*, January 2, 1938.

40. *New York Times*, February 22, 1938, p. 3.

41. Max R. Grossman, *Boston Post*, December 12, 1937, p. A3.

42. Kennedy to Roosevelt, January 13, 1938, MS. at Roosevelt Library, Hyde Park, N.Y., in President's Secretary's Files, I, Dip. Correspondence, Great Britain, Box 8.

43. Mrs. Kennedy to Roosevelt, undated, MS. at Roosevelt Library, Hyde Park, N.Y., in President's Personal File 207.

44. Roosevelt to Mrs. Kennedy, January 27, 1938, MS. at Roosevelt Library, Hyde Park, N.Y., in President's Personal File 207.

45. Kennedy requested that the British postpone passage of a proposed act until he arrived to personally complete negotiations. Lindsay was favorably disposed—"with his great energy and resourcefulness he would be at his best in attacking a complicated and difficult task like this and he might well do wonders"—but practicalities of the British situation made compliance impossible. Lindsay to Foreign Office, February 1, 1938, and response, MSS. Public Record Office, London, FO371/21530/A791/175/45.

46. Joseph F. Thorning, *Builders of the Social Order* (Ozone Park, N.Y.: Catholic Literary Guild, 1941), p. 71.

47. Daniel Marx, Jr., "The United States Maritime Commission, 1936–1940," (Doctoral thesis, University of California at Berkeley, 1946), p. 109.

48. *The Secret Diary of Harold L. Ickes*, Vol II: *The Inside Struggle, 1936–1939* (New York: Simon & Schuster, 1954), p. 340.

49. *Ibid.* Also, Emory S. Land, *Winning the War with Ships* (New York: Robert M. McBride Co., 1958), p. 11; and, *New York Times*, February 19, 1938, p. 1.

50. *Ickes Diary*, II, 340.

51. Frederick C. Lane, *Ships for Victory* (Baltimore, Maryland: Johns Hopkins Press, 1951), pp. 11–12; Marx, "The U.S. Maritime Commission, 1936–1940," p. 93.

52. *New York Times*, February 24, 1938, p. 8.

53. *Time*, March 7, 1938, p. 143.

54. *N.M.U. Pilot*, March 25, 1938, p. 1.

AN IMMEDIATE SUCCESS

1. Weather report in *Manchester Guardian*, March 1, 1938.

2. *New York Times*, March 2, 1938, p. 14.

3. Comments on page are based for the most part on sketches of him in the *Dictionary of American Biography* and the *Encyclopaedia Britannica*.

4. One of the better articles debunking Page is C. H. Grattan, "The Walter Hines Page Legend," *American Mercury*, September, 1925.

5. State Department folk myth has it that Ambassador Choate was once mistaken for a footman by a formal Englishman who asked the ambassador to "call me a cab." Choate responded that the gentleman was "a cab."

6. Kennedy to James Roosevelt, March 3, 1938, MS. in Hull Papers, Box 42, File 104, at Library of Congress Manuscript Division, Washington, D.C. (Hereafter cited as Hull Papers.)

7. Though her biographer says that Mrs. Kennedy does not like dogs—"a characteristic she has gone to great lengths to conceal." Gail Cameron, *Rose* (London: Michael Joseph, 1972), p. 31.

8. Howard Fyfe to Harry A. Havens, February 27, 1938, State Department MS. 123 Kennedy, Joseph P./35 at National Archives, Washington, D.C. (Such material hereafter cited as "S.D.MS." followed by document numbers.)

9. Harry A. Havens to Howard Fyfe, February 28, 1938, S.D.MS., same file, document 36.

10. Kennedy interview with W. P. Crozier of the *Manchester Guardian*, May 26, 1938; MS. notes at the Beaverbrook Library, London.

11. It is funny to see "bloody" in typescripts of transcribed telephone calls, as, for instance, Kennedy-Hull conversation, April 24, 1939, MS. in Hull Papers.

12. *New York Times*, March 6, 1938, p. 1.

13. Joe McCarthy, *The Remarkable Kennedys* (New York: Popular Library, paperback ed., 1960), p. 55.

14. Kennedy to Landis, March 22, 1938, MS. in James M. Landis Papers, Library of Congress Manuscript Division, Washington, D.C. (hereafter cited as "Landis Papers"), Office Files Box 24.

15. *New York Times*, March 9, 1938, p. 1. Though foreign diplomats generally wore knickers, most of Kennedy's predecessors as American Ambassadors in London had presented their credentials in trousers. McCarthy, *The Remarkable Kennedys*, p. 56.

16. Randolph Churchill, *Evening Standard* (London), March 9, 1938.

17. James M. Landis, untitled, unpublished manuscript intended by Landis to constitute Kennedy's diplomatic memoirs, copy at Joseph P. Kennedy offices, 230 Park Avenue, New York City, p. 8. (Hereafter cited as "Landis MS.") Over a period of years, Landis worked on Kennedy's diplomatic dispatches, correspondence, and diary notes, preparing a draft of the Ambassador's memoirs. The project was abandoned short of completion, Landis told the author, because he concluded that publication of the memoirs would cause embarrassment to John Kennedy. The author believes the draft at the Kennedy offices to be the most nearly finished version of Landis's work. Chunks of an earlier draft of the Landis MS. are to be found in the Landis Papers, Box 51. That set consists of six chapters numbered 17, 18, 36, 37, 40, and 41. While these six chapters cover a relatively small portion of the Ambassador's diplomatic career, for the period that each segment covers, the Library of Congress's drafts of chapters are much fuller than the corresponding portions of the later "Landis MS." located at the Kennedy offices. Hereafter, "Landis MS., Library of Congress," will refer to the Library's earlier draft. In those few instances in which parallel citations are possible, both will be given.

18. E. Wilder Spaulding, *Ambassadors Ordinary and Extraordinary* (Washington: Public Affairs Press, 1961), pp. 218–19.

19. *The Times* (London), March 19, 1938, p. 17.

20. Anecdote from Balderston correspondence, MS. at Library of Congress Manuscript Division, Washington, D.C.

21. Andrew Boyle, *Montagu Norman* (New York: Weybright and Talley, 1967), p. 315 cites interview with Norman's widow.

22. Lord Francis-Williams, *Nothing So Strange* (New York: American Heritage Press, 1970), p. 155.

23. Leonard Mosley, *Backs to the Wall* (New York: Random House, 1971), p. 36n.

24. *Secret Diary of Harold L. Ickes*, Vol. II: *The Inside Struggle, 1936–1939* (New York: Simon & Schuster, 1954), diary entry of April 17, 1938, p. 370. Ickes himself, ever wary of Wall-Streeter Kennedy, suspected that Kennedy had been taken in hand by Lady Astor's "Cliveden Set." Diary entry of April 23, 1938, II, 377.

25. Phillips diary entry of April 22, 1938, MS. at Houghton Library, Harvard University, Cambridge, Mass., pp. 2526–27. (Hereinafter cited as "Phillips Diary MS.") On his own part, Phillips remained enthusiastic for Kennedy. See Phillips to Roosevelt, June 23, 1938, MS. in Phillips file, 1937–1941, Roosevelt Library, Hyde Park, N.Y.

26. Lindsay to Eden, April 13, 1937, Foreign Office MS., FO371/20655/A2944/88/45 at Public Record Office, London. (Foreign Office Manuscripts at the Public Record Office are hereafter cited merely with their document numbers, beginning with the initials "FO".)

27. Lindsay dispatch 122, May 6–7, 1937, FO371/20655/A3354/80/45.

28. Foreign Office minute of March 14, 1938, FO371/21530/A2151.

29. Lord Riverdale to Thomas J. Watson, March 24, 1938, MS. at Roosevelt Library, Hyde Park, N.Y., in Roosevelt Office File 3060.

30. *The Diaries & Letters of Harold Nicolson*, Vol. II: *The War Years, 1939–1945*, ed. Nigel Nicolson (New York: Atheneum, 1967), diary entry of December 3, 1940, p. 130.

31. Franklin Gunther to Roosevelt, April 19, 1938, MS. at Roosevelt Library, Hyde Park, N.Y., in President's Secretary's File: State Department, 1938.

32. Asserted as having been the case by a leading British diplomat of the day, London, July, 1972.

33. Asserted by a different British diplomat of the day. Interview, London, July, 1972.

34. *The Diaries of Sir Alexander Cadogan, 1938–1945*, ed. David Dilks (London: Cassell, 1971), diary entry of March 14, 1938, p. 62.

35. J. J. Astor to Brendon Bracken, February 19, 1941, FO371/26217/A348/339/45. By the time of this letter Astor had conluded that Kennedy was "a bad man." *Ibid.*

36. Interview, August 7, 1965.

37. Interview in London with leading British diplomat of the day, July, 1972.

38. *Ibid.*

39. Joseph Alsop and Robert Kintner, *Evening Star* (Washington), December 18, 1939.

40. Kennedy to Beaverbrook and Beaverbrook to Kennedy, May, 1938, MSS. at Beaverbrook Library, London.

41. Notwithstanding which, Kennedy was capable of describing "Beaver," who inspired hotly mixed feelings, as a "treacherous little bastard." *The London Journal of General Raymond E. Lee, 1940–41*, ed. James Leutze (Boston: Little, Brown and Company, 1971), diary entry of October 14, 1940, p. 92.

42. Interview, August 7, 1965.

43. *The Times* (London), March 31, 1938, p. 8.

44. See Krock, *New York Times*, April 12, 1938, p. 22, for the fullest story of how the decision came about. Kennedy had originally planned to have Krock break the story after Kennedy's letter and Lodge's response, but perhaps (only perhaps) through a slip, the Ambassador's letter to Lodge was released before Lodge even received it. This created the impression that Kennedy was snubbing the Massachusetts Brahmin and annoyed the Senator. See *New York Times*, April 10, 1938, p. 2; and, Moffat Diary MS., Houghton Library, Harvard University, Cambridge, Mass., April 10, 1938. (Hereafter cited as "Moffat Diary MS.")

45. *New York Times*, April 11, 1938, p. 2, quotes the headlines from the English papers, none of which are available at either the New York City Public Library or the Library of Congress. The restrained London *Times* and the *Manchester Guardian* gave the story the more routine coverage it warranted. Most diplomats approved of Kennedy's decision, though Sir Sidney Clive, Marshal of the Diplomatic Corps, feared that it might be taken as an affront to the Monarchs. Kennedy to Hull, March 11, 1938. Hull Papers, Box 42, File 104.

46. Appeared as an editorial in several papers, most prominent of them being the *New York World Telegram and Sun*, April 11, 1938, p. 16, and the *Washington Daily News*, same day.

47. James Roosevelt to Kennedy, April 12, 1938, MS. at Roosevelt Library, Hyde Park, N.Y., in President's Personal File 207.

48. Kent to Kennedy, April 12, 1938, MS. in Frank Kent Papers, Maryland Historical Society, Baltimore, Md.

49. *Boston Post*, May 17, 1938, p. 1, given currency in the *New York Times* of the following day, p. 19.

50. James MacGregor Burns, *John Kennedy: A Political Profile* (New York: Harcourt, Brace & Company, 1959), p. 37.

51. The author believes the earliest source for this much-quoted line to be Walter Vincent Carty, "Kennedy's Father," *This Month*, February, 1962, p. 11.

52. Dilks, *Cadogan Diary*, entry of April 11, 1938, pp. 67–68.

53. Kennedy wire of March 21, 1939, S.D.MS. 123 Kennedy, Joseph P./180.

54. Interview, London, July, 1972.

55. Randolph Churchill to C. L. Sulzberger, in Sulzberger's *The Last of the Giants* (New York: The Macmillan Company, 1970), p. 629. Later Kennedy warned others against just such tactics. Landis MS., p. 405.

56. Same interview as cited in note 54.

57. Interview, September 20, 1973.

58. Kennedy wire of March 10, 1938, S.D.MS. 123 Kennedy, Joseph P./42.

59. Revisions in Hull to Kennedy, March 11, 1938, S.D.MS. 123 Kennedy, Joseph P./44.

60. Moffat Diary MS., entry of March 12, 1938. p. 2.

61. Hull to Roosevelt, March 13, 1938, Hull Papers, Correspondence: March 1–31, 1938.

62. Hull to Kennedy, March 14, 1938, S.D.MS. 123 Kennedy, Joseph P./45.

63. Moffat Diary MS., entry of March 11, 1938, after the first set of revisions. Even in its final version, though, the speech struck Abraham Flexner, Director of Princeton's Institute for Advanced Study, as "the most isolationist utterance that has come from an American Ambassador in many years." Thomas Jones, *A Diary With Letters, 1931–1950* (London: Oxford University Press, 1954), p. 398. The liberal

Protestant journal *Christian Century* also found it too isolationist. *Christian Century*, March 31, 1938.

64. Moffat Diary MS., entry of March 15, 1938.

65. *Ibid.*

66. Edward Lee Henson, Jr., "Britain, America and the European Crisis, 1937–1938" (Ph.D. thesis at University of Virginia, 1969), p. 176.

67. *The Times* (London), March 19, 1938, p. 17. The speech was widely reported. More readily available sources for it are *New York Times*, March 19, 1938, p. 1; and, *Vital Speeches*, April 1, 1938, pp. 355–56.

68. Landis MS., p. 16.

69. Kennedy to Baruch, March 21, 1938, MS. in Baruch Papers at Princeton University Library, Princeton, N.J. (Hereafter cited as "Baruch Papers.") Throughout this text, material cited from Kennedy-to-Baruch letters might alternately be cited from Kennedy-to-Frank Kent letters, same dates, MSS., Frank Kent Papers, Maryland Historical Society, Baltimore. Presumably the same quotations appear in Kennedy-to-Krock letters, probably the same dates. The Krock letter files at Princeton are "closed" as of this writing. No doubt similar language is included in letters of the same date from Kennedy to countless others. See page 140 *infra.*

70. Comment of Hans Dieckhoff, the German Ambassador to Washington, his wire of March 22, 1938 to Foreign Secretary Joachim von Ribbentrop. In *Documents on German Foreign Policy, 1918–1945*, Series D (1937–1945) (Washington, Department of State, published various dates) I, 694. (Hereafter cited as *German Documents.*) Dieckhoff, strangely, saw the speech as being far from isolationist, because of its indication that in the event of a German war with Great Britain, the United States would intervene when its parallel interests were threatened. I, 694.

71. Kennedy to Hull, March 22, 1938, p. 4, MS. in Hull Papers. See also Kennedy to Hull, October 27, 1938, S.D.MS. 841 George VI/267.

72. Kennedy to Baruch, March 21, 1938, MS. in Baruch Papers.

73. The Earl of Birkenhead, *Halifax* (Boston: Houghton Mifflin Company, 1966), p. 418.

74. William C. Bullitt, American Ambassador in France during Kennedy's period in London, explained to the author that he knew little about Kennedy because the two had been interested in different things—"I was always interested in international relations, and he, well . . . everyone knows what he was interested in." Telephone conversation with Ambassador Bullitt, March 20, 1962. See Adolf A. Berle, *Navigating the Rapids, 1918–1971*, ed. Beatrice Bishop Berle and Travis Beal Jacobs (New York: Harcourt Brace Jovanovich, Inc., 1973), p. 311, on the relations between Kennedy and Bullitt.

75. The author has no documentation for this assertion. Viewed in the totality of their relationship, the Earl of Birkenhead is probably correct in concluding "There is no doubt that Halifax had little use for him." Letter to the author, July 4, 1972.

76. Halifax to Lindsay, April 6, 1938, FO371/21494/A2707/1/45.

77. Halifax to Lindsay, September 5, 1938, FO371/21504/A6875/1/45.

78. Kennedy to Roosevelt, March 11, 1938, MS. at Roosevelt Library, Hyde Park, N.Y., in President's Personal File 207.

79. Kennedy to Baruch, March 21, 1938, MS. in Baruch Papers, and the same letter in the Kent files, both say "foreseen," not "unforeseen."

80. *Ibid.*

81. Kennedy-Hull phone conversation, March 15, 1938, transcript in Hull Papers, Box 66.

82. *Ibid.*

83. Before the American Club of London, *New York Times*, March 25, 1938, p. 1.

84. Kennedy to Baruch, March 28, 1938, MS. in Baruch Papers.

85. Halifax to Lindsay, April 6, 1938, FO371/21494/A2707/1/45.

86. Roger Bjerk, "Kennedy at the Court of St. James" (Ph.D. thesis at Washington State University, 1971), p. 71.

87. Kennedy to Baruch, April 14, 1938, MS. in Baruch Papers.

88. Welles to Kennedy, April 19, 1938, *Foreign Relations of the United States, 1938* (Washington, D.C.: U.S. Government Printing Office, 1955), I, 148. (Volumes from this series hereafter cited as *F.R.U.S.*) D. C. Watt minimizes Kennedy's influence on Roosevelt's position on the Anglo-Italian agreement. "Roosevelt and Neville Chamberlain: two appeasers," *International Journal*, Spring, 1973, p. 197.

89. The Earl of Longford and Thomas P. O'Neill, *Eamon DeValera* (London: Hutchinson & Co., 1970), p. 318, cite Roosevelt to DeValera, February 22, 1938.

90. Interview with a Colonial Office employee, London, July, 1972.

91. Halifax to Malcolm Macdonald, FO800/310, XI, 187 (p. 206); and, Halifax to Lindsay, April 6, 1938, FO371/21494/6544.

92. Lindsay to Halifax, May 9, 1938, FO371/21496/A3834/1145.

93. Interview, London, July, 1972.

94. *Ickes Diary*, entry of July 3, 1938, II, 416.

95. Lancelot Oliphant memorandum, FO371/21495/6543, pp. 121, 171.

96. A. J. P. Taylor, *English History, 1914–1945* (London: Penguin Books, paperback ed., 1970), p. 499.

97. Kennedy to Baruch, May 3, 1938, MS. in Baruch Papers.

98. Winston S. Churchill, *The Second World War*, Vol I: *The Gathering Storm* (Boston: Houghton Mifflin Company, 1948), p. 278. One leading British diplomat with whom the author spoke took strenuous objection to this conclusion, and insisted that but for the settlement, Ireland would have actively sabotaged Britain in the war, hurting the Allies much much more than the loss of the ports had hurt them.

99. Kennedy to Baruch, May 3, 1938, MS. in Baruch Papers.

100. *Ibid.*

101. Morris DeHaven Tracy, *Boston Herald*, June 22, 1938.

102. Halifax to Malcolm Macdonald and Halifax to Lindsay, April 6, 1938, FO800/310, XI, 187 (p. 206); and, FO371/21494/6544.

103. Oliphant memorandum and Oliphant to Kennedy, April 22, 1938, FO371/21495/6543, 171 (p. 121); and FO371/21495/6531, p. 173.

104. Suggested in interview, London, July, 1972.

105. Longford and O'Neill, *Eamon DeValera*, p. 323. On their own part, Longford and O'Neill are unsatisfied as to the significance of Kennedy's participation. *Ibid.*

106. Morgenthau Presidential Diary, MS. at Roosevelt Library, Hyde Park, N.Y., I, 41.

107. Kingsley Martin, *Editor: "New Statesman" Years, 1931–1945* (Chicago: Henry Regnery Company, 1970), pp. 213–14.

108. *The Week*, May 17, 1939, p. 6, and June 14, 1939, p. 2; Robert Bendiner,

The Riddle of the State Department (New York: Farrar & Rinehart, Inc., 1942), p. 59.

109. Josiah C. Wedgwood attributes the suggestion to Zionist leader Rabbi Stephen Wise in letter to Lord Halifax, October 3, 1938, FO371/22453/R1177/153/37.

110. Kennedy to Hull, May 9, 1938, *F.R.U.S.*, 1938, I, 188, 192.

111. F. Jay Taylor, *The United States and the Spanish Civil War, 1936–1939* (New York: Bookman Associates, 1956), p. 186.

112. *Ibid.*

113. Halifax to Lindsay, April 6, 1938, FO371/21494/A2707/1/45.

114. Kennedy to Hull, April 9, 1938, and Kennedy to Welles, April 19, 1938, S.D.MSS. 852.00/7717 and 7785—"It seems to me a strategic stroke to get this class of person out of Spain."

115. See also *New York Times*, July 22, 1938, p. 1 and July 23, 1938, p. 2.

116. Burns, *John Kennedy*, p. 32.

117. See Hank Searls, *The Lost Prince* (New York: The World Publishing Company, 1969), pp. 136 ff.

118. Kennedy to Baruch, March 28, 1938, MS. in Baruch Papers.

119. Kennedy-Hull conversation, March 30, 1938, typescript in Hull Papers. See also Moffat Diary MS., March 30, 1938.

120. Correct speculation as to the bankers' opinions is in *New York Times*, March 30, 1938, p. 8.

121. Kennedy to Norman Davis, May 20, 1938, MS. at Library of Congress Manuscript Division, Washington, D.C., in Norman Davis Box 32, "Kennedy, Joseph P., 1922–1938."

122. Kennedy to Borah, April 28, 1938, MS. at Library of Congress Manuscript Division, Washington, D.C., in Borah's Scrapbooks, Second Series, XXIII, 184. Kennedy was also in touch with isolationist Senator Key Pittman. See Fred L. Israel, *Nevada's Key Pittman* (Lincoln: University of Nebraska Press, 1963), pp. 155–57.

123. Ickes saw Kennedy in June and made this comment in his diary. *Ickes Diary*, entry of June 26, 1938, II, 406.

124. Dirksen to Ernst von Weizsäcker, May 31, 1938, *German Documents*, II, 368–69.

125. Dirksen to Weizsäcker, June 13, 1938, *German Documents*, I, 713–18.

126. *Ibid.*, pp. 714–15.

127. Kennedy was not so anxious to visit Germany during this interview as he was at previous and later meetings. Compare *German Documents*, I, 715, with II, 368–69; I, 723; and IV, 633.

128. *Ibid.*, I, 715.

129. Churchill, *The Gathering Storm*, p. 223.

130. *German Documents*, I, 717.

131. *Ibid.*, at 718.

132. *Ibid.* Also, *German Documents*, I, 723.

133. See Weizsäcker's margin note on Dirksen's dispatch of July 20, 1938, *German Documents*, I, 723. Also, Dieckhoff to von Dirksen, November 2, 1938, IV, 637. For more German reactions to Kennedy and his doings, see the Dieckhoff wire quoted by Marian C. McKenna, *Borah* (Ann Arbor: University of Michigan Press, 1961), p. 358; and, Woermann to Kordt, August 16, 1938, in *German Documents*, I, 725.

134. Dieckhoff to von Dirksen, November 2, 1938, *German Documents*, IV, 637.

135. Dirksen to Weizsäcker, July 20, 1938, *German Documents*, I, 723.

136. Joseph E. Davies, *Mission to Moscow* (New York: Simon & Schuster, 1941), diary entry of June 14, 1938, p. 370.

137. Kennedy's address at the annual University of London dinner, May 13, 1938, *New York Times*, May 14, 1938, p. 15.

138. Kennedy's speeches at two cathedral dedications, *New York Times*, July 13, 1938, p. 23, and September 3, 1938, p. 2.

139. Davies, *Mission to Moscow*, p. 370.

140. *Boston Globe* (evening edition), June 20, 1938, p. 1; *New York Times*, June 21, 1938, p. 6.

141. *New York Times*, June 22, 1938, p. 4.

142. Presidential Press Conference 468, June 21, 1938, typescript at Roosevelt Library, Hyde Park, New York, Press Conferences, XI, 479–81.

143. *Boston Globe* (evening edition), June 22, 1938, p. 1.

144. On Oglethorpe honorary, see Thornwell Jacobs to Baruch, February 2, 1937; Kennedy reponse written on the same letter; and, Baruch to Jacobs, February 18, 1937, MSS. in Baruch Papers, Vol. 40. On Trinity honorary, see *Ickes Diary*, II, 416. According to Ickes, Kennedy told Roosevelt that he had been offered the degree from Trinity College, but had not made up his mind whether to go to the trouble of accepting. *Ibid.* On Princeton honorary, see Breckenridge Long Diary MS. at Library of Congress Manuscript Division, Washington, D.C. (hereafter cited as "Long Diary MS."), diary entry of February 15, 1939, pp. 163–64.

145. *Boston Globe* (evening edition), May 17, 1938, p. 24, and *Boston Globe* (evening edition), June 22, 1938, p. 5.

146. See the Boston papers of June 22, 23, 1938. The author is not convinced by this explanation: Kennedy had sought the leave time expressly so that he could attend the graduation. He did not have to attend to Jack's ill health during the precise hours of the graduation ceremony. Perhaps Kennedy had privately expected the "kudos"—such honors are kept highly secret until long after Kennedy had had to arrange for his leave time—and then, after having made arrangements for the trip, learned that the honor was not to be forthcoming. That being the case, he avoided the graduation ceremony in order to save himself the embarrassment of being passed over in his very presence.

147. *New York Times*, June 25, 1938, p. 3, and June 26, 1938, p. 25.

148. Arthur Krock, *Memoirs: Sixty Years on the Firing Line* (New York: Funk & Wagnalls, 1968), p. 341. The author wonders whether the "curfew" might have been imposed with a wink, purely for the impression to be made on the strait-laced Krock, or possibly so that Kennedy could tell his sons' mother that, for whatever it might have been worth, he had imposed a curfew.

149. *Ibid.*

150. British Embassy in Washington to American Department at Foreign Office, February 17, 1938, FO371/21524/A1564/60/45.

151. Pointed out by columnist Heywood Broun in the *New York World-Telegram and Sun*, April 13, 1938, p. 23.

152. James Roosevelt to Kennedy, April 12, 1938, MS. at Roosevelt Library, Hyde Park, N.Y., in President's Personal File 207.

153. Landis MS., p. 36. Reports in *New York Times*, July 22, 1938, p. 1, and July 23, 1938, p. 2.

154. Moffat Diary MS., entry of November 22, 1938.

155. Anecdote in Sulzberger, *The Last of the Giants*, pp. 630–31.

156. Krock, *Memoirs*, p. 334.

157. The author compared Kennedy-to-Baruch with Kennedy-to-Kent, March 21, March 28, April 14, May 2–3, May 17, May 31, all 1938.

158. Richard Whalen writes that one of the recipients had never met Kennedy. *The Founding Father* (New York: The New American Library of World Literature, Inc., 1964), p. 222 cites anonymous interview.

159. Kent to Baruch, May 25, 1938, in Baruch Papers.

160. Interview with Walter Trohan, longtime Washington Bureau Chief for the *Chicago Daily Tribune*, Washington, March 22, 1962. See Trohan's column of June 23, 1938, in the *Chicago Daily Tribune*, p. 1. See also pages 235–36 *infra*.

161. Kennedy to James Roosevelt, March 3, 1938, p. 5, MS. in Hull Papers, Correspondence: March 1–31, 1938.

162. *Boston Globe*, June 20, 1938, p. 1; and, *New York Times*, June 21, 1938, p. 6. Neither paper says that the statement was in response to a question.

163. Trohan, *Chicago Daily Tribune*, June 23, 1938, p. 1. A parallel article is in the *Philadelphia Public Ledger*, same day. See also Alsop and Kintner, *Evening Star*, (Washington), September 19, 1938; Krock, *New York Times*, December 13, 1938, p. 24; and, McCarthy, *The Remarkable Kennedys*, pp. 60–61.

164. *Ickes Diary*, entry of July 3, 1938, II, 415. Cf. Roosevelt to Morgenthau, pages 116–17 *supra*. When first appointed, Kennedy wrote James Roosevelt, "I may not last long over here, but it is going to be fast and furious while it's on." Kennedy to James Roosevelt, March 3, 1938, p. 5, copy in Hull Papers, Correspondence: March 1–31, 1938.

MUNICHTIME

1. *New York Times*, July 8, 1938, and July 11, 1938, p. 11. Apparently, a Trinity degree could not be produced on short notice, but Ireland's National University, being connected with the government, was amenable to diplomatic pressure.

2. Cudahy to State Department, July 11, 1938, S.D.MS. 123 Kennedy, Joseph P./97.

3. Notably, the first major piece on Kennedy, "Joe Kennedy Has Never Liked Any Job He's Tackled," *American Magazine*, May, 1928, pp. 32 ff., quoted extensively in earlier chapters.

4. Minute in FO371/21548/A5134/5134/45.

5. Cudahy wire, *op. cit.*

6. *New York Times*, July 9, 1938, p. 14; *Irish Press*, July 9, 1938. See also Edward A. Lawler, *Boston Sunday Post*, July 24, 1938, and Harry Henry, *Sunday Globe* (Boston), July 24, 1938.

7. *The Secret Diary of Harold L. Ickes*, Vol. II: *The Inside Struggle, 1936–1939* (New York: Simon & Schuster, 1954), entry of July 16, 1938, p. 420.

8. It turned out that the fall meeting was not held in Germany, and Kennedy missed it.

9. *German Documents*, I, 721–23. For German reactions to the proposed visit, see p. 723, bottom, for margin note by Weizsäcker, and p. 725 for a wire from Woermann to Kordt.

10. Kennedy's wire of July 20, 1938, 8 P.M., S.D.MS. 741.62/280. This is the only wire the author was able to locate at the State Department reporting the von

Dirksen-Kennedy conversations. Apparently Kennedy did not report his other visits with the German Ambassador.

11. Von Dirksen, before his June thirteenth visit with Kennedy, asked for instructions. *German Documents*, II, 368–69. The ideas sent him provided the basis for much of his talk on the thirteenth. *Ibid.*, I, 713.

12. *The Times* (London), August 4, 1938, p. 13. The rest of the family had been at the Riviera playground at least since July 24, 1938. *New York Times*, July 24, 1938, II, 2.

13. Kennedy to Land, August 8, 1938, MS. at Library of Congress Manuscript Division, Washington, D.C., Emory S. Land Collection, Container 2, Personal Letter File H to K.

14. *New York Times*, August 11, 1938, p. 2.

15. Perhaps he returned earlier. On that day he gave an interview to Father Thorning. (Date in letter from Rev. Thorning to the author, February 20, 1962.)

16. Roosevelt to Kennedy, August 25, 1938, MS. at Roosevelt Library, Hyde Park, President's Secretary's File, I, Diplomatic Correspondence, Great Britain, 1933–1945, Box 7.

17. Halifax to Lindsay, September 2, 1938, in *Documents on British Foreign Policy, 1919–1939*, 3rd series, ed. E. L. Woodward and Rohan Butler (London: H.M.'s Stationery Office, 1949), II, 212–13. (Hereafter cited as "British Documents.")

18. Kennedy wire of August 30, 1938, *F.R.U.S.*, 1938, I, 560–61.

19. Ione Robinson, *A Wall to Paint On* (New York: E. P. Dutton and Company, Inc., 1946), letter of September 2, 1938, p. 311.

20. Halifax to Lindsay, September 2, 1938, *British Documents*, 1938, II, 213.

21. Kennedy telegram, August 30, 1938, *F.R.U.S.*, 1938, I, 560–61.

22. Robinson, *A Wall to Paint On*, letter of September 2, 1938, p. 311.

23. Halifax to Lindsay, September 2, 1938, *British Documents*, 1938, II, 212–13.

24. See page 158 *infra*, and Robinson, *A Wall to Paint On*, p. 367.

25. Robinson, *A Wall to Paint On*, letter of September 2, 1938, p. 311. The sincerity with which he held this belief is attested to by the fact that at the time his own wife was shopping in Paris, and several of his children were at Cannes. Joseph F. Dinneen, *The Kennedy Family* (Boston: Little, Brown and Company, 1959), p. 66.

26. See page 292 *infra*.

27. Wire printed in *F.R.U.S.*, 1938, I, 565–66. No clue is given in this document as to Kennedy's views or reactions.

28. Joseph A. Frankland, *Boston Evening American*, August 31, 1938, p. 1.

29. Roosevelt to Hull, September 1, 1938, S.D.MS. 123 Kennedy, Joseph P./108.

30. Draft of Hull to Kennedy, September 1, 1938, S.D.MS. 123 Kennedy, Joseph P./109.

31. Hull to Kennedy, September 1, 1938, *F.R.U.S.*, 1938, I, 568–69.

32. Roosevelt to Kennedy, September 7, 1938, *F.D.R., His Personal Letters, 1928–1945*, ed. Elliott Roosevelt (New York: Duell, Sloan and Pearce, 1950), II, 809.

33. Morgenthau Diary MS. at Roosevelt Library, Hyde Park, N.Y., entry of September 1, 1938, Vol. 138, p. 33.

34. Later comment to Morgenthau about Kennedy and Bullitt, in Morgenthau diary entry of October 3, 1939, Morgenthau Presidential Diary MS., II, 317.

35. Edward L. Henson, Jr., "Britain, America, and The European Crisis, 1937–1938" (Ph.D thesis at University of Virginia, 1969), p. 230. Henson continues: "Had it been interpreted correctly and presented truthfully, American public opinion would have provided a powerful deterrent to Mr. Chamberlain's type of appeasement.

Ambassador Kennedy, however, apparently on his own initiative, presented Chamberlain with a picture of American opinion which could serve only to reinforce his ideas and hasten him and his Government down the tragic path."

36. *The Moffat Papers: Selections from the Diplomatic Journals of Jay Pierrepont Moffat, 1919–1943*, ed. N. H. Hooker (Cambridge, Mass.: Harvard University Press, 1956), p. 203 note 23, diary entry of September 1, 1938. (Hereafter cited as "Hooker, *Moffat Papers*," to distinguish it from the unpublished sections of the Moffat Diary MS. cited as "Moffat Diary MS." Wherever possible the published citation will be given.)

37. *In Search of Light: The Broadcast of Edward R. Murrow, 1938–1961*, ed. Edward Bliss, Jr. (New York: Alfred A. Knopf, 1967), p. 7, for Murrow broadcast of September 17, 1938.

38. *New York Times* comments on *Yorkshire Post*, September 3, 1938, p. 3.

39. *The Times* (London) September 2, 1938.

40. "Cuss out the press": Roosevelt's phrase, Morgenthau Diary MS., September 1, 1938, Vol. 138, p. 20. "In his process of playing the Chamberlain game": Morgenthau's phrase. *Ibid.*, p. 34. See also John M. Blum, *From the Morgenthau Diaries*, Vol. I: *Years of Crisis, 1928–1938* (Boston: Houghton Mifflin Company, 1959), p. 518. (Blum hereafter cited as "Blum, *Morgenthau Diary*," to distinguish it from the unpublished portions of Morgenthau's several-hundred-volume diary, which is cited as "Morgenthau Diary MS.")

41. Morgenthau Diary MS., entry of September 1, 1938, Vol. 138, p. 35.

42. *Ibid.*

43. Hull to Kennedy, *F.R.U.S.*, 1938, I, 568–69.

44. *The Times* (London), September 2, 1938.

45. Hooker, *Moffat Papers*, entry of September 9, 1938, p. 199.

46. Walter Lippmann, *New York Herald-Tribune*, October 20, 1938, p. 25.

47. Moffat Diary MS., entry of September 1, 1938.

48. See Adolph A. Berle, *Navigating the Rapids, 1918–1971*, ed. Beatrice Bishop Berle and Travis Beal Jacobs (New York: Harcourt Brace Jovanovich, Inc., 1973), diary entry of September 1, 1938, p. 184.

49. Halifax to Lindsay, September 10, 1938, *British Documents*, II, 284–85. Lindsay agreed with Kennedy's analysis. Lindsay to Foreign Office, September 12, 1938, FO371/21737/C9711/1941/18. The author suspects that Churchill read the Halifax wire containing Kennedy's prediction; he seems to have made the same arguments back to Kennedy. *F.R.U.S.*, 1940, III, 35, 37.

50. Kennedy to Hull, September 10, 1938, *F.R.U.S.*, 1938, I, 585–86.

51. Kennedy told Lindbergh that the Ambassador himself had had the cruisers sent to England, simply for the effect that their presence might have on Germany. *The Wartime Journal of Charles A. Lindbergh* (New York: Harcourt Brace Jovanovich, Inc., 1970), diary entry of September 29, 1938, p. 79.

52. Halifax to Lindsay, September 11, 1938, *British Documents*, II, 296.

53. Halifax at Cabinet meeting, September 12, 1938, Cabinet Minutes, Cab. 23, Vol. 95, p. 9, MS. at Public Record Office, London.

54. Lippmann's analysis of the speculation was that it stiffened Czech resistance but did not fool Hitler, thus increasing the risk of war, rather than decreasing it. It was therefore counter-productive of Kennedy's desired goal. By hindsight that analysis looks rather convincing. *New York Herald-Tribune*, October 20, 1938, p. 25.

55. Landis MS., p. 61.

56. Lindbergh, *Wartime Journal*, entry of September 29, 1938, p. 79.

57. Kordt to Ribbentrop, September 12, 1938, *German Documents*, II, 743.

58. Memorandum of a conversation between the two in a different wire from Kordt to Ribbentrop of September 12, 1938, *German Documents*, II, 744.

59. Hooker, *Moffat Papers*, entry of September 14, 1938, p. 202.

60. Kennedy to Hull, September 17, 1938, *F.R.U.S.*, 1938, I, 609–12.

61. Kennedy to Hull, September 19, 1938, *F.R.U.S.*, 1938, I, 622.

62. Kennedy to Hull, September 21, 1938, *F.R.U.S.*, 1938, I, 631–32.

63. Lindbergh, *Wartime Journal*, entry of May 5, 1938, p. 26. Later that month, Kennedy hosted a dinner for Halifax to which the Lindberghs and the Luces were invited. *New York Times*, May 22, 1938, VI, 4.

64. Indeed, many suspect that Goering showed Lindbergh more of the German Air Force than in fact existed. One of Britain's most respected historians of modern Britain insisted to the author that Goering had had the planes shown Lindbergh at airfield "A" flown out to arrive at airfield "B" in advance of Lindbergh, where the American was shown the same airplanes all over again, and then on to airfield "C" and so on, thus grossly exaggerating the size of the armada, and the impression made upon the unsuspecting American. When I asked the historian for his documentation, he assured me that it was "very well known," but the author is unaware of the documentation and believes that Lindbergh was too sophisticated to be duped by such a ploy.

65. Phipps to Foreign Office, September 13, 1938, FO371/21737/C9704/1941/18.

66. Lindbergh, *Wartime Journal*, entry of September 19, 1938, p. 71.

67. Lindbergh's full statement to Kennedy in Truman Smith, "Air Intelligence Activity," MS. at Yale University, New Haven, Conn. Kennedy's wire in *F.R.U.S.*, 1938, I, 72–73. See also *Memoirs of Cordell Hull* (New York: The Macmillan Company, 1948), I, 590.

68. Kenneth S. Davis, *The Hero: Charles A. Lindbergh and the American Dream* (Garden City, N.Y.: Doubleday and Company, Inc., 1959), p. 378.

69. Walter Winchell, *Providence Journal* (Providence, R.I.), January 2, 1939.

70. See John Evelyn Wrench, *Geoffrey Dawson and Our Times* (London: Hutchinson, 1955), p. 337. Also, Sir John Slessor, *The Central Blue* (New York: Frederick A. Praeger, 1957), p. 218.

71. As Kennedy pointed out to Walter Winchell, *Providence Journal*, January 2, 1939.

72. Wrench, *Geoffrey Dawson*, p. 377.

73. Interview, London, July 26, 1972.

74. H. C. Hole to H. L. Hopkinson, October 24, 1938, FO371/21710/C13219/1425/18, p. 224.

75. Loening to Kennedy, October 17, 1938, p. 1, MS. at Library of Congress Manuscript Division, Washington, D.C. in Grover Loening Box 12, File "January–October, 1938."

76. Burton Klein, *Germany's Economic Preparations for War* (Cambridge, Mass.: Harvard University Press, 1959), pp. 19–20.

77. A. J. P. Taylor, *English History, 1914–1945* (London: Penguin Books, paperback ed., 1970), pp. 503, 535.

78. John E. Wood, "The *Luftwaffe* as a Factor in British Policy, 1935–1939" (Ph. D. thesis, Tulane University, 1965), p. 345.

79. *Ibid.*, p. 348.

80. Hugh Dalton diary entry of September 24, 1938, MS. at London School of Economics, London, England.

81. Vachell to Foreign Office, October 19, 1938, FO371/21710/C13079/ 1425/18.

82. Slessor, *The Central Blue*, p. 218. Ultimately, Roosevelt drew the uncharitable conclusion that Lindbergh himself was a Nazi. Morgenthau Presidential Diary MS., entry of May 20, 1940, III, p. 0563.

83. Taylor, *English History*, p. 520.

84. Kennedy-Hull phone conversation, September 24, 1938, typescript in Hull Papers, Box 66, Folder 289; *The Memoirs of Cordell Hull*, I, 590.

85. Hull, *Memoirs*, I, 590. Duff Cooper led the opposition in the cabinet to Chamberlain's policies, and at this time even Halifax sided with him.

86. William L. Shirer, *The Rise and Fall of the Third Reich* (New York: Simon & Schuster, 1960), pp. 391 ff.

87. Kennedy to Hull, September 25, 1938, *F.R.U.S.*, 1938, I, 652.

88. Hooker, *Moffat Papers*, entry of September 26, 1938, p. 214.

89. Landis MS., pp. 58–59.

90. Kennedy to Hull, September 26, 1938, *F.R.U.S.*, 1938, I, 659.

91. Shirer, *Rise and Fall*, p. 403. Before the speech, Kennedy took steps to see to it that the address received a wide American audience, by calling Welles to seek permission for it to be broadcast on American radio. Welles declined to permit a direct broadcast; indeed, the President himself, according to Welles, had said that he did not want the speech broadcast directly, lest it be construed as being an appeal beamed in part to the United States. Kennedy said that he would arrange for a rebroadcast. Kennedy-Welles phone conversation, September 26, 1938, S.D.MS. 760F62/1117 2/10, published in part in *F.R.U.S.*, 1938, I, 568–69. Roosevelt himself had made suggestions for possible incorporation into Chamberlain's address. Landis MS., pp. 59–60.

92. Shirer, *Rise and Fall*, pp. 410–11.

93. Kennedy to Hull, September 28, 1938, *F.R.U.S.*, 1938, I, 692–93.

94. Wire of September 28, 1938, in *F.R.U.S.*, 1938, I, 688. Years later, Halifax mentioned to Kennedy that the Foreign Office could never locate its copy of the easy-to-remember wire, and Kennedy explained to him "I had delivered the message orally as I felt that the President was riding the fence on the issue of Munich and seemed to be going in two directions at once." Landis MS., p. 64. But to a reporter in 1960, Kennedy gave a somewhat different explanation: "I went over to 10 Downing Street the day I received the cable, but instead of handing the cable to Chamberlain, as is customary, I read it to him. I had a feeling that cable would haunt Roosevelt some day, so I kept it." *New York World-Telegram and Sun*, April 11, 1960, p. 3. See page 165 *infra*.

95. Hull to Kennedy, September 27, 1938, S.D.MS. 123 Kennedy, Joseph P./120, with marginal notation about the other recipients of the wire.

96. Halifax to Lindsay, September 29, 1938, *British Documents*, II, 625.

97. Landis MS., p. 63.

98. Lindbergh, *Wartime Journal*, entry of September 29, 1938, p. 79.

99. "In whose warm and endearing character an intense *joie de vivre* was secretly

in conflict with a profound Slav melancholy." The Earl of Birkenhead, *Halifax* (Boston: Houghton Mifflin Company, 1966), pp. 385–86.

100. Kennedy to Hull, September 28, 1938, *F.R.U.S.*, 1938, I, 692–93.

101. Germany's calculations, repeated by Shirer, *Rise and Fall*, pp. 421–22.

102. "In this strange way, the British Government guaranteed a weak, defenceless Czechoslovakia, where they had previously declared it impossible to assist a heavily armed one." Taylor, *English History*, p. 523.

103. Shirer, *Rise and Fall*, p. 437.

104. The Earl of Birkenhead, *Halifax*, p. 406.

105. Page one headline of the *Daily Herald* (London), October 1, 1938, and countless other newspapers.

106. James Laver, *Between the Wars* (Boston: Houghton Mifflin Company, 1961), p. 225. Years later, Masaryk, who was wounded deeply by Munich, would talk about the lighthearted way Kennedy had taken the pact: "My God, he didn't even have any tact or sympathy about it!" Dorothy Thompson, *Tampa Morning Tribune* (Tampa, Florida), March 19, 1948. On his own part, Kennedy liked Masaryk, but thought that the Czech was "not realistic enough."

107. Robinson, *A Wall to Paint On*, letter of November 4, 1938, p. 367.

108. Shirer, *Rise and Fall*, pp. 420, 423.

109. Landis MS., Library of Congress, Chap. 17, p. 1.

110. Hull, *Memoirs*, I, 596.

111. Landis MS., p. 65; slightly different phrasing in Library of Congress draft, Chap. 17, p. 2.

112. He made this argument, both publicly and privately, on countless occasions, most recently in a speech at the University of Virginia in 1950 (pages 353 ff., *infra*) after virtually all scholars had seen the truth of what Munich meant. The argument was a leitmotif in John Kennedy's 1939 best seller, *Why England Slept*.

113. Shirer, *Rise and Fall*, pp. 423, 425 ff.; Peter Calvocoressi and Guy Wint, *Total War: Causes and Courses of the Second World War* (London: The Penguin Press, 1972), pp. 92–96; B. H. Liddell Hart, *History of the Second World War* (London: Cassell, 1970), pp. 22–23. For the most nearly respectable contrary thesis see Keith Eubank, *Munich* (Norman: University of Oklahoma Press, 1963), pp. 278, 286–87.

114. Shirer, *Rise and Fall*, p. 424.

115. *Ibid.*, p. 425.

116. Cf. speech of December 12, 1950, in *Vital Speeches*, January 1, 1951, pp. 170 ff., and John W. Wheeler-Bennett, *Munich, Prologue to Tragedy* (London: Macmillan & Co., 1948).

117. See Kennedy to Hull, September 21, 1938, *F.R.U.S.*, 1938, I, 631–32, and *Hearings before the House Committee on Foreign Affairs on H.R. 1776*, January 21, 1941, pp. 270, 312. See also, Kennedy's wire of August 24, 1939, quoted in Arthur Krock, *New York Times Magazine*, July 18, 1943, p. 37.

118. For most concise analysis of the "bought time" theory see Calvocoressi and Wint, *Total War*, pp. 92–96. To same extent is Martin Gilbert and Richard Gott, *The Appeasers* (Boston: Houghton Mifflin Company, 1963), xi–xii.

119. Kennedy to Hull, September 21, 1938, *F.R.U.S.*, 1938, I, 631–32, and Landis MS., p. 52. In contemporary conversations with journalists, however, Kennedy had insisted that Munich really had meant "peace in our time." Interview, August 7, 1965.

120. Halifax to Lindsay, September 29, 1938, *British Documents*, II, 625.

121. Robinson, *A Wall to Paint On*, letter of November 4, 1938, p. 367. Joe Jr., had visited Germany about that time and had been extremely impressed. Hank Searls, *The Lost Prince* (New York: The World Publishing Company, 1969), p. 123; see also Minute by Berkeley Gage, September 26, 1939, FO371/22827/A6561/1090/45.

122. Draft of speech in Kennedy to Hull, August 31, 1938, S.D.MS. 123 Kennedy, Joseph P./106.

123. Cf. Chamberlain's later "quarrel in a far away country speech," page 153 *supra*.

124. Moffat Diary MS., entry of August 31, 1938, p. 3; to roughly the same extent, see Berle, *Navigating the Rapids*, entry of September 1, 1938, p. 182.

125. Hull to Kennedy, August 31, 1938, S.D.MS. 123 Kennedy, Joseph P./107.

126. See page 206 *infra*.

127. Blum, *Morgenthau Diary*, I, 518.

128. *New York Herald-Tribune*, October 20, 1938, p. 9.

129. *Ibid.* Halifax believed that Eden's resignation as foreign secretary had been caused partly because of "Anthony's natural revulsion from Dictators, which I have always told him was too strong inasmuch as you have got to live with the devils whether you like them or not." The Earl of Birkenhead, *Halifax*, p. 380.

130. See Phillips Diary MS., entry of October 23, 1938, p. 2801, and Moffat Diary MS., entry of October 26, 1938, p. 2. For the Roosevelt speech see *The Public Papers and Addresses of Franklin D. Roosevelt*, ed. Samuel I. Rosenman (New York: The Macmillan Company, 1941), VI (1937 volume), pp. 406–11; or, *F.R.U.S., Japan, 1931–1941*, I, 379–83.

131. Moffat Diary MS., entry of October 26, 1938, p. 1.

132. *The Times* (London), October 21, 1938, p. 15. Less friendly was the *News Chronicle* (London), October 20, 1938, p. 15. Most of the British papers ignored the speech editorially. This author checked the *Daily Herald*, the *Daily Telegraph and Morning Post*, and the *Manchester Guardian*. The *Guardian*, a liberal paper, did not even include the pro-appeasement statements in their account of the speech; probably they were not included in the version distributed to the press in advance of delivery.

133. The author saw no American editorials approving the speech or defending Kennedy.

134. *New York Herald-Tribune*, October 22, 1938, p. 14.

135. *Washington Post*, October 21, 1938, p. 10.

136. *New York Post*, October 21, 1938, p. 18.

137. Walter Lippmann, *New York Herald-Tribune*, October 22, 1938, p. 17.

138. Frankfurter to Roosevelt, October 27, 1938, in *Roosevelt and Frankfurter: Their Correspondence, 1928–1945*, ed. Max Freedman (Boston: Little, Brown and Company, 1967), pp. 463–64.

139. Knox to Hull, October 25, 1938, MS. in Hull Papers, Box 43, File 107.

140. Hull memorandum of October 28, 1938, S.D.MS. 123 Kennedy, Joseph P./136.

141. Messersmith to Raymond H. Geist, November 7, 1938, MS. in Messersmith Papers at University of Delaware, Newark, Del., Box I, File E.

142. James MacGregor Burns, *John Kennedy: A Political Profile* (New York: Harcourt Brace & Company, 1959), p. 37.

143. Landis MS., Library of Congress, Chap. 18, p. 4: and while he could appreciate their personal stances, he could not accept what he took to be their "slander

and falsification to achieve their aims," and he was unprepared for "the full viciousness of this onslaught."

144. Hooker, *Moffat Papers*, entry of October 21, 1938, pp. 220–21.

145. Moffat Diary MS., entry of October 18, 1938.

146. Hooker, *Moffat Papers*, entry of October 21, 1938, p. 221.

147. *Ibid.* Breckenridge Long's diary includes a parallel comment in an entry of 1940: "[Hull] has not liked the action of either of them [Kennedy or Bullitt] for a long time. They have a custom of going over his head and talking to the President, and he has found it necessary to secure agreement with the President about his intended instructions to them before they are issued in order that he and the President will find themselves in perfect agreement and that the President will stand hitched." Long Diary MS., entry of March 29, 1940. For Roosevelt's reaction to the speech see Press Conference 493, October 21, 1938, typescript at Roosevelt Library, Hyde Park, N.Y., Press Conferences, XII, 176.

148. See also E. Wilder Spaulding, *Ambassadors Ordinary and Extraordinary* (Washington, D.C.: Public Affairs Press, 1961), p. 13.

149. Phillips Diary MS., entry of March 14, 1939, pp. 3056–57. Actually, the State Department did not deny that it had given advance approval for the speech, but merely made clear that the speech did not represent State Department policy. *New York Times*, October 21, 1938, p. 8.

150. Kennedy speech before the Worchestershire Association dinner honoring Lord Baldwin, *The Times* (London), October 27, 1938, p. 16.

151. *Manchester Guardian*, November 24, 1938, p. 11, for the fullest account. Also *New York Times*, November 24, 1938, p. 1; and, *New York Times*, December 8, 1938.

152. The author saw the Hays response only in the *Daily Telegraph and Morning Post* (London), November 24, 1938, p. 18.

153. *New York Times*, November 24, 1938, p. 22; *Boston Globe*, same day.

154. Joseph F. Dinneen, *Boston Globe* (morning edition), December 16, 1938, p. 9.

155. Most of the British papers commented editorially on either November 24, 25, 26, or December 8, 9, or 10.

156. The *New York Post* at least began its editorial with "Ambassador Joseph P. Kennedy's motives may have been of the highest, but . . ." See its issue of November 26, 1938, p. 6.

157. *Chicago Daily Tribune*, December 5, 1938, p. 14.

158. *New York Times*, December 13, 1938, p. 24.

159. Not surprisingly, Kennedy had no high regard for professional diplomats. See the *Chicago Daily Tribune*, August 20, 1938, p. 3.

160. Morris DeHaven Tracy, *Boston Traveler*, June 22, 1938, p. 2.

161. Landis MS., p. 36. The other reason: page 179 *infra*.

162. *German Documents*, I, 721–23.

163. *New York Times*, December 8, 1938.

164. Kenneth Crawford, *New York Post*, December 9, 1938.

165. *New York Times*, December 8, 1938.

166. Walter Lippmann, *New York Herald-Tribune*, October 22, 1938, p. 17.

167. Morris DeHaven Tracy, *Boston Herald*, June 22, 1938.

168. Robinson, *A Wall to Paint On*, letter of November 4, 1938, p. 367.

169. *Memoirs of Dr. Eduard Beneš*, trans. G. Lias (Boston: Houghton Mifflin Company, 1954), p. 172.

170. Ivan Maisky, *Kto Pomogal Gitleru* (Moscow: Izdatelstvo Instituta Mezhdunarodnykh Otnoshenii, 1962), p. 125, trans. *The Times* (London), February 5, 1962, p. 9, slightly different translation in Ivan Maisky, *Who Helped Hitler?*, trans. Andrew Rothstein (London: Hutchinson & Co., 1964), p. 136.

171. *British Documents*, VII, 627.

172. Landis MS., pp. 58–59; see also Halifax to Lindsay, September 29, 1938, *British Documents*, II, 625.

173. William L. Langer and S. Everett Gleason, *The Challenge to Isolation, 1937–1940* (New York: Harper & Brothers Publishers, 1952), p. 35, footnote, citing telegram to Kennedy of October 5, 1938.

174. Daniels' note of January 14, 1939, in *Roosevelt and Daniels*, ed. Carroll Kilpatrick (Chapel Hill: University of North Carolina Press, 1952), p. 182. D. C. Watt, the British historian, calls Roosevelt "an accessory before and after the fact to the Munich settlement." "Roosevelt and Neville Chamberlain: two appeasers," *International Journal*, Spring, 1973, p. 199.

175. Blum, *Morgenthau Diary*, I, 518; parallel comment to Breckenridge Long quoted page 563, note 17, *infra*.

176. Blum, *Morgenthau Diary*, I, 518.

177. Langer and Gleason, *Challenge to Isolation*, p. 58, though see Watt's provocative article, *op. cit.*, to the contrary, p. 207.

178. Alsop and Kintner, *Evening Star* (Washington), September 19, 1938, p. A11. While Kennedy's views frequently parallel those of the Clivedeners, the author has found no evidence that he was ever a "participating" member of the reactionary Cliveden Set. That he had not become an intense Anglophile became clear after the war actually began.

179. *New York Times*, May 14, 1938, p. 15; *Boston Globe*, same day, with a United Press byline.

180. *New York Times*, September 3, 1938, p. 2. See also a speech reported in *New York Times* on July 13, 1938, p. 23.

181. *The Times* (London), November 25, 1938, p. 16.

182. *Baltimore Sun*, December 16, 1938, p. 1.

183. Blum, *Morgenthau Diary*, I, 502.

184. Page 276 *infra*.

185. Winston S. Churchill, *The Second World War*, Vol. I: *The Gathering Storm* (Boston: Houghton Mifflin Company, 1948), p. 221.

186. Or (excepting "businesslike") to Churchill himself.

187. Krock, *New York Times*, December 13, 1938, p. 24.

188. Derek Walker-Smith, *Neville Chamberlain: Man of Peace* (London: Robert Hale Limited, n.d.), pp. 380–81.

189. Kennedy to Baruch, March 28, 1938, MS. in Baruch Papers.

190. Landis MS., pp. 5–6.

191. Quoted in Freda Kirchway, "Watch Joe Kennedy," *The Nation*, December 14, 1940, p. 593.

192. Marginal notation by Vansittart on a January, 1940 "minute," FO371/24248/A825/434/45.

193. Kennedy to Hull, April 14, 1939, and Hull to Kennedy, April 17, 1939 ("I

am, therefore, fearful that your writing such a foreword at this time might lead to inferences which, however unfounded, might be embarrassing to you or to this Government"), S.D.MS. 123 Kennedy, Joseph P./189 and 192.

194. *The Times* (London), November 12, 1940, p. 4.

195. *Baltimore Sun*, December 16, 1938, p. 1. To H. V. Kaltenborn, Kennedy observed that "anything that keeps Britain at peace is in the interest of the United States." Kaltenborn, *Fifty Fabulous Years* (New York: G. P. Putnam's Sons, 1950), p. 215.

REFUGEES,
TRADE, AND A HOLIDAY

1. Robert P. Post, *New York Times*, July 23, 1939, IV, 5.

2. *F.R.U.S.*, 1938, I, 660–61.

3. Krock, *New York Times*, December 13, 1938, p. 24.

4. Comments on the Hull trade policy are based principally on a *Fortune* article, September, 1937, pp. 90 ff. See also Julius W. Pratt, *Cordell Hull*, Vol. XII of *The American Secretaries of State and their Diplomacy*, ed. Robert H. Ferrell (New York: Cooper Square Publishers, Inc., 1964), p. 125 ff; or, Arthur W. Schatz, "Cordell Hull and the Struggle for the Reciprocal Trade Agreements Program, 1932–1940" (Ph.D. thesis, University of Oregon, 1965).

5. Hull to Johnson, January 31, 1938, *F.R.U.S.*, 1938, II, 10.

6. Baruch to Kent, December 16, 1937, MS. in Baruch Papers, Vol. 40.

7. Hull to Johnson, January 31, 1938, *F.R.U.S.*, 1938, II, 10.

8. *The Times* (London), April 29, 1938, p. 18.

9. *The Times* (London), July 5, 1938, p. 16.

10. Landis MS., Library of Congress, Chap. 18, p. 5.

11. Chamberlain report of discussion with Kennedy at cabinet meeting of July 28, 1938, MS. at Public Record Office, London, Cab. 23, Vol. 94, p. 264. It is unclear from the minutes whether the quotation is supposed to be Kennedy's words or the Prime Minister's paraphrase of the gist of his argument.

12. *New York Times*, July 27, 1938, p. 8.

13. ". . . He felt himself that through this, however it could be developed, it might be possible for the United States to exercise some influence with both Germany and Italy in favour of more sensible and more steady international relations." Halifax to Lindsay, October 6, 1938, FO371/22661/W13347/86/41. The discussion reported was about the European situation in general, and not about trade or trade agreements in particular, but occurred at the time of apparent impasse in the negotiations on the Anglo-American trade agreement.

14. Lindsay to Foreign Office, February 1, 1938, FO371/21530/A791/175/45, and Hull to Johnson, January 31, 1938, *F.R.U.S.*, 1938, II, 10.

15. Hull to Johnson, February 15, 1938, *F.R.U.S.*, 1938, II, 19.

16. Landis MS., p. 54.

17. Hugh Dalton's characterization. Dalton Diary MS. at London School of Economics, entry of October 9, 1940. Lord Strang noted on a foreign office minute, "Mr. Butterworth is always worth listening to." FO371/24418/C2461/1285/18. At the State Department, Moffat suspected that Butterworth was "the only one of the staff [in London] who made good." Moffat Diary MS., entry of January 7–8, 1939, p. 3.

18. Interview, July 26, 1972.

19. Morgenthau Diary MS., entry of December 5, 1938, Vol. 157, p. 367.

20. Interview, August 7, 1965.

21. *The Times* (London), June 14, 1938, p. 16.

22. Kennedy to Hull, October 7, 1938, *F.R.U.S.*, 1938, II, 59–60.

23. Landis MS., Library of Congress, Chap. 18, pp. 5, 7.

24. Kennedy to Hull, October 18, 1938, and Hull to Kennedy, same day, are in *F.R.U.S.*, 1938, II, 65–66.

25. "The offer of my services, however, evoked no enthusiasm." Landis MS., Library of Congress, Chap. 18, p. 7.

26. Hooker, *Moffat Papers*, entry of October 21, 1938, p. 221.

27. Landis MS., Library of Congress, Chap. 18, p. 8.

28. Hull to Kennedy, November 3, 1938, *F.R.U.S.*, 1938, II, 70.

29. Landis MS., Library of Congress, Chap. 18, p. 7.

30. *Manchester Guardian* (weekly ed.), November 25, 1938, p. 421.

31. Before American Chamber of Commerce in London, *The Times* (London), November 29, 1938, p. 9.

32. Speech before joint meeting of the Manchester Chamber of Commerce and the English Speaking Union, in *Manchester Guardian* (weekly ed.), December 3, 1938, p. 453. Reported without the shouts in *The Times* (London), November 30, 1938, p. 9. For other Kennedy statements on commerce, see his speech before the Plymouth Chamber of Commerce, *The Times* (London), December 7, 1938, p. 10, or less fully in *New York Times*, same day, p. 15.

33. *New York Times*, July 16, 1938, p. 4.

34. Lord Strang visit with Polish Ambassador Count Edward Raczyński, December 9, 1938, FO371/22540/W16615.

35. Documents in FO371/22553, *passim.*

36. Minute on discussion with Raczyński and M. Balinski of the Polish Embassy, November 18–19, 1938, FO371/22537/W15316/104/98.

37. Lindsay to Foreign Office, November 18, 1938, FO371/21637/C14092. Lindsay expressed surprise at Welles' characterization of the position of the "Jewish leaders," and one does wonder as to what Jewish leaders Welles had consulted.

38. Visit of May 28, 1938, FO371/21749/C5319/2289/18. Kennedy had Harold Ickes with him on the visit, who, according to Halifax, shared Kennedy's view (sic, Ickes). Roosevelt once remarked to Kennedy, "if there was a demagogue around here of the type of Huey Long to take up anti-Semitism, there would be more blood running in the streets of New York than in Berlin." Landis MS., p. 80.

39. Myron C. Taylor to Hull, August 12, 1938, *F.R.U.S.*, 1938, I, 764; and, Taylor and Rublee to Hull, August 29, 1938, *ibid.*, 776–78.

40. Memorandum of telephone call between Rublee and Welles on October 10, 1938, *F.R.U.S.*, 1938, I, 795–96.

41. Kennedy's choice of emphasis is inherent in the fact that he himself conducted aspects of the trade negotiations, assisted by the "crackerjack" Butterworth, leaving matters on refugees to be handled, for the most part, by the embassy's chargé, the well-respected but traditional Herschel Johnson.

42. Long Diary MS., entry of March 8, 1939, p. 167.

43. Minute of May 28, 1938, FO371/21749/C5319/2289/18.

44. "Mr. Kennedy had not attempted to conceal his low opinion of Mr. Myron

Taylor, who had not only no knowledge of the problem, but was making no attempt to get it." On his own part, Bearsted thought Kennedy's ideas on the problem "somewhat hazy." Minute of June 9, 1938, FO371/21749/C5681/2289/18, p. 459.

45. Rublee-Welles telephone call, October 10, 1938, *F.R.U.S.*, 1938, I, 795–96.

46. Macdonald memorandum of visit of October 13, 1938, FO371/21882/ E6035/10/31.

47. *The Times* (London), October 15, 1938, p. 11; *New York Times* same day and October 25, 1938, p. 17.

48. Halifax at Cabinet Meeting, p. 9 in FO371/21658.

49. *New York Times*, November 15, 1938, p. 6.

50. See Moffat Diary MS., entries of November 15, 16, 17 and 22, 1938.

51. *New York Times*, November 16, 1938, p. 1.

52. Moffat Diary MS., entry of November 16, 1938, p. 4.

53. *New York Times*, November 18, 1938, p. 3.

54. Lindsay to Halifax, November 17, 1938, FO371/C14147/1667/62.

55. Moffat Diary MS., entry of November 17, 1938, p. 2.

56. McCarthy, *The Remarkable Kennedys*, p. 62.

57. *Life* quoted in Joe McCarthy, *The Remarkable Kennedys* (New York: Popular Library, paperback ed., 1960), p. 62.

58. McCarthy, *ibid.*, p. 62.

59. Lindsay to Foreign Office, November 19, 1938, FO371/22537/ W15183/104/98.

60. "Kennedy and the Jews," *The Nation*, November 26, 1938, pp. 548, 555. The issue was apparently circulated several days before publication date.

61. Landis MS., p. 36.

62. *New York Times*, November 23, 1938, p. 3.

63. Ione Robinson, *A Wall to Paint On* (New York: E. P. Dutton and Company, Inc., 1946), letter of December 25, 1938 p. 380.

64. Moffat Diary MS., entry of November 22, 1938.

65. Interview, London, July, 1972.

66. Halifax to Lindsay, November 16, 1938, FO371/21637/C13900/1667/62.

67. Interview, London, July 17, 1972.

68. "The Reminiscences of George Rublee" (1950–51), pp. 283–84, typescript in The Oral History Collection of Columbia University.

69. In a late October, 1938, meeting with Lindsay, Roosevelt made the remarkable suggestion that the trans-Jordanian desert be irrigated and the Palestine Arabs be enticed to move there, and forced to do so if necessary, freeing their Palestine lands for Jews. Jews would be prohibited from emigrating to Jordan, and Arabs forbidden from emigrating to Palestine. The Foreign Office thought the proposal to be unfeasible both politically and also from an engineering standpoint. Lindsay to Lancelot Oliphant, November 3, 1938, reporting visit of October 25, 1938, and minute thereon, FO371/21883/F6606/10/31.

70. Rublee oral history typescript, pp. 283–85.

71. Memo to German Ambassadors in London, Paris, Rome, Warsaw, and Washington, dated July 8, 1938, *German Documents*, V, 894–95.

72. Memo dated October 20, 1938, *German Documents*, V, 901–02.

73. Ribbentrop to von Dirksen, December 23, 1938, *German Documents*, V, 919.

74. Memo dated November 12 and November 14, 1938, in *German Documents*, V, 904–05.

75. *German Documents*, V, 920–21.

76. Rublee oral history typescript, p. 302.

77. *Ibid.*, p. 304.

78. *Ibid.*, p. 285.

79. Interview, London, July 17, 1972.

80. *The Times* (London), November 29, 1938, p. 14.

81. *New York Times*, November 29, 1938, p. 18.

82. Presidential Press Conference 504, November 29, 1938, typescript at Roosevelt Library, Hyde Park, N.Y., Press Conferences, XII, 268.

83. *New York Times*, November 30, 1938, p. 14.

84. Kenneth Crawford, *New York Post*, December 9, 1938.

85. Morgenthau Diary MS., entry of December 5, 1938, Vol. 154, p. 367.

86. Cabinet Meeting, minutes in FO371/21658.

87. *Baltimore Sun*, December 7, 1938, p. 7.

88. *New York Times*, December 7, 1938, p. 15.

89. *New York Times*, December 16, 1938, p. 13.

90. *Ibid.*

91. *The Times* (London), December 19, 1938, p. 21. The author did not find this advice in other accounts of the interview. For a third report, see the *Baltimore Sun*, December 16, 1938.

92. Landis MS., pp. 74–75.

93. Landis MS., pp. 72, 73, 78, 80. Kennedy was particularly upset at being bypassed on arrangement-making for a proposed Royal Tour of the United States. See Landis MS., pp. 72, 73; Landis MS., Library of Congress, Chap. 18, p. 12; Moffat Diary MS., entry of November 4, 1938; and, S.D.MS. 841.001 George VI/269 and 274.

94. Landis MS., pp. 78, 80.

95. *New York Times*, December 17, 1938, p. 8.

96. See the Moffat Diary MS., entry of December 16, 1938, for notes on Kennedy's visit with the European Bureau Chief.

97. *New York Times*, December 19, 1938. The rest of the family was vacationing in Switzerland. *The Times* (London), December 12, 1938, p. 14.

98. Among the reports was one that Kennedy had prophesized that the next move in the appeasement policy was to grant Germany military bases in Canada or the West Indies. For a denial, see *New York Times*, January 14, 1939, p. 3.

99. Lord Strang's note on the reports: "I fear that the Ambassador's pessimism is justified on the whole." Minute of January 13, 1939, FO371/22961/C425/C715/15/18.

100. *The Times* (London), January 11, 1939, p. 9, and January 12, 1939, p. 10; Landis MS., p. 79.

101. *New York Times*, January 10, 1939, p. 1.

102. *The Secret Diary of Harold L. Ickes*, Vol. II: *The Inside Struggle, 1936–1939* (New York: Simon & Schuster, 1954), entry of January 22, 1939, p. 562.

103. *New York Times*, January 11, 1939, p. 13.

104. *Congressional Record*, February 1, 1939, XXCIV, 1014.

105. *New York Times*, February 17, 1939, p. 3.

106. Henry Ehrlich, *Boston Herald*, March 26, 1939.

107. Cadogan memorandum, apparently of February 2, 1939, FO371/22827/A1090/1090/45.

108. Halifax note of February 3, 1939, same file. Halifax took it to mean that the less said in England about Roosevelt the better.

109. Roosevelt's explanation to Kennedy. Landis MS., p. 80.

110. Long Diary MS., entry of February 9, 1939.

111. Moffat Diary MS., entry of February 9, 1939.

112. *New York Times*, February 10, 1939, p. 3.

113. Long Diary MS., entry of February 9, 1939.

114. Moffat Diary MS., entry of February 9, 1939.

115. Boake Carter, *Boston Globe*, April 20, 1939, p. 1; see also Carter's earlier piece, *New York Daily Mirror*, November 12, 1938.

116. Harry Henry, *Boston Globe* (morning edition), April 25, 1939, p. 1.

117. *Ibid.*

118. Moffat Diary MS., entry of November 22, 1938.

119. *Ickes Diary*, entry of July 16, 1938, II, 420. Farley doubts that Roosevelt was thinking in such terms. Interview, New York, March 3, 1962.

120. Edward T. Folliard, *Washington Post*, February 22, 1939, p. 9.

THE
INTERCRISIS PERIOD

1. Ione Robinson, *A Wall to Paint On* (New York: E. P. Dutton and Company, Inc., 1946), letter of November 4, 1938, p. 367.

2. Landis MS., pp. 75–76, 77, 123–24.

3. Halifax to Lindsay, February 17, 1939, FO371/22829/A1385/1292/45.

4. William W. Kaufman, "Two American Ambassadors," in *The Diplomats*, ed. Gordon A. Craig and Felix Gilbert (Princeton, N.J.: Princeton University Press, 1953), p. 667.

5. *The Memoirs of Cordell Hull* (New York: The Macmillan Company, 1948), I, 623.

6. Kennedy to Hull, February 23, 1939, *F.R.U.S.*, 1939, I, 22.

7. Bullitt to Hull, March 11, 1939, *F.R.U.S.*, 1939, I, 32.

8. Kennedy to Hull, February 23, 1939, *F.R.U.S.*, 1939, I, 22.

9. *New York Times*, February 25, 1939, p. 6.

10. *New York Times*, February 28, 1939, p. 1.

11. Kennedy to Hull, February 27, 1939, S.D.MS. 867N.01/1449. Halifax's wire to Lindsay after the conference suggests, "It would probably be well for your Excellency to make certain that the State Department has received from the United States Ambassador an accurate version of the tentative suggestions put forward by H.M.G." Halifax to Lindsay, February 27, 1939, FO414/276/E1505/6/31.

12. Unidentified clipping dated February 28, 1939, in the *Boston Herald* archives.

13. *New York Times*, March 10, 1939.

14. *New York Times*, May 18, 1939.

15. Interview, London, July 17, 1972.

16. Halifax to Lindsay, May 25, 1939, FO371/22797/A3920. Shades of Walter Hines Page.

17. Moffat to Kennedy, March 2, 1939, MS. in Moffat Papers at Houghton Library, Harvard University, Cambridge, Mass.

18. *New York Times*, November 6, 1936.

19. Assumed on the basis of a March 6, 1939, wire to Welles: "Dear Sumner: I cannot tell you how much I appreciate your kindness. If I have one real virtue I never forget." S.D.MS. 123 Kennedy, Joseph P./171.

20. Long Diary MS., entry of March 8, 1939, p. 167.

21. Moffat Diary MS., entry of March 6, 1939.

22. Gail Cameron, *Rose* (London: Michael Joseph Ltd., 1972), p. 102.

23. Kennedy to Moffat, March 17, 1939, MS. in Moffat Papers.

24. Actually, eight children plus two nurses and the Eddie Moores. Joe, Jr., was in Spain at the time, touring the battlefront.

25. Pope Paul VI, recorded interview, typescript at John F. Kennedy Library, Oral History Program.

26. Phillips Diary MS., entry of March 10, 1939.

27. Landis MS., p. 92. A leading writer on the subject of American-Vatican relations told the author that Kennedy's interest in the establishment of recognition of the Vatican, his meddling in internal Church politics, and his frequent phone calls, were not welcomed in either the Vatican or the United States, but Churchmen on both sides of the Atlantic put up with it because Kennedy was a wealthy contributor. Many noted inaccuracies in memoranda he provided at the time of recognition of the Vatican. Interview, New York, March 11, 1962.

28. Landis MS., p. 92.

29. *New York Herald-Tribune*, March 14, 1939, p. 20.

30. Stephen Hess, *American Political Dynasties, from Adams to Kennedy* (Garden City, N.Y.: Doubleday & Company, Inc., 1966), p. 518.

31. *New York Herald-Tribune*, March 14, 1939, p. 20.

32. Years later he would repeat the thought: "There is no use in being an Ambassador today. The Secretary of State now runs the whole works. An Ambassador doesn't amount to that," he said, snapping his fingers, before the Providence, Rhode Island, Chamber of Commerce. *Providence Bulletin*, October 31, 1946, p. 14.

33. Phillips Diary MS., entry of March 13, 1939, pp. 3054–55.

34. Kennedy to Hull, March 17, 1939, S.D.MS. 865.00/1805.

35. Interview, September 20, 1973.

36. Kennedy to Hull, March 17, 1939, S.D.MS. 865.00/1805.

37. Landis MS., p. 94.

38. Kennedy to Hull, March 17, 1939, S.D.MS. 865.00/1805.

39. Robert Graves and Alan Hodge, *The Long Week-End* (London: Faber & Faber, Ltd., 1940), p. 448.

40. Kennedy's Roman holiday was to have lasted until March 20. *The Times* (London), March 16, 1939, p. 19. It was cut short by events.

41. Halifax to Lindsay, March 17, 1939, in *British Documents*, IV, 364.

42. Templewood Papers, University Library, Cambridge, Eng., XIX: (B) 5, March 17, 1939.

43. William L. Shirer, *The Rise and Fall of the Third Reich* (New York: Simon & Schuster, 1960), p. 454.

44. Kennedy to State Department, February 17, 1939, *F.R.U.S.*, 1939, I, 14–17.

45. Halifax to Lindsay, March 18, 1939, *British Documents*, IV, 380.

46. *Ibid.*

47. Kennedy to Hull, March 24, 1939, *F.R.U.S.*, 1939, I, 98–99. Cf. Halifax to

Lindsay, March 24, 1939, *British Documents*, IV, 499–500: "It seemed to him that considerable doubt emerged as to the willingness of Poland and Rumania to defend themselves against German encroachment or attack, and, in short, he seemed to detect some doubt in many quarters, firstly, as to whether those Governments were likely to mean business, and, further, whether His Majesty's Government and France really meant business." See also Count E. Raczyński to Beck, March 29, 1939, in *Polish Documents Relative to the Origin of the War*, 1st Series (Berlin: Auswartiges Amt, 1940), No. 3, p. 32 (Hereafter cited as *"Polish Documents"*).

48. *Providence Journal* (Providence, R.I.), March 25, 1939, p. 1, under an Associated Press byline. *The Times* (London), reported Kennedy's presence but not his comment, March 25, 1939, p. 14, and the *New York Times* had no report.

49. Joseph E. Davies, *Mission to Moscow* (New York: Simon & Schuster, 1941), diary entry of April 3, 1939, p. 440.

50. Kennedy-Hull phone conversation, April 24, 1939, typescript in Hull Papers; see also Memorandum by Jan Wszelaki after conference with Kennedy, June 16, 1939, *Polish Documents*, pp. 42–43.

51. *The Diaries of Sir Alexander Cadogan, 1938–1945*, ed. David Dilks (London: Cassell, 1971), entry of March 31, 1939, p. 167.

52. Halifax to Lindsay, March 31, 1939, FO414/276 part 51, p. 67, for C4529/54/18.

53. *Ibid.*

54. Halifax to Lindsay, April 11, 1939, *British Documents*, V, 169.

55. *New York Times*, April 15, 1939, p. 3.

56. Halifax to Lindsay, April 11, 1939, *British Documents*, V, 169.

57. Kennedy to Hull, April 17, 1939, *F.R.U.S.*, 1939, I, 139–40.

58. *Ibid.*

59. Butterworth made clear to the British that purchase of strategic materials was not the only consideration; disposal of American commodities was an essential element. Minute of April 29, 1939, FO371/22797/A3122.

60. Bernard M. Baruch, *My Own Story*, Vol. II: *The Public Years* (New York: Holt, Rinehart & Winston, 1960), p. 301.

61. Lindsay to Halifax, May 17, 1939, FO371/22797/A3554.

62. Moffat Diary MS., entry of April 14, 1939, p. 2.

63. Hull to Kennedy, April 18, 1939, *F.R.U.S.*, 1939, II, 234–36.

64. Hull to Kennedy, May 10, and May 12, 1939, *F.R.U.S.*, 1939, II, 241–43, 246–47.

65. As to Byrnes, minute of April 29, 1938, FO371/22797/A3122. For Baruch, *The Public Years*, p. 301.

66. Landis MS., pp. 80–81.

67. Documents in F0371/22797, *passim*.

68. Perowne minute, May 23, 1939, FO371/22797/A3664/26/45.

69. *Ibid.* Perowne cites a Sir W. Brown, p. 87.

70. Kennedy to Hull, June 2, 1939, *F.R.U.S.*, 1939, II, 248–49.

71. Perowne minute, May 23, 1939, FO371/22797/A3664/26/45; Halifax to Lindsay, May 25, 1939, same volume, A3920 (E3875/6/31).

72. Halifax to Lindsay, May 25, 1939, FO371/22797/A3920 (E3875/6/31).

73. Lindsay to Halifax, May 17, 1939, FO371/22797/A3554.

74. *Ibid.* For Halifax, Halifax to Lindsay, May 16, 1939, FO371/22797/A3446/26/45.

75. Perowne minute, *op. cit.*

76. Lindsay to Halifax, May 17, 1939, *op. cit.*

77. Feis to Butterworth, May 9, 1939, in Feis Papers at Library of Congress Manuscript Division, Washington, D.C., Box 12, File "W. W. Butterworth."

78. Perowne minute, *op. cit.*

79. Halifax to Lindsay, May 15, 1939, in FO371/22797.

80. Lindsay to Halifax, May 25, 1939, in FO371/22797/A3781. Minute of June 23, 1939, FO371/22798/A4374.

81. Perowne minute, *op. cit.* Many of the more unfriendly references to Kennedy appear in minutes by Perowne. Victor Perowne, of the Foreign Office's American Department, was described to the author by one of his colleagues as a "very intelligent, highly nervous type, who traveled in gossipy circles, but I should think he had his reasons for any minute he wrote." Perowne died in an equestrian accident around 1950. His widow told the author that he had left no papers. Interview, London, July, 1972.

82. Halifax to Simon and Stanley, June 13, 1939, FO371/22797/A4202, pp. 154/55.

83. Cabinet Meeting of June 14, 1939, Cab. 23, Vol. 99, p. 367.

84. Cabinet Meeting of June 21, 1939, Cab. 23, Vol. 100, p. 23.

85. *The Times* (London), July 24, 1939, p. 12; 54 U.S. Stat. 1411, or Department of State Treaty Series 947.

86. Hull to Kennedy, June 20, 1939, *F.R.U.S.*, 1939, II, 256–57.

87. Ferdinand Kuhn, Jr., *New York Times*, June 24, 1939, p. 5.

88. Interview, August 17, 1965.

89. *The Times* (London), April 22, 1939. This author has not seen the original text of the speech, but it must have been very different; Berle regarded the draft of it as "a more than usually foolish speech," and got the President to personally approve the Department's veto. Adolf A. Berle, *Navigating the Rapids, 1918–1971*, ed. Beatrice Bishop Berle and Travis Beal Jacobs (New York: Harcourt Brace Jovanovich, 1973), diary entry of April 20, 1939, p. 214; Berle to Roosevelt, April 20, 1939, S.D.MS. 123 Kennedy, Joseph P./195. En route to Edinburgh the Ambassador wired Hull and Roosevelt: "On my way to Edinburgh with speech. All international affairs omitted, talking about flowers, birds and trees. The only thing I am afraid of is that instead of giving me the freedom of the city they will make me Queen of the May." Kennedy to Hull and Roosevelt, April 20, 1939, MS. at Roosevelt Library, Hyde Park, N.Y., in President's Secretary's Files, I, Diplomatic Correspondence, Great Britain, Box 8, Folder on Joseph P. Kennedy, 1938–1940; or in State Department Files, 123 Kennedy, Joseph P./195.

90. *The Times* (London), May 18, 1939, p. 18.

91. *The Times* (London), May 19, 1939, p. 18.

92. *Ibid.*, editorial on p. 17.

93. *The Times* (London), May 26, 1939, p. 16.

94. Harry Henry, *Boston Sunday Globe*, June 11, 1939, p. 21.

95. Landis MS., p. 28.

96. Eleanor Roosevelt, *This I Remember* (New York: Harper & Brothers, 1949), pp. 183–84.

97. Interview, August 17, 1965.

98. Landis MS., p. 72.

99. Moffat Diary MS., entry of November 4, 1938, and Memorandum from Moffat to Welles, November 4, 1938, S.D.MS. 841.001 George VI, 274.

100. Landis MS., pp. 72–73. According to Krock, Kennedy in great part planned the tour. Krock, *New York Times*, July 18, 1939, p. 18.

101. Kennedy to Hull, October 28, 1938, S.D.MS. 841.001 George VI, 269.

102. *Ibid.*

103. Roosevelt to Kennedy, November 2, 1938, MS. at Roosevelt Library, Hyde Park, N.Y., in President's Secretary's File, I, Diplomatic Correspondence, Great Britain, 1933–1945, Box 7, King & Queen folder for 1938.

104. *The Times* (London), June 8, 1939, p. iii.

105. Kennedy before the Institute of Mechanical Engineers, *The Times* (London), June 10, 1939, p. 17.

106. *New York Times*, June 23, 1939.

107. *New York Times*, July 5, 1939, p. 8.

108. Will Durant to Steve Early, October 19, 1939, MS. at Roosevelt Library, Hyde Park, N.Y., in President's Personal File 5660. See also Walter Lippmann, *New York Herald-Tribune*, October 20, 1938, p. 25.

109. When Madame Ciano asked Kennedy whether the United States would enter the threatening European war, Kennedy answered a firm "Positively," thinking that that was the answer most likely to have a pacifying effect on Mussolini. Landis MS. p. 94.

110. *New York Times*, February 26, 1939, p. 24.

111. *The Times* (London), April 19, 1939, p. 14.

112. Interview, London, July, 1972.

113. *The Times* (London), April 21, 1939, p. 15.

114. *Boston Globe*, April 19, 1939, and April 20, 1939 (morning edition), p. 1.

115. Hearing before the Senate Committee on Foreign Relations, April 24, 1939, p. 227. Reported *New York Times*, April 25, 1939, p. 12.

116. *The Times* (London), April 21, 1939, p. 15; *New York Times*, April 21, 1939, p. 8.

117. *New York Times* editorial, April 27, 1939, p. 24.

118. Kennedy-Hull phone call, April 24, 1939, MS. in Hull Papers.

119. Krock, *New York Times*, May 4, 1939, p. 22.

120. See Raczyński to Beck, March 29, 1939, *Polish Documents*, p. 34.

121. *The Week*, May 17, 1939, p. 6, edited differently in *The Secret Diary of Harold L. Ickes*, Vol. II: *The Inside Struggle, 1936–1939* (New York: Simon & Schuster, 1954), p. 676.

122. *New York Post*, June 1, 1939.

123. See, for example, Moffat to Leah Elkin, June 17, 1939, S.D.MS. 123 Kennedy, Joseph P./212.

124. *The Week*, June 14, 1939, p. 2.

125. *Ickes Diary*, entry of July 2, 1939, II, 676. See also Ickes' entry of September 27, 1939, *The Secret Diary of Harold L. Ickes*, Vol. III: *The Lowering Clouds, 1939–1941* (New York: Simon & Schuster, 1954), pp. 22–23.

126. Krock, *New York Times*, July 18, 1939, p. 18.

127. Halifax to Lindsay, June 7, 1939, *British Documents*, V, 793.

128. Kennedy to Hull, June 7, 1939, quoted in Arthur Krock, "How War Came: Extracts from the Hull Files," *New York Times Magazine*, July 18, 1943, p. 34.

129. George Bilainkin, *Maisky* (London: George Allen & Unwin Ltd., 1944), p. 266.

130. Davies, *Mission to Moscow*, diary entry of April 3, 1939, p. 440. Kennedy's account of the conversation, in Landis MS., pp. 106–107, is substantially parallel.

131. Robert Bendiner, *Riddle of the State Department* (New York: Farrar & Rinehart, Inc., 1942), p. 9.

132. *Ibid.* Later, in 1945, Kennedy expounded this line of argument to Forrestal—which does not necessarily mean that he had subscribed to it in 1938–39. *Forrestal Diaries*, ed. Walter Millis (New York: The Viking Press, 1951), pp. 121–22.

133. *F.R.U.S.*, 1939, I, 282–83.

134. *New York Times* reported that Kennedy was taking a "short vacation." July 21, 1939, p. 8. *The Times* (London) said that the holiday was to last to the end of August—which would make it a six-week vacation. July 22, 1939, p. 11.

135. Balfour minute of September 30, 1939, FO371/22827/A6635/1090/45, p. 160.

136. Charles Loch Mowat, *Britain Between the Wars* (Chicago: University of Chicago Press, 1955), p. 643.

137. Kennedy wire in *F.R.U.S.*, 1939, I, 341, 342. In June, Jack Kennedy had visited Poland and had conlcuded that Poland would fight. James MacGregor Burns, *John Kennedy: A Political Profile* (New York: Harcourt, Brace & Company, 1959), p. 38.

138. Wire of August 23, 8:00 P.M., *F.R.U.S.*, 1939, I, 355–56.

139. Interview, London, July 31, 1972.

140. Charles Peake account of lunch with Hillman on October 11, 1939, FO371/22827/A7195/1090/45. Hillman, a Hearst correspondent, was Kennedy's only close friend among the American press corps in London.

141. H. V. Kaltenborn, *Fifty Fabulous Years* (New York: G. P. Putnam's Sons, 1950), p. 215.

142. *Ibid.*

143. Wire of the twenty-fourth in Krock, *New York Times Magazine*, July 18, 1943, p. 37.

144. Landis MS., p. 149.

145. Kennedy to Hull, August 24, 1939, S.D.MS. 760C.62/943.

146. Moffat Diary MS., entry of August 25, 1939.

147. Hooker, *Moffat Papers*, entry of August 24, 1939, p. 253.

148. Hull, *Memoirs*, I, 662.

149. Landis MS., pp. 150–51; parallel material in Berle, *Navigating the Waters*, diary entry of August 24, 1939, p. 243.

150. Kennedy to Hull, August 25, 1939, *F.R.U.S.*, 1939, I, 369–70.

151. *Ibid.*

152. Landis MS., p. 162.

153. Landis MS., p. 154.

154. Memorandum by Jan Wszelaki after conference with Kennedy, June 16, 1939, *Polish Documents*, pp. 42–43; Kennedy-Hull phone conversation, April 24, 1939, typescript in Hull Papers.

155. Landis MS., p. 155.

156. Hearings on H.R. 1776 (Lend-Lease), p. 289.

157. Burton K. Wheeler with Paul F. Healy, *Yankee From the West* (Garden City, N.Y.: Doubleday & Company, Inc., 1962), p. 27.

158. Millis, *The Forrestal Diaries*, pp. 121–22.

159. Years later, Kennedy attributed the Japanese attack on Pearl Harbor as in part having been provoked by American economic policies. Arthur Krock, *Memoirs: Sixty Years on the Firing Line* (New York: Funk & Wagnalls, 1968), pp. 337–38.

160. Kennedy wire quoted in Krock, *New York Times Magazine*, July 18, 1943, p. 37.

161. Kennedy to Hull, August 30, 1939, 5:00 P.M., *F.R.U.S.*, 1939, I, 386 f.

162. Kennedy to Hull, August 30, 1939, 8:00 P.M. *ibid.*, p. 392.

163. Joseph Alsop and Robert Kintner, *American White Paper* (New York: Simon & Schuster, 1940), p. 59.

164. Hull *Memoirs*, I, 672. According to the Landis MS., Hull himself "sounded like a tired old man." Landis MS., p. 164.

165. When Labour M.P. Arthur Greenwood rose during the debate of September 2, 1939, to demand on behalf of the Labour party that war be declared, Leo Amery, a respected Conservative party member, cried out to him, "Speak for England, Arthur!" A.J.P. Taylor, *English History, 1914–1945* (London: Penguin Books, paperback ed., 1970), p. 552, or virtually any other account of the session. According to Taylor, Greenwood "did his best," the meaning of which is unclear from Taylor's account, but in any event, the house broke up in confusion from his speech.

166. Sir Reginald Dorman-Smith, Chamberlain's Minister of Agriculture, recounts the Cabinet session at which the decision was virtually taken away from the exhausted and pathetic Prime Minister: ". . . facing a Cabinet on a 'sit-down strike' he had no alternative. The climax came most dramatically. The P.M. said quietly: 'Right, gentlemen, this means war.' Hardly had he said it, when there was the most enormous clap of thunder and the whole Cabinet Room was lit up by a blinding flash of lightning." Michael Moynihan *Sunday Times* (London), September 6, 1964, p. 3.

167. The Earl of Birkenhead, *Halifax* (Boston: Houghton, Mifflin Company, 1966), p. 423.

168. Alsop and Kintner, *American White Paper*, p. 68. In the morning, Missy LeHand called to tell Kennedy that the President would try to talk with Kennedy later, but that Roosevelt wanted Kennedy to know he was thinking of him. Landis MS., p. 67.

DURING
THE PHONY WAR

1. Edward Raczyński, *In Allied London* (London: Weidenfeld and Nicolson, 1962), pp. 33–34.

2. John W. Wheeler-Bennett, *King George VI* (New York: St. Martin's Press, 1958), p. 419.

3. Balfour minute of September 20, 1939, FO371/22827/A6561/1090/45, p. 157.

4. Gage, the minute writer, describes his informant as a friend in the Coldstream Guards on close terms with one or all of Kennedy's daughters. Hartington meets that description. Generally, private informants are not named in the written minutes, though those with access to the minutes were told the identity orally.

5. This author doubts the informant's interpretation. By the time of this incident, friction had developed between Kennedy and the leaders of the British war effort, and

this author suspects that Kennedy's apparent attitude was a momentary manifestation of simple soreness at the British heads of state.

6. Gage minute, September 20, 1939, FO371/22827/A6561/1090/45, p. 156.

7. Continuation of the same minute, dated September 26, 1939, same citation, p. 154 f.

8. Lord Francis-Williams, *Nothing So Strange* (New York: American Heritage Press, 1970), pp. 155–56. According to Lord Francis-Williams, John Kennedy did not adopt his father's defeatist views, though the Hartington account quoted in the text would seem to point to the contrary.

9. Kennedy to Hull, September 11, 1939, *F.R.U.S.*, 1939, I, 421–24.

10. Kennedy to Hull, September 15, 1939, *F.R.U.S.*, 1939, I, 426–27. See also Kennedy to Hull, September 12, 1939, *ibid.*, pp. 551–52.

11. Landis MS., p. 191.

12. Kennedy to Hull, October 4, 1939, *F.R.U.S.*, 1939, I, 501–502.

13. Landis MS., p. 188.

14. Kennedy to Hull, September 18, 1939, 11:00 A.M., *F.R.U.S.*, 1939, I, 439 at 441.

15. *Ibid.*, p. 440.

16. Kennedy to Roosevelt, September 30, 1938, in William L. Langer and S. Everett Gleason, *The Challenge to Isolation, 1937–1940* (New York: Harper & Brothers, 1952), p. 252.

17. Page 206 *supra*.

18. Landis MS., Library of Congress, p. 467.

19. Kennedy to Hull, September 11, 1939, *F.R.U.S.*, 1939, I, 421–24. This document was wired at 2:00 P.M. London time, but because of the time differential was received in Washington before 2:00 P.M. Washington time.

20. Langer and Gleason, *The Challenge to Isolation*, pp. 247, 255.

21. Hull to Kennedy, September 11, 1939, 5:00 P.M., *F.R.U.S.*, 1939, I, 424.

22. John M. Blum, *From the Morgenthau Diaries*, Vol. II: *Years of Urgency, 1938–1941* (Boston: Houghton Mifflin Company, 1965), p. 102.

23. Lothian to Halifax, September 14, 1939, FO800/324/XXXVII/26.

24. Chamberlain's report of September 18 meeting at Cabinet Meeting of September 19, 1939, Cab. 65, Vol. 1, p. 116, MS. at Public Record Office, London.

25. Halifax to Lothian, September 25, 1939, FO371/22816/A6586/98/45, p. 251 (p. 56). After the conference, Kennedy wired Hull, "I would be very much surprised if Britain's war aims for the future were not put on a high idealistic plane with very general and less particular specifications as to what is going to be done for Poland," not mentioning his own suggestions on the war aims. Kennedy to Hull, September 25, 1939, *F.R.U.S.*, 1939, I, 453–55.

26. Responding to Kennedy's fear about Germany "going Communist," the President wrote him that "I do not think people in England should worry about Germany going Communist in the Russian manner. They might blow up and have chaos for awhile but the German upbringing for centuries, their insistence on independence of family life, and the right to hold property in a small way, would not, in my judgement, permit the Russian form of brutality for any length of time." Roosevelt to Kennedy, October 30, 1939, in *F.D.R., His Personal Letters, 1928–1945*, ed. Elliott Roosevelt (New York: Duell, Sloan and Pearce, 1950), II, 949.

27. Langer and Gleason, *The Challenge to Isolation*, pp. 251–52, cite Kennedy to Roosevelt, September 30, 1939.

28. Same wire, portion not quoted by Langer and Gleason. MS. at Roosevelt Library, Hyde Park, N.Y.

29. Bastiani to Ciano, October 24, 1939, *I Documenti Diplomatici Italiani*, 9th Series: 1939–1943 (Rome: Ministero degli Affari Esteri, 1954), I, 567.

30. Halifax to Lothian, October 31, 1939, FO414/276, No. 41, A7516/1292/45.

31. Balfour comment of November 4, 1939, on the Halifax wire of October 31. FO371/22830/A7516/1292/45.

32. *The Diaries of Sir Alexander Cadogan, 1938–1945*, ed. David Dilks (London: Cassell, 1971), entry of September 9, 1939, p. 215.

33. *Chips: The Diaries of Sir Henry Channon*, ed. Robert Rhodes James (London: Weidenfeld and Nicolson, 1967), p. 225.

34. Kennedy to Hull, September 18, 1939, 11:00 A.M., *F.R.U.S.*, 1939, I, 439.

35. Thomsen to German Foreign Office, paraphrased in *New York Herald Tribune*, April 26, 1961, p. 7.

36. Scott minute, September 26, 1939, FO371/22827/A6561/1090/45, page following page numbered 155.

37. Perowne minute, January 29, 1940, FO371/24248/A825/434/45, page following page numbered 147 (370).

38. *Ibid.*

39. *Ibid.*

40. Perowne minute, January 25, 1940, FO371/24251/A605/605/45.

41. Perowne minute, January 29, 1940, *op. cit.*, p. 147 (370) and following page. Perowne was wrong. A curious flaw in Kennedy's generally warranted reputation as one of the most calculating of men, was the capacity for loose talk that remained within him.

42. Interview, August 7, 1965.

43. Lord —— to the author, August 20, 1965.

44. Interview, August 17, 1965. The author has seen documentary evidence that one of the embassy staff members close to Kennedy did adjust his investments shortly after the outbreak of the war, and thereafter traded in British pounds on the New York market, but not in such magnitude as to seem horribly sinister.

45. Perowne minute, September 27, 1939, FO371/22827/A6635/1090/45, p. 161 and following page.

46. Balfour minute, September 27, 1939, same citation, page following p. 161.

47. Possibly Vansittart's hand. Same citation, p. 161. Baron Palmstierna is long deceased. One of his close friends told the author that the Baron was "an aristocrat, but nonetheless a leftish sort of man." The two men had been very close, but he did not recall ever having discussed Ambassador Kennedy with the Baron. Interview, London, July 30, 1972.

48. Interview, London, July 30, 1972.

49. Cf. Cadogan's "[Kennedy] sees everything from the angle of his own investments," Dilks, *Cadogan Diary*, entry of September 9, 1939, p. 215, with Vansittart's attitude quoted page 239 *infra*.

50. Scott, dated 30/? /39, FO371/22827/A8763/1090/45, last page of paper.

51. Interview, London, July 26, 1972.

52. "I am sorry to inform you that any correspondence between my father, the late Elisha Walker, and Mr. Joseph P. Kennedy has been destroyed and, therefore, I cannot help you in your research." Elisha Walker, Jr., to the author, October 26, 1972.

53. Interview, London, July 17, 1972.

54. Perowne minute, January 29, 1940, FO371/24248/A825/434/45, p. 148 (371).

55. Perowne minute, September 20, 1939, FO371/22827/A6561/1090/45, page following page 156 and page 157.

56. Balfour minute, same date, same citation.

57. Gage minute, September 26, 1939, same citation, p. 155.

58. Perowne minute, January 29, 1940, FO371/24248/A825/434/45, p. 148 (371).

59. Foreign Office to Lothian, October 3, 1939, FO371/22827/A6635/1090/45, p. 162.

60. A. J. P. Taylor, *English History, 1914–1945* (London: Penguin Books, paperback ed., 1970), p. 568.

61. Roosevelt prophetically responded, "While the World War did not bring forth strong leadership in Great Britain, this war may do so." Roosevelt to Kennedy, October 30, 1939, in *F.D.R., His Personal Letters, 1928–1945*, II, 949.

62. Kennedy to Hull, September 25, 1939, *F.R.U.S.*, 1939, I, 453–55.

63. Peter Fleming, Operation Sea Lion (New York: Simon & Schuster, 1957), p. 91.

64. Perowne minute, September 4, 1939, FO371/22816/A6016/98/45, p. 25.

65. Kennedy to Hull, October 2, 1939, *F.R.U.S.*, 1939, I, 500.

66. Kennedy to Roosevelt, September 30, 1939, in Landis MS., pp. 192–93.

67. Same wire, Landis MS., pp. 193–94.

68. Von Dirksen to Weizsäcker, October 13, 1939, *German Documents*, IV, 634.

69. Dieckhoff to von Dirksen, November 2, 1939, *German Documents*, IV, 637.

70. *German Documents*, IV, 636, note 4.

71. For similar tactic by Kennedy, see Montagu Norman's diary note of a visit with Kennedy on May 6, 1940 in Andrew Boyle, *Montagu Norman* (New York: Weybright and Talley, 1967), p. 314.

72. Kennedy to Welles, May 4, 1939, S.D.MS. 123 Kennedy, Joseph P./199.

73. Welles to Kennedy, May 4, 1939, S.D.MS. 123 Kennedy, Joseph P./201.

74. Page 292 *infra*.

75. *New York Times*, August 25, 1939, p. 7.

76. Kennedy to Hull, September 3, 1939, *F.R.U.S.*, 1939, I, 596.

77. Moffat Diary MS., entry of September 2–3, 1939.

78. Hull to Kennedy, September 3, 1939, *F.R.U.S.*, 1939, I, 597.

79. Landis MS., p. 175.

80. Phrase applied both to Kennedy and Bullitt, Moffat Diary MS., entry of September 9–10, 1939, p. 2.

81. Moffat Diary MS., entry of September 3, 1939.

82. *The Memoirs of Cordell Hull* (New York: The Macmillan Company, 1948), I, 674.

83. *The War Diary of Breckenridge Long: Selections from the Years 1939–1944*, ed. Fred L. Israel (Lincoln: University of Nebraska Press, 1966), entry of September 7, 1939, p. 10. (Hereafter cited as "Israel, *Long Diary*," to distinguish it from the unpublished portions of the Long Diary, cited as "Long Diary MS." The published citation is given where existent.)

84. Landis MS., p. 175.

85. Israel, *Long Diary*, entry of September 7, 1939, p. 10. To the Department,

Kennedy denied having leaked the gist of his conversations with Truitt to the press. Moffat Diary MS., entry of September 8, 1939.

86. Landis MS., p. 175. This author has not seen the document.

87. Moffat Diary MS., entry of September 3, 1939.

88. Long Diary MS., entry of October 4, 1939, p. 238.

89. Kennedy to Hull, September 15, 1939, *F.R.U.S.*, 1939, I, 603–04.

90. Hull to Kennedy, September 16, 1939, *F.R.U.S.*, 1939, I, 605–06.

91. Kennedy to Hull, September 26, 1939, and Hull to Kennedy, September 27, 1939, *F.R.U.S.*, 1939, I, 613–16.

92. *F.R.U.S.*, 1939, I, 621–22.

93. Interview with the mother of a beneficiary, London, July 25, 1972.

94. Kennedy told Halifax that the incident had resulted in a stiffening of anti-German feelings in America, and urged Halifax to use this fact in his attempts to keep Italy "neutral." Halifax note of September 4, 1939, FO371/22981/C12953.

95. Kennedy to Hull and Hull to Kennedy, September 8, 1939, *F.R.U.S.*, 1939, I, 598–99.

96. *New York Times*, September 17, 1939, p. 45. "I have never seen such bad mob psychology in all my life of professional theatre-going," said Robert J. Landry, a *Variety* editor on board. *Ibid.*

97. Simon suspected that that was the motive, and, erroneously, that the decision to proceed had been Hull's. Cabinet Meeting, September 13, 1939, Cab. 65, Vol. I, p. 105, MS. at Public Record Office, London.

98. Kennedy to Hull, October 13, 1939, *F.R.U.S.*, 1939, II, 219–20. The Landis MS. explains the problem thus: British exhibitors paid American film producers a percentage of gross which was payable in dollars. These payments "spelled the difference between profit and loss." On the outbreak of the war, the British put a maximum on dollar outgo for films, which Kennedy negotiated very much upwards, to the point where film producers would receive almost as much as if there had been no restrictions at all. Landis MS., Library of Congress, p. 469.

99. Kennedy to Hull, October 13, 1939, *F.R.U.S.*, 1939, II, 219–20.

100. Hull to Kennedy, October 12, 1939, *F.R.U.S.*, 1939, II, 219. In 1943, a film journal complained about the uncooperative treatment American film interests had traditionally received from all of the United States' embassies. They saw only one exception—"During Joe Kennedy's stay in London, EVERY request was given IMMEDIATE action." (Their emphasis.) *The Hollywood Reporter*, September 22, 1943.

101. Hull to Kennedy, October 16, 1939, *F.R.U.S.*, 1939, II, 221–22.

102. Kennedy to Hull, October 18, 1939, *F.R.U.S.*, 1939, II, 222f.

103. Minute, FO371/24348, p. 165 (p. 398).

104. Interview, London, July 26, 1972.

105. Minute, FO371/24348, p. 165 (p. 398).

106. See *F.R.U.S.*, 1939, II, 215–18.

107. Kennedy to Hull, November 13, 1939; Welles to Kennedy, November 14, 1939; and Kennedy to Hull, November 15, 1939, *F.R.U.S.*, 1939, II, 226–28.

108. Hull to Kennedy, October 14, 1939, *F.R.U.S.*, 1939, II, 221.

109. Minute, FO371/24348, p. 165 (p. 398).

110. Kennedy to Hull, October 19, 1939, *F.R.U.S.*, 1939, I, 884.

111. Hull to Kennedy, October 31, 1939, *F.R.U.S.*, 1939, I, 885.

112. Kennedy to Hull, November 8, 1939, *F.R.U.S.*, 1939, I, 892.

113. Hull to Kennedy, November 13, 1939, *F.R.U.S.*, 1939, I, 893–95.

114. Hull to Kennedy, November 24, 1939, *F.R.U.S.*, 1939, I, 898–99.

115. Kennedy to Hull, November 28, 1939, *F.R.U.S.*, 1939, I, 899–900.

116. Hull to Kennedy, November 28, 1939, *F.R.U.S.*, 1939, I, 902–04.

117. Kennedy to Hull, November 29, 1939, *F.R.U.S.*, 1939, I, 904.

118. Kennedy to Morgenthau, September 6, 1939, S.D.MS. 841.852 Queen Mary/2.

119. "Kennedy will claim all the credit" was only part of Hull's reasoning. Blum, *Morgenthau Diaries*, II, 96.

120. Morgenthau Diary MS., entry of September 19, 1938, Vol. 141, p. 115.

121. See Donald Watt, "Roosevelt and Chamberlain: two appeasers," *International Journal*, Spring, 1973.

122. Landis MS., pp. 173–74.

123. Landis MS., p. 196; Landis MS., Library of Congress, p. 462.

124. William W. Kaufmann, "Two American Ambassadors," in *The Diplomats, 1919–1939*, ed. Gordon A. Craig and Felix Gilbert (Princeton, N.J.: Princeton University Press, 1953), p. 668.

125. Interview, London, July 30, 1972.

126. Landis MS., p. 181.

127. *The Secret Diary of Harold L. Ickes*, Vol. II: *The Inside Struggle, 1936–1939* (New York: Simon & Schuster, 1954), entry of July 15, 1939, p. 685.

128. *The Secret Diary of Harold L. Ickes*, Vol. III: *The Lowering Clouds 1939–1941* (New York: Simon & Schuster, 1954), entry of March 10, 1940, p. 147. When the author asked Ambassador Bullitt to confirm or deny the accuracy of this quotation, Bullitt begged off: it had been so long that he was not in a position to confirm or deny—"So many things happen in a life; it's funny the things one remembers and the things one doesn't remember." He paused and then added "Harold [Ickes] and I were quite close." Telephone conversation with Ambassador Bullitt on March 20, 1962.

129. *Ickes Diary*, entry of August 29, 1939, II, 707.

130. Morgenthau Diary MS., entry of September 19, 1938, Vol. 141, p. 115.

131. Alsop and Kintner, *Boston Globe* (evening edition), October 7, 1940, p. 1.

132. *The Times* (London), December 7, 1939, p. 8.

133. Selby to Halifax, January 25, 1940, FO371/24492/C1641/1641/36.

134. *Philadelphia Inquirer*, December 7, 1939, p. 3.

135. Joseph F. Dinneen, *Washington Evening Star*, December 7, 1939.

136. *Detroit News*, December 7, 1939.

137. Doris Fleeson, *Times-Herald* (Washington), December 7, 1939, p. 1.

138. Presidential Press Conference 604, December 8, 1939, typescript at Roosevelt Library, Hyde Park, N.Y., XIV, 349–51.

139. *The Times* (London), December 9, 1939, p. 5.

140. *Washington Daily News*, December 9, 1939, p. 5. Ickes noted in his diary a day later that Kennedy "believes that Germany and Russia will win the war and that the end of the world is just down the road." *Ickes Diary*, III, 85.

141. *New York Times*, December 9, 1939, p. 1.

142. *New York Herald Tribune*, December 9, 1939, p. 1.

143. *The Times* (London), December 9, 1939, p. 5.

144. *Ickes Diary*, entry of December 10, 1939, III, 85.

145. Krock, *New York Times*, December 12, 1939, p. 26.

146. *Ibid.*

147. See *Ickes Diary*, entry of August 29, 1939, II, 707.

148. John O'Conner, *Boston Herald*, December 11, 1939, p. 4.

149. *Ibid.*

150. Cadogan comment dated December 14, 1939, FO371/22827/A8763/1090/45.

151. Same minute, Balfour note dated December 13, 1939.

152. *The Spectator*, December 15, 1939, p. 854; or, see extensive quotations in *New York Herald Tribune*, December 16, 1939.

153. *New York Sun*, December 13, 1939, p. 1.

154. Alsop and Kintner, *Evening Star* (Washington), December 18, 1939, p. A11.

155. Moffat Diary MS., entry of December 15, 1939; Langer and Gleason, *The Challenge to Isolation*, p. 345.

156. Butler to Halifax, November 13, 1940, FO414/277 Part 54, p. 76.

157. John O'Conner, *Boston Herald*, December 11, 1939, p. 4; Landis MS., Library of Congress, p. 487.

158. *New York Times*, February 13, 1940.

159. *Evening Standard* (London), January 25, 1940.

160. *Ibid.*

161. Lothian to Halifax, February 27, 1940, FO800/324/XXXVII/55.

162. Perowne, January 25, 1940, FO371/24251/A605/605/45, p. 55 (p. 162).

163. Balfour, January 25, 1940, same citation.

164. Vansittart, January 26, 1940, same citation. Vansittart was probably correct: Kennedy long suffered "the normal stomach disorder to which the successful American businessmen are so prone." Irwin Ross, *New York Post*, January 10, 1961, p. 25.

165. *New York Journal–American*, February 10, 1940, p. 2.

166. Inez Robb, *Chicago Daily Tribune*, February 12, 1940. It was, on the whole, an accurate prediction.

167. *Boston Post*, February 12, 1940, p. 1.

168. *New York Daily News*, December 10, 1937, p. 22.

169. *Boston Sunday Post*, May 29, 1938; *Boston American*, May 28, 1938.

170. For example: the *Kansas City Star* (Kansas City, Mo.) commented that but for his fortune and his yacht, Kennedy would be a powerful likely. July 8, 1937. The *Fort Worth Star-Telegram* (Fort Worth, Tex.) lamented that Kennedy's great wealth would bar the possibility of his being a Presidential candidate. August 1, 1937. The *Columbia Daily Record* (Columbia, S.C.) endorsed him for President on September 20, 1937. *Washington Post* columnist Harlan Miller wrote that Kennedy had an excellent chance of being the first Roman Catholic President. March 15, 1938. After Kennedy began his ambassadorial career, press support increased all over.

171. Arthur Krock, *The Consent of the Governed* (Boston: Little, Brown and Company, 1971), p. 148.

172. Leeper to Perowne, October 16, 1939, FO371/22817/A7270, p. 270.

173. Henry Luce, recorded interview by John L. Steele, November 11, 1965, p. 8, typescript at John F. Kennedy Library, Oral History Program. See also W. A. Swanberg, *Luce and His Empire* (New York: Charles Scribner's Sons, 1972), p. 154.

174. Louis Fischer, *Men and Politics* (New York: Duell, Sloan and Pearce, 1941, 1946), pp. 123–24.

175. Minute, FO371/616/P3516.

176. Henry Ehrlich, *Boston Herald*, March 26, 1939.

177. See, for example, Blum, *Morgenthau Diary*, II, 96 or Moffat Diary MS., entry of November 22, 1938.

178. According to Harold Hinton, FO371/616/P3516, p. 435.

179. Interview, Washington, D.C., September 24, 1973.

180. Leeper, December 28, 1939, FO371/616/P3516, p. 432.

181. Charles Peake minute, October 12, 1939, FO371/22827/A7195/1090/45, p. 164.

182. Interview, September 24, 1973.

183. Hugh Johnson, *New York World-Telegram*, June 17, 1938, p. 21. At the time, Johnson was favorably disposed to Kennedy; he later soured on the Ambassador because of suspicion that Kennedy had "gone British." See page 201 *supra*.

184. Blum, *Morgenthau Diary*, II, 37. James Roosevelt told the author, "We all knew that Krock was Kennedy's mouthpiece." Interview, Washington, March 20, 1962.

185. Dorothy G. Wayman, *David I. Walsh: Citizen-Patriot* (Milwaukee, Wis.: Bruce Publishing Company, 1952), p. 278.

186. Oliver McKee, Jr., *Boston Transcript*, suggested that Kennedy might emerge as a coalition candidate. August 30, 1938.

187. Loening to Kennedy, October 17, 1938, p. 1, MS. at Library of Congress Manuscript Division, Washington, D.C., in Loening Papers, Box 12, File "January–October, 1938."

188. *Evening Star* (Washington), February 13, 1940.

189. *The Times* (London), February 14, 1940, p. 7.

190. *New York Journal-American*, February 16, 1940, p. 2. Also "mourning" was General Hugh Johnson, who had soured on Kennedy, and implored "take Greatheart away." He made the sensible observation that Kennedy's decision not to run was based on the realization that he did not have "a Chinaman's chance." *New York World-Telegram*, February 15, 1940, p. 17.

191. *Boston Herald*, February 14, 1940.

192. Landis MS., p. 226.

193. *Boston Evening American*, August 21, 1938, p. 4.

194. *Boston Globe* (morning edition), February 14, 1940, p. 1.

195. Interview with Mr. Farley, New York City, March 3, 1962.

196. Krock, *New York Times*, December 13, 1938, p. 24.

197. *New York Times*, February 16, 1940. According to a later John O'Donnell piece, the Massachusetts Farley forces rallied around the Ambassador's son. *Times-Herald* (Washington), July 14, 1947.

198. Hank Searls, *The Lost Prince* (New York: The New American Library, Inc., 1969), p. 154, apparently based on interview with Burke.

199. *Ibid.*, p. 154.

200. *Ibid.*, p. 156.

201. *Ibid.*, p. 163.

202. *Jim Farley's Story* (New York: McGraw-Hill Book Company, Inc., 1948), p. 264.

203. Fullest account of the visit in Krock's essay in *As We Remember Joe*, ed. John F. Kennedy (privately printed, Cambridge, Mass.: University Press, 1945), pp. 39–41; minor variations in Krock's *Memoirs: Sixty Years on the Firing Line* (New York: Funk & Wagnalls, 1968), pp. 340–41.

204. Searls, *The Lost Prince*, p. 164, apparently based on interview with Joseph Timilty, who was listening on an extension. Krock was apparently unaware that the telephone call had been made.

205. Halifax to Lothian, July 31, 1940 (a couple of weeks after the convention), FO414/277, p. 20 at p. 21.

OUR MOST
BOMBED AMBASSADOR

1. *New York Journal-American*, February 25, 1940, p. L7.

2. Robert Murphy, *Diplomat Among Warriors* (Garden City, N.Y.: Doubleday & Company, Inc., 1964), p. 38. When Kennedy's boat docked in Europe, he had a long visit with Ambassador Phillips, who found him deeply depressed and unwell. Phillips Diary MS., entries of March 4 and 5, 1940, pp. 3757–58.

3. Lothian to Halifax, February 27, 1940, FO800/324/XXXVII/55.

4. Interview, London, July 30, 1972.

5. Harold Nicolson, *The Diaries and Letters of Harold Nicolson*, Vol. II: *The War Years, 1939–1945*, ed. Nigel Nicolson (London: Collins, 1967), diary entry of February 29, 1940, p. 60.

6. Perowne and Balfour notes, March 2, 1940, FO371/24251/A1945, p. 86 (p. 194).

7. Vansittart note, January 22, 1940, FO371/24251/A605/605/45. "Van's" note of early March is surprisingly mild: "Mr. Kennedy only cares about our condition in so far as it affects his pocket and well-being. He has liquidated all his holdings, I am told, and has most of his fortune now in cash." Same volume, A1945, page following page numbered 85.

8. In particular, Perowne felt that "our cupboard and the skeletons in it have been far too freely exposed to the kindly but searching glance of Mr. Butterworth. But I don't know how we are to stop the Board of Trade high officials from indulging in the delights of the confessional with so engaging an interrogator." Perowne, March 2, 1940, same citation, p. 86.

9. Scott's phrase, March 3, 1940, same citation, page following page numbered 86.

10. So secret as to have been omitted from the minute books, though copies of responses received from other departments are included, which give indication as to the text of Cadogan's note. Same citation, p. 87 ff.

11. Interview, September 20, 1973, and September 24, 1973.

12. Leeper to Perowne, October 16, 1939, FO371/22817/A7270, p. 270.

13. Mr. Jebb's report dated February 14, 1940, in FO371/24418/C2461/1285/18.

14. Gage minute, March 2, 1940, FO371/24251/A1945, p. 85 (p. 193).

15. Lee's diary entry of September 17, 1940, of a discussion with Major General Delos Emmons: "Emmons expressed a great admiration of Kennedy. A damned smart man. A clever man. I finally said that we needed, in all our great diplomatic positions, wise and sagacious men. 'That's just it,' he said, 'That's what he is. A damned smart fellow.' I had to drop the subject." *The London Journal of General Raymond E. Lee, 1940–1941*, ed. James Leutze (Boston: Little, Brown and Company, 1971), p. 62.

16. Both February 3, 1940, FO371/24251/A1945, p. 86 (p. 194). Those to whom the author spoke certainly did.

17. *The Spectator*, March 8, 1940 (but circulated a few days in advance), p. 327. Scott found it "quite amusing and quite offensive." FO371/24251/A2013/605/45, p. 90 (p. 201).

18. *The Times* (London), March 8, 1940, p. 8.

19. This quotation, which caused considerable controversy, was not included in *The Times* account cited above. See *Daily Express* (London), March 8, 1940. The report of the interview in the Landis MS. has Kennedy having said, "we had no desire to participate in war, particularly since we seemed to be learning less and less of what it was all about," which may or may not have been what Kennedy meant. If so, Kennedy's penchant for overstatement led to considerable embarrassment. Landis MS., Library of Congress, p. 542.

20. See *Daily Herald* (London), March 11, 1940; *News Chronicle* (London), March 14, 1940. Lothian's weekly political summary of May 18, 1940, says that a few months prior, "An American Ambassador could state publicly that his countrymen did not know what the war is all about. . . . today only Colonel Lindbergh doesn't know." FO371/24234/A3223/39/45. There remained at least one other.

21. *Sunday Graphic* (London), March 10, 1940, p. 15, reprinted in Congressional Record XXCVI, A1881. "Very nicely put!" was the reaction of T. North Whitehead at the Foreign Office. FO371/24238/A1904/131/45.

22. Congressman Fred L. Crawford, Congressional Record, XXCVI, A1881.

23. Landis MS., Library of Congress, Chap. 41, seventh page. Bilainkin was one with whom Kennedy remained friendly over the years. He helped ghost-write the Ambassador's speeches. See his "Joseph P. Kennedy: The Truth," in *Contemporary Review*, February, 1970, p. 67.

24. George Bilainkin, *Diary of a Diplomatic Correspondent* (London: George Allen & Unwin Ltd., 1942), entry of April 8, 1940, p. 59.

25. Kennedy to Baruch, March 21, 1938, MS., Baruch Papers; Kennedy to Hull, March 22, 1938, MS., Hull Papers.

26. John W. Wheeler-Bennett, *King George VI* (New York: St. Martin's Press, 1958), p. 419.

27. Bilainkin, *Diary of a Diplomatic Correspondent*, entry of April 8, 1940, pp. 59–60.

28. *Daily Telegraph* (London), March 18, 1940.

29. Landis MS., p. 236; Landis MS., Library of Congress, p. 542. Chamberlain was not one of those who cooled. Landis MS., Library of Congress, p. 548.

30. None is claimed for him in the Landis MS., and none is ascribed to him in any of the principal literature on the mission.

31. Moffat Diary MS., entry of February 3–12, 1940.

32. Landis MS., p. 233. Moffat Diary MS., entry of February 3–12, 1940, says that Kennedy disliked the proposed trip, as does Julius W. Pratt, *Cordell Hull*, Vol. XII in *The American Secretaries of State and Their Diplomacy*, ed. Robert H. Ferrell (New York: Cooper Square Publishers, Inc., 1964), 340. This author accepts the assertion of the Landis MS. to the contrary.

33. As Halifax made clear to Kennedy on the eve of Welles' arrival. Halifax to Lothian, March 8, 1940, FO800/324/XXXVII/61.

34. British documents summarized in *New York Times*, January 1, 1971.

35. Scott minute, February 7, 1940, FO371/24238/A1309/131/45.

36. Vansittart minute, February 9, 1940, FO371/24238/A1309/131/45.

37. Such was the crux of the terms set out by Chamberlain to Welles, March 13, 1940 note, FO800/326/H/XL/47.

38. Hoare to Lothian, February 14, 1940, MS. in Templewood Papers, University Library, Cambridge, England, Vol. XI:5.

39. Sumner Welles, *The Time for Decision* (New York: Harper & Brothers, 1944), p. 130.

40. Landis MS., pp. 238 ff.; Landis MS., Library of Congress, p. 551.

41. Hooker, *Moffat Diary*, entry of March 10, 1940, pp. 297–98. Of course, as far as Kennedy was concerned, that really wasn't good enough.

42. Landis MS. pp. 244–45; Landis MS., Library of Congress, p. 557. Kennedy noted that the Queen wore a purple dress, pearls, and a diamond bracelet, and looked as charming as ever. Landis MS., p. 251; Landis MS., Library of Congress p. 562. Quite a contrast to Italian society: at an opera in Rome, the Ambassador found "the homeliest group [of women] that I had ever seen. . . . five thousand dollars could have bought all the jewelry in the house." Landis MS., p. 235; cf. Landis MS., Library of Congress, p. 540: ". . . five thousand dollars could have bought all the jewelry that any of them was wearing."

43. Hooker, *Moffat Diary*, entry of March 13, 1940, p. 303.

44. *Ibid.*

45. Kennedy to Hull, March 14, 1940, S.D.MS. 121.840 Welles/123.

46. Kennedy thought that Welles' second interview with Chamberlain had left room for hope, Landis MS., p. 267; Landis MS., Library of Congress, p. 577, though the conversations Kennedy reports don't seem to leave much room for his brief optimism.

47. Bilainkin, *Diary of a Diplomatic Correspondent*, p. 244.

48. William L. Langer and S. Everett Gleason, *The Challenge to Isolation, 1937–1940* (New York: Harper & Brothers, 1952), p. 715. See also H. Montgomery Hyde, *Room 3603: The Story of the British Intelligence Center in New York During World War II* (New York: Farrar, Straus and Company, 1963), p. 37.

49. State Department to Kennedy, July 11, 1940, S.D.MS. 740.0011 European War 1939/4570A.

50. Kennedy to Hull, July 12, 1940, same file, 4571 1/3.

51. Kennedy to Hull and Welles, July 13, 1940, S.D.MS. 841/00N/9½.

52. Welles memorandum to Roosevelt, July 12, 1940, S.D.MS. 740.0011 European War 1939/4571 1/3.

53. Leutze, *Lee Journal*, p. 19, note 22, cites memo Roosevelt to Knox, July 13, 1940, FDRL, PSF: Knox.

54. Kennedy to Hull, July 31, 1940, S.D.MS. 740.0011 European War 1939/4929 2/4, Section Two. According to the Landis MS., Kennedy wired Washington: "The least, it seems to me, that can be done for the American Ambassador in London is to let him, subject to the State Department's policy, run his own job. . . . Now there is probably a good reason why it is necessary to go around the Ambassador in London and take up the matter with the British before he knows about it. However, I do not like it and I either want to run this job or get out. At this time, this job is a delicate one and to do the job well, requires that I know what is going on. Not to know what is going on causes embarrassment and confusion. I want to know, in other words, what is going to happen before the British are notified. . . ." Landis MS., p. 393. The author was unable to locate this wire in either the Hull Papers, State Department Archives, or Roosevelt Library files and suspects that the portion quoted in the Landis MS. may come from a discarded draft of the wire quoted in the main body of the text.

Hyde writes, incorrectly, that the Donovan mission was kept secret from Kennedy as a "calculated snub." Page 37. Perhaps Hyde had the Ghormley mission in mind.

55. Thomsen to Foreign Office, August 19, 1940, *German Documents*, X, 510.

56. *New York Post*, October 23, 1940.

57. J. C. W. Reith, *Into the Wind* (London: Hodder and Stoughton, 1949), meeting of April 25, 1940, p. 371.

58. Kennedy to Roosevelt and Hull, April 26, 1940, S.D.MS. 841.00/1464.

59. *Ibid.* Taylor says the Norwegian campaign loss was "after all a comparatively trivial affair—not even a Gallipoli, let alone a threat of total defeat." Taylor, *English History, 1914–1945* (London: Pelican Books, paperback ed., 1970), p. 588.

60. *The Memoirs of Cordell Hull* (New York: The Macmillan Company, 1948), I, 763.

61. Morgenthau Presidential Diary MS., entry of April 29, 1940, p. 0471.

62. Roosevelt to Kennedy, May 3, 1940, in *F.D.R., His Personal Letters, 1928–1945*, ed. Elliott Roosevelt (New York: Duell, Sloan and Pearce, 1950), II, 1020.

63. Kennedy to Hull, May 9, 1940, S.D.MS. 841.00/1466.

64. *Ibid.*

65. *Ibid.*

66. The Earl of Birkenhead, *Halifax* (Boston: Houghton Mifflin Company, 1966), p. 452.

67. Landis MS., p. 290, relying on Kennedy to Welles, May 7, 1940, a document not seen by this author. The embassy's staff member whose views most closely paralleled the Ambassador's, was Naval Attaché Alan Kirk. Curiously, Kirk wrote Admiral W. S. Anderson, Director of Naval Intelligence in Washington, in substantially the same terms on May 1, 1940. Kirk Papers, Division of Naval History, Washington Navy Yard. Until Kennedy's departure from London, the Ambassador's telegrams to Washington and Kirk's reports to Anderson show that the two were thinking along the same lines. Kirk became Kennedy's only close friend among the embassy's high-level personnel; continued to speak highly of the Ambassador in his letters to Anderson; and remained friendly to Kennedy over the years.

68. The Earl of Birkenhead, *Halifax*, p. 453.

69. In October, 1940, Chamberlain described the fateful evening to Kennedy: "Realizing the necessity of a change, he had wanted Halifax as Prime Minister, but Halifax, as might be expected, began to say, 'Perhaps I can't handle it, being in the House of Lords—' Whereupon Churchill broke in, saying 'I don't think you could—' and that settled it." Landis MS., p. 432. Cf. The Earl of Birkenhead, *Halifax*, pp. 454–55 ("Winston, with suitable expressions of regard and humility, said he could not but feel the force of what I had said") and Churchill, *The Second World War*, Vol. I: *The Gathering Storm* (Boston: Houghton Mifflin Company, 1948), p. 663 ("Usually I talk a great deal, but on this occasion I was silent.").

70. Churchill, *The Gathering Storm*, p. 666.

71. Taylor, *English History*, p. 579.

72. Cf. "Chips" Channon's reaction, in Leonard Mosley, *Backs to the Wall* (New York: Random House, 1971), p. 35.

73. Landis MS., pp. 390–91. While it would be unfair to heap the entire blame on Churchill, Taylor calls it "a nice twist that a campaign directed largely by Churchill, should bring Chamberlain down and raise Churchill up." *English History*, p. 575.

74. Halifax to Lothian, May 13, 1940, FO371/24239/A3242/131/45. Landis MS.

includes an account of this conversation, p. 302, from a different slant, but not at variance.

75. Landis MS., pp. 207–08, 214.

76. Landis MS., p. 297. In a later discussion with Churchill, Kennedy commented to the Prime Minister, "Well, you certainly picked a nice time to be Prime Minister," to which Churchill responded, "They wouldn't have given me the prime ministership if there had been any meat left on the bone." Landis MS., p. 339.

77. H. C. Allen, *Great Britain and the United States* (New York: St. Martin's Press, 1955), p. 787.

78. Robert E. Sherwood, *Roosevelt and Hopkins* (New York: Grosset & Dunlap, paperback ed., 1948), p. 238.

79. Kennedy to Roosevelt, July 20, 1939, p. 2, copy in Hull Papers, Correspondence: July 2–31, 1939.

80. Kennedy to Roosevelt, November 3, 1939, MS. at Roosevelt Library, Hyde Park, N.Y., President's Secretary's File, Box 8, Great Britain.

81. Landis MS., p. 174. In fact, Churchill was not slighting Cobh; at the time, "Queenstown" was still an appropriate reference to Cobh's harbor, to which Churchill was referring. Kennedy was oversensitive on the matter.

According to Whalen, an unnamed friend of the Ambassador quoted Kennedy to the extent that he "could not forgive those who had been responsible for sending the infamous Black and Tans into rebellious Ireland"—an apparent reference to Churchill, who was involved in the Irish problem at the time of the "Black and Tans." Richard J. Whalen, *The Founding Father* (New York: The New American Library of World Literature, Inc., 1964), p. 231.

82. Kennedy's note of a visit of Welles and himself with Churchill: "He grew eloquent in talking of Germany and her misdeeds. He characterized the Nazi Government as ' a monster born of hatred and of fear.' Of England and the last war, he said: 'The victor forgot, the vanquished plotted on.' Only Welles and I were his audience, but his language, his emphasis, his gestures were as if he were speaking to thousands." Landis MS., Library of Congress, p. 568. This is the same interview of which Welles' account is cited in note [87] *infra*. Welles was also influenced by Churchill's eloquence; the phrase "cascade of oratory" is his.

83. An interviewer in 1959 noted that Kennedy "is repetitious and repeated everything that follows two or three times. It's always a shock to me when a highly successful man is unable to express himself fairly well and he often gropes for simple words." Ed Plaut, notes of interview with Kennedy October 29, 1959.

84. Landis MS., pp. 346, 379.

85. *Ibid.*, p. 337.

86. *Ibid.*, p. 402.

87. Bill Cunningham, *Boston Herald*, April 7, 1957, V, 19. Welles noted that when he went to see Churchill at his office, "Mr. Churchill was sitting in front of the fire, smoking a 24″ cigar, and drinking a whiskey and soda. It was quite obvious that he had consumed a good many whiskeys before I arrived." Nonetheless, in the course of their visit, Churchill made a highly favorable impression on Welles, and "became quite sober." Welles memorandum of March 12, 1940, copy in Hull Papers, Subject File: Welles, Sumner, European trip, 1940.

88. Cunningham article, *Boston Herald*, April 7, 1957, V, 19. Taylor would say

that Kennedy was on point: that Churchill's great work was to have kept the war going until the United States was drawn in. Taylor, *English History*, p. 651.

89. Landis MS., Library of Congress, p. 485; different reference in Landis MS., pp. 269–70.

90. Landis MS., p. 292.

91. Landis MS., pp. 390–91. See also Leutze, *Lee Journal*, p. 36. At a meeting of United States military officers Kennedy commented, "Anything the Navy does well is credited to Churchill; any mistakes it makes is attributed to the Admirals." Moffat Diary MS., entry of December 15, 1939.

92. One senses something of a loss of perspective in a line such as "Churchill's talk had convinced me that he had no scruples about ordering anything from us without paying for it." Landis MS., p. 405.

93. Moffat Diary MS., entry of December 8, 1939.

94. Landis MS., pp. 196–97; Landis MS., Library of Congress, p. 463.

95. Moffat Diary MS., entry of December 8, 1939, perhaps a reference to Churchill's friend Baruch.

96. See, for example, Churchill to Roosevelt, May 20, 1940, S.D.MS. 811.34544/1 3/12.

97. Echoes of Taylor, *English History*, p. 579.

98. "The Reminiscences of Alan Kirk" (1962), p. 147, typescript in The Oral History Collection of Columbia University.

99. Kennedy to Hull, May 15, 1940, *F.R.U.S.*, 1940, III, 29–30. This author is unsatisfied that Kennedy had been so steely with Churchill. See page 266 *infra*.

100. Kennedy to Hull, May 16, 1940, *F.R.U.S.*, 1940, I, 224–25.

101. In fact, Perowne, and probably Vansittart himself, by this time did regard Kennedy as anti-British. Perowne noted on May 22, 1940, that Kennedy "thinks and hopes that we shall be defeated," and believed Kennedy responsible for spreading stories not only that Britain would not win, but that Britain did not deserve to win. Perowne minute, May 22, 1940, FO371/24251/A1945, p. 79 (p. 187).

102. In his edition of Bullitt's papers, Bullitt's brother includes the Foreign Office's report of Roché's comments, but does not indicate whether or not the French actually called the matter to Bullitt's attention. *For the President, Personal and Secret: Correspondence Between Franklin D. Roosevelt and William C. Bullitt*, ed. Orville H. Bullitt (Boston: Houghton Mifflin Company, 1972), p. 436.

103. Comments of Perowne and Balfour, May 22, 1940; Balfour and Halifax, May 23, 1940; and Balfour, May 24, 1940, all in FO371/24251/A1945, pp. 78–80 (pp. 186–88).

104. Kennedy to Hull, May 24, 1940, *F.R.U.S.*, 1940, III, 31–32.

105. Kennedy to Hull, May 27, 1940, *F.R.U.S.*, 1940, I, 233.

106. See William L. Shirer, *The Rise and Fall of the Third Reich* (New York: Simon & Schuster, 1960), pp. 729–30. Shirer himself seems to be in agreement with the King's critics.

107. Bilainkin, *Diary of a Diplomatic Correspondent*, entry of August 20, 1940, p. 190. B. H. Liddell Hart, the distinguished British military historian, is also sympathetic to King Leopold's decision. See his *History of the Second World War* (Cassell: London, 1970), pp. 77–78. In 1950, the Joseph P. Kennedy, Jr., Foundation published *The Surrender of King Leopold*, by Joseph P. Kennedy and James M. Landis, a long pamphlet in which Landis uses papers from Kennedy's files to defend the King from his critics.

The pamphlet's line of argument is to the extent that English blundering made King Leopold's action inevitable. See also Landis to Kennedy, February 18, 1949, in which Landis brings Kennedy up-to-date on the debate over Leopold's actions, essentially explaining what the controversy was all about. Landis Papers, Box 173. *The Surrender of King Leopold* came out in time to affect the Belgium plebiscite to decide whether Leopold's family should be restored to the monarchy. The pamphlet was privately circulated by the Kennedy offices to a long and distinguished mailing list, copy of which is in Landis Papers, Box 173. Later, Belgium awarded Kennedy the "Leopold III Medal."

108. Bilainkin, *Diary of a Diplomatic Correspondent*, entry of June 11, 1940, p. 106.

109. *Ibid.*, p. 105.

110. Landis MS., p. 323. Kennedy was especially eager to have the gold and the family in Canada so that Churchill would have an impetus to see that the fleet ended up there too, rather than in the hands of Adolph Hitler. Kennedy to Hull, May 27, 1940, S.D.MS. 740.0011 European War 1939/3018 3/10.

111. Landis MS., p. 371.

112. *Ibid.*, pp. 341–42.

113. Kennedy to Hull, May 27, 1940, S.D.MS. 740.0011 European War 1939/3018 3/10; Landis MS., p. 323. So, when Kennedy told Churchill "You haven't got enough here to whip the New York police force," he was quick to add, "and we haven't got enough to send you to make certain both of us could do it." Bill Cunningham, *Boston Herald*, April 7, 1957, V, 19.

114. See communications of June 6, 7, 10, 1940, in *F.R.U.S.*, 1940, III, 32–35.

115. Kennedy to Hull, August 2, 1940, S.D.MS. 740.0011 European War 1939/5480½.

116. Kennedy to Hull, June 14, 1940, S.D.MS. 740.0011 European War 1939/3786½. To the same extent is Kennedy wire of August 15, 1940, S.D.MS. 811.34544/1 10/12.

117. Kennedy to Hull, June 14, 1940, S.D.MS. 740.0011 European War 1939/3786½.

118. Shirer, *Rise and Fall*, p. 746.

119. Ivan Maisky, *Kto Pomogal Gitleru* (Moscow: Izdatelstvo Instituta Mezdunarodnykh Otnoshenii, 1962), p. 125, trans. *The Times* (London), February 5, 1962, p. 9, slightly different translation in Ivan Maisky, *Who Helped Hitler?*, trans. Andrew Rothstein (London: Hutchinson & Co., 1964), pp. 135–36. Kennedy's account of the interview, not strikingly different, is in Landis MS., p. 372. Visit also referred to in Bilainkin, *Diary of a Diplomatic Correspondent*, entry of July 8, 1940, p. 152.

120. The Earl of Birkenhead, *Halifax*, p. 459; parallel comments to Kennedy, Landis MS., p. 400.

121. Lothian's wires of June 23, 1940, June 26, 1940, and July 19, 1940, FO371/24230/A3464/26/45, quote from last cited, p. 466.

122. Perowne minute, FO371/24230/A3464/26/45.

123. Perowne, *ibid.*, confirms speculation of Langer and Gleason, *The Challenge to Isolation*, p. 715.

124. For Donovan's evaluations see Langer and Gleason, *The Challenge to Isolation*, p. 715; Leutze, *Lee Journal*: p. 27; Corey Ford, *Donovan of OSS* (Boston: Little, Brown and Company, 1970), pp. 91–94; Herbert Wilcox, *Twenty-Five Thousand Sunsets* (New York: A.S. Barnes and Company, 1967), p. 127.

125. Or so Donovan told Lee. Leutze, *Lee Journal*, entry of August 3, 1940, p. 28.

126. Balfour note of August 22, 1940, FO371/24251/A1945, p. 77 (p. 185).

127. Kennedy's historically sound analysis in Halifax to Lothian, July 31, 1940, FO414/277, p. 20 at p. 21.

128. See page 251 *supra*.

129. Perowne minute, August 22, 1940, FO371/24251/A1945, p. 77 (p. 185); interview, August 7, 1965.

130. Interview, London, July 17, 1972.

131. Interview, London, July 30, 1972.

132. Interview, August 7, 1965.

133. Scott memorandum, October 15, 1940, FO371/24251/A4485/605/45, identifies "a highly reputable member of the American Embassy, who has now left London." One of the embassy staff members with whom the author spoke told the author that he had never "darkened the doors" of the "safe" house provided for the staff in the country; another said that he could not have repaired to the country "because my wife didn't want to miss a bombing." Interviews, September 20, 1973, and September 24, 1973.

134. Perowne's note of September 3 says that Kennedy's defeatism was "no longer so noxious to our cause. The harm has been done and there are now practically no neutrals in Europe left whose views and attitude could possible be influenced by any views or attitude of Mr. Kennedy. On the other hand, his known views and attitude have earned him the dislike and contempt not only of the British but also of the U.S. nationals and press in this country, by whom he is regarded apparently as little better than a Fifth Columnist. If he repents him of the evil, the effect, though belated, will be all the more considerable, and if he persists in his pessimism this will affect his position in the U.S. as things are at present, as he very well knows, without affecting us very much." FO371/24251/A1945, p. 76 f (p. 184 f).

135. Because of his talks to neutral journalists, the diplomatic correspondent of London's *Daily Mail* came to regard Kennedy as "the biggest Fifth Columnist in the country." Perowne minute, August 22, 1940, FO371/24251/A1945, p. 77 (p. 185).

136. Letter to the author. Actually, Sunningdale was the location of the home that, at Kennedy's request, the State Department maintained for the embassy staff. Kennedy's retreat was located farther out, at St. Leonards. It was Kennedy's St. Leonards home that was nearly struck by a bomb. Landis MS., p. 415; Kirk to Mrs. Kirk, September 9, 1940, Kirk Papers, Naval History Division, Washington Navy Yard; Landis MS., Library of Congress, Chap. 41, fifth page.

137. Bilainkin, *Diary of a Diplomatic Correspondent*, entry of June 28, 1940, pp. 134–35.

138. Iain Macleod, *Neville Chamberlain* (London: Frederick Muller, Ltd., 1961), p. 279, cites Chamberlain's diary entry of July 1, 1940. It is possible that Kennedy made the comment with relative innocence. According to the account of the meeting in the Landis MS., the two were discussing Ireland's attitude towards the war, and Chamberlain had said that the Irish firmly believed Britain would lose. Landis MS., p. 377.

139. Perowne notes of talk with the diplomatic correspondent of the *Daily Mail* minute of August 22, 1940, FO371/24251/A1945/1945, p. 77 (p. 185).

140. Kennedy to State Department, August 2, 1940, 7:00 P.M., S.D.MS. 740.0011

European War 1939/4929 3/4, Section Ten. Similar comments in Kennedy to Landis, August 6, 1940, Landis Papers, Box 24.

141. Kennedy to State Department, August 2, 1940, S.D.MS. 740.0011 European War 1939/4929 3/4.

142. Kennedy to Hull, August 15, 1940, *F.R.U.S.*, 1940, III, 67–68.

143. Perowne minute, August 22, 1940, FO371/24251/A1945, p. 77 (p. 185).

144. Bilainkin, *Diary of a Diplomatic Correspondent*, entry of August 20, 1940, p. 189.

145. *Ibid.*, entry of August 27, 1940, p. 195.

146. Kennedy to Roosevelt and Hull, September 7, 1940, S.D.MS. 740.0011 European War 1939/5413 GMR.

147. Kennedy to Hull, September 11, 1940, S.D.MS. 740.0011 European War 1939/5480½.

148. *Sun* (New York), September 23, 1940, p. 3. The author doubts the report because Kennedy never wired the incident to the State Department; because Krock did not report it in the *New York Times*; and because it was not one of the anecdotes that Kennedy repeated in his later years. Landis, who perhaps picked it up from the press, includes it in the first draft of his manuscript (Landis MS., Library of Congress, Chap. 41, sixth page) but it does not appear in the later draft, and so was presumably edited out as error. A military superstition has it that if a soldier be missed by a shell with his initials on it, he is safe for the duration of the conflict.

149. Landis MS., p. 415.

150. Israel, *Long Diary*, entry of October 11, 1940, p. 141.

151. Krock, *New York Times*, October 8, 1940, p. 24.

152. Actually, German losses far exceeded British losses.

153. September 11, 1940, Kennedy to Roosevelt and Hull, S.D.MS. 740.0011 European War 1939/5480½.

154. Bilainkin, *Diary of a Diplomatic Correspondent*, entry of September 12, 1940, p. 208.

155. *Ibid.*, p. 213.

156. September 20, 1940, Kennedy to Roosevelt and Hull, S.D.MS. 740.0011 European War 1939/5609½.

157. Halifax to Lothian, September 26, 1940, FO371/24242/A4338/131/45, p. 137, paragraph 4.

158. Kennedy to Roosevelt and Hull, September 19, 1940, S.D.MS. 740.0011 European War 1939/5585.

159. Taylor, *English History*, p. 627.

160. September 27, 1940, *F.R.U.S.*, 1940, III, 48–49. The contents of this wire accurately found their way to the Germans, and thence to the Italians. See Alfieri to Ciano, October 2, 1940, in *I Documenti Diplomatici Italiani*, 9th Series, 1939–1945 (Rome: Ministero degli Affari Esteri, 1965), V, 641.

161. Landis MS., pp. 418–19. A hint of this is contained in Kennedy to Hull, September 27, 1940, *F.R.U.S.*, 1940, III, 48. Kennedy's analysis of the military factors is arguable.

162. Langer and Gleason, *The Challenge to Isolation*, p. 744; Leutze, *Lee Journal*, pp. 27–28.

163. Halifax to Lothian, October 10, 1940, FO371/24251/A4485/605/45.

164. Alsop and Kintner, *Boston Globe* (morning edition), October 7, 1940, p. 3.

165. Perowne minute, August 22, 1940, FO371/24251/A1945.

166. Alsop and Kintner, *Boston Globe* (morning edition), October 7, 1940, p. 3.

167. Strong's report quoted in Winston S. Churchill, *The Second World War*, Vol. II: *Their Finest Hour* (Boston: Houghton Mifflin Company, 1949), p. 338.

168. James R. Leutze, "If Britain Should Fall: Roosevelt and Churchill and British-American Naval Relations, 1938–1940" (Doctoral dissertation at Duke University, 1970), p. 319.

169. Leutze, *Lee Journal, passim*.

170. Cf. Kirk to Anderson, December 13, 1939 and June 11, 1940, MSS., Kirk Papers, Washington Navy Yard, Washington, D.C.

171. *German Documents*, X, 510; XI, 227.

172. *The Secret Diary of Harold L. Ickes*, Vol. II: *The Inside Struggle, 1936–1939* (New York: Simon & Schuster, 1954), entry of August 29, 1939, p. 707.

173. Landis MS., p. 252; Landis MS., Library of Congress, p. 564.

174. Landis MS., p. 328.

175. *Ibid.*, p. 260; Landis MS., Library of Congress, p. 572.

176. Kennedy to Hull, May 16, 1940, *F.R.U.S.*, 1940, I, 224–25. The friend is not identified.

177. "H.F.B." to Sir Eric Machtig, February 4, 1941, recounting conversation with Carroll Binder of the *Chicago Daily News*, FO371/26217.

178. Bilainkin, *Diary of a Diplomatic Correspondent*, entry of August 27, 1940, p. 195.

179. Sherwood, *Roosevelt and Hopkins*, p. 150.

180. Kennedy to Hull, May 15, 1940, *F.R.U.S.*, 1940, III, 29–30.

181. Hull, *Memoirs*, I, 766.

182. Kennedy to Hull, June 12, 1940, *F.R.U.S.*, 1940, III, 37.

183. Kennedy to Hull, June 14, 1940, *F.R.U.S.*, 1940, I, 248–49. Roosevelt was not ready to make known to the American public that he was giving this kind of encouragement to the Allies. Publication of the note would be embarrassing to him during his campaign for reelection; he refused to permit it.

184. Kennedy to Hull, July 31, 1940, S.D.MS. 740.0011 European War 1939/4929¼, Section Four.

185. Kennedy to Hull, August 2, 1940, and September 11, 1940, S.D.MS. 740.0011 European War 1939/4929 3/4, Section Twelve, and 5480½.

186. Kennedy to Hull, September 27, 1940, *F.R.U.S.*, 1940, III, 48.

187. Alfieri, Italian Ambassador in Berlin, to Ciano, Italian Secretary of State, October 2, 1940, *I Documenti Diplomatici Italiani*, 1939–45, V, 641.

188. Landis MS., pp. 219, 283.

189. Kennedy to Roosevelt, April 11, 1940, MS. at Roosevelt Library, Hyde Park, N.Y., in Office File 299 Money, May-December 1940; copy also in Hull Papers. Morgenthau told his staff that it was "one of those typical asinine Joe Kennedy letters" (which it was not). Morgenthau Diary MS., entry of April 29, 1940, Vol. 258, page 123. More to the point, Morgenthau-Blum writes, "Perhaps the Ambassador . . . was trying to protect American interests, but his recommendation, which Roosevelt ignored, could have had the effect only of impairing England's capacity to obtain dollars with which to buy the means for continuing the war." John M. Blum, *From the Morgenthau Diaries*, Vol. II: *Years of Urgency, 1938–1941* (Boston: Houghton Mifflin Company, 1965), p. 109.

190. Morgenthau, at least momentarily, misunderstood Kennedy's position and thought he was urging the contrary—that Britain dump all its securities on the market without regard for its effect on the market. Morgenthau's explanation for what he took to be Kennedy's position was that Kennedy was "short" on the market, and was trying to depress the market for his own personal gain. Morgenthau Diary MS., Vol. 258, pp. 123, 129. Speculation as to motives omitted in Blum, *Morgenthau Diary*, II, 104–105.

191. Landis MS., Library of Congress, p. 471; Moffat Diary MS., entries of February 13, 14, 1940.

192. Blum, *Morgenthau Diaries*, II, 105.

193. Landis MS., pp. 228–29.

194. Landis MS., pp. 300–301, apparently relying on Kennedy to Hull, May 13, 1940, S.D.MS. 740.00111A Financial/141, in which Kennedy reports that he had set forth to Churchill his reasons for opposing credits.

195. Kennedy to Hull, August 2, 1940, and Kennedy to Hull and Roosevelt, September 11, 1940, S.D.MSS. 740.0011 European War 1939/4929 3/4 and 5480½.

196. Kennedy to Hull, August 2, 1940, S.D.MS. 740.0011 European War 1939/4929 3/4, Section Eleven.

197. Kennedy to Roosevelt and Hull, September 11, 1940, S.D.MS. 740.0011 European War 1939/5480½, Section Four.

198. Morgenthau soured on Butterworth, the Treasury Department's contact in London, over Butterworth's closeness with his London chief, the Ambassador: "He had his choice as between reporting to the Treasury and Mr. Kennedy, and he chose Mr. Kennedy, so I don't want him. . . . One of the reasons that Gifford didn't take my advice is because he took Kennedy's, and Butterworth was in a position where he could have helped the Treasury, and I don't think I am being unfair when I say that he let me down." Morgenthau Diary MS., Vol. 337, pp. 38H and 38I; Vol. 338, p. 246.

Kennedy, on the other side of the Atlantic, badly wanted "in" in discussions of the problem, and wired that his position would be compromised in the eyes of the British were he to be frozen out. Morgenthau Diary MS., Vol. 218, pp. 48, 112–18, see also Vol. 206, pp. 333 ff. He was frozen out.

199. *British Documents*, IV, 364–66; see also, Chamberlain at Cabinet Meeting of July 6, 1938, Cab. 23, Vol. 94, 31 (38) 6, p. 15, MS. at Public Record Office, London.

200. The author has found no documentation as to what Kennedy's real attitude was towards repeal of the Neutrality Act and the Landis MS. gives no clues. Repeal, however, brought the country a step closer to war, a matter that Kennedy appreciated. Page 219 *supra*.

201. Halifax to Lothian, November 27, 1939, FO414/276, part 52, p. 182.

202. Andrew Boyle, *Montagu Norman* (New York: Weybright and Talley, 1967), quotes Norman diary entry of May 6, 1940, pp. 314–15.

203. Landis MS., pp. 354–56. Churchill does not mention the phone call in *Their Finest Hour*, which makes the author suspect that his presence during the call was "secret."

204. Halifax at Cabinet Meetings of June 1 and June 4, 1940, Cab. 65, Vol. 7, pp. 222, 243; Leutze, *Lee Journal*, pp. 20–21.

205. There is much in Kennedy's dispatches to the State Department that might warrant a conclusion that Kennedy favored providing Britain with destroyers. May 31, 1940: "The situation here as regards destroyers is getting rather desperate. They have lost three outright in this withdrawal from Dunkirk and thirteen have been damaged. If

it were practical or possible to get any legislation that would give them destroyers or some aircraft immediately the psychological effect would be of even more value than the actual help." Kennedy to Hull, May 31, 1940, S.D.MS. 740.0011 European War 1939/3018 7/10. June 6, 1940: "I suggest (action) in order to save a great deal of ill-will towards the United States which will arise if nothing is done since refusal to give them destroyers or planes will unfortunately appear to the British public as American unwillingness to help them in their battle of death. We do not want in England a united hostile people." Kennedy wire of June 12, 1940, quoted in memorandum, Fayne to Kennedy, July 15, 1958, MS. at Beaverbrook Library, London, original document not seen by the author. June 12, 1940: "[Churchill] needs destroyers more than anything else including planes. The gap is by no means being filled by repairs and replacements." *Ibid.* June 17, 1940: "[Churchill] would like to know one way or the other whether there is any chance of the British getting the destroyers they have requested. I think this is a fair request. . . ." Wire quoted in Landis MS., p. 368; copy in National Archives, S.D.MS. 740.0011 European War 1939/3882½ reads simply "I think this is a request," omitting the word "fair." A transmission failure?

Nonetheless, by the time that the "Destroyer Deal" got down to the negotiating stages, Kennedy took a hard-nosed approach to it. August 2, 1940: "They have not demonstrated one thing that would justify us in assuming any kind of a partnership with them or any kind of an agreement with them. . . . If we are going to give them destroyers, might not we ask them for assurances that if they are defeated the fleet or what is left of it must of necessity come to our shores? And numerous other considerations of this kind. The staff talks which I understand from the British are to take place here with our navy group should not be undertaken by us as the potential partner of England on any enterprise but rather as the man who owns 51 percent of the stock of the company. . . . I think you will find them not disposed to give up anything. . . . As I view it, they have not got a Chinaman's chance if they do not get help from us. If they do get assurances of help from us, in our present ridiculously weak position I do not think it will do them any good; it will only do us the harm of signing a blank check on all our resources—financial, industrial and man power." Kennedy to Hull, August 2, 1940, S.D.MS. 740.0011 European War 1939/4929 3/4, Sections 12 and 13. This wire, sent while Washington decision-makers were formulating their ultimate position on the destroyer deal, seems to say "don't."

After the deal was consummated, Kennedy seemed to share Churchill's view in a wire to Washington: "As [Churchill] says, it puts a ring of steel around the United States that it would be impossible for Germany to penetrate and what could the President of the United States accomplish for his country greater than this? And no matter what criticism may be leveled at the giving of a few destroyers, the President can very properly say: 'At least I have conducted the affairs of this country in such a manner that it has been possible to obtain these important bases for 99 years with no real loss of anything worthwhile to America.'" Kennedy to Hull, August 29, 1940, 11:00 P.M., *F.R.U.S.*, 1940, III, 72–73. The Landis MS. sheds no light on Kennedy's position.

206. According to Krock, who was probably closest in tune at the time with the Ambassador's real attitude, Kennedy thought the Destroyer Deal " 'the worst ever,' that we have no contract for the bases, and that when 'all the facts are known,' they will 'shock the American people.' " Arthur Krock, *Memoirs: Sixty Years on the Firing Line* (New York: Funk & Wagnalls, 1968), p. 336.

207. Scott minute, October 19, 1940, FO371/24251/A4485/605/45. To same

extent, Kennedy comments in Halifax to Lothian, October 31, 1939, FO414/276, p. 154 at 155. More candid is Kennedy comment that "there might be a question of the United States giving [Britain] financial help, but there could be no question of lending." Halifax to Lothian, May 13, 1940, FO371/24239/A3243/131/45. Midway between is "if and when France and Great Britain were in real need and difficulty, the right course would be for the United States to *give* them any supplies that they could, rather than go through the form of selling material for which everybody knew no payment could be made." Halifax to Lothian, September 14, 1939, FO414/276, p. 126.

208. Landis MS., p. 427.

209. Butler, in Washington, to Foreign Office, November 3, 1940, FO371/24234/A4627/39/45.

210. Bilainkin, *Diary of a Diplomatic Correspondent*, entry of June 11, 1940, p. 104. See also, John deCourcy, *Behind the Battle* (London: Eyre and Spottiswoode, 1942), p. 193.

211. Bilainkin, *ibid.*, entry of August 20, 1940, p. 189.

212. See, for example, minute of May, 1940, FO371/24239/A3242/131/45.

213. Landis MS., p. 419.

214. Churchill to Halifax, October 4, 1940, in Churchill, *Their Finest Hour*, p. 675.

215. Robert T. Brady, *Boston Post*, July 21, 1940; Charles S. Groves, *Boston Globe*, July 28, 1940.

216. Landis MS., pp. 386–87. Roosevelt told Jimmy Byrnes that Kennedy had declined the post. Byrnes, *All In One Lifetime* (New York: Harper & Brothers, 1958), p. 125.

217. *Boston Post* editorial, August 25, 1940, reprinted in *Congressional Record*, XXCVI, A5478.

218. *Boston Globe*, September 30, 1940.

219. Arthur Krock, *New York Times*, October 8, 1940, p. 24.

220. Harry Henry, *Boston Globe* (morning edition), April 25, 1939, p. 1.

221. Landis MS., p. 423.

222. "Kennedy likes the limelight too much to be satisfied with this." Lee to Mrs. Lee, October 5, 1940, in Leutze, *Lee Journal*, p. 81.

223. See, for example, William H. Stoneman, *New York Post*, October 4, 1940, or Frederick Sondern, Jr., *New York Post*, October 23, 1940.

224. Landis MS., p. 387.

225. *Ibid.*, p. 407, and *F.D.R., His Personal Letters*, II, 1061–62.

226. Landis MS., p. 407.

227. *F.D.R., His Personal Letters*, II, 1061–62.

228. Churchill to Roosevelt, July 31, 1940, *F.R.U.S.*, 1940, III, 58.

229. Hull to Kennedy, September 21, 1940, S.D.MS., 123 Kennedy, Joseph P.

230. Landis MS., p. 389.

231. Landis MS., pp. 417–19.

232. Page 245 *supra*.

233. Landis MS., p. 417.

234. *Ibid.*, p. 436.

235. *Ibid.*, p. 337.

236. *Ibid.*, p. 344.

237. *Ibid.*, p. 349.

238. *Ibid.,* pp. 341–42. The press reported that Kennedy was only staying until he had been in the bombings, so that people would not think him a coward.

239. See, for example, Foreign Office to Lothian, October 6, 1940, FO371/24384/C10148, p. 60.

240. Joe McCarthy, *The Remarkable Kennedys* (New York: Popular Library, paperback ed., 1960), p. 65.

241. William V. Nessly, *Washington Post,* October 27, 1940, III, 3.

242. Alsop and Kintner, *Boston Globe* (morning edition), October 7, 1940, p. 3.

243. *New York Times,* October 8, 1940, p. 24.

244. *The Times* (London), October 12, 1940, p. 4.

245. Krock, recorded interview by Charles Bartlett, May 10, 1964, p. 6, typescript at John F. Kennedy Library, Oral History Program; cf. Krock's *Memoirs,* p. 334.

246. Halifax to Lothian, October 10, 1940, FO371/24251/A4485/605/45. In an analysis of this news, the Foreign Office's Graham Hutton wrote: "This confirms what we have heard at various times, namely that Mr. Kennedy's interests in Wall Street have been attracting him back to that sphere; and that as Wall Street is supporting Mr. Willkie, Mr. Kennedy has decided to go along with it." Halifax's wire said that Kennedy sought fuller data on Britain's finances before he left, to which Hutton's memorandum counsels against, on the theory that Kennedy would only use the data to hurt Roosevelt and the British. Memorandum dated October 18, 1940, same citation, p. 97 (p. 208).

247. Kennedy to Beaverbrook, November 5, 1940, MS. at Beaverbrook Library, London.

248. Landis MS., pp. 429–30.

249. Kennedy to Beaverbrook, November 5, 1940, MS. at Beaverbrook Library, London.

250. Landis MS., p. 429.

251. Memorandum, Lauchlin Currie to Missy LeHand, October 26, 1940, MS. at Roosevelt Library, Hyde Park, N.Y., references comments of Arthur Goldsmith, one of Kennedy's close friends.

252. Randolph Churchill in the *Press-Scimitar,* April, 1947; see also Randolph Churchill comments to C. L. Sulzberger, diary entry of January 15, 1960, in Sulzberger's *The Last of the Giants* (New York: The Macmillan Company, 1970), pp. 629–30. The author wrote Mr. Luce requesting that the publisher confirm, deny, or elaborate on Randolph Churchill's story. Luce kindly replied: "For various reasons, quite a few people expected Joe Kennedy to oppose Roosevelt in 1940, but he did not do so. He purchased radio time for himself and, if memory serves, he recommended the reelection of Roosevelt on the grounds that Roosevelt would keep us out of war." Luce to the author, July 9, 1963. He did not, however, confirm or deny Randolph Churchill's report.

253. Interview, New York, November 18, 1972.

254. Landis MS., p. 424, exactly on point with Roosevelt's comments to Breck Long, Israel, *Long Diary,* p. 141.

255. Krock, *Memoirs,* p. 335. The threat is not mentioned in either the Landis MS. or the *Long Diary,* but in view of Kennedy's comments to Lord Halifax, the author credits it.

256. *Daily Mail* (London), October 9, 1940, p. 3.

257. Alsop and Kintner, *Boston Globe* (evening edition), October 7, 1940, p. 1.

258. Kennedy to Welles, October 11, 1940, S.D.MS. 123 Kennedy, Joseph

P./300½. The Department's wire to Kennedy said they wanted him back around October 21.

259. Leutze, *Lee Journal*, entry of October 17, 1940, p. 96.

260. *Ibid.*, letter to Mrs. Lee of October 24, 1940, p. 105.

261. *Ibid.*, entry of October 7, 1940, p. 82.

262. *Ibid.*, entry of October 16, 1940, p. 95.

263. *Ibid.*

264. Reith, *Into the Wind*, p. 411.

265. Dalton Diary MS., London School of Economics, entry of October 15, 1940. Given Dalton's Ickes-like disposition and diction, the comment must be read to be a mild condemnation.

266. According to Bilainkin, *Diary of a Diplomatic Correspondent*, p. 241.

267. Johnson to Hull, S.D.MS. 123 Kennedy, Joseph P./302.

AMBASSADOR
KENNEDY

1. *The Times* (London), May 26, 1939, p. 16.

2. *The Times* (London), May 3, 1939, p. 16.

3. *The Times* (London), July 19, 1938, p. 11.

4. *The Times* (London), May 19, 1939, p. 18.

5. Ralph Ingersoll and Ben Robertson, *P.M.* (defunct New York daily newspaper), January 19, 1941, p. 11.

6. *Time*, November 4, 1940, p. 19, for the *Daily Herald*'s editorial and reprints of several other similar editorials, such as that of the London *Evening News*: "It is Mr. Kennedy single-handed who has strengthened Anglo-American friendship in London." The comment that meant most to Kennedy was that of *The Times* (London): "He has earned the respect due to a great *American* Ambassador who never for a moment mistook the country to which he was accredited for the country of his birth." For Kennedy's reaction to *The Times* editorial see John Evelyn Wrench, *Geoffrey Dawson and Our Times* (London: Hutchinson, 1955), p. 431. For another favorable editorial see the London *Daily Mail*, October 23, 1940 (not quoted in *Time*). London's *News Chronicle*, which was never particularly favorable to Kennedy, and which became most bitter towards him in the period November, 1940 to January, 1941, editorially ignored his departure. Interestingly enough, London press comments on Kennedy's retirement were published at the time of his return from London, and long before his retirement was officially announced.

7. T. J. Hamilton, Jr., *New York Times*, March 27, 1938, IV, 4; Krock, *New York Times*, December 13, 1938, p. 24; conceded by the left-wing *P.M.* (New York), January 19, 1941, pp. 10–12; questioned by Harold Laski, *Harper's*, April, 1941, p. 464.

8. George Bilainkin, *Diary of a Diplomatic Correspondent* (London: George Allen & Unwin Ltd.), entry of August 27, 1940, p. 195. An Ed Sullivan column years later, no doubt based on information Kennedy provided the columnist, has Bevin reminding Kennedy that "In the old days, before I was 'fashionable' you were the only one to invite me to the American Embassy." Sullivan, *New York Daily News*, November 11, 1946, p. 41. Not even Kennedy, though, invited Bevin to the embassy until after Bevin had entered Churchill's cabinet as Minister of Labour and National Service—by which point Bevin had become "fashionable." Landis MS., p. 369.

9. Interview with James Roosevelt, Washington, March 20, 1962.

10. The Landis MS. records a touching visit between Kennedy and the dying and discredited Neville Chamberlain, at which the two closed-out men discussed who had the less competent cabinet, Roosevelt or Churchill. Landis MS., p. 420. Also on the subject of Kennedy's circle of associations in the late ambassadorial period see Andrew Boyle, *Montagu Norman* (New York: Weybright and Talley, Inc., 1967), p. 315.

11. *The London Journal of General Raymond E. Lee, 1940–41*, ed. James Leutze (Boston: Little, Brown and Company, 1971), entry of June 3, 1940, p. 4.

12. William W. Kaufmann, "Two American Ambassadors: Bullitt and Kennedy," in *The Diplomats*, ed. Gordon A. Craig and Felix Gilbert (Princeton, N.J.: Princeton University Press, 1953), p. 660.

13. Moffat to Kennedy, September 20, 1938, MS. in Moffat Papers, Houghton Library, Harvard, Cambridge, Mass.

14. Messersmith to Raymond H. Geist, November 7, 1938, MS. in Messersmith Papers, Box I, File E, at University of Delaware, Newark, Del. Messersmith and Kennedy were of greatly different general outlook on the world situation. Later, when Roosevelt suggested Messersmith as a possible successor for the London Embassy, Kennedy objected; if a "career man" was to be named, those already serving in London were more entitled to consideration. Landis MS., p. 446.

15. *Boston Sunday Advertiser*, December 12, 1937, p. 1.

16. *P.M.* (New York), January 19, 1940, p. 11.

17. John M. Blum, *From the Morgenthau Diaries*, Vol. I: *Years of Crisis, 1928–1938* (Boston: Houghton Mifflin Company, 1959), p. 518. Breck Long noted, "it is my understanding from several persons close to the White House that they think that Kennedy has become injected with the same social virus which most of his predecessors have suffered from and that it has changed his point of view." Long Diary MS., entry of February 15, 1939.

18. Blum, *Morgenthau Diary*, I, 518.

19. FO395/616/P2367 and P3015/1157/150.

20. *The Secret Diary of Harold L. Ickes*, Vol. II: *The Inside Struggle, 1936–1939* (New York: Simon & Schuster, 1954), entry of July 3, 1938, p. 415.

21. *The Memoirs of Anthony Eden, Earl of Avon: The Reckoning* (Boston: Houghton Mifflin Company, 1965), pp. 46–47.

22. *The Diplomatic Diaries of Oliver Harvey, 1937–1940*, ed. John Harvey (London: Collins, 1970), p. 225.

23. Arthur Krock, *Memoirs: Sixty Years on the Firing Line* (New York: Funk & Wagnalls, 1968), p. 167.

24. Pages 199–200 *supra*.

25. FO800/324/VII/19–22.

26. Landis MS., p. 29.

27. Interview, London, July 30, 1972. Kennedy was the proud purchaser of a tea set donated by the Queen to a Red Cross benefit auction at Christie's. *The Times* (London), July 16, 1940, p. 2.

28. Pages 263, 266, *supra*.

29. Halifax to Lindsay, September 29, 1938, *British Documents*, II, 625.

30. Halifax to Lindsay, September 11, 1938, *British Documents*, II, 295–96.

31. Halifax to Lindsay, March 18, 1939, *British Documents*, IV, 380.

32. Landis MS., p. 71.

33. Kennedy to Moffat, September 27, 1938, MS. in Moffat Papers.

34. See Kennedy speeches reported in *New York Times*, May 14, 1938, p. 15; July 13, 1938, p. 23; September 3, 1938, p. 2; and, November 25, 1938, p. 7.

35. W. A. Swanberg, *Luce and his Empire* (New York: Charles Scribner's Sons, 1972), p. 305.

36. Stephen Shadegg, *Clare Boothe Luce* (New York: Simon & Schuster, 1970), p. 114.

37. Kennedy speech reported in *New York Times* of January 19, 1941, p. 35.

38. Page 179 *supra*.

39. Moffat Diary MS., entries of December 16, 1938, p. 5, and December 8, 1939; Landis MS., Library of Congress, Chap. 18, p. 4.

40. Baruch to Kennedy, March 30, 1938, MS. in Baruch Papers.

41. Hank Searls, *The Lost Prince* (New York: The New American Library, Inc., 1969), p. 123, cites letter Joseph P. Kennedy, Jr., to Tom Schriber, November 5, 1938.

42. Balfour minute, September 4, 1939, FO371/22816/A6016/98/45, page following page 25; Gage minute, September 26, 1939, FO371/22827/A6561/1090/45, page following page 154.

43. Ione Robinson, *A Wall to Paint On* (New York: E. P. Dutton and Company, Inc., 1946), letter of November 4, 1938, p. 367.

44. Landis MS., p. 375.

45. Israel, *Long Diary*, entry of November 6, 1940, p. 147.

46. Page 313 *infra*.

47. Transcript of phone conversation of March 16, 1938, Morgenthau Diary MS., Vol. 115, pp. 183–89.

48. *The Diplomats*, p. 659.

49. See page 242 *supra*.

50. *P.M.* (New York), January 19, 1941, pp. 10–12. See page 241 *supra*.

51. Halifax to Lothian, September 26, 1940, FO414/277, part 54, pp. 58–59. Halifax wired Lindsay that it was a view that Kennedy had more than once expressed to the Foreign Secretary, and judging from the comments quoted in the text, to many others.

52. Interview with James M. Landis, March 3, 1962.

53. Balfour minute, September 4, 1939, FO371/22816/A6016/98/45.

54. Scott minute, September 21, 1939, FO371/22827/A6561/1090/45, page following p. 157.

55. Leutze, *Lee Journal*, entry of September 17, 1940, p. 62.

56. Louis Fischer, *Men and Politics* (New York: Duell, Sloan and Pearce, 1941), p. 625.

57. Letter from "H.F.B." to Sir Eric Machtig, February 4, 1941, in FO371/26217/A1160/339/45.

58. ". . . the quintessence of the 'go-getter'; the American businessman to whom the world of art and the science of politics and diplomacy was a much restricted one. One always felt that 'Joe' traveled widely with eyes that took in too little. . . . Idealism had passed him by and sentimentality, rather than sentiment, tinged much of his outlook." Newcastle *Journal*, March 3, 1941.

59. Sir John Balfour, letter to the author, August 6, 1972.

60. Interview, July 17, 1972.

61. This quotation is the summation of the memorandum in the Landis MS., p. 75. The memo itself, dated December 19, 1938, is at Roosevelt Library, Hyde Park, N.Y., in President's Secretary's Files, I, Diplomatic Correspondence, Great Britain, Box 8, Joseph P. Kennedy, 1938–1940, and uses slightly different language. Shortly after the war began, Kennedy requested the Foreign Office to provide him with a memorandum on the adverse consequences to the United States of a British defeat. As to his request, the Foreign Office records are somewhat confusing, but apparently they decided not to cooperate, largely because they feared the conclusions that might be drawn by the public in the event that it should be leaked that they were even willing to think in such terms. Anyway, "we know that Mr. Roosevelt no longer has confidence in [Kennedy]," Vansittart concluded. FO371/22816/A6586/98/45 and FO371/22817/A6886, A6891 and A7270.

62. See *F.R.U.S.*, 1938, I, 754.

63. *F.D.R., His Personal Letters, 1928–1945*, ed. Elliott Roosevelt (New York: Duell, Sloan and Pearce, 1950), II, 780.

64. Kennedy's Foreword to a special United States-Canadian supplement of London's *Financial News*, April 16, 1939. William Phillips, United States Ambassador to Italy, noted a conversation with Kennedy on March 5, 1940, in his diary: "No one at home fully realizes, [Kennedy] thinks, how closely the United States is tied up with British prosperity, and as the Empire will be exhausted in the not distant future, we shall be caught in the crash." Phillips Diary MS., p. 3758.

65. *The Times* (London), July 5, 1938.

66. Kennedy to Roosevelt, September 30, 1938, MS. at Roosevelt Library, Hyde Park, N.Y.

67. *P.M.* (New York), January 19, 1941, p. 10.

68. Unnamed friend (sounds like Landis) quoted by Richard Whalen, *Fortune*, January, 1963, p. 160.

69. Joseph F. Dinneen, *The Kennedy Family* (Boston: Little Brown & Co., 1959), p. 79.

70. *New York Post*, January 11, 1961, p. 37, makes the assertion, but does not identify the friends. See also memorandum in *German Documents*, Series D, II, 744.

71. Kennedy to Beaverbrook, October 23, 1944, MS. at Beaverbrook Library, London.

72. Peake memorandum dated October 12, 1939, of visit with Hillman on October 11, 1939, FO371/22827/A7195/1090/45, p. 164.

73. Landis MS., p. 420.

74. Channon's diary entry of November 4, 1940 of a visit with Lothian, *Chips: The Diaries of Sir Henry Channon*, ed. Robert Rhodes James (London: Weidenfeld and Nicolson, 1967), p. 272. Oliver Harvey, November 1, 1939: "I'm afraid [Kennedy] only thinks of his wealth and how capitalism will suffer if the war should last long." *Diplomatic Diaries of Oliver Harvey*, p. 326. Balfour, January 29, 1940: ". . . concerned, for financial reasons of his own, to see an early end to the war." FO371/24248/A825/434/45. Kingsley Martin: ". . . a self-centred, frightened rich man who thought only in terms of money." Kingsley Martin, *Editor: "New Statesman" Years, 1931–1945* (Chicago: Henry Regnery Company, 1970), p. 313.

75. Landis MS., p. 421.

76. Leutze, *Lee Journal*, entry of October 24, 1940, p. 105.

77. Bill Cunningham, *Boston Herald*, March 28, 1941, p. 30.

78. Page 517 *supra*, note 74.

79. Interview, August 7, 1965.

80. Leutze, *Lee Journal*, entry of June 3, 1940, p. 4.

81. See Lend-Lease Hearings, pp. 236, 264.

82. Rev. Joseph F. Thorning, *Builders of the Social Order* (Ozone Park, N.Y.: Catholic Literary Guild, 1941), p. 68. The date of the interview is not given in Father Thorning's book; Father Thorning supplied it in letter to this author dated February 20, 1962.

83. Kennedy to Hull, August 2, 1940, S.D.MS. 740.0011 European War 1939/4929 3/4. See also *Boston Globe*, November 8, 1940, and Long Diary MS., entry of November 6, 1940, p. 259. According to A. J. P. Taylor, war production "produced a revolution in British economic life, until in the end direction and control turned Great Britain into a country more fully socialist than anything achieved by the conscious planners of Soviet Russia." A. J. P. Taylor, *English History, 1914–1945* (London: Penguin Books, paperback ed., 1970), p. 616.

84. Kennedy to State Department, September 27, 1940, *F.R.U.S.*, III, 48–49.

85. See Kennedy's later thoughts along these lines in Dinneen, *Kennedy Family*, p. 110.

86. Robinson, *A Wall to Paint On*, letter of November 4, 1938, p. 367.

87. Kennedy to Roosevelt, September 30, 1939, in Landis MS., p. 194.

88. Landis MS., p. 27.

89. Kennedy to Roosevelt, September 30, 1939, in Landis MS., pp. 192–93. The author was unable to ascertain which articles in *The Times* Kennedy was comparing.

90. Balfour minutes, September 20, 1939, FO371/22827/A6561/1090/45, p. 157; and, January 29, 1940, FO371/24248/A825/434/45, page following page 145 (p. 368). Also, Lothian comment to "Chips" Channon of November 4, 1940, *Chips: The Diaries of Sir Henry Channon*, p. 272.

91. As did Dean Landis. "The Reminiscences of James M. Landis" (1964), p. 250, typescript in The Oral History Collection of Columbia University.

92. Morris DeHaven Tracy, *Boston Traveler*, June 22, 1938, p. 1.

93. Kennedy to Roosevelt, September 30, 1939, in Landis MS., p. 192.

94. Kennedy to Hull, August 29, 1940, MS. in Hull Papers, Correspondence: August 1–31, 1940.

95. Clare Boothe Luce, *Europe in the Spring* (New York: Alfred A. Knopf, 1940), this quotation is reprinted in Lend-Lease Hearings, p. 276.

96. Balfour's characterization, FO371/26217/A1160/339/45.

97. J. J. Astor to Brendon Bracken, February 19, 1941, quotes extract from letter of unidentified friend in America, FO371/26217/A1160/339/45.

98. See page 219 *supra*.

99. Landis MS., p. 286.

100. Kennedy speech to the American public on January 18, 1941, *New York Times*, January 19, 1941, p. 35.

101. Louis Lyons, *Boston Globe*, November 10, 1940.

102. But cf. Kennedy's comments to a group of United States military officers in December, 1939: that if Britain lost, "Europe would be so exhausted that we would have nothing to fear." Moffat's phrase, in Moffat Diary MS., entry of December 15, 1939, p. 4.

103. See, for example, Kennedy's comments in Halifax to Lothian, September 26, 1940, FO414/277, Part 54, pp. 58–59.

104. Lend-Lease hearings, p. 230.

105. In a speech of January, 1941, Joseph P. Kennedy, Jr., endorsed barter with a Nazi-conquered Europe as a preferable alternative to engaging in total war on Britain's side. *New York Times*, January 7, 1941, p. 7.

106. It could only have had that effect. Lothian was much concerned that "defeatism now rampant in high American circles, is strengthening the hands of those who are now trying to withdraw supplies promised to Britain for their own armament, on the ground that everything sent to us will be lost within a few weeks." Lothian to Foreign Office, July 19, 1940, FO371/24230, p. 466. Similar analysis in Haggard, from New York, to Foreign Office, June 14, 1940, FO371/24239/A3242/131/45. Perowne attributed the "defeatism now rampant in high American circles" to Kennedy's influence. Minute attached to Lothian wire, *op. cit.*

107. Kennedy to Roosevelt, March 3, 1939, MS. at Roosevelt Library, Hyde Park, N.Y., in President's Secretary's File, Great Britain, Kennedy.

108. Israel, *Long Diary*, entry of November 6, 1940, p. 148.

109. According to interventionist newsman Carroll Binder, Kennedy "was all out to save capitalism from socialism and that from this point of view he would prefer the Germany of Hitler to the England of Churchill and Bevin." "H.F.B." to Sir Eric Machtig, February 4, 1941, FO371/26217.

110. Kennedy to Hull, July 20, 1938, S.D.MS. 741.62/280 makes an interesting comparison with von Dirksen to Weizsäcker of the same date in *German Documents*, Series D, I, 721, especially p. 723 subsection 5.

111. Israel, *Long Diary*, entry of November 7, 1940, p. 148.

112. Halifax to Sir Ronald Lindsay, September 2, 1938, *British Documents*, II, 212–13.

113. Kennedy to Hull, August 31, 1938, *F.R.U.S.*, 1938, I, 565.

114. Hull to Kennedy, September 1, 1938, *F.R.U.S.*, 1938, I, 568–69.

115. Page 149 *supra*.

116. Hooker, *Moffat Papers*, p. 199.

117. Long Diary MS., entry of March 29, 1940.

118. Hooker, *Moffat Papers*, pp. 197, 221.

119. See *The Diplomats*, pp. 679–80.

120. See page 182 *supra*.

121. Leutze, *Lee Journal*, letter of October 5, 1940, p. 81.

122. Bilainkin, *Diary of a Diplomatic Correspondent*, p. 257.

123. Parallel observation by Perowne, March 9, 1940, in FO371/24251/A1848/605/45, page following page 66 (p. 174).

124. *Jim Farley's Story* (New York: McGraw-Hill Book Company, Inc., 1948), p. 199. See also Long Diary MS., entry of March 15, 1939.

125. Bilainkin, *Diary of a Diplomatic Correspondent*, p. 60.

THE
GREATEST CAUSE

1. Randolph Churchill conversation with C. L. Sulzberger, latter's diary entry of January 15, 1960, in his *The Last of the Giants* (New York: The Macmillan Company, 1970), p. 630.

2. Memorandum, "E.M.W." (presumably Colonel Edwin Martin Watson, a secretary to Roosevelt) to Roosevelt, October 25, 1940, MS. at Roosevelt Library, Hyde Park, N.Y.

3. Memorandum, Lauchlin Currie to Missy LeHand, October 26, 1940, MS at Roosevelt Library, Hyde Park, N.Y.

4. *New York Post*, October 23, 1940, same in *Pittsburgh Post-Gazette*, October 24, 1940; Carroll Binder in *Chicago Daily News* and *St. Louis Post-Dispatch*, both October 23, 1940, and in *Baltimore Sun*, October 24, 1940. Also, *Bristol News Bulletin* (Bristol, Va.), October 28, 1940. Papers friendly to Kennedy, the *New York Times* and the Hearst journals, apparently did not report the rumor, realizing, even if the Ambassador did not, that it would cause him embarrassment.

5. Roosevelt conversation with Breckenridge Long, October 11, 1940, in Israel, *Long Diary*, pp. 141–42.

6. Interview, July 26, 1972.

7. Arthur Krock, *Memoirs: Sixty Years on the Firing Line* (New York: Funk & Wagnalls, 1968), p. 334. Krock expected Kennedy to "sit out" the campaign.

8. On October 21, 1940, Joe, Jr., spoke for Roosevelt in a radio broadcast sponsored by "The Massachusetts Independent Voters Committee for Roosevelt and Wallace." *Boston Globe* (morning edition), October 22, 1940, p. 4. He was scheduled to participate in a "Youth for Roosevelt" rally at Faneuil Hall, Boston, on October 23, 1940, and presumably did. *Boston Evening Transcript*, October 23, 1940, p. 9.

9. An unsigned and undated handwritten note in the Foreign Office minute books, appearing on the same page as a note dated October 19, 1940, and in the hand possibly of either Vansittart or Halifax, says "When he came to see me 2 days ago, Kennedy said he was *not* going to do anything to embarrass Roosevelt." FO371/24251/A4485/605/45, page between page 95 (p. 206) and page 96 (p. 207). This news was apparently not forwarded to Lothian.

10. Alsop and Kintner, *Boston Globe*, October 7, 1940.

11. "E.M.W." to Roosevelt, October 25, 1940, MS. at Roosevelt Library, Hyde Park, N.Y.

12. Landis MS., p. 433, says Kennedy was indignant at receiving the note, perhaps because it heightened his suspicion that Roosevelt himself was behind Alsop and Kintner's barbs.

13. Landis MS., pp. 433–34; to same extent, Krock's contemporary memorandum in his *Memoirs*, p. 335.

14. George Bilainkin, *Diary of a Diplomatic Correspondent* (London: George Allen & Unwin Ltd., 1942), p. 252.

15. Landis MS., p. 434. Compare chronology in Joe McCarthy, *The Remarkable Kennedys* (New York: Popular Library, paperback ed., 1960), p. 67, and Whalen, *Founding Father* p. 334.

16. Krock, *Memoirs*, p. 399. The significance of drawing the forefinger across the throat is subject to interpretation. Krock disbelieves the reported anecdote on the theory that the motion must have meant that Roosevelt would extract Kennedy's resignation from him—which Krock knew was not at all the President's intention at that moment. The motion, however, is subject to other interpretation which would be consistent with the President's aims: "Boy, am I going to take advantage of Kennedy." Roosevelt's appointment book for the day in question, October 27, 1940, indicates that

he spent time that day with "Speaker Rayburn and Rep. L. Johnson." President's Appointment Book, MS. at Roosevelt Library, Hyde Park, N.Y.

17. Landis MS., pp. 434–38, 441, substantially in accord with the account of the meeting in James F. Byrnes, *All in One Lifetime* (New York: Harper & Brothers, 1958), p. 125.

18. Stewart Alsop, "Kennedy's Magic Formula," *Saturday Evening Post*, August 13, 1960, p. 59.

19. Victor Lasky, *Robert F. Kennedy: The Myth and the Man* (New York: Trident Press, 1968), p. 57.

20. McCarthy, *The Remarkable Kennedys*, p. 50.

21. Landis MS., p. 439. It was a sound conclusion too; Willkie was a flaming "internationalist," who had early assured the British of his sympathies and willingness to help Britain. Lothian to Halifax, August 29, 1940, FO800/324/xxxvii/90.

22. Krock, *Memoirs*, p. 335; see also Randolph Churchill's comments to C. L. Sulzberger, Sulzberger's diary entry of January 15, 1960, *Last of the Giants*, p. 630.

23. *New York Journal-American*, October 30, 1940.

24. *The Times* (London), October 29, 1940, p. 3.

25. Landis MS., pp. 270, 423; Landis MS., Library of Congress, Chap. 41, pp. 4–5. In March, 1940, Kennedy "couldn't help but remember what Roosevelt had said to me over a year before—that he would be a bitter isolationist, then help with arms and money and later, depending on the state of affairs, get into the fight." Landis MS., p. 270. And so it came to pass.

26. Speech reported in *New York Times*, October 30, 1940, pp. 1, 8.

27. Krock, *Memoirs*, p. 336.

28. Typescript of telephone conversation in Morgenthau Diary MS., Vol. 326, p. 252. A great number of Morgenthau's telephone calls, such as this one, were monitored by his long-time personal secretary, Mrs. Henrietta Klotz, who, unannounced, listened in on an extension telephone and made stenographic notes of the conversation. This practice was widely known and resented in government circles. Once when a government associate had to place a call to Morgenthau, Kennedy insisted on opening the conversation with the Secretary of Treasury: "Hello, Henry?" Kennedy began, and quickly followed up with a torrent of lurid language. Placing his hand over the telephone mouthpiece, Kennedy whispered to his companion, "A couple of more sentences, and Mrs. Klotz will hang up." Interview, September 20, 1973.

29. *New York Times*, October 31, 1940, p. 19. Republican editorial writers criticized the "experience" argument. See *Wall Street Journal*, October 31, 1940, p. 4, and *Washington Post*, same day, p. 10.

30. *Washington Post*, November 1, 1940, p. 11.

31. *Life* quoted in McCarthy, p. 67.

32. *The London Journal of General Raymond E. Lee, 1940–41*, ed. James Leutze (Boston: Little, Brown and Company, 1971), entry of October 30, 1940, p. 115.

33. Castle interview of November 19, 1940, typescript in Morgenthau Diary MS., Vol. 340, p. 266.

34. Krock, *Memoirs*, p. 337.

35. Landis MS., p. 440, says, "I went to see the President the day after the election." This is probably error. Roosevelt spent the day after the election in Hyde Park, but was back in Washington the following day, November 7, and according to his

appointment book, he saw Kennedy that day. President's appointment calendar, MS. at Roosevelt Library, Hyde Park, N.Y.

36. Landis MS., p. 442.

37. Page 269 *supra*.

38. Landis MS., pp. 440–41.

39. *Boston Globe* (morning edition), November 8, 1940, p. 1.

40. President's Appointment Book, November 7, 1940, p. 15.

41. Israel, *Long Diary*, entry of November 6, 1940, p. 148.

42. Interview with Louis Lyons, Boston, July 28, 1961.

43. Ed Plaut, who interviewed Kennedy 19 years later, found him an easy mark for an experienced journalist; "a garrulous bloke," who "could have been made to gush plenty of information just as he did in that historic interview about the King and Queen of England which Louis Lyons wrote." Plaut's notes of interview of October 29, 1959.

44. Louis M. Lyons, *Newspaper Story: One Hundred Years of the Boston Globe* (Cambridge, Mass.: The Belknap Press, 1971), pp. 290–94.

45. Lyons told that author that he had been proceeding quite innocently, thinking that all the story amounted to was a colorful feature article—"Hometown boy comes home." He was, he said, politically unsophisticated at the time, did not appreciate the implications of the piece, and did not expect the article to create the furor that it did. Interview, July 28, 1961.

46. The previous day, Kennedy had told Breck Long that "he was going to the West Coast and would see Hearst and try to set him right and see other publishers like McCormick." Israel, *Long Diary*, p. 148. Much of the other substantive matter in the Lyons article was told Long as well. *Ibid.*

47. Lyons, *Boston Sunday Globe*, November 10, 1940, p. 1, reprinted and more readily available in *Congressional Record*, XXCVI, A6622.

48. Luther Conant, Jr., *Boston Evening Transcript*, November 13, 1940, reprinted in *Congressional Record*, XXCVI, A6624. Cf. Dinneen's first-hand account in *The Kennedy Family* (Boston: Little, Brown and Company, 1959), pp. 84–86.

49. *New York Herald Tribune*, November 14, 1940, p. 26.

50. *New York Herald Tribune*, November 12, 1940, p. 22.

51. *New York Herald Tribune*, November 14, 1940, p. 26.

52. Kennedy to Beaverbrook, November 13, 1940, MS. at Beaverbrook Library, London.

53. *News Chronicle* (London), November 21, 1940, p. 5; see also *Daily Herald* (London), November 12, 1940, p. 2. The less respectable British press was more curt. The London *Tribune*: "I can tell President Roosevelt of one person who is not grata at all; and that is Mr. J. P. (call me Joe) Kennedy. . . . Mr. Kennedy is a very rich man and a Catholic, with the prejudices which accompany those two characteristics when their possessor is not particularly cultured or intelligent." With regard to Kennedy's comments about Lyons' untrustworthiness, the *Tribune* said: "A reporter's job is not to protect but to get the stuffed shirt to talk more and worse nonsense; it makes a better story." Their editorial ends, "There's your hat, Mr. Kennedy." November 15, 1940.

54. Dorothy Thompson, *New York Herald Tribune*, November 15, 1940, p. 19; Walter Lippmann, *New York Herald Tribune*, December 5, 1940.

55. Harold Laski, "British Democracy and Mr. Kennedy," *Harper's*, April, 1941, pp. 464 ff.

56. Castle interview, November 19, 1940, typescript in Morgenthau Diary MS., Vol. 340, p. 266. Castle thought it particularly tasteless that Kennedy told "all the dirty stuff about his relations with the President which he had been doing privately." *Ibid.*

57. The author found no defenders.

58. Quoted in *New York Times*, December 23, 1940, p. 3.

59. Edward M. Gallagher, recorded interview by Ed Martin, January 8, 1965, typescript at John F. Kennedy Library, Oral History Program.

60. Interview with Joseph F. Dinneen, Needham, Mass., July 29, 1961.

61. Lyons, *Newspaper Story*, pp. 290–94.

62. Dinneen interview.

63. Kennedy to Beaverbrook, November 13, 1940, MS. at Beaverbrook Library, London.

64. Frankfurter denied it to Dinneen. Dinneen interview.

65. Frankfurter to Roosevelt, November 11, 1940, *Roosevelt and Frankfurter: Their Correspondence, 1928–1945*, ed. Max Freedman (Boston: Little Brown and Company, 1967), p. 553.

66. Irwin Ross, *New York Post Magazine*, January 9, 1961, p. 1.

67. Except see Harold Nicolson's *Diaries and Letters of Harold Nicolson*, Vol. II, *The War Years, 1939–1945*, ed. Nigel Nicolson (London: Collins, 1967), entry of December 3, 1940, p. 130.

68. Whitehead minute, November 15, 1940, FO371/24251/A4485/605/45.

69. Perowne minute, November 26, 1940, FO371/24251/A1945/605/45, p. 72 (p. 180).

70. Lady Astor to Lothian, November 21, 1940, in Christopher Sykes, *Nancy* (New York: Harper & Row, 1973), p. 426.

71. *News Chronicle* (London), November 15, 1940, p. 4.

72. *Chips: The Diaries of Sir Henry Channon*, ed. Robert Rhodes James (London: Weidenfeld and Nicolson, 1967), diary entry of November 4, 1940, p. 272.

73. *The Times* (London), November 26, 1940, p. 4.

74. Gore Vidal reports that years later, Eleanor Roosevelt recollected for guests about the time that Kennedy "came back to Boston and gave that *unfortunate* interview in which he was . . . well, somewhat *critical* of us." "Well, *my* Franklin said, 'We better have him down here.'—we were at Hyde Park—'and see what he has to say.' So Mr. Kennedy arrived at Rhinecliff on the train and I met him and took him straight to Franklin. Well, ten minutes later one of the aides came and said, 'The President wants to see you right away.' This was unheard of. So I *rushed* into the office and there was Franklin, white as a sheet. He asked Mr. Kennedy to step outside and then he said, and his voice was *shaking*, 'I never want to see that man again as long as I live. . . . get him out of here. . . .' ". Gore Vidal, *New York Review of Books*, November 18, 1971, p. 8. The author includes the anecdote in footnote, rather than in the body of the text, because he suspects that the story is in large part erroneous. The story may be true *if* Kennedy's first visit with Roosevelt subsequent to the *Globe* interview took place in Hyde Park, but the author doubts that it did. Kennedy did see Roosevelt in Washington on December 1, 1940; according to the President's appointment book, between the *Globe* interview and December 1, the President was in Hyde Park only from November 20 to November 24. Kennedy went to California on November 13, and while the author does not know the date of Kennedy's return to the East, the author believes that Kennedy was probably still on the West Coast during the November 20–24 period.

75. Associated Press dispatch from San Francisco, November 14, 1940, in

Congressional Record, XXCVI, A6622. See the *Boston Herald*, November 14, 1940, for a somewhat different account of his comments.

76. Sources for the comments in the text on the meetings with the moguls are numerous and consistent, but uniformly sketchy. The author is aware of the following, in chronological order: (a) John L. Balderston to Ulrich Bell, both active in interventionist activity, November 18, 1940, MS. in Balderston Papers, Library of Congress Manuscript Division, Box 1; (b) Douglas Fairbanks to Roosevelt, Mellett Correspondence, November 19, 1940, Bureau of Motion Pictures, Domestic Radio Bureau, Office of War Information, National Archives, Washington (not seen by the author, cited in Richard R. Lingeman, *Don't You Know There's A War On?: The American Home Front, 1941–1945*, New York: G. P. Putnam's Sons, 1970, p. 172); (c) Memorandum, "Small Dinner Meeting, Century Club," November 22, 1940, MS. at Princeton University Library (not seen by the author, cited in Mark Lincoln Chadwin, *The Hawks of World War II*, Chapel Hill: University of North Carolina Press, 1968, p. 126); (d) E. A. Cleaugh, at British Consulate, Los Angeles, to Richard Ford, at British Library of Information, New York, November 22, 1940, FO371/26217; (e) first published account: Pearson and Allen column, *Times-Herald* (Washington) and *Boston Evening Transcript*, November 26, 1940; (f) Balderston to Bell, November 27, 1940, MS. at Princeton University Library (not seen by the author, cited in Chadwin, *op. cit.*, p. 126; (g) *Newsweek*, December 16, 1940; (h) Kenneth Crawford, *P.M.* (New York), December 26, 1940; (i) Ben Hecht, *P.M.* (New York), January 16, 1941 (substantially repeated in Hecht's autobiographical *A Child of the Century*, New York: Simon & Schuster, 1954, p. 520). See also *Ickes' Diary*, December 1, 1940, *The Secret Diary of Harold L. Ickes*, Vol. III, *The Lowering Clouds, 1939–1941* (New York: Simon & Schuster, 1954), p. 386.

77. This attitude was no doubt sincerely held by Kennedy. As early as February, 1939, Kennedy told Halifax "that he had observed a considerable development of anti-Jewish feeling in the United States. This was in part due to the constant suggestion that the Jews were trying to get America into war." Halifax to Lindsay, February 17, 1939, FO371/22829/A1385/1292/45.

78. E. A. Cleaugh to Richard Ford, November 22, 1940, FO371/26217.

79. Alsop and Kintner, *New York Herald Tribune*, December 3, 1940, p. 14. See also Ickes' extended comments along the same line, in III, 386, 387, for a diary entry of December 1, 1940.

80. John L. Balderston to Ulrich Bell, December 4, 1940, MS. in Balderston Papers, Library of Congress, Manuscript Division, says, "I have myself seen a private letter from Kennedy in which he referred to himself as the 'Number One Appeaser.' "

81. Alsop and Kintner, *New York Herald Tribune*, December 5, 1940, p. 4.

82. *The Times* (London), December 3, 1940, p. 4.

83. Landis MS., p. 443.

84. *The Times* (London), December 2, 1940, p. 4.

85. *New York Herald Tribune*, December 3, 1940, p. 26.

86. Alsop and Kintner, *New York Herald Tribune*, December 5, 1940, p. 4.

87. Dorothy Thompson, *New York Herald Tribune*, December 6, 1940, p. 21.

88. Seymour to Kennedy, December 8, 1940, copy in FO371/24251/A1945/605/45.

89. *The Spectator*, December 6, 1940, p. 601, reprinted in England as an editorial in the *Huddersfield Daily Examiner*, December 10, 1940.

90. *News Chronicle* (London), December 6, 1940, p. 4.

91. Kennedy to Seymour, stamped with date December 9, 1940, FO371/24251/A1945/605/45.

92. See page 154 *supra*.

93. Krock, *New York Times*, December 8, 1940, IV, p. 3; editorials in the *Boston Post*, December 10, 1940; Hearst's *Los Angeles Examiner* and *New York Journal American*, both December 11, 1940; *Kansas City Times*, reprinted in the *St. Louis Post-Dispatch* of December 16, 1940. Most of these took the line that Kennedy was being attacked because he wanted to keep the United States out of war. But as Frank Kent wrote in his *Baltimore Sun-Wall Street Journal* column, Kennedy was being attacked "not because he wants to keep this country out of war—most people take that stand—but because of the character of his remarks and general attitude, prior to his resignation as well as now." *Wall Street Journal*, December 9, 1940. Krock, more sophisticated than the Hearst editorial writers, did not take that line, but instead went about to prove that "appeaser" was misapplied to Kennedy. In response to Krock, see Pearson and Allen, *Daily Mirror* (New York), January 1, 1941.

94. *Daily Express* (London), reprinted Hearst's editorial in its issue of December 12, 1940. Viscount Castlerosse defended Kennedy in his *Sunday Express* column of December 15, 1940.

95. Bilainkin wrote in his diary on December 23, 1940, "Let us be just to Kennedy, wait till fuller records are available. I have never doubted his friendship for the people of this country." *Diary of a Diplomatic Correspondent*, p. 262.

96. The *Daily News* editorial was reprinted in the *Times-Herald* and the *Congressional Record*, XXCVII, 92–93, at the request of Senator Vandenberg, and in the *Congressional Record*, XXCVII, A107, at the request of another congressman.

97. Mark Sullivan, *New York Herald Tribune*, December 3, 1940. See also Walter Lippmann's negative response to Sullivan, *New York Herald Tribune*, December 5, 1940.

98. *Congressional Record*, XXCVII, 92.

99. *The Sign*, January, 1941.

100. James L. Kilgallen, *Boston Herald*, December 3, 1940. See also *Ickes' Diary*, December 1, 1940, III, 386–87.

101. Nonetheless, Kennedy remained one of the primary targets in the interventionist press. The *New York Post* identified him as "the ex-officio braintruster directing the isolationist fight." February 6, 1941. When Senator Tydings, a down-the-line reactionary, entered the great foreign policy debate, the left-wing *P.M.* headlined that Tydings "NOW IS PITCHING APPEASEMENT ON THE KENNEDY TEAM." To the left it was "Kennedy's team." Kenneth Crawford, *P.M.* (New York), January 15, 1941. On Kennedy's relations with Tydings, see also Alsop and Kintner, *New York Herald Tribune*, January 9, 1941.

102. Wayne S. Cole, *America First* (Madison: The University of Wisconsin Press, 1953), p. 17, cites Kennedy to Mrs. M. P. Weedy, December 31, 1940, America First MSS., Hoover Library, Stanford University. There is little available on Kennedy's relations with "America First" or its leaders. See *The Wartime Journals of Charles A. Lindbergh* (New York: Harcourt Brace Jovanovich, Inc., 1970), entry of December 12, 1940, p. 427. He appears to have been close to Laurence Dennis, intellectual leader of America's far-right isolationists. "The Reminiscences of Laurence Dennis" (1967), p. 24, typescript in The Oral History Collection of Columbia University.

103. *Congressional Record*, December 19, 1940, XXCVI, 13983.

104. Alsop and Kintner, *New York Herald Tribune*, January 9, 1941; *New York Times*, February 2, 1941, p. 18.

105. Krock, *New York Times*, December 8, 1940, IV, 3; Pearson and Allen, *Daily Mirror* (New York), January 1, 1941.

106. *Ickes Diary*, entry of December 21, 1940, III, 395; Pearson and Allen, *Daily Mirror* (New York), January 1, 1941.

107. *The Scotsman*, November 13, 1940.

108. Robert Bendiner, *Riddle of the State Department* (New York: Farrar & Rinehart, Inc., 1942), p. 207.

109. Landis MS., p. 445. A note from Steve Early to the President, though, reads: "You said you would see Joe Kennedy. Is it possible that you can see him before this broadcast, Saturday night?" which sounds as if the interview had been requested by Kennedy, not Roosevelt. Early memo, January 15, 1941, MS. at Roosevelt Library, Hyde Park, N.Y., in President's Personal File 207.

110. Account of the visit based on Landis MS., pp. 445–46. Doris Fleeson and John O'Donnell, *Washington Times-Herald*, January 17, 1941, p. 1, report its occurrence.

111. Anecdote told the author by Wheeler's close friend, Walter Trohan, Chief of the Washington Bureau of the *Chicago Daily Tribune*. Interview, Washington, March 22, 1962. Whalen reports the same anecdote citing interview with Wheeler. Richard J. Whalen, *The Founding Father* (New York: The New American Library of World Literature, Inc., 1964), p. 356. Fleeson and O'Donnell reported that Wheeler and Kennedy had met immediately after Kennedy's conference with the President to confer on rebuffing the President's plans. *Times-Herald* (Washington), January 17, 1941, p. 1.

112. *Chicago Daily Tribune*, January 19, 1941, p. 1, and editorial, January 21, 1941; *Chicago Herald American*, January 19, 1941, p. 1.

113. *News Chronicle* (London), January 20, 1941, p. 3.

114. *News Chronicle* (London), January 21, 1941, p. 4.

115. Ivan Maisky, *Memoirs of a Soviet Ambassador: The War 1939–1943*, trans. Andrew Rothstein (London: Hutchinson, 1967), p. 133.

116. Full text in *Washington Post*, January 19, 1941, p. 5.

117. *Daily Telegraph and Morning Post* (London), January 20, 1941, p. 4.

118. *The Times* (London), January 23, 1941, p. 3.

119. Dorothy Thompson, *New York Herald Tribune*, January 22, 1941, p. 17.

120. Trohan interview. Whalen, *Founding Father*, p. 354, to same effect, cites unnamed interview, perhaps also Trohan.

121. *The Nation*, February 1, 1941. The *News Chronicle* headlined its report of Kennedy's testimony with MR. KENNEDY SAYS "YES SIR!" TO AID FOR BRITAIN. *News Chronicle* (London), January 22, 1941, p. 1.

122. As late as 1944, Joseph Kennedy rejected the term "isolationist" as inappropriate for himself. Dinneen, *The Kennedy Family*, p. 106. But by 1947, Kennedy was ready to acknowledge that "isolationist" was a shoe that fit him, and he began to wear it proudly. Frank Conniff, *New York Journal-American*, April 30, 1947, p. 21.

123. Harry Golden, *The Right Time* (New York: G. P. Putnam's Sons, 1969), p. 433.

124. Paul Mallon, *New York Journal-American*, January 2, 1941.

125. Leonard Baker, *Roosevelt and Pearl Harbor* (New York: The Macmillan

Company, 1970), p. 30, cites O'Connor to Amos Pinchot, January 24, 1941, Pinchot Papers, Library of Congress Manuscript Division, Box 71.

126. Whalen, *Founding Father*, p. 356, cites interview with Wheeler.

127. Trohan interview. The author wrote Dean Clarence Manion, one-time Dean of the Notre Dame law school and one of those to whom the comment was supposed to have been made, in July, 1963, and again in October, 1972, soliciting confirmation or denial. The author's queries went unanswered.

128. Landis MS., p. 447.

129. *Ibid.*

130. He expressed some interest in a statement isolationist leaders were drafting in opposition to the President's policies in the summer of 1941, but ultimately declined to sign it himself. Donald R. McCoy, *Landon of Kansas* (Lincoln: University of Nebraska Press, 1966), p. 472.

131. Bill Cunningham, *Boston Herald*, March 28, 1941, p. 30.

132. Helen Essary, *Times-Herald* (Washington), May 9, 1941, p. 10.

133. Wheeler, May 26, 1941, in *Congressional Record*, XXCVII, A2510.

134. Kennedy's views coincided neatly with those of Colonel Lindbergh; the rhetoric of his "tides of the mighty revolution" is reminiscent of Anne Morrow Lindbergh's *The Wave of the Future*, published the year before. (New York: Harper and Brothers, 1940).

135. Reprinted twice in the *Congressional Record*, XXCVII, A2510, A2492.

136. Claude Bowers to Roosevelt, June 9, 1941, MS. at Roosevelt Library, Hyde Park, New York, in Office File 303, Claude G. Bowers, 1940–1943 Chile.

137. *Washington Post*, May 30, 1941, p. 6. The Hearst press continued to be enthusiastically isolationist, and asserted that "There has been no more masterful summation of logical and patriotic reasons for keeping the United States out of war." *Boston American*, June 11, 1941, p. 20; *San Francisco Examiner* and *Chicago Herald American*, June 12, 1941; *New York Journal-American*, June 20, 1941. But the temper of the country was going against Kennedy, even in the traditionally isolationist Midwest. The *Milwaukee Post* asserted that the speech revealed "a fatal misunderstanding of what is going on in Europe." As to Kennedy's comment about the "mighty revolution," it suggested that Kennedy was mistaking invasion, depredation, and subjection for revolution. May 30, 1941, p. 4. The Green Bay, Wisconsin *Press Gazette* said, "Treason bubbled further to his lips." May 27, 1941. Kennedy's position was in no way aided by the applause of Fascist editor Virginio Gayda, who paid tribute to Kennedy for seeing "the reality of the new European revolution" and "telling his countrymen what they ought to know." *New York Herald Tribune*, May 27, 1941, p. 2.

138. *New York Times*, June 2, 1941, p. 20.

POST-MORTEM
ON A FRIENDSHIP

1. Kennedy to Roosevelt, December 7, 1941, in *F.D.R., His Personal Letters, 1928–1945*, ed. Elliott Roosevelt (New York: Duell, Sloan and Pearce, 1950), II, 1290.

2. *Ibid.*, p. 1289.

3. Robert E. Sherwood, *Roosevelt and Hopkins* (New York: Grosset & Dunlap, paperback ed., 1948), p. 230.

4. Memorandum dated January 13, 1941, in Hull Papers, Subject File: Great Britain, 1941.

5. *Ibid.*

6. Landis MS., p. 446.

7. *Boston Traveler*, January 14, 1942, reprinted in *Congressional Record*, Vol. XXCVIII, A221.

8. *New York Times*, February 20, 1942.

9. *Liberty*, February 14, 1942.

10. *New York Enquirer*, February 23, 1942.

11. Pearson and Allen, *Daily Mirror* (New York), February 10, 1942.

12. Kennedy to Roosevelt, March 4, 1942, MS. at Roosevelt Library, Hyde Park, N.Y., President's Personal File 207.

13. Roosevelt to Kennedy, March 7, 1942, *ibid.*

14. Frederick C. Lane, *Ships for Victory* (Baltimore: Johns Hopkins Press, 1951), p. 167. After some search, I have not been able to find this letter. Lane's citation is unclear, but refers to a letter of March 12, 1942.

15. Emory Scott Land, *Winning the War with Ships* (New York: Robert M. McBride Co., Inc., 1958), p. 211. It is not clear that Kennedy made these statements in the letter of March 12 cited by Lane. Admiral Land does not date the letter he refers to, but it seems reasonable to conclude that it was the letter of March 12.

16. Lane, *Ships for Victory*, p. 167.

17. *Ibid.*, p. 168.

18. *Ibid.*, p. 167.

19. President's Press Conference 819, April 14, 1942, typescript at Roosevelt Library, Hyde Park, N.Y., Press Conferences, XIX, 278–79.

20. *Washington Post*, April 16, 1942, p. 3. Also, *New York Times*, same day, p. 23.

21. *F.D.R., His Personal Letters*, II, 1290.

22. Pearson and Allen, *Daily Mirror* (New York), April 25, 1942, *Times Herald* (Washington), June 15, 1942. Leonard Lyons wrote that Kennedy refused three different jobs offered him. *New York Post*, January 25, 1943.

23. Interview with Mr. Woodward by Chester L. Guthrie and Allan M. Ross, June 7, 1946, MS. notes of which are at the National Archives, Maritime Commission, Historian's Collection, Research File 105.

24. ". . . and if it was merely an excuse for putting me under cover, I resented that equally, so that didn't work out very well, and I am still in the leper colony." Kennedy to Kent, March 2, 1943, MS. in Kent Papers, Maryland Historical Society, Baltimore, Md.

25. President's Press Conference 820, April 21, 1942, typescript at Roosevelt Library, Hyde Park, N.Y., Press Conferences, XIX, 290–91.

26. *Boston Herald*, April 22, 1942.

27. *New York Times*, April 22, 1942, p. 12.

28. *New York Times*, April 26, 1942, p. 35.

29. Pearson and Allen, *Daily Mirror* (New York), February 10, 1942, and April 25, 1942; also, Kenneth Crawford, *P.M.* (New York), April 16, 1942.

30. Kennedy's old antagonist Joe Curran charitably said simply that "shipping czar" was no job for a "defeatist" like Kennedy. Clem Norton, *Telegram-News* (Lynn, Mass.) October 17, 1943. The New York *Daily Worker*, organ of the Communist Party,

discussed Kennedy's job prospects in an article headlined "IS THERE A PLOT AGAINST U.S. SHIPPING?" *Daily Worker*, May 4, 1942.

31. Interview with James Roosevelt, Washington, March 20, 1962.

32. *New York Post*, April 21, 1942, p. 5.

33. *Boston Herald*, August 16, 1942, p. 1. Krock decried "the organized New Deal attack" on his friend. *New York Times*, May 10, 1942. Boake Carter explained that Kennedy's "talents are not wanted by the management of the nation, he told the truth too often." *Daily Mirror* (New York), March 28, 1942, p. 8.

34. Kennedy to Beaverbrook, August 12, 1942, MS. at Beaverbrook Library, London.

35. *Ibid.*

36. James O'Hanlon, *P.M.* (New York), September 15, 1942, p. 13.

37. John Henry Cutler, *"Honey Fitz": Three Steps to the White House*, (Indianapolis, Ind.: Bobbs-Merrill Company, Inc., 1962), p. 295.

38. Kennedy to Beaverbrook, August 12, 1942, MS. at Beaverbrook Library, London.

39. *Boston Herald*, August 23, 1942; *Boston American*, August 31, 1942; and *P.M.* (New York), September 15, 1942, p. 13. Farley's candidate for Governor of New York, John J. Bennett, got the nod.

40. W. E. Mullins, *Boston Herald*, August 23, 1942.

41. O'Hanlon, *P.M.* (New York), September 15, 1942, p. 13.

42. Cutler, *"Honey Fitz,"* p. 296. Kane made similar recitation to the author, April 5, 1962.

43. Cutler, *"Honey Fitz"*, p. 295.

44. Interview with Joseph Kane, Boston, April 5, 1962.

45. Arthur Krock, *Memoirs: Sixty Years on the Firing Line* (New York: Funk & Wagnalls, 1968), p. 357.

46. Kennedy to Beaverbrook, December 31, 1942, MS. at Beaverbrook Library, London.

47. *New York Times*, December 9, 1942, p. 14.

48. Kennedy to Beaverbrook, December 31, 1942, MS. at Beaverbrook Library, London. To substantially the same extent is the *Times-Herald* (Washington), January 3, 1943.

49. *New York Times*, December 9, 1942, p. 14.

50. *St. Louis Post-Dispatch*, January 2, 1943.

51. *Boston Herald*, February 16, 1943.

52. Robert C. Albright, *Chicago Daily Tribune*, April 27, 1943. Halifax, then serving as British Ambassador in Washington, reported the speculation to the Foreign Office, where a minute writer jotted down, "The President would probably be wise to put Joe Kennedy to work somewhere before he goes to work for Farley & Co." FO371/34159/A4148/144/45. It was already too late.

53. Clem Norton, *Telegram-News* (Lynn, Mass.), October 17, 1943.

54. *Boston Herald*, February 21, 1944. Given currency in the *New York Times*, February 22, 1944, p. 40. Also, *New York Sun*, February 22, 1944. The story was quickly denied by all concerned. *New York Times*, February 23, 1944, p. 12.

55. Richard J. Whalen, *Fortune*, January, 1963, p. 160.

56. *Financial Chronicle* (New York), March 11, 1943.

JOE KENNEDY
IN THE POSTWAR WORLD

1. *New York Times*, March 8, 1946, p. 1, and March 14, 1946; p. 11; Doris Fleeson, *New York Post*, March 14, 1946; Lyle C. Wilson, *Boston Globe*, March 14, 1946.

2. *Time*, June 17, 1946, says Kennedy was touted for the post by Democratic National Chairman Robert Hannegan, but that Byrnes nixed Kennedy out of loyalty to the memory of FDR.

3. Wilton Vaugh, *Boston Post*, April 25, 1945, p. 1; *Boston Herald*, May 26, 1945; Joseph F. Dinneen, *Boston Globe*, August 19, 1945, pp. 1, 18; W. E. Playfair, *Boston Herald*, August 19, 1945; *Time*, September 24, 1945, p. 17; *Life*, October 1, 1945, p. 38; Arthur Krock, *New York Times*, November 8, 1945, p. 18. The job was to "sell" the idea of a Department of Commerce throughout the state, a task that Kennedy accepted because of its promise of bringing him in contact with the "grass-roots" business community across Massachusetts, enabling him to scout out political opportunities for his son John, then still in a Navy uniform. Edward M. Gallagher, recorded interview by Ed Martin, January 8, 1965, p. 10, typescript at John F. Kennedy Library, Oral History Program; Robert Healy, *Boston Globe*, November 19, 1969, p. 27.

4. Page 345 *infra*.

5. Page 345 *infra*.

6. Pages 369–70 *infra*.

7. Interview with Dinneen, July 29, 1961.

8. Landis quoted in the *New York Post*, January 10, 1961, p. 25.

9. Joe McCarthy, *The Remarkable Kennedys* (New York: Popular Library, paperback ed., 1960), p. 11.

10. The *Fortune* list is more readily available in the *New York Times*, October 28, 1957, p. 20.

11. Harold Lavine and Jess Stearn, *Newsweek*, September 12, 1960, p. 26; *Pageant*, June, 1962.

12. *Newsweek*, September 12, 1960, p. 29, quotes Reynolds as saying "in New York real estate alone." Mr. Reynolds told the author that his actual estimate had been $100 million in real estate. Interview with John J. Reynolds, New York, May 28, 1962.

13. Interview with Jess Stearn, New York, March 14, 1962. While bargaining for a house in 1960, John Kennedy commented to Fay, "That much for a house and one acre of land! People must still be reading that article in *Fortune*." Paul B. Fay, Jr., *The Pleasure of His Company* (New York: Harper & Row, 1966), p. 246.

14. Fay, *The Pleasure of His Company*, p. 158.

15. While the author was at 230 Park Avenue in the early '60s, a call came in from a Secret Service man: the First Lady had just purchased some horses and wanted to know what address to use in order to minimize taxes on the transaction.

16. Inventory shows Florida real estate valued at $345,000; equity, not "priced" in a ranch in Corpus Christi, Texas, in real estate in Hyannis Port, in Albany's "Standard Building," and in a one-eighth interest in the Merchandise Mart; unvalued oil interests; $36,000 in cash; clothing of approximately $100.00; a Chrysler Imperial later sold for $4,500; "Jewelry consisting of 3 pairs of cufflinks and a Movado Pocket Watch"; accounts receivable of $83,000; and memberships in various golf clubs. Inventory dated

November 4, 1970, Palm Beach County Judge's Court, Vol. 460 at page 629. Kennedy left modest $25,000 bequests to his sisters, Loretta Connelly and Margaret Burke (if they should outlive him, which they did, but otherwise not to their families); to his rich-enough wife he left Albany's "Standard Building" plus a half-million dollars; all the rest, after taxes and costs, he left to the Joseph P. Kennedy, Jr., Foundation. Will dated December 30, 1955, in Clerk's Volume 395 at page 652.

17. Speech in Buffalo, New York, to Catholic clergy; quotation is the *Times*'s paraphrase of Kennedy's comment. *New York Times*, September 25, 1947, p. 32. Fuller report, *New York Herald Tribune*, same day.

18. See Landis' analysis of the trusts in Landis Papers, Box 52, Library of Congress Manuscript Division, Washington, D.C.

19. Reynolds interview.

20. W. Clifford Harvey, *Christian Science Monitor*, May 26, 1943.

21. Reynolds interview.

22. *Christian Science Monitor*, May 26, 1943.

23. *New York Herald Tribune*, June 30, 1943.

24. Leonard Lyons, *New York Post*, September 2, 1948.

25. *New York Times*, July 19, 1945, p. 35.

26. *New York Times*, May 15, 1943, p. 18, reports that Kennedy purchased the largest single block of Hialeah shares.

27. Colonel John R. Stingo, *New York Enquirer*, March 4, 1946.

28. Leonard Lyons, *New York Post*, January 20, 1948.

29. Inventory, Palm Beach County Judge's Court, Vol. 480, p. 629, values Kennedy's interest in the 2,740 acres at $27,319.60.

30. Richard J. Whalen, *Fortune*, January, 1963, p. 167; Whalen, *The Founding Father* (New York: New American Library of World Literature, Inc., 1964), pp. 409–410.

31. Inventory, *op. cit.*

32. Reynolds interview.

33. *Ibid.*

34. *New York Times*, July 22, 1945, p. 35.

35. *Ibid.*, p. 32; *Time*, July 30, 1945, p. 84.

36. Whalen, *Fortune*, January, 1963, p. 162.

37. *New York Times*, September 29, 1944, p. 23, and October 6, 1944, p. 36.

38. *Ibid.*

39. *New York Post*, March 6, 1946.

40. *Chicago Daily Tribune*, September 29, 1944.

41. *New York Times*, October 6, 1944, p. 36.

42. Associated Press story in *Boston Globe* and *Boston Herald*, August 6, 1945.

43. All of the many publicly reported sales and purchases included the line "John J. Reynolds was the broker."

44. Reynolds interview.

45. *New York Post*, March 6, 1946.

46. The principle is fully outlined in William Nickerson's widely read "How-To," *How I Turned $1000 into a Million in Real Estate in My Spare Time* (New York: Simon & Schuster, 1959).

47. *New York Post*, March 6, 1946.

48. Whalen, *Fortune*, January, 1963, p. 111.

49. While other papers later commented, the *New York World-Telegram and Sun* exposed the situation and gave it the fullest coverage. See that paper for October 11, 1957, p. 1; August 18, 1958, p. 17; November 12, 1959, p. 39.

50. Danton Walker, *New York Daily News*, June 21, 1946, p. 37.

51. *New York Post*, January 10, 1961, p. 25, says $8,500,000; Whalen says "some $8,000,000," *Fortune*, January, 1963, p. 167. The author saw an estimate giving the sale price as a mere $5,000,000, but has lost the citation. See also page 53 *supra*, for further account of the sale of Somerset.

52. *New York Times*, January 8, 1946, p. 32.

53. *Peacock Alley*, April, 1946.

54. *New York Times*, October 7, 1943, p. 21.

55. Hedda Hopper, *New York Daily News*, October 8, 1943.

56. Walter Winchell, *Daily Mirror* (New York), September 16, 1946.

57. *New York Post*, June 29, 1942. The State Department asked its Mexico City Embassy to scout out the reports. S.D.MS. 811.503112/201.

58. Landis to Kennedy, June 28, 1949, Landis Papers, Box 51.

59. *Variety*, June 3, 1942; *Motion Picture Hearld*, June 6, 1942; Landis to Kennedy, June 30, 1949, Landis Papers, Box 51.

60. Whalen, *Founding Father*, pp. 411–12, cites unnamed interview.

61. *Ibid.*, p. 411, on *New York Sun* and *Boston Post*.

62. Dinneen interview, July 29, 1961. Kennedy reportedly told a friend, "Economically, Boston is a monopoly newspaper city, like almost every city in this country. The Hearst papers [in Boston] are going to fold within a couple of years and that will leave the *Globe* and *Herald-Traveler* to fight it out. After they've ruined each other, I'll come in and pick up the winner." Edward Linn, "The Truth About Joe Kennedy," *Saga*, July, 1961, p. 88.

63. *The Autobiography of William Zeckendorf* (New York: Holt, Rinehart and Winston, 1970), pp. 162–65.

64. Whalen, *Founding Father*, p. 411, does not cite his source.

65. Stearns interview.

66. The British Catholic Film Institute approved "Baby Doll" for adults only, and it was accepted in Italy on the authority of Fr. John A. Burke of the British Catholic Film Institute. See *New York Times*, December 27, 1956, p. 21; *Variety*, January 2, 1957, p. 5 and January 9, 1957, p. 1.

67. Kennedy was made a Knight of Malta by the Pope in January, 1942. *Boston Herald*, January 3, 1942.

68. The Kennedys generally showed excellent timing for their generosity. During the 1960 Presidential election, a large number of African students were unable to obtain funds for transportation to pursue their studies in the United States. With considerable publicity, the Joseph P. Kennedy, Jr., Foundation supplied the rides. The foundation had been previously unknown for any interest in international relations or African affairs. Its generosity, however, certainly did not cost John Kennedy any black votes or zeal. In 1958, Republican National Chairman, H. Meade Alcorn, made his "too-much-profile, not-enough-courage" speech in Boston, a devastating, carefully documented analysis of John Kennedy's Congressional record. Before the speech was delivered, one Republican National Committee employee predicted, "Jack will not reply in any way, but two weeks later, Joe will donate a huge amount to some charity." And so it came to pass. Interview with H. Meade Alcorn, Hartford, April, 1962. Kennedy's contributions

to "Jewish" charities were most unspectacular, and may or may not have been politically motivated.

69. Hank Searls, *The Lost Prince* (New York: The New American Library, Inc., 1969), p. 178.

70. *Ibid.*, p. 189.

71. *As We Remember Joe*, ed. John F. Kennedy (Cambridge, Mass., University Press, privately printed, 1945), p. 2.

72. Arthur Krock, *Memoirs: Sixty Years on the Firing Line* (New York: Funk & Wagnalls, 1968), pp. 348–49.

73. Searls, pp. 270–71.

74. Edward T. Folliard, *Washington Post*, November 19, 1969, p. A29. Similar comments, with tears, to Bob Considine. *It's All News to Me* (New York: Meredith Press, 1967), pp. 375–82.

75. Searls, *The Lost Prince*, p. 118.

76. Nancy Randolph, *New York Daily News*, December 27, 1940.

77. Gail Cameron, *Rose* (London: Michael Joseph, 1972), p. 139.

78. Whalen, *Founding Father*, pp. 369–70.

79. *Ibid.*, p. 370; Ralph de Toledano, *R.F.K.: The Man Who Would be President* (New York: Putnam's, 1967), p. 32.

80. Cameron, *Rose*, p. 139.

81. Kennedy to Beaverbrook, May 24, 1944, MS. in Beaverbrook Library, London.

82. Kennedy to Beaverbrook, October 23, 1944, MS. in Beaverbrook Library, London.

83. Bookman interview with Kennedy, June 3, 1960, quoted in Whalen, *Founding Father*, p. 92.

84. *Ibid.*

85. Interview with James M. Landis, March 3, 1962.

86. As, no doubt, did tax planning. Philanthropy is a must in modern-day tax planning, sometimes constituting positive financial *advantage* to the rich man and, in any event, not costing the rich man significantly. The minimal personal cost to a rich man of some fabulous charity is a small price to pay for the heaping portion of public admiration and self-satisfaction that it purchases. The Boston Irish laborer who tithes himself to the Church makes real personal sacrifice to charity with his relatively modest contribution.

87. *Boston Globe*, August 12, 1946, p. 1; *New York Times*, August 13, 1946, p. 15.

88. According to *Newsweek*, by 1951, it had already given away $43,000,000; September 12, 1960, p. 30. As of 1956, it had given almost $3,000,000 to the Archdiocese of Boston alone. *Christian Science Monitor*, February 10, 1956. In August, 1960, the foundation made a spectacular grant of $12,000,000 for research into problems of mental retardation. *Chicago Daily Tribune*, August 24, 1960.

89. *Boston Herald*, March 22, 1947.

90. Will dated December 30, 1955, Palm Beach County Judge's Court, Vol. 395, page 652.

91. *The Pilot*, February 11, 1956, reprinted in *Congressional Record*, CII, 2559.

92. *New York Times*, July 28, 1957, p. 48.

93. *Chicago Daily Tribune*, August 24, 1960.

94. *Boston Herald*, September 1, 1951.

95. *New York Times*, August 21, 1951, p. 1; August 23, 1951; August 31, 1951, pp. 22, 39.

96. *Newsweek*, September 12, 1960, p. 27.

97. *New York Times*, August 24, 1960.

98. Interview with the beneficiary.

99. Clem Norton, *Telegram-News* (Lynn, Mass.), April 28, 1953.

100. Whalen includes several in *Founding Father*, pp. 381–83. One of the more commonly reported of such examples was included, uncritically, in a 1963 draft of this book: "When Kennedy was bidding for the old Ziegfeld Theatre, one of the other interested parties asked him to abstain from further bids. It was Billy Rose, showman and one-time secretary to Bernard Baruch. Rose said he wanted the theatre for sentimental reasons. Kennedy dropped out of the bidding." *Newsweek*, September 12, 1960, p. 27. The author removed the anecdote after reading Rose's very different account to the extent that Kennedy told Rose he would abstain from bidding only to throw Rose off the track, and then actually bid higher. On Baruch's advice that Kennedy was not to be trusted, Rose bid higher than he would have had he counted on Kennedy abstaining, and so managed to get the building anyway. Polly Rose Gottlieb, *The Nine Lives of Billy Rose* (New York: Crown Publishers, Inc., 1968), pp. 172–74. Some (but surely not all) of this type of story may be less than fully candid.

101. Landis interview.

FIGHTING
FOR THE OLD ORDER

1. Quoted in Cleveland Amory, *The Last Resorts* (New York: Harper & Brothers, 1952), p. 393.

2. William H. A. Carr, *Those Fabulous Kennedy Women* (New York: Wisdom House, 1961), p. 115.

3. Kennedy to Palmer, March 25 and September 27, 1955, MSS. at Yale University, New Haven, Connecticut. Kennedy regarded Beaver as "a great hustler." In 1956, he established the Lord Beaverbrook Chair of Journalism at Notre Dame, in honor of the Canadian-born Press Lord. Beaverbrook's newspapers, notably the *Express* (London), were in the Hearst-Patterson vein, with crime and scandal taking considerably greater precedence over stories of world developments.

4. Stevenson: Stevenson to Kennedy, June 29, 1954, in Stevenson Papers, Princeton University Library, Princeton, N.J. Baruch: Despite a fawning note from the Ambassador, Baruch declined to give any date on which it would be possible for him to appear, inasmuch as "at his age" he could never know if he'd feel up to anything at any given future time. Kennedy to Baruch, April 8, 1955, in Baruch Papers, Princeton University Library, Princeton, N.J. Perhaps some declined because of the blatant merchandising aspects of the project: the Merchandisers Hall of Fame was situated on the premises of (you guessed it) the Merchandise Mart.

5. Herbert Hoover, *Addresses Upon the American Road, 1950–55* (Stanford, Calif.: Stanford University Press, 1955), pp. 171–72. Even Hoover may have been a little uncomfortable about it. In his address at the Merchandisers Hall of Fame, Hoover mentioned that Kennedy had just contributed $25,000 to Hoover's favorite charity.

6. James A. Fayne, recorded interview by Raymond Henle (for the Hoover

Library), August 8, 1968, p. 8, typescript available also at John F. Kennedy Library, Oral History Program.

7. Edward M. Gallagher, recorded interview by Ed Martin, January 8, 1965, p. 30, typescript at John F. Kennedy Library, Oral History Program. Kennedy apparently made something of a pest of himself with the telephone. See page 366 *supra*, and page 535, note 27, *infra*.

8. The inscription, on a photo of the "Hoover Commission," read "To Joe Kennedy, our greatest member." Fayne oral history typescript, p. 3.

9. Joseph F. Dinneen, *The Kennedy Family* (Boston: Little, Brown and Company, 1959), p. 110.

10. *Ibid.*

11. Speeches reported in *Washington Herald*, October 20, 1946; *Evening Bulletin* (Providence, R.I.), October 31, 1946; *Chicago Herald-American*, November 20, 1946; and, *Chicago Herald-American* January 8, 1948.

12. Reprinted in *Congressional Record*, XCIII, A2488. See also Kennedy statements in *Herald-American* (Chicago), November 20, 1946; *New York Times* or *Chicago Daily Tribune*, both May 19, 1946; and speech reported in *Congressional Record*, XC, A3792.

13. The careers of men like Xerox's Sol M. Linowitz have belied such gloomy forecasts.

14. Speech May 19, 1946, to Illinois Junior Association of Commerce, *New York Times*, May 19, 1946, p. 32, or *Chicago Daily Tribune*, same day.

15. Speech to Boy Scout Commissioners, *New York Times*, October 7, 1945, p. 45; reprinted in full in *Vital Speeches*, November 15, 1945, pp. 88–90.

16. Illinois Junior Association of Commerce speech, *op. cit.*

17. *Boston Traveler*, June 17, 1946, p. 17.

18. *Journal of Commerce* (Chicago), November 21, 1946. Significantly, he did not mention John L. Lewis, a friend of his, by name.

19. Krock, *New York Times*, January 8, 1946, p. 22.

20. Speeches to Illinois Junior Association of Commerce, *op. cit.*, and others reported in *Journal of Commerce* (Chicago), November 21, 1946, and *Evening Bulletin* (Providence, R.I.), October 31, 1946.

21. Ferrel Heady, "The Hoover Commission: A Symposium," *American Political Science Review*, Vol. 43, p. 948. In boosting the "conservationists" in 1951, Congressman Paul W. Shafer told Congress of Kennedy's contributions to the First Commission: "Mr. Kennedy was the activating force in the Hoover plan. . . . (He was) just the man to furnish the string to Mr. Hoover's bow." *Congressional Record*, XCVII, 2207.

22. Kennedy to Landis, October 19, 1951, MS. in Landis Box 51 at Library of Congress Manuscript Division, Washington, D.C.

23. On the First Hoover Commission study of the public power field, Hoover drafted a separate opinion through which ran an undertone of criticism of government participation in the field. Kennedy had concurred in Hoover's special opinion. Frank Gervasi, *Big Government* (New York: Whittlesey House, 1949), pp. 150–51.

24. *New Republic*, May 21, 1956, p. 20. Besides Holifield, the Commission's most frequent dissenters were Republicans Herbert Brownell and Arthur Flemming, joined occasionally by Farley.

25. Interview with a Hoover Commission staff member, Washington, March 22, 1962.

26. *Ibid.*

27. Kennedy's dissent said: "In my opinion, the importance of this program as an instrumentality of our foreign policy has not been sufficiently considered. Although the volume of these loans may be small compared to the volume of total export-import trade, their usefulness in implementing our national policy should not be overlooked." *Report on Lending Agencies* (Washington: Commission on Organization of the Executive Branch of the Government, March, 1955), p. 123. On the balance, Kennedy wanted to trade with the world but take no part in activities which might be classified as "peace-keeping."

28. The task force that gathered the "facts" for this report was composed of 11 members: five bankers; a partner from Price, Waterhouse; the business manager of the *Reader's Digest*; a past president of the United States Chamber of Commerce, and three others.

29. Interview with Hoover Commission staff member.

30. *Washington Post*, May 15, 1955, p. 16. Public reactions to the report followed liberal-conservative cleavages. Conservative columnist George Sokolsky endorsed it while the liberal *Washington Post* found it "difficult to escape Representative Holifield's conclusions." *Ibid.*; also, Sokolsky column in the *Washington Post*, March 25, 1955.

31. *The Times* (London), May 19, 1939, p. 18.

32. Dinneen, *The Kennedy Family*, p. 106.

33. *New York Journal-American*, April 30, 1947, p. 21.

34. Speech of September, 1942, reprinted in *Congressional Record*, XXCVIII, A3467.

35. Complete text in *Boston Globe*, May 23, 1944, p. 13, or *Congressional Record*, XC, A2588.

36. Krock, *New York Times*, May 23, 1944, p. 22. See also editorial comment in *Wall Street Journal*, May 24, 1944, p. 6.

37. Speech of June 12, 1944, reprinted in *Congressional Record*, XC, A3792.

38. Full text in *Boston Sunday Globe*, May 30, 1943, p. 5; also reported in *New York Times*, May 30, 1943, p. 16.

39. *Congressional Record*, XC, 3792.

40. *Boston Globe* (morning edition), October 24, 1945, p. 6.

41. *New York Times*, March 4, 1946, pp. 1, 3.

42. See sentiments along the line of "shoring up British socialism" in Kennedy's speech to the Boy Scout Commissioners, October 6, 1945, in *Vital Speeches*, November 15, 1945, p. 89, and more explicit in his speech to the Illinois Junior Association of Commerce, reported *Chicago Daily Tribune*, May 19, 1946.

43. Hugh Dalton misread the press and took Kennedy's stand as a manifestation of the wish to defeat communist influence, which he attributed to papal influence. Dalton, *High Tide and After: Memoirs, 1945–1960* (London: Frederick Muller Limited, 1962), p. 108.

44. *New York Times*, March 4, 1946, p. 1.

45. *The Times* (London), March 5, 1946, p. 3.

46. Mark Sullivan, *New York Herald Tribune*, March 6, 1946. Sullivan, a prewar isolationist, was favorably disposed to the suggestion.

47. Joseph P. Kennedy, "The U.S. and the World," *Life*, March 18, 1946, pp. 106 ff.

48. *Ibid.*

49. Hearst syndicate article, May 25, 1947, reprinted in *Congressional Record,* XCIII, A2488.

50. Conniff, *New York Journal-American,* April 30, 1947, p. 21.

51. Hearst article of May 25, 1947, *Congressional Record,* XCIII, A2488; also see *Christian Science Monitor,* October 24, 1947.

52. Kennedy's comments on the Marshall Plan were much milder than his comments on the Truman Doctrine. Krock explains that Kennedy became convinced that the nation would adopt a foreign economic aid program of some sort; that being the case, it was best for Kennedy to "go along" with the Marshall Plan and try to add desired safeguards. Krock, *New York Times,* September 4, 1947, IV, 3. Kennedy made numerous statements on or about the Marshall Plan. Germany should be included in Marshall Plan: *Boston Post,* October 24, 1947 (vis-à-vis John Kennedy's contrary position). Skeptical about Marshall Plan and opposed to inclusion of U.S.S.R. while excluding Spain: *Boston Globe,* same day. "Mr. Kennedy is agin' the Plan as a rat-hole expedient destined to drain away the resources America may yet sorely need": Frank Conniff, *New York Journal-American,* March 26, 1948, p. 17. Kennedy on European study tour of Marshall Plan operation: William J. Humphreys, *New York Herald Tribune,* April 24, 1948; Charles A. Merrill, *Sunday Globe* (Boston), April 25, 1948; Bill Cunningham, *Boston Herald,* April 25, 1948; Grace Davidson, *Boston Post,* April 27 and 30, 1948. General disapproval: Robert S. Allen, *New York Journal-American,* June 13, 1948, reprinted in *Congressional Record,* XCIV A3913.

It was Joseph Kennedy who designed the family strategy, employed by all of his sons, of making foreign tours as a ploy to obtain bigger and better press coverage at home.

53. *Pic,* October, 1948, pp. 31 ff., reported in some detail in *Chicago Daily Tribune,* September 21, 1948.

54. Kennedy might have said that Southern Africa was controlled by people whose support for the United States and for the capitalistic system was unquestionable. But he erred when he identified the Boers of the Union of South Africa, the Belgians of the Congo, the White Supremecists of the Rhodesias, the Portuguese of Angola and Mozambique, as "friendly to democratic ideals." Only one to whom "democracy" had become a near-synonym for "capitalism" could have made such an error in diction.

55. Asserted by Danton Walker, *New York Daily News,* January 24, 1951, and confirmed by Dean Landis in interview, March 3, 1962.

56. Reprinted in full in *Vital Speeches,* January 1, 1951, pp. 170 ff.

57. Kennedy closed his Hearst syndicate article with speculation that his comments would bring "name calling." For such a widely circulated piece, it brought surprisingly little attention. The author saw only one editorial comment, though that one bore out Kennedy's prediction of name-calling: "The point most salient in Mr. Kennedy's long article is that he has no moral responsibility. That is not news to us. There is nothing in his background to indicate that anything but money and what can be had with money ever motivated the whiz from Boston. . . . The Fitzgeralds, the Curleys, and the Kennedys of Boston would not know anything about international obligations or moral obligations. Outside of their own family relationship there is no glaring evidence that they and their kind of get-rich-quicks know anything about any kind of morals. . . . Mr. Kennedy is either intellectually dishonest and/or fearfully ignorant of almost everything except how to negotiate a deal as an investment banker. It

is this kind of ignoramus with an ignorant political following that can mess up American foreign policy. . . . If we take Mr. Kennedy's advice, the Politburo will have all Europe and Asia with which to fight us. If we give them all that, the last great war will be inevitable." *Argonaut* (San Francisco), May 30, 1947.

58. See *New York Times*, December 18, 1950, p. 15.

59. *New York Daily News*, December 19, 1950.

60. *Daily Mirror* (New York), editorial, December 13, 1950.

61. *New York Journal-American* editorial, December 18, 1950, p. 18.

62. Lippmann criticized both the Kennedy and Truman approaches, *New York Herald-Tribune*, December 19, 1950.

63. *Wall Street Journal*, December 14, 1950, p. 10.

64. *Wall Street Journal*, December 20, 1950, p. 10. The same day, the *New York Times* reported that letters were running ten-to-one in favor of Acheson's aid-and-containment policy. See *U.S. News and World Reports*, December 29, 1950, p. 12, for comment on the comments.

65. *New York Herald Tribune*, December 24, 1950, II, 27.

66. *Congressional Record*, XCVI, 16513, 16515.

67. *Ibid.*, p. A7909. A lot Rankin would have known.

68. *Ibid.*, XCVII, A2207.

69. *Wall Street Journal*, December 22, 1950, p. 4; December 27, 1950, p. 4; December 28, 1950, p. 6.

70. Americans were largely unaware of Britain's war against communism in Malaya, or France's war in Indo-China.

71. The speech is printed in Hoover's *Addresses Upon The American Road*, pp. 3–10. Also *New York Times*, December 21, 1950.

72. *Life*, January 8, 1951, pp. 12–13.

73. *New York Journal-American*, April 21, 1951.

74. *Boston American*, May 14 and May 15, 1951; *Boston Globe*, May 21, 1951.

75. *New York Times*, December 18, 1951, p. 4; *Sun-Times* (Chicago) December 18, 1951, p. 5.

76. *New York Journal-American*, December 19, 1951, p. 28.

77. *New York Daily News*, December 30, 1951, p. 11C.

78. *Chicago Daily Tribune*, December 20, 1951.

79. *Evening Star* (Washington), December 31, 1951, p. A10.

80. Typical was the *Boston Herald* editorial, December 19, 1951, p. 30: "Mr. Kennedy is seductive in his argument, because he is a little right . . . Yet on the total problem, Mr. Kennedy is wrong."

81. Kennedy kept up a personal debate with the Chicago *Sun-Times* for some time after the speech. See the *Sun-Times* editorial pages of December 19, 1951, January 5, 1952, January 10, 1952, and January 18, 1952.

82. Article for the Hearst syndicate, May 25, 1947, reprinted in *Congressional Record*, XCIII, A2488.

83. Speech to Illinois Junior Association of Commerce, *Chicago Daily Tribune* and *New York Times*, May 19, 1946.

84. Hearst syndicate article, May 25, 1947, *op. cit.*

85. *Congressional Record*, XXCVII, A2492, A2510.

86. Hearst syndicate article, May 25, 1947, *op. cit.*

87. *Pic*, October, 1948.

88. Kennedy letters to Paul Palmer, MSS., Yale University, New Haven, Conn.

89. Hanson W. Baldwin, "Dissection of the 'Fortress America' Idea," *New York Times Magazine*, August 17, 1952, pp. 7, 54.

90. *Ibid.*, p. 54; Samuel Lubell, *Revolt of the Moderates* (New York: Harper & Brothers, 1956), p. 46.

91. Quoted by Baldwin, *New York Times Magazine*, August 17, 1952, p. 55.

92. Selig Adler, *The Isolationist Impulse: Its Twentieth-Century Reaction* (London: Abelard-Schuman Limited, 1957), p. 95.

93. *Partisan Review*, May-June, 1947, pp. 233–34, 240. Schlesinger identified Joseph Kennedy in his article as "That *doyen* of American capitalists," and asserted that Kennedy exemplified the "death wish."

94. It is ironic that some 20 years later, many of the same arguments which Joseph Kennedy expressed against internationalist foreign policy were used with more telling effect against the specific military application of it by the advisors and successors of President John F. Kennedy. What is a perversion of a policy orientation, and what is its "logical" conclusion?

95. *Boston Post*, October 24, 1947, p. 12.

96. Krock, *New York Times*, March 12, 1947, p. 18.

97. Cleveland Amory, *The Proper Bostonians* (New York: E. P. Dutton & Co., Inc., 1947), p. 346. It is interesting that Kennedy avoided typically "Irish" names for his sons. He had very great respect for his father Pat, and the family is famed for its closeness. One of his sons was named for Honey and one for himself, but he named none of his sons in honor of his own beloved father. Nor were there any Kevins, Brians, or even a Michael. Rather, he chose Joseph, John, Robert, and Edward. Four less imaginative names could hardly be found, nor could four names more typically "American" be found.

The choice of names probably also had something to do with social acceptability. Kennedy always felt his social position was insecure, and probably wanted to spare his children social difficulties by giving them "American" names. In 1963 John Kennedy was the first of Joe's sons to use the name Patrick, which he gave to his second and short-lived son. By then the social position of the Kennedy's was secure and few questioned the President's Americanism.

98. As Ambassador, Joseph Kennedy always insisted on doing things "American" from the day when he wore trousers to present his credentials. Though he himself had a high appreciation of things gourmet, he served typical American food to embassy visitors, rather than the French cuisine to which the diplomatic circles were accustomed. The menus were printed in English, rather than French, another violation of diplomatic tradition. When he left England, the editorial that pleased Kennedy the most was the London *Times*' assertion that he had "remained an American."

99. Adler, *The Isolationist Impulse*, p. 298.

100. Schlesinger grouped Kennedy with the "fellow travelers" and inferred that there was little meaningful difference between them. *Partisan Review*, May-June, 1947, pp. 234, 240.

101. Interview with a former McCarthy aide, Washington, March 27, 1962.

102. Ralph G. Martin and Ed Plaut, *Front Runner, Dark Horse* (Garden City, N.Y.: Doubleday & Company, Inc., 1960), p. 202.

103. Interview with McCarthy aide.

104. Roy Cohn, *McCarthy* (New York: The New American Library, 1968), p. 66.

105. Arthur Krock, *Memoirs: Sixty Years on the Firing Line* (New York: Funk & Wagnalls, 1968), p. 343.

106. Drew Pearson cited in Fred J. Cook, *The Nightmare Decade* (New York: Random House, 1971), p. 283.

107. Cohn, *McCarthy*, p. 66.

108. *Ibid.*, p. 48.

109. Mr. and Mrs. John H. Kelso, recorded interview by John F. Stewart, September 6, 1967, typescript at John F. Kennedy Library, Oral History Program.

110. Irwin Ross, *New York Post*, January 12, 1961, p. 25. Not surprisingly, Joseph Kennedy denied the story cold. *Ibid.*

111. Irwin Ross, *New York Post Magazine*, January 9, 1961, p. 1.

112. Kennedy to Beaverbrook, December 18, 1943, MS. at Beaverbrook Library, London.

113. *New York Times*, October 27, 1944, p. 1. See also, William D. Hassett, *Off the Record with F.D.R., 1942–1945* (New Brunswick, N.J.: Rutgers University Press, 1958), pp. 23, 284. Thomas Pappas, a sixty-year friend of Kennedy and erstwhile Republican National Committeeman from Massachusetts told the author that he had heard from "thoroughly reliable sources" that Kennedy contributed to Dewey in 1944. Interview with Mr. Pappas, Boston, April 3, 1962. James Roosevelt told the author that he thought it unlikely that Kennedy would have failed to contribute to Dewey that year. Interview with James Roosevelt, Washington, March 20, 1962.

114. *Boston Herald*, April 16, 1945, p. 3.

115. A Kennedy eulogy (of sorts) is in *Evening Star* (Washington), April 13, 1945. With time, Kennedy's feelings toward Roosevelt so hardened that when his sons' friend Kenny O'Donnell offered vigorous defense of Roosevelt at the dinner table, Kennedy became deeply angered. Arthur M. Schlesinger, Jr., *A Thousand Days: John F. Kennedy in the White House* (Boston: Houghton Mifflin Company, 1965), p. 93.

116. Kennedy to Beaverbrook, May 13, 1946, MS. at Beaverbrook Library, London.

117. Doris Fleeson, *New York Post*, March 14, 1946, p. 7.

118. *Washington Herald*, October 20, 1946.

119. *New York Daily News*, January 10, 1947.

120. *New York Journal-American*, March 4, 1947, p. 8.

121. Krock, *New York Times*, January 14, 1952, p. 1.

122. Interview with James M. Landis, March 3, 1962.

123. Thomas Pappas told the author that "he understood" that Kennedy again helped the Dewey forces financially. Interview.

124. Kennedy to Beaverbrook, March 23, 1948, MS. at Beaverbrook Library, London.

125. Quoted in *Standard-Times* (New Bedford, Mass.), July 31, 1953. Basil Brewer, head of the *Standard-Times* was a Bob Taft Democrat and a friend of Kennedy.

126. Quoted in *Newsweek*, September 12, 1960, p. 29.

127. O'Donnell, *New York Daily News*, December 20, 1951, p. 4.

128. *Chicago Daily Tribune*, December 20, 1951, reprinted in John O'Donnell, *New York Daily News*, December 21, 1951.

129. Knickerbocker, *New York Journal-American*, February 5, 1952.

130. Kennedy's longtime business associate James Fayne says, "In spite of the fact that his sons have always been representatives of the Democratic party, (Kennedy)

himself was without party designation. I'd say he was almost without national designation." James A. Fayne, recorded interview by Raymond Henle (for the Hoover Library), August 8, 1968, p. 1, typescript also available at the John F. Kennedy Library, Oral History Program.

131. Arthur Krock, recorded interview by Charles Bartlett, May 10, 1964, p. 15, typescript at John F. Kennedy Library, Oral History Program.

132. Stevenson apparently never understood Kennedy's support for him, and incorrectly attributed John Kennedy's reserve towards himself to the fact that "Joe Kennedy hated me because of his Catholicism." Harry Golden, *The Right Time* (New York: Putnam's, 1969), p. 286.

133. Kennedy to Beaverbrook, September 6, 1952, MS. at Beaverbrook Library, London. The author was surprised that no copy of this letter appears in the Stevenson letter files at Princeton University.

134. *Ibid.*

135. Landis interview. At the same time, Kennedy led Republican friends to think he was quietly backing their candidate. Pappas interview.

136. Kennedy speeches at Boston Latin School Association and the Oysterville, Mass. Rotary Club, *Boston Herald*, November 25, 1952, and *Standard-Times* (New Bedford, Mass.), November 27, 1952.

137. Hal Foust, *Chicago Sunday Tribune*, February 15, 1953, I, 2.

138. *New York Times*, January 14, 1956, p. 1.

139. Interview with Dr. James Killian, Jr., Cambridge, Mass., April 6, 1962.

140. Bill Cunningham, *Boston Herald*, April 7, 1957.

141. Landis interview.

THE
FAMILY

1. Whalen quotes an unnamed Kennedy intimate as saying that Kennedy "had the progenitor's sense; to him, his children were an extension of himself. Therefore, what he did, he did with them always in mind. He played the game differently than if he had been after something entirely for himself." Richard J. Whalen, "Joseph P. Kennedy: A Portrait of the Founder," *Fortune*, January, 1963, p. 111. According to sociologist Hazel Kyrk, "Self-interest is not, as is commonly said, the motivation for economic endeavor but family interest. It is not so much love for self as love for one's children that is the obstacle to the application of the golden rule." Hazel Kyrk, *The Family in the American Economy* (Chicago: University of Chicago Press, 1957), pp. 12–17.

2. John Griffin, *Boston Sunday Post*, July 1, 1934.

3. *The Secret Diary of Harold L. Ickes*, Vol. 1: *The First Thousand Days, 1933–1936* (3 Vols., New York: Simon & Schuster, 1953), I, 173.

4. *Literary Digest*, December 25, 1937, p. 6.

5. Fletcher Knebel, "Pulitzer Prize Entry—John F. Kennedy," *Candidates 1960*, editor Eric Sevareid (New York: Basic Books, Inc., 1959), p. 183.

6. See note 1, *supra*.

7. See Laski's essay in *As We Remember Joe*, ed. John F. Kennedy (Cambridge, Mass.: University Press, privately printed, 1945), pp. 43–44.

8. Hank Searls, *The Lost Prince* (New York: The New American Library, Inc., 1969), p. 88.

9. *Ibid.*, pp. 102 ff.

10. Harold Laski in *As We Remember Joe*, p. 43; Searls, *The Lost Prince*, pp. 75, 77.

11. Searls, *The Lost Prince*, p. 169; see page 568 note 8, *supra*.

12. *New York Herald-Tribune*, December 18, 1940, p. 2; *Newsweek*, December 30, 1940, p. 9; *New York Times*, January 7, 1941, p. 7.

13. Searls, *The Lost Prince*, p. 171.

14. *Ibid.*, p. 122. For Joe Junior on Jews see also Searls, p. 123, and Laski in *As We Remember Joe*, p. 44.

15. Searls, *The Lost Prince*, pp. 183–84.

16. Searls, *passim*.

17. *Ibid.*, p. 93.

18. *Ibid.*, pp. 40, 61.

19. *Ibid.*

20. *Ibid.*, p. 99

21. *Ibid.*, p. 63.

22. *Ibid.*, pp. 95, 115.

23. *Ibid.*, pp. 183, 239; Frank More O'Ferrall in *As We Remember Joe*, pp. 65–66.

24. Searls, pp. 93, 120.

25. *Ibid.*, p. 211.

26. *Ibid.*, pp. 166, 181.

27. *Ibid.*, p. 74.

28. *Ibid.*, p. 181.

29. Edgar Ansel Mowrer, *Triumph and Turmoil* (New York: Weybright and Talley, 1968), p. 289.

30. Timothy J. Reardon, in *As We Remember Joe*, pp. 13–14.

31. Frankfurter, recorded interview by Charles McLaughlin (Landis' son-in-law), June 10, 1964, p. 5, typescript at John F. Kennedy Library, Oral History Program.

32. Joe McCarthy, *The Remarkable Kennedys* (New York: Popular Library, paperback ed., 1960), pp. 16–17.

33. Father Maurice Sheehy in *As We Remember Joe*, p. 36.

34. For Joe Junior and Teddy, see Searls, *The Lost Prince*, p. 117.

35. *Ibid.*, p. 168; cf. John F. Kennedy in *As We Remember Joe*, pp. 1–2.

36. Kirk to Joseph P. Kennedy, Jr., April 8, 1941, MS. in Kirk Papers, Naval History Division, Washington Navy Yard, Washington, D.C.

37. Searls, *The Lost Prince*, pp. 193, 212, 257.

38. *Ibid.*, p. 223.

39. *Ibid.*, p. 181.

40. *Ibid.*, pp. 202–203.

41. *The Times* (London), October 25, 1945, p. 3.

42. Kennedy to Grace Tully, August 29, 1944, MS. at Roosevelt Library, Hyde Park, N.Y., in President's Personal File 207.

43. McCarthy, *The Remarkable Kennedys*, p. 81.

44. *Ibid.*, p. 79; Bob Considine, *It's All News to Me* (New York: Meredith Press, 1967), pp. 375–82.

45. Family friend Dinah Bridge recalls: "One more episode which stands out vividly in my memory is the morning that Eunice rang up and said Kick (Kathleen) was

dead, and would I go round. As far as I remember, Eunice, Pat and Jack were there and there was a grim, tragic restlessness about the atmosphere, with the gramophone playing, and a closing-in of the ranks of family and friends, but no emotional collapse. There was a disciplinary fortitude about them and inborn courage." Dinah Bridge recorded interview by Joseph E. O'Connor, October 30, 1966, p. 12, typescript at John F. Kennedy Library, Oral History Program.

46. Dinneen, *Boston Globe* (morning edition), May 28, 1948, p. 3.

47. Bridge oral history typescript, p. 2.

48. Kennedy to Beaverbrook, July 27, 1948, MS. at Beaverbrook Library, London.

49. *Standard Times* (New Bedford, Mass.), September 12, 1943.

50. Harold H. Martin, "The Amazing Kennedys," *Saturday Evening Post*, September 7, 1957, pp. 19, 48.

51. *Collected Papers of Sigmund Freud* (1914), IV, 48.

52. Another Freudian concept. *Ibid.*

53. McCarthy, *The Remarkable Kennedys*, p. 28.

54. Searls, *The Lost Prince*, p. 107.

55. T. J. Hamilton, *New York Times*, June 9, 1939, VII, 6.

56. FO371/24139/W2642/103/41.

57. *New York Times*, February 17, 1939, p. 8.

58. *Boston Herald*, February 24, 1939.

59. Thurston to Hull, April 11, 1939, S.D.MS. 123 Kennedy, Joseph P./187.

60. Feis to Arthur M. Schlesinger, Jr., May 23, 1966, MS. in Feis Papers, Box 20, File "Kennedy, John F.," at Library of Congress Manuscript Division, Washington, D.C.

61. Kennedy to Arthur Bliss Lane (United States Ambassador to Yugoslavia), June 16, 1939, MS. at Yale University, New Haven, Conn.

62. *For the President, Personal and Secret: Correspondence Between Franklin D. Roosevelt and William C. Bullitt*, ed. Orville H. Bullitt (Boston: Houghton Mifflin Company, 1972), p. 273.

63. George F. Kennan, *Memoirs, 1925–1950* (Boston: Little, Brown and Company, 1967), pp. 91–92.

64. Frankfurter to Kennedy, January 8, 1938, MS. in Frankfurter Papers, Library of Congress Manuscript Division, Washington, D.C.

65. Harry Henry, *Boston Globe* (evening edition), December 3, 1938, p. 10.

66. *New York Times*, January 24, 1939, p. 12.

67. Rex Leeper to Victor Perowne, October 16, 1939, FO371/22817/A7270, p. 270.

68. Jan Wszelaki memorandum of conversation with Kennedy on June 16, 1939, *Polish Documents Relative to the Origin of the War*, 1st series (Berlin: Auswartiges Amt, 1940) #3, pp. 42–43. At the time of publication of the Polish Documents, many doubted their authenticity. Joseph Kennedy did not. In the first draft of the Landis MS., Dean Landis would have Kennedy explain, "With considerable paternal pride, I had sent some of young Joe's observations to the President, and I could easily have bragged about the interest that I thought the President took in them." Landis MS., Chap. 41, p. 12. This line was edited out of the later draft of the Landis MS., perhaps by the sensitive Krock, who did some revisions after Landis was through.

69. T. J. Hamilton, *New York Times*, June 4, 1939, VII, 6.

70. Fayne to Landis, August 22, 1951, Landis Papers, Box 51, at Library of Congress Manuscript Division, Washington, D.C.

71. Theodore H. White, *The Making of the President, 1960* (New York: Atheneum, 1961), p. 5; Cleveland Amory, *The Last Resorts* (New York: Harper & Brothers, 1952), p. 373.

72. Gail Cameron, *Rose* (London: Michael Joseph, 1972), pp. 41, 66.

73. McCarthy, *The Remarkable Kennedys*, p. 13.

74. *Parents Magazine*, September, 1939, pp. 26, 62.

75. James MacGregor Burns, *John Kennedy: A Political Profile* (New York: Harcourt, Brace & Company, 1959), pp. 24–27.

76. *Ibid.*, p. 44.

77. D. W. Brogan, *Politics in America* (New York: Harper & Brothers, 1954), p. 109.

78. McCarthy, *The Remarkable Kennedys*, p. 72. A "real" Brahmin with whom the author spoke tossed off that Dever's characterization was "a contradiction in terms," as she plucked withered petals from her huge potted geraniums. Interview, September 20, 1973.

79. Bill Cunningham, *Boston Herald*, May 20, 1948, p. 30. Kennedy apparently subscribed to the continental concept of the aristocracy running the government.

80. *Ibid.*

81. Speech to the Providence, R.I. Chamber of Commerce, in the *Providence Bulletin*, October 31, 1946, p. 1.

82. Joseph P. Kennedy, *I'm For Roosevelt* (New York: Reynal & Hitchcock, 1936), p. 3.

83. William H. A. Carr, *Those Fabulous Kennedy Women* (New York: Wisdom House, Inc., paperback ed., 1961), p. 141.

84. *Time*, February 16, 1962, p. 19.

85. Victor Lasky, *Robert F. Kennedy: The Myth and the Man* (New York: Trident Press, 1968), p. 67.

86. Mary Barelli Gallagher, *My Life with Jacqueline Kennedy*, ed. Frances Spatz Leighton (New York: David McKay Company, Inc., 1969), p. 162.

87. Cameron, *Rose*, pp. 175–76, apparently in reliance on Gallagher.

88. Frank L. Kluckhohn, *America: Listen!* (Derby, Conn.: Monarch Books, Inc., paperback ed., 1961), p. 56.

89. Cameron, *Rose*, p. 209.

90. *Ibid.*, p. 208. The parallels between the careers and life-styles of Onassis and Joseph Kennedy are obvious.

91. Carr, *Those Fabulous Kennedy Women*, pp. 99–100.

92. Sue Seay, "A New Mrs. Kennedy in Washington," *Look*, February 26, 1963, p. 25.

93. Harold H. Martin, *Saturday Evening Post*, September 7, 1957, pp. 19, 46–47. See also the parallel thought in Victor Navasky, *Kennedy Justice* (New York: Atheneum, 1971), p. 330.

94. Harold Martin, *op. cit.*, pp. 46–47.

95. Ed DeBlasio, *Photoplay*, August, 1962, p. 93.

96. Interview with Landis, March 3, 1962; Burns, pp. 160–61.

97. Landis Papers, Box 50, File "Kennedy, Eunice," at Library of Congress Manuscript Division, Washington, D.C.

98. Theodore C. Sorensen, *Kennedy* (New York: Harper & Row, 1965), p. 91.

99. Alsop, "What Made Teddy Run?," *Saturday Evening Post*, October 27, 1962, p. 17.

100. Lasky, *R.F.K.*, p. 128.

101. Burns, *John Kennedy*, pp. 92–93. Burns interprets Kennedy's refusal to cooperate with Curley's backers as a manifestation of John Kennedy's "distaste for the Curley element in the party," but John Kennedy's distaste for the boss-element was never operative against Bronx Boss Buckley or Chicago Mayor Daley.

102. McCarthy, *The Remarkable Kennedys*, p. 130. John Kennedy, however, tried not to inherit his father's press enemies and was on good terms with both Louis Lyons (page 300 *supra*) and Joseph Alsop (page 354 *supra*), two influential journalists who were hostile to his father. Joseph Kennedy always stressed the importance of good press relations and would have been the first to condone his son's relations with the two.

103. *Life*, January 26, 1962, p. 82.

104. Lasky, *R.F.K.*, pp. 175–76.

105. Landis interview.

106. William O. Douglas, recorded interview by John F. Stewart, November 9, 1967, p. 8, typescript at John F. Kennedy Library, Oral History Program.

107. Page 366 *supra*.

108. Robert A. Leston, *Sargent Shriver: A Candid Portrait* (New York: Farrar, Straus & Co., no date, but prior to Shriver's emergency of 1972), p. 59.

109. Lasky, *R.F.K.*, p. 129.

110. Arthur Krock, recorded interview by Charles Bartlett, May 10, 1964, p. 20, typescript at John F. Kennedy Library, Oral History Program.

111. *Ibid.*, p. 21.

112. Cardinal Spellman was confronted with a parallel problem. His history of intimacy with Joseph Kennedy parallelled Krock's, but he was charged with the duty of furthering the interests of his own constituency, and on "Catholic" issues he had every reason to suspect that Protestant Nixon would be more solicitous of the Church's position than Catholic Kennedy, who would be apt to take the Church "for granted." Ultimately the Cardinal permitted himself to be photographed during the campaign with President Eisenhower and Jack's opponent, Richard Nixon. There ended his lifelong friendship with Joseph P. Kennedy.

113. *New York Times*, September 21, 1962. This author does not entirely subscribe to Reston's column. Reston says that John Kennedy generally adhered to the policy of appointing on the basis of competence, making his departure from that policy for the family more blatant. He cites the Cabinet appointments and Kennedy's ambassadorial appointments as examples. Both could certainly be argued. Kennedy's appointments to federal judgeships numbered among the least able in a century, with a healthy sprinkling of nods going to plain old party hacks. On the whole, Eisenhower's judicial appointees were men of greater legal competence.

114. Stephen Hess, *America's Political Dynasties from Adams to Kennedy* (Garden City, N.Y.: Doubleday & Company, Inc., 1966), p. 515.

115. John Henry Cutler, *"Honey Fitz": Three Steps to the White House* (Indianapolis, Ind.: The Bobbs-Merrill Company, Inc., 1962), pp. 104–105.

116. Dan Wakefield, *Esquire*, April, 1962, p. 128.

117. McCarthy, *The Remarkable Kennedys*, p. 110.

118. D. W. Brogan, *Punch*, April 17, 1963, p. 546; Francis Williams, *Punch*, May 15, 1963, p. 691.

119. *Saturday Evening Post*, October 27, 1962, p. 16.

120. Sorensen, *Kennedy*, p. 34.

121. Private source.

122. Kluckhohn, *America: Listen!*, p. 28.

123. Marguerite Higgins, *McCalls*, May, 1960, p. 104.

124. Landis interview.

125. *Time*, July 5, 1963, p. 20. Other comments on Shriver based principally on Leston, *Sargent Shriver: A Candid Portrait.*

126. Eunice certainly needed no help in attracting a husband. Hers is a dignified and mature, womanly beauty, like that of Katherine Hepburn. Her social-service work has been more meaningful than that of the other Kennedy women, who have generally devoted their efforts to projects of remote social utility. Eunice did social work in a federal prison for women; she helped the Sisters of Good Shepherd in their work with unwed mothers; she participated in Justice Department studies of juvenile delinquency.

127. Leston, *Sargent Shriver*, p. 59.

128. Says Joan Kennedy, quoted in *Time*, September 28, 1962, p. 15.

129. Cameron, *Rose*, p. 95.

130. McCarthy, *The Remarkable Kennedys*, p. 23.

131. Myra MacPherson, *Washington Post*, November 19, 1969, Section B, p. 1.

132. Victor Lasky, *J.F.K.: The Man and the Myth* (New York: The Macmillan Company, 1963), p. 457.

133. Burns, *John Kennedy*, p. 26.

134. McCarthy, *The Remarkable Kennedys*, p. 24.

135. Burns, *John Kennedy*, pp. 26–27.

136. Jack Newfield, *Robert Kennedy: A Memoir* (New York: E. P. Dutton & Co., Inc., 1969), p. 42.

137. Ralph Horton Jr., recorded interview by Joseph Dolan, June 1, 1964, typescript at John F. Kennedy Library, Oral History Program.

138. McCarthy, *The Remarkable Kennedys*, pp. 43–44.

139. See, for example, *New York Times*, January 20, 1935, IV, 7.

140. See *Business Week*, July 14, 1934, p. 20.

141. Joseph F. Dinneen, *The Kennedy Family* (Boston: Little, Brown and Co., 1959), p. 110.

142. Baruch's remembrances of Joseph Kennedy, Sr., dated January 26, 1965, written for inclusion in *The Fruitful Bough*, MS. in Baruch Papers, Princeton University Library, Princeton, N.J.

143. Kennedy to Frankfurter, July 31, 1934, in Frankfurter Papers, Library of Congress Manuscript Division, Washington, D.C.

144. Landis interview.

145. Denis W. Brogan, *Esquire*, November, 1969, p. 163.

146. Searls, *The Lost Prince*, p. 72.

147. *Ibid.*, p. 79.

148. Kay Halle, recorded interview by William M. McHugh, February 7, 1967, p. 3, typescript at John F. Kennedy Library, Oral History Program.

149. Krock oral history typescript, p. 10. Alfred Steinberg recounts this anecdote:

while Joseph Kennedy and Senator George Aiken were serving together on the First Hoover Commission in the late 1940s, Kennedy confided to Aiken that Jack hoped to make a political career beyond the House of Representatives. Aiken, with a wry smile, asked what advice the reactionary isolationist had given his thirty-year-old son. "I told him," the patriarch replied, "Just stand for everything your old man's against and you might even become President." Alfred Steinberg, *Sam Johnson's Boy* (New York: The Macmillan Company, 1968), p. 585. He did and he did.

150. Rose Kennedy, recorded interview by Raymond Henle (for the Hoover Library), February 1, 1968, p. 18, typescript available at John F. Kennedy Library, Oral History Program.

151. London: Michael Joseph, 1972.

152. Comments on handwriting based on round-table discussion with handwriting expert Dan Anthony and Associates, New York, October 11, 1972.

153. Cameron, *Rose*, p. 173.

154. Phrase "iron hand in a velvet glove" borrowed from Florence Anthony of the New School. Cameron quotes Pierre Salinger as describing Rose as "half Irish charm and all business." *Rose*, p. 216.

155. Cameron, *Rose*, p. 35.

156. *Ibid.*, pp. 163, 169–70.

157. Burns, *John Kennedy*, p. 21.

158. Cameron, *Rose*, p. 20.

159. Burns, *John Kennedy*, p. 25.

160. See, for example, Cameron, *Rose*, p. 20.

161. Luella R. Hennessey, *Good Housekeeping*, August, 1961.

162. Cameron, *Rose*, p. 172.

163. *Boston Post*, December 17, 1951, reprinted in *Congressional Record*, IIC, A17.

164. Cameron, *Rose*, p. 42.

165. McCarthy, *The Remarkable Kennedys*, p. 43.

166. See his somewhat superficial article, "What My Religion Means to Me," *Miami Herald*, March 11, 1952, p. 1.

167. Arthur Krock, *Memoirs: Sixty Years On the Firing Line* (New York: Funk & Wagnalls, 1968), pp. 353–54.

168. Krock, oral history typescript, p. 9.

169. Burns, *John Kennedy*, p. 21.

170. Ralph G. Martin and Ed Plaut, *Front Runner, Dark Horse* Garden City, N.Y.: Doubleday & Company, Inc., 1960), p. 177.

171. Cameron, *Rose*, p. 159.

172. Kluckhohn, *America: Listen!*, p. 51, quotes *Life*.

173. Speech in Hartford, Conn. during the campaign. Teddy's opponent, Republican George Lodge, never did make his position clear on the French-Canadian issue.

174. Cameron, *Rose*, p. 156.

175. Lasky, *R.F.K.*, p. 404, cites *Chicago Daily Tribune*, May 11, 1968; slightly different in David Halberstam, *The Unfinished Odyssey of Robert Kennedy* (New York: Bantam Books, 1969), p. 172.

176. Cameron, *Rose*, p. 207.

177. *Ibid.*, p. 173.

178. *Ibid.*, p. 104.

179. *Ibid.*, p. 194.

180. The author saw a letter from Mrs. Kennedy to Beaverbrook saying that she would prefer that his papers "leave her out."

181. Cameron, *Rose*, p. 86.

182. Mrs. George H. DePinto, in *As We Remember Joe*, p. 25.

183. McCarthy, *The Remarkable Kennedys*, p. 15.

184. Henry R. Luce, recorded interview by John L. Steele, November 11, 1965, p. 8, typescript at John F. Kennedy Library, Oral History Program. An embassy associate recalls that when the Kennedys entertained in London, they showed movies after dinner, and "Englishmen enjoy after-dinner conversation; they're not interested in seeing some movie that they wouldn't pay two-and-six to see." Interview, September 20, 1973.

185. Horton, oral history typescript, pp. 3–4.

186. *Newsweek*, September 12, 1960, p. 30.

187. Landis interview.

188. Burns, *John Kennedy*, p. 196.

189. There are countless examples of paternal morale boosting in the Kennedy literature. See, for example, Paul B. Fay, Jr., *The Pleasure of His Company* (New York: Harper & Row, 1966), p. 9; Sorensen, *Kennedy*, p. 31; Lasky, *R.F.K.*, p. 171.

190. Arthur Schlesinger Jr.'s article in *Randolph Churchill: The Young Unpretender*, ed. Kay Halle (London: Heineman, 1971), p. 282.

191. Ray Moley, who knew them all, says that the sons were but "pale progeny" of their father in personal force and determination. *The First New Deal* (New York: Harcourt, Brace & World, 1966), p. 379.

192. Interview, London, July 17, 1972.

193. Edward M. Gallagher, recorded interview by Ed Martin, January 8, 1965, p. 17, typescript at John F. Kennedy Library, Oral History Program; or, in his often quoted comment, "I happen to be the most average guy in this whole damned outfit." McCarthy, *The Remarkable Kennedys*, p. 143; different phrasing, Sorensen, *Kennedy*, p. 32.

FATHER AND SONS

1. See the charming letter from Jack at fifteen to Jeffrey Roche, reproduced in Charles Hamilton, *The Robot That Helped to Make a President* (New York: privately printed, 1965), p. 39.

2. Classmate Ralph Horton, Jr., a fellow "Mucker," recorded interview by Joseph Dolan, June 1, 1964, p. 5, typescript at the John F. Kennedy Library, Oral History Program.

3. James MacGregor Burns, *John Kennedy: A Political Profile* (New York: Harcourt, Brace & Company, 1959), p. 26.

4. Hank Searls, *The Lost Prince* (New York: The New American Library, Inc., 1969), p. 68.

5. Horton oral history typescript, p. 6.

6. E. J. Kahn, Jr., *The World of Swope* (New York: Simon & Schuster, 1965), pp. 380–81.

7. Burns, *John Kennedy*, p. 39.

8. Payson S. Wild, recorded interview by Larry J. Hackman, November 25, 1968, p. 12, typescript at the John F. Kennedy Library, Oral History Program. See also Arthur M. Schlesinger, Jr., *A Thousand Days: John F. Kennedy in the White House* (Boston: Houghton Mifflin Company, 1965), p. 85.

9. Schlesinger, p. 80, cites William G. Carleton, "Kennedy in History: An Early Appraisal," *Antioch Review,* Fall, 1964.

10. Kennedy to Lothian, December 27, 1939, MS. in Lothian Papers, Scottish Record Office, Edinburgh, GD40/17/402 No. 16.

11. Interview with one such, August 7, 1965.

12. "Appeasement at Munich," MS. at Harvard University Library, Cambridge, Mass.

13. Hank Searls, *The Lost Prince,* p. 156.

14. Arthur Krock, *Memoirs: Sixty Years on the Firing Line* (New York: Funk & Wagnalls, 1968), p. 350.

15. *Ibid.*

16. John F. Kennedy, *Why England Slept* (New York: Wilfred Funk, Inc., 1940, 1961), p. 191.

17. Burns, *John Kennedy,* p. 43.

18. Lord Lothian to John Kennedy, August 7, 1940, Lothian Papers, GD40/17/402 No. 22.

19. Burns, *John Kennedy,* p. 44.

20. Kennedy to Laski, August 20, 1940, and Laski to Kennedy, undated, both in *Roosevelt and Frankfurter: Their Correspondence, 1928–1945,* ed. Max Freedman (Boston: Little, Brown and Company, 1967), pp. 589–90. Frankfurter later told an interviewer, "I was very proud of Harold for writing that letter." Felix Frankfurter, recorded interview by Charles McLaughlin, June 10, 1964, p. 40, typescript at John F. Kennedy Library, Oral History Program. Laski must have been proud of it too, inasmuch as he sent a copy of it to Frankfurter. According to Mrs. Laski, Jack Kennedy told her husband in 1948, "How right you were about my book. I do wish I had never written it." Victor Lasky, *Robert F. Kennedy: The Myth and the Man* (New York: Trident Press, 1968), p. 56, cites *Washington Post Sunday Supplement,* December 3, 1967.

21. For Jack at Stanford, see Harry Muheim, "When JFK was Rich, Young and Happy," *Esquire,* August, 1966, pp. 64 ff.

22. Kirk to Capt. C. W. Carr, in Kirk Papers, Washington Navy Yard, Washington, D.C.

23. Joe McCarthy, *The Remarkable Kennedys* (New York: Popular Library, paperback ed. 1960), p. 73.

24. John Kennedy's PT boat (numbered, we are told, 109) was cut in two by a Japanese destroyer, and John Kennedy risked his own life by saving one of his injured men, conduct which was unarguably exemplary and heroic. In view of which, it seems nit-picky to point out that the PT boat is perhaps the most maneuverable of navy vessels. Even in a deep fog, it takes real negligence for a PT boat to get inexorably into a runover-position.

25. Krock, recorded interview by Charles Bartlett, May 10, 1964, p. 12, typescript at John F. Kennedy Library, Oral History Program. See also anecdote in Krock's *Memoirs,* pp. 350–51.

26. Paul B. Fay, Jr., *The Pleasure of His Company* (New York: Harper & Row,

1966), p. 152. Cf. Kenneth P. O'Donnell and David F. Powers with Joe McCarthy, *"Johnny, We Hardly Knew Ye,"* (Boston: Little, Brown and Company, 1972), p. 46.

27. Eleanor Harris, "The Senator is in a Hurry," *McCall's,* August, 1957, p. 123.

28. Though accepted "as is" as part of Boston political legend.

29. Only his Sorenson (or his O'Donnell or Powers), however, could explain the entrance in terms of "an expression of his own ideals and interests in an arena thereby opened to him." Theodore C. Sorensen, *Kennedy* (New York: Harper & Row, 1965), p. 15. O'Donnell and Powers, *Johnny, We Hardly Knew Ye,* p. 45.

30. McCarthy, *The Remarkable Kennedys,* p. 89.

31. James A. Reed, recorded interview by Robert J. Donovan, June 16, 1964, p. 13 typescript at John F. Kennedy Library, Oral History Program.

32. *Item* (Lynn, Mass.), February 7, 1946.

33. McCarthy, *The Remarkable Kennedys,* p. 90.

34. Ralph G. Martin and Ed Plaut, *Front Runner, Dark Horse* (Garden City, New York: Doubleday and Company, Inc., 1960), pp. 131–32.

35. Robert L. Lee, recorded interview by Ed Martin, May 19, 1964, p. 1, typescript at John F. Kennedy Library, Oral History Program.

36. Lee recalls that the day of the Bunker Hill Day parade in June, 1946, "was a very very hot day, and Jack was exhausted and collapsed at the very end. He was brought to my home." Lee oral history typescript, pp. 4–5.

37. John Henry Cutler, *"Honey Fitz": Three Steps to the White House* (Indianapolis, Ind.: The Bobbs-Merrill Company, Inc., 1962), p. 308.

38. Martin and Plaut, *Front Runner, Dark Horse,* p. 139.

39. Cutler, *"Honey Fitz",* p. 308.

40. Robert Bendiner, "Bay State Prospects," *Nation,* October 12, 1946, p. 402.

41. Burns, *John Kennedy,* p. 67.

42. Martin and Plaut, *Front Runner, Dark Horse,* p. 140.

43. Interview with Joseph Kane, Boston, April 5, 1962. To Martin and Plaut: ". . . everything his father got . . . he bought and paid for." Martin and Plaut, *Front Runner, Dark Horse,* p. 133.

44. Martin and Plaut, *Front Runner, Dark Horse,* p. 133.

45. In the '46 campaign, Honey sometimes accompanied his grandson on the hustings, but had a hard time remembering that his grandson, not himself, was the candidate, and was frequently upstaging the less flamboyant hopeful. See anecdote in Fay, *The Pleasure of His Company,* p. 155.

46. Martin and Plaut, *Front Runner, Dark Horse,* p. 131.

47. *Ibid.,* p. 140.

48. Burns, *John Kennedy,* p. 69.

49. Martin and Plaut, p. 134.

50. Kahn, *The World of Swope,* p. 34. Perhaps everyone elected to Congress for the first time gets a note from someone forecasting greater things, but few such notes are so nicely phrased.

51. See Kennedy's explanation for dissenting Congressman in Sorensen, *Kennedy,* p. 346; cf. his view of himself as a dissenting Congressman, in Burns, *John Kennedy,* p. 93.

52. Burns, *John Kennedy,* p. 80. See Schlesinger's apologia, p. 13.

53. *John Kennedy,* p. 80.

54. During his first term in Congress, John Kennedy denounced the Yalta Pact

for its "betrayal" of Poland. Most scholars today regard such conclusions as historically unsound.

55. Burns, *John Kennedy*, p. 80.

56. John P. Mallan, "Massachusetts: Liberal and Corrupt," *New Republic*, October 13, 1952, pp. 10–12. Presumably, this is the material that Sorensen describes as "thoroughly discredited." Sorensen, *Kennedy*, pp. 4, 136. How? Where? Surely, Professor Arthur Holcombe's disclaimer published in *New Republic*, November 3, 1952, p. 2, falls far short of thoroughly discrediting anything. The thrust of Kennedy's "alleged" comments (as Sorensen describes them) is perfectly consistent with John Kennedy's contemporary statements on foreign policy and his attitude towards the internal Communist plot. As for John Kennedy on Nixon's triumph over Douglas in one of the most vicious campaigns in American history, Paul Fay's documentation confirms Mallan's notes. Fay, *The Pleasure of His Company*, p. 62.

57. Burns, *John Kennedy*, p. 80.

58. *Ibid.*, p. 84.

59. *Ibid.*, p. 146.

60. Charles Spalding, recorded interview (J.F.K. section), p. 35, typescript at John F. Kennedy Library, Oral History Program.

61. Fullest source on the writing of *Profiles* is Sorensen, *Kennedy*, pp. 67–70. To some extent all senatorial writing is ghost-written—by researchers, by those who prepare memorandum, and by editors. It seems that *Profiles* was more nearly written by John Kennedy than most senatorial books are written by their "authors," and according to Sorensen, John Kennedy was far-and-away the fellow who put in the most time on the book and played the largest part in assembling the words. That answers all the questions except: whose contributions gave the book such literary merit as it may have had? Halberstam insists that with Sorensen's "soggy" prose, it couldn't have been Ted. David Halberstam, "Ask Not What Ted Sorensen Can Do for You . . . ," *Harper's*, November, 1969, p. 91.

62. Schlesinger, *A Thousand Days*, p. 14.

63. Krock quoted in William Manchester, *Portrait of a President* (Boston: Little, Brown and Company, 1962, 1967), p. 112.

64. Arthur M. Schlesinger, Jr., *Kennedy or Nixon: Does it Make Any Difference?* (New York: The Macmillan Co., 1960), p. 22.

65. John Kennedy remained extremely touchy about his stand on McCarthy. On the hustings for President in 1960, a questioner asked Kennedy to comment on Mrs. Roosevelt's assertion that he had been soft on McCarthyism. With apparent irritation, Kennedy replied that his civil liberties record was clear—and "I am not ready to accept any indictment from you or Mrs. Roosevelt on that score." Burns, *John Kennedy*, p. 154. John Kennedy's civil liberties record was never at all clear.

66. Evelyn Lincoln, *My Twelve Years With John F. Kennedy* (New York: David McKay Company, Inc., 1965), p. 46.

67. Sorensen, *Kennedy*, p. 45.

68. Schlesinger, *A Thousand Days*, p. 16.

69. Tully, *New York World-Telegram and Sun*, April 7, 1960.

70. Bill Cunningham, *Boston Herald*, April 7, 1957.

71. Sorensen, *Kennedy*, pp. 30–31.

72. Krock, oral history typescript, p. 14.

73. Burns, *John Kennedy*, p. 99.

74. Krock, *Memoirs*, p. 357, for commentary.

75. Gail Cameron, *Rose* (London: Michael Joseph, 1972), p. 146.

76. Most chroniclers accept the view put forth by Burns: that John Kennedy's race against Lodge was an uphill fight. The late Joseph F. Dinneen, though, was a longtime Boston political commentator with vast sensitivity for Massachusetts politics, and he saw the 1952 race exactly the other way around. According to Dinneen, "Long before election Kennedy was, in the jargon of the day, 'home free'. . . . Early in September the odds quoted by Boston gamblers on Kennedy to win were 10 to 1. They would climb to 20 to 1. He could not lose." *The Kennedy Family* (Boston: Little, Brown and Co., 1959), p. 145.

The Kennedys have unquestionably misled commentators on occasion, particularly by exaggerating the power of their opponents, so that their victories would appear all the more stunning. The Kennedys, for example, confidently expected to sweep the West Virginia primary of 1960 from beginning to end, but privately they led the press to believe that they expected to be shellacked, so that when their true expectations were fulfilled, they could use West Virginia to show either that the "religious issue" could be overcome; that their strength was surprising even to themselves; or that the will of the people was unmistakable. George R. Snider, Jr., "The Kennedy Buildup: A Study of the Press in Campaign Politics" (Senior thesis at Yale University, 1962). It is possible that the notion of the 1952 Senate campaign as an uphill fight had the same kind of origin. By 1968, the press had caught on. David Halberstam, *The Unfinished Odyssey of Robert Kennedy* (New York: Bantam Books, paperback ed. 1969), pp. 110–11.

77. Acknowledged even by Sorensen? *Kennedy*, p. 27.

78. Lincoln, *My Twelve Years*, p. 13.

79. Joseph Kennedy to Lord Beaverbrook, September 6, 1952, MS. at Beaverbrook Library, London.

80. *Ibid.*

81. Krock, *Memoirs*, p. 342.

82. Sargent Shriver memorandum dated September 15, 1952, p. 2., MS. in Stevenson Papers, Princeton University Library, Princeton, N.J. The memo suggests, by way of overall approach, that Stevenson identify Jack as "Stevenson's type of man." Page 1. Stevenson took this advice in his strong endorsement of Kennedy as "my type of guy." Burns, *John Kennedy*, p. 112. The author has not researched whether or not Stevenson picked up "this anti-communist business" that Shriver saw as "a good thing to emphasize."

83. Lasky, *R.F.K.*, pp. 73–74.

84. Eleanor Harris, *McCall's*, August, 1957, p. 118.

85. Burns, *John Kennedy*, p. 108. See also Ralph M. Blagden, "Cabot Lodge's Toughest Fight," *Reporter*, September 30, 1952, p. 12.

86. After his election, Kennedy hired a New Bedford girl who was a friend of Brewer's, and like him, a "Kennedy Republican" for his staff. Lincoln, *My Twelve Years*, p. 18.

87. McCarthy, *The Remarkable Kennedys*, p. 104.

88. *Facts on File*, 1958, p. 211C2.

89. McCarthy, *The Remarkable Kennedys*, p. 106.

90. Lee, oral history typescript, p. 11.

91. *Facts on File*, 1958, p. 211C2.

92. Martin and Plaut, *Front Runner, Dark Horse*, p. 181.

93. Sorensen, *Kennedy*, p. 78. The two were only temporarily allied. See Sorensen, pp. 78–79.

94. Burns, *John Kennedy*, p. 107.

95. Martin and Plaut, *Front Runner, Dark Horse*, p. 183; McCarthy, *The Remarkable Kennedys*, p. 105.

96. McCarthy, *The Remarkable Kennedys*, p. 105.

97. *Ibid.*

98. Mallan, *New Republic*, October 13, 1952, p. 12.

99. Richard J. Whalen, *The Founding Father*, (New York: The New American Library of World Literature, Inc., 1964), p. 420, cites interview with Dalton.

100. Martin and Plaut, *Front Runner, Dark Horse*, p. 161.

101. Men like Krock, Swope, Baruch, or Morgenthau—largely "white," or assimilated Jews, rather than successful "new" Jews, the Jewish equivalents of that "striver" Joseph Kennedy.

102. Not impressive in size except insofar as it involved grants to Jewish institutions for research into mental retardation.

103. Dinneen, who knew Kennedy intimately for years, and whose extensive for-publication interview with Kennedy on the subject of anti-Semitism is published in full in Whalen, *Founding Father*, pp. 388–89, personally regarded Kennedy as a rabid anti-Semite. Interview with Joseph F. Dinneen, Needham, Mass., July 29, 1961. That may reflect nothing more than the fact that Kennedy "let himself go" in the presence of men of similar ethnic background.

John Gunther wrote in 1947, "Popularly Boston is supposed to be the most anti-Semitic town in the United States." *Inside U.S.A.* (New York: Harper & Brothers, 1947), pp. 515–16. Boston Coughlinites were always unrestrained in their vicious anti-Semitic tirades, and the city was racked by anti-Semitic rioting in 1944.

104. Sorensen, *Kennedy*, p. 74.

105. Schlesinger, *John Kennedy*, p. 99.

106. Krock, *Memoirs*, p. 338.

107. Joseph Kennedy to Beaverbrook, June 15, 1956, MS. at Beaverbrook Library, London.

108. Interview with James M. Landis, March 3, 1962.

109. Martin and Plaut, *Front Runner, Dark Horse*, p. 68; Bill Cunningham, *Boston Herald*, April 7, 1957.

110. According to O'Donnell and Powers, the die was not finally cast until the convention, at which time the Ambassador denounced the decision to seek the nod over trans-Atlantic telephone in what they call "blue language." *"Johnny, We Hardly Knew Ye,"* p. 122.

111. Martin and Plaut, *Front Runner, Dark Horse*, p. 68.

112. Sorensen, *Kennedy*, pp. 81, 83.

113. Lincoln, *My Twelve Years*, p. 75.

114. Sorensen, *Kennedy*, pp. 80–81.

115. Minow to Stevenson, memo dated March 30, 1956, MS. in Stevenson Papers, Princeton University Library.

116. John Kennedy to Minow, April 16, 1956, MS. in Stevenson Papers, Princeton University Library.

117. Lincoln, *My Twelve Years*, p. 73.

118. Sorensen, *Kennedy*, pp. 82–83.

119. Shriver to Joseph Kennedy, July 18, 1956, MS. at Kennedy Library, Waltham, Mass. File Box 586.

120. Martin and Plaut, *Front Runner, Dark Horse*, p. 68.

121. *Ibid.*, p. 106.

122. McCarthy, *The Remarkable Kennedys*, p. 79.

123. Spalding, oral history typescript, p. 43.

124. Sorensen, *Kennedy*, p. 99.

125. Schlesinger, *A Thousand Days*, pp. 92–93.

126. William O. Douglas, recorded interview by John F. Stewart, November 9, 1967, pp. 9, 18, typescript at John F. Kennedy Library, Oral History Program. Another sympathetic observer, Tom Wicker, concedes Kennedy's Senate career to have been "generally lackluster." *Esquire*, June, 1964, p. 111.

127. Cf. Schlesinger, *A Thousand Days*, p. 100.

128. "No congressional leader of the very first rank save James Madison has been elected Pres.," was a marginal note he made in one of his notebooks during his illnesses of the '50s. Schlesinger, *ibid.*, p. 98.

129. Lincoln, *My Twelve Years*, p. 52.

130. Douglas's quoted comment is conditioned with a "Well, up to 1958 . . ." Page 18.

131. According to O'Donnell and Powers, the father's role was never central in any of the son's campaigns; their styles and modus operandi were radically at variance, and the son, according to them, ignored the father's advice with consistency.

132. *New York Post Magazine*, January 13, 1961, p. 1.

133. Kennedy to Beaverbrook, February 18, 1960, MS. at Beaverbrook Library, London.

134. *New York Post Magazine*, January 13, 1961, p. 1.

135. Charles Bartlett, *Evening Star* (Washington), January 14, 1962.

136. Sorensen, *Kennedy*, p. 119.

137. Ed Plaut, notes of interview with Sorensen.

138. *Newsweek*, September 12, 1960, p. 30.

139. Plaut, notes of interview with Sorensen, p. 12.

140. Plaut notes of interview with Joseph Kennedy, October 29, 1959, pp. 7, 10. On the early organization of the Kennedy campaign, Sorensen agrees with Joseph Kennedy. Sorensen, *Kennedy*, p. 121.

141. Sorensen, *Kennedy*, p. 30.

142. David MacDonald, recorded interview by Charles T. Morrissey, February 15, 1966, p. 3, typescript at John F. Kennedy Library, Oral History Program; David J. MacDonald, *Union Man* (New York: E. P. Dutton & Co., Inc., 1969), p. 283.

143. Fay, *The Pleasure of His Company*, p. 26.

144. Krock, *Memoirs*, p. 330.

145. *Boston Herald*, July 3, 1959.

146. MacDonald, oral history typescript, p. 8.

147. Theodore H. White, *The Making of the President, 1960* (New York: Atheneum, 1961), p. 179.

148. *The Ideas of Henry Luce*, ed. John K. Jessup (New York: Atheneum, 1969), pp. 367–68.

149. Henry Luce, recorded interview by John L. Steele, November 11, 1965, p. 12, typescript at John F. Kennedy Library, Oral History Program.

150. *The Ideas of Henry Luce*, pp. 367–68. Was it mere seller's talk?

151. Spalding, oral history typescript, p. 68.

152. Philip Potter, "How LBJ Got the Nomination," *Reporter*, June 18, 1964, pp. 16–17.

153. Schlesinger, *A Thousand Days*, p. 25.

154. Senator George Smathers, recorded interview, p. 15F, typescript at John F. Kennedy Library, Oral History Program.

155. Jack Newfield, *Robert Kennedy: A Memoir* (New York: E. P. Dutton & Co., Inc., 1969), p. 182.

156. Sorensen, *Kennedy*, p. 156.

157. Peter Lisagor, recorded interview by Ronald J. Grele, April 22, 1966, p. 25, typescript at John F. Kennedy Library, Oral History Program.

158. Lisagor told him. *Ibid.*

159. Philip Potter, *Reporter*, June 18, 1964, p. 17.

160. *Ibid.*

161. Lasky, *R.F.K.*, p. 147, does not identify his source.

162. Lisagor, oral history typescript p. 25.

163. William W. Prochnau and Richard W. Larsen, *A Certain Democrat: Senator Henry M. Jackson* (Englewood Cliffs, N.J.: Prentice-Hall, Inc., 1972), p. 60.

164. Schlesinger, *A Thousand Days*, p. 58.

165. In May of 1960, Joseph Kennedy wrote Beaverbrook: "The only thing troubling me was to have that lovely Miss Leibly of your staff thinking that Humphrey deserved better than he got. He went into the primaries for no other reason than to head up the stop-Kennedy movement." Kennedy to Beaverbrook, May 27, 1960, MS. at Beaverbrook Library, London.

166. Kennedy to Beaverbrook, September 9, 1960, MS. at Beaverbrook Library, London.

167. Sorensen, *Kennedy*, p. 34.

168. White, *The Making of the President, 1960*, p. 109. William Benton, whose experience is detailed by White, later denied that Bailey had threatened him. William Benton, recorded interview, p. 34, typescript at John F. Kennedy Library, Oral History Program.

169. White, *The Making of the President, 1960*, p. 110.

170. George R. Snider, Jr., "The Kennedy Buildup: A Study of the Press in Campaign Politics," (Senior thesis, Yale University, 1962), p. 18.

171. *Ibid.*

172. William H. A. Carr, *J.F.K.: An Informal Biography* (New York: Lancer Books, Inc., 1962), p. 117.

173. Frank L. Kluckhohn, *America: Listen!* (New York: Monarch Books, Inc., 1961), p. 68.

174. Interview with James M. Landis, March 3, 1962.

175. Sorensen, *Kennedy*, p. 311.

176. Ultimately Krock proved of no use in the 1960 campaign. See page 386 *supra.*

177. For Kennedy's comment on Patterson's death, see *New York Daily News*, May 28, 1946.

178. Curiously, Krock was one of the first to speak out against the Kennedy

Administration's "News Management"; he did so in much these terms. See Krock in *Fortune*, February, 1963.

179. Snider, "The Kennedy Buildup," p. 59.

180. Martin and Plaut, *Front Runner, Dark Horse*, p. 462.

181. Snider, "The Kennedy Buildup," p. 67. Harry Golden, no mean observer, is just as certain that Luce was in the Nixon corner, and reports an anecdote that seems to back up his side. See *You're Entitle'* (New York: Fawcett World Library, 1963), p. 125 ff., or "Billy Graham—Partisan for God" in other editions.

182. Richard M. Nixon, *Six Crises* (Garden City, New York: Doubleday & Company, Inc., 1962), p. 420. Nixon and Joseph Kennedy were friends for many years. The rumor persists that Joseph Kennedy money helped finance Nixon's early campaigns. The author has heard it asserted as fact by don't-quote-me's that John Kennedy, as well as his father, contributed to Nixon's U.S. Senate campaign against Helen G. Douglas, a matter denied by Theodore Sorensen. Burns, *John Kennedy*, p. 184, Sorensen, *Kennedy*, p. 136. Sorensen, of course, wasn't with Jack at that time, and so wouldn't know first hand, and close as he was to the President, John Kennedy had no confessors.

183. Pearson, *North Star* (Oklahoma City, Kan.), October 13, 1960.

184. See the *New York World-Telegram and Sun*, October 11, 1957, p. 1; August 18, 1958, p. 17; and, November 12, 1959, p. 39. Political opponents attributed John Kennedy's vote on the Saint Lawrence Seaway to the fact that the seaway would benefit Chicago-area businesses like the Merchandise Mart. But Jack worked quite hard to do away with the oil depletion allowances, and so worked against the family's financial interests.

After the election, embarrassments arising from the family businesses continued to occur. On the day that President John Kennedy berated the steel interests for their inflationary price rises, Joseph Kennedy's bureaucracy raised all the rents in the Merchandise Mart, the world's largest privately owned office building, by 5 percent.

The embarrassments worked both ways, however. In 1953, the father passed up purchasing control of Litton Industries for $250,000, because the company did considerable work for the government, and Joe, Sr., feared that his ownership of Litton might prove politically embarrassing for Jack. Today, Litton's annual sales exceed $250,000,000. Richard J. Whalen, "Joseph P. Kennedy: A Portrait of the Founder," *Fortune*, January, 1963, pp. 167–68.

185. Schlesinger's phrase, *A Thousand Days*, pp. 27–28.

186. *Ibid.*, p. 26.

187. O'Donnell and Powers attribute Truman's opposition to John Kennedy entirely to the fact, they tell us, that Joseph Kennedy had refused to contribute to Truman's reelection bid in 1948. *Johnny, We Hardly Knew Ye*, pp. 10, 151. Something of an oversimplification.

188. *New York Times*, January 8, 1961, p. 36.

189. *New York Times*, February 23, 1959. In fact, Mrs. Roosevelt's charge was apparently premature. See Sorensen, *Kennedy*, p. 119.

190. Lawrence Fuchs, recorded interview by John F. Stewart, November 26, 1966, p. 10, typescript at John F. Kennedy Library, Oral History Program.

191. Andrew Tully, *New York World-Telegram and Sun*, April 7, 1960, p. 3. Two things about the 1960 election surprised the Ambassador: "First, I thought he would get a bigger Catholic vote than he did. Second, I did not think so many would vote against

him because of his religion." Or so he told Time-Life reporter Hugh Sidey. *Life*, December 19, 1960, p. 32.

192. Schlesinger, *A Thousand Days*, p. 119.

193. *New York Post Magazine*, January 9, 1961, p. 1.

194. For Kennedy, see page 444 *infra*; for Verdon, see Mary Barelli Gallagher, *My Life With Jacqueline Kennedy*, ed. Frances Spatz Leighton (New York: David McKay Company, Inc., 1969), p. 122; and, Pierre Salinger, *With Kennedy* (Garden City, N.Y.: Doubleday & Company, Inc., 1966), p. 86.

195. Lisagor, oral history typescript, second interview, May 12, 1966, p. 56, told with less color in Peter Lisagor and Marguerite Higgins, *Overtime in Heaven: Adventures in the Foreign Service* (Garden City, N.Y.: Doubleday & Company, Inc., 1964), pp. 1–2.

196. Spalding, oral history typescript, p. 77.

197. Dwight David Eisenhower, *The White House Years: Waging Peace, 1956–1961* (Garden City, N.Y.: Doubleday & Company, Inc., 1965), p. 603.

198. *The Ideas of Henry Luce*, p. 368.

199. Gallagher, *My Life with Jacqueline Kennedy*, p. 162.

200. Stewart Alsop quoted in Kluckhohn, *America: Listen!*, p. 52.

201. Spalding, oral history typescript, p. 102.

202. Landis interview.

203. John Burns to Felix Frankfurter, November 6, 1935, MS. in Frankfurter Papers, Box 135, at Library of Congress Manuscript Division, Washington, D.C.

204. Krock, oral history typescript, p. 9; Krock's *Memoirs*, p. 349.

205. Spalding, oral history typescript, p. 48.

206. *Ibid.*, pp. 64–65.

207. Spalding, recorded interview by Larry J. Hackman (R.F.K. sections), March 22, 1969, pp. 30–31, typescript at John F. Kennedy Library, Oral History Program.

208. Smathers, oral history typescript, p. 4D.

209. Eleanor Harris, *McCall's*, August, 1957, p. 118.

210. Sorensen, *Kennedy*, p. 33.

211. Pearson, *North Star* (Oklahoma City, Kan.), October 13, 1960.

212. Martin and Plaut, *Front Runner, Dark Horse*, p. 175.

213. Same quotation in Sorensen, *Kennedy*, p. 33, and Schlesinger, *A Thousand Days*, p. 74.

214. Spalding, J.F.K. oral history typescript, pp. 26, 102.

215. Sorensen, *Kennedy*, pp. 367–68; Pierre Salinger, *With Kennedy*, pp. 84–85, 100–101.

216. O'Donnell and Powers, *"Johnny, We Hardly Knew Ye,"* p. 39.

217. Nicely capsulated in Sorensen's observation that "The father's normal conversation was often filled with hyperbole—his son's speech, in private as in public, was more often characterized by quiet understatement." *Kennedy*, p. 31.

218. Interview, August 17, 1965.

219. See, for example, Henry Fairlie, *The Kennedy Promise: The Politics of Expectation* (Garden City, N.Y.: Doubleday & Company, Inc., 1973), pp. 21, 181, 182, 185.

220. Denied by Sorensen, *Kennedy*, p. 757.

221. And are, by the President's close friend Charles Bartlett, *Evening Star* (Washington), January 14, 1962.

222. Sorensen and Schlesinger attribute John Kennedy's "seeming distance" from the burning questions of the day to a maturity of political judgment—an admirable and desirable willingness to see both sides without any doctrinaire adherence to left or right. Perhaps.

223. Martin and Plaut, *Front Runner, Dark Horse*, p. 206. Parallel comment in Sorensen, *Kennedy*, p. 46.

224. Sorensen, *Kennedy*, pp. 26, 470, 471, 477.

225. See Sorensen's explanation, *Kennedy*, p. 50.

226. A qualification with significance?

227. Krock, oral history typescript, pp. 17–18.

228. Daniel A. Poling, *Mine Eyes Have Seen*, (New York: McGraw-Hill Book Company, Inc., 1959), p. 257; see explanation in Sorensen, *Kennedy*, p. 192, and rejoinder in Victor Lasky, *J.F.K., The Man and the Myth* (New York: The Macmillan Company, 1963), pp. 279–80.

229. Sorensen, *Kennedy*, p. 111.

230. Burns, *John Kennedy*, p. 88.

231. Cf. Fairlie, *The Kennedy Promise*, pp. 138–39.

232. Schlesinger's explanation: timing. *A Thousand Days*, pp. 721, 966.

233. Burns, *John Kennedy*, p. 128.

234. Douglas, oral history typescript, pp. 29–30.

235. *Ibid.*, p. 28. See also Sorensen, *Kennedy*, p. 754; Schlesinger, *A Thousand Days*, pp. 1016, 1030.

236. William Manchester, *Portrait of a President* (Boston: Little, Brown and Company, 1962, 1967) p. 237. Virtually identical comment to Dave Powers, O'Donnell and Powers, *"Johnny, We Hardly Knew Ye"*, p. 102.

237. William Manchester, *Death of a President* (New York: Harper & Row, 1967), pp. 372–73, 500–502.

238. Beaverbrook to Rose Kennedy, November 24, 1963, MS. at Beaverbrook Library, London.

239. Jack Newfield, *Robert Kennedy: A Memoir* (New York: E. P. Dutton & Co., Inc., 1969), p. 44.

240. William V. Shannon, *The Heir Apparent* (New York: The Macmillan Company, 1967), p. 45.

241. Nick Thimmesch and William Johnson, *Robert Kennedy at 40* (New York: W. W. Norton & Company, Inc., 1965), p. 28.

242. Krock, *Memoirs*, p. 342.

243. For Joseph Kennedy on Yalta, see William Cunningham, *Boston Herald*, April 25, 1948, and Hal Faust, *Chicago Daily Tribune*, February 15, 1953; for John Kennedy, see Burns, *John Kennedy*, p. 80.

244. Fay, *The Pleasure of His Company*, pp. 156–58, 161.

245. Krock, *Memoirs*, p. 342. According to Lasky, Kennedy's admiration for McCarthy was so great that he named McCarthy godfather to one of his children. Lasky, *R.F.K.*, pp. 77, 90. Lasky does not identify his source, and this author tends to doubt the assertion but only because it does not occur in other Robert Kennedy literature.

246. Shannon, *The Heir Apparent*, p. 57.

247. Vidal's mother was once married to Jacqueline Onassis's step-father.

248. Gore Vidal, "The Best Man: 1968," *Esquire*, March, 1963, p. 61.

249. Burns, *John Kennedy*, p. 154.

250. It is difficult to see how Shannon can conclude that "The consensus in the legal community is that Kennedy did not impair the rights of witnesses before the committee." *The Heir Apparent*, p. 65. The overwhelming weight of lawyerly opinion seems to be to the contrary. See Paul Jacobs, "Extra-curricular Activities of the McClellan Committee," *California Law Review* (May, 1963), or Yale Law Professor Alexander M. Bickel, *New Republic*, January 9, 1961, pp. 15 ff.

251. Monroe H. Freedman, "The Professional Responsibility of the Prosecuting Attorney," *Georgetown Law Journal* (May, 1967), p. 1035.

252. Newfield, *Robert Kennedy*, p. 66.

253. Draft, Beaverbrook to Robert Kennedy, May 11, 1961, MS. at Beaverbrook Library, London. Ultimate wire, also dated May 11, 1961, also at Beaverbrook Library.

254. Edward Lynn, "The Truth About Joe Kennedy," *Saga*, July 1961, p. 87.

255. Lasky, *J.F.K.*, cites Bishop column in Longview *Daily News*, October 25, 1960. It was that kind of attitude that prompted Massachusetts Governor Paul Dever to throw Bobby out of his office during the '52 campaign, and to complain to the Ambassador, "I know you're an important man around here and all that, but I'm telling you this and I mean it. Keep that fresh kid of yours out of sight from here on in." *Saga*, July 1961, p. 87.

256. David Halberstam, *The Unfinished Odyssey of Robert Kennedy* (New York: Bantam Books, paperback ed., 1969), pp. 138–39.

257. Snider, "The Kennedy Buildup," pp. 72, 66. The Ambassador himself wrote Beaver, "We have a few troubles in West Virginia. Only about 3% of the State is Catholic . . . and they are passing out religious leaflets up and down the line." Kennedy to Beaverbrook, April 20, 1960, MS. at Beaverbrook Library, London. Beaverbrook's Canadian newspapers carried some influence in the border states.

258. *New York Times*, May 31, 1928, p. 1.

259. Shannon, *The Heir Apparent*, p. 185. According to O'Donnell and Powers, recruitment of F.D.R., Jr., was the Ambassador's idea. *"Johnny, We Hardly Knew Ye,"* p. 165.

260. Newfield, *Robert Kennedy*, pp. 28, 181.

261. Spalding's R.F.K. oral history typescript, p. 34.

262. Newfield, *Robert Kennedy*, p. 28; Laski, *R.F.K.*, slightly different wording, p. 143, cites *Baltimore Sun*, July 14, 1960.

263. Lester David, *Ted Kennedy* (New York: Grosset & Dunlap, 1971), pp. 88–89.

264. Shannon, *The Heir Apparent*, p. 69.

265. Schlesinger, *A Thousand Days*, p. 129.

266. *Ibid.*, p. 142.

267. *Ibid.*

268. Fay, *The Pleasure of His Company*, p. 11.

269. Hugh Sidey, *John F. Kennedy, President* (New York: Atheneum, 1963), p. 15.

270. Halberstam, *The Unfinished Odyssey*, p. 139.

271. Schlesinger, *A Thousand Days*, p. 142.

272. Sidey, *John F. Kennedy*, p. 15.

273. Victor S. Navasky, *Kennedy Justice* (New York: Atheneum, 1971), p. xviii.

274. And Sidey, *John F. Kennedy*, p. 15; Schlesinger, *A Thousand Days*, p. 142, and most other accounts.

275. Bob Considine, *New York Journal-American*, January 8, 1961, p. 12L.

276. Schlesinger, *A Thousand Days*, p. 142; similar comment in Halberstam, *The Unfinished Odyssey*, p. 140.

277. *New York Times*, November 23, 1961.

278. *New York Journal-American*, January 8, 1961, p. 12L.

279. Bickel, *New Republic*, January 9, 1961, p. 15.

280. Navasky, *Kennedy Justice*, p. 5.

281. Vidal, *Esquire*, March, 1963, p. 61. None of the Kennedys ever demonstrated any real appreciation for civil liberties. Way back in the early part of the century, Mayor John F. Fitzgerald was refusing parade permits for socialists, and banning "obscene" dancing like the "Turkey Trot."

282. Newfield, *Robert Kennedy*, p. 40.

283. Navasky, *Kennedy Justice*, pp. 52–53.

284. *Ibid.*, p. 60.

285. Krock, *Memoirs*, p. 344; cf. Schlesinger, *A Thousand Days*, p. 932 (nothing political about it at all).

286. Navasky, *Kennedy Justice*, p. 227.

287. *Ibid.*, p. 254.

288. Sorensen, *Kennedy*, p. 277.

289. Navasky, *passim*.

290. Given his famous Bay-of-Pigs confrontation with Chester Bowles, one can only imagine his reaction had a Junior Senator questioned the President's Vietnam policy.

291. Acknowledges Sorensen backhandedly, *Kennedy*, p. 268.

292. *Newsweek*, March 18, 1963.

293. *Time*, February 16, 1962, p. 19.

294. *Ibid.*, p. 21.

295. *Saturday Evening Post*, September 22, 1962, p. 16.

296. *Esquire*, March 1963, p. 61.

297. *Newsweek*, March 18, 1963, p. 26.

298. Newfield, *Robert Kennedy*, pp. 30–31. Newfield confuses inner torture with growth. There was surely an element of both in Robert Kennedy, but the one was not the other.

299. *Ibid.*, p. 66.

300. Krock, *Memoirs*, p. 328.

301. Newfield, *Robert Kennedy*, p. 31.

302. Shannon, *The Heir Apparent*, p. 255.

303. Lasky, *R.F.K.*, p. 32, cites several sources. "News management" becomes a two-way street: Bobby himself was manipulated by the media and reduced, at least during his period of mourning, to thinking of himself and of the heroic in terms of clichés and media images.

304. Shannon, *The Heir Apparent*, p. 9.

305. Lasky, *R.F.K.*, p. 195 cites various press reports.

306. Halberstam, *The Unfinished Odyssey*, p. 35.

307. *New York Times*, June 22, 1964.

308. *Newsweek*, August 24, 1964, p. 23.

309. *New York Times*, August 12, 1964, p. 34.

310. Shannon, *The Heir Apparent*, p. 17; Newfield, *Robert Kennedy*, p. 157.

311. Shannon, *The Heir Apparent*, pp. 35–38; Bruce L. Felknor, *Dirty Politics* (New York: W. W. Norton & Company, Inc., 1966), pp. 182 ff.

312. Stephen Hess, *America's Political Dynasties From Adams to Kennedy* (Garden City, N.Y.: Doubleday & Company, Inc., 1966), pp. 524–25.

313. Gail Cameron, *Rose* (London: Michael Joseph, 1972), p. 193.

314. Shannon, *The Heir Apparent*, p. 245; Newfield, *Robert Kennedy*, pp. 19–20.

315. Hess, *America's Political Dynasties*, p. 526.

316. David Susskind thought it "a terrible violation of good taste." Lasky, *R.F.K.*, p. 218 cites *New York World-Telegram and Sun*, October 28, 1964.

317. *New York Times*, November 4, 1964, p. 38.

318. Shannon, *The Heir Apparent*, p. 88.

319. Anthony Lewis, *New York Times Magazine*, April 7, 1963, p. 59; Dan Wakefield quotes Arthur Schlesinger, Jr., *Esquire*, April, 1962, p. 126.

320. Shannon, *The Heir Apparent*, p. 76.

321. Shannon, *The Heir Apparent*, pp. 95, 286.

322. Arthur Krock, *New York Times*, May 26, 1966, p. 46.

323. Lasky, *R.F.K.*, p. 335.

324. Shannon, *The Heir Apparent*, p. 284.

325. William vanden Heuvel and Milton Gwirtzman, *On His Own: Robert F. Kennedy, 1964–1968* (Garden City, N.Y.: Doubleday & Company, Inc., 1970), p. 214.

326. Shannon's phrase, *The Heir Apparent*, p. 112; parallel material in most R.F.K. literature.

327. While he named one child Matthew Maxwell Taylor Kennedy, he also named a child in honor of the more dovish Averell Harriman.

328. See Halberstam, *The Unfinished Odyssey*, p. 32.

329. *New York Times*, February 11, 1962, p. 14.

330. "I have to go all the way with this one," John Kennedy told a friend about Vietnam. Lasky, *R.F.K.*, p. 14.

331. Halberstam, *The Unfinished Odyssey*, p. 23.

332. Says Newfield, *Robert Kennedy*, p. 121; see also Schlesinger, *A Thousand Days*, p. 170.

333. Shannon, *The Heir Apparent*, p. 110; see also Newfield, *Robert Kennedy*, p. 133.

334. Shannon views Bobby's turn to the dove position more cynically than this author does. *The Heir Apparent*, pp. 109–110.

335. In response to which Administration spokesmen resurrected John Kennedy's comment on coalition governments with communists: "No Democrat can ride the back of that tiger." *New York Times*, February 19, 1966.

336. Theodore H. White, *The Making of the President, 1968* (New York: Atheneum, 1969), p. 74; Halberstam, *The Unfinished Odyssey*, p. 11.

337. "Gene McCarthy felt he should have been the first Catholic President just because he knew more St. Thomas Aquinas than my brother." Newfield, *Robert Kennedy*, p. 212.

338. Halberstam, *The Unfinished Odyssey*, pp. 48–53.

339. Burton Hersh, *The Education of Edward Kennedy: A Family Biography* (New York: William Morrow & Company, Inc., 1972), p. 294.

340. Halberstam, *The Unfinished Odyssey*, pp. 16–17.

341. *The Times* (London), January 9, 1968, p. 4, no doubt in American papers same day or preceding day.

342. Halberstam, *The Unfinished Odyssey*, p. 63.

343. Newfield, *Robert Kennedy*, p. 195, relying on Schlesinger.

344. Newfield, *Robert Kennedy*, pp. 211–12; Halberstam, *The Unfinished Odyssey*, p. 64, is more definite.

345. Krock, *Memoirs*, p. 345.

346. Lasky, *R.F.K.*, p. 28, cites Paul Hope, *Washington Star*, March 18, 1968; another McCarthyite reaction: Murray Kempton, "The Emperor's Kid Brother," *Esquire*, July, 1968.

347. Newfield, *Robert Kennedy*, p. 186.

348. Newfield, *Robert Kennedy*, p. 30.

349. Newfield observes that Bobby was the one politician of his time who might have united black and white poor into a new majority. *Robert Kennedy*, p. 12. This author agrees: blacks, because of his policy appeal; whites, largely in spite of it.

350. See Hersh, *The Education of Edward Kennedy*, p. 300.

351. Ron Rosenbaum, "Kretchmer couldn't: Notes on a 12-day campaign," *Village Voice*, March 15, 1973, p. 30.

352. Newfield, *Robert Kennedy*, p. 20.

353. *Ibid.*, p. 245.

354. White, *The Making of the President, 1968*, pp. 170–71; Lasky, *R.F.K.*, p. 405; cf. Newfield, p. 41 with Newfield, pp. 36, 37.

355. Halberstam, *The Unfinished Odyssey*, p. 121.

356. Lasky, *R.F.K.*, p. 7, cites Newfield article in *Village Voice*, June 13, 1968; same quotation somewhat edited in Newfield's *Robert Kennedy*, p. 20; different account with somewhat parallel quotation in Halberstam, *The Unfinished Odyssey*, p. 214.

357. *New York Times*, June 16, 1968, p. 1.

358. Photo in *Newsweek*, June 24, 1968, p. 28.

359. Newfield, *Robert Kennedy*, p. 29.

360. See discussion in Shannon, *The Heir Apparent*, p. 250.

361. Newfield, *Robert Kennedy*, p. 49.

362. *Ibid.*, p. 58.

363. *Ibid.*, p. 49.

364. *Ibid.*, pp. 31, 69.

365. Notwithstanding his plaintive you-still-love-me? to Newfield on the occasion of his announcement for the Presidency. Newfield, *Robert Kennedy*, p. 17.

366. *Ibid.*, p. 165.

367. *Newsweek*, March 18, 1963, p. 28.

368. Gallagher, oral history typescript, p. 26.

369. Krock, oral history typescript, p. 2.

370. Bernard Baruch, article drafted for inclusion in *The Fruitful Bough*, MS. in Baruch Papers, Vol. 48, at Princeton University Library, Princeton, N.J.

371. Gore Vidal, "The Best Man, 1968," *Esquire*, March, 1963.

372. The Ambassador, for example, publicly endorsed the Kennedy Administration's minimum-wage proposals. *New York Post Magazine*, January 13, 1961, p. 1.

373. Sorensen, *Kennedy*, p. 32.

374. *Life*, January 26, 1962, p. 90.

375. Thimmesch and Johnson, *Robert Kennedy at 40*, p. 134.

376. *Life*, January 26, 1962, cover.

377. Sorensen's observation, *Kennedy*, p. 35, perhaps his conscious commentary on "he hates the same way I do."

378. *Newsweek*, March 18, 1963, p. 28. ". . . and when it comes to hating, Joseph P. Kennedy has had few peers," adds Victor Lasky, *R.F.K.*, p. 17. Navasky doubts the quotation. *Kennedy Justice*, p. 332.

379. Thimmesch and Johnson, *Robert Kennedy at 40*, pp. 24–25.

380. Robert E. Thompson and Hortense Myers, *Robert F. Kennedy: The Brother Within* (New York: Dell Publishing Co., Inc., paperback ed., 1962), p. 107.

381. Lasky, *R.F.K.*, p. 35.

382. Shannon, *The Heir Apparent*, p. 51.

383. Thompson and Myers, *Robert F. Kennedy*, p. 39.

384. "Bobby Kennedy: He Hates to be Second," *Look*, May 21, 1963, pp. 94 ff.

385. *Life*, January 26, 1962, p. 80.

386. Newfield doesn't seem to see any cynicism whatsoever in the fact that Robert Kennedy "nevertheless later invited Harwood to stay the night in his private suite, the only daily reporter given that special favor." *Robert Kennedy*, p. 262.

387. *New Republic*, January 9, 1961, p. 18.

388. Nixon, *Six Crises*, pp. 365 ff. Sorensen takes strenuous exception. *Kennedy*, pp. 176, 217, 219.

389. Thompson and Myers, pp. 207, 209.

390. Lasky, *R.F.K.*, p. 155.

391. Spalding, R.F.K. oral history typescript, p. 18.

392. *Ibid.*, p. 16.

393. See, for example, Lasky, *R.F.K.*, pp. 22, 227, 381.

394. *Ladies Home Journal*, February, 1939, p. 23.

395. See novelist John O'Hara quoted in Lasky's *R.F.K.*, p. 19, for which Lasky cites *Town & Village*, July 15, 1965.

396. Lasky, *R.F.K.*, p. 34.

397. Lester David, *Ted Kennedy: Triumphs and Tragedies* (New York: Grosset & Dunlap, 1971), pp. 53–54.

398. Burton Hersh, *The Education of Edward Kennedy: A Family Biography* (New York: Morrow, 1972), pp. 82–83.

399. *Ibid.*, pp. 78, 85.

400. *Time*, September 28, 1962, p. 15.

401. Hersh, *The Education of Edward Kennedy*, pp. 103–104.

402. David, *Ted Kennedy*, pp. 75–76.

403. *Time*, October 27, 1961, p. 25 and September 28, 1962, p. 14; Joe McCarthy, *Look*, November 6, 1962, p. 24.

404. David, *Ted Kennedy*, pp. 88–89; parallel anecdote in Hersh, *The Education of Edward Kennedy*, pp. 154–55. As they wrote at the same time it seems unlikely that either took it from the other. The author doubts that the father ever seriously considered the seat for Bobby, and suspects that he used Bobby's name only to test Ward's general receptivity to Kennedy-family influence.

405. Curiously, hinted at in Sorensen, *Kennedy*, p. 228.

406. *Wall Street Journal*, June 1, 1962, p. 18.

407. Edward McCormack, recorded interview, p. 9, typescript at John F. Kennedy Library, Oral History Program.

408. Hersh, *The Education of Edward Kennedy*, p. 149.

409. *Time*, September 28, 1962, pp. 14, 16.

410. Luce, oral history typescript, p. 7.

411. Hersh, *The Education of Edward Kennedy*, p. 153.

412. *Ibid.*

413. Garrett Byrne, recorded interview by John Stewart, September 28, 1967, p. 45, typescript at John F. Kennedy Library, Oral History Program.

414. Thomas B. Morgan, *Esquire*, April, 1962, p. 60.

415. *Time*, September 28, 1962, p. 14 and *Saturday Evening Post*, October 27, 1962, p. 16. One editor gave it emphasis with the explanation that "Rose and Joe Kennedy share this simple conviction that what's right is right." *The First Family Album* (New York: Macfadden-Bartlett Corp., 1963).

416. Stewart Alsop, *Saturday Evening Post*, October 27, 1962, p. 17; Joe McCarthy, *Look*, November 6, 1962, p. 23.

417. Lincoln, *My Twelve Years*, pp. 307–308.

418. Reed, oral history typescript, p. 57.

419. Hersh, *The Education of Edward Kennedy*, pp. 159–160.

420. David, *Ted Kennedy*, p. 64.

421. Hersh, *The Education of Edward Kennedy*, p. 165.

422. *Time*, June 15, 1962, p. 14, September 28, 1962, p. 16.

423. Paul Driscoll, " 'Jack Was Asking About You,' " *New Republic*, June 4, 1962, p. 8.

424. *Time*, September 28, 1962, p. 16.

425. *New Republic*, June 4, 1962, p. 9.

426. *Ibid.*

427. The *Wall Street Journal* speculated that if he lost, Ted might find that at the next family dinner he would have to eat in the kitchen. March 15, 1962, p. 14.

428. See, for example, the report of the "National Committee for an Effective Congress," headed by Arthur Schlesinger, Sr., and Hans Morgenthau, in *Time*, August 24, 1962, p. 12. The two exceptions were ADA-head Samuel Beer and Kennedy-biographer James MacGregor Burns, who sided with Edward Kennedy on the grounds that only he could clean up Massachusetts corruption and the Massachusetts Democratic Party.

But the governorship was the office from which such laudable goals might have been accomplished, and Edward Kennedy had pointedly passed up the governorship— as much because of the corruption pitfalls as anything else. Over the many years that the Kennedy family has been in a position to control the Massachusetts Democratic Party, at least since 1956, they have made not the slightest effort to clean up the party or the state, despite occasional eloquence on the low state of Massachusetts public morality.

429. *The Reporter*, July 5, 1962, p. 15; Hersh, *The Education of Edward Kennedy*, pp. 176–77.

430. Sorensen, *Kennedy*, p. 355; Hersh, *The Education of Edward Kennedy*, p. 177.

431. *Time*, June 15, 1962, p. 14.

432. *The Nation*, March 10, 1962, p. 212.

433. David, *Ted Kennedy*, p. 111, no doubt in reliance on Murray B. Levin,

Kennedy Campaigning (Boston: Beacon Press, 1966), the basic text on the 1962 campaign.

434. *Time*, September 28, 1962, p. 14.

435. *The Nation*, March 10, 1962, p. 212.

436. *Newsweek*, October 30, 1961, p. 16.

437. *Time*, September 28, 1962, p. 18.

438. *Time*, September 28, 1962, p. 14.

439. Edward M. Kennedy to Beaverbrook, December 17, 1962, MS. at Beaverbrook Library, London.

440. Thompson and Myers, *Robert F. Kennedy*, p. 216.

441. Bickel comment, New Haven, Conn., 1963.

442. Stewart Alsop, *Saturday Evening Post*, October 27, 1962, p. 16.

443. *New York Times*, September 19, 1962, p. 38.

444. *Punch*, April 17, 1963, p. 548.

445. Stewart Alsop, *Saturday Evening Post*, October 27, 1962, p. 16.

446. Hersh, *The Education of Edward Kennedy*, p. 188.

447. Lord Beaverbrook to Edward M. Kennedy, December 31, 1962, MS. at Beaverbrook Library, London.

448. Hersh, *The Education of Edward Kennedy*, p. 217.

449. William H. Honan, *Ted Kennedy: Profile of a Survivor* (New York: Quadrangle Books, 1972), p. 146.

450. *Newsweek*, January 17, 1966.

451. Navasky, *Kennedy Justice*, p. 363. According to Cardinal Cushing, Joseph Kennedy was bitter that J.F.K. had passed up Morrissey, and through Cushing, approached Morrissey to accept a $75,000 trust fund for his children, as consolation. Morrissey declined the offer. John Henry Cutler, *Cardinal Cushing of Boston* (New York: Hawthorn Books, Inc., 1970), p. 293.

452. *Newsweek*, October 11, 1965, p. 35.

453. *Newsweek*, January 17, 1966, p. 19.

454. Fullest account in Hersh, *The Education of Edward Kennedy*, pp. 233–49.

455. *Ibid.*, p. 248.

456. *Ibid.*, p. 311.

457. Honan, *Ted Kennedy*, p. 130.

458. Fullest discussion in Lewis Chester, Godfrey Hodgson and Bruce Page, *An American Melodrama: The Presidential Campaign of 1968* (New York: The Viking Press, 1969), pp. 572–74. Nor Bobby for McCarthy: Kennedy loyalists turned to the last-minute, futile protest candidacy of Bobby's friend George McGovern, or returned to the organization fold behind Humphrey, rather than back Bobby's ideological parallel but personal rival McCarthy.

459. Honan, *Ted Kennedy*, pp. 130–31.

460. Hersh, *The Education of Edward Kennedy*, p. 351; see also Honan, *Ted Kennedy*, pp. 126, 130–31.

461. Chester, Hodgson and Page, *An American Melodrama*, p. 576.

462. Hersh, *The Education of Edward Kennedy*, p. 354.

463. *Ibid.*, p. 332.

464. Honan, *Ted Kennedy*, p. 138.

465. Hersh, *The Education of Edward Kennedy*, p. 334.

466. David, *Ted Kennedy*, p. 239; Hersh, *The Education of Edward Kennedy*, pp. 379–80.

467. See *Newsweek*, July 28, 1969, p. 33.

468. *Wall Street Journal*, April 30, 1970, p. 1.

469. David Halberstam, "Ask Not What Ted Sorensen Can Do For You . . ." *Harpers*, November, 1969, p. 90.

470. *Newsweek*, January 12, 1970.

471. Sorensen, *Kennedy*, pp. 141, 146.

472. Hersh, *The Education of Edward Kennedy*, pp. 357–59, 455–57; Honan, *Ted Kennedy*, pp. 106, 121, 137.

473. *Hartford Courant* (Hartford, Conn.), November 12, 1972.

474. *Hartford Courant*, July 15, 1973, p. 35.

475. Says the Associated Press, *Hartford Courant*, November 9, 1972 and columnist Warren Rogers, *Hartford Courant*, November 14, 1972.

476. Honan, *Ted Kennedy*, pp. 56, 119.

477. *Ibid.*, p. 133.

478. *Ibid.*, p. 171.

479. *Ibid.*, pp. 171–72.

480. Hersh, *The Education of Edward Kennedy*, p. 206.

481. Honan, *Ted Kennedy*, p. 171.

482. David, *Ted Kennedy*, pp. 241–42 to the contrary.

483. Honan, *Ted Kennedy*, p. 172.

484. *Ibid.*, p. 165.

485. Lee oral history typescript, p. 16.

486. *Newsweek*, June 24, 1968, p. 28.

487. Hersh's comparison, *The Education of Edward Kennedy*, p. 255.

488. Rita Dallas, *The Kennedy Case* (New York: Putnam's, 1973), pp. 254–55; see also curious observation in Hersh, *Education of Edward Kennedy*, p. 186.

489. Honan, *Ted Kennedy*, p. 128.

490. Dallas, *The Kennedy Case*, p. 316.

491. David, *Ted Kennedy*, p. 21.

492. *Ibid.*, p. 22, quoting Joe McCarthy.

493. *Ibid.*, p. 57, for example.

494. Dallas, *The Kennedy Case*, pp. 338–39. According to obituaries published of the father, he was never told of the incident at all. *New York Post*, November 18, 1969, p. 5.

495. *Ibid.*, p. 342.

EPILOGUE

1. Years before, Kennedy's dear friend, Prime Minister Neville Chamberlain, had reflected on death—Chamberlain's own impending death and the death of Chamberlain's father: "I can tell you, though I haven't told my wife—I want to die. I saw my father live on for eight years after a stroke and I often wished he were dead. Now I only worry about my family, I can't do any work—I can't even visit my friends." Landis MS., p. 432. The parallels were obvious.

2. Francis I. Broadhurst, *Boston Herald-Traveler* November 17, 1969, p. 1, quoted slightly differently in the *Boston Globe*, same day, p. 1.

3. *Ibid.*

4. The Associated Press photo is reproduced in Gail Cameron, *Rose* (London: Michael Joseph, 1972), centerfold.

5. Mary Barelli Gallagher, *My Life With Jacqueline Kennedy*, ed. Frances Spatz Leighton (New York: David McKay Company, Inc., 1969), p. 162.

6. *Evening Standard* (London), November 17, 1969, p. 1; *Daily Telegraph* (London), November 18, 1969, p. 3; a later glowing Jacqueline Onassis photo is in *Boston Herald-Traveler*, November 20, 1969, p. 1.

7. *Boston Globe* headline, November 18, 1969, p. 1.

8. See, for example, the *Boston Herald-Traveler*, November 18, 1969, p. 12.

9. See, for example, Sargent Shriver in the *Evening Standard* (London), November 17, 1969, p. 1.

10. *Boston Herald-Traveler*, November 19, 1969, p. 1.

11. *Boston Herald-Traveler* and *Boston Globe*, both November 20, 1969, p. 1.

12. While preparing herself for the funeral of Robert Kennedy in 1968, Rose Kennedy was heard to murmur, "Oh, why did it have to be Bobby? Why couldn't it have been Joe?" Cameron, *Rose*, pp. 166–67, quotes unnamed Bergdorf-Goodman saleslady.

13. For the Cardinal at the inauguration: Paul B. Fay, Jr., *The Pleasure of His Company* (New York: Harper & Row, 1966) p. 91; Arthur M. Schlesinger, Jr., *A Thousand Days: John F. Kennedy in the White House* (Boston: Houghton Mifflin, 1965), p. 2; Theodore C. Sorensen, *Kennedy* (New York: Harper & Row, 1965), p. 244.

14. The author checked every major public and university library in the United States and found that none of them had a copy of *The Fruitful Bough*. Senator Edward Kennedy's office declined to give the author access to a copy. Fullest source on *The Fruitful Bough* is *Newsweek*, November 1, 1965.

15. Funeral reported *Boston Herald-Traveler* and *Boston Globe*, November 21, 1969, p. 1.

16. Cameron, *Rose*, p. 71.

17. Nixon's phrase, *Washington Post*, November 19, 1969, p. 1.

18. Fullest collection of tributes is in *Boston Heard-Traveler*, November 19, 1969, pp. 16, 27.

19. *Boston Herald-Traveler*, November 19, 1969, p. 18.

20. *Chicago Daily Tribune*, November 20, 1969, p. 20.

21. *Newsweek*, December 1, 1969, pp. 28–30.

22. *New York Times*, December 9, 1969, p. 60; *Newsweek*, December 15, 1969, p. 15. Edward Kennedy took issue with most of the nastier items in the obituary, but did not mention *Newsweek*'s imputation to his father of marital infidelity.

23. The Ambassador and his family had encouraged reference to himself in the third person as "the Ambassador."

24. Macleod, *Spectator*, June 25, 1965, p. 811.

25. *Observer*, November 23, 1969, p. 23. Most English newspapers gave Kennedy's death modest coverage, some of them giving him less space than was allotted to the death of "The King of Swing," popular English bandleader Ted Heath, who died at the same time. London's *Daily Express*, once owned by Kennedy's last English friend Lord Beaverbrook, for example, put Ted Heath on page one of its November 19, 1969 issue and did not even mention the passing of the Ambassador. See also London's *Sun*, November 19, 1969, pp. 2, 7; and, *Daily Telegraph*, same date, p. 1.

BIBLIOGRAPHY

NEWSPAPERS AND MAGAZINE ARTICLES HAVE GENERALLY BEEN identified fully with each citation and are not included in this bibliography. Interviews have also been omitted from the list. The author's interview notes will ultimately be made available to the Kennedy Library.

MANUSCRIPTS AND UNPUBLISHED MATERIALS

Manuscripts have been fully identified only in the first citation of them, and thereafter have been identified only with short descriptions, as in "Baruch Papers."

Included in this section of the bibliography are manuscript collections and repositories visited by the author, with commentary on the fruitfulness of each collection consulted; reports on the present status of a few collections not yet available, but which should prove fruitful to future students of Joseph Kennedy's career; and all academic dissertations cited, whether or not available in xerographic copies through University Microfilms of Ann Arbor, Michigan.

Amery Diaries: Leo Amery, influential Conservative Party member of Parliament during Kennedy's tenure as Ambassador, kept a voluminous diary, which, when his family determines to make it available, should contain a wealth of Joseph Kennedy material.

Balderston Papers: The papers of "interventionist" John L. Balderston, at the Library of Congress's Manuscript Division, Washington, contain only passing references to Joseph Kennedy. Another set of Balderston materials, at Princeton, was not perused by the author.

Baruch Papers: The papers of Bernard Baruch, at Princeton University, Princeton, New Jersey, include some Joseph Kennedy letters and commentary about him in the correspondence of others.

Beaverbrook Library: The Beaverbrook Library, London, has an interesting series of later letters from Joseph Kennedy to Beaverbrook; the author suspects that when Kennedy's own letter files are opened, the correspondence already available at the Beaverbrook Library will prove to be among the most revealing letters Kennedy ever wrote.

Bjerk, Roger. "Kennedy at the Court of St. James." Ph.D. dissertation, Washington State University. One of several doctoral dissertations done on the ambassadorial career of Joseph Kennedy, but the only one to date to become available. Written before the opening of the Foreign Office papers, it is generally sympathetic to Kennedy.

Bullitt Papers: Ambassador William C. Bullitt, Kennedy's counterpart in Paris in the early-war period, probably had little or no correspondence with Kennedy, but his letters to third parties may report information about Kennedy. The Ambassador's family has not yet seen fit to make his papers available to researchers.

Cadogan Papers: Sir Alexander Cadogan's papers are still held tightly within the familial bosom, notwithstanding David Dilk's published edition of Cadogan's *Diaries*.

Chamberlain Papers: Prime Minister Neville Chamberlain's papers at the University of Birmingham have not yet been opened for general research. They are currently being "gone through" for an authorized biography by Leeds Professor David Dilks, ghost to the great.

Churchill Papers: Prime Minister Churchill's papers are being worked on by Professor Martin Gilbert, and perhaps when he is finished with them, decades hence, they may be opened to others. Churchill's son Randolph's papers, which might well contain fascinating Joseph Kennedy material, Randolph's son writes me, "are housed in a large number of steel boxes, which are as yet unsorted, so unfortunately I am unable to let you have access to them."

Columbia University: Columbia's fascinating collection of oral history transcripts is constantly growing. As of this writing, the most useful of them on Joseph Kennedy are the interviews with Eddie Dowling, Alan Kirk, Arthur Krock, James M. Landis, Chester T. Lane, George Rublee, and James P. Warburg. Other than the oral history materials, Columbia does not have any significant Joseph Kennedy material.

Dalton Diary MS.: Much of the diary of Labour party theoretician Hugh Dalton remains unpublished and is available to researchers at the London School of Economics. There is very little Joseph Kennedy material in it.

Davis Papers: The Norman Davis papers at the Library of Congress's Manuscript Division have a few Joseph Kennedy references.

Feis Papers: Herbert Feis's papers at the Library of Congress's Manuscript Division, Washington, do not have much Kennedy material in them, though they are fascinating reading in general. Anyone who gets to the Manuscript Division should make a point to read the beautiful unpublished letter to Feis from Harold Laski dated November 3, 1921.

Foreign Office Papers: The bound memoranda of the staff of the British Foreign Office are available at the Portugal Street branch of the Public Record Office in London, and, for the period when Joseph Kennedy served, are fully open to researchers. Of course, they constitute a must in any research on the Ambassador.

Frankfurter Papers: The papers of Supreme Court Justice Felix Frankfurter are open and available at the Library of Congress's Manuscript Division. There is not much Joseph Kennedy material in them.

Halifax Papers: There are two batches of papers of Foreign Secretary Lord Halifax. The smaller group, at the Public Record Office, London, has little or no Joseph Kennedy material in it. The larger set, amongst the "Hickleton Papers" at the

Yorkshire estate of the Halifax family, was unavailable when the author was in
England due to the vacation of the family librarian. The author understands that
there is surprisingly little Joseph Kennedy material in them.

Harvey Diaries: The diaries of Oliver Harvey of the Foreign Office have been largely
published, and the manuscript diary itself, housed in the Manuscript Division of
the British Museum, is in an indecipherable hand.

Henson, Edward Lee, Jr. "Britain, America and the European Crisis, 1937–1938." Ph.D.
dissertation, University of Virginia, 1969. Not too valuable for Joseph Kennedy
insights.

Hoare Papers: Sir Samuel Hoare's papers are available at University Library,
Cambridge, England, catalogued as "Templewood Papers," but did not prove
too fruitful.

Hull Papers: Secretary of State Cordell Hull's papers, at the Library of Congress's
Manuscript Division, have a wealth of Joseph Kennedy material in them, much
of it duplicated in the State Department Archives or at the Roosevelt Library at
Hyde Park, New York.

Ickes Diary Manuscript: The many-volumed diaries of Harold Ickes are housed at the
Library of Congress's Manuscript Division and will be opened sometime during
this decade. They should contain much more of what filled the three published
volumes of *The Secret Diary of Harold L. Ickes*.

Kennedy, John F. "Appeasement at Munich." Undergraduate thesis, Harvard University, Cambridge, Massachusetts. Interesting only as a curiosity.

Kennedy Library: The John F. Kennedy Library, currently housed at the Federal
Records Center, 380 Trapelo Road, Waltham, Massachusetts, does not have very
much material opened to researchers yet, other than its huge and growing set of
oral history transcripts. Those cited in this book include the interviews of
William Benton, Dinah Bridge, Garrett Byrne, Joseph E. Casey, William O.
Douglas, James Fayne (done for the Hoover Library), Felix Frankfurter,
Lawrence Fuchs, Edward M. Gallagher (especially good on Joseph Kennedy)
Ralph Horton, Jr., Kay Halle, Mr. and Mrs. John H. Kelso, Rose Kennedy (done
for the Hoover Library), Arthur Krock (material largely covered in Krock's later
Memoirs), Robert L. Lee, Peter Lisagor, Henry Luce, David MacDonald, Pope
Paul VI, James A. Reed, George Smathers, Charles Spalding (two interviews, one
on John Kennedy and one on Robert Kennedy, both insightful), and Payson
Wild.

Kennedy Papers: The Kennedy Library is obviously the logical recipient of Joseph
Kennedy's papers, but they are still within the family's custody and are not likely
to be opened to the public until long after the end of the Presidential tenure of
some Kennedy yet unborn.

Kent Papers: Journalist Frank Kent's papers, at the Maryland Historical Society,
Baltimore, contain a set of Kennedy's "syndicated Private and Confidential
letters," as Kent described them (also available in the Baruch papers) and a little
more.

Kirk Papers: The papers of Admiral Alan Kirk, at the Washington Navy Yard,
Washington, D.C., contain a little Joseph Kennedy material, and much useful
background on London in the early-war period.

Krock Papers: As Kennedy's closest confidant in the fourth estate, Arthur Krock's
papers at Princeton University are likely to have valuable Joseph Kennedy

material (perhaps largely revealed in Krock's *Memoirs*), but are currently closed to researchers.

Land Papers: Admiral Emory S. Land's papers at the Library of Congress's Manuscript Division have very little in them about Joseph Kennedy.

Landis Manuscript: James M. Landis's unpublished work on the diplomatic career of Joseph Kennedy is a valuable if not indispensable tool. More fully described in footnote 17, page 514 *infra.*

Landis Papers: Dean Landis's papers at the Library of Congress's Manuscript Division are less fruitful than I might have expected, but still worth consulting.

Lane Papers: There is a little Joseph Kennedy material in the papers of Ambassador Arthur Bliss Lane at Yale University, New Haven, Connecticut.

Leutze, James R. "If Britain Should Fail: Roosevelt and Churchill and British-American Naval Relations, 1938–1940." Ph.D. dissertation, Duke University, 1970. Exhaustively researched and interesting study of its topic, though not too valuable for Joseph Kennedy insights.

Loening Papers: The papers of aviator Grover Loening at the Library of Congress's Manuscript Division contain just a little Joseph Kennedy material; the existence of any correspondence with Kennedy at all attests to the limitlessness of the Ambassador's circle.

Long Diary MS.: The most explosive sections of Breckenridge Long's Diary have now been published in Professor Fred Israel's edition, but there is still more Joseph Kennedy material in the unpublished portions at the Library of Congress's Manuscript Division.

Lothian Papers: Lord Lothian, British Ambassador to the United States while Kennedy was Ambassador in England, had little written communication with his American counterpart. A few pieces, mostly with regard to *Why England Slept*, are among Lothian's papers at the Scottish Record Office, Edinburgh.

Marx, Daniel, Jr. "The U.S. Maritime Commission, 1936–1940." Ph.D. dissertation, University of California at Berkeley, 1946. The author does not believe this dissertation to be available through University Microfilms, but it is worth writing the University of California for it.

Messersmith Papers: George Messersmith's papers are at the University of Delaware; the author was surprised at the paucity of references to Joseph Kennedy in them.

Moffat Diary MS: Nancy Hooker's edition of *The Moffat Papers* largely covers the ground, but there are many more Joseph Kennedy references in the unpublished portions of the diary of European Bureau Chief Jay Pierrepont Moffat at Houghton Library, Harvard University, Cambridge, Massachusetts, and the papers also include a few letters to, or referring to, Ambassador Kennedy.

Morgenthau Diary MS.: There are fewer references to Joseph Kennedy than one might expect in the several hundred volumes of Henry Morgenthau's bound memoranda, fully open to researchers at the Roosevelt Library, Hyde Park, New York.

National Archives: The National Archives at Washington, D.C., include the essential State Department Papers (see below) and also some material relating to Kennedy's career at the Maritime Commission.

Palmer Papers: The papers of *Readers Digest* editor Paul Palmer are available at Yale University and include some interesting Joseph Kennedy correspondence from the 1940s.

Phillips Diary MS.: The unpublished diary of U.S. Ambassador to Italy William Phillips, at the Houghton Library, Cambridge, Massachusetts, has some valuable Kennedy material in it.

Public Record Office: The locus of the indispensable Foreign Office Papers, Cabinet minutes, and the smaller group of Halifax Papers referred to above.

Roosevelt Library: At Hyde Park, New York, the Roosevelt Library has a fair number of Kennedy letters in the President's and President's Secretary's Files, as well as the Morgenthau Diary MS. discussed above.

Samuel Papers: The papers of Herbert, Viscount Samuel, are available at the House of Lords Library, London, but are not very valuable for those tracing Ambassador Kennedy's career.

Schatz, Arthur W. "Cordell Hull and the Struggle for the Reciprocal Trade Agreements Program, 1932–1940." Ph.D. dissertation, University of Oregon, 1965. As interesting as it could possibly have been, given the topic.

Smith, Truman. "Air Intelligence Activities, Office of the Military Attaché, American Embassy, Berlin, Germany, August, 1935–April, 1939." MS. at Yale University, New Haven, Connecticut. Includes Lindbergh's report to Kennedy on Germany's air strength.

Snider, George R., Jr. "The Kennedy Buildup: A Study of the Press in Campaign Politics." Undergraduate dissertation, Yale University, 1962. An excellent study of the press in the West Virginia primary of 1960.

Stanley Papers: Oliver Stanley, President of Britain's Board of Trade during Kennedy's tenure as Ambassador in England, had a great deal of contact with the American Ambassador. He left no papers, his daughter told the author.

State Department MSS.: The State Department files housed in the National Archives, Washington, are now open for the period of Kennedy's ambassadorship, including all of his wires and his personal file. Naturally, indispensable.

Stevenson Papers: Adlai Stevenson's papers at Princeton University are open but not very useful for Joseph Kennedy material.

Vansittart Papers: Sir Robert Vansittart's papers are available, but he and Kennedy had little contact, and the archivist in charge discouraged the author from coming to peruse them.

Welles Papers: Under Secretary of State Sumner Welles' family has not yet let researchers into his papers. When they do, there should be valuable Kennedy material.

Wood, John E. "The Luftwaffe as a Factor in British Policy, 1935–1939." Ph.D. dissertation, Tulane University, 1965. Conclusion: it played too great a factor.

BOOKS

The author has generally identified a published source fully in its first citation in each chapter in which it is cited. Subsequent references to the same source in the same chapter have referred to author, short form of title, and page number (e.g., "Newfield, *Robert Kennedy*, p. 19"). The author has included in the following roster all books cited in the text and a very few books not cited but which the author feels to be particularly useful.

Most of the peaks and many of the valleys that go to make up the mountain of Kennedy family literature are included below; in the face of powerful temptation, the author has refrained from distinguishing the ones from the others.

Adams, William Forbes. *Ireland and Irish Emigration to the New World.* New Haven, Conn.: Yale University Press, 1932

Adler, Selig. *The Isolationist Impulse: Its Twentieth Century Reaction.* London: Abelard-Schuman Limited, 1957.

Ainley, Leslie G. *Boston Mahatma: A Biography of Martin M. Lomasney.* Boston: Bruce Humphries, Inc., 1949.

Allen, H. C. *Great Britain and the United States.* New York: St. Martin's Press Inc., 1955.

Alsop, Joseph and Robert Kintner. *American White Paper.* New York: Simon & Schuster, 1940.

Amory, Cleveland. *The Last Resorts.* New York: Harper & Brothers, 1952.

———. *The Proper Bostonians.* New York: E. P. Dutton & Co., Inc., 1947.

Avon, The Earl of. *Memoirs of Anthony Eden, Earl of Avon: The Reckoning.* Boston: Houghton Mifflin Company, 1965.

Baker, Leonard. *Roosevelt and Pearl Harbor.* New York: The Macmillan Company, 1970.

Baruch, Bernard M. *My Own Story.* Vol. II: *The Public Years.* New York: Holt, Rinehart & Winston, 1960.

Bendiner, Robert. *The Riddle of the State Department.* New York: Farrar & Rinehart, Inc., 1942.

Beneš, Eduard. *Memoirs of Dr. Eduard Beneš.* Translated by Godfrey Lias. Boston: Houghton Mifflin Company, 1954.

Berle, Adolf A. *Navigating the Rapids, 1918–1971.* Edited by Beatrice Bishop Berle and Travis Beal Jacobs. New York: Harcourt Brace Jovanovich, Inc., 1973.

Bilainkin, George. *Diary of a Diplomatic Correspondent.* London: George Allen & Unwin Ltd., 1942.

———. *Maisky.* London: George Allen & Unwin, Ltd., 1944.

Birkenhead, The Earl of. *Halifax.* Boston: Houghton Mifflin Company, 1966.

Blum, John M. *From the Morgenthau Diaries.* Vol. I: *Years of Crisis, 1928–1938.* Boston: Houghton Mifflin Company, 1959.

———. *From the Morgenthau Diaries.* Vol. II: *Years of Urgency, 1938–1941.* Boston: Houghton Mifflin Company, 1965.

Boyle, Andrew. *Montagu Norman.* New York: Weybright and Talley, 1967.

Brogan, Denis W. *The Era of Franklin D. Roosevelt.* New Haven, Conn.: Yale University Press, 1951.

———. *Politics In America.* New York: Harper & Brothers, 1954.

Bullitt, Orville H., ed. *For the President, Personal and Secret: Correspondence Between Franklin D. Roosevelt and William C. Bullitt.* Boston: Houghton Mifflin Company, 1972.

Burns, James MacGregor. *John Kennedy: A Political Profile.* New York: Harcourt, Brace & Company, 1959.

Byrnes, James F. *All in One Lifetime.* New York: Harper & Brothers, 1958.

Cadogan, Alexander. *The Diaries of Sir Alexander Cadogan, 1938–1945.* Edited by David Dilks. London: Cassell, 1971.

Calvocoressi, Peter, and Guy Wint. *Total War: Causes and Courses of the Second World War*. London: The Penguin Press, 1972.

Cameron, Gail. *Rose*. London: Michael Joseph, 1972.

Carr, William H. A. *J.F.K.: An Informal Biography*. Paperback edition. New York: Lancer Books, Inc., 1962.

——. *Those Fabulous Kennedy Women*. Paperback edition. New York: Wisdom House, Inc., 1961.

Chadwin, Mark Lincoln. *The Hawks of World War II*. Chapel Hill, N.C.; University of North Carolina Press, 1968.

Chamberlain, John. *The American Stakes*. New York: Carrick & Evans, Inc., 1940.

Channon, Sir Henry. *Chips: The Diaries of Sir Henry Channon*. Edited by Robert Rhodes James. London: Weidenfeld and Nicolson, 1967.

Charles, Searle F. *Minister of Relief: Harry Hopkins and the Depression*. Syracuse, N.Y.: Syracuse University Press, 1963.

Chester, Lewis, Geoffrey Hodgson, and Bruce Page. *An American Melodrama: The Presidential Campaign of 1968*. New York: The Viking Press, 1969.

Churchill, Winston S. *The Second World War*. Vol. I: *The Gathering Storm*. Boston: Houghton Mifflin Company, 1948.

——. *The Second World War*. Vol. II: *Their Finest Hour*. Boston: Houghton Mifflin Company, 1949.

Cohn, Roy. *McCarthy*. New York: New American Library, Inc., 1968.

Cole, Wayne S. *America First*. Madison, Wis.: The University of Wisconsin Press, 1953.

Congressional Record.

Considine, Bob. *It's All News To Me*. New York: Meredith Press, 1967.

Cook, Fred J. *The Nightmare Decade*. New York: Random House, 1971.

Cramer, C. H. *Newton D. Baker*. Cleveland: The World Publishing Company, 1961.

Crown, James Tracy. *The Kennedy Literature: A Bibliographical Essay on John F. Kennedy*. New York: New York University Press, 1968.

Crowther, Bosley. *Hollywood Rajah: The Life and Times of Louis B. Mayer*. New York: Henry Holt and Company, 1960.

Curley, James Michael. *I'd Do It Again*. Englewood Cliffs, N.J.: Prentice-Hall, Inc., 1957.

Curtis, Thomas Quinn. *Von Stroheim*. New York: Farrar, Straus and Giroux, 1971.

Cutler, John Henry. *Cardinal Cushing of Boston*. New York: Hawthorn Books, Inc., 1970.

——. *"Honey Fitz": Three Steps to the White House*. Indianapolis, Ind.: The Bobbs-Merrill Company, Inc., 1962.

Dallas, Rita, with Jeanira Ratcliffe. *The Kennedy Case*. New York: G. P. Putnam's Sons, 1973.

Dalton, Hugh. *High Tide and After: Memoirs, 1945–1960*. London: Frederick Muller Limited, 1962.

Damore, Leo. *The Cape Cod Years of John Fitzgerald Kennedy*. Englewood Cliffs, N.J.: Prentice-Hall, Inc., 1967.

David, Lester. *Ted Kennedy: Triumphs and Tragedies*. New York: Grosset & Dunlap, 1971.

Davies, Joseph E. *Mission to Moscow*. New York: Simon & Schuster, 1941.

Davis, Kenneth S. *The Hero: Charles A. Lindbergh and the American Dream*. Garden City, N.Y.: Doubleday & Company, Inc., 1959.

Day, J. Edward. *My Appointed Rounds*. New York: Holt, Rinehart & Winston, 1965.

deCourcy, John. *Behind the Battle*. London: Eyre and Spottiswoode, 1942.

deToledano, Ralph. *R.F.K.: The Man Who Would Be President*. New York: G. P. Putnam's Sons, 1967.

Dinneen, Joseph F. *The Kennedy Family*. Boston: Little, Brown and Company, 1959.

————. *The Purple Shamrock*. New York: W. W. Norton & Company, Inc., 1949.

Documents on British Foreign Policy, 1919–1939. Third Series. Edited by E. L. Woodward and Rohan Butler. London: Her Majesty's Stationery Office, 1949.

Documents on German Foreign Policy, 1918–1945. Series D (1937–45). Washington: Department of State, various dates.

Douglas, William O. *Democracy and Finance*. Edited by James Allen. New Haven, Conn.: Yale University Press, 1940.

Eisenhower, Dwight David. *The White House Years: Waging Peace, 1956–1961*. Garden City, N.Y.: Doubleday & Company, Inc., 1965.

Encyclopædia Britannica. 13th ed. Vol. XXI.

Eubank, Keith. *Munich*. Norman, Okla.: University of Oklahoma Press, 1963.

Fairlie, Henry. *The Kennedy Promise: The Politics of Expectation*. Garden City, N.Y.: Doubleday & Company, Inc., 1973.

Farley, James A. *Jim Farley's Story*. New York: McGraw-Hill Book Company, Inc., 1948.

Fay, Paul B., Jr. *The Pleasure of His Company*. New York: Harper & Row, 1966.

Felknor, Bruce L. *Dirty Politics*. New York: W. W. Norton & Company, Inc., 1966.

Film Year Book, 1927. New York: The Film Daily, undated.

Fischer, Louis. *Men and Politics*. New York: Duell, Sloan and Pearce, 1941 and 1946.

Fleming, Peter. *Operation Sea Lion*. New York: Simon & Schuster, 1957.

Flynn, Edward J. *You're the Boss*. New York: The Viking Press, 1947.

Ford, Corey. *Donovan of OSS*. Boston: Little, Brown and Company, 1970.

Foreign Relations of the United States. Washington: Government Printing Office.

Forrestal, James. *The Forrestal Diaries*. Edited by Walter Millis. New York: The Viking Press, 1951.

Francis-Williams, Lord. *Nothing So Strange*. New York: American Heritage Press, 1970.

Freedman, Max, ed. *Roosevelt and Frankfurter: Their Correspondence, 1928–1945*. Boston: Little, Brown and Company, 1967.

Gainard, Joseph A. *Yankee Skipper*. New York: Frederick A. Stokes Company, 1940.

Gallagher, Mary Barelli. *My Life With Jacqueline Kennedy*. Edited by Frances Spatz Leighton. New York: David McKay Company, Inc., 1969.

Gervasi, Frank. *Big Government*. New York: Whittlesey House, 1949.

Gilbert, Douglas. *American Vaudeville*. New York: McGraw-Hill Book Company, Inc., 1940.

Gilbert, Martin, and Richard Gott. *The Appeasers*. Boston: Houghton Mifflin Company, 1963.

Goldberg, Joseph P. *The Maritime Story: A Study in Labor-Management Relations*. Cambridge, Mass.: Harvard University Press, 1958.

Golden, Harry. *The Right Time*. New York: G. P. Putnam's Sons, 1969.

Goldman, Eric F. *The Tragedy of Lyndon Johnson*. London: Macdonald, 1969.

Gottlieb, Polly Rose. *The Nine Lives of Billy Rose*. New York: Crown Publishers, Inc., 1968.

Grange, Red. *The Red Grange Story.* As told to Ira Morton. New York: G. P. Putnam's Sons, 1953.

Graves, Robert, and Alan Hodge. *The Long Week-end: A Social History of Great Britain, 1919–1939.* London: Faber & Faber Limited, 1941.

Green, Abel, and Joe Laurie, Jr. *Show Biz.* New York: Henry Holt and Company, 1951.

Gunther, John. *Inside U.S.A.* New York: Harper & Brothers, 1947.

Gussow, Mel. *Don't Say Yes Until I Finish Talking: A Biography of Darryl F. Zanuck.* Garden City, N.Y.: Doubleday & Company, Inc., 1971.

Halberstam, David. *The Unfinished Odyssey of Robert Kennedy.* Paperback edition. New York: Bantam Books, 1969.

Halle, Kay, ed. *Randolph Churchill: The Young Unpretender.* London: Heineman, 1971.

Hamilton, Charles. *The Robot That Helped to Make a President.* New York: privately printed, 1965.

Handlin, Oscar. *Boston's Immigrants.* Revised edition. Cambridge, Mass.: Belknap Press, 1959.

Hansen, Marcus Lee. *The Atlantic Migration.* Cambridge, Mass.: Harvard University Press, 1940.

———. *The Immigrant In American History.* Cambridge, Mass.: Harvard University Press, 1940.

Harvard Class Book, 1912.

Harvey, Oliver. *The Diplomatic Diaries of Oliver Harvey, 1937–1940.* Edited by John Harvey. London: Collins, 1970.

Hasset, William D. *Off the Record With F.D.R., 1942–1945.* New Brunswick, N.J.: Rutgers University Press, 1958.

Hays, Will H. *The Memoirs of Will H. Hays.* Garden City. N.Y.: Doubleday & Company, Inc., 1955.

Hecht, Ben. *A Child of the Century.* New York: Simon & Schuster, 1954.

Hersh, Burton. *The Education of Edward Kennedy: A Family Biography.* New York: William Morrow & Company, Inc., 1972.

Hess, Stephen. *America's Political Dynasties from Adams to Kennedy.* Garden City, N.Y.: Doubleday & Company, Inc., 1966.

Honan, William H. *Ted Kennedy: Profile of a Survivor.* New York: Quadrangle Books, 1972.

Hoover, Herbert. *Addresses Upon the American Road, 1950–55.* Stanford, Calif.: Stanford University Press, 1955.

———. *Memoirs of Herbert Hoover.* Vol. 3: *The Great Depression, 1929–1941.* New York: The Macmillan Company, 1952.

Hopper, Hedda. *From Under My Hat.* Garden City, N.Y.: Doubleday & Company, Inc., 1952.

Hudson, Richard M., and Raymond Lee. *Gloria Swanson.* South Brunswick, N.J.: A. S. Barnes and Company, 1970.

Hull, Cordell. *The Memoirs of Cordell Hull.* Two volumes. New York: The Macmillan Company, 1948.

Hyde, H. Montgomery. *Room 3603: The Story of the British Intelligence Center in New York During World War II.* New York: Farrar, Straus and Company, 1963.

Ickes, Harold L. *The Secret Diary of Harold L. Ickes.* Vol. I: *The First Thousand Days, 1933–1936.* New York: Simon & Schuster, 1953.

————. *The Secret Diary of Harold L. Ickes*. Vol. II: *The Inside Struggle, 1936–1939*. New York: Simon & Schuster, 1954.

————. *The Secret Diary of Harold L. Ickes*. Vol III: *The Lowering Clouds, 1939–1941*. New York: Simon & Schuster, 1954.

I Documenti Diplomatici Italiani. 8th Series: 1935–1939 and 9th Series: 1939–1945. Rome: Ministero degli Affari Esteri, various dates.

Israel, Fred L. *Nevada's Key Pittman*. Lincoln, Neb.: University of Nebraska Press, 1963.

James, Marquis, and Bessie Rowland James. *Biography of a Bank: The Story of Bank of America*. New York: Harper & Brothers, 1954.

Jones, Thomas. *A Diary With Letters, 1931–1950*. London: Oxford University Press, 1954.

Josephson, Matthew. *Infidel In the Temple: A Memoir of the Nineteen-Thirties*. New York: Alfred A. Knopf, 1967.

Journal of the House. Commonwealth of Massachusetts.

Journal of the Senate. Commonwealth of Massachusetts.

Kahn, E. J., Jr. *The World of Swope*. New York: Simon & Schuster, 1965.

Kaltenborn, H. V. *Fifty Fabulous Years*. New York: G. P. Putnam's Sons, 1950.

Kaufman, William W. "Two American Ambassadors." *The Diplomats*. Edited by Gordon A. Craig and Felix Gilbert. Princeton, N.J.: Princeton University Press, 1953.

Kennedy, John F., ed. *As We Remember Joe*. Cambridge, Mass. University Press (privately printed), 1945.

————. *Why England Slept*. New York: Wilfred Funk, Inc., 1940.

Kennedy, Joseph P. *I'm For Roosevelt*. New York: Reynal & Hitchcock, 1936.

————, ed. *The Story of the Films*. Chicago: A. W. Shaw Company, 1927.

————, and James M. Landis. *The Surrender of King Leopold*. New York: privately printed, 1950.

Kennan, George F. *Memoirs, 1925–1950*. Boston: Little, Brown and Company, 1967.

Kilpatrick, Carroll, ed. *Roosevelt and Daniels*. Chapel Hill, N.C.: University of North Carolina Press, 1952.

Klein, Burton H. *Germany's Economic Preparations for War*. Cambridge, Mass.: Harvard University Press, 1959.

Kluckhohn, Frank L. *America: Listen!* Paperback edition. Derby, Conn.: Monarch Books, Inc., 1961.

Krock, Arthur. *The Consent of the Governed*. Boston: Little, Brown and Company, 1971.

————. *Memoirs: Sixty Years on the Firing Line*. New York: Funk & Wagnalls, 1968.

Kronenberger, Louis. *No Whippings, No Gold Watches*. Boston: Little, Brown and Company, 1970.

Kyrk, Hazel. *The Family In the American Economy*. Chicago: University of Chicago Press, 1957.

Land, Emory S. *Winning the War with Ships*. New York: Robert M. McBride Co., Inc., 1958.

Lane, Frederic C. *Ships for Victory*. Baltimore: Johns Hopkins Press, 1951.

Langer, William L., and S. Everett Gleason. *The Challenge to Isolation, 1937–1940*. New York: Harper & Brothers, 1952.

————. *The Undeclared War, 1940–41*. New York: Harper & Brothers, 1953.

Lasky, Victor. *J.F.K.: The Man and the Myth.* New York: The Macmillan Company, 1963.

———. *Robert F. Kennedy: The Myth and the Man.* New York: Trident Press, 1968.

Laurie, Joe, Jr. *Vaudeville.* New York: Henry Holt and Company, 1953.

Laver, James. *Between the Wars.* Boston: Houghton Mifflin Company, 1961.

Lee, Raymond E. *The London Journal of General Raymond E. Lee, 1940–41.* Edited by James Leutze. Boston: Little, Brown and Company, 1971.

Leston, Robert A. *Sargent Shriver: A Candid Portrait.* New York: Farrar, Straus and Company, n.d.

Leuchtenburg, William E. *The Perils of Prosperity, 1914–1932.* Chicago: The University of Chicago Press, 1958.

Liddell-Hart, B. H. *History of the Second World War.* London: Cassell, 1970.

Lief, Alfred. *Democracy's Norris.* New York: Stackpole Sons, 1939.

Lincoln, Evelyn. *My Twelve Years with John F. Kennedy.* New York: David McKay Company, Inc., 1965.

Lindbergh, Charles A. *The Wartime Journals of Charles A. Lindbergh.* New York: Harcourt Brace Jovanovich, Inc., 1970.

Lingeman, Richard R. *Don't You Know There's A War On?: The American Home Front, 1941–1945.* New York: G. P. Putnam's Sons, 1970.

Lisagor, Peter, and Marguerite Higgins. *Overtime in Heaven: Adventures in the Foreign Service.* Garden City, N.Y.: Doubleday & Company, Inc., 1964.

Long, Breckenridge. *The War Diary of Breckenridge Long: Selections From the Years, 1939–1944.* Edited by Fred L. Israel. Lincoln, Neb.: University of Nebraska Press, 1966.

Longford, The Earl of, and Thomas P. O'Neill. *Eamon DeValera.* London: Hutchinson & Co., 1970.

Lubell, Samuel. *Revolt of the Moderates.* New York: Harper & Brothers, 1956.

Luce, Clare Boothe. *Europe in the Spring.* New York: Alfred A. Knopf, 1940.

Luce, Henry. *The Ideas of Henry Luce.* Edited by John K. Jessup. New York: Atheneum, 1969.

Lyons, Eugene. *David Sarnoff.* New York: Harper & Row, 1966.

Lyons, Louis M. *Newspaper Story: One Hundred Years of the Boston Globe.* Cambridge, Mass.: The Belknap Press, 1971.

Maisky, Ivan. *Kto Pomogal Gitleru.* Moscow: Izdatelstvo Instituta Mezhdunarodnykh Otnoshenii, 1962.

———. *Memoirs of a Soviet Ambassador: The War, 1939–1943.* Translated by Andrew Rothstein. London: Hutchinson, 1967.

———. *Who Helped Hitler?* Translated by Andrew Rothstein. London: Hutchinson & Co., 1964.

Manchester, William. *The Death of a President.* New York: Harper & Row, 1967.

———. *Portrait of a President.* Boston: Little, Brown and Company, 1962, 1967.

Markman, Charles Lam. *The Buckleys.* New York: William Morrow & Company, 1973.

Martin, Kingsley. *Editor: "New Statesman" Years, 1931–45.* Chicago: Henry Regnery Company, 1970.

Martin, Ralph G., and Ed Plaut. *Front Runner, Dark Horse.* Garden City, N.Y.: Doubleday & Company, Inc., 1960.

McCarthy, Joe. *The Remarkable Kennedys.* Paperback edition. New York: Popular Library, 1960.

McCoy, Donald R. *Landon of Kansas*. Lincoln, Neb.: University of Nebraska Press, 1966.

MacDonald, David J. *Union Man*. New York: E. P. Dutton & Co., Inc., 1969.

McKenna, Marian C. *Borah*. Ann Arbor, Mich.: University of Michigan Press, 1961.

Macleod, Iain. *Neville Chamberlain*. London: Frederick Muller, Ltd., 1961.

Moffat, Jay Pierrepont. *The Moffat Papers: Selections from the Diplomatic Journals of Jay Pierrepont Moffat, 1919–1943*. Edited by N. H. Hooker. Cambridge, Mass.: Harvard University Press, 1956.

Moley, Raymond. *After Seven Years*. New York: Harper & Brothers, 1939.

————. *The First New Deal*. New York: Harcourt, Brace & World, Inc., 1966.

Mooney, Booth. *Roosevelt and Rayburn*. Philadelphia: J. B. Lippincott Company, 1971.

Mosley, Leonard. *Backs To the Wall*. New York: Random House, 1971.

Mowat, Charles Loch. *Britain Between the Wars*. Chicago: University of Chicago Press, 1955.

Mowrer, Edgar Ansel. *Triumph and Turmoil*. New York: Weybright and Talley, 1968.

Murphy, Robert. *Diplomat Among Warriors*. Garden City, N.Y.: Doubleday & Company, Inc., 1964.

Murrow, Edward R. *In Search of Light: The Broadcasts of Edward R. Murrow, 1938–1961*. Edited by Edward Bliss, Jr. New York: Alfred A. Knopf, 1967.

Namier, L. B. *Diplomatic Prelude, 1938–39*. London: Macmillan & Co., Ltd., 1948.

Navasky, Victor. *Kennedy Justice*. New York: Atheneum, 1971.

The New Dealers. By Unofficial Observer. New York: Simon & Schuster, Inc., 1934.

Newfield, Jack. *Robert Kennedy: A Memoir*. New York: E. P. Dutton & Co., Inc., 1969.

Nicolson, Harold. *The Diaries & Letters of Harold Nicolson*. Vol. II. *The War Years, 1939–1945*. Edited by Nigel Nicolson. New York: Atheneum, 1967.

Nixon, Richard. *Six Crises*. Garden City, N.Y.: Doubleday & Company, Inc., 1962.

Noble, Peter. *Hollywood Scapegoat*. London: The Fortune Press, 1950.

O'Donnell, Kenneth P., and David F. Powers, with Joe McCarthy. *"Johnny, We Hardly Knew Ye."* Boston: Little, Brown and Company, 1972.

Parliamentary Papers.

Pawle, Gerald. *The War and Colonel Warden*. London: George G. Harrap & Co., 1963.

Peel, Roy V., and Thomas C. Donnelly. *The 1932 Campaign*. New York: Farrar & Rinehart, Inc., 1935.

Poling, Daniel A. *Mine Eyes Have Seen*. New York: McGraw-Hill Book Company, Inc., 1959.

Polish Documents Relative to the Origin of the War. 1st Series, #3. Berlin: Auswartiges Amt, 1940.

Pratt, Julius W. *Cordell Hull*. Vol. XII: *The American Secretaries of State and Their Diplomacy*. Edited by Robert H. Ferrell. New York: Cooper Square Publishers, Inc., 1964.

Prochnau, William W., and Richard W. Larsen. *A Certain Democrat: Senator Henry M. Jackson*. Englewood Cliffs, N.J.: Prentice-Hall, Inc., 1972.

Raczyński, Count Edward. *In Allied London*. London: Weidenfeld and Nicolson, 1962.

Reith, J. C. W. *Into the Wind*. London: Hodder & Stoughton, 1949.

Robinson, Ione. *A Wall to Paint On*. New York: E. P. Dutton & Company, Inc., 1946.

Roosevelt, Eleanor. *This I Remember*. New York: Harper & Brothers, 1949.

Roosevelt, Elliott, and James Brough. *An Untold Story: The Roosevelts of Hyde Park*. New York: G. P. Putnam's Sons, 1973.

Roosevelt, Franklin D. *F.D.R., His Personal Letters, 1928–1945.* Edited by Elliott Roosevelt. New York: Duell, Sloan and Pearce, 1950.

———. *The Public Papers and Addresses of Franklin D. Roosevelt.* Edited by Samuel Rosenman. New York: The Macmillan Company, various dates.

Rosenman, Samuel I. *Working With Roosevelt.* New York: Harper & Brothers, 1952.

Salinger, Pierre. *With Kennedy.* Garden City, N.Y.: Doubleday & Company, Inc., 1966.

Schlesinger, Arthur M., Jr. *The Coming of the New Deal.* Boston: Houghton Mifflin Company, 1959.

———. *Kennedy or Nixon: Does It Make Any Difference?* New York: The Macmillan Company, 1960.

———. *The Politics of Upheaval.* Boston: Houghton Mifflin Company, 1960.

———. *A Thousand Days: John F. Kennedy In the White House.* Boston: Houghton Mifflin Company, 1965.

Schrier, Arnold. *Ireland and the American Emigration, 1850–1900.* Minneapolis, Minn.: University of Minnesota Press, 1958.

Searls, Hank. *The Lost Prince.* New York: The World Publishing Company, 1969.

Sevareid, Eric, ed. *Candidates, 1960.* New York: Basic Books, Inc., 1959.

Shadegg, Stephen, *Clare Boothe Luce.* New York: Simon & Schuster, 1970.

Shannon, William V. *The Heir Apparent.* New York: The Macmillan Company, 1967.

Sherwood, Robert E. *Roosevelt and Hopkins.* Paperback edition. New York: Grosset & Dunlap, 1948.

Shirer, William L. *The Rise and Fall of the Third Reich.* New York: Simon & Schuster, 1960.

Sidey, Hugh. *John F. Kennedy, President.* New York: Atheneum, 1963.

———. *A Very Personal Presidency.* New York: Atheneum, 1968.

Slessor, Sir John. *The Central Blue.* New York: Frederick A. Praeger, 1957.

Sorensen, Theodore C. *Kennedy.* New York: Harper & Row, 1965.

Spalding, E. Wilder. *Ambassadors Ordinary and Extraordinary.* Washington: Public Affairs Press, 1961.

Steffens, Lincoln. *The Autobiography of Lincoln Steffens.* New York: Harcourt, Brace and Company, 1931.

Steinberg, Alfred. *Sam Johnson's Boy.* New York: The Macmillan Company, 1968.

Stiles, Lela. *The Man Behind Roosevelt: The Story of Louis McHenry Howe.* Cleveland: The World Publishing Company, 1954.

Sulzberger, C. L. *The Last of the Giants.* New York: The Macmillan Company, 1970.

Swanberg, W. A. *Citizen Hearst.* New York: Charles Scribner's Sons, 1961.

———. *Luce and His Empire.* New York: Charles Scribner's Sons, 1972.

Sykes, Christopher. *Nancy.* New York: Harper & Row, 1973.

Talese, Gay. *The Kingdom and the Power.* New York: The World Publishing Company, 1969.

Taylor, A. J. P. *English History, 1914–1945.* Paperback edition, London: Penguin Books, 1970.

———. *The Origins of the Second World War.* Second edition. Paperback. Greenwich, Conn.: Fawcett Publications, Inc., 1961.

Taylor, F. Jay. *The United States and the Spanish Civil War, 1936–1939.* New York: Bookman Associates, 1956.

Thimmesch, Nick, and William Johnson. *Robert Kennedy At 40.* New York: W. W. Norton & Company, Inc., 1965.

Thompson, Robert E., and Hortense Myers. *Robert F. Kennedy: The Brother Within.* Paperback edition. New York: Dell Publishing Co., Inc., 1962.

Thorning, Joseph F., Fr. *Builders of the Social Order.* Ozone Park, N.Y.: Catholic Literary Guild, 1941.

Tull, Charles J. *Father Coughlin and the New Deal.* Syracuse, N.Y.: Syracuse University Press, 1965.

Tully, Grace. *F.D.R. My Boss.* New York: Charles Scribner's Sons, 1949.

United States Congress. House of Representatives. *Hearings Before House Committee on Foreign Affairs on HR1776 (Lend-Lease), January 21, 1941.*

United States Congress. House of Representatives. *Hearings Before House Committee on Merchant Marine & Fisheries on HR8532, 1937.*

United States Congress. House of Representatives. *Hearings Before the Sub-committee of the Committee of Appropriations, House of Representatives, 75th, 1st session on the 3rd Deficiency Approval Bill for 1937.*

United States Maritime Commission. *Economic Survey of the American Merchant Marine.* Washington: Government Printing Office, November, 1937.

United States Senate. *Hearings Before the Senate Committee on Banking & Currency on Senate Resolution 84 and Senate Resolutions 56 & 94, Part 14, 1933.*

United States Senate. *Hearings Before the Senate Committee on Commerce and the Committee on Education and Labor on S3078, 1937.*

United States Senate. *Hearings Before Senate Committee on Commerce and the Committee on Education and Labor on S3078, 1938.*

United States Senate. *Hearings Before Committee on Foreign Relations, April 24, 1939.*

vanden Heuvel, William, and Milton Gwirtzman. *On His Own: Robert F. Kennedy, 1964–1968.* Garden City, N.Y.: Doubleday & Company, Inc., 1970.

Walker-Smith, Derek. *Neville Chamberlain: Man of Peace.* London: Robert Hale Limited, undated.

Wayman, Dorothy G. *David I. Walsh: Citizen-Patriot.* Milwaukee, Wis.: Bruce Publishing Company, 1952.

Welles, Sumner. *Time for Decision.* New York: Harper & Brothers, 1944.

Whalen, Richard J. *The Founding Father.* New York: The New American Library of World Literature, Inc., 1964.

Wheeler, Burton K., with Paul F. Healy. *Yankee From the West.* Garden City, N.Y.: Doubleday & Company, Inc., 1962.

Wheeler-Bennett, John W. *King George VI.* New York: St. Martin's Press, 1958.

———. *Munich, Prologue to Tragedy.* London: Macmillan & Co., Ltd., 1948.

White, Theodore H. *The Making of the President, 1960.* New York: Atheneum, 1961.

———. *The Making of the President, 1968.* New York: Atheneum, 1969.

Wilcox, Herbert. *Twenty-Five Thousand Sunsets.* New York: A. S. Barnes and Company, 1967.

Wrench, John Evelyn. *Geoffrey Dawson and Our Times.* London: Hutchinson, 1955.

Zeckendorf, William, with Edward McCreary. *The Autobiography of William Zeckendorf.* New York: Holt, Rinehart & Winston, 1970.

INDEX

631